NEHRU
THE FIRST SIXTY YEARS

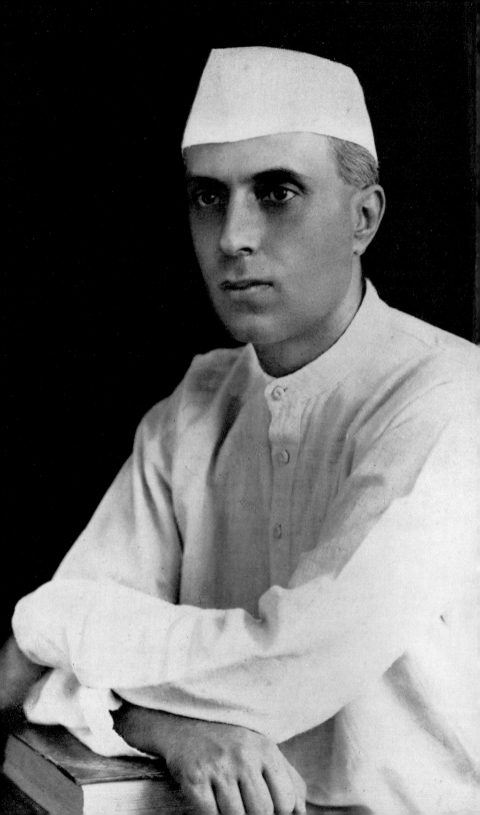

Nehru

THE FIRST SIXTY YEARS

Presenting in his own words the
development of the political thought
of Jawaharlal Nehru and the
background against
which it evolved

Including significant passages from
Nehru's writings, speeches, statements
before the court, press conferences,
conversations, interviews and other
documents, up to the founding of
the Republic of India, 1950

*Selected and edited, with introductory, historical
and other interpretative commentary by*

DOROTHY NORMAN

with a foreword by

JAWAHARLAL NEHRU

———✳———

VOLUME

ONE

———✳———

THE JOHN DAY COMPANY
NEW YORK

To

JAWAHARLAL NEHRU

To the first sixty years—a great period in a life dedicated to the struggle for independence from colonial rule; to democracy and equality of opportunity; to the obliteration of communalist hatred, and of poverty and hunger; to a concentrated effort to reduce international misunderstandings and tensions; above all, to humanism: to the *dignity of man*. To a voice that has played a significant role in helping to transform the conscience of my own generation. To the young in spirit, everywhere, in the hope that they may find some inspiration in these pages.

D.N.

ACKNOWLEDGMENTS

I wish to extend warmest thanks to Richard J. Walsh Jr, of John Day, Max Reinhardt and Barney Blackley, of The Bodley Head, Mrs Laura Cohn, Professor Amiya Chakravarty, Professor Ainslee Embree and Natwar Singh for reading these volumes in manuscript, and for their valuable suggestions. I should like to express my gratitude also to M. A. Vellodi, Narendra Singh and Z. L. Kaul for their generous cooperation in determining the accuracy of various facts and documents; to Stephen Koss for his help in further checking; to Janet Dowd and Anne Salomon for their devoted secretarial assistance, especially in the final phase of preparing so extensive and exacting a work; to Elinor Weis for her excellent aid in reading proofs; to Nehru's assistant, N. K. Seshan, for his numerous courtesies.

I also gratefully acknowledge the permission kindly given by the publishers of the many works on which I have drawn to reprint copyright material. The sources of quotations are given in the footnotes. Full details of all works cited are given in the Bibliography at the end of Volume II.

FOREWORD

Over four years ago, Dorothy Norman told me that she intended writing a book about me. It was proposed that this should contain extracts from my writings and speeches. I welcomed the idea. I had no conception of how arduous this undertaking would be.

She referred to me from time to time to find out some fact or to verify what she was collecting. I discovered then that she had cast her net rather wide and that her work was much more difficult than I had imagined. During these years, she has laboured hard and has discovered many statements made by me which I had almost forgotten.

An unfortunate occurrence confined me to bed during the early days of this year. I took advantage of this to glance through some of the manuscripts of this book. They brought back to my memory incidents that had happened long ago and I lived for the moment in the past. Indeed, the pre-independence past remains vivid in my mind. Many difficult problems have come to me since independence. And yet the impact of the past, and especially of Gandhiji, is greater on me than all these present problems. Often I have wondered how Gandhiji would have dealt with these problems of today and what advice he would have given. The fact that sometimes we have not followed his directions has troubled me. And yet it is difficult to know what his advice would have been in existing circumstances.

It is often said that Gandhiji and his views are gradually fading out from the minds of people in India. To a slight extent, that might be true. But I do not think this is basically so. Especially those of us who had the privilege of working with them can never forget his towering personality. But apart from personal reactions to him, he has become embedded in India's history and in the thinking of millions of our people.

Thirteen years ago, in June 1951, I wrote something about Gandhi in a foreword to his life—*Mahatma* by D. G. Tendulkar. I give below the last paragraph from this foreword:

"People will write the life of Gandhi and they will discuss and criticise him and his theories and activities. But to some of us he will remain something apart from theory—an ardent and beloved figure who ennobled and gave some significance to our petty lives, and whose passing away has left us with a feeling of emptiness and loneliness. Many pictures rise in my mind of this man, whose eyes were often full of laughter and yet were pools of infinite sadness. But the picture that is dominant and most significant is, as I saw him marching, staff in hand, to Dandi on the salt march in 1930. Here was a pilgrim on his quest of Truth, quiet, peaceful, determined and fearless, who would continue that quest and pilgrimage, regardless of consequences."

New Delhi,
March 23, 1964

Jawaharlal Nehru

INTRODUCTION
by Dorothy Norman

I

The time: January, 1950. The month during which the newly liberated
Republic of India was to be formally inaugurated. Exhilarating excitement
in the air. Indians massing. Visitors gathering from the far corners of the
world to join in celebration of the auspicious occasion.

The scene: New Delhi. The residence of Jawaharlal Nehru, first Prime
Minister of Free India.

As the Prime Minister walked away from a group of guests he concealed
his amusement with difficulty. A woman with whom he had just spoken,
who had only recently arrived in India, and whom he had never met
before, had informed him that what he had been saying had so impressed
her, she wondered whether he had ever written anything. The world-
renowned author smiled his shy, fleeting smile.

As Nehru spoke, I realized that, despite my own long-standing interest
in his writings, it had not occurred to me to inquire during just that period
whether he happened to be working on some new publication. I asked
him whether he was. My question aroused still further laughter: "How
could I be? I've not been in jail of late."

As I smiled in response, I was startled to discover that I had myself
temporarily forgotten—before even the birth of the Indian Republic—
that the major writings of this extraordinarily gifted and courageous man
had come into being precisely during those long and lonely, wearying
terms of imprisonment, suffered for no other crime than the sincere and
passionate desire to see colonial India liberated from foreign rule.

I was also moved by the gentle humor and exemplary lack of bitterness
displayed, both so clearly stemming from a generous ability to ignore
already past issues, in order to concentrate upon more pressing problems
involving the future fate of over three hundred million fellow-countrymen.

II

The Delhi incident continued to haunt me. And then at a later time,
while reading Nehru's almost daily utterances as Prime Minister, and

ix

re-reading his pre-independence writings, it struck me as singularly unfortunate that so much of what he had said over the years should be unknown to the world at large; that a preponderance of his work should be available only in obscure and out-of-print publications; that there should be no single volume in which one could trace the evolution of his ideas and acts, described in his own words, in orderly fashion.

The more I contemplated this regrettable situation, the more valuable I felt it might be to prepare a book that would present the history Nehru had both made and written; that would indicate the manner in which his political philosophy had developed over the years, and the background against which his attitudes and actions had evolved. I came to believe, with a sense of mounting urgency, that the West, in particular, must pay greater heed to the forces responsible for moulding the viewpoint of so outstanding a twentieth-century spokesman for the oppressed millions not only of India, but of all other lands yearning passionately for peace, freedom, equality of opportunity and a higher standard of living. Unless we did so we would be in gravest danger of closing our minds and our hearts to the aspirations and sufferings of the major part of the human race. We would run the risk of remaining insensitively unaware of how crucially necessary it is to re-evaluate any exclusively Western-oriented view of both world history and contemporary events. I discovered that many of Nehru's writings were also currently difficult to obtain even in India. Hence I addressed myself to the task of preparing these volumes.

III

Although Mohandas K. Gandhi was both primary architect of India's freedom movement, and father of contemporary India, it was against his nature to accept political office. As long ago as the late nineteen twenties he expressed the wish that the then still young Jawaharlal Nehru should become the political leader of India, a hope that could not possibly have come to fruition had Nehru himself not had a mass following; had he not been profoundly concerned about the intolerable conditions under which the majority of Indians lived; and had he not, simultaneously, been an independent yet nevertheless loyal follower of the Mahatma.

In 1929, a little over ten years after the two men first had met, Gandhi characterized Nehru as " pure as crystal . . . truthful beyond suspicion . . . a knight *sans peur et sans reproche.*" [1]

Gandhi early recognized his youthful colleague's natural political

[1] H.I.N.C. (Vol. II), p. 9.

talent; his effortless ability to lead; his selfless dedication, idealism, honesty and openness to the need for change. The Mahatma was as deeply impressed by Jawaharlal's stalwart courage, as by his intransigent efforts on behalf of India's freedom; as much by the breadth of his views about international affairs, as by his ability to combat the institution of British imperialism, without, at the same time, feeling hatred for the British as individuals. Gandhi was moved by Nehru's eloquence, his lack of pettiness, his passionate and enlightened devotion to the Indian people. Equally commendable were Jawaharlal's faith in the democratic way of life and his clear-cut desire for an undivided, secular India; his fervent mistrust of all forms of blind and confining tradition, and his firm rejection of the divisive, destructive tendencies of India's communalists.[1] Most appealing of all, perhaps, were young Nehru's enormous capacity for constructive work; his sustained will-power and drive; his ability to conceive of concrete, long-range plans for the future development of his still so greatly underdeveloped and oppressed land.

IV

Gandhi has long been likened to the crest of a vast wave, the Indian people having been the wave itself. He has long been revered in India as a great and unique saint. Nehru was to become the nation's most beloved and respected political leader many years before independence was achieved in 1947.

Despite their profound attachment to one another, the relationship between these two remarkable men was by no means ever a simple one. Inevitable differences of opinion were bound to arise between personalities of such markedly divergent temperaments. Yet, although both Gandhi and Nehru have written with candor—and sadness—about their periodic disagreements, each was to cherish the other with utmost devotion to the very end of Gandhi's life. It even may be that their dialogue was to be quite as significant to each of them as was the love that they bore for one another, and that it was of equal moment in shaping the destiny of modern India.

As late as 1946 the Mahatma acknowledged with respect that it was,

---

[1] In India the word communalism has connoted the opposition of religious groups within the country, in connection with political and other matters. India's communalists have not only laid stress upon differences (alleged or real) among religious, linguistic, social, political and economic groups; they have often tended to exacerbate and create tensions and antagonisms, even when none has existed.

after all, Jawaharlal who had accustomed the country to look "at everything in the international light, instead of the parochial." [1] (Since Gandhi's
death in 1948 Nehru, in turn, has described how his already overwhelming
admiration for the Mahatma increased a thousand-fold.)

V

In a compilation chosen from such voluminous writings and statements
covering so many years, it has not been possible to include what Nehru
has said about subjects not directly germane to the general theme of these
particular volumes. Neither has it been feasible, in a publication designed
primarily to include observations *by* Nehru, to indicate how others have
interpreted major decisions he made, or various critical situations he has
discussed, save in scattered instances or, at times, when he himself has
done so.

Since *The First Sixty Years* consists essentially of Nehru's political
testament from his own youth to the founding of the Indian Republic in
1950, his general view of past historical events, together with his literary
commentaries, have had to be almost totally disregarded. So too have
virtually all references to his personal life, and what he has had to say
about it. Since, however, Nehru's autobiographical writings have become
rather generally available since these volumes were undertaken, they can
be readily consulted, whereas the major part of the material herewith
presented has been neither similarly organized nor published elsewhere.
What Nehru has said or done since 1950 lies outside the scope of this
publication.

With respect to Nehru's general "philosophy", since one of its dominant features has been its undogmatic character, no attempt has been
made to summarize it in doctrinaire terms. As for Nehru's acts in relationship to his "philosophy", whenever he was in conflict about anything he
did, or critical of it, he confessed his attitude with extraordinary frankness. He took the consequences of his deeds throughout his life with
fortitude; without attempting to shirk responsibility, or to "tidy up"
facts at a later time in his own favor. When he outgrew or modified a
point of view he did not hesitate to say so. Thus, since the following pages
include many passages that would most assuredly be phrased differently
had they been uttered at a later period, the dates when they were written
or spoken might be carefully noted.

Nehru consistently felt compassion for the oppressed and the poor. He

[1] Harijan, 1946.

believed with unswerving intensity in world peace, freedom and democracy, striving ever valiantly to attain dignity for the world's subject
peoples. He was opposed to imperialism, regimentation and injustice in
all forms, to the very end of his life. Yet certain other attitudes inevitably
changed, at times in almost imperceptible fashion.

Despite his early attraction to Marxist Socialism as a possible cure for
India's economic ills, at no time did Nehru favor Communism as a
desirable form of government for India. It was, after all, the humane
aspect of Socialism that aroused his enthusiasm. He had no interest,
whatever, in mere dogma or theory, nor did he wish to exercise brutality,
in order to bring about needed social and economic reforms in a colonial,
largely feudalistic society. Most important of all, perhaps, he hoped to
alter the hearts of men, not to establish a dictatorship. It should be
remembered also that, under Nehru, India has consistently attempted to
carry out programs for the development of both a Private and a Public
Sector in her Five Year Plans. In any case, since Nehru's ideas concerning
economic questions, as well as numerous other topics, did change, it is of
utmost importance to take this fact into consideration. Just as he was
fully aware that life is not static, at any level, so he was not, himself, static.

Finally, also, contemplation of the precise evolution of Nehru's thought
over the years should help make it possible not only to comprehend the
significance of a unique and magnanimous individual with increased
clarity, but to see an entire era with greater perspective.

VI

Because Nehru so often spoke extemporaneously, it has not been
possible to find complete texts of all of his addresses. Moreover, so many
different versions of a few of his earlier utterances are on record that one
cannot be entirely certain about which of them is totally accurate. Fortunately, the variations to be found are uniformly minor; in no case do
they affect the essential meaning of what was said. Moreover, despite the
fact that various early documents either no longer exist, or could not be
found—even when I asked Nehru himself about them—there doubtless
would have been insufficient space for all of them. In similar fashion it
has been impossible to utilize everything of a later date that I did succeed
in locating. Not only space has been a necessary consideration in this
connection, but also the desire to portray the developments of events,
year by year, with a certain proportion.

Every effort has been made to consult and compare extant texts, in
order to make the most careful possible presentation of the passages

chosen. Material has been arranged essentially in chronological order, although occasionally it has been deemed preferable to group certain sequences according to subject-matter.

Choices of what to stress and what to omit necessarily have been as seemingly arbitrary as they have been difficult. It is hoped that what is included gives a fair portrait, lends insight into a personality at once complex, yet ever seeking greater self-clarification, and that it will be of historical value. (On the whole, topics of general historical interest, rather than of merely local or momentary significance, have been included, save in instances where a seemingly trivial occurrence has seemed to cast light upon an issue of greater importance.)

Text by Nehru is printed without quotation marks, and is more widely spaced than the explanatory sections in brackets preceding and following it. Words spoken by Nehru that appear in bracketed sequences, or in various conversations included in passages not written by him, have been placed in quotation marks. Congress resolutions and related committee declarations are similarly printed with quotation marks, but are not bracketed, even when not specifically attributed to Nehru, although in most cases when out of prison—especially after 1940—he played an important role in writing or helping to draft such statements.

In order not to interrupt the main flow of the publication, several relevant documents, too detailed to place in the main body of the text, are included in an appendix. Missing words and descriptive or qualifying phrases throughout both volumes have been placed in brackets. A key to the abbreviations of book titles, etc., placed at the beginning of footnotes is to be found on pages xix to xxi.

Despite the fact that brief historical summaries have been interpolated throughout the text for the reader's convenience, the major purpose of these volumes remains the presentation of Nehru's own view of the events chronicled up to 1950.

Notations relating to individuals not described by Nehru have been provided, except when the personalities mentioned are widely known. A glossary is appended, as is a list of members of Nehru's immediate family circle. (Definitions of many Indian and specialized terms appear throughout the text.)

Initially the reader may be somewhat bewildered because such words as the following are variously rendered: lathi, taluqdar, zamindar, Czechoslovakia, traveling, labor, Muslim, non-cooperation, etc. Since isolated passages inevitably will be quoted afresh from these volumes, as from the many sources from which they are taken, I have considered it generally inadvisable to regularize spelling, sentence structure and punctuation that have appeared differently in different major publications, even in those by Nehru himself. In certain cases, however, typographical form and punctuation have had to be altered in the interest of a certain conformity, even though content has not been affected thereby. (In several early, as well as other, documents originally published without benefit of sufficient editorial attention, or Nehru's own corrections, punctuation and sentence structure also have, at times, been altered for the sake of clarification, and typographical errors have been corrected, without comment. A few historical facts, as written by Nehru while in prison, when he did not have adequate source material at hand, may be questioned, but they have not been changed.)

Although the greatest of care has been exercised in order not to introduce new typographical or other errors, it is doubtless inevitable that some should occur, in spite of all precautions, in a publication of such vast proportions, derived from so many diverse sources.

No references have been given for several brief passages that I had collected before undertaking these volumes, and it has been impossible to *double*-check a few texts, because of present unavailability of original documents in which they first appeared. (The passages in question are, however, considered to be correct.) With respect to quotations from various newspapers, periodicals, pamphlets and other such material, it has not always been possible to give page numbers.

In the last four parts I have included more explanatory material than in earlier sections, both because of the complexity of the events that occurred between 1946 and 1950, and because Nehru himself did less writing during those years than in previous periods.

In the first volume, since both Jawaharlal and his father, Motilal Nehru, are so frequently mentioned, I have preferred in most cases to refer to the former simply as Jawaharlal, in the interest of brevity, and in order to avoid confusion. After the death of Motilal in 1930, the name Nehru almost invariably refers to Jawaharlal, unless otherwise noted.

I should like to note that I had no suggestions, either from Nehru or from anyone else, concerning what to include in these pages. In fact, as Nehru has indicated in his Foreword—one of the last documents he wrote during the final months of his life—he saw a copy of my manuscript (except for Part One) only after its completion. Even then, he wrote that

there was nothing he felt needed correction, and he made no effort whatever to influence what I had undertaken to do.

VII

I should like to suggest in conclusion that, whatever one's disagreements
or criticisms, Nehru emerges as both an outstanding literary figure of our
epoch, and as an important political force. This is so whether one considers his exposition of his evolving credo, so often formulated during
periods of greatest stress, or his writings about modern history; his commentaries on political events up to 1950, or on the background against
which such happenings may be viewed. For he has, after all, been
responsible for helping bring to fruition the greatest peaceful, democratic, social revolution of our time, and for long headed the largest democracy in the world.

I should like to suggest further that, in reading these volumes, the
history of India, as well as her geographical situation, be kept in mind;
that it be recalled that the major part of what is included here was set down
while India was still under foreign rule, and that the heritage of colonialism inevitably influenced decisions Nehru made even after India gained
her freedom.

Despite the fact that Nehru so consistently functioned at the storm
center of life, he once noted with profound interest how greatly Buddhist
monks in Ceylon were respected wherever they went. He was deeply
impressed by their peace and calm, by their "strange detachment from
the cares of the world". Yet, even while regarding "them with some
envy, with just a faint yearning for a haven", he realized fully that his
own "lot was a different one cast in storms and tempests". He saw
clearly that there was, in fact, no possible haven for him, since even "the
tempests within" him were quite "as stormy as those outside".[1]

Thus it is that, despite the painful sense of loneliness Nehru experienced, beginning in his childhood, and the many risks he endured—without
complaint or self-pity—he steadfastly faced the inexorable fact that had
he found himself protected in any seemingly "safe harbor", he would
have been neither contented nor happy there. Inevitably, he had to pay
the price demanded of all who take complex public responsibility over a
long period of time, buffeted by the often furious and cruelly shifting
winds of reality.

[1] T.F., p. 198-99.

A Postscript : Although these volumes are going to press just after Nehru's death, no alteration has been made in the text or dedication (but excerpts from his extraordinary will have been added to the appendix). It was always intended that the publication should appear in the fall-winter of 1964–65, on the occasion of Nehru's seventy-fifth birthday (November 14, 1964) and the fifteenth anniversary of the birth of the Republic of India (January 26, 1950). It is with the deepest sorrow that these additional lines are being appended on the very day on which the extraordinary man whom this publication honors is being cremated. Perhaps the very fact of his death may serve to heighten the world's understanding of the significance of Nehru's noble battle for the freedom not only of India but of mankind as a whole.

New York,
May 28, 1964

KEY TO ABBREVIATIONS
USED IN FOOTNOTES

A.	*Asia Magazine.*
A.B.P.	*Amrita Bazar Patrika.*
A.C.B.	Connell, John. *Auchinleck—A Critical Biography.*
A.I.C.C.	All India Congress Committee Report.
B.A.I.	Bright, J. S. *Before and After Independence.*
B.I.S.J.N. (I).	Bright, J. S. *Important Speeches of Jawaharlal Nehru* (1922–1946).
B.I.S.J.N. (II).	Bright, J. S. *Important Speeches of Jawaharlal Nehru* (1946–1957).
B.J.	Bolitho, Hector. *Jinnah.*
B.L.J.N.	Bright, J. S. *The Life of Jawaharlal Nehru.*
B.O.L.	Nehru, Jawaharlal. *A Bunch of Old Letters.*
B.S.I.	Brailsford, H. N. *Subject India.*
B.S.W.J.N.	Bright, J. S. *Selected Writings of Jawaharlal Nehru* (1916–1950).
C.A.D.	Constituent Assembly Debates.
C.B.	Congress Bulletin.
C.D.N.	Narasimhaiah, C.D. *Jawaharlal Nehru.*
C.I.G.T.	Nehru, Jawaharlal. *Can Indians Get Together?*
C.M.	*Jawaharlal Nehru on The Cripps Mission.*
C.M.N.	Chablani and Chablani. *Motilal Nehru.*
C.S.W.	Nehru, Jawaharlal. *China, Spain and the War.*
D.A.F.R. (IV).	Goodrich, Leland M., ed. *Documents on American Foreign Relations.*
D.I.	Nehru, Jawaharlal. *The Discovery of India.*
D.Q.	Moon, Penderel. *Divide and Quit.*
E.I.P.	Philips, C. H. *The Evolution of India and Pakistan.*
E.M.I.	Nehru, Jawaharlal. *Eighteen Months in India.*
F.	Nehru, Jawaharlal. "India's Day of Reckoning," *Fortune Magazine.*
F.A.	Nehru, Jawaharlal. "Changing India", *Foreign Affairs.*
F.E.S.	*Far Eastern Survey.*
F.F.Y.P.	*The First Five Year Plan.*
F.O.I.	*Facts on India.*
G.I.A.	Gunther, John. *Inside Asia.*
G.I.I.S.	Government of India Information Services.
G.W.H.	Nehru, Jawaharlal. *Glimpses of World History.*
H.I.N.C. (I).	Sitaramayya, Dr. Pattabhi. *The History of the Indian National Congress, 1885–1935.*

H.I.N.C. (II).	Sitaramayya, Dr. Pattabhi. *The History of the Indian National Congress, 1935–1947.*
I.A.	Nehru, Jawaharlal. *Independence and After (1946–1949).*
I.A.A.	*India and the Aggressors.*
I.A.R.	*Indian Annual Register.*
I.C.L.C.	Nehru, Jawaharlal. "India Can Learn From China", *Asia and the Americas.*
I.F.P.	Nehru, Jawaharlal. *India's Foreign Policy.*
I.G.M.	*Indiagram.*
I.I.	Nehru, Jawaharlal. *Letter to African Leaders.*
I.N.	*India News.*
I.P.C.	Brown, W. Norman. *India, Pakistan, Ceylon.*
I.Q.R.	*Indian Quarterly Register.*
I.T.	*India Today.*
I.T.W.	Nehru, Jawaharlal. *India and the World.*
I.W.C.	Nehru, Jawaharlal. *Indian Writers in Council.*
I.W.F.	Azad, Maulana Abul Kalam. *India Wins Freedom.*
I.W.N.	*India What Next?*
J.N.A.	Nehru, Jawaharlal. *An Autobiography.*
K.F.S.	*Kashmir—A Factual Survey.*
K.U.N.	*Kashmir and the United Nations.*
L.	Nehru, Jawaharlal. "Letter to a Young Chinese Journalist", *Life Magazine.*
L.M.	*Labour Monthly.*
L.M.G.	Fischer, Louis. *The Life of Mahatma Gandhi.*
L.T.P.I.	Lumby, E. W. R. *The Transfer of Power in India.*
M.B.	Brecher, Michael. *Nehru: A Political Biography.*
M.G.L.I.	Ismay, Lord. *The Memoirs of General Lord Ismay.*
M.H.I.	Krishnamurti, Y. G. *Jawaharlal Nehru: The Man and His Ideas.*
M.J.N.	Moraes, Frank. *Jawaharlal Nehru.*
M.L.P. (I), (II).	Pyarelal. *Mahatma Gandhi—The Last Phase.*
M.M.	Campbell-Johnson, Alan. *Mission with Mountbatten.*
M.R.	"Chanakya" (Jawaharlal Nehru). "The Rashtrapati", *Modern Review.*
N.H.	*National Herald.*
N.I.A.	Nehru, Jawaharlal. *Inside America.*
N.L.H.S.	Hutheesing, Krishna Nehru. *Nehru's Letters to His Sister.*
N.O.G.	Nehru, Jawaharlal. *Nehru on Gandhi.*
N.R.S.	Singh, Anup. *Nehru the Rising Star of India.*
N.S.	*Jawaharlal Nehru's Speeches, 1949–1953.*
N.Y.T.	*The New York Times.*
N.Y.T.M.	Nehru, Jawaharlal. "Colonialism Must Go", *The New York Times Magazine.*
P.A.	*Pacific Affairs.*

P.A.I.	Nehru, Jawaharlal. *Peace and India.*
P.H.	Nehru, Jawaharlal. *Prison Humours.*
P.M.U.N.	*Correspondence between the Prime Ministers of Pakistan and India regarding Peaceful Settlements of Indo-Pakistan Disputes.*
R.E.W.	Nehru, Jawaharlal. *Recent Essays and Writings.*
R.H.C.	Rao, M. V. Ramana. *A Short History of the Indian National Congress.*
R.I.N.C.	*Report of the 42nd Indian National Congress.*
R.M.L.V.	Murphy, Ray. *Last Viceroy.*
R.T.C.	*Rabindranath Tagore. A Centenary Volume (1861–1961).*
S.A.B.P.	*Sunday Amrita Bazar Patrika.*
S.D.A.A. (II).	Poplai, S. L. *Selected Documents on Asian Affairs.*
S.D.I.C. (I), (II).	Gwyer, Sir Maurice, and A. Appadorai. *Speeches and Documents on the Indian Constitution 1921–47.*
S.I.	Spear, Percival. *India—A Modern History.*
S.N.	Zakaria, Rafiq. *A Study of Nehru.*
S.R.	Nehru, Jawaharlal. *Soviet Russia.*
T.A.R.	*The Asiatic Review.*
T.A.Y.	*Twice A Year.*
T.D.G.	Tendulkar, D. G. *Mahatma.*
T.F.	Nehru, Jawaharlal. *Toward Freedom.*
T.I.	*Times of India.*
T.L.	*The Leader.*
T.M.	Mende, Tibor. *Nehru: Conversations on India and World Affairs.*
T.N.	Nanda, B. R. *The Nehrus—Motilal and Jawaharlal.*
T.N.R.	"A Cable From Pandit Nehru", *The New Republic.*
T.P.I.	Menon, V. P. *The Transfer of Power in India.*
T.R.	Chakravarty, Amiya. *A Tagore Reader.*
T.T.N.	Gopal, Ram. *The Trials of Nehru.*
U.I.	Nehru, Jawaharlal. *The Unity of India.*
V.B.Q.	Nehru, Jawaharlal. "Tagore and Gandhi", *Visva-Bharati Quarterly.*
V.I.	*Voice of India.*
V.M.M.	Isherwood, Christopher. *Vedanta for Modern Man.*
V.S.N.	Sheean, Vincent. *Nehru: The Years of Power.*
V.T.A.	Nehru, Jawaharlal. *Visit to America.*
W.P.A.U.N.	Holborn, Louise W. *War and Peace Aims of the United Nations.*
W.P.J.K.	*White Paper on Jammu and Kashmir.*

CONTENTS OF VOLUME ONE

PART TWO

1930–1933

PART THREE
1934–1936

PART FOUR
1937–1938

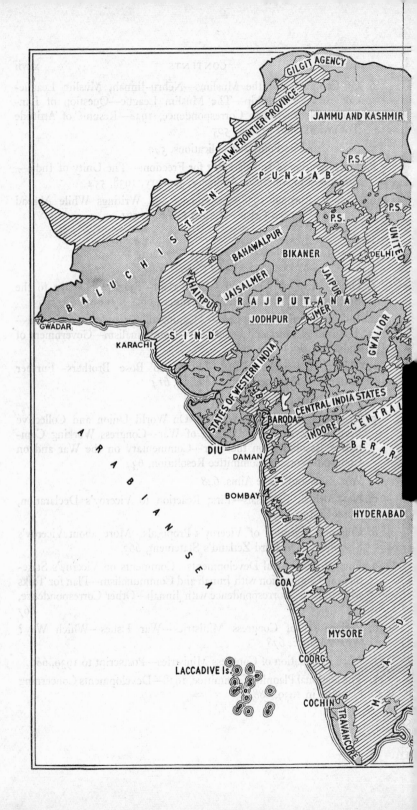

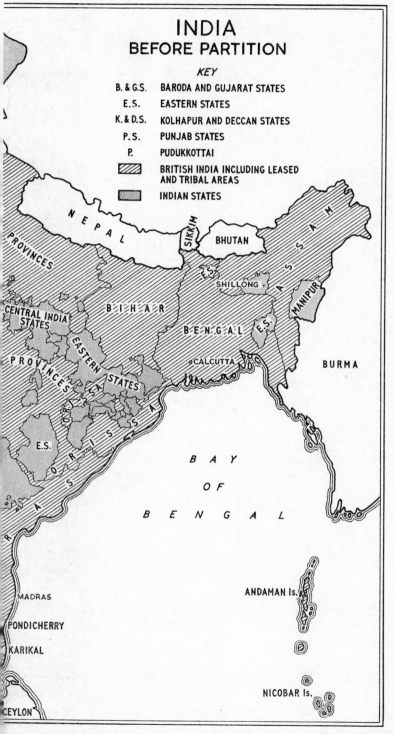

INDIA
BEFORE PARTITION

KEY

B. & G.S.	BARODA AND GUJARAT STATES
E.S.	EASTERN STATES
K. & D.S.	KOLHAPUR AND DECCAN STATES
P.S.	PUNJAB STATES
P.	PUDUKKOTTAI
	BRITISH INDIA INCLUDING LEASED AND TRIBAL AREAS
	INDIAN STATES

NEPAL

PROVINCES

SIKKIM

BHUTAN

A S S A M

SHILLONG

MANIPUR

B I H A R

CENTRAL INDIA STATES

E.S.

B E N G A L

EASTERN STATES

E.S.

CALCUTTA

BURMA

PROVINCES

O R I S S A

E.S.

B A Y

O F

B E N G A L

ANDAMAN Is.

MADRAS

PONDICHERRY

KARIKAL

NICOBAR Is.

CEYLON

Government of India

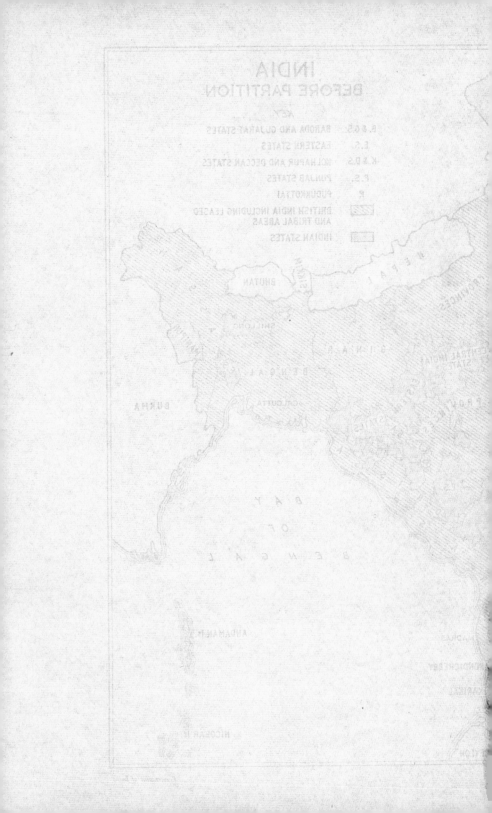

PART ONE

Youth—Early Political Development
(to 1929)

Two things are . . . dear to me . . . independence for
[India] and equality between man and man.[1]

*

Whatever you . . . write . . . never write out of fear.[2]

*

I suppose my father and Gandhiji have been the chief
personal influences in my life. But outside influences
do not carry me away. There is a tendency to resist
being influenced. Still influences do work slowly and
unconsciously.[3]

[1] Quoted in M.B., p. 125.
[2] M.J.N., p. 488.
[3] A. (Feb., 1939), p. 95.

I

Family Background—Early Childhood and Influences—Dawn of Nationalist Aspirations, 1899-1904—Political Developments

Family Background

[Jawaharlal Nehru was born in Allahabad, India, on November 14, 1889. The eldest child of Motilal and Swaruprani Nehru—distinguished Indians of Kashmiri Brahmin descent—he was educated at home by English governesses and private tutors, before being taken to England to continue his studies at the age of fifteen. Passionately eager to provide the finest possible education for his only son, Motilal sent Jawaharlal to Harrow in the autumn of 1905; Trinity College, Cambridge, in 1907.

During Jawaharlal's childhood, Motilal Nehru was a brilliantly successful, affluent and influential lawyer who, although deeply versed in Indo-Persian culture, greatly admired the British and was strongly attracted by the West. At first convinced that "a progressive Westernization" combined with "constitutional evolution" would bring freedom to his beleaguered and beloved land, by 1919-1920 Motilal had sharply altered his views, thereafter becoming a devoted supporter of Mohandas K. Gandhi, foremost figure in India's non-violent struggle for independence.

Terming himself a born rebel, Motilal ardently claimed that as long as one drop of Nehru blood remained in any living child, there would not and could not be any surrender.[1]]

Early Childhood and Influences

My childhood [Jawaharlal was to observe many years later, during one of his numerous imprisonments] was . . . a sheltered and uneventful one. I listened to the grown-up talk of my cousins without always understanding all of it. Often this talk related to the overbearing character and insulting manners of the English people, as well as Eurasians, toward Indians, and how it was the duty of every Indian to stand up to this and not to tolerate

[1] C.M.N., unnumbered introductory p.

3

it. Instances of conflicts between the rulers and the ruled were common and were fully discussed. It was a notorious fact that whenever an Englishman killed an Indian he was acquitted by a jury of his own countrymen. In railway trains compartments were reserved for Europeans, and, however crowded the train might be—and they used to be terribly crowded —no Indian was allowed to travel in them, even though they were empty. Even an unreserved compartment would be taken possession of by an Englishman, and he would not allow any Indian to enter it. Benches and chairs were also reserved for Europeans in public parks and other places. I was filled with resentment against the alien rulers of my country who misbehaved in this manner; and, whenever an Indian hit back, I was glad. Not infrequently one of my cousins or one of their friends became personally involved in these individual encounters, and then of course we all got very excited over it. One of the cousins was the strong man of the family, and he loved to pick a quarrel with an Englishman, or more frequently with Eurasians, who, perhaps to show off their oneness with the ruling race, were often even more offensive than the English official or merchant. Such quarrels took place especially during railway journeys.

Much as I began to resent the presence and behavior of the alien rulers, I had no feeling whatever, so far as I can remember, against individual Englishmen. I had had English governesses, and occasionally I saw English friends of my father's visiting him. In my heart I rather admired the English.[1]

Dawn of Nationalist Aspirations, 1899–1904

When I was ten years old ... the Boer War was ... going on; this interested me, and all my sympathies were with the Boers. ...

Father was then in Europe. ... [His] visit ... led to an internal storm in the Kashmiri [Brahmin] community in India. He refused to perform any *prayashchit* or purification ceremony on his return. Some years previously another Kashmiri [Brahmin] had gone to England to be called to the Bar. On his return the orthodox members of the community had refused to have anything to do with him, and he was outcast, although he performed the *prayashchit* ceremony. This had resulted in the splitting up of the community into two more or less equal halves. Many Kashmiri young men went subsequently to Europe for their studies and on their return joined the reformist section, but only after a formal ceremony of

[1] T.F., pp. 20–21.

purification. This ceremony itself was a bit of a farce, and there was little of religion in it. It merely signified an outward conformity and a submission to the group will. Having done so, each person indulged in all manner of heterodox activities and mixed and fed with [non-Brahmins] and non-Hindus.

Father went a step further and refused to go through any ceremony or to submit in any way, even outwardly and formally, to a so-called purification. A great deal of heat was generated, chiefly because of father's aggressive and rather disdainful attitude, and ultimately a considerable number of Kashmiris joined father, thus forming a third group. Within a few years these groups gradually merged into one another as ideas changed and the old restrictions fell. Large numbers of Kashmiri young men and girls have visited Europe or America for their studies, and no question has arisen of their performing any ceremonies on their return. Food restrictions have almost entirely gone, except in the case of a handful of orthodox people, chiefly old ladies, and interdining with non-Kashmiris, Moslems, and non-Indians is common. Purdah has disappeared among Kashmiris even as regards other communities. . . . Intermarriage with other communities is still not popular, although (increasingly) instances occur. Both my sisters have married non-Kashmiris. . . .

When I was about eleven, a new resident tutor, Ferdinand T. Brooks, came and took charge of me. . . . He was a keen theosophist who had been recommended to my father by Mrs Annie Besant. For nearly three years he was with me, and in many ways he influenced me greatly. The only other tutor I had at the time was a dear old Pandit who was supposed to teach me Hindi and Sanskrit. . . . Brooks developed in me a taste for reading . . . [and] also initiated me into the mysteries of science. . . .

Apart from my studies, . . . Brooks brought a new influence to bear upon me which affected me powerfully for a while. This was theosophy. He used to have weekly meetings of theosophists in his rooms, and I attended them and gradually imbibed theosophical phraseology and ideas. There were metaphysical arguments, and discussions about reincarnation and the astral and other supernatural bodies, and auras, and the doctrine of karma, and references not only to big books by Madame Blavatsky and other theosophists but to the Hindu scriptures, the Buddhist *Dhammapada*, Pythagoras, Apollonius Tyanaeus, and various philosophers and mystics. I did not understand much that was said, but it all sounded very mysterious and fascinating, and I felt that here was the key to the secrets of the universe. For the first time I began to think, consciously and deliberately, of religion and other worlds. The Hindu religion especially went up in my estimation; not the ritual or ceremonial part, but its great books, the *Upanishads* and the *Bhagavad Gita*. I did not understand them, of course, but they seemed very wonderful. I dreamed of astral bodies and imagined myself flying vast distances. This dream of flying high up in the air (without any appliance) has indeed been a frequent one throughout my life; and sometimes it has been vivid and realistic and the countryside seemed to lie underneath me in a vast panorama. I do not know how the modern interpreters of dreams, Freud and others, would interpret this dream.

Mrs Annie Besant visited Allahabad in those days and delivered several addresses on theosophical subjects. I was deeply moved by her oratory and returned from her speeches dazed and as in a dream. I decided to join the Theosophical Society, although I was only thirteen then. When I went to ask father's permission, he laughingly gave it; he did not seem to attach importance to the subject either way. I was a little hurt by his lack of feeling. Great as he was in many ways in my eyes, I felt that he was lacking in spirituality. As a matter of fact he was an old theosophist, having joined the Society in its early days when Madame Blavatsky was in India. Curiosity probably led him to it more than religion, and he soon dropped out of it; but some of his friends, who had joined with him, persevered and rose high in the spiritual hierarchy of the Society.

So I became a member of the Theosophical Society at thirteen, and Mrs Besant herself performed the ceremony of initiation, which consisted of good advice and instruction in some mysterious signs, probably a relic of freemasonry. . . .

Soon after F. T. Brooks left me I lost touch with theosophy, and in a remarkably short time (partly because I went to school in England) theosophy left my life completely. But I have no doubt that those years with F. T. Brooks left a deep impress upon me, and I feel that I owe a debt to him and to theosophy. But I am afraid that theosophists have since then gone down in my estimation. Instead of the chosen ones they seem to be very ordinary folk, liking security better than risk, a soft job more than the martyr's lot. But for Mrs Besant I always had the warmest admiration.

The next important event that I remember affecting me was the Russo–Japanese War. Japanese victories stirred up my enthusiasm, and I waited eagerly for the papers for fresh news daily. . . .

Nationalistic ideas filled my mind. I mused of Indian freedom and

Asiatic freedom from the thralldom of Europe. I dreamed of brave deeds, of how, sword in hand, I would fight for India and help in freeing her.[1]

Political Developments

[It is within this context—against this background—that we see young Jawaharlal's life unfold. We perceive swiftly that great as was Motilal's love for and effect upon his spirited and talented son, painful differences of opinion inevitably were to arise between two individuals possessed of such extraordinarily passionate convictions.

Despite Motilal's exceptional independence of mind and spirit; his fearless defiance of confining orthodoxies, stultifying superstitions and blind prejudice within India—as well as his equally courageous opposition to the manifold indignities of foreign rule—he was, by nature, far more of a "moderate" than Jawaharlal ever was to become. Thus it is perhaps to the credit of both father and son that, when the latter was still quite youthful, he not only should have opposed so commanding a figure as Motilal on any number of occasions, but even, at times, have influenced him. (Ultimately, Jawaharlal similarly was to help alter the entire course of contemporary Indian history, his role in so doing becoming second only to that of the other paramount influence on his early life: Mahatma Gandhi.

In the period just before Jawaharlal left for England in May, 1905, at the age of fifteen, tensions between "colonial" India and Britain became sharply intensified. Although later sections will describe political developments in greater detail, a brief elucidation of what was occurring during Jawaharlal's childhood may help to clarify the general situation in India at the time.

Lord Curzon, appointed Viceroy for India toward the end of the nineteenth century, bluntly stated in 1900 that, in his view, the nationalist-minded Indian Congress Movement (founded in 1885), was "tottering to its fall", one of his "great ambitions while in India" being "to assist it to a peaceful demise".[2]

By 1905, when Lord Curzon resigned, he had succeeded in administering a severe shock to India, by way of his ill-fated measure of partitioning the province of Bengal. Whether or not, as Viceroy, he viewed himself as concerned with reorganizing the administration of India merely in the interest of improved efficiency and coordination, as he claimed, in the eyes of India's nationalist leaders he seemed intent upon centralizing Britain's power in India at the expense of local or provincial legislatures. His patronizing, often arrogant attitude toward Indians proved equally infuriating and insulting.

[1] Ibid., pp. 26–30.
[2] S.I., p. 318. Copyright © by the University of Michigan 1961.

Rajendra Prasad, an influential member of Congress—later to become free India's first President—has recorded how decisively Lord Curzon's act of partitioning Bengal destroyed confidence in British rule: "The great agitation that followed . . . was an index of the rising tide of popular national consciousness which had not a little been influenced by world events, such as the victory of Japan over Russia in the beginning of the 20th century."[1]

Ironically, Lord Curzon's repressive action with respect to Bengal served to give added stimulus to the Indian nationalist movement, as did his "Official Secrets Act whereby anybody could be arrested on suspicion" (the proof of innocence being "the responsibility of the accused, while the prosecution was relieved of the duty of proving the guilt").[2]

While Lord Curzon was Viceroy, not only did local self-government in India become a mere sham in the eyes of Congress leaders, but education was both crippled and mutilated. Once Curzon's régime was terminated, attempts were made to achieve improvement of the country's administration, to press for increased substitution of Indians for Europeans in government, and to alleviate the poverty of the Indian people.[3]

Although Motilal Nehru had been briefly involved in Indian National Congress activities in the late nineteenth century, he was no longer a Congress delegate during the period immediately preceding Lord Curzon's raising of India's "political temperature". The partition of Bengal not only drew Motilal back into the political arena, but inspired the also moderate Gopal Krishna Gokhale to initiate a constitutional reform movement—or "agitation", as it was called—which succeeded admirably in "voicing the sentiments . . . hopes and . . . illusions of the first generation of Congressmen".[4] As a result of such developments, the already outstanding Gokhale became the respected leader of the Moderates in Congress, and, for the time being, "the mentor of Gandhi and the idol of Motilal."[5]

Lord Curzon's ironic aptitude in galvanizing those forces in India opposed to British Imperialism helped also to widen the gulf between the Moderates and Extremists within Congress—a breach soon to become increasingly pronounced. It was, in fact, widely felt that Lord Curzon served as "a godsend to the Extremists", who began seriously to ponder "whether self-government within the Empire was at all a practicable ideal."[6] Under the circumstances, the Extremists, led by Bal Gangadhar Tilak—with whom Motilal initially disagreed, but whom Jawaharlal was greatly to admire—were swift to advocate such vigorous measures as the

---

[1] H.I.N.C. (Vol. I), Introduction, 1st p., unnumbered.
[2] R.H.C., p. 50
[3] Ibid., p. 52.
[4] T.N., p. 55.
[5] Ibid., p. 54.
[6] Ibid., p. 56.

boycotting of British goods, and the promotion of India's own industries, two decisively important planks in the mounting campaign against British rule in India.]

My father was a rebel against many social customs. That, of course, had some influence on me in my early days. By modern standards, my father would be called a conservative in many ways. But in those days he was a great rebel. And a man of very strong character. That influenced me greatly and so I grew up in this rather composite environment with the steadily increasing influence of the West, or rather of the English West, through the reading of books ... stories and ... magazines. With that I went to England.[1]

---

2 | The Goal of Swaraj—Harrow, 1905–1907— Political Background of the Period— Cambridge, 1907–1910—Events in India— Brief Altercations with Motilal Nehru

The Goal of Swaraj

[Early in 1906, soon after Jawaharlal had left for England, Congress activities entered upon a new phase. So also did Indo–British relations. The President of the 1906 Calcutta session of Congress, Dadabhai Naoroji, decided to work toward Swaraj, or self-government, a goal far more radical than that advocated previously by such Moderates as Gokhale and Motilal.

Since, at the time, identification with Gokhale's "constitutional methods of agitation" seemed quite natural for Motilal, in view of his "legal training and background",[2] he was swift to deplore "the fact that the subversive ideas of the Extremists" were building a ready response in "the young blood of schools and colleges. . . . Little did he know that the contagion had travelled to England where his only son was at school at Harrow."[3]]

---

[1] T.M., p. 10. Reprinted from *Nehru: Conversations on Indian and World Affairs* by Tibor Mende, with the permission of the publisher, George Braziller, Inc. © 1956.
[2] T.N., p. 59. [3] Ibid., p. 61.

1*

Harrow, 1905–1907

[Immediately after Jawaharlal entered Harrow, Motilal wrote that the "pangs of separation" he was suffering were for his son's "own good"; to make "a real man of you, which you are bound to be. . . . I look upon you, my dear son, as the man who will build upon the foundations I have laid and have the satisfaction of seeing a noble structure of renown rearing up its head to the skies. . . . I have not the slightest doubt that you will rise to all my expectations and more. You have enough work to keep you engaged . . . work includes the preservation of health. Be perfect in body and mind and this is the only return we seek for tearing ourselves from you."[1]

Dr Joseph Wood, Headmaster of Harrow, wrote to Motilal in November, 1905: "Every master speaks well of your boy, both as to his work and his conduct. He has distinct ability, is already ahead of his form. . . . I am fully satisfied with him in every way."[2]]

I was greatly interested in the [British] General Election, which took place, as far as I remember, at the end of 1905 and which ended in a great Liberal victory. Early in 1906 our form master asked us about the new Government, and, much to his surprise, I was the only boy in his form who could give him much information on the subject.[3]

[Jawaharlal to Motilal, March 4, 1906.] I must confess, I cannot mix properly with English boys. My tastes and inclinations are quite different. Here boys, older than me and in higher forms . . ., take great interest in things which appear to me childish. . . . I almost wish sometimes that I had not come to Harrow, but gone straight to the 'Varsity. I have no doubt that public schools are excellent things and their training essential to every boy, but I have come here very late to really enjoy the life.[4]

[From answer to a letter from Motilal about tensions between the Moderates and Extremists at the 1906 Calcutta Congress Session, which gives an early intimation of Jawaharlal's later preoccupation with Congress "harmony".] I am sorry to hear . . . that the Congress was not a success. I am impatiently waiting . . . to know the result of the proceedings. I do hope the different parties worked smoothly together, and there were no dissensions among the delegates. A most foolish thing this seems to me; for not only do they do no good to themselves but they do harm

[1] Ibid., p. 68.
[2] Ibid., p. 70.
[3] T.F., p. 31.
[4] T.N., pp. 79–80.

to their country they both pretend to serve. There couldn't have been any great difference or disagreement among the delegates, as our friends the Anglo-Indians would hardly have failed to wire the fact over here.[1]

Political Background of the Period

[Throughout 1906–1907 the slogan Swaraj—self-rule, or self-government —began to fire the imagination of the Indian people. Annulment of Lord Curzon's partition of Bengal also was demanded. Swadeshi—the doctrine of promoting and encouraging indigenous industries, an offshoot of anti-partition agitation—gained impetus, as did the struggle for widespread national education.]

Right through the years . . . 1906 and 1907 news from India had been agitating me. I got meager enough accounts from the English papers; but even that little showed that big events were happening at home. There were deportations, and Bengal seemed to be in an uproar, and Tilak's name was often flashed from [India], and there was Swadeshi [meaning literally, "of one's own country"; thus, the encouragement of Indian trade and industry, associated with the boycotting of British products] and boycott. All this stirred me tremendously; but there was not a soul in Harrow to whom I could talk about it. . . .

A prize I got for good work at school was one of G. M. Trevelyan's Garibaldi books. This fascinated me, and soon I obtained the other two volumes of the series and studied the whole Garibaldi story . . . carefully. Visions of similar deeds in India came before me, of a gallant fight for freedom, and in my mind India and Italy got strangely mixed together. Harrow seemed a rather small and restricted place for these ideas, and I wanted to go to the wider sphere of the university. So I induced father to agree to this and left Harrow after only two years' stay, which was much less than the usual period.[2]

Cambridge, 1907–1910

Cambridge, Trinity College, the beginning of October 1907, my age seventeen, or rather approaching eighteen. I felt elated at being an under-graduate with a great deal of freedom, compared to school, to do what I

[1] Ibid., p. 81.
[2] T.F., p. 32.

chose. I had got out of the shackles of boyhood and felt at last that I could claim to be a grown-up.[1]

I paid a visit to Ireland at the beginning of Sinn Fein. I was much interested in it.[2]

[Jawaharlal to Motilal, from Dublin, September 12, 1907.] In your last letter . . . you asked me not to go near Belfast on account of the riots, but I would have dearly liked to have been there for them. About a fortnight ago, there was a chance of our having similar scenes here, but to my mortification the whole thing ended in a fiasco. The tramway employees were on the point of striking, and if they had done so, there would have been a little fighting in the streets of Dublin.

Have you heard of the Sinn Fein in Ireland ? . . . It is a most interesting movement and resembles very closely the so-called Extremist movement in India. Their policy is not to beg for favours but to wrest them. They do not want to fight England by arms, but "to ignore her, boycott her, and quietly assume the administration of Irish affairs". . . . Among people, who ought to know, this movement is causing . . . consternation. They say that if its policy is adopted by the bulk of the country, English rule will be a thing of the past.[3]

The Indians in Cambridge had a society called the "Majlis". We discussed political problems there often but in somewhat unreal debates. More effort was spent in copying parliamentary and the University Union style and mannerisms than in grappling with the subject. Frequently I went to the Majlis, but during my three years I hardly spoke there. I could not get over my shyness and diffidence. . . .

In the Majlis and in private talks Indian students often used the most extreme language when discussing Indian politics. They even talked in terms of admiration of the acts of violence that were then beginning in Bengal. Later I was to find that these very persons were to become members of the Indian Civil Service, High Court judges, very staid and sober lawyers, and the like. Few of these parlor firebrands took any effective part in Indian political movements subsequently.

In London there was the student center opened by the India Office. This was universally regarded by Indians, with a great deal of justifica-

[1] Ibid., p. 32.
[2] T.M., p. 15. Reprinted from *Nehru: Conversations on Indian and World Affairs* by Tibor Mende, with the permission of the publisher, George Braziller, Inc. © 1956.
[3] T.N., pp. 89–90.

tion, as a device to spy on Indian students. Many Indians, however, had to put up with it, whether they wanted to or not, as it became almost impossible to enter a university without its recommendation.[1]

[When Motilal visited Jawaharlal at Cambridge in 1907, he warned: "Do not go near the Majlis." Jawaharlal's reply: "I went the other day to a meeting of the Majlis here . . . just to see if they were as bad as they were painted. I failed to discover anything reprehensible."[2]]

[Jawaharlal to Motilal, October 24, 1907.] I have just come back . . . from a lecture on "Socialism and the University Man". . . . The lecturer was George Bernard Shaw, about whom you must have heard a good deal. I was more interested in the man than in the subject of the lecture, and that was the reason of my going there."[3]

Many of the people I met at Cambridge or during the vacations in London or elsewhere talked learnedly about books and literature and history and politics and economics.[4]

I would say that it was really at Cambridge that, broadly speaking, certain socialistic ideas—partly Fabian Socialism, partly some slightly more aggressive socialistic ideas—developed. But it was all very academic. . . .

I do not think I can mention any particular person who had a very marked influence on me. But men like Bernard Shaw, Bertrand Russell, Keynes the economist, who were lecturing there. . . .

I was against British rule in India; very strongly so. . . . Any book . . . that was written about India by either an Indian or an Englishman, which brought out the harm done to India by British rule, immediately appealed to me. . . .

In England, in my early days, too, I was much influenced by things like the story of the Italian Republic, by Mazzini, Cavour and Garibaldi; by the Irish struggle. . . .

I have always been interested in the French Revolution. I read . . . books on that, too, and it excited me. [As did a] kind of vague . . . national-ism . . . [and] freedom movement . . . aiming at some kind of equality . . . these broad things, . . . a kind of Utopian Socialism, not scientific at all really.[5]

[1] T.F., p. 35.   [2] T.N., p. 89.   [3] Ibid., p. 96.   [4] T.F., p. 33.
[5] T.M., pp. 13–15. Reprinted from *Nehru: Conversations on Indian and World Affairs* by Tibor Mende, with the permission of the publisher, George Braziller, Inc. © 1956.

Events in India—Brief Altercations with Motilal Nehru

[The influence of the Extremists, which had increased during 1906, waned considerably in 1907. Subsequently the measures they had been promulgating, such as Swaraj and the boycott, were swiftly disavowed by the Moderates, as the power of the latter mounted. Although an open break had been avoided between the two wings of Congress in 1906, inter-group tensions reached a "bursting point" during the following year. (The Extremists did not become active again until the Home Rule Leagues were founded a decade later, and as a result of Gandhi's influence in 1916. In the early 1900s it was quite naturally the Extremists, however, rather than the Moderates, whom the British sought to suppress.)

Already aroused by the constitutional reform movement of the Moderates, Motilal Nehru was pushed "to the center of the political stage" early in 1907. Asked to be President of a Provincial Conference, he accepted the invitation with some misgivings. He knew that he was more moderate than the Moderates, whereas even the students in his province —whom the Extremist leader Tilak recently had addressed—were opposed even to the Moderates.]

[Jawaharlal to Motilal, February 19, 1907.] I am sure . . . you will be as successful in the new line as you have been in other fields. You have already kept away from [politics] far too long, but that, I hope, will add a new zest to it. . . . However you disagree with the details of the Congress programme . . . you cannot but agree with its general aim. . . . Your [presidential] address is certain to be a brilliant one; only I hope it will not be too moderate. Indians are as a rule too much so, and require a little stirring up.[1]

Father was never moderate in anything except his politics, and step by step his nature drove him from even that remnant of moderation. A man of strong feelings, strong passions, tremendous pride, and great strength of will, he was very far from the moderate type. And yet in 1907 and 1908 and for some years afterward, he was undoubtedly a moderate of Moderates, and he was bitter against the Extremists, though I believe he admired Tilak.[2]

The political situation in India had drawn my father into more active

[1] T.N., p. 86.
[2] T.F., p. 36.

politics, and I was pleased at this although I did not agree with his politics.[1]

[Jawaharlal to Motilal. Reaction to article by Motilal that had appeared in the *Pioneer* (India).] I had till now an idea that you were not so very moderate as you would have me believe. [Your] article almost makes me think that you are "immoderately Moderate". I would have said that the article had been written by a person with strong loyalist tendencies if I had not known you better.[2]

[Jawaharlal to Motilal, January 2, 1908. Of the current split between the Moderates and Extremists in Congress.] It is of course a great pity that such a split should have occurred. But it was sure to come and the sooner we have it, the better. You will most probably throw all the blame on Tilak and the Extremists. They may have been to blame for it, but the Moderates had certainly a lot to do with it.... The Moderates may represent part of the country, but they seem to think, or at any rate try to make others believe, that they are the "natural leaders" and representatives of the whole country. The manner in which some of them try to ignore and belittle all those who differ from them would be annoying, if it was not ridiculous. I firmly believe ... that there will hardly be any so-called Moderates left in a very few years' time. By the methods they are following at present, they are simply hastening the doom of their party.

[From Motilal to Jawaharlal, January 24, 1908: "I am favoured with your views as to the conduct of the Moderates and Extremists ... and feel flattered by the compliment you have paid to the Moderates, knowing of course that your father is one."]

[Jawaharlal to Motilal.] You don't approve of my opinions, but really I can't help holding them in the present state of affairs ... anyhow I have not the presumption of imagining that my opinions are infallible.... The Government must be feeling very pleased with you at your attitude.

[The storm between father and son abated by April, 1908. Motilal to Jawaharlal: "I do not of course approve of your politics and have on certain occasions expressed myself very strongly, as you know, I can, when I wish to. This is, however, neither here nor there. My love for you knows

[1] Ibid., pp. 35–36.
[2] T.N., p. 90.

no bounds, and unless there is some very remarkable change in me, I do not see how it can be affected." [1]]

[Jawaharlal to Motilal, June 4, 1908.] *The Saturday Review* . . . made a very wise remark a few weeks ago. It said that Indians were bound to have self-government but—and herein lies the difficulty—not before a few aeons of geological time! This may mean anything between a few million years and a wholly incomprehensible period. The chief difficulty was the want of education and some million generations will be required to educate them (Indians) up to the Colonial standard.

[Jawaharlal to Motilal, 1909? After hearing Haldane, the British Secretary of State for War, on the new Officers' Training Corps.] If I were an Englishman, I should certainly take advantage of it [the Officers' Training Corps]. At the end of his speech [Haldane] was asked a number of questions, among them being one concerning Indians. The question was whether Indians could join the Officers' Training Corps and, at the end of their 'Varsity life, go out to India as officers. His answer to this was rather evasive. He said that it was an excellent idea . . . but, as the Indian army was quite separate from the English army, he could not say anything definite about it. The Corps here, as you know, does not take Indians. [2]

[Of further "thoughts" and "moods" while at Cambridge.] So far as political matters were concerned, I was . . . an Indian nationalist desiring India's freedom and rather inclined, in the context of Indian politics, to the more extreme wing. . . . I felt like any average Indian student would feel. There was nothing peculiar about it. [3]

During my stay at Cambridge the question [arose] as to what career I should take up. For a little while the Indian Civil Service was contemplated; there was a glamour about it still in those days. But this idea was dropped as neither my father nor I was keen on it. . . .

It is curious that, in spite of my growing extremism in politics, I did not then view with any strong disfavor the idea of joining the Indian Civil Service and thus becoming a cog in the British Government's administrative machine in India. Such an idea in later years would have been repellent to me. [4]

[1] Ibid., pp. 91–92.
[2] Ibid., pp. 97–98.
[3] Quoted in M.B., p. 49.
[4] T.F., p. 37.

3 | Return to India, 1912: First Interest in Politics

[After receiving his degree at Cambridge in June, 1910, Jawaharlal expressed a desire to go to Oxford instead of London, "to study something besides law. 'Law and Science are all very well in their own way [he informed his father], but no man, however great a lawyer he may be, will or should be excused for his want of knowledge in certain other subjects. I would much rather risk my success at the Bar than go through life as a mere lawyer with no interest in anything save the technicalities and trivialities of law.'"

Since Motilal disagreed with his son's preference for Oxford, London's Inner Temple was chosen as an alternative. The plan to attend the London School of Economics was denied because of Motilal's fear that "the study of economics . . . might distract" from concentration on the law.[1]

Upon his return to India in 1912, Jawaharlal joined the Allahabad High Court Bar, his first active interest in politics dating from that time.]

As I grew up and became engaged in activities which promised to lead to India's freedom, I became obsessed with the thought of India. What was this India that possessed me and beckoned to me continually, urging me to action so that we might realize some vague but deeply felt desire of our hearts? The initial urge came to me, I suppose, through pride, both individual and national, and the desire, common to all men, to resist another's domination and have freedom to live the life of our choice. It seemed monstrous to me that a great country like India, with a rich and immemorial past, should be bound hand and foot to a faraway island which imposed its will upon her. It was still more monstrous that this forcible union had resulted in poverty and degradation beyond measure. That was reason enough for me and for others to act.

But it was not enough to satisfy the questioning that arose within me. What is this India, apart from her physical and geographical aspects? What did she represent in the past; what gave strength to her then? How did she lose that old strength, and has she lost it completely? Does she represent anything vital now, apart from being the home of a vast number of human beings? How does she fit in to the modern world?

[1] T.N., pp. 119–20.

This wider international aspect of the problem grew upon me as I realized more and more how isolation was both undesirable and impossible. The future that took shape in my mind was one of intimate co-operation, politically, economically, culturally, between India and the other countries of the world. . . .

India was in my blood and there was much in her that instinctively thrilled me. . . . Yet I approached her almost as an alien critic, full of dislike for the present as well as for many of the relics of the past that I saw. To some extent I came to her via the West and looked at her as a friendly Westerner might have done. I was eager and anxious to change her outlook and appearance and give her the garb of modernity. And yet doubts rose within me. Did I know India, I who presumed to scrap much of her past heritage? There was a great deal that had to be scrapped, that must be scrapped; but surely India could not have been what she undoubtedly was, and could not have continued a cultured existence for thousands of years, if she had not possessed something very vital and enduring, something that was worth while. What was this something? . . .

Gradually a sense of reality began to creep into my mental picture of India and the land of my forefathers became peopled with living beings, who laughed and wept; loved and suffered; and among them were men who seemed to know life and understand it, and out of their wisdom they had built a structure which gave India a cultural stability which lasted for thousands of years. . . .

Slowly the long panorama of India's history unfolded itself before me, with its ups and downs, its triumphs and defeats. There seemed to me something unique about the continuity of a cultural tradition through five thousand years of history, of invasion and upheaval, a tradition which was widespread among the masses and powerfully influenced them. . . . And this panorama of the past gradually merged into the unhappy present, when India, for all her past greatness and stability, was a slave country, an appendage of Britain, and all over the world terrible and devastating war was raging and brutalizing humanity. But that vision of five thousand years gave me a new perspective, and the burden of the present seemed to grow lighter. The hundred and eighty years of British rule in India were just one of the unhappy interludes in her long story; she would find herself again; already the last page of this chapter was being written.[1]

[1] D.I., pp. 37-40.

4 | Of India before World War I— Morley-Minto Reforms

Of India before World War I

[In order to comprehend Jawaharlal's attitude concerning the general situation in India before World War I, it is essential to understand something of his own historical view of the cultural, economic and political background against which the Indian Nationalist Movement had been developing.]

It is interesting to note that the early waves of nationalism in India in the nineteenth century were religious and Hindu. The Muslims naturally could take no part in this Hindu nationalism. They kept apart. Having kept away from English education, the new ideas affected them less, and there was far less intellectual ferment amongst them. Many decades later they began to come out of their shell, and then, as with the Hindus, their nationalism took the shape of a Muslim nationalism, looking back to Islamic traditions and culture, and fearful of losing these because of the Hindu majority. But this Muslim movement became evident much later, towards the end of the century.

Another interesting thing to note is that these reform and progressive movements in Hinduism and Islam tried to fit in, as far as possible, the new scientific and political ideas derived from the West with their old religious notions and habits. They were not prepared to challenge and examine fearlessly these old notions and habits; nor could they ignore the new world of science and political and social ideas which lay around them. So they tried to harmonize the two by trying to show that all modern ideas and progress could be traced back to the old sacred books of their religions. This attempt was bound to end in failure. It merely prevented people from thinking straight. Instead of thinking boldly and trying to understand the new forces and ideas which were changing the world, they were oppressed by the weight of ancient habit and tradition. Instead of looking ahead and marching ahead, they were all the time furtively looking back. It is not easy to go ahead, if the head is always turned and looks back.

The English-educated class grew slowly in the cities, and at the same time a new middle class arose consisting of professional people—that is, lawyers and doctors and the like, and merchants and traders. There had been, of course, a middle class in the past, but this was largely crushed by the early British policy. The new *bourgeoisie*, or middle class, was a direct outcome of British rule; in a sense they were the hangers-on of this rule. They shared to a small extent in the exploitation of the masses; they took the crumbs that fell from the richly laden table of the British ruling classes. They were petty officials helping in the British administration of the country; many were lawyers assisting in the working of the law courts and growing rich by litigation; and there were merchants, the go-betweens of British trade and industry, who sold British goods for a profit or commission.

The great majority of these people of the new *bourgeoisie* were Hindus. This was due to their somewhat better economic condition, as compared to the Muslims, and also to their taking to English education, which was a passport to government service and the professions. The Muslims were generally poorer. Most of the weavers, who had gone to the wall on account of the British destruction of Indian industries, were Muslims. In Bengal, which has the biggest Muslim population of any Indian province, they were poor tenants or small land-holders. The landlord was usually a Hindu, and so was the village *bania*, who was the money-lender and the owner of the village store. The landlord and the *bania* were thus in a position to oppress the tenant and exploit him, and they took full advantage of this position. It is well to remember this fact, for in this lies the root cause of the tension between Hindu and Muslim.

In the same way the higher-caste Hindus, especially in the south, exploited the so-called " depressed " classes [untouchables] who were mostly workers on the land. . . . The untouchables have been agricultural serfs who were not allowed to own land. They had other disabilities also.

Although India as a whole and the masses grew poorer, the handful of people comprising the new *bourgeoisie* prospered to some extent because they shared in the country's exploitation. The lawyers and other professional people and the merchants accumulated some money. They wanted to invest this, so that they could have an income from interest. Many of them bought up land from the impoverished landlords, and thus they became themselves landowners. Others, seeing the wonderful prosperity of English industry, wanted to invest their money in factories in India. So Indian capital went into these big machine factories and an Indian industrial capitalist class began to rise. This was . . . after 1880.

As this *bourgeoisie* grew, their appetite also grew. They wanted to get on, to make more money, to have more posts in government service, more facilities for starting factories. They found the British obstructing them in every path. All the high posts were monopolized by the British, and industry was run for the profit of the British. So they began agitating, and this was the origin of the new nationalist movement. After the revolt of 1857 and its cruel suppression, people had been too much broken up for any agitation or aggressive movement. It took them many years to revive a little. . . .

Meanwhile the power of Indian capital was also increasing, and it demanded more elbow-room to grow. At last in 1885 all these various elements of the new *bourgeoisie* determined to start an organization to plead their cause. Thus was the Indian National Congress founded in 1885. This organization . . . has become in recent years great and powerful. It took up the cause of the masses and became, to some extent, their champion. It challenged the very basis of British rule in India, and led great mass movements against it. It raised the banner of independence and fought for freedom manfully. And . . . it is still carrying on the fight. But all this is subsequent history. The National Congress when it was first founded was a very moderate and cautious body, affirming its loyalty to the British and asking, very politely, for some petty reforms. It represented the richer *bourgeoisie*; even the poorer middle classes were not in it. As for the masses, the peasants and workers, they had nothing to do with it. It was the organ of the English-educated classes chiefly, and it carried on its activities in our step-mother tongue—the English language. Its demands were the demands of the landlords and Indian capitalists and the educated unemployed seeking for jobs. Little attention was paid to the grinding poverty of the masses or their needs. It demanded the " Indianization " of the services—that is to say, the greater employment of Indians in government service in place of Englishmen. It did not see that what was wrong with India was the machine which exploited the people, and that it made no difference who had charge of the machine, Indian or foreigner. The Congress further complained of the huge expenses of the English officials in the military and civil services, and of the " drain " of gold and silver from India to England.

Do not think that in pointing out how moderate the early Congress was I am criticizing it or trying to belittle it. That is not my purpose, for I believe that the Congress in those days and its leaders did great work. The hard facts of Indian politics drove it step by step, almost unwillingly, to a more and more extreme position. But in the early days it could not

have been anything but what it was. And in those days it required great
courage for its founders to go ahead. It is easy enough for us to talk
bravely of freedom when the crowd is with us and praises us for it. But
it is very difficult to be the pioneer in a great undertaking. . . .

The Congress grew, but even faster than the Congress grew the ideas
of nationality and the desire for freedom. The Congress appeal was
necessarily limited because it was confined to the English-knowing people.
To some extent this helped in bringing different provinces nearer to each
other and developing a common outlook. But because it did not go down
deep to the people, it had little strength. . . . An occurrence which stirred
Asia greatly . . . was the victory of little Japan over giant Russia in 1904–5.
India, in common with other Asiatic countries, was vastly impressed,
that is, the educated middle classes were impressed, and their self-
confidence grew. If Japan could make good against one of the most
powerful European countries, why not India? For long the Indian people
had suffered from a feeling of inferiority before the British. The long
domination by the British, the savage suppression of the Revolt of 1857,
had cowed them. By an Arms Act they were prevented from keeping
arms. In everything that happened in India they were reminded that they
were the subject race, the inferior race. Even the education that was given
to them filled them with this idea of inferiority. Perverted and false
history taught them that India was a land where anarchy had always
prevailed, and Hindus and Muslims had cut each other's throats, till the
British came to rescue the country from this miserable plight and give it
peace and prosperity. Indeed, the whole of Asia, the Europeans believed
and proclaimed, regardless of fact or history, was a backward continent
which must remain under European domination.

The Japanese victory, therefore, was a great pick-me-up for Asia. In
India it lessened the feeling of inferiority, from which most of us suffered.
Nationalist ideas spread more widely. . . . An event took place which
shook Bengal to the depths and stirred the whole of India. The British
Government divided up the great province of Bengal (which at that time
included Bihar) into two parts, one of these being Eastern Bengal. The
growing nationalism of the *bourgeoisie* in Bengal resented it. It suspected
that the British wanted to weaken them by thus dividing them. Eastern
Bengal had a majority of Muslims, so by this division a Hindu–Muslim
question was also raised. A great anti-British movement rose in Bengal.
Most of the landholders joined it, and so did Indian capitalists. The cry
of *Swadeshi* was first raised then, and with it the boycott of British goods,

which of course helped Indian industry and capital. The movement even spread to the masses to some extent, and partly it drew its inspiration from Hinduism. Side by side with it there arose in Bengal a school of revolutionary violence, and the bomb first made its appearance in Indian politics. . . .

In western India, in the Maharashtra country, there was also a great ferment at this time and a revival of an aggressive nationalism, tinged also with Hinduism. A great leader arose there, Bal Gangadhar Tilak, known throughout India as the Lokamanya, the "Honoured of the People". Tilak was a great scholar, learned alike in the old ways of the East and the new ways of the West; he was a great politician; but, above all, he was a great mass leader. The leaders of the National Congress had so far appealed only to the English-educated Indians; they were little known by the masses. Tilak was the first political leader of the new India who reached the masses and drew strength from them. His dynamic personality brought a new element of strength and indomitable courage, and, added to the new spirit of nationalism and sacrifice in Bengal, it changed the face of Indian politics.

What was the Congress doing during these stirring days of 1906 and 1907 and 1908? The Congress leaders, far from leading the nation at the time of this awakening of the national spirit, hung back. They were used to a quieter brand of politics in which the masses did not intrude. They did not like the flaming enthusiasm of Bengal, nor did they feel at home with the new unbending spirit of Maharashtra, as embodied in Tilak. They praised *Swadeshi* but hesitated at the boycott of British goods. Two parties developed in the Congress—the extremists under Tilak and some Bengal leaders and the moderates under the older Congress leaders. The most prominent of the moderate leaders was, however, a young man, Gopal Krishna Gokhale, a very able man who had devoted his life to service. . . . Tilak and he faced each other from their rival groups and, inevitably, the split came in 1907 and the Congress was divided. The moderates continued to control the Congress, the extremists were driven out. The moderates won, but it was at the cost of their popularity in the country, for Tilak's party was far the more popular with the people. The Congress became weak and for some years had little influence.

And what of the government during these years? How did it react to the growth of Indian nationalism? Governments have only one method of meeting an argument or a demand which they do not like—the use of the bludgeon. So the government indulged in repression and sent people to prison, and curbed the newspapers with Press laws, and let loose crowds of secret policemen and spies to shadow everybody they did not like. Since those days the members of the C.I.D. in India have been the constant companions of prominent Indian politicians. . . .

But repression did not succeed in crushing Bengal. So a measure of reform in the administration was hurried up to appease some people at least. The policy was then, as it was later and is now, to split up the nationalist ranks. The moderates were to be " rallied " and the extremists crushed. In 1908 these new reforms, called the Morley-Minto reforms, were announced. They succeeded in " rallying the moderates ", who were pleased with them. The extremists, with their leaders in gaol, were demoralized and the national movement weakened. In Bengal, however, the agitation against the partition continued and ended with success. In 1911 the British Government reversed the partition of Bengal. This triumph put new heart in the Bengalis. But the movement of 1907 had spent itself, and India relapsed into political apathy.

In 1911 also it was proclaimed that Delhi was to be the new capital— Delhi, the seat of many an empire, and the grave also of many an empire.

So stood India in 1914 when the World War broke out in Europe and ended the 100-year period. That war also affected India tremendously.[1]

Morley-Minto Reforms

[Tilak, who believed in subjecting Britain to the greatest possible pressure, had been advocating an all-India boycott of foreign goods. He hoped that such a measure would weaken the British economy while simultaneously strengthening India's self-reliance and her hand-loom industry. Because of Tilak's efforts in behalf of a foreign boycott—and British charges that he was inciting to revolution—he was imprisoned in 1908. He was not released until 1914.

Although Britain's Morley-Minto Reforms followed closely upon Tilak's imprisonment, the changes they proposed allegedly owed their origin to a memorandum furnished by the moderate Gokhale to the Secretary of State for India, Lord Morley. To add to the irony, the new reforms, which might not have been introduced at all save for the activities of the Extremist Tilak, proved, in certain respects, to be actually retrogressive. Even such British statesmen as Edwin S. Montagu and Lord Chelmsford, later themselves to introduce what they considered still further " reforms ", felt it but fair to concede that the Morley-Minto

[1] G.W.H., pp. 437-42.

proposals failed to " satisfy Indian opinion ". They cautioned that continuance of the new reforms could but " lead to a further cleavage between the Indian members and the Government and a further cultivation of criticism unchecked by Responsibility ".[1]

Although it is generally agreed that Lord Morley, who became Secretary of State for India in 1905, sincerely desired Indian political reform and, by 1907, had secured appointment of two Indians—a Hindu and a Muslim—to the Indian Council (the advisory body of the Secretary of State), these new representatives apparently enjoyed " neither an effective voice in the Council, nor the support of their countrymen at home ".[2] (Lord Minto, Viceroy from 1905 to 1910, further proposed inclusion of an Indian in his Executive Council and, after passage of the Morley-Minto Act, one was so appointed. Simultaneously Indians were included in the Provincial Executive Councils.)

Although the Morley-Minto Indian Councils Act was intended to prepare " the way for the first major step toward Indian self-government ",[3] among the features of the new reforms that most displeased Congress leaders was the fact that " six constituencies were created for Muslim landholders on the plea that [Muslims] were underrepresented on the various electoral bodies, and that on a general electoral roll based on a property franchise they would be underrepresented on the score of property ".

British recognition of such electoral claims—first put forward in 1906 by the newly organized Muslim League—has long been considered as the first opening of the door to communal representation, "which eventually spread throughout Indian political life, often reducing it to questions of percentages and reserved seats"[4] for minorities, or what came to be called separate electorates.

Whereas Congress leadership was primarily responsible for the positive aspects of the Morley-Minto attempts at reform, for the time being, at any rate, the autocratic nature of the British Government in India remained virtually unaltered.[5]

Even as a student in England, Jawaharlal was by no means pleased by the Morley-Minto Reforms.]

[Jawaharlal to Motilal, after the above reforms were introduced, December, 1908.] Do you not think he [Morley] has got a strange sense of humour?

[Jawaharlal to Motilal, November 19, 1908.] [Gokhale] thinks [the new

---

[1] H.I.N.C. (Vol. I), p. 26.
[2] B.J., p. 60.
[3] I.P.C., p. 164.
[4] S.I., p. 327. Copyright © by the University of Michigan 1961.
[5] Based on I.P.C., p. 165.

proposals] . . . fairly liberal. This evidently is not the opinion of the
Government of India, who think that they are far and away too liberal.
Great pressure is being brought to bear on Lord Morley.

[Jawaharlal to Motilal, March 12, 1909.] . . . Morley is coming up to
Cambridge today, presumably to confer with the dons on the Indian
question. There was a meeting here a few days ago of Masters of colleges
and others to discuss the same question. Various resolutions were passed
which, I am told, were to the effect that no other college should take in
an Indian who had been forcibly made to leave his college. The Master
of Downing was the only person who objected to this. He told them
plainly that if an Indian was expelled through spite and without sufficient
reason from the college, he would take him.

Morley was asked to come to the Indian Majlis dinner here which
takes place tonight. His answer, of course, was that he was too busy.[1]

[After King Edward VII died in 1910, Lord Hardinge became Viceroy
of India. It was at this time that Gandhi achieved growing prominence
as leader of the Indians of South Africa. He returned to India in 1915.]

5

Early Political Activity and View of Scene in India, 1912—Bankipore Congress Session

Early Political Activity and View of Scene in India, 1912

I felt . . . . dissatisfied with life in those early years after my return from
England [in 1912]. My profession did not fill me with a wholehearted
enthusiasm. Politics, which to me meant aggressive nationalist activity
against foreign rule, offered no scope for this. I joined the Congress and
took part in its occasional meetings. When a special occasion arose, like
the agitation against the Fiji indenture system for Indian workers, or the

[1] T.N., pp. 97–98.

South African Indian question, I threw myself into it with energy and worked hard. But these were only temporary occupations. . . .[1]

Socially, the Indian national revival in 1907 [had been] definitely reactionary. Inevitably, [the] new nationalism in India, as elsewhere in the East, was a religious nationalism. The Moderates thus represented a more advanced social outlook, but they were a mere handful on the top out of touch with the masses. They did not think much in terms of economics, except in terms of the new upper middle class which they partly represented and which wanted room for expansion. They advocated also petty social reforms to weaken caste and do away with old social customs which hindered growth.[2]

From 1907 onward for several years India was seething with unrest and trouble. For the first time since the Revolt of 1857, India was showing fight and not submitting tamely to foreign rule. . . . Almost without . . . exception we were Tilakites or Extremists.[3]

I was attracted in those early years to Mr Gokhale's Servants of India Society. I never thought of joining it, partly because its politics were too moderate for me, and partly because I had no intention then of giving up my profession. But I had a great admiration for the members of the society, who had devoted themselves for a bare pittance to the country's service. Here at least, I thought, was straight and single-minded and continuous work even though this might not be on wholly right lines.[4]

Toward the end of 1912 India was, politically, very dull. Tilak was in jail, the Extremists had been sat upon and were lying low without any effective leadership . . . and the Moderates had been effectively " rallied " to the Minto-Morley scheme of councils. There was some interest in Indians overseas, especially in the condition of Indians in South Africa. The Congress was a moderate group, meeting annually, passing some feeble resolutions, and attracting little attention.[5]

Bankipore Congress Session

I attended the Bankipore [1912] Congress as a delegate. . . . It was very much an English-knowing upper-class affair where morning coats and

[1] T.F., p. 41.
[2] Ibid., pp. 36–37.
[3] Ibid., pp. 34–35.
[4] Ibid., p. 41.
[5] Ibid., p. 39.

well-pressed trousers were greatly in evidence. Essentially it was a social gathering with no political excitement or tension. . . .

The official and Service atmosphere invaded and set the tone for almost all Indian middle-class life, especially the English-knowing intelligentsia. . . .

Professional men, lawyers, doctors, and others succumbed to it, and even the academic halls of the semiofficial universities were full of it. All these people lived in a world apart, cut off from the masses and even the lower middle class. Politics was confined to this upper stratum. The nationalist movement in Bengal from 1906 onward had for the first time shaken this up and infused a new life in the Bengal lower middle class and to a small extent even the masses. The process was to grow rapidly in later years under Gandhiji's leadership.[1]

6 | India During World War I

[In the period immediately preceding the outbreak of World War I, Jawaharlal undertook Red Cross work. With Mr K. N. Knox of the Indian Civil Service, who was later to try him for sedition, he became the joint secretary of the Allahabad branch of the St John Ambulance Brigade. When Gokhale appealed for help for Gandhi's South African struggle, Jawaharlal threw himself wholeheartedly into the campaign, becoming secretary of the organization set up for the collection of funds.[2]

Although Jawaharlal had joined the United Provinces Congress organization by 1913, he remained politically rather inactive for some time thereafter. He did, however, become involved in the agitation on behalf of the Indians of Fiji, which aimed at abolishing the system of indentured labor to which they were subjected.]

India, as a part of the British Empire, was of course directly involved in the World War. But there was no actual fighting in or near India. Nonetheless the war influenced developments in India in a variety of ways, both directly and indirectly, and thus brought about considerable

[1] Ibid., pp. 39–40.
[2] T.N., p. 124.

changes. Her resources were used up to the fullest extent to help the Allies.

It was not India's war. India had no grievance against the German Powers, and, as for Turkey, there was great sympathy for her. But India had no choice in the matter. She was but a dependency of Britain, forced to toe the line of her imperialist mistress. And so, in spite of much resentment in the country, Indian soldiers fought against Turks and Egyptians and others, and made India's name bitterly disliked in western Asia. . . .

Politics were at a low ebb in India on the eve of the war. The coming of the war still further diverted attention from them, and numerous war measures, taken by the British Government, made real political activity difficult. A war period is always considered by governments a sufficient excuse for suppressing everybody else and doing just what they like themselves. The only licence permitted is licence for themselves. A censorship is established which suppresses truth, often spreads falsehoods, and prevents criticism. Special acts and regulations are passed to control almost every form of national activity. This was done in all the warring countries, and, naturally, it was done in India also, where a " Defence of India Act " was passed. Public criticism of the war or anything connected with it was thus effectively checked. Yet in the background there was universal sympathy with Turkey, and a desire that Britain should get a hard knock from Germany. This impotent wish was natural enough among those who had themselves been knocked about sufficiently. But there was no public expression of it.

In public, loud shouts of loyalty to Britain filled the air. Most of this shouting was done by the ruling princes, and some of it by the upper middle classes who came into contact with the government. To a slight extent the *bourgeoisie* was also taken in by the brave declarations of the Allies about democracy and liberty and the freedom of nationalities. Perhaps, it was thought, this might apply to India also, and it was hoped that help rendered then to Britain, in her hour of need, might meet with a suitable reward later. In any event, there was no choice in the matter, and there was no other safe way; so they made the best of a bad job.

This outward display of loyalty in India was much appreciated in England in those days, and there was many an expression of gratitude. It was stated by those in authority that, after this, England would look at India with a " new angle of vision ".

But there were some Indians, both in India and in foreign countries, who did not adopt this " loyal " attitude. They did not even remain quiet and passive as the great majority did. They believed, according to the old Irish maxim, that England's difficulty was their country's opportunity. In particular, some Indians in Germany and other countries of Europe gathered together in Berlin to devise means to help England's enemies, and formed a committee for this purpose. The German Government was naturally eager to accept help of every kind, and they welcomed these Indian revolutionaries. A regular written agreement was arrived at and signed by the two parties—the German Government and the Indian Committee—in which, among other things, the Indians promised to help the German Government during the war on the understanding that, in the event of victory, Germany would insist on Indian freedom. This Indian Committee thereupon worked on behalf of Germany throughout the war. They carried on propaganda among the Indian troops that were sent abroad, and their activities spread right up to Afghanistan and the north-west frontier of India. But, apart from causing a great deal of anxiety to the British, they did not succeed in doing much. An attempt to send arms to India by sea was frustrated by the British. The German defeat in the war put an end automatically to this committee and its hopes.

In India also there were some instances of revolutionary activity, and special tribunals were appointed to try conspiracy cases, and many were sentenced to death and many to long terms of imprisonment. Some of the persons sentenced then are . . . in prison—after eighteen years!

As the war proceeded, a handful of people made huge profits, as elsewhere, but the great majority felt the strain more and more and discontent grew. The demand for more men for the front went on growing, and recruiting for the army became very intense. All manner of inducements and rewards were offered to those who brought in recruits, and *zamindars* were made to supply fixed quotas of recruits from among their tenants. . . .

It is difficult to know all that happened in those war days, because the censorship would not allow many kinds of news to appear, and consequently wild rumours used to spread. It is known, however, that a big mutiny in an Indian regiment took place in Singapore, and there was trouble on a smaller scale in many other places.

Apart from supplying men for the war and helping in other ways, India was also made to provide hard cash. This was called a " gift " from India. A hundred million pounds was paid in this way on one occasion and, later, another big sum. To call this enforced contribution from a poor country a "gift" does credit to the sense of humour of the British Government.

All this ... consisted of the less important consequences of the war, so far as India was concerned. But a far more fundamental change was being brought about by the wartime conditions. During the war, India's foreign trade, like the foreign trade of other countries, was wholly upset. The vast quantity of British goods that used to come to India was now very largely cut off. The German submarines were sinking ships in the Mediterranean and the Atlantic, and trade could not be carried on under these conditions. India had thus to provide for herself and supply her own needs. She had also to supply the government with all manner of things needed for the war. So that Indian industries grew rapidly, both the old industries, like the textile and jute, and new war-time industries. Tata's iron and steel works, which had so far been cold-shouldered by the government, now assumed tremendous importance, as they could produce war material. They were more or less run under government control.

For the war years, therefore, capitalists in India, both British and Indian, had an open field and little competition from abroad. They made full use of this opportunity and profited by it at the cost of the poor Indian masses. Prices of goods were put up and incredible dividends were declared. But the workers, whose labour produced these dividends and profit, saw little change in their miserable conditions. Their wages went up a little, but the prices of the necessities of life went up far more, and so their position actually became worse.[1]

In Bombay ... an inquiry commission found in one room, fifteen feet by twelve, six families, in all thirty adults and children, living together. Three of these women were expecting a confinement soon, and each family had a separate oven in that one room. These are special cases, but they are not very exceptional. ...

I remember visiting some of these slums and hovels of industrial workers, gasping for breath there, and coming out dazed and full of horror and anger. I remember also going down a coal mine ... and seeing the conditions in which our womenfolk worked there. I can never forget that picture or the shock that came to me that human beings should labor thus. Women were subsequently prohibited from working underground. But ... they have been sent back there. ... Yet millions of men are starving and unemployed; there is no lack of men. But the wages are so low and the conditions of work so bad that they do not attract.[2]

[1] G.W.H., pp. 667–70.
[2] D.I., p. 359.

The capitalists prospered greatly and accumulated huge profits, which they wanted to invest again in industry. For the first time Indian capitalists were strong enough to exert pressure on the government. Even apart from this pressure, the force of events had forced the British Government to help Indian industry during war time. The demand for further industrialization of the country led to the importation of more machinery from abroad, as such machinery could not then be made in India. So that in place of manufactured goods coming from England to India, we find now more machinery coming.

All this involved a great change in British policy in India; a century-old policy was given up and a new one adopted in its place. British imperialism, adapting itself to changing conditions, changed its face completely.[1]

There was little sympathy with the British [in India] in spite of loud professions of loyalty. [Moderates] and Extremists alike learned with satisfaction of German victories. There was no love for Germany, of course, only the desire to see our own rulers humbled. It was the weak and helpless man's idea of vicarious revenge. I suppose most of us viewed the struggle with mixed feelings. Of all the nations involved my sympathies were probably most with France. The ceaseless and unabashed propaganda on behalf of the Allies had some effect, although we tried to discount it greatly.[2]

[In December, 1914, Congress members resolved to "put a price" on their cooperation in the war effort, precisely because of the type of misgivings described by Nehru. In view of the profound and avowed loyalty the Indian people were manifesting during the war crisis, they declared that the British Government should take such measures as might "be necessary for the recognition of India as a component part of a Federated Empire, in the full and free enjoyment of the rights belonging to that status".[3]]

[1] G.W.H., p. 670.
[2] T.F., pp. 41–42.
[3] Quoted in B.J., p. 62.

Evolution and Motivation of British
Rule in India—Revival of Nationalist
Movement and Formation of Home Rule
Leagues—Lucknow Congress of 1916—

7 | Background of Congress-Muslim League
Frictions and Attempts at Amity—
Accusations by Hindu Mahasabha—
Intensified Involvement in Nationalist
Movement

Evolution and Motivation of British Rule in India

[The first phase of British rule in India involved] the eighteenth-century stage of plunder. . . . Then came the second stage when British rule was firmly established, and which lasted for over 100 years—right up to the war. This was to keep India as a field of raw material and a market for Britain's manufactured goods. Big industry was discouraged here in every way, and India's economic development prevented. Now, during war-time, comes the third stage, when big industry in India is encouraged by the British Government, and this is done in spite of the fact that it conflicts to some extent with Britain's manufacturers. . . . Why then should the British Government make this change in its policy to the detriment of . . . British industries? . . . Let us consider [the] reasons for the change in detail:

1. War-time demands automatically force the issue and push on industrialization in India.

2. This increases the Indian capitalist class and strengthens it, so that they demand more and more facilities for the growth of industry, to afford them an opportunity to invest their surplus funds. Britain is no longer in a position to ignore them completely, as this might alienate them and lead them to support the more extreme and revolutionary elements in the country, which are growing stronger. Therefore, it is

2+N.

desirable to keep them, if possible, on the British side by giving them some opportunities for growth.

3. The surplus money of the capitalist class in England also seeks opportunities for the investment in undeveloped countries, as profits are greater there. England itself being highly industrialized there are no such favourable opportunities of investment there. Profits are not so great and, owing to the strength of the organized labour movement, labour troubles are frequent. In undeveloped areas labour is weak, and hence wages are low and profits high. British capitalists naturally prefer investing in undeveloped areas under British control, such as India. Thus British capital comes to India, and this leads to still further industrialization.

4. The experience of the war showed that only highly industrialized countries can carry on a war effectively. Tsarist Russia broke down ultimately in the war because it was not sufficiently industrialized and had to rely on other countries. England fears that the next war may be a war with Soviet Russia at the Indian frontier. If India has not got her own big industries, the British Government will not be able to carry on the war properly on the frontier. This is too great a risk. Therefore, again, India should be industrialized.

For these reasons, inevitably, British policy changed and the industrialization of India was decided upon. The larger imperial policy of Britain demanded it, even at the cost of Lancashire and some other British industries. Of course Britain made out that this change was due to the British Government's exceeding love of India and her welfare. Having decided upon this policy, Britain took steps to ensure that the real control of the new industry in India would remain in the hands of British capitalists. The Indian capitalist is obligingly taken as a very junior partner in the concern.

In 1916, during war-time, an Indian Industrial Commission was appointed, and two years later it reported, recommending that industries should be encouraged by government, and that new industrial methods should be introduced in agriculture. It also suggested that an attempt should be made to give universal primary education. As in the early days of factory development in England, mass elementary education was considered necessary in order to produce skilled labour.

This commission was [to be] followed after the war by a host of other commissions and committees. It was even suggested that Indian industries should be protected by duties or tariffs. All this was considered a great victory for Indian industry. And so, to some extent, it was. But a closer analysis revealed certain interesting features. It was proposed to encourage foreign capital, which meant in effect British capital, to come to India; and British capital poured in. It was not only predominant, but overwhelmingly so. The vast majority of the big concerns were financed by British capital. So that tariff duties and protection in India resulted in protecting British capital in India! The great change in British policy in India had not proved so bad after all for the British capitalist. He had got a good sheltered market to spread out in and make his dividends with the help of low wages to his workers. This proved to be advantageous to him in another way also. Having invested his capital in India, China, Egypt, and such countries, where wages were low, he threatened the English workers in England with a reduction of wages. He told them that he could not otherwise compete with the products of low wages in India, China, etc. And if the English workman objected to having his wages cut down, the capitalist told him that he would be regretfully compelled to shut up his factory in England and invest the capital elsewhere.

The British Government in India also took many other steps to control industry in India. This is a complicated subject. . . . But one thing I might mention. Banks play a very important part in modern industry, because big business often requires credit. The best of businesses may fail suddenly if these credit facilities are denied it. As the banks give this credit, you can appreciate what a lot of power they must have. They can make or mar a business. Soon after the war the British Government brought the entire banking system of the country under its control. In this way, and by the manipulation of the currency, the government can exercise vast power over Indian industries and firms. Further, in order to encourage British trade in India, they introduced "imperial preference". This meant that if foreign goods are taxed for tariff purposes, British goods should be taxed less or not taxed at all, so that British goods may have an advantage over the others.[1]

Revival of Nationalist Movement and Formation of Home Rule Leagues

The growing strength of the Indian capitalist classes and upper *bourgeoisie* during the war began to show itself in the political movement also. Politics gradually came out of the pre-war and early war lull, and various demands for self-government and the like began to be made. Lokamanya Tilak came out of prison after completing his long term. The National

[1] G.W.H., pp. 670–72.

Congress then ... was in the hands of the moderate group, and was a small uninfluential body having little touch with the people. As the more advanced politicians were not in the Congress, they organized Home Rule Leagues. Two such leagues were started, one by Lokamanya Tilak and the other by Mrs Annie Besant. [Jawaharlal joined both, but worked more ardently for Mrs Besant's League.] For some years Mrs Besant played an important part in Indian politics, and her great eloquence and powerful advocacy did much to revive interest in politics. The government considered her propaganda so dangerous that they even interned her ... for some months. She presided over a session of the Congress in Calcutta, and was its first woman president.[1]

[Mrs Besant's internment] stirred even the older generation, including many of the Moderate leaders. The home rule leagues were attracting not only all the old Extremists who had been kept out of the Congress since 1907 but large numbers of newcomers from the middle classes. They did not touch the masses.

Mrs Besant's internment also resulted in my father and other Moderate leaders joining the Home Rule League. Some months later most of these Moderate members resigned from the league. My father remained in it and became the president of the Allahabad branch.

Gradually my father had been drifting away from the orthodox Moderate position. His nature rebelled against too much submission and appeal to an authority which ignored us and treated us disdainfully. But the old Extremist leaders did not attract him; their language and methods jarred upon him. The episode of Mrs Besant's internment and subsequent events influenced him considerably, but still he hesitated before definitely committing himself to a forward line. Often he used to say in those days that moderate tactics were no good, but nothing effective could be done till some solution for the Hindu–Muslim question was found. If this was found, then he promised to go ahead with the youngest of us.[2]

[Compromise in 1916 between Extremists and Moderates] was of short duration, for within two years there was another split, and the Moderates, now calling themselves Liberals, walked away from the Congress, and they have kept away.[3]

[1] Ibid., p. 672.
[2] T.F., p. 42.
[3] G.W.H., p. 672.

The Lucknow Congress of 1916

The Lucknow Congress of 1916 marks the revival of the National Congress. From that time onwards it grew in strength and importance and, for the first time in its history, began to be really a national organization of the *bourgeoisie* or middle classes. It had nothing to do with the masses as such, and they were not interested in it till Gandhiji came. . . .

The essential difference between the Moderates and the Extremists was that the former were a prosperous party of the Haves and some hangers-on of the Haves, and the Extremists had a number of Have-nots also and, as the more extreme party, naturally attracted the youth of the country, most of whom thought that strong language was a sufficient substitute for action. . . . But neither the Moderates nor the Extremists had anything to do with the real Have-nots, the workers and the peasants. . . .

The Lucknow Congress of 1916 was notable for another reunion, a Hindu–Muslim one. The Congress had always clung to a national basis, but in effect it was predominantly a Hindu organization, because of the overwhelming majority of Hindus in it. Some years before the war [1906] the Muslim intelligentsia, egged on to some extent by the government, had organized a separate body for themselves, called the All-India Muslim League. This was meant to keep the Muslims away from the Congress, but soon it drifted towards the Congress, and at Lucknow there was an agreement between the two about the future constitution of India. This was called the Congress-League Scheme, and it laid down, among other things, the proportion of seats to be reserved for the Muslim minorities. This Congress-League Scheme then became the joint programme which was accepted as the country's demand. It represented the views of the *bourgeoisie*, who were the only politically minded people at the time. Agitation grew on the basis of this scheme.

The Muslims had grown more politically minded, and had joined hands with the Congress largely because of their exasperation at the British fighting Turkey. Because of sympathy for Turkey and a vigorous expression of it, two Muslim leaders . . . had been interned early in the war. . . . All this served to irritate and annoy the Muslims, and they turned away from the government more and more.[1]

[1] Ibid., pp. 672–74.

Background of Congress-Muslim League Frictions and Attempts at Amity

[In 1906, when the All-India Muslim League had been founded, its future leader, M. A. Jinnah, was private secretary to the great Parsi Congress leader, Naoroji, during the Calcutta Congress Session of the same year. The Muslim League was founded at Dacca, on December 30, 1906. Its three main objectives were: "(a) To promote, amongst the Mussalmans of India, feelings of loyalty to the British Government and to remove any misconception that may arise as to the intentions of Government with regard to Indian measures. (b) To protect and advance the political rights of the Mussalmans of India and respectfully represent their needs and aspirations to the Government. (c) To prevent the rise among the Mussalmans of any feeling of hostility towards other communities without prejudice to the other aforesaid objects of the League."[1]

As early as 1909, Indian nationalists had become increasingly outraged by what they felt to be the playing up of differences between Hindus and Muslims by British officials and their protégés. Motilal to Jawaharlal, March 25, 1909: "An open rupture between the leaders of the two communities is imminent. Nothing short of a miracle can save it. I do not attach much importance to the differences of opinion among the leaders as there has never been much love lost between the two. The masses of both communities have, however, always been good friends and neighbours, and what I dread is the day when the tension of feeling filters down to the lower classes. Nation-building will then be a thing of the past. . . . Our Anglo-Indian friends have distinctly scored in this matter."[2]

The President of the Allahabad Congress, Sir William Wedderburn, subsequently had convened a Hindu–Muslim conference on unity in 1910—one of many similar meetings to be held during the next thirty years—all of which, unfortunately, were to produce "a harmony of phrases rather than of minds and hearts". Tragically, too, at the 1910 Congress, a number of Hindu leaders had "conceived the Hindu Mahasabha [a right-wing Hindu organization], as a communal counter-blast to the . . . Muslim League . . .", after which Motilal wrote to Jawaharlal (January 6, 1911) that this occurrence would "not only minimize the chance of the [Wedderburn] Hindu–Muslim Committee doing any good, but sap the foundation of the Congress itself. I opposed [its] formation."[3]

"In 1913, the goal of the Muslim League . . . was enlarged to include the attainment of self-government. The outbreak in 1914 of a war in which Turkey was ranged on the side of Germany created a painful dilemma for the devout: as a Muslim leader put it, 'the Government of our Caliph is at war with the Government of our King-Emperor'.

[1] B.J., p. 45.
[2] T.N., p. 109.
[3] Ibid., p. 114.

"The political consciousness of the Muslim middle class was thus heightened by events abroad. The Hindu middle class had already been made sensitive by bureaucratic sins of omission and commission at home. The two streams of discontent converged at Lucknow, where the Congress and the League held their annual sessions in December, 1916. M. A. Jinnah, who presided over the League, spoke of a new India under the influence of Western education fast ' growing in identity of thought, purpose and outlook '. ' We have found luck in Lucknow,' declared Tilak, ' we are now united in every way in the United Provinces.' History was to make a mockery of this optimism. The Lucknow Pact did not prove the turning point in the nationalist movement it was expected to be. Separate electorates failed to win lasting adherence of the Muslim middle class to Indian nationalism and in fact turned out to be the thin end of the wedge which was to split India apart thirty years later. And ironically enough, Jinnah, one of the chief architects of the Lucknow Pact, was to become the prophet of Muslim separatism. All this was of course in the womb of the future. In 1916 the [temporary] fraternization between Moderates and the Extremists as well as between Muslims and Hindus warmed the hearts of all patriotic Indians." [1]

It was in 1913 that Jinnah decided to join the Muslim League. During the same period Congress placed on record its warm appreciation of the adoption by the " Muslim League of the ideal of Self-Government for India, within the British Empire; and of the belief which the League had so emphatically declared at its last session ' that the political future of the country depends upon the harmonious working and cooperation of the two great communities '." [2]

Despite occasional periods of relative amity, Muslim League disagreements with the goals and activities of Congress were nevertheless to increase in intensity over the years. Although the efforts of the Lucknow Congress of 1916 to achieve harmony between India's Hindus and Muslims were of great historic importance, leading to at least a temporary reduction of communal tensions, the Congress-League scheme unfortunately failed to achieve the long-range results envisaged at the time.]

Accusations by Hindu Mahasabha

I have been accused by some leaders of the Hindu *Mahasabha* of my ignorance of Hindu sentiments because of my defective education and general background of " Persian " culture. What culture I possess, or whether I possess any at all, is a little difficult for me to say. Persian, as a language, unhappily, I do not even know. But it is true that my father had grown up in an Indo-Persian cultural atmosphere, which was the

[1] Ibid., pp. 125-26.
[2] B.J., p. 58.

legacy in north India of the old Delhi court, and of which, even in these degenerate days, Delhi and Lucknow are the two chief centers. Kashmiri [Brahmins] had a remarkable capacity for adaptation, and coming down to the Indian plains and finding that this Indo-Persian culture was predominant at the time, they took to it, and produced a number of fine scholars in Persian and Urdu. Later they adapted themselves with equal rapidity to the changing order, when a knowledge of English and the elements of European culture became necessary.[1]

Intensified Involvement in Nationalist Movement

My own political and public activities in the early war years were modest, and I kept away from addressing public gatherings. I was still diffident and terrified of public speaking. Partly also I felt that public speeches should not be in English, and I doubted my capacity to speak at any length in Hindustani. . . .

At home, in those early years, political questions were not peaceful subjects for discussion, and references to them, which were frequent, immediately produced a tense atmosphere. Father had been closely watching my growing drift toward Extremism, my continual criticism of the politics of talk, and my insistent demand for action. What action it should be was not clear, and sometimes father imagined that I was heading straight for the violent courses adopted by some of the young men of Bengal. This worried him very much. As a matter of fact I was not attracted that way, but the idea that we must not tamely submit to existing conditions and that something must be done began to obsess me more and more. Successful action, from the national point of view, did not seem to be at all easy, but I felt that both individual and national honor demanded a more aggressive and fighting attitude to foreign rule. Father himself was dissatisfied with the Moderate philosophy, and a mental conflict was going on inside him. He was too obstinate to change from one position to another until he was absolutely convinced that there was no other way. Each step forward meant for him a hard and bitter tussle in his mind, and, when the step was taken after that struggle with part of himself, there was no going back. He had not taken it in a fit of enthusiasm but as a result of intellectual conviction, and when he had done so, all his pride prevented him from looking back.

The outward change in his politics came about the time of Mrs

[1] T.F., pp. 130-31.

Besant's internment, and from that time onward step by step he went ahead, leaving his old Moderate colleagues far behind, till the tragic happenings in the Punjab in 1919 finally led him to cut adrift from his old life and his profession and throw in his lot with the new movement started by Gandhiji. . . .

I was a pure nationalist, my vague socialist ideas of college days having sunk into the background. . . . The Easter Week rising in Ireland by its very failure attracted, for was that not true courage which mocked at almost certain failure and proclaimed to the world that no physical might could crush the invincible spirit of a nation? . . .

Fresh reading was again stirring the embers of socialistic ideas in my head. They were vague ideas, more humanitarian and utopian than scientific. A favorite writer of mine during the war years and after was Bertrand Russell.

These thoughts and desires produced a growing conflict within me and a dissatisfaction with my profession of the law. I carried on with it because there was nothing else to be done, but I felt more and more that it was not possible to reconcile public work, especially of the aggressive type which appealed to me, with the lawyer's job.[1]

8 | Jawaharlal's Marriage and First Meeting with Gandhi, 1916

[Two events of crucial importance for Jawaharlal took place in 1916. He married Kamala Kaul. He met Mohandas K. Gandhi. Although the Gandhian era of Congress did not actually begin until 1919–1920, the Mahatma so moved and overwhelmed Jawaharlal after their initial encounter that his entire life was changed thereby.]

My first meeting with Gandhiji was about the time of the Lucknow Congress during Christmas, 1916. All of us admired him for his heroic fight in South Africa, but he seemed very distant and different and unpolitical to many of us young men. He refused to take part in Congress

[1] Ibid., pp. 42–44.

2*

or national politics then and confined himself to the South African Indian question. Soon afterward [1917] his adventures and victory in Champaran [in the district of Bihar, India] on behalf of the tenants of . . . [European] planters, filled us with enthusiasm. We saw that he was prepared to apply his methods in India also, and they promised success.[1]

I was simply bowled over by Gandhi, straight off. . . . I worked as a kind of secretary to [him]. . . . I was searching for some [satisfying] method of action.[2]

[Gandhi] was like a powerful current of fresh air that made us stretch ourselves and take deep breaths, like a beam of light that pierced the darkness and removed the scales from our eyes, like a whirlwind that upset many things but most of all the working of people's minds. He did not descend from the top; he seemed to emerge from the millions of India, speaking their language and incessantly drawing attention to them and their appalling condition. Get off the backs of these peasants and workers, he told us, all of you who live by their exploitation; get rid of the system that produces this poverty and misery.

Political freedom took new shape then and acquired a new content. Much that he said we only partially accepted or sometimes did not accept at all. But all this was secondary. The essence of his teaching was fearlessness and truth and action allied to these, always keeping the welfare of the masses in view. The greatest gift for an individual or a nation, so we had been told in our ancient books, was *abhaya*, fearlessness, not merely bodily courage but the absence of fear from the mind. . . .that it was the function of the leaders of a people to make them fearless. But the dominant impulse in India under British rule was that of fear, pervasive, oppressing, strangling fear; fear of the army, the police, the widespread secret service; fear of the official class; fear of laws meant to suppress, and of prison; fear of the landlord's agent; fear of the moneylender; fear of unemployment and starvation, which were always on the threshold. It was against this all-pervading fear that Gandhi's quiet and determined voice was raised: Be not afraid.

Was it so simple as all that? Not quite. And yet fear builds its phantoms which are more fearsome than reality itself, and reality when calmly analyzed and its consequences willingly accepted loses much of its terror. So, suddenly as it were, that black pall of fear was lifted from the

[1] T.F., p. 44.
[2] T.M., pp. 23–24. Reprinted from *Nehru: Conversations on Indian and World Affairs* by Tibor Mende, with the permission of the publisher George Braziller, Inc. © 1956.

people's shoulders, not wholly, of course, but to an amazing degree. As fear is close companion to falsehood, so truth follows fearlessness. The Indian people did not become much more truthful than they were, nor did they change their essential nature overnight; nevertheless a sea change was visible as the need for falsehood and furtive behavior lessened. It was a psychological change, almost as if some expert in psychoanalytical method had probed deep into the patient's past, found out the origins of his complexes, exposed them to his view, and thus rid him of that burden.

There was that psychological reaction also, a feeling of shame at our long submission to an alien rule that had degraded and humiliated us, and a desire to submit no longer, whatever the consequences might be. We did not grow much more truthful, perhaps, than we had been previously, but Gandhi was always there as a symbol of uncompromising truth to pull us up and shame us into truth.

What is truth? I do not know for certain, and perhaps our truths are relative and absolute truth is beyond us. Different persons may and do take different views of truth, and each individual is powerfully influenced by his own background, training, and impulses. So also Gandhi. But truth is at least for an individual what he himself feels and knows to be true. According to that definition I do not know of any person who holds to the truth as Gandhi does. That is a dangerous quality in a politician, for he speaks out his mind and even lets the public see its changing phases.

Gandhi influenced millions of people in India in varying degrees; some changed the whole texture of their lives, others were only partly affected, or the effect wore off, and yet not quite, for some part of it could not be wholly shaken off.[1]

| 9 | Montagu Declaration, 1917—Expectations of Change—Montagu-Chelmsford Reforms, 1918 |

Montagu Declaration, 1917

[In 1916–1917 Jawaharlal became so profoundly aroused by political developments in India that he began to devote an increasing amount of time to the freedom movement.

[1] D.I., pp. 361–62.

The Montagu Declaration of 1917 (announced to the British Parliament by the Secretary of State for India, Edwin Montagu) was designed to improve the political situation that had resulted from introduction of the earlier Morley-Minto Reforms. The 1917 Declaration was, however, received without enthusiasm by India's Congress leaders.

During the same period Jawaharlal was elected Secretary of the Home Rule League in Allahabad, and first became a member of the All-India Congress Committee. Events abroad continued to have a decisive effect upon the evolution of his political views.]

Expectations of Change

As the demand for self-government grew in India, the British Government made various promises and started inquiries in India which occupied the people's attention. [During] 1918 the then Secretary of State for India and the Viceroy presented a joint report—[referred to as] the Montagu-Chelmsford Report—which embodied certain proposals for reforms and changes in India. Immediately a great argument arose in the country over these tentative proposals. The Congress strongly disapproved of them and considered them insufficient. The Liberals welcomed them, and, because of this, they parted company with the Congress. . . .

Everywhere there was a lively expectation of change. The political barometer was rising, and the mild and soothing, the somewhat apologetic and ineffective, whispers of the Moderates were giving place to the more confident, aggressive, direct, and truculent shouts of the Extremists. But both the Moderates and Extremists thought and talked in terms of politics and the outward structure of government; behind them British imperialism went on quietly strengthening its hold on the economic life of the country.[1]

Montagu-Chelmsford Reforms, 1918

[Sir Reginald Craddock, the Home Member of the Government of India, summed up the complex political situation: "'The position is one of great difficulty, the Moderate leaders can command no support among the vocal classes who are being led at the heels of Tilak and Besant. The great figures among the Moderates have passed away [Gokhale had died in 1915] and so far they have no successors. Home Rule is pressed for not so much as constitutional reform now becoming due, but as the only salvation from innumerable wrongs and grievances under which India is

[1] G.W.H., p. 674.

suffering . . . under cover of constitutional agitation, the minds of the people who read newspapers are being poisoned against the British Government. . . .'

"'Sedition in India,' Craddock wrote [still further], 'is like the tides which erode a coastline as the sea encroaches. The last high tide was in 1907-8. The tide then went out, but it is flowing in now rapidly, and it will reach a point now higher than it ever reached before. We must have our dam in order lest it inundate sound land.'

"The projected dam against the seditious flood was a declaration of policy." [1]

On August 20, 1917, the Montagu Declaration stated: "The policy of His Majesty's Government . . . is that of increasing association of Indians in every branch of the administration, and gradual development of self-governing institutions with a view to the progressive realization of responsible government in India as an integral part of the British Empire." [2]

Not only were India's Congress leaders unimpressed by the Declaration, but even such a British Conservative as Austen Chamberlain—a member of the India Office in 1917—was moved to say at the time: "After all, we must take into account the changes produced by [the] war . . . the constant emphasis laid upon the fact that the Allies are fighting for freedom and nationality . . . the revolution in Russia, and the way it has been hailed throughout Europe . . . the effect of all these things on Indian opinion and on our own attitude to Indian questions. What would have seemed a great advance a little time ago, would now satisfy no one and we should, I think, be prepared for bold and radical measures." [3]

When Montagu arrived in India in 1917 he, too, was intent upon doing "something big" and "epoch-making". He set himself "to the task of outlining a new constitution which would set India on the road to self-government". [4] Yet, despite his hopes, and the issuing of the Montagu-Chelmsford Report of 1918 (Lord Chelmsford was Viceroy of India from 1916 to 1921), the fates were to decree otherwise.

From the Montagu-Chelmsford Report, 1918: "There should be, as far as possible, complete popular control in local bodies and the largest possible independence for them of outside control. . . .

"The provinces are the domain in which the earlier steps towards the progressive realisation of responsible government should be taken. Some measure of responsibility should be given at once, and our aim is to give complete responsibility as soon as conditions permit. This involves at once giving the provinces the largest measure of independence, legislative, administrative, and financial, of the Government of India which is compatible with the due discharge by the latter of its own responsibilities. . . .

"The Government of India must remain wholly responsible to Parliament, and saving such responsibility, its authority in essential matters

---

[1] T.N., p. 133.
[2] Ibid., p. 140.
[3] Ibid., p. 142.
[4] Ibid., pp. 144-45.

must remain indisputable, pending experience of the effect of the changes now to be introduced in the provinces. In the meantime the Indian Legislative Council should be enlarged and made more representative and its opportunities of influencing Government increased. . . .

"In proportion as the foregoing changes take effect, the control of Parliament and the Secretary of State over the Government of India and provincial Governments must be relaxed."[1]

The Montagu-Chelmsford Report commentary on Communal Electorates included at least one observation deserving of special attention: "We regard any system of communal electorates . . . as a very serious hindrance to the development of the self-governing principle. The evils of any extension of the system are plain."[2] (The introduction of separate electorates for members of different communal or religious groups already had seemed distinctly objectionable—because divisive—to those Congress leaders overwhelmingly in favor of a modern, secular democracy.)

As Michael Brecher has noted, although, to the British, the Montagu-Chelmsford Report seemed an appropriate introduction to responsible self-government in the Indian sub-continent, "to most Indian nationalists . . . it was a paltry concession, far short of the expectations raised by the Montagu Declaration". Hence Congress, demanding self-government within the Empire, "asserted that India was ready for responsible government, and requested the abandonment of the notion of dyarchy, which would have left the central government and most vital provincial matters under the exclusive jurisdiction of the existing régime.[3] It also demanded fiscal autonomy for India and a declaration of Indian rights", while reaffirming the 1916 Lucknow Pact with the Muslim League "as the preferred basis for the composition of the legislatures, federal and provincial".[4] In other words, "the principle of self-determination for all peoples, proclaimed by President Wilson in his Fourteen Points",[5] had stirred the imagination of the intelligentsia throughout the world.

According to Rajendra Prasad, "The announcement made by the Secretary of State for India on behalf of the British Government in 1917 promising Self-Government by stages occasioned differences of opinion amongst Indians which became more and more acute as the result of investigations undertaken by the Secretary of State and the Viceroy became known and [a] Bill, which ultimately became the Government of India Act in 1920, took shape and form. During this time of incubation of the Bill the war had ended in a victory for the British, and the feeling grew in India that as the pressure in Europe had relaxed on account of the success-

---

[1] E.I.P., pp. 267-68.

[2] Ibid., p. 209.

[3] Only certain so-called "safe" departments were to be turned over to "Indian ministers responsible to majorities in the lower houses of the provincial legislatures" under dyarchy, a system destined to frustrate the aspirations of nationalist leaders (I.P.C., p. 168).

[4] M.B., p. 61.

[5] Ibid., p. 60.

ful termination of the war for Britain, the British attitude had changed for the worse towards India."[1]

The Montagu-Chelmsford Reforms, in fact, "set the pattern which was to determine the actual administration of India from 1919 until the eve of independence [in 1947]. The central government at New Delhi underwent almost no change between 1919 and 1946; [even] the system by which the British Crown's paramountcy over Indian princely states was exercised changed [only] slightly in form but not in substance."[2]

	Post-World War I Period: Rowlatt Act—
	Beginning of Gandhian Non-Cooperation
10	Movement—Amritsar Massacre: Martial
	Law—A Crucial Turning Point

Post-World War I Period: Rowlatt Act

[Résumé 1919–1921: Although, when Congress met in 1919, it agreed to "cooperate" with the Montagu-Chelmsford Reforms, subsequent passage of the repressive Rowlatt Acts, and the tragic Amritsar—or Jallianwala Bagh—Massacre in the Punjab, described in the following pages, greatly antagonized nationalists throughout India.

During 1920, Britain's exoneration of (British) General Dyer—despite his cruel and unfeeling role at the time of the above Massacre—followed, as it was, by the Khilafat Movement (see Section 12), further infuriated Congress to such a degree that, when it met later in the same year, it reversed its previous acceptance of the Montagu-Chelmsford Reforms. It was at this point that Gandhi first persuaded Congress to adopt non-violent non-cooperation as a method of protesting against British policy.

The Defence of India Act, which provided India's colonial rulers with "wide arbitrary powers, was to lapse after six months of the termination of the war. A case was sought to be made out to justify the enactment of a new law, and with this end in view, Government appointed an inquiry committee, named the Rowlatt Committee after its chairman, a British

[1] H.I.N.C. (Vol. I), Introduction, p. 2.
[2] I.P.C., p. 167.

judge. The Committee's recommendations ... announced in January, 1919, were interpreted by national leaders as the death-warrant of civil liberties. There was widespread indignation, and Gandhi became the focal point of the campaign against the recommendations.

"When the recommendations were embodied in a Bill, popularly known as the Rowlatt Bill, and there remained no doubt that it would soon become law, Gandhi resolved to organise a countrywide protest. A day was appointed for general closing of shops, suspension of all business activity, fasting, prayers and public meetings throughout the country. Both Hindus and Muslims responded to his call. The forces, released by the protest day demonstrations, became uncontrollable, and the terror-stricken Government met them with firings, killing thousands of people." [1]

Of the Rowlatt Bills, which "sought to arm the executive with special powers to suppress political violence", [2] Gandhi wrote that they were, in fact, "designed to rob the people of all freedom". One of the Rowlatt Bills "referred to trial of [anarchical] crimes by a court of three judges and provided no right of appeal. The other Bill provided for a change in the Criminal Law of the land. The former was intended to be a temporary measure while the latter would be permanent and ... provided for punishment for possession of any seditious document with intent to circulate or publish it. The Second Bill was ... dropped while the first was passed in March 1919." [3]]

The end of the World War found India in a state of suppressed excitement. Industrialization had spread. ... [The] handful at the top had prospered and were greedy for more power and opportunity to invest their savings and add to their wealth. The great majority, however, were not so fortunate and looked forward to a lightening of the burdens that crushed them. Among the middle classes there was everywhere an expectation of great constitutional changes which would bring a large measure of self-rule and thus better their lot by opening out many fresh avenues of growth to them.

Political agitation, peaceful and wholly constitutional as it was, seemed to be working itself to a head, and people talked with assurance of self-determination and self-government. Some of this unrest was visible also among the masses, especially the peasantry. ...

The dominant note all over India was one of waiting and expectation, full of hope and yet tinged with fear and anxiety. Then came the Rowlatt Bills with their drastic provisions for arrest and trial without any of the checks and formalities which the law is supposed to provide. A wave of anger greeted them all over India, and even the Moderates joined in this

[1] T.T.N., pp. 1–2.
[2] T.N., p. 157.
[3] R.H.C., p. 84.

and opposed the measures with all their might. Indeed there was universal opposition on the part of Indians of all shades of opinion. Still the Bills were pushed through by the officials and became law, the principal concession made being to limit them to three years.[1]

Beginning of Gandhian Non-Cooperation Movement

Gandhiji had passed through a serious illness early in 1919. Almost from his sick bed he begged the Viceroy not to give his consent to the Rowlatt Bills. That appeal was ignored as others had been, and then, almost against his will, Gandhiji took the leadership in his first all-India [non-violent mass] agitation. He started the *Satyagraha Sabha* [Satyagraha—adherence to truth; Sabha—organization], the members of which were pledged to disobey the Rowlatt Act, if it was applied to them, as well as other objectionable laws to be specified from time to time. In other words, they were to court jail openly and deliberately.

When I first read about ... [the *Satyagraha Sabha*] proposal in the newspapers, my reaction was one of tremendous relief. Here at last was a way out of the tangle, a method of action which was straight and open and possibly effective. I was afire with enthusiasm and wanted to join the *Satyagraha Sabha* immediately. I hardly thought of the consequences—law-breaking, jail-going, etc.—and if I thought of them I did not care. [However] suddenly my ardor was damped, and I realized that all was not plain sailing. My father was dead against this new idea. He was not in the habit of being swept away by new proposals; he thought carefully of the consequences before he took any fresh step. And the more he thought of the *Satyagraha Sabha* and its program, the less he liked it. What good would the jail-going of a number of individuals do, what pressure could it bring on the Government? Apart from these general considerations, what really moved him was the personal issue. It seemed to him preposterous that I should go to prison. The trek to prison had not then begun, and the idea was most repulsive. Father was intensely attached to his children. He was not showy in his affection, but behind his restraint there was a great love.

For many days there was this mental conflict, and because both of us felt that big issues were at stake involving a complete upsetting of our lives, we tried hard to be as considerate to each other as possible. I wanted

[1] T.F., pp. 47-48.

to lessen his obvious suffering if I could, but I had no doubt in my mind that I had to go the way of *Satyagraha*. Both of us had a distressing time, and night after night I wandered about alone, tortured in mind and trying to grope my way out. Father—I discovered later—actually tried sleeping on the floor to find out what it was like, as he thought that this would be my lot in prison.

Gandhiji came to Allahabad at father's request, and they had long talks at which I was not present. As a result Gandhiji advised me not to precipitate matters or to do anything which might upset father. I was not happy at this, but other events took place in India which changed the whole situation, and the *Satyagraha Sabha* stopped its activities.[1]

Amritsar Massacre : Martial Law

Satyagraha Day—all-India *hartals* and complete suspension of business —firing by the police and military at Delhi and Amritsar, and the killing of many people—mob violence in Amritsar and Ahmedabad—the massacre of Jallianwala Bagh—the long horror and terrible indignity of martial law in the Punjab. The Punjab was isolated, cut off from the rest of India; a thick veil seemed to cover it and hide it from outside eyes. There was hardly any news, and people could not go there or come out from there.

Odd individuals, who managed to escape from that inferno, were so terror-struck that they could give no clear account. Helplessly and impotently, we who were outside waited for scraps of news, and bitterness filled our hearts. Some of us wanted to go openly to the affected parts of the Punjab and defy the martial law regulations. But we were kept back, and meanwhile a big organization for relief and inquiry was set up on behalf of the Congress.

As soon as martial law was withdrawn from the principal areas and outsiders were allowed to come in, prominent Congressmen and others poured into the Punjab offering their services for relief or inquiry work....

Most of the evidence relating to Jallianwala Bagh and that terrible lane where human beings were made to crawl on their bellies, that subsequently appeared in the Congress Inquiry Report, was taken down in our presence. We paid numerous visits to the so-called Bagh itself and examined every bit of it carefully.

[1] Ibid., pp. 48–49.

A suggestion has been made . . . that General Dyer was under the impression that there were other exits from the Bagh and it was because of this that he continued his firing for so long. Even if that was Dyer's impression, and there were in fact some exits, that would hardly lessen his responsibility. But it seems very strange that he should have such an impression. Any person, standing on the raised ground where he stood, could have a good view of the entire space and could see how shut in it was on all sides by houses several stories high. Only on one side, for a hundred feet or so, there was no house, but a low wall about five feet high. With a murderous fire mowing them down and unable to find a way out, thousands . . . rushed to this wall and tried to climb over it. The fire was then directed, it appears (both from our evidence and the innumerable bullet marks on the wall itself), toward this wall to prevent people from escaping over it. And when all was over, some of the biggest heaps of dead and wounded lay on either side of this wall.

Toward the end of that year (1919) I traveled from Amritsar to Delhi by the night train. The compartment I entered was almost full, and all the berths, except one upper one, were occupied by sleeping passengers. I took the vacant upper berth. In the morning I discovered that all my fellow passengers were military officers. They conversed with each other in loud voices which I could not help overhearing. One of them was holding forth in an aggressive and triumphant tone, and soon I discovered that he was Dyer, the hero of Jallianwala Bagh, who was describing his Amritsar experiences. He pointed out how he had the whole town at his mercy and he had felt like reducing the rebellious city to a heap of ashes, but he took pity on it and refrained. . . . I was greatly shocked to hear his conversation and to observe his callous manner. He descended at Delhi station in pyjamas with bright pink stripes, and a dressing gown. . . .

The Punjab happenings and the inquiry into them had a profound effect on father. His whole legal and constitutional foundations were shaken by them, and his mind was gradually prepared for that change which was to come a year later. He had already moved far from his old moderate position. Dissatisfied with the leading Moderate newspaper, the *Leader* of Allahabad, he had started another daily, the *Independent*, from Allahabad early in 1919. This paper met with great success, but from the very beginning it was handicapped by quite an amazing degree of incompetence in the running of it. Almost everybody connected with it—directors, editors, managerial staff—had their share of responsibility for this. I was one of the directors, without the least experience of the job, and the troubles and the squabbles of the paper became quite a nightmare to me. Both my father and I were, however, soon dragged away to the Punjab.[1]

[For many years after 1919, the period from April 6 to 13 was observed annually in India as National Week. It was marked by "fasting on the opening and closing days", and the "engaging in intensive constructive work during the week. In 1919, [the] 6th of April [was] observed as a day of protest to mark the launching of all-India Satyagraha against the repressive 'seditious crimes' legislation known as the Rowlatt Act by fasting, prayer and hartal. April 13, the 'Black Friday', witnessed the Jallianwala Bagh massacre."[2]]

A Crucial Turning Point

[Having joined the Besant Home Rule League in 1917, Motilal Nehru had gone still further in 1918, making a final break with his moderate friends over the Montagu-Chelmsford Declaration.[3] In 1919 he became so deeply influenced by Gandhi—after the Jallianwala Bagh massacre, and passage of the Rowlatt Act—that he soon voluntarily gave up both his luxurious way of life and his lucrative profession.

Since austerity is respected in India far more than is wealth, the fact that a rich and successful lawyer should sacrifice his flourishing legal career in order to follow the Mahatma had profound significance. (Jawaharlal: "It was . . . a tremendous struggle for [my father] to uproot himself and to fit himself into [the] new environment."[4])

Although, periodically, Motilal was to have severe clashes of opinion with Gandhi, in much the same manner in which he was to disagree with Jawaharlal, he was to remain an ardent Swarajist (nationalist) throughout the remainder of his life.

There can be little doubt that, since the Mutiny of 1857, no event had caused so tumultuous a reaction in India as the Amritsar tragedy. Its effect upon Jawaharlal, coupled with Gandhi's influence, caused him also to give up his legal practice and, henceforth, to become totally involved in the Nationalist Movement. Jallianwala Bagh (or the Amritsar Massacre) was an important turning point in Indo–British relations in general, among other reasons because it revealed in such shattering manner that the British who appeared before the Hunter Commission looked upon Indians as an inferior race.]

[1] Ibid., pp. 49–51.
[2] M.L.P. (Vol. I), pp. 715–16.
[3] T.N., p. 182.
[4] Quoted in M.B., p. 65.

Direct Contact with Poverty of India, 1920—Early Experience in Dealing with Indian Masses—First Reactions to Russian Revolution

11

Direct Contact with Poverty of India, 1920

In 1920 I was totally ignorant of labor conditions in factories or fields, and my political outlook was entirely bourgeois. I knew, of course, that there was terrible poverty and misery, and I felt that the first aim of a politically free India must be to tackle this problem of poverty. But political freedom, with the inevitable dominance of the middle class, seemed to me the obvious next step. I was paying a little more attention to the peasant problem since Gandhiji's agrarian movements. But my mind was full of political developments and of noncooperation, which was looming on the horizon.

Just then a new interest developed in my life which was to play an important part in later years. I was thrown . . . into contact with the peasantry. . . . I got entangled in the kisan (peasant) movement. That entanglement grew in later years and influenced my mental outlook greatly. . . .

Early in June 1920 (so far as I can remember), about two hundred *kisans* marched fifty miles from the interior of Partabgarh district to Allahabad city with the intention of drawing the attention of the prominent politicians there to their woebegone condition. . . .

I learned that these *kisans* were squatting on the river bank, on one of the Jumna ghats, and, accompanied by some friends, went to see them. They told us of the crushing exactions of the talukdars, of inhuman treatment, and that their condition had become wholly intolerable. They begged us to accompany them back to make inquiries as well as to protect them from the vengeance of the talukdars, who were angry at their having come to Allahabad on this mission. They would accept no denial and literally clung onto us. At last I promised to visit them two days or so later. . . .

That visit was a revelation to me. We found the whole countryside afire with enthusiasm and full of a strange excitement. Enormous gatherings would take place at the briefest notice by word of mouth. One village would communicate with another, and the second with the third, and so on; and presently whole villages would empty out, and all over the fields there would be men and women and children on the march to the meeting place. Or, more swiftly still, the cry of *Sita-Ram—Sita-Ra-a-a-a-m*— would fill the air, and travel far in all directions and be echoed back from other villages, and then people would come streaming out or even running as fast as they could. They were in miserable rags, men and women, but their faces were full of excitement and their eyes glistened and seemed to expect strange happenings which would, as if by a miracle, put an end to their long misery. . . .

Looking at them and their misery and overflowing gratitude, I was filled with shame and sorrow—shame at my own easygoing and comfortable life and our petty politics of the city which ignored this vast multitude of semi-naked sons and daughters of India, sorrow at the degradation and overwhelming poverty of India. A new picture of India seemed to rise before me, naked, starving, crushed, and utterly miserable. And their faith in us, casual visitors from the distant city, embarrassed me and filled me with a new responsibility that frightened me.

I listened to their innumerable tales of sorrow, their crushing and ever-growing burden of rent, illegal exactions, ejectments from land and mud hut, beatings; surrounded on all sides by vultures who preyed on them— zamindar's agents, moneylenders, police; toiling all day to find what they produced was not theirs and their reward was kicks and curses and a hungry stomach. Many of those who were present were landless people who had been ejected by the landlords and had no land or hut to fall back upon. The land was rich, but the burden on it was very heavy, the holdings were small, and there were too many people after them. Taking advantage of this land hunger, the landlords, unable under the law to enhance their rents beyond a certain percentage, charged huge illegal premiums. The tenant, knowing of no other alternative, borrowed money from the moneylender and paid the premium, and then, unable to pay his debt or even the rent, was ejected and lost all he had.

This process was an old one, and the progressive pauperization of the peasantry had been going on for a long time. What had happened to bring matters to a head and rouse up the countryside? Economic conditions, of course. . . .

What amazed me . . . was our total ignorance in the cities of this great agrarian movement. No newspaper had contained a line about it; they were not interested in rural areas. I realized more than ever how cut off we were from our people and how we lived and worked and agitated in a little world apart from them. . . .

Even before my visit to Partabgarh in June 1920, I had often passed through villages, stopped . . . and talked to the peasants. I had seen them in their scores of thousands on the banks of the Ganges during the big *melas*, and we had taken our home rule propaganda to them. But somehow I had not fully realized what they were and what they meant to India. Like most of us, I took them for granted. This realization came to me during these Partabgarh visits, and ever since then my mental picture of India always contains this naked, hungry mass. . . .

I resumed my visits to the villages and watched the agrarian movement grow in strength. The downtrodden *kisan* began to gain a new confidence in himself and walked straighter with head up. His fear of the landlords' agents and the police lessened, and, when there was an ejectment from a holding, no other *kisan* would make an offer for that land. Physical violence on the part of the zamindars' servants and illegal exactions became infrequent, and, whenever an instance occurred, it was immediately reported and an attempt at an inquiry was made. This checked the zamindars' agents as well as the police.

The talukdars and the big zamindars, the lords of the land, the "natural leaders of the people", as they are proud of calling themselves, are the spoiled children of the British Government; but that Government had succeeded, by the special education and upbringing it provided or failed to provide for them, in reducing them, as a class, to a state of complete intellectual impotence. They do nothing at all for their tenantry, and are complete parasites on the land and the people. Their chief activity lies in endeavoring to placate the local officials, without whose favor they could not exist for long, and demanding ceaselessly a protection of their special interests and privileges.

Right through the year 1921 I continued my visits to the rural areas, but my field of activity grew till it comprised the whole of the United Provinces. Nonco-operation had begun in earnest, and its message had reached the remotest village. A host of Congress workers in each district went about the rural areas with the new message, to which they often added, rather vaguely, a removal of *kisan* grievances. *Swaraj* was an all-embracing word to cover everything. Yet the two movements—nonco-operation and the agrarian—were quite separate, though they overlapped and influenced each other greatly. . . . As a result of Congress preaching, litigation went down with a rush and villages established their *panchayats* to deal with their disputes. Especially powerful was the influence of the Congress in favor of peace, for the new creed of nonviolence was stressed wherever the Congress worker went. This may not have been fully appreciated or understood, but it did prevent the peasantry from taking to violence.[1]

Early Experience in Dealing with Indian Masses

"Go to the villages" was the slogan, and we trudged many a mile across fields and visited distant villages and addressed peasant meetings. I experienced the thrill of mass feeling, the power of influencing the mass. I began to understand a little the psychology of the crowd, the difference between the city masses and the peasantry, and I felt at home in the dust and discomfort, the pushing and jostling of large gatherings, though their want of discipline often irritated me. Since those days I have sometimes had to face hostile and angry crowds, worked up to a state when a spark would light a flame, and I found that that early experience and the confidence it begot in me stood me in good stead. Always I went straight to the crowd and trusted it, and so far I have always had courtesy and appreciation from it, even though there was no agreement. But crowds are fickle, and the future may have different experiences in store for me.

I took to the crowd, and the crowd took to me, and yet I never lost myself in it; always I felt apart from it. From my separate mental perch I looked at it critically, and I never ceased to wonder how I, who was so different in every way from those thousands who surrounded me, different in habits, in desires, in mental and spiritual outlook, had managed to gain good will and a measure of confidence from these people. Was it because they took me for something other than I was? Would they bear with me when they knew me better? Was I gaining their good will under false pretenses? I tried to be frank and straightforward to them.[2]

First Reactions to Russian Revolution

[From Conversation with Tibor Mende.]
J.N.: "When we first heard the news [in India] of the first [Russian]

[1] T.F., pp. 54–57, 59–61.
[2] Ibid., pp. 75–76.

Revolution, the Kerensky Revolution, we naturally were very happy. I had read some books and accounts about previous attempts in Russia and about Czarist rule being very oppressive and very autocratic. I reacted against that type and I sympathized with the revolutionary movement there. There was no Marxism attached to it in any way. So, the Kerensky Revolution created a great deal of interest not only in me but in India in general. Then followed the Bolshevik Revolution, which was a very exciting episode indeed. We did not get much information about it at the time, it was just after the war and that, of course, was a very absorbing factor. Our sympathies were very much with Lenin and the others, without knowing much about Marxism. I had not read anything about Marxism by then."

T.M.: "At that time, your sympathies with the Russian events were simply in . . . chronological order, following [those] for the Italian Republic, for the Irish revolutionaries or for the Kerensky Revolution. . . ."

J.N.: "Yes, plus [a] new socialistic element. Because Lenin was the representative of this socialistic urge. . . ."

T.M.: "At that stage this was still rather vague. You did not know much about their ideology. . . ."

J.N.: "[It was] vague, yes . . . but it [had to do with] bringing up the underdog and . . . equalizing people, removing vested interests and all that. . . . [After that] . . . our sympathies, mine at any rate, were entirely with Lenin and the others. Again, without knowing much about what was happening. . . . Also, you will remember, perhaps . . . what Lenin did . . . in regard to China. He immediately gave up extra-territoriality and the special privileges of the Russians there. His movement in Russia powerfully affected parts of Asia. I am not talking of the Soviet parts of it but those countries toward the Middle East.

"After the First World War, Mr Churchill had actually talked about a great Middle-Eastern empire of the British stretching from India to Constantinople. And after the war they were practically in possession of these countries. Now, I did not like that. So, I liked the developments in Russia as a counterpoise to all this. I have no doubt that it made a great difference to Iran and Turkey and all those countries, in those days."

T.M.: "At that stage . . . the Russian experiment did not imply to you any applicability to the Indian situation? Or was it a purely international phenomenon?"

J.N.: "Except that it made me think of politics much more in terms of social change.

"It was not merely a nationalist upsurge, or one against autocracy like the Czars' rule, but a social change coming up in the people. It meant more equality. The precise problems of democracy and authoritarianism did not trouble me, they did not come up before me. These developed in me only later. . . .

"After the Russian Revolution the thing that impressed us most was [the] idea of planning; and more especially the stories we heard of the tremendous changes in the Central Asian parts which were very, very backward. . . .

"I am . . . referring to the early 'twenties, to 1921, 1922, when changes were taking place in all these areas to the north of Afghanistan; in Uzbekistan, Samarkand and Bukhara. But precise news we did not have. Anyhow, the general impression was created that great social and political changes were taking place there and one rather discounted the violence in them. That was partly because war was going on, [which] one could not help; but partly also because we discounted the stories that came to us, as propaganda."[1]

[It was not until his initial visit to the U.S.S.R. in 1927 that Jawaharlal was to have his first direct contact with Soviet Russia, and to see Communism in action.]

12 | Inception of Gandhian Era of Congress, 1919–1920: Khilafat Committee— Development of Muslim League— The Early 1920s

Inception of Gandhian Era of Congress, 1919–1920 : Khilafat Committee

[When Gandhi's leadership became firmly established in Congress in 1920, the Indian Nationalist Movement entered upon an entirely new phase, utilizing hitherto untried, novel and unorthodox political methods.

[1] T.M., pp. 16–18. Reprinted from *Nehru: Conversations on Indian and World Affairs* by Tibor Mende, with the permission of the publisher, George Braziller, Inc. © 1956.

Its middle-class, bourgeois character was almost entirely transformed. The masses became strongly attracted to it. Its spirit was daring, courageous, "revolutionary"—the "revolution" involved being that of Gandhian non-violence.

In certain respects, what the Mahatma advocated seemed somewhat negative, initially, to those who failed to comprehend his larger purpose. Gandhi's program at first appeared to involve a mere boycott, even though a quadruple one: of foreign goods, of impending elections under the Government of India Act of 1919, of schools and colleges, of the law courts. Yet, to "the surprise of many, both officials and Congressmen, almost two-thirds of the electors stayed away from the polls in November 1920". This, in itself, had spectacular repercussions. Subsequently at the 1920 Nagpur Congress session, the entire Congress goal was officially changed, entirely because of Gandhi's influence, to "'the attainment of Swaraj [freedom] . . . by all legitimate and peaceful means', a radical departure from the previous goal of 'self-government within the Empire'".[1]

With respect to the Khilafat Committee: the Turkish Sultan had been "regarded by the Muslim world as their Caliph or spiritual head. During World War I . . . Lloyd George [as British Prime Minister] gave a pledge that the integrity of Turkey would be maintained and [that] the sacred places of Islam would remain with the acknowledged head of the Muslim religion." The Muslims of India consequently gave their loyal support to the British during the war, even agreeing to fight against their "brothers in Islam". After the war, however, the promises that had been made were unfulfilled. The Ottoman Empire was dismembered. Turkey was deprived of her Arabian provinces, in which Islam's holy places are located. India's Muslims regarded what had occurred as a breach of faith, which constituted for them what they termed the Khilafat Wrong.[2]]

The Amritsar Congress [of 1919–1920] was the first Gandhi Congress. Lokamanya Tilak was also present and took a prominent part in the deliberations, but there could be no doubt about it that the majority of the delegates, and even more so the great crowds outside, looked to Gandhi for leadership. The slogan *Mahatma Gandhi ki jai* [Victory to Gandhi] began to dominate the Indian political horizon. The Ali brothers [prominent Muslim leaders], recently discharged from internment, immediately joined the Congress, and the national movement began to take a new shape and develop a new orientation.

M. Mohamad Ali went off soon on a Khilafat deputation to Europe. In India the Khilafat Committee came more and more under Gandhiji's influence and began to flirt with his ideas of nonviolent noncooperation.

[1] M.B., p. 71.
[2] M.L.P. (Vol. I), pp. 712–13.

I remember one of the earliest meetings of the Khilafat leaders and Moulvies and Ulemas in Delhi in January 1920. A Khilafat deputation was going to wait on the Viceroy, and Gandhiji was to join it. Before he reached Delhi, however, a draft of the proposed address was, according to custom, sent to the Viceroy. When Gandhiji arrived and read this draft, he strongly disapproved of it and even said that he could not be a party to the deputation if this draft was not materially altered. His objection was that the draft was vague and wordy, and there was no clear indication in it of the absolute minimum demands which the Moslems must have. He said that this was not fair to the Viceroy and the British Government, or to the people, or to themselves. They must not make exaggerated demands which they were not going to press, but should state the minimum clearly and without possibility of doubt, and stand by it to the death. If they were serious, this was the only right and honorable course to adopt.

This argument was a novel one in political or other circles in India. We were used to vague exaggerations and flowery language, and always there was an idea of a bargain in our minds. Gandhiji, however, carried his point; and he wrote to the private secretary of the Viceroy, pointing out the defects and vagueness of the draft address sent, and forwarding a few additional paragraphs to be added to it. These paragraphs gave the minimum demands. The Viceroy's reply was interesting. He refused to accept the new paragraphs and said that the previous draft was, in his opinion, quite proper. Gandhiji felt that this correspondence had made his own position and that of the Khilafat Committee clear, and so he joined the deputation after all.

It was obvious that the Government were not going to accept the demands of the Khilafat Committee, and a struggle was therefore bound to come. There were long talks with the Moulvies and the Ulemas, and nonviolence and noncooperation were discussed, especially nonviolence. Gandhiji told them that he was theirs to command, but on the definite understanding that they accepted nonviolence with all its implications. There was to be no weakening on that, no temporizing, no mental reservations. It was not easy for the Moulvies to grasp this idea, but they agreed, making it clear that they did so as a policy only and not as a creed, for their religion did not prohibit the use of violence in a righteous cause.

The political and the Khilafat movements developed side by side during 1920, both going in the same direction and eventually joining hands with the adoption by the Congress of Gandhiji's nonviolent noncooperation. . . .

The Moslem League did not represent . . . any considerable section of

Moslem opinion. It was the Khilafat Committee of 1920 that was a powerful and far more representative body, and it was this Committee that entered upon the [non-violent] struggle with enthusiasm.[1]

[In the Khilafat issue were also "involved the conflicting ambitions of the Turks, the Greeks and the Arabs and the clash of interests—strategic as well as economic—of the Allies at the end of the First World War. The Muslim divines and politicians who had Gandhi's ear were unable to see that the Khilafat was a moribund institution, that the Turks themselves were thoroughly sick of it, that the Ottoman Empire had to go the way of the Hapsburg Empire, that the smaller nations, Arab and non-Arab, were struggling to shake off the Turkish yoke."[2]]

Development of Muslim League

[Founded] in 1906 with British encouragement and in order to keep away the new generation of Moslems from the National Congress, [the Moslem League] remained a small upperclass organization controlled by feudal elements. It had no influence on the Moslem masses and was hardly known by them. By its very constitution it was limited to a small group and a permanent leadership which perpetuated itself. Even so, events and the growing middle class among the Moslems pushed it in the direction of the Congress. World War I and the fate of the Turkish [Khilafat] and the Moslem holy places produced a powerful impression on the Moslems of India and made them intensely anti-British. The Moslem League, constituted as it was, could not offer any guidance or leadership to these awakened and excited masses; indeed the League suffered from an attack of nerves and practically faded away.... The Moslem masses drifted [away] from political activity, as also the Hindu masses to a lesser extent. But a very considerable number of Moslems, chiefly of the middle classes, continued to function through the Congress.

During this period a number of petty Moslem organizations functioned spasmodically, often coming into conflict with each other. They had no mass affiliations, no political importance except such as was given to them by the British government. Their chief function was to demand special privileges and protection for the Moslems in the legislatures and services. In this matter they did represent a definite Moslem viewpoint, for there was a background of resentment and fear among the Moslems at the

[1] T.F., pp. 51-53.
[2] T.N., pp. 173-74.

superior position of the Hindus in education, services, and industry, as well as numbers.[1]

[After the Muslim agitation relating to the Khilafat issue had lost its *raison d'être*, hence its momentum, Hindu–Muslim tensions reappeared. Serious communal disturbances occurred in 1923.]

The Early 1920s

I saw a great deal of Gandhiji. Very often his proposals seemed novel. . . . But almost always he argued his way to their acceptance, and subsequent events showed the wisdom of his advice. Faith in his political insight grew in me. . . .[2]

In the autumn of 1920 a special session of . . . Congress met at Calcutta. . . . This special session . . . began the Gandhi era in Congress politics. . . . The whole look of the Congress changed; European clothes vanished, and soon only *khadi* [hand-spun, hand-woven cloth of Indian-grown thread] was to be seen; a new class of delegate, chiefly drawn from the lower middle classes, became the type of Congressman; the language used became increasingly Hindustani, or sometimes the language of the province where the session was held, as many of the delegates did not understand English, and there was also a growing prejudice against using a foreign language in our national work; and a new life and enthusiasm and earnestness became evident in Congress gatherings.[3]

Gandhi . . . immediately brought about a complete change in [the Congress] constitution. He made it democratic and a mass organization. Democratic it had been previously also, but it had so far been limited in franchise and restricted to the upper classes. Now the peasants rolled in, and in its new garb it began to assume the look of a vast agrarian organization with a strong sprinkling of the middle classes. This agrarian character was to grow. Industrial workers also came in, but as individuals and not in their separate, organized capacity.

Action was to be the basis and objective of this organization, action based on peaceful methods. Thus far the alternatives had been: just talking and passing resolutions, or terroristic activity. Both of these were set aside, and terrorism was especially condemned as opposed to the basic policy of the Congress. A new technique of action was evolved which,

[1] D.I., pp. 384–85.
[2] T.F., p. 50.
[3] Ibid., pp. 65–67.

though perfectly peaceful, yet involved nonsubmission to what was considered wrong, and as a consequence, a willing acceptance of the pain and suffering involved in this. Gandhi was an odd kind of pacifist, for he was an activist full of dynamic energy. There was no submission in him to fate or anything that he considered evil; he was full of resistance, though this was peaceful and courteous.

The call of action was twofold. There was of course the action involved in challenging and resisting foreign rule; there was also the action which led us to fight our own social evils. Apart from the fundamental objective of the Congress—the freedom of India—and the method of peaceful action, the principal planks of the Congress were national unity, which involved the solution of the minority problems, and the raising of the depressed classes and the ending of the curse of untouchability.

Realizing that the main props of British rule were fear, prestige, the cooperation, willing or unwilling, of the people, and certain classes whose vested interests were centered in British rule, Gandhi attacked these foundations. Titles were to be given up, and though the title-holders responded to this only in small measure, the popular respect for these British-given titles disappeared and they became symbols of degradation. New standards and values were set up, and the pomp and splendor of the viceregal court and the princes, which used to impress so much, suddenly appeared supremely ridiculous and vulgar and rather shameful, surrounded as they were by the poverty and misery of the people. Rich men were not so anxious to flaunt their riches; outwardly at least many of them adopted simpler ways, and in their dress became almost indistinguishable from humbler folk.

The older leaders of the Congress, nurtured in a different and more quiescent tradition, did not take easily to these new ways and were disturbed by the upsurge of the masses. Yet so powerful was the wave of feeling and sentiment that swept through the country that some of that intoxication filled them also. A very few fell away, and among them was Mr M. A. Jinnah. He left the Congress [in 1920] not because of any difference of opinion on the Hindu–Moslem question but because he could not adapt himself to the new and more advanced ideology, and even more because he disliked the crowds of ill-dressed people, talking in Hindustani, who filled the Congress. His idea of politics was of a superior variety, more suited to the legislative chamber or to a committee room. For some years he felt completely out of the picture and even decided to leave India for good. He settled down in England and spent several years there.[1]

[1] D.I., pp. 363-64.

[Despite his sojourn in England, Mohammed Ali Jinnah was to become India's most influential Muslim League leader. After his withdrawal from the Home Rule League and Congress in 1920, he began increasingly to rebel against the philosophy of both groups, especially against Gandhi's credo of satyagraha.

In Jawaharlal's view, since Jinnah's policies basically were in harmony with those of India's large landowners, it seemed inevitable that he should oppose the social reforms advocated by a Gandhi-oriented Congress. Becoming an ardent opponent of a united, secular India, Jinnah ultimately favored Muslim separatism—or partition—through the founding of a new nation, Pakistan.]

It is said, and I think with truth, that the Indian habit of mind is essentially one of quietism. Perhaps old races develop that attitude to life; a long tradition of philosophy also leads to it. And yet Gandhi, a typical product of India, represents the very antithesis of quietism. He has been a demon of energy and action, a hustler, and a man who not only drives himself but drives others. He has done more than anyone I know to fight and change the pietism of the Indian people.[1]

[Gandhi] . . . didn't shout. . . . He spoke softly and gently, and put forward what he thought were his minimum demands, and stuck to them. There was an element of great strength about it.[2]

He sent us to the villages, and the countryside hummed with the activity of innumerable messengers of the new gospel of action. The peasant was shaken up and he began to emerge from his quiescent shell. The effect on us was different but equally far-reaching, for we saw, for the first time as it were, the villager in the intimacy of his mud hut and with the stark shadow of hunger always pursuing him. We learned our Indian economics more from these visits than from books and learned discourses. The emotional experience we had already undergone was emphasized and confirmed, and henceforward there could be no going back for us to our old life or our old standards, howsoever much our views might change subsequently.

Gandhi held strong views on economic, social, and other matters. He did not try to impose all of these on the Congress, though he continued to develop his ideas, and sometimes in the process varied them, through his writings. But some he tried to push into the Congress. He proceeded cautiously, for he wanted to carry the people with him. Sometimes he went too far for the Congress and had to retrace his steps. Not many

[1] Ibid., p. 364.
[2] Quoted in M.B., p. 75.

accepted his views in their entirety; some disagreed with that fundamental outlook. But many accepted them in the modified form, in which they came to the Congress as being suited to the circumstances then existing. In two respects the background of his thoughts had a vague but considerable influence: the fundamental test of everything was how far it benefited the masses, and the means were always important and could not be ignored even though the end in view was right, for the means governed the end and varied it.

Gandhi was essentially a man of religion, a Hindu to the innermost depths of his being, and yet his conception of religion had nothing to do with any dogma or custom or ritual. It was basically concerned with his firm belief in the moral law, which he calls the Law of Truth or Love. Truth and nonviolence appear to him to be the same thing or different aspects of one and the same thing, and he uses these words almost interchangeably.

Claiming to understand the spirit of Hinduism, he rejects every text or practice which does not fit in with his idealist interpretation of what it should be, calling it an interpolation or a subsequent accretion. "I decline to be a slave," he has said, "to precedents or practice I cannot understand or defend on a moral basis." And so in practice he is singularly free to take the path of his choice, to change and adapt himself, to develop his philosophy of life and action, subject only to the overriding consideration of the moral law as he conceives this to be. Whether that philosophy is right or wrong may be argued, but he insists on applying the same fundamental yardstick to everything, and himself specially. In politics, as in other aspects of life, this creates difficulties for the average person, and often misunderstanding. But no difficulty makes him swerve from the straight line of his choosing, though within limits he is continually adapting himself to a changing situation. Every reform that he suggests, every advice that he gives to others, he straightway applies to himself. He is always beginning with himself, and his words and actions fit into each other like a glove on the hand. And so, whatever happens, he never loses his integrity and there is always an organic completeness about his life and work. Even in his apparent failures he has seemed to grow in stature.

What was his idea of India which he was setting out to mold according to his own wishes and ideals? "I shall work for an India in which the poorest shall feel that it is their country, in whose making they have an effective voice, an India in which there shall be no high class and low class of people, an India in which all communities shall live in perfect harmony. . . . There can be no room in such an India for the curse of untouchability or

3+N.

the curse of intoxicating drinks and drugs. . . . Women . . . will enjoy the same rights as men. . . . This is the India of my dreams."

Proud of his Hindu inheritance as he was, he tried to give to Hinduism a kind of universal attire and included all religions within the fold of truth. He refused to narrow his cultural inheritance. "Indian culture," he wrote, "is neither Hindu, Islamic nor any other, wholly. It is a fusion of all." Again he said: "I want the culture of all lands to be blown about my house as freely as possible. But I refuse to be blown off my feet by any. I refuse to live in other peoples' houses as an interloper, a beggar or a slave." Influenced by modern thought currents, he never let go of his roots and clung to them tenaciously.

And so he set about to restore the spiritual unity of the people and to break the barrier between the small westernized group at the top and the masses, to discover the living elements in the old roots and to build upon them, to waken these masses out of their stupor and static condition and make them dynamic. In his single-track and yet many-sided nature the dominating impression that one gathered was his identification with the masses, a community of spirit with them, an amazing sense of unity with the dispossessed and poverty-stricken not only of India but of the world. Even religion, as everything else, took second place to his passion to raise these submerged people. "A semi-starved nation can have neither religion nor art nor organization." "Whatever can be useful to starving millions is beautiful to my mind. Let us give today first the vital things of life, and all the graces and ornaments of life will follow. . . . I want art and literature that can speak to millions." These unhappy dispossessed millions haunted him, and everything seemed to revolve round them. "For millions it is an eternal vigil or an eternal trance." His ambition, he said, was "to wipe every tear from every eye".

It is not surprising that this astonishingly vital man, full of self-confidence and an unusual kind of power, standing for equality and freedom for each individual, but measuring all this in terms of the poorest, fascinated the masses of India and attracted them like a magnet. He seemed to them to link up the past with the future and to make the dismal present appear just as a steppingstone to that future of life and hope. And not the masses only, but intellectuals and others also, though their minds were often troubled and confused and the changeover for them from the habits of lifetimes was more difficult. Thus he effected a vast psychological revolution not only among those who followed his lead but also among his opponents and those many neutrals who could not make up their minds what to think and what to do.

Congress was dominated by Gandhi, and yet it was a peculiar domination, for the Congress was an active, rebellious, many-sided organization, full of variety of opinion, and not easily led this way or that. Often Gandhi toned down his position to meet the wishes of others; sometimes he accepted even an adverse decision. On some vital matters for him he was adamant, and on more than one occasion there came a break between him and the Congress. But always he was the symbol of India's independence and militant nationalism, the unyielding opponent of all those who sought to enslave her, and it was as such a symbol that people gathered to him and accepted his lead, even though they disagreed with him on other matters. They did not always accept that lead when there was no active struggle going on, but when the struggle was inevitable, that symbol became all-important and everything else was secondary.

Thus in 1920 the National Congress, and to a large extent the country, took to this new and unexplored path and came into conflict repeatedly with the British power. That conflict was inherent both in these methods and the new situation that had arisen; yet back of all this was not political tactics and maneuvering but the desire to strengthen the Indian people, for by that strength alone could they achieve independence and retain it. Civil disobedience struggles came one after the other, involving enormous suffering, but that suffering was self-invited and therefore strength-giving, not the kind which overwhelms the unwilling, leading to despair and defeatism. The unwilling also suffered, caught in the wide net of fierce governmental repression, and even the willing sometimes broke and collapsed. But many remained true and steadfast, harder for all the experience they had undergone. At no time, even when its fortunes were low, did Congress surrender to superior might or submit to foreign authority. It remained the symbol of India's passionate desire for independence and her will to resist alien domination. It was because of this that vast numbers of the Indian people sympathized with it and looked to it for leadership, even though many of them were too weak and feeble, or so circumstanced as to be unable to do anything themselves. The Congress was a party in some ways; it has also been a joint platform for several parties; but essentially it was something much more, for it represented the innermost desire of vast numbers of our people. The number of members on its rolls, large as this was, was only a feeble reflection of this widespread representative character, for membership depended not on the people's desire to join but on our capacity to reach remote villages. Often . . . we have been an illegal organization, not existing at all in the eyes of the law, and our books and papers have been taken away by the police.

Even when there was no civil disobedience struggle going on, the general attitude of non-co-operation with the British apparatus of government in India continued, though it lost its aggressive character. That did not mean, of course, non-co-operation with Englishmen as such. When Congress governments were installed in many provinces, there was inevitably much co-operation in official and governmental work. Even then, however, that background did not change much, and instructions were issued regulating the conduct of Congressmen apart from official duties. Between Indian nationalism and an alien imperialism there could be no final peace, though temporary compromises and adjustments were sometimes inevitable. Only a free India could co-operate with England on equal terms.[1]

[August 1, 1920 was proclaimed the date for inaugurating the Noncooperation Movement. At just that time the last serious rival to Gandhi's leadership in Congress—Lokamanya Tilak—died in Bombay.]

13 | First Police Action against Jawaharlal, 1920—Correspondence Relating Thereto

First Police Action against Jawaharlal, 1920

[First sentenced to jail in the early twenties, Jawaharlal was to be imprisoned nine times before the end of World War II and once briefly thereafter in Kashmir, before India finally gained her independence in 1947. His actual "sentences" totalled over fourteen years, plus one term of "indefinite detention". An initial order of externment, issued against him in Mussoorie in 1920 for allegedly being in contact with a visiting Afghan delegation, was withdrawn by the Government.]

My mother and Kamala (my wife) were both unwell, and early in May 1920 I took them up to Mussoorie. Peace negotiations were proceeding between the Afghan and British envoys (this was after the brief Afghan War in 1919 when Amanullah came to the throne) at Mussoorie, and the

[1] D.I., pp. 364-68.

Afghan delegation were stopping at the same hotel. They kept to themselves, however, fed separately, and did not appear in the common rooms. I was not particularly interested in them, and for a whole month I did not see a single member of their delegation, or if I saw them I did not recognize them. Suddenly one evening I had a visit from the superintendent of police, who showed me a letter from the local government asking him to get an undertaking from me that I would not have any dealings or contacts with the Afghan delegation. This struck me as extraordinary since I had not even seen them during a month's stay and there was little chance of my doing so. The superintendent knew this, as he was closely watching the delegation, and there were literally crowds of secret service men about. But to give any undertaking went against the grain, and I told him so. He asked me to see the district magistrate, the superintendent of the Dun, and I did so. As I persisted in my refusal to give an undertaking, an order of externment was served on me, calling upon me to leave the district of Dehra Dun within twenty-four hours, which really meant within a few hours from Mussoorie. I did not like the idea of leaving my mother and wife, both of whom were ailing; and yet I did not think it right to break the order. There was no civil disobedience then. So I left Mussoorie.

My father had known Sir Harcourt Butler, who was then Governor of the United Provinces, fairly well, and he wrote to him a friendly letter saying that he was sure that he (Sir Harcourt) could not have issued such a stupid order; it must be some bright person in Simla who was responsible for it. Sir Harcourt replied that the order was quite a harmless one and Jawaharlal could easily have complied with it without any injury to his dignity. Father, in reply, disagreed with this and added that, although there was no intention of deliberately breaking the order, if my mother's or wife's health demanded it I would certainly return to Mussoorie, order or no order. As it happened, my mother's condition took a turn for the worse, and both father and I immediately started for Mussoorie. Just before starting, we received a telegram rescinding the order.

When we reached Mussoorie the next morning, the first person I noticed in the courtyard of the hotel was an Afghan who had my baby daughter in his arms! I learned that he was a minister and a member of the Afghan delegation. It transpired that immediately after my externment the Afghans had read about it in the newspapers, and they were so much interested that the head of the delegation took to sending my mother a basket of fruit and flowers every day.[1]

[1] T.F., pp. 54–55.

[It is generally agreed that it was Jawaharlal's interest in the Kisan Movement—already referred to—rather than any possible contact he might have had with the Afghans, that aroused the British against him in 1920.]

Correspondence Relating to First Police Action

[To Motilal—May 14, 1920.] Greatness is being thrust on me. I have just had a visit from the Superintendent of Police. He showed me a letter from the Government addressed to him in which he was asked to take a positive undertaking from me to the effect that I would refrain from seeing or having any communication with the Afghan delegates. In case I refused to give this undertaking, an externment order was to be served on me. I told him that as a matter of fact I had no intention of having anything to do with the Afghan delegation. I had not even seen any of them from a distance so far. He said this was so. He knew it perhaps from various C.I.D. sources. But I told him that on principle I was opposed to giving any undertaking. He was very courteous.[1]

[To M. L. Oakes, Superintendent of Police, Mussoorie, May 14, 1920.] I have carefully thought over the conversation we had this morning and the question of my giving a "Positive undertaking", as required by Government, not to see or have any communication with the Afghan delegates now at Mussoorie. I regret I am unable to change my opinion on the subject.

As you are aware, I came to Mussoorie with my mother, wife and sisters solely on account of my wife's ill health. It was my intention to stay here with my family till such time as my father was free to come up. I have no concern with the Afghan delegation and it was an accident that we both happened to be in the same hotel. As a matter of fact their presence here has put me out to a certain extent as I was looking forward to taking possession of the rooms at present occupied by them. I am of course interested in the delegation, as every intelligent person must be, but I had or have not the slightest intention of going out of my way to meet them. We have been here now for the last seventeen days and during this period I have not seen a single member of the delegation even from a distance. You are yourself aware of this fact as you told me this morning.

But, although I have no intention whatever of seeing the Afghans or

[1] T.N., pp. 178–79.

having any communication with them, I utterly dislike the idea of binding myself down to any course of action at the instance of the Government, even though such action may not prove irksome. It is really a question of principle or conscience. You will, I feel sure, appreciate my position. I am therefore unable, I am sorry to say, to accept your courteous advice and give an undertaking to Government.

If the Government chooses to serve any order on me, I am, for the present, prepared to obey it. It will be a great inconvenience to me to have to go down suddenly and leave my family by themselves here. The condition of my wife's health requires the most careful attention and my mother is a confirmed invalid, and it is most difficult to leave them uncared for. My sudden departure will upset my father's and my plans entirely and cause us any amount of trouble and anxiety. But I suppose individual conveniences cannot be considered in high matters of state.[1]

[To G. F. Adams, District Magistrate, Mussoorie, May 15, 1920.] I have again fully considered the matter and I regret that I am unable to give the undertaking required by Government. Under the circumstances I am prepared to go down from Mussoorie if the Government orders me to do so. I was at first inclined to accept your suggestion and go down of my own accord without any written order from Government, but on further consideration, I do not think it will be right for me to do so. I shall therefore await the formal notice.

[First Externment Order against Jawaharlal—May 16, 1920: "Whereas in the opinion of the Local Government there are reasonable grounds for believing that Jowahir [sic] Lal Nehru of Allahabad is acting, or is about to act in a manner prejudicial to the public safety, Now Therefore the Lieutenant Governor of the United Provinces in exercise of the powers conferred on him by rule 3 of the Defence of India (Consolidation) Rules, 1915, is pleased to direct that the said Jowahir Lal Nehru of Allahabad shall not enter, reside, or remain, in any area within the limits of the district of Dehra Dun in the United Provinces and the said Jowahir Lal Nehru is hereby warned that if he knowingly disobeys the direction in this order he will be liable to the penalty prescribed by sub-section (i) of rule 5 of the Defence of India (Consolidation) Rules, 1915, a copy of which rule is attached to this order.

M. KEANE
Chief Secretary to Government.
United Provinces.

[1] B.O.L., pp. 7–8.

Mr J. L. Nehru will leave the Dehra Dun District this day. By order of Supdt. Dun.

M. L. OAKES
S. P. Dehra Dun,
16.5.20."

Letter from Motilal Nehru to Sir Harcourt Butler, Lieutenant Governor, United Provinces, May 19, 1920:

"Jawaharlal was attending to my work in the High Court besides his own and it involved no little sacrifice to give up both and accompany the ladies to the hills. He was busy in making various arrangements when the peace of the family was suddenly disturbed 'for reasons of State'. He had put his little sister to school the very morning when the Superintendent of Police paid his first visit to him, and as he was going down after service of the order he met the riding ponies sent for his use from Allahabad going up to Mussoorie.

"These are the circumstances under which 'in the opinion of the Local Government there are reasonable grounds for believing that Jawaharlal Nehru of Allahabad is acting or is about to act in a manner prejudicial to the public safety'. From the conversation which the Superintendent of Police had with Jawaharlal it would appear that the 'reasonable grounds' would have ceased to exist if Jawaharlal had degraded himself by giving a 'positive undertaking' not to do a thing which he had not the faintest idea of doing. I need hardly say that I wholly approve of Jawaharlal's action. It was indeed the only course open to him. His politics and mine are well known. We have never made any secret of them. We know they are not of the type which finds favour with the Government and we are prepared to suffer any discomfort which may necessarily flow from them. But the imputation made against Jawaharlal runs directly counter to the very principles we stand for and are prepared to suffer for. . . . [Young] Jawaharlal is known throughout India and I can confidently say that there is not a man, excepting perhaps in the C.I.D., who will believe that he is capable of carrying on a secret intrigue of the nature apprehended from him. You have yourself had a long talk with him and knowing as I do the vast and varied knowledge of human nature you possess I cannot easily believe that you could for a moment doubt the material he is made of. I am therefore inclined to think that one of two alternatives has happened: either the order has been issued by some mistake or inadvertence or under pressure from above. If neither alternative is true, I shall be driven to the painful conclusion that the policy of leaving well alone so far followed by your Government is now undergoing a change.

"We have known each other for over 30 years and I have thought it best to express my feelings frankly and unreservedly. All I desire is to know whether the order was issued after due consideration by the Local Government and if so on what grounds. I shall feel grateful if you will kindly direct that this information may be supplied to me."[1]

[1] Ibid., pp. 9-11.

From Sir Harcourt's reply to Motilal: "I am really very sorry that you and your son, and especially the ladies of your family, should have been inconvenienced by an official act which your son made it a matter of conscience not to fall in with. . . . I hope, whatever views we may hold on public matters . . . in private life . . . nothing will interfere with the friendly relations that have existed between us for thirty years."

From Motilal to Jawaharlal, June 14: "It was necessary to let Master Butler know, that we are not the people to be overawed by him into servility. I have written to him exactly as I felt and knew how you would feel."[1]

On June 15, the externment order against Jawaharlal was unconditionally revoked.]

14 | 1921: The Non-Cooperation Campaign Gains Impetus

About this time or a little later, C. F. Andrews wrote a pamphlet advocating independence for India. I think it was called *Independence—the Immediate Need*. This was a brilliant essay . . . and it seemed to me not only to make out an unanswerable case for independence but also to mirror the inmost recesses of our hearts. The deep urge that moved us and our half-formed desires seemed to take clear shape in his simple and earnest language. There was no economic background or socialism in what he had written; it was nationalism pure and simple, the feeling of the humiliation of India and a fierce desire to be rid of it and to put an end to our continuing degradation. It was wonderful that C. F. Andrews, a foreigner and one belonging to the dominant race in India, should echo that cry of our inmost being.[2]

Many of us who worked for the Congress program lived in a kind of intoxication during the year 1921. We were full of excitement and optimism and a buoyant enthusiasm. We sensed the happiness of a person crusading for a cause. We were not troubled with doubts or hesitation;

[1] T.N., pp. 179–80.
[2] T.F., p. 67.

3*

our path seemed to lie clear in front of us, and we marched ahead, lifted up by the enthusiasm of others, and helping to push on others. We worked hard, harder than we had ever done before, for we knew that the conflict with the Government would come soon, and we wanted to do as much as possible before we were removed.

Above all, we had a sense of freedom and a pride in that freedom. The old feeling of oppression and frustration was completely gone. There was no more whispering, no round-about legal phraseology to avoid getting into trouble with the authorities. We said what we felt and shouted it out from the housetops. What did we care for the consequences? Prison? We looked forward to it; that would help our cause still further. The innumerable spies and secret-service men who used to surround us and follow us about became rather pitiable individuals as there was nothing secret for them to discover. All our cards were always on the table.

We had not only a feeling of satisfaction at doing effective political work which was changing the face of India before our eyes and, as we believed, bringing Indian freedom very near, but also an agreeable sense of moral superiority over our opponents, in regard to both our goal and our methods. We were proud of our leader and of the unique method he had evolved, and often we indulged in fits of self-righteousness. In the midst of strife, and while we ourselves encouraged that strife, we had a sense of inner peace.

As our morale grew, that of the Government went down. They did not understand what was happening; it seemed that the old world they knew in India was toppling down. There was a new aggressive spirit abroad and self-reliance and fearlessness, and the great prop of British rule in India—prestige—was visibly wilting. Repression in a small way only strengthened the movement, and the Government hesitated for long before it would take action against the big leaders. It did not know what the consequences might be. . . .

The nerves of many a British official began to give way. The strain was great. There was this ever-growing opposition and spirit of defiance which overshadowed official India like a vast monsoon cloud, and yet because of its peaceful methods it offered no handle, no grip, no opportunity for forcible suppression. The average Englishman did not believe in the *bona fides* of nonviolence; he thought that all this was camouflage, a cloak to cover some vast secret design which would burst out in violent upheaval one day. Nurtured from childhood in the widespread belief that the East is a mysterious place, and in its bazaars and narrow lanes secret conspiracies are being continually hatched, the Englishman can seldom think straight on matters relating to these lands of supposed mystery. He never makes an attempt to understand that somewhat obvious and very unmysterious person, the Easterner.[1]

There was a strange mixture of nationalism and politics and religion and mysticism and fanaticism. Behind all this was agrarian trouble and, in the big cities, a rising working-class movement. Nationalism and a vague but intense countrywide idealism sought to bring together all these various, and sometimes mutually contradictory, discontents, and succeeded to a remarkable degree. And yet this nationalism itself was a composite force, and behind it could be distinguished a Hindu nationalism, a Moslem nationalism partly looking beyond the frontiers of India, and, what was more in consonance with the spirit of the times, an Indian nationalism. For the time being they overlapped and pulled together. . . .

Even more remarkable was the fact that these desires and passions were relatively free from hatred of the alien rulers against whom they were directed. Nationalism is essentially an anti-feeling, and it feeds and fattens on hatred and anger against other national groups, and especially against the foreign rulers of a subject country. There was certainly this hatred and anger in India in 1921 against the British, but, in comparison with other countries similarly situated, it was extraordinarily little. Undoubtedly this was due to Gandhiji's insistence on the implications of nonviolence. It was also due to the feeling of release and power that came to the whole country with the inauguration of the movement and the widespread belief in success in the near future. Why be angry and full of hate when we were doing so well and were likely to win through soon? We felt that we could afford to be generous.

We were not so generous in our hearts, though our actions were circumspect and proper, toward the handful of our own countrymen who took sides against us and opposed the national movement. It was not a question of hatred or anger, for they carried no weight whatever and we could ignore them. But deep within us was contempt for their weakness and opportunism and betrayal of national honor and self-respect.

So we went on, vaguely but intensely, the exhilaration of action holding us in its grip. But about our goal there was an entire absence of clear thinking. It seems surprising . . . how completely we ignored the theoretical aspects, the philosophy of our movement as well as the definite objective that we should have. Of course we all grew eloquent about *Swaraj*, but each one of us probably interpreted the word in his or her own way. To most of

[1] Ibid., pp. 69-70.

the younger men it meant political independence, or something like it, and a democratic form of government, and we said so in our public utterances. Many of us also thought that inevitably this would result in a lessening of the burdens that crushed the workers and the peasantry. But it was obvious that to most of our leaders *Swaraj* meant something much less than independence. Gandhiji was delightfully vague on the subject, and he did not encourage clear thinking about it either. But he always spoke, vaguely but definitely, in terms of the underdog, and this brought great comfort to many of us, although, at the same time, he was full of assurances to the top dog also. Gandhiji's stress was never on the intellectual approach to a problem but on character and piety. He did succeed amazingly in giving backbone and character to the Indian people.

It was this extraordinary stiffening-up of the masses that filled us with confidence. A demoralized, backward and broken-up people suddenly straightened their backs and lifted their heads and took part in disciplined, joint action on a countrywide scale. This action itself, we felt, would give irresistible power to the masses. We ignored the necessity of thought behind the action; we forgot that without a conscious ideology and objective the energy and enthusiasm of the masses must end largely in smoke. To some extent the revivalist element in our movement carried us on; a feeling that nonviolence as conceived for political and economic movements or for righting wrongs was a new message which our people were destined to give to the world. We became victims to the curious illusion of all peoples and all nations that in some way they are a chosen race. Nonviolence was the moral equivalent of war and of all violent struggle. It was not merely an ethical alternative, but it was effective also. Few of us, I think, accepted Gandhiji's old ideas about machinery and modern civilization. We thought that even he looked upon them as utopian and as largely inapplicable to modern conditions. Certainly most of us were not prepared to reject the achievements of modern civilization, although we may have felt that some variation to suit Indian conditions was possible. Personally, I have always felt attracted toward big machinery and fast traveling. Still, there can be no doubt that Gandhiji's ideology influenced many people and made them critical of the machine and all its consequences. So, while some looked to the future, others looked back to the past. And, curiously, both felt that the joint action they were indulging in was worth while, and this made it easy to bear sacrifice and face self-denial.

I became wholly absorbed and wrapped in the movement, and large numbers of other people did likewise. I gave up all my other associations and contacts, old friends, books, even newspapers, except in so far as they dealt with the work in hand.[1]

15 | First Imprisonment, 1921

[The Prince of Wales paid a " good-will " visit to India during a period of great tension: November, 1921. A highly successful hartal, organized by Gandhi, occurred on the day the Prince was to arrive (not in order to dramatize or inspire hatred of either the Prince or the English, but rather to register protest against Britain's repressive measures in India). Nationalists were arrested by the thousands, among them Jawaharlal and his father, Motilal.

Before his first imprisonment, Jawaharlal had been appointed Secretary of the United Provinces Congress. In April, 1921, Lord Reading succeeded Lord Chelmsford as Viceroy.]

Right through the year 1921 individual Congress workers were being arrested and sentenced, but there were no mass arrests. . . . I was threatened in the summer with proceedings for sedition because of some speeches I had delivered. No such step, however, was taken then. The end of the year brought matters to a head. . . .

The inevitable conflict between the Congress and the Government was about to break out. Prison was still an unknown place, the idea of going there still a novelty. I was sitting rather late one day in the Congress office at Allahabad trying to clear up arrears of work. An excited clerk told me that the police had come with a search warrant and were surrounding the office building. I was, of course, a little excited also, for it was my first experience of this kind, but the desire to show off was strong, the wish to appear perfectly cool and collected, unaffected by the comings and goings of the police. So I asked a clerk to accompany the police officer in his search round the office rooms and insisted on the rest of the staff carrying on their usual work and ignoring the police. A little later a friend and a colleague, who had been arrested just outside the office, came to me, accompanied by a policeman, to bid me good-by. I was so

[1] Ibid., pp. 73-75

full of the conceit that I must treat these novel occurrences as everyday happenings that I treated my colleague in a most unfeeling manner. Casually I asked him and the policeman to wait till I had finished the letter I was writing. Soon [the] news came of other arrests in the city. I decided at last to go home and see what was happening there. I found the inevitable police searching part of the large house and learned that they had come to arrest both father and me. . . .

There was an orgy of arrests and convictions.[1]

[Arrested at Allahabad, Jawaharlal was confined to Lucknow District Jail for his first term in prison, from December 6, 1921 to March 3, 1922.]

Both my father and I . . . [were] . . . sentenced to six months' imprisonment on different charges and by different courts. The trials were farcical . . . we took no part in them. It was easy enough, of course, to find enough material in our speeches or other activities for a conviction. But the actual choice was amusing. Father was tried as a member of an illegal organization, the Congress volunteers, and to prove this a form with his signature in [Hindi] was produced. The signature was certainly his, but, as it happened, he had hardly ever signed in [Hindi] before, and very few persons could recognize his [Hindi] signature. A tattered gentleman was then produced who swore to the signature. The man was quite illiterate, and he held the signature upside down when he examined it. . . .

My offense was distributing notices for a *hartal*. This was no offense under the law then. . . . However, I was sentenced [to six months' imprisonment]. Three months later I was informed in the prison . . . that some revising authority had come to the conclusion that I was wrongly sentenced and I was to be discharged.[2]

[Jawaharlal's first trial was quite as farcical as was his father's. Charged with having appealed to shopkeepers to observe a complete hartal, he was originally to have been convicted under Section 17(2) of Act XIV of 1908. The magistrate discovered, however, that that section was not applicable in his case. Thus the conviction was handed down instead under section 17(1).

Immediately after the charge against Jawaharlal was read out, the examination of the accused began. Magistrate: "Are you a member of the Central Volunteer Board, appointed on 24th or 25th November 1921, to organize [a] Volunteer Corps in the United Provinces?" Jawaharlal: "I do not recognize the British Government in India, and I do not regard this as a court. I regard these proceedings as farce or show. This

[1] T.F., pp. 77–78.
[2] Ibid., pp. 83–84.

court carries out what has already been decided." Question: "Did you attend a meeting of the Congress Committee on the 3rd of December, 1921 in Lucknow?" Answer: "I do not wish to give a reply to this question, or to any question."

"When the magistrate asked the accused to elucidate what he meant by his answer to the first question, [Jawaharlal] said he had decided not to answer any question."

The judgment handed down stated: "The accused does not plead and the only statement he makes is that he does not recognize the Government of India and the court, and regards his trial as a farce.

"The evidence that has been adduced consists of a statement . . . [that the accused was seen] with others distributing notices for [a] *hartal* and boycott of the Prince's visit. There is no evidence to show what part he played in the Lucknow meeting, and as regards his pledge in Allahabad, it is an offence triable there."[1]

In addition to being sentenced to jail, Motilal and Jawaharlal also were fined. Though the fines were small, "both father and son refused to pay them: as non-co-operators they could not admit the jurisdiction of British courts. This gave the local police a pretext for making raids on Anand Bhawan [the Nehru residence] and carrying away . . . furniture and carpets worth thousands in lieu of fines of a few hundreds."[2]]

In the early 'twenties when we had our first experience of prison . . . we were intensely occupied with our own struggle. Everything else was interesting in a distant way only. . . . But we were so very conscious of ourselves and so confident in ourselves that external occurrences did not disturb us. . . .

We had so much faith in Gandhiji and in Gandhiji's methods. . . . [We] felt that we were on the right path. So we were not really exploring. We were not in a frustrated mind as to what to do. We knew that we were right and rather—if I may say so, egotistically—we *were* right. It was a combination, which is always a happy combination, of feeling that you are morally right and yet you are effective. It is a very happy combination which seldom comes and which gives one strength.

Secondly, going to prison made us discuss among ourselves in jail and . . . read books for which we had no time outside. And, of course . . . Gandhi was always talking of the underdog. He was doing it in his own way; not in the Socialist way, not in the class-struggle way, but just always talking about the underdog: especially of the peasants of India. So, our thinking became more and more conditioned to the peasantry of India; not so much to the industrial workers, though to some extent to them too. It was rather to the peasants and very much against the land-lords and the rest. So, in that sense, socially speaking, all of us were powerfully conditioned. Now, the Russian example did not come in much; it helped us in thinking. We thought we could learn much from it—but merely to adapt our thinking . . . not to change it basically.[1]

Imprisonment for political offenses was not a new thing in the India of 1921. From the time of the [1905] Bengal partition agitation especially, there had always been a continuing stream of men going to prison, sentenced often to very long terms. There had been internments without trial also. . . . The Great War speeded up this process of internment and imprisonment, and conspiracy cases became frequent, usually resulting in death sentences or life terms. . . .

But still in 1921 prison was an almost unknown place, and very few knew what happened behind the grim gates that swallowed the new convict. Vaguely we imagined that its inhabitants were desperate people and dangerous criminals. In our minds the place was associated with isolation, humiliation, and suffering, and, above all, the fear of the unknown. Frequent references to jail-going from 1920 onward, and the march of many of our comrades to prison, gradually accustomed us to the idea and took away the edge from that almost involuntary feeling of repugnance and reluctance. But no amount of previous mental preparation could prevent the tension and nervous excitement that filled us when we first entered the iron gates. Since those days, thirteen years ago, I imagine that at least three hundred thousand men and women of India have entered those gates for political offenses, although often enough the actual charge has been under some other section of the criminal code. Thousands of these have gone in and out many a time; they have got to know well what to expect inside; they have tried to adapt themselves to the strange life there, as far as one can adapt oneself to an existence full of abnormality and a dull suffering and a dreadful monotony. We grow accustomed to it, as one grows accustomed to almost anything; and yet, every time that we enter those gates again, there is a bit of the old excitement, a feeling of tension, a quickening of the pulse. And the eyes turn back involuntarily to take a last good look outside at the greenery and wide spaces, at people and conveyances moving about, at familiar faces that they may not see again for a long time. . . .[2]

[1] T.M., pp. 19–20. Reprinted from *Nehru: Conversations on India and World Affairs* by Tibor Mende, with the permission of the publisher, George Braziller, Inc. © 1956.
[2] T.F., pp. 85–86.

In ... jail every effort was made to keep us apart from the ordinary nonpolitical convicts, special jails being as a rule preserved for politicals. But complete segregation was impossible, and we often came into touch with those prisoners and learned from them, as well as directly, the realities of prison life in those days. It was a story of violence and widespread graft and corruption. The food was quite amazingly bad; I tried it repeatedly and found it quite uneatable. The staff was usually wholly incompetent and was paid very low salaries, but it had every opportunity to add to its income by extorting money on every conceivable occasion from the prisoners or their relatives. The duties and responsibilities of the jailer, and his assistants, and the warders, as laid down by the Jail Manual, were so many and so various that it was quite impossible for any person to discharge them conscientiously or competently. The general policy of the prison administration in the United Provinces (and probably in other provinces) had absolutely nothing to do with the reform of the prisoner or of teaching him good habits and useful trades. The object of prison labor was to harass the convict. He was to be frightened and broken into blind submission; the idea was that he should carry away from prison a fear and a horror of it, so that he might avoid crime and a return to prison in the future.[1]

The restrictions on us gradually grew in number, and stricter rules were enforced. The government, having got the measure of our movement, wanted us to experience the full extent of its displeasure with our temerity in having dared to challenge it. . . .[2]

The days lengthened themselves into weeks, and the weeks became months. We grew accustomed to our routine existence. But in the world outside the real burden fell on our womenfolk, our mothers and wives and sisters. They wearied with the long waiting, and their very freedom seemed a reproach to them when their loved ones were behind prison bars.[3]

16 | Suspension of Civil Disobedience, 1922

[Despite Nehru's love of and admiration for Gandhi, and his essential respect for utilizing the technique of non-violent civil resistance, it was

[1] Ibid., p. 91.
[2] Ibid., p. 89.
[3] Ibid., p. 91.

in 1922 that he first disagreed with the Mahatma about the strategy to be used in conjunction with employing it. The disagreement was to recur.]

Gradually the Government gave up the policy of indiscriminate arrests; only noted workers were picked out. Gradually also the first flush of enthusiasm of the people cooled down, and, owing to the absence in prison of all the trusted workers, a feeling of indecision and helplessness spread. But the change was superficial only; there was still thunder in the air, and the atmosphere was tense and pregnant with revolutionary possibilities. During the months of December 1921 and January 1922 it is estimated that about thirty thousand persons were sentenced to imprisonment in connection with the nonco-operation movement. But, though most of the prominent men and workers were in prison, the leader of the whole struggle, Mahatma Gandhi, was still out, issuing from day to day messages and directions which inspired the people, as well as checking many an undesirable activity. The Government had not touched him so far, for they feared the consequences, the reactions on the Indian Army and the police.

Suddenly, early in February 1922, the whole scene shifted, and we in prison learned, to our amazement and consternation, that Gandhiji had stopped the aggressive aspects of our struggle, that he had suspended civil resistance. We read that this was because of what had happened near the village of Chauri Chaura, where a mob of villagers had retaliated on some policemen by setting fire to the police station and burning half a dozen or so policemen in it.

We were angry when we learned of this stoppage of our struggle at a time when we seemed to be consolidating our position and advancing on all fronts. But our disappointment and anger in prison could do little good to anyone; civil resistance stopped, and nonco-operation wilted away. After many months of strain and anxiety the Government breathed again, and for the first time had the opportunity of taking the initiative. A few weeks later they arrested Gandhiji and sentenced him for a long term of imprisonment.

The sudden suspension of our movement . . . was resented, I think, by almost all the prominent Congress leaders—other than Gandhiji, of course. My father (who was in jail at the time) was much upset by it. The younger people were naturally even more agitated. Our mounting hopes tumbled to the ground, and this mental reaction was to be expected. What troubled us even more were the reasons given for this suspension and the consequences that seemed to flow from them. . . .

[The incident that caused the suspension] may have been and was a deplorable occurrence and wholly opposed to the spirit of the nonviolent movement; but were a remote village and a mob of excited peasants in an out-of-the-way place going to put an end, for some time at least, to our national struggle for freedom? If this was the inevitable consequence of a sporadic act of violence, then surely there was something lacking in the philosophy and technique of a nonviolent struggle. For it seemed to us to be impossible to guarantee against the occurrence of some such untoward incident. Must we train the three hundred and odd millions of India in the theory and practice of nonviolent action before we could go forward? And, even so, how many of us could say that under extreme provocation from the police we would be able to remain perfectly peaceful? But even if we succeeded, what of the numerous *agents provocateurs*, stool pigeons, and the like who crept into our movement and indulged in violence themselves or induced others to do so? If this was the sole condition of its function, then the nonviolent method of resistance would always fail.

We had accepted that method, the Congress had made that method its own, because of a belief in its effectiveness. Gandhiji had placed it before the country not only as the right method but as the most effective one for our purpose. In spite of its negative name it was a dynamic method, the very opposite of a meek submission to a tyrant's will. It was not a coward's refuge from action, but the brave man's defiance of evil and national subjection. But what was the use of the bravest and the strongest if a few odd persons—maybe even our opponents in the guise of friends— had the power to upset or end our movement by their rash behavior?

Gandhiji had pleaded for the adoption of the way of nonviolence, of peaceful nonco-operation, with all the eloquence and persuasive power which he so abundantly possessed. His language had been simple and unadorned, his voice and appearance cool and clear and devoid of all emotion, but behind that outward covering of ice there was the heat of a blazing fire and concentrated passion, and the words he uttered winged their way to the innermost recesses of our minds and hearts, and created a strange ferment there. The way he pointed out was hard and difficult, but it was a brave path, and it seemed to lead to the promised land of freedom. . . .

We were moved by [Gandhiji's] arguments, but for us and for the National Congress as a whole the nonviolent method was not, and could not be, a religion or an unchallengeable creed or dogma. It could only be a policy and a method promising certain results, and by those results it would have to be finally judged. Individuals might make of it a religion or incontrovertible creed. But no political organization, so long as it remained political, would do so.

[The cause of the suspension of civil resistance] and its consequences made us examine [the] implications of nonviolence as a method, and we felt that, if Gandhiji's argument for the suspension of civil resistance was correct, our opponents would always have the power to create circumstances which would necessarily result in our abandoning the struggle. Was this the fault of the nonviolent method itself or of Gandhiji's interpretation of it? After all, he was the author and originator of it, and who could be a better judge of what it was and what it was not? And without him where was our movement?

Many years later, just before the 1930 civil disobedience movement began, Gandhiji, much to our satisfaction, made this point clear. He stated that the movement should not be abandoned because of the occurrence of sporadic acts of violence. If the nonviolent method of struggle could not function because of such almost inevitable happenings, then it was obvious that it was not an ideal method for all occasions, and this he was not prepared to admit. For him the method, being the right method, should suit all circumstances and should be able to function, at any rate in a restricted way, even in a hostile atmosphere. Whether this interpretation, which widened the scope of nonviolent action, represented an evolution in his own mind or not I do not know.

It may be that the decision to suspend civil resistance in 1922 was a right one, though the manner of doing it left much to be desired and brought about a certain demoralization.

It is possible, however, that this sudden bottling up of a great movement contributed to a tragic development in the country. The drift to sporadic and futile violence in the political struggle was stopped, but the suppressed violence had to find a way out, and in the following years this perhaps aggravated the communal trouble. The communalists of various denominations, mostly political reactionaries, had been forced to lie low because of the overwhelming mass of support for the nonco-operation and civil disobedience movement. They emerged now from their retirement. Many others, secret-service agents and people who sought to please the authorities by creating communal friction, also worked on the same theme.[1]

[1] T.F., pp. 79-83.

[From Gandhi to Jawaharlal—Bardoli, February 19, 1922: "I see that all of you are terribly cut up over the resolutions of the Working Committee. I sympathise with you, and my heart goes out to Father. . . . I received letters both from Hindus and Mohammedans . . . telling me . . . that our people were becoming aggressive, defiant and threatening, that they were getting out of hand and were not non-violent in demeanor. . . .

"With all [such] news in my possession and much more . . . the Chauri Chaura news came like a powerful match to ignite the gunpowder, and there was a blaze. I assure you that if the [civil resistance movement] had not been suspended we would have been leading not a non-violent struggle but essentially a violent struggle. It is undoubtedly true that non-violence is spreading like the scent of the otto [sic] of roses throughout the length and breadth of the land, but the foetid smell of violence is still powerful, and it would be unwise to ignore or underrate it. The cause will prosper by this retreat. The movement had unconsciously drifted from the right path. We have come back to our moorings, and we can again go straight ahead."[1]]

| 17 | On Gandhi's Religious Outlook— On Organized Religion |

On Gandhi's Religious Outlook

[As already indicated, in spite of his life-long devotion to Gandhi, Jawaharlal occasionally was to be somewhat critical of his beloved colleague.]

To some extent I resented Gandhiji's preoccupation with nonpolitical issues, and I could never understand the background of his thought. . . . [When] he was collecting funds for *khadi* work . . . he would say frequently that he wanted money for *Daridranarayan*, the "Lord of the Poor," or "God that resides in the poor"; meaning thereby, presumably, that he wanted it to help the poor to find employment and work in cottage industries. But behind that word there seemed to be a glorification of poverty; God was especially the Lord of the poor; they were His

[1] B.O.L., pp. 23–24.

chosen people. That, I suppose, is the usual religious attitude every-where. I could not appreciate it, for poverty seemed to me a hateful thing, to be fought and rooted out and not to be encouraged in any way. This inevitably led to an attack on a system which tolerated and produced poverty, and those who shrunk from this had of necessity to justify poverty in some way. They could only think in terms of scarcity and could not picture a world abundantly supplied with the necessaries of life; probably, according to them, the rich and the poor would always be with us.

Whenever I had occasion to discuss this with Gandhiji, he would lay stress on the rich treating their riches as a trust for the people; it was a viewpoint of considerable antiquity, and one comes across it frequently in India as well as medieval Europe. I confess that I have always been wholly unable to understand how any person can reasonably expect this to happen, or imagine that therein lies the solution of the social problem.[1]

Gandhiji was continually laying stress on the religious and spiritual side of the movement. His religion was not dogmatic, but it did mean a definitely religious outlook on life, and the whole movement was strongly influenced by this and took on a revivalist character so far as the masses were concerned. The great majority of Congress workers naturally tried to model themselves after their leader and even repeated his language. And yet Gandhiji's leading colleagues in the Working Committee [including Motilal Nehru] were not men of religion in the ordinary sense of the word, and they considered political problems on the political plane only. In their public utterances they did not bring in religion. But what-ever they said had far less influence than the force of their personal example—had they not given up a great deal that the world values and taken to simpler ways of living? This in itself was taken as a sign of religion and helped in spreading the atmosphere of revivalism.

I used to be troubled sometimes at the growth of this religious element in our politics, both on the Hindu and the Moslem side. I did not like it at all. Much that Moulvies and Maulanas and Swamis and the like said in their public addresses seemed to me most unfortunate. Their history and sociology and economics appeared to me all wrong, and the religious twist that was given to everything prevented all clear thinking. Even some of Gandhiji's phrases sometimes jarred upon me—thus his frequent reference to *Rama Raj* as a golden age which was to return. But I was powerless to intervene, and I consoled myself with the thought that

[1] T.F., p. 143.

Gandhiji used the words because they were well known and understood by the masses. He had an amazing knack of reaching the heart of the people.

But I did not worry myself much over these matters. I was too full of my work and the progress of our movement to care for such trifles, as I thought at the time they were. A vast movement had all sorts and kinds of people in it, and, so long as our main direction was correct, a few eddies and backwaters did not matter. As for Gandhiji himself, he was a very difficult person to understand; sometimes his language was almost incomprehensible to an average modern. But we felt that we knew him quite well enough to realize that he was a great and unique man and a glorious leader, and, having put our faith in him, we gave him an almost blank check, for the time being at least. Often we discussed his fads and peculiarities among ourselves and said, half-humorously, that when *Swaraj* came these fads must not be encouraged.

Many of us, however, were too much under his influence in political and other matters to remain wholly immune even in the sphere of religion. Where a direct attack might not have succeeded, many an indirect approach went a long way to undermine the defenses. The outward ways of religion did not appeal to me, and above all I disliked the exploitation of the people by the so-called men of religion, but still I toned down toward it. I came nearer to a religious frame of mind in 1921 than at any other time since my early boyhood. Even so I did not come very near.

What I admired was the moral and ethical side of our movement and of *Satyagraha*. I did not give an absolute allegiance to the doctrine of nonviolence or accept it forever, but it attracted me more and more, and the belief grew upon me that, situated as we were in India and with our background and traditions, it was the right policy for us. The spiritualization of politics, using the word not in its narrow religious sense, seemed to me a fine idea. A worthy end should have worthy means leading up to it. That seemed not only a good ethical doctrine but sound, practical politics, for the means that are not good often defeat the end in view and raise new problems and difficulties.[1]

On Organized Religion

Organized religion, whatever its past may have been, today is very largely an empty form devoid of real content. It has been filled up by some

[1] Ibid., pp. 71–72.

totally different substance. And, even where something of value still remains, it is enveloped by other and harmful contents.

That seems to have happened in our Eastern religions as well as in the Western. The Church of England is perhaps the most obvious example of a religion which is not a religion in any real sense of the word. Partly that applies to all organized Protestantism, but the Church of England has probably gone further because it has long been a State political department. [In India the Church of England has been almost indistinguishable from the Government. The officially paid (out of Indian revenues) priests and chaplains are the symbols of the Imperial power just as the higher services are.][1]

Many . . . votaries [of the Church of England] are undoubtedly of the highest character, but it is remarkable how that Church has served the purposes of British imperialism and given both capitalism and imperialism a moral and Christian covering. It has sought to justify, from the highest ethical standards, British predatory policy in Asia and Africa and given that extraordinary and enviable feeling of being always in the right to the English. Whether the Church has helped in producing this attitude of smug rectitude or is itself a product of it, I do not know. Other less favored countries on the continent of Europe and in America often accuse the English of hypocrisy—*perfide Albion* is an old taunt—but the accusation is probably the outcome of envy at British success, and certainly no other imperialist Power can afford to throw stones at England, for its own record is equally shady. No nation that is consciously hypocritical could have the reserves of strength that the British have repeatedly shown, and the brand of "religion" which they have adopted has apparently helped them in this by blunting their moral susceptibilities where their own interests were concerned. Other peoples and nations have often behaved far worse than the British have done, but they have never succeeded, quite to the same extent, in making a virtue of what profited them. All of us find it remarkably easy to spot the mote in the other's eye and overlook the beam in our own, but perhaps the British excel at this performance.

Protestantism tried to adapt itself to new conditions and wanted to have the best of both worlds. It succeeded remarkably so far as this world was concerned, but from the religious point of view it fell, as an organized religion, between two stools, and religion gradually gave place to sentimentality and big business. Roman Catholicism escaped this fate,

[1] Ibid., p. 241; material in brackets from footnote on same page.

as it stuck on to the old stool, and, so long as that stool holds, it will flourish. Today it seems to be the only living religion, in the restricted sense of the word, in the West. A Roman Catholic friend sent me in prison many books on Catholicism and papal encyclicals, and I read them with interest. Studying them, I realized the hold it had on such large numbers of people. It offered, as Islam and popular Hinduism offer, a safe anchorage from doubt and mental conflict, an assurance of a future life which will make up for the deficiencies of this life.

I am afraid it is impossible for me to seek harborage in this way. I prefer the open sea, with all its storms and tempests. Nor am I greatly interested in the afterlife, in what happens after death. I find the problems of this life sufficiently absorbing to fill my mind. The traditional Chinese outlook, fundamentally ethical and yet irreligious or tinged with religious skepticism, has an appeal for me, though in its application to life I may not agree. It is the *Tao*, the path to be followed and the way of life, that interests me; how to understand life, not to reject it but to accept it, to conform to it, and to improve it. But the usual religious outlook does not concern itself with this world. It seems to me to be the enemy of clear thought, for it is based not only on the acceptance without demur of certain fixed and unalterable theories and dogmas, but also on sentiment and emotion and passion. It is far removed from what I consider spiritual and things of the spirit, and it deliberately or unconsciously shuts its eyes to reality lest reality may not fit in with preconceived notions. It is narrow and intolerant of other opinions and ideas; it is self-centered and egotistic; and it often allows itself to be exploited by self-seekers and opportunists.

This does not mean that men of religion have not been and are not still often of the highest moral and spiritual type. But it does mean that the religious outlook does not help, and even hinders, the moral and spiritual progress of a people, if morality and spirituality are to be judged by this world's standards, and not by the hereafter. Usually religion becomes an asocial quest for God or the Absolute, and the religious man is concerned far more with his own salvation than with the good of society. The mystic tries to rid himself of self, and in the process usually becomes obsessed with it. Moral standards have no relation to social needs but are based on a highly metaphysical doctrine of sin. And organized religion invariably becomes a vested interest and thus inevitably a reactionary force opposing change and progress.[1]

[1] Ibid., pp. 241–43.

18 | Boycott of Foreign Cloth— Second Arrest—Statement in Court at Allahabad—Jail, 1922

Boycott of Foreign Cloth

[After Jawaharlal was released from Lucknow District Jail on March 3, 1922, he became intensely interested in the boycott of foreign cloth. "It was this activity which became the cause of his arrest for the second time. On May 11, [1922] he had gone to visit his father in . . . Lucknow jail, and while there, he was asked by the superintendent to come out with him. . . . [At] the jail gate he was put under arrest and taken to Allahabad where, on May 13, he was produced before the district magistrate." [1]]

I interested myself in the boycott of foreign cloth. This item of our program still continued in spite of the withdrawal of civil resistance. Nearly all the cloth merchants in Allahabad had pledged themselves not to import or purchase foreign cloth, and had formed an association for the purpose. The rules of this association laid down that any infringement would be punished by a fine. I found that several of the big dealers had broken their pledges and were importing foreign cloth. This was very unfair to those who stuck to their pledges. We remonstrated with little result, and the cloth dealers' association seemed to be powerless to take action. So we decided to picket the shops of the erring merchants. Even a hint of picketing was enough for our purpose. Fines were paid, pledges were taken afresh. The money from the fines went to the cloth merchants' association.

Two or three days later I was arrested, together with a number of colleagues who had taken part in the negotiations with the merchants. We were charged with criminal intimidation and extortion! I was further charged with some other offences, including sedition. I did not defend myself, but I made a long statement in court. I was sentenced on at least three counts, including intimidation and extortion, but the sedition charge was not proceeded with, as it was probably considered that I had already got as much as I deserved. As far as I remember there were three sentences, two of which were for eighteen months and were concurrent.

[1] T.T.N., p. 10.

In all, I think, I was sentenced to a year and nine months. That was my second sentence. I went back to prison after about six weeks spent outside it.[1]

[From translation from Urdu of relevant portion of speech on picketing Allahabad cloth dealers (who refused to cease importing foreign cloth)—April, 1922.]

People come to me these days, cloth merchants of your city come and take out their scales and say that this is profitable to us and this is unprofitable to us, and that if they do not sell foreign cloth they will sustain a great loss. What should I say to you and them? I have said much to these sellers of foreign cloth. I have seen them many a time. During the last month, i.e. ever since my release [from jail], I have visited them nearly every week. I have told them that they would agree to what I have said when I would picket their shops. But I do not want to exert pressure upon them. I [have] wanted [them to agree] of their own accord. . . . Some persons [have broken] their pledges which they signed before God saying that they would not import foreign cloth. . . . They imported foreign cloth, and if you go to the bazaar you will see how they are importing foreign cloth. For the last one and a half months I bore this.

What I had to say I have said. Now I tell you and any one of them who may be present here, that there will be picketing from tomorrow. (Cheers). . . . Why are you clapping? I have told you this simply because you know that picketing is a thing which is impossible as long as you or the shop-keepers do not sympathise with us. It is not possible that two or three men should picket shops so long as the public is not with them. Therefore, I have perfect faith in our success, because as your clapping indicates, I find that you sympathise with us. But you should not sympathise with us only to the extent of saying 'hear-hear'. Rather you should in sympathising with us . . . become volunteers, enlist others as volunteers and make this picketing successful. I have pondered over it before starting it.[2]

Second Arrest

[At the time charges were brought against Jawaharlal, the following interchange took place: The Magistrate: "Do you plead guilty?" Jawaharlal: "I refuse to plead."

[1] T.F., pp. 84–85.
[2] T.T.N., pp. 22–23.

Q. "Do you wish to cross-examine the prosecution witnesses?" A. "I do not wish to cross-examine the witnesses." Q. "Do you wish to produce any defence?" A. "No. I do not wish to produce any defence." Q. "Do you wish to make any statement?" A. "As I said yesterday, I wish to make a comprehensive statement, and that is the only part that I propose to take in the proceedings. I will require some time to prepare my statement, and it would be convenient to me if the next hearing is postponed till Wednesday." [1]]

From Statement in Court Before District Magistrate of Allahabad—May 17, 1922

I am making this statement not in order to defend myself against the various charges brought against me but to define my position and to state the motives which have induced me to act in the manner I have done. I have refused to plead guilty or not guilty, and I have declined to participate in the trial by cross-examination of witnesses or otherwise. I have done so because I do not recognise this court as a court where justice is administered. I mean no disrespect to the presiding officer when I say that so far as political offences are concerned the courts in India merely register the decrees of the executive. They are being used today more than ever before to prop up the fabric of a Government which has misgoverned India long enough and of which the prestige is gone for ever.

I stand here charged with criminal intimidation and abetment of an attempt to extort. The warrant of my arrest bears also the familiar section 124A, although I am not being tried for it today. I propose however to make a comprehensive statement. I cannot divide myself up into various compartments, one for picketing, another for sedition and yet another perhaps for volunteering. All my activities have but one end in view, and that end I have striven to attain with all the strength and energy that is in me. Less than ten years ago I returned from England and after a lengthy stay there, I had passed through the usual course of public school and university. I had imbibed most of the prejudices of Harrow and Cambridge, and in my likes and dislikes I was perhaps more an Englishman than an Indian. I looked upon the world almost from an Englishman's standpoint. And so I returned to India as much prejudiced in favour of England and the English as it was possible for an Indian to be.

Today, ten years later, I stand here in the dock charged with two offences and with a third hovering in the background—an ex-convict who has been to jail once already for a political offence, and rebel against the present system of Government in India. That is the change which the years have brought in me. It is not necessary for me to recite the reasons for this change. Every Indian knows them; every Indian has felt them and has hung his head in shame for them. And if he has retained a spark of the old fire in him, he has taken a solemn pledge to strive unceasingly for India's freedom, so that his countrymen may never again be subjected to the miseries and humiliations that are the lot of a subject race. Today, sedition against the present Government in India has become the creed of the Indian people; to preach and practise disaffection against the evil which it represents has become their chief occupation.

I am charged with criminal intimidation, and attempted extortion. I have wondered if these charges were seriously meant. The sections of the Code which have been applied bear no relation to the facts even as disclosed by the prosecution evidence. I presume that the signal success that has attended our efforts in Allahabad has induced the authorities to take some action against the picketers. If peaceful picketing for a lawful object is a crime then indeed I am guilty of having advised it and helped in it. But I have yet to learn that peaceful picketing has become an offence even under the laws of British India. Our object in picketing was to make the cloth dealers adhere to the pledges they had jointly taken. Does anyone believe that we could achieve success in this by criminal intimidation and extortion? All the world knows that our strength lies in the support of our people and the good-will of our countrymen. Our weapons are not the old time ones of force and coercion. The weapons which our great leader has put in our hands are those of love and self-sacrifice. We suffer ourselves and by our suffering seek to convert our adversary.

Criminal intimidation involves a threat of injury to a person or his property, and injury denotes harm "illegally" caused. So also extortion must include the putting of any person in fear of "injury" and thereby "dishonestly" inducing him to part with property. I have listened to the prosecution evidence with interest in order to find out on what ground these novel charges are based. What was the injury to any person or property that was threatened? What was the harm "illegally" caused? Wherein lay the dishonesty of any of us? I have not heard a single allegation yet made, much less proved, which suggests that we have caused injury to any person or property, caused any harm illegally or acted dishonestly. Not a single prosecution witness including the police and the C.I.D. has made such an allegation. In the whole of Allahabad there was found no person of the thousands who must have witnessed the picketing, who could bring the charge of any intimidation against us, or even a harsh word uttered by one of our picketers. No greater proof of our triumph can be given than this unsought testimony of the police and the C.I.D. Our picketing has been, I make bold to say, a model of its kind, perfectly peaceful, perfectly courteous, relying on entreaties and exhortations, and not even hinting at force or intimidation. The cloth dealers, who are alleged to have been intimidated by us, are presumably the aggrieved party. But not one of them has complained.

Ten months ago, the cloth dealers of Allahabad took a solemn pledge to refrain from purchasing foreign cloth till the end of 1922. All the signatories to the pledge, and they included almost every cloth-merchant in the city, constituted themselves into an association styled the Vyapar Mandal and elected office-bearers and a committee. The first business of the Mandal was to lay down that every member who broke his pledge and purchased foreign cloth would have to pay a certain penalty and in case he refused to do this, picketing would be resorted to. The Committee of the Mandal was to determine in each individual case how much foreign cloth had been bought and what the penalty was to be. On several occasions during the past year the Mandal committee considered such breaches of the pledge and imposed and recovered fines in accordance with their rules. Occasionally, at their request, picketing was also resorted to. Two months ago a large quantity of foreign cloth was purchased by some of the cloth-dealers in Allahabad. This was in contravention of the pledge, and the shops of some of these cloth-dealers were picketed. Later, a committee of the Vyapar Mandal, newly reconstituted, assessed the fines on the merchants who had broken their pledges, and themselves collected this money, which lies at the disposal of the Mandal. To the best of my knowledge two of the gentlemen, who have given evidence for the prosecution in this case, are members of the committee of the Mandal, and as such they must have themselves helped in the assessment and collection of the fines.

These are the facts relating to picketing in Allahabad. It is clear beyond doubt that there was neither intimidation nor any attempt at [extortion]. The present prosecution is really an attempt to suppress lawful and peaceful picketing under cover of charges of intimidation and extortion. Picketing has been going on all over India for many months. It has taken place in many cities and bazaars in the province. Here in this very city of Allahabad we have repeatedly resorted to it. And yet Government took no action against it as such. They knew well that in India, as in England, peaceful picketing is no crime. Of course, it is open to them by a stroke of the pen to make even peaceful picketing illegal. But whether they do so or not we shall not give it up. To entreat and exhort and advise others to follow a certain line of action or to abstain from doing something is a right which we will not abandon, whatever the Government may do. We have few rights and privileges left in this country and even these are sought to be taken away. We have shown to the world how we value the right of free association, and we have continued our efforts in spite of thousands of arrests and all Government notifications to the contrary. We will not and we cannot submit to any restriction of our right of free speech.

A quarter of a century ago, a great British judge stated in the House of Lords with reference to this right of free speech: "A man has a right to say what he pleases to induce, to exhort, to command, provided he does not slander or deceive or commit any other of the wrongs known to the law of which speech may be the medium. Unless he is thus shown to have abused his right, why is he to be called upon to excuse or justify himself because his words may interfere with some one else and his calling?" This right of free speech we shall cling to, whatever the cost.

I am glad for many reasons that I am being tried for picketing. My trial will bring the question of the boycott of foreign cloth even more to the fore, and the people of Allahabad and of the province will realise the full significance of it. They will discard all foreign cloth as unholy and treat the touch of it almost as a pollution. If they pondered over the evils and the misery and the poverty that foreign cloth has brought to this long suffering country, perhaps they would feel some of the horror I feel at the thought of wearing it. They will not bring forth arguments that old clothes have to be worn out or that festivities require fine clothing. They would know that the salvation of India and of her hungry millions demand the use of the *charkha* and the wearing of *khaddar* and they would cast out all foreign clothes and consign them to the flames or to the dustbin. I pray that the cloth merchants of Allahabad will adhere to their sacred pledge twice taken, and do their utmost to bring about a complete boycott of foreign cloth in this ancient and holy city. Some of these cloth-dealers have given evidence for the prosecution in this case. I have no grievance against them. I shall suffer most gladly any imprisonment that may be awarded me if I know that thereby I have touched their hearts and won them over to the great cause. And I would appeal to the public of this city and province and earnestly request them to do this much for their country —wear *khaddar* and ply the *charkha*. . . .

I should like the police and Government officials to examine their own conscience, to go deep down into their hearts and say what many of them have done during the past year and a half. Intimidation and terrorism, bribery and extortion have been going on over the length and breadth of the province. And the persons guilty of them have not been Congressmen or our volunteers, but the underlings of Government who have indulged in them frequently with the knowledge and approval of their superiors. Yet they are not tried or punished. They are patted on the back and praised and promoted.

My colleagues and I have seen and personally investigated acts of terrorism and inhumanity. We have seen how men and women have been subjected to uttermost humiliation. We have seen how terror reigns. . . . We have investigated . . . brutalities . . . and we know how hundreds of . . . gallant workers have been sent to jail for the sole offence of being Congress office-bearers or other principal workers of the Congress. And the poor down-trodden kisans with the haunted hopeless look in their eyes, work-ing away like beasts of the field from morning to night-fall, so that others may enjoy the fruits of their labour—we have seen them harassed and made utterly miserable till life became a burden almost too heavy to be borne. I need not refer to individual districts. Almost every one of them has the same sad and splendid tale to tell.

Intimidation and terrorism have become the chief instruments of Government. By these methods they seek to keep down a people and to suppress their disaffection. Do they imagine that they will thus instil affection for themselves in the people or make them loyal instruments of their Imperialism? Affection and loyalty are of the heart. They cannot be purchased in the market place, much less can they be extorted at the point of the bayonet. Loyalty is a fine thing. But in India some words have lost their meaning and loyalty has come to be almost a synonym for treason to the Motherland, and a loyalist is he who is not loyal to his God or his country but merely hangs on to the coat-tails of his alien master. Today, however, we have rescued the word from the depths, and in almost every jail in India will be found true loyalists who have put their cause and their faith and their country above everything else and have been true to them despite all consequences. To them has come the great call; they have seen the vision of freedom and they will not rest or turn away till they have achieved their heart's desire. England is a mighty country with her armies and her navy, but today she is confronted with something that is mightier. Her armies and her navy have to face the suffering and the self-sacrifice of a nation determined to be free, and no man can doubt what the issue of such a struggle must be. We are fighting for our freedom, for the freedom of our country and faith. We desire to injure no nation or people. We wish to have no dominion over others. But we must be perfectly free in our own country. England has cruelly wronged us during the past one hundred and fifty years or more. And even yet she has not repented and mended her ways. India gave her a chance a year and a half ago, but in the pride and arrogance of her physical might she has not taken it. The people of India have tried her and they have passed judgment and from that decree there is no turning back. India will be free; of that there is no doubt, but if England seeks the friendship of a free India she must repent and purge herself of her many sins, so that she may be worthy of a place in the coming order of things.

I shall go to jail again most willingly and joyfully. Jail has indeed become a heaven for us, a holy place of pilgrimage since our saintly and beloved leader was sentenced. . . . One feels almost lonely outside . . . jail, and selfishness prompts a quick return. Perhaps I shall be awarded a long term of imprisonment this time. Whether this is so or not, I shall go with the conviction that I shall come out to greet Swaraj in India.

I have said many hard things about the British Government. For one

I marvel at my good fortune.
To serve India in the battle for
freedom is honour enough!
To serve her under a leader like
Mahatma Gandhi is doubly fortunate.
But to suffer for the dear country!!
What greater good could befall an
Indian unless it be Death for the
Cause or the Full Realisation of
our Glorious Dream !!!

Jawaharlal

4+N.

thing however I must offer it my grateful thanks. It has given us a chance of fighting in this most glorious of struggles. Surely few people have had such an opportunity given them. And the greater our suffering, the more difficult the test we have to pass, the more splendid will be the future of India. India has not sent the noblest and best twenty-five thousand of her sons to the jails to give up the struggle. India's future is assured. Some of us, men and women of little faith, doubt and hesitate occasionally. But those who have vision can almost see the glory that is to be India.

I marvel at my good fortune. To serve India in the battle of freedom is honour enough. To serve her under a leader like Mahatma Gandhi is doubly fortunate. But to suffer for the dear country: what greater good fortune could befall an Indian unless it be death for the cause or the full realization of our glorious dream.[1]

Jail, 1922

[Jawaharlal to Motilal, September 1, 1922.] My mind is full of books I ought to read and it is with great difficulty that I refrain from sending you even longer lists than I have done so far. . . . I wonder often how I shall be able to compress so much reading, spinning, writing, etc., as I have to do before discharge.

Ever since my return from England I had done little reading, and I shudder to think, what I was gradually becoming, before politics and N.C.O. [Non-Co-Operation] snatched me away from the doom that befalls many of us . . . the life I led and that so many of us led, the atmosphere of the lower courts, the uninspiring conversation of the Bar Library, the continuous contact with the sordid side of human nature—all this and the absence of any organized intellectual life—gradually kill . . . the power of free thought. We dare not think or follow up the consequences of our thought. We remain in the ruts and valleys, incapable almost of looking up towards the mountain-tops. And the finer side of life escapes us, we cannot even appreciate art or beauty, for everything that is outside the ruts and the valleys terrifies us. We cling to our physical comfort, and a very second-rate bourgeois comfort at that. We do not even know how to live well or to enjoy ourselves. Few of us have any *joie de vivre* left. And so we live out our lives with little said or little done, that beautifies existence for us or for others, or that will be remembered by anyone after we are dead and gone. That was the fate reserved for us also, till the high

[1] Ibid., pp. 14-21.

gods took us in hand, and removed us from the ruts, and placed us on the mountain side. We may not reach the top yet awhile, but the glory of wide vision is ours, and sometimes the rays of the morning sun reach us sooner than those in the valleys.

Many years ago [an acquaintance] told me that, after he had finished his academical career, he gave a year or two to reading and thinking and did nothing else during that period. I envied him that year or two. And now the chance has been given to me. Shall I not rejoice?[1]

[From prison in 1922, Jawaharlal sent 10,570 yards of yarn to his family home, Anand Bhawan—Abode of Happiness.] It took me . . . a considerable time to spin, chiefly because I tried to spin fine yarn. Spinning coarse yarn does not interest me.[2]

19 | Congress Activities, 1923— The Delhi Congress

Congress Activities, 1923

[After his release from prison early in 1923, Jawaharlal continued with his Congress activities. The 1923 controversy between the "no-changers" and "pro-changers" within Congress marked his "*entrée*" into the inner politics of the party. Until then he was merely one of the Mahatma's bright young disciples and the son of Pandit Motilal Nehru, entirely overshadowed by his elders. Now, for the first time, he showed initiative and dexterity in weaving his way through the intricacies of factional dissension. Far more important, this episode witnessed Nehru's earliest performance as a mediator, a role which he was to play with increasing skill in the struggle for national freedom, in independent India, and in world affairs after 1947. Frequently during the 'thirties and 'forties he was to provide a formula which reflected the consensus within the Congress High Command. . . . This penchant for honourable compromise, derived from the

[1] T.N., p. 213.
[2] Ibid., p. 215.

Mahatma, and his talent for mediation found their earliest expression during the party squabbles of 1922 and 1923."[1]

Originally the "pro-changers" favored essentially uniform, continuous and consistent obstruction, through participation in elections to be held for the Legislative Assemblies, in order "to carry the good fight into the enemy's camp".

During the period of which Jawaharlal writes, Motilal was a leading member of the Swaraj party, a group of "pro-changers" within Congress. Thus the current political attitudes of father and son on this particular subject were sharply at odds, Jawaharlal being an ardent "no-changer". There were, at times, also disagreements between the two groups concerning Gandhian, non-violent non-co-operation.]

The Delhi Congress

The Delhi Congress [of 1923], it is said, has brought [about] a compromise between the two rival schools of thought [pro-changers and no-changers]. . . . If the Congress results in ending bitterness and suspicion and re-introducing in our politics charity of judgment and non-violence in our thought, then indeed it has largely succeeded. . . . I do not think there can be any real or stable compromise between the two principal view points which have been fighting for mastery in the country. They are fundamentally different. They are both honourable methods and their advocates are brave men and keen thinkers but nonetheless they differ radically.

The Delhi Congress, it has been remarked, marks the end of non-co-operation. I wonder at any one who [has] lived through the last three or four years in India making this assertion. It passes my comprehension, how even a resolution of the Congress can put an end to a mighty movement. If India has at all imbibed the teaching of Mahatma Gandhi, if even a group of men remain true to that gospel, then non-co-operation cannot die. And if all of us are utterly unworthy of this teaching and incapable of acting in accordance with it, even then a subsequent generation will wield the mighty weapon and prove . . . that this is the only and the best way which ensures true freedom and ends strife. Non-violent non-co-operation cannot die. It has gone beyond the boundaries of our country and is the property of the world. . . .

I am not in the least afraid of . . . difference of opinion amongst ourselves. That must continue. But I confess . . . [I] experienced a feeling

[1] M.B., p. 88.

of humiliation, when I saw that our noble movement, nurtured on high ideals and voluntary suffering, was being converted into . . . [two parties, composed of those who did, and those who did not, favor abandoning the policy of non-violent non-co-operation], each devoting its money and energy to raising delegates who would lift up their hands at the bidding of their leaders. Non-co-operation will prosper not by resorting to such western political methods and manœuvres, but by its utter purity and straightness and by its appeal to the masses. I almost wish that the Calcutta Special Congress in 1920 had not accepted the non-co-operation policy and programme. This acceptance overwhelmed us from the very beginning, and the weight of numbers paralysed us. We could then have marched in a compact body, strong in our faith and in our discipline, and at the right moment have converted the masses and the Congress to our view-point. The process was reversed and we have suffered accordingly. The basis of non-co-operation is direct action, and this involves continuous suffering. No one can expect large masses of people to suffer. Only the elect can do that, and the masses can sympathize with them occasionally for a short while. If the Congress really represents the people, it is natural that it should attempt to go back a little to some kind of constitutional action, whenever large numbers of people are tired of direct action. To the eager, ever ready for the fray, this is painful. But there is no room for despondency. Only a heavier burden is cast on those who have to keep the method of direct action always before the people; they have to fight on.[1]

20 | Third Arrest, 1923—Experiences in Nabha Jail—Further Political Activities

Third Arrest, 1923

In [September] 1923 I was suddenly arrested by the Nabha State authorities and later charged with various offences, including conspiracy.[2]

[1] B.S.W.J.N., pp. 145–46.
[2] B.O.L., p. 28.

[Jawaharlal to Motilal, immediately after his September, 1923 arrest.] We have been fortunate enough to be arrested. . . . We have been waiting here for the last few hours in the police station, and do not know what is going to happen. Whatever that may be, we are thoroughly satisfied. . . . Do not worry.[1]

[My father] when he heard of [my arrest] was greatly upset, more especially as many of the Indian states of those days functioned according to no known or accepted laws. He paid me a visit in prison and was most anxious to get me out. I was distressed at this because I did not want him to ask for any favour from the government.[2]

Experiences in Nabha Jail

In the evening we were marched to the [police] station. [One of my co-workers] . . . and I were handcuffed together, his left wrist to my right one, and a chain attached to the handcuff was held by the policeman leading us. [Our other colleague], also handcuffed and chained, brought up the rear. This march of ours down the streets . . . reminded me forcibly of a dog being led on by a chain. We felt somewhat irritated to begin with, but the humor of the situation dawned upon us, and on the whole we enjoyed the experience. We did not enjoy the night that followed. This was partly spent in crowded third-class compartments in slow-moving trains, with, I think, a change at midnight, and partly in a lock-up at Nabha. All this time, till the forenoon of next day, when we were finally delivered up at the Nabha Jail, the joint handcuff and the heavy chain kept us company. Neither of us could move at all without the other's co-operation. To be handcuffed to another person for a whole night and part of a day is not an experience I should like to repeat.

In Nabha Jail we were all three kept in a most unwholesome and insanitary cell. It was small and damp, with a low ceiling which we could almost touch. At night we slept on the floor, and I would wake up with a start, full of horror, to find that a rat or a mouse had just passed over my face.

Two or three days later we were taken to court for our case, and the most extraordinary and Gilbertian proceedings went on there from day to day. The magistrate or judge seemed to be wholly uneducated. He knew no English, of course, but I doubt if he knew how to write the court

[1] T.N., p. 218.
[2] B.O.L., p. 28.

language, Urdu. We watched him for over a week, and during all this time he never wrote a line. If he wanted to write anything, he made the court reader do it. We put in a number of small applications. He did not pass any orders on them at the time. He kept them and produced them the next day with a note written by somebody else on them. We did not formally defend ourselves. We had got so used to not defending cases in court during the nonco-operation movement that the idea of defense, even when it was manifestly permissible, seemed almost indecent. But I gave the court a long statement containing the facts, as well as my own opinion about Nabha ways, especially under British administration.

Our case was dragging on from day to day although it was a simple enough affair. Suddenly there was a diversion. One afternoon after the court had risen for the day we were kept waiting in the building; and late in the evening, at about seven P.M., we were taken to another room where a person was sitting by a table and there were some other people about. One man, our old friend, the police officer who had arrested us . . . was there, and he got up and began making a statement. I inquired where we were and what was happening. I was informed that it was a courtroom and we were being tried for conspiracy. This was an entirely different proceeding from the one we had so far attended, which was for breach of the order not to enter Nabha territory. It was evidently thought that the maximum sentence for this breach, being only six months, was not enough punishment for us and a more serious charge was necessary. Apparently three were not enough for conspiracy, and so a fourth man, who had absolutely nothing to do with us, was arrested and put on his trial with us. This unhappy man, a Sikh, was not known to us, but we had just seen him in the fields on our way to Jaito.

The lawyer in me was rather taken aback by the casualness with which a conspiracy trial had been started. The case was a totally false one, but decency required that some formalities should be observed. I pointed out to the judge that we had had no notice whatever and that we might have wanted to make arrangements for our defense. This did not worry him at all. It was the Nabha way. If we wanted to engage a lawyer for our defense we could choose someone in Nabha. When I suggested that I might want some lawyer from outside, I was told that this was not permitted under the Nabha rules. We were further enlightened about the peculiarities of Nabha procedure. In some disgust we told the judge to do what he liked, but so far as we were concerned we would take no part in the proceedings. I could not wholly adhere to this resolve. It was difficult to listen to the most astounding lies about us and remain silent, and so occasionally we expressed our opinion, briefly but pointedly, about the witnesses. We also gave the court a statement in writing about the facts. [The] second judge, who tried the conspiracy case, was more educated and intelligent than the other one.

Both these cases went on and we looked forward to our daily visits to the two courtrooms, for that meant a temporary escape from the foul cell in jail. Meanwhile, we were approached, on behalf of the Administrator, by the superintendent of the jail and told that if we would express our regret and give an undertaking to go away from Nabha, the proceedings against us would be dropped. We replied that there was nothing to express regret about, so far as we were concerned; it was for the administration to apologize to us. We were also not prepared to give any undertaking.

About a fortnight after our arrest the two trials at last ended. All this time had been taken up by the prosecution, for we were not defending. Much of it had been wasted in long waits, for every little difficulty that arose necessitated an adjournment or a reference to some authority behind the scenes—probably the English Administrator. On the last day, when the prosecution case was closed, we handed in our written statements. The first court adjourned and, to our surprise, returned a little later with a bulky judgment written out in Urdu. Obviously this huge judgment could not have been written during the interval. It had been prepared before our statements had been handed in. The judgment was not read out; we were merely told that we had been awarded the maximum sentence of six months for breach of the order to leave Nabha territory.

In the [Nabha] conspiracy case we were sentenced the same day to either eighteen months or two years, I forget which. This was to be in addition to the sentence for six months. Thus we were given in all either two years or two and a half years.

Right through our trial there had been any number of remarkable incidents which gave us some insight into the realities of Indian state administration, or rather the British administration of an Indian state. The whole procedure was farcical. Because of this I suppose no newspaperman or outsider was allowed in court. The police did what they pleased, and often ignored the judge or magistrate and actually disobeyed his directions. The poor magistrate meekly put up with this, but we saw no reason why we should do so. On several occasions I had to stand up and insist on the police behaving and obeying the magistrate. Sometimes there was an unseemly snatching of papers by the police, and, the magistrate being incapable of action or of introducing order in his own court, we had partly to do his job! The poor magistrate was in an unhappy position. He was afraid of the police, and he seemed to be a little frightened of us, too, for our arrest had been noised in the press. If this was the state of affairs when more or less prominent politicians like us were concerned, what, I wonder, would be the fate of others less known?

My father knew something of Indian states, and so he was greatly upset at my unexpected arrest in Nabha. Only the fact of arrest was known; little else in the way of news could leak out. In his distress he even telegraphed to the Viceroy for news of me. Difficulties were put in the way of his visiting me in Nabha, but he was allowed at last to interview me in prison. He could not be of any help to me, as I was not defending myself, and I begged him to go back to Allahabad and not to worry. He returned, but he left a young lawyer colleague of ours . . . in Nabha to watch the proceedings. [His] . . . knowledge of law and procedure must have been considerably augmented by his brief experience of the Nabha courts. The police tried to deprive him forcibly in open court of some papers that he had.

Most of the Indian states are well known for their backwardness and their semifeudal conditions. They are personal autocracies, devoid even of competence or benevolence. Many a strange thing occurs there which never receives publicity. And yet their very inefficiency lessens the evil in some ways and lightens the burden on their unhappy people. For this is reflected in a weak executive, and it results in making even tyranny and injustice inefficient. That does not make tyranny more bearable, but it does make it less far-reaching and widespread. The assumption of direct British control over an Indian state has a curious result in changing this equilibrium. The semifeudal conditions are retained, autocracy is kept, the old laws and procedure are still supposed to function, all the restrictions on personal liberty and association and expression of opinion (and these are all-embracing) continue, but one change is made which alters the whole background. The executive becomes stronger, while a measure of efficiency is introduced, and this leads to a tightening-up of all the feudal and autocratic bonds. In course of time the British administration would no doubt change some of the archaic customs and methods, for they come in the way of efficient government as well as commercial penetration. But to begin with they take full advantage of them to tighten their hold on the people, who have now to put up not only with feudalism and autocracy, but with an efficient enforcement of them by a strong executive.

I saw something of this in Nabha. The state was under a British Administrator, a member of the Indian Civil Service, and he had the full powers of an autocrat, subject only to the Government of India. And yet

4*

at every turn we were referred to Nabha laws and procedure to justify the denial of the most ordinary rights. We had to face a combination of feudalism and the modern bureaucratic machine with the disadvantages of both and the advantages of neither.

So our trial was over and we had been sentenced. We did not know what the judgments contained, but the solid fact of a long sentence had a sobering effect. We asked for copies of the judgments, and were told to apply formally for them.

That evening in jail the superintendent sent for us and showed us an order of the Administrator under the Criminal Procedure Code suspending our sentences. There was no condition attached, and the legal result of that order was that the sentences ended so far as we were concerned. The superintendent then produced a separate order called an executive order, also issued by the Administrator, asking us to leave Nabha and not to return to the state without special permission. I asked for the copies of the two orders, but they were refused. We were then escorted to the railway station and released there. We did not know a soul in Nabha, and even the city gates had been closed for the night. . . .

[Later] I wrote to the Administrator requesting him to send me copies of his two orders, so that I might know exactly what they were, also copies of the two judgments. He refused to supply any of these copies. I pointed out that I might decide to file an appeal, but he persisted in his refusal. In spite of repeated efforts I have never had the opportunity to read these judgments, which sentenced me and my two colleagues to two years or two and half years. For aught I know, these sentences may still be hanging over me, and may take effect whenever the Nabha authorities or the British Government so choose.[1]

[His sentence suspended, Jawaharlal was in Nabha jail only from September 22 to October 4, 1923. Expelled from the State, he was informed that if he were to return, he would immediately be sent back to jail.

"The Nabha episode, which gave Jawaharlal a glimpse of the administration of an Indian State, even under the aegis of a senior British officer, turned him into a stout champion of the rights of the people in 'Princely States'. British officials had unwittingly rounded off [his] political education. The externment from Mussoorie had given him an insight into the problems of the peasantry in 'British India'; the trial in Nabha suddenly illuminated the arbitrary régimes thriving in 'Indian India'."[2]]

[1] T.F., pp. 98–102.
[2] T.N., p. 223.

Further Political Activities

[After his release from jail, when Jawaharlal became Congress Chairman of the Allahabad Municipality in 1923, "he tried to rouse the enthusiasm of the citizens, to accelerate the tempo of the municipal organization and to pull the city fathers out of the well-worn ruts in which many of them had moved all their lives.

"In Allahabad, as in many other Indian towns, membership of civic bodies was ... regarded as a sinecure, yielding prestige, profit and patronage without definite responsibility. But Jawaharlal made surprise inspections, called for quarterly reports from the standing committees of the Board, set precise targets for performance and prescribed codes of conduct. He frowned upon nepotism. 'Members will remember,' he wrote on April 19, 1924, 'that last year I wrote a note on patronage. I was, and am, very much against chits and testimonials and recommendations. We discussed this matter, and it was felt that where a recommendation had to be made it should be in writing and reasons should be given. On no account should a recommendation be made orally.' He encouraged the idea of a municipal volunteer corps, 'a strong civic guard, open to all classes and communities ... thus a spirit of *camaraderie*, which has been lacking amongst our citizens of late, might develop.' He discouraged extravagance. ...

"There was hardly a civic issue on which Jawaharlal did not try to educate his colleagues. He wrote a long minute on a proposal for segregation of prostitutes: 'Last year the Board made a brave effort to abolish prostitution by passing a resolution and appointing a committee.' Segregation of prostitutes, even if feasible (he wrote) was as undesirable as segregation of criminals. 'I do not believe in issuing a fiat that prostitutes must not live in any part of Allahabad except a remote corner. If this is done, I would think it equally reasonable to reserve another part of Allahabad for men who exploited women and because of whom prostitutes flourish.' The solution lay not merely in punitive measures but in socioeconomic reforms. He suggested a number of constructive measures such as educative propaganda on venereal disease, the building of 'homes' for widows and helpless women and improvement in the legal and economic status of women.

"This enthusiasm and industry did not produce the results young Nehru had expected. Many of his colleagues on the Municipal Board were more interested in securing appointments for friends and relatives than in making Allahabad a model city. The powers of the Municipal Board were circumscribed by the Government, and almost every important reform faced administrative or financial hurdles. Between the hopeless apathy of his colleagues and the nagging interference of hide-bound officials Jawaharlal felt frustrated. In April, 1924, he felt he had had enough of the Municipal Board and resigned from the chairmanship. He was persuaded to continue, but finally resigned in February, 1925. ...
[The] British Commissioner of Allahabad, asked him to reconsider his

decision. 'You have had a very difficult and uphill task . . . and everyone recognizes that you have carried it out with much ability and conspicuous fairness to all parties in the board. . . .' The U.P. Government formally regretted 'Pandit Jawaharlal's decision to vacate a post he has filled with great ability and fairness'. However, Jawaharlal had no intention of losing himself permanently in the local affairs of Allahabad. 'I feel that it is within the power of a [Municipal] Board,' he wrote to an officer of the Board from Nabha gaol in September, 1923, 'to make life a little more bearable, a little less painful to the inhabitants of Allahabad. This is worthy work. To me . . . it is only secondary work. My real passion, as I have repeatedly informed the Board, lies in a different direction, and, God-willing, I shall go that way till my purpose is achieved'." [1]

Jawaharlal was General Secretary of the All-Indian Congress Committee from 1923 to 1925. He was President of the United Provinces Political Conference held at Benares in October, 1923.]

21 | Ends and Means, 1923— Muslim-Hindu Tensions, 1923

Ends and Means—from Presidential Address at United Provinces Political Conference, Benares, October 13, 1923

[The Fascists took power in Italy on October 28, 1922, with Mussolini assuming dictatorial powers. The reference to Mussolini in the following speech indicates Jawaharlal's early and clear understanding of the brutal, reactionary and increasingly totalitarian nature of Italian Fascism. His sense of repugnance concerning the violent methods of "Bolshevism" is equally marked.]

What . . . is our aim and what should be our means? Our creed is short and simple, but it shelters many interpretations. We have made it abundantly clear that we have not the slightest interest in provincial autonomy or the transfer of subjects in the Government of India. Full internal freedom means that we must control the finances and the army and the police. So long as we do not control these, we have no freedom in India. This is

[1] Ibid., pp. 248-49.

the minimum. But the question has arisen whether we should not define Swaraj in our creed as independence. Personally I shall welcome the day when the Congress declares for independence. I am convinced that the only proper and right goal for India is independence. . . .

I believe in the Non-co-operation Movement as inaugurated by Mahatma Gandhi. I believe that the salvation of India and, indeed, of the world will come through non-violent non-co-operation. Violence has had a long career in the world. It has been weighed repeatedly and found wanting. The present condition of Europe is eloquent testimony of the inefficiency of violence to settle anything. I believe that violence in Europe will go from excess to excess and will perish in the flames it has itself kindled and be reduced to ashes. Many people smile and fling cheap sneers at the prospect of non-violence ever coming into its own and directing the affairs of men and nations. They point to the frailty of human nature, and the universal prevalence of anger and hatred and violence. I am afraid few of us are free from these. I know to my sorrow that I am full of violent thoughts and can with difficulty drag myself back to this straight and narrow path. But those who mock and smile would do well if they realised the power of the idea, and if they studied the progress of this particular idea. For it has already caught the imagination of the thinkers of the world and the Indian masses have been wonderfully affected by it.

Non-co-operation and non-violence, these are the two essential ingredients of this movement. The idea of non-co-operation is simple enough and clear to the meanest intellect, but nonetheless few of us had realised it, excepting partly during the Bengal partition days, till Mahatmaji issued his call to action. Evil flourishes only because we tolerate and assist it. The most despotic and tyrannical government can only carry on because the people it governs themselves submit to it. England holds India in bondage because Indians co-operate with the Englishmen and thereby strengthen British rule. Withdraw the co-operation and the fabric of foreign rule collapses. That follows automatically and requires no proof.

But in spite of the logic and of the inevitability of the result, many of us cannot adopt this obvious method. The subtle position of the British rule has enervated us and emasculated us and made cowards of us all. We have lost the spirit of adventure and we cannot take a risk even though the prize be so splendid as the freedom of India. The idea of non-co-operation has taken root and has sunk down to the masses, but sustained courage is lacking to give outward expression to this idea. With many it is an economic question. But what shall we say of those who even without this incentive give their time, energy and money to organise the innumerable functions for the honour and glory of English officials? To such a depth we have sunk that men of intelligence and education among us think it no shame to help in their own dishonour. I make no complaint of the English officials. They are brave men serving their country to the best of their ability. I wish our men were equally brave and would think as often of the honour and dignity of their own country.

I firmly believe in the efficiency of non-violence. But non-violence has nothing to do with cowardice or weakness. Mahatmaji repeatedly stated that even violence is preferable to cowardice. Fear and cowardice are the greatest sins and unhappily we have enough of them in our country. Our anger and hatred are really the outcome of our fear and impotence. If we could get rid of this fear and cowardice, there would be little hatred left or any other obstacle to our onward march. Let us, therefore, root out this cowardice and give it no shelter. Above all let it not masquerade, as it unfortunately often does, as non-violence. "A world of evil" says a great Frenchman "is preferable to emasculated good." There is too much sappiness and softness in us, too much emasculated good. One is almost driven to the conclusion that we are inanely and passively good, if good that is, because this is the path of least resistance and because we have not the courage to be evil. We dare not sin, though we think of it often enough and would like to do so.

This is a hateful condition. It is dishonest, neuter and hypocritical. Better the honest man of evil who sins consciously and knowingly and with the strength that is in him. When he reforms, he will be a tower of strength to the cause of good, because his foundations are strong. But the inanely and hypocritically good can be of use to no cause. There is no strength in them, their foundations are laid upon the shifting sands. And so there is no place for the cowardly in the non-violent movement.

I am laying stress on this question of non-violence for it is well that we should be clear about it. After some years of suspension there has apparently been a recrudescence of the violent revolutionary movement in Bengal. I can appreciate the impatience and longing for freedom which impels many a young man to violent action. I can admire the reckless courage which does not count the cost. But I cannot understand how anyone imagines that sporadic violence can bring freedom nearer to us. Freedom is our right; and according to old customs and ordinary law of nations, we are entitled even to resort to violence to achieve it. But even freedom would be a doubtful and a tainted thing if we have to resort to foul means to gain it. I pray that this fate may never overtake our great movement.

Violence may be justified under certain circumstances, but it must be open and above-board and straight-forward. But no circumstance will justify secret killing, the dagger of the assassin and the stab in the dark. No nation has yet profited by these methods. They but sully a great cause and alienate world sympathy. On no account, therefore, can we take to the bomb and the dagger. And those who unthinkingly adopt these methods injure the cause they have at heart. We cannot even think of open and organised violence. We have really little choice left in the matter and even if we did not and on other grounds preferred it, we would be driven to non-violent non-co-operation. Bolshevism and Fascism are the waves of the West to-day. They are really alike and represent different phases of insensate violence and intolerance. The choice for us is between Lenin and Mussolini on the one side, and Gandhi on the other. Can there be doubt as to who represents the soul of India to-day?

India made her choice more than three years ago. She chose the path of non-violence and suffering, of direct action and peaceful revolution. From that there is no going back. There may occasionally appear to be some slackness or some change. We may have our bad patches and our moments of despondency, but the vision once seen cannot be forgotten and the glory of suffering for a great cause cannot be given up. Again and again the chance will come to us and while the wise argue, the brave will go forth heeding not the consequences, full of joy at the thought that they have been privileged to serve the great cause. Learned disputations take place frequently in the country for the preparation of civil disobedience. Much can be done in disciplining the people and creating a favourable atmosphere. But courage and [a] will to suffer cannot be instilled into the people by lectures or tours. Personal examples alone can do it and it may be that [a] little incident may electrify the whole of India and make us launch a mighty campaign of civil disobedience. Till that time comes, we may have many opportunities given us of testing our mettle and hardening our fibre. Let us take advantage of them and keep the practice and ideal of direct action and peaceful revolution ever before the people. We need not worry about the opportunities and chances. They will surely come to us. Let us see to it that they find us ready when they do come.

But our suffering would serve little purpose if we cannot deal sanely with our communal questions and exorcise the spirit of strife and bigotry. A few broken heads matter little, but the reason for this does matter. It is most strange that for the most trivial things, for childish superstitions or silly prejudices, people take [risks] and lose their reason in the sea of anger. The vital things, the real things that matter, pass unnoticed.

Ignorance and bigotry put an end to all rational thoughts. It is almost useless to argue or convince. Religion is sacred and in its name are done the most shameful things. Indeed religion has become the excuse for many sins. It has little sanctity left and it is trotted out in season and out of season and all agreement naturally ends. We seem to have drifted back to a state of affairs which prevailed in Europe during the dark ages, when to think rationally was considered an evil. I think it is time for persons who regard religion as something good and sacred, and the exercise of rational thought as essential for human progress, to protest with all their might against all kinds of bigotry and superstition. . . .

I have had my say. I wish to assure you in all honesty and I am full of hope. I have little patience with the pessimists. . . . I am convinced that political freedom will come to us before long, if not entirely through our strength, then through the weakness of Europe and England. For Europe is in the melting pot and England with all her seeming might cannot but be affected by the collapse of the continent. Wars and rumours of . . . wars follow each other in quick succession. They will continue till the lesson of non-violence is learnt by bitter experience. So political freedom for India is certain. But I sometimes fear that when it comes to us it may find us lacking in true strength and the greater qualities. And instead of leaving a shining example to the rest of the world, India may become a cheap and inefficient replica of the countries of the West. Let us take the longer view from now [on] and try to avoid this and build up a great and strong India worthy of the great leader whom God has blessed us with.[1]

Muslim–Hindu Tensions, 1923

[For some time after the 1916 Lucknow Pact, the relationship between India's Hindus and Muslims was relatively amicable. Up to 1920, as has been noted, the Muslim leader, M. A. Jinnah, had remained a Congress member. By 1923, however, renewed tensions had begun to flare up between the various communal groups and, in Jawaharlal's view, the major goals of Congress were in grave danger of being jeopardized.]

[Of 1923]: [There was a] progressive deterioration of Hindu–Moslem relations, in North India especially. In the bigger cities a number of riots took place, brutal and callous in the extreme. The atmosphere of distrust and anger bred new causes of dispute which most of us had never heard of before. Previously a fruitful source of discord had been the question of

[1] B.A.I., pp. 38–43.

cow sacrifice, especially on the *Bakr-id* day. There was also tension when Hindu and Moslem festivals clashed.

But now a fresh cause of friction arose, something that was ever present, ever recurring. This was the question of music before mosques. Objection was taken by the Moslems to music or any noise which interfered with their prayers in their mosques. In every city there are many mosques, and five times every day they have prayers, and there is no lack of noises and processions (including marriage and funeral processions). So the chances of friction were always present. In particular, objection was taken to processions and noises at the time of the sunset prayer in the mosques. As it happens, this is just the time when evening worship takes place in the Hindu temples, and gongs are sounded and the temple bells ring. *Arti*, this is called, and *arti-namaz* disputes now assumed major proportions.

It seems amazing that a question which could be settled with mutual consideration for each other's feelings and a little adjustment should give rise to great bitterness and rioting. But religious passions have little to do with reason or consideration or adjustments, and they are easy to fan when a third party in control can play off one group against another.

One is apt to exaggerate the significance of these riots in a few northern cities. Most of the towns and cities and the whole of rural India carried on peacefully, little affected by these happenings, but the newspapers naturally gave great prominence to every petty communal disturbance. It is perfectly true, however, that communal tension and bitterness increased in the city masses. This was pushed on by the communal leaders at the top, and it was reflected in the stiffening-up of the political communal demands. Because of the communal tension, Moslem political reactionaries, who had taken a back seat during all these years of nonco-operation, emerged into prominence, helped in the process by the British Government. From day to day new and more far-reaching communal demands appeared on their behalf, striking at the very root of national unity and Indian freedom. On the Hindu side also political reactionaries were among the principal communal leaders, and, in the name of guarding Hindu interests, they played definitely into the hands of the Government. They did not succeed, and indeed they could not, however much they tried by their methods, in gaining any of the points on which they laid stress; they succeeded only in raising the communal temper of the country.

The Congress was in a quandary. Sensitive to and representative of national feeling as it was . . . communal passions were bound to affect it. Many a Congressman was a communalist under his national cloak. But the Congress leadership stood firm and, on the whole, refused to side with either communal party, or rather with any communal group, for now the Sikhs and other smaller minorities were also loudly voicing their particular demands. Inevitably this led to denunciation from both the extremes.

Long ago, right at the commencement of nonco-operation or even earlier, Gandhiji had laid down his formula for solving the communal problem. According to him, it could only be solved by good will and the generosity of the majority group, and so he was prepared to agree to everything that the Moslems might demand. He wanted to win them over, not to bargain with them. With foresight and a true sense of values he grasped at the reality that was worth while; but others, who thought they knew the market price of everything and were ignorant of the true value of anything, stuck to the methods of the market place. They saw the cost of purchase with painful clearness, but they had no appreciation of the worth of the article they might have bought.

It is easy to criticize and blame others, and the temptation is almost irresistible to find some excuse for the failure of one's plans. Was not the failure due to the deliberate thwarting of others, rather than to an error in one's own way of thinking or acting? We cast the blame on the Government and the communalists; the latter blame the Congress. Of course, there was thwarting of us, deliberate and persistent thwarting, by the Government and their allies. Of course, British governments in the past and the present have based their policy on creating divisions in our ranks. Divide and rule has always been the way of empires, and the measure of their success in this policy has been also the measure of their superiority over those whom they thus exploit. We cannot complain of this, or, at any rate, we ought not to be surprised at it. To ignore it and not to provide against it is in itself a mistake in one's thought.

How are we to provide against it? Not, surely, by bargaining and haggling and generally adopting the tactics of the market place, for whatever offer we make, however high our bid might be, there is always a third party which can bid higher and, what is more, give substance to its words. If there is no common national or social outlook, there will not be common action against the common adversary. If we think in terms of the existing political and economic structure and merely wish to tamper with it here and there, to reform it, to "Indianize" it, then all real inducement for joint action is lacking. The object then becomes one of sharing in the spoils, and the third and controlling party inevitably plays the dominant role and hands out its gifts to the prize boys of its choice. Only by thinking in terms of a different political framework—and even more so a different social framework—can we build up a stable foundation for joint action. The whole idea underlying the demand for independence was this: to make people realize that we were struggling for an entirely different political structure and not just an Indianized edition (with British control behind the scenes) of the present order, which Dominion status signifies. Political independence meant, of course, political freedom only, and did not include any social change or economic freedom for the masses. But it did signify the removal of the financial and economic chains which bind us to the City of London, and this would have made it easier for us to change the social structure. So I thought then. I would add now that I do not think it is likely that real political freedom will come to us by itself. When it comes, it will bring a large measure of social freedom also.

But almost all our leaders continued to think within the narrow steel frame of the existing political, and of course the social, structure. They faced every problem—communal or constitutional—with this background, and, inevitably, they played into the hands of the British Government, which controlled completely that structure. They could not do otherwise, for their whole outlook was essentially reformist and not revolutionary, in spite of occasional experiments with direct action. But the time had gone by when any political or economic or communal problem in India could be satisfactorily solved by reformist methods. Revolutionary outlook and planning and revolutionary solutions were demanded by the situation. But there was no one among the leaders to offer these.

The want of clear ideals and objectives in our struggle for freedom undoubtedly helped the spread of communalism. The masses saw no clear connection between their day-to-day sufferings and the fight for *Swaraj*. They fought well enough at times by instinct, but that was a feeble weapon which could be easily blunted or even turned aside for other purposes. There was no reason behind it, and in periods of reaction it was not difficult for the communalists to play upon this feeling and exploit it in the name of religion. It is nevertheless extraordinary how the bourgeois classes, both among the Hindus and the Moslems, succeeded, in the sacred name of religion, in getting a measure of mass sympathy and support for programs and demands which had absolutely nothing to do with the masses, or even the lower middle class. Every one of the communal demands put forward by any communal group is, in the final analysis, a demand for jobs, and these jobs could only go to a handful of the upper middle class. There is also, of course, the demand for special and additional seats in the legislatures, as symbolizing political power, but this too is looked upon chiefly as the power to exercise patronage. These narrow political demands, benefiting at the most a small number of the upper middle classes, and often creating barriers in the way of national unity and progress, were cleverly made to appear the demands of the masses of that particular religious group. Religious passion was hitched on to them in order to hide their barrenness.

In this way political reactionaries came back to the political field in the guise of communal leaders, and the real explanation of the various steps they took was not so much their communal bias as their desire to obstruct political advance. We could only expect opposition from them politically, but still it was a peculiarly distressing feature of an unsavory situation to find to what lengths they would go in this respect. Moslem communal leaders said the most amazing things and seemed to care not at all for Indian nationalism or Indian freedom; Hindu communal leaders, though always speaking apparently in the name of nationalism, had little to do with it in practice and, incapable of any real action, sought to humble themselves before the Government, and did that too in vain. Both agreed in condemning socialistic and suchlike "subversive" movements; there was a touching unanimity in regard to any proposal affecting vested interests.[1]

22 | Gandhi in the Mid-Twenties— Hindu–Muslim Relations

Gandhi in the Mid-Twenties

Ever since Gandhiji appeared on the Indian political scene, there has been no going back in popularity for him, so far as the masses are concerned. . . . They may not carry out his wishes, for human nature is often weak, but their hearts are full of good will for him. When objective conditions help, they rise in huge mass movements; otherwise they lie low. A leader does not create a mass movement out of nothing, as if by a stroke of the magician's wand. He can take advantage of the conditions themselves when they arise; he can prepare for them, but not create them.

[1] T.F., pp. 112–16.

There is a waning and a waxing of Gandhiji's popularity among the intelligentsia. In moments of forward-going enthusiasm they follow him; when the inevitable reaction comes, they grow critical. But even so the great majority of them bow down to him. Partly this has been due to the absence of any other effective program. The Liberals and various groups resembling them do not count; those who believe in terroristic violence are completely out of court in the modern world and are considered ineffective and out of date. The socialist program is still little known, and it frightens the upper-class members of the Congress.[1]

Hindu–Muslim Relations

[A Unity Conference of the mid-twenties urged Hindus and Muslims to be more tolerant and respectful of one another's religious practices and beliefs. Although, temporarily, conditions became more peaceful, they were not long to remain so.

By the time Lord Irwin replaced Lord Reading as Viceroy in 1926—a year during which elections were held in India—communal tensions had reached a new peak. Voting based on separate electorates served further to exacerbate the situation.]

The Delhi Unity Conference of 1924 was hardly over when a Hindu-Moslem riot broke out in Allahabad. It was not a big riot, as such riots go, in so far as casualties were concerned; but it was painful to have these troubles in one's home town. I rushed back with others from Delhi to find that the actual rioting was over; but the aftermath, in the shape of bad blood and court cases, lasted a long time.[2]

[From Letter to Congress Colleague, Dr Syed Mahmud, May 24, 1926.] I do not attach very much importance to political squabbles, but the communal frenzy is awful to contemplate. We seem to have been caught in a whirlpool of mutual hatred and we go round and round and down and down this abyss. . . . For months or even a year or more we have thought that the situation was so bad that it could not become worse. . . . But it does [grow] worse and heaven knows where it will end.[3]

[To Dr Mahmud—1926-27.] No country or people who are slaves to dogma . . . can progress, and unhappily our country and people have

[1] T.F., pp. 108-09.
[2] Ibid., p. 116.
[3] Quoted in M.B., pp. 98-99.

ecome extraordinarily dogmatic and little-minded. . . . Religion as practised in India has become the old man of the sea for us, and it has not only broken our backs but stultified and almost killed all originality of thought and mind. Like Sinbad the sailor we must get rid of this terrible burden before we can aspire to breathe freely or do anything useful. . . . I have no patience left with the legitimate and illegitimate offspring of religion.[1]

23 | Voyage to Europe, 1926— Remarks at Brussels Congress, 1927

Voyage to Europe, 1926

[Jawaharlal remained General Secretary of Congress in 1926. During the mid-twenties he also became Secretary of the Spinners Association. By the end of 1925 his wife Kamala had become dangerously ill. Because European medical care was recommended, a trip to Switzerland was decided upon. Since Jawaharlal was himself weary and discouraged by political developments at home, he was grateful for the prospect of a change of scene. Complications arose, however: first, over the issuing of his passport; next, because of his refusal to give an undertaking that during his stay in Europe he would not take part in politics.[2] Finally the departure for Europe was arranged without an undertaking being required.]

I wanted . . . to go out of India myself. My mind was befogged, and no clear path was visible. . . . I thought that, perhaps, if I was far from India I could see things in better perspective and lighten up the dark corners of my mind.[3]

[The downheartedness was to be of but brief duration. August 11, 1926.] The outlook in India is dark enough, but somehow I do not feel as

[1] Ibid., pp. 99.
[2] T.N., pp. 251–52.
[3] T.F., p. 121.

pessimistic as the news would warrant. . . . We shall . . . see swaraj. . . .
As for me, I am flourishing like the proverbial green bay tree![1]

[From letter from Europe, December 1, 1926.] I am beginning to feel
a bit restive and I wish I could hurl myself into the whirlpool of Indian
politics. The suppressed energy of some months wants an outlet. I should
have liked to be at the Gauhati Congress [the annual session held towards
the end of 1926]. Not that I think I would have done any good to anybody, but I would feel better for a little aggressiveness. And there seem
to be so many people about in India whom I should like to go for! There
is nothing to be downhearted about. . . . We are passing through an
inevitable phase and we shall be the better for it.[2]

[Jawaharlal's journey was made after "years of war, and revolution,
and tremendous change."[3] During 1926–1927 he visited Italy, Switzerland, England, Belgium, France, Germany, Holland, Ceylon and Russia.
His nearly two years' sojourn contributed to his ever-growing awareness
of international affairs.]

Toward the end of 1926 I happened to be in Berlin. . . . I learned there
of a forthcoming Congress of Oppressed Nationalities,[4] which was to be
held at Brussels. The idea appealed to me, and I wrote home, suggesting
that the Indian National Congress might take official part in the Brussels
Congress. My suggestion was approved, and I was appointed the Indian
Congress representative for this purpose.

The Brussels Congress was held early in February 1927. I do not know
who originated the idea. . . . [It is averred that it was born in] Berlin . . .
at the time a center which attracted political exiles and radical elements
from abroad; it was gradually catching up [with] Paris in that respect.
The communist element was also strong there. Ideas of some common
action between oppressed nations *inter se*, as well as between them and
the labor left wing, were very much in the air. It was felt more and more
that the struggle for freedom was a common one against the thing that
was imperialism; and joint deliberation and, where possible, joint action
were desirable. The colonial Powers—England, France, Italy, etc.—were

[1] Quoted in M.B., pp. 106–07.
[2] Ibid., p. 107.
[3] T.F., p. 121.
[4] Variously termed as above, or as the International League against Imperialism (or of
Oppressed Nations). The Congress of Oppressed Nationalities is said to have established the League against Imperialism in 1927.

naturally hostile to any such attempts being made; but Germany was, since the war, no longer a colonial Power, and the German Government viewed with a benevolent neutrality the growth of agitation in the colonies and dependencies of other Powers. This was one of the reasons which made Berlin a center for advanced and disaffected elements from abroad. Among these the most prominent and active were the Chinese belonging to the left wing of the Kuomintang, which was then sweeping across China, the old feudal elements rolling down before its irresistible advance. Even the imperialist Powers lost their aggressive habits and minatory tone before this new phenomenon. It appeared that the solution of the problem of China's unity and freedom could not long be delayed. The Kuomintang was flushed with success, but it knew the difficulties that lay ahead, and it wanted to strengthen itself by international propaganda. Probably it was the left wing of the party, co-operating with communists and near-communists abroad, that laid stress on this propaganda, both to strengthen China's national position abroad and its own position in the party ranks at home. The party had not split up at the time into two or more rival and bitterly hostile groups, and presented, to all outward seeming, a united front.

The European representatives of the Kuomintang, therefore, welcomed the idea of the Congress of Oppressed Nationalities; perhaps they even originated the idea jointly with some other people. Some communists and near-communists were also at the back of the proposal right from the beginning, but, as a whole, the communist element kept in the background. Active support and help also came from Latin America, which was then chafing at the economic imperialism of the United States. Mexico, with a radical President and policy, was eager to take the lead in a Latin-American *bloc* against the United States; and Mexico, therefore, took great interest in the Brussels Congress. Officially the Government could not take part, but it sent one of its leading diplomats to be present as a benevolent observer.

There were also present at Brussels representatives from the national organizations of Java, Indo-China, Palestine, Syria, Egypt, Arabs from North Africa, and African Negroes. Then there were many left-wing labor organizations represented; and several well-known men who had played a leading part in European labor struggles for a generation, were present. Communists were there also, and they took an important part in the proceedings; they came not as communists but as representatives of trade-unions or similar organizations.[1]

[1] T.F., pp. 123-25.

From Remarks at International League Against Imperialism (or
Congress of Oppressed Nationalities)—Brussels, February 9,
1927

I.

I am glad to have the opportunity to associate myself on behalf of the
Indian National Congress and the people of India whom it represents,
with the aims and [objectives] of this international Congress. The Indian
National Congress stands for the freedom of India; freedom for the poor
and the oppressed from all exploitation. We welcome this International
Congress because, as we understand it, it has been called together to
further these aims and objects in the international sphere. We realise that
there is much in common in the struggle which various subject and semi-
subject and oppressed peoples are carrying on to-day. Their opponents
are often the same, although they sometimes appear in different guises
and the means employed for their subjection are often similar. Contact
between the various peoples will lead to a better understanding of each
other's problems and difficulties, and is bound to result in closer co-operation which must bring success nearer to all. The fabric of imperialism
looks imposing and appears to hold together, but any rent in it will
automatically lead to its total destruction.

The Indian National Congress is necessarily national and has nationalism as its basis, but as our great leader Mahatma Gandhi [has] said, our
nationalism is based on the most intense internationalism. The problem
of Indian freedom is for us a vital and urgently essential one; but at the
same time it is not merely a purely national problem. India is a world
problem and as in the past so in the future other countries and peoples
will be vitally affected by the condition of India.

To-day the strongest and the most far-reaching imperialism is that of
Britain, and British imperialism and policy always [have] had India as
their corner stone. Both Egypt and other parts of Africa have suffered
domination because British imperialism wanted to strengthen its hold on
India and to protect its sea routes to that country. The importance of
India and her future for this International Congress is thus obvious.

The Indian National movement has welcomed with the liveliest sympathy and hope the successes of the Nationalists in China. It has been a
matter of shame and sorrow to us that the British Government should
venture to send Indian troops to China in an attempt to coerce the
Chinese people. You are probably aware that the Indian National Congress
has protested in the strongest language against this and the Nationalist

members of the Indian Legislature wanted to raise this question in the Legislative Assembly, but the English Viceroy exercised his veto on the ground that it raised matters of foreign policy. Mahatma Gandhi and [other] Indian leaders have emphatically on behalf of the people of India expressed their ardent hope that the Chinese Nationalists will bring about the final emancipation of China. The Indian press have condemned the Government's action and mass meetings have been held in various parts of the country for the [same] purpose. India to-day is with China, not only because she has every sympathy for her but because she feels that China's successful fight is the most hopeful sign of the future downfall of imperialism. As of old, imperialism is trying to utilise one subject country to coerce another, but in spite of her weakness India is not so weak to-day as to permit herself to be employed as a pawn in the imperialist game.

The attempts [so] to use India . . . make it all the more necessary for the forces of nationalism in the subject nations to co-operate together for their common good. And I trust that this Congress will help us to bring about this co-operation and will thus bring nearer the freedom of oppressed nationalities.[1]

II. (February 10, 1927).

With the greatest pleasure I bring the warm and hearty greetings of the Indian National Congress which has commissioned me to link our national movement with this international united effort to fight imperialism. . . . We know accurately what it means and we are naturally interested in every movement which is directed against imperialism. In fact if you want a typical example that will help you to understand the nature and consequence of imperialism, I think you will find nothing better than India. From the internal condition of India . . . it may be understood in what manner . . . English imperialism represses and exploits workers. In India you will find a wonderful instance of every phase of imperialism that you may wish to study. Whether you come from China, Egypt or other distant lands, your interests are bound up with ours. And the Indian problem, too, is of interest and importance for you.

I cannot tell you . . . the whole history of Indian exploitation—how India is maltreated, repressed and plundered. It is a long and very sad story. . . . You have heard of various disturbances, massacres and random butcheries. . . . [The British] came to us . . . by putting one province against another until they finally established themselves firmly.

During the whole period of their stay they have followed the old policy

[1] I.Q.R. (1927, Vol. I), pp. 204–05.

of "Divide and Rule". I regret to . . . say that they still follow this policy. The early history of their occupation is one of the wildest and . . . most shameless examples we have ever seen in the history of the world. Even the British historians, who are certainly not impartial, admit that the early history of India under . . . British rule represents an epoch of predatory war—a period in which free-booters prowled about and committed plunder and robberies in the land in an unbridled manner. You know perhaps . . . the event . . . known as the Sepoy Mutiny . . . which took place seventy years ago. It is called so, but if fate had willed otherwise, and the so-called rebels had been crowned with success, then to-day it would have been called the Indian War of Independence. . . . Even to-day random firing is not infrequent. Numberless comrades and friends of ours are detained in prison without any accusation and without any trial. Many of our best comrades in India have made jail their real home, or they are in exile and cannot come back to their fatherland. . . . But the real injury by the [British] in India, the real exploitation, is much more severe than the shootings and hangings. . . .

We read [of the riches of India in the] history, not only of . . . ancient [but also of modern] times. . . . India has allured, by [way of] her riches, the most different people from the . . . extremities of the world. But now, if one goes to India, the most horrible poverty stares [one] in the face. There [one] finds [that the majority of the people] do not know where they will get their next meal, and frequently they do not get it at all. Everywhere one meets these hungry people, or these half-fed people. This is the India of to-day. No statistics, facts or numbers are [required] to convince you of this, that India has suffered [a] terrible economic decline, and that if definite steps are not taken to prevent this process, India will altogether cease to exist as a nation.

You know perhaps how [recently the British] applied the most ruthless methods to render their industries profitable for themselves. . . .

In multifarious ways the spirit of [the] Indian people was destroyed, and [an attempt was made] to take away from them every capacity for active and constructive work. The conscious policy of [the] British . . . in India was to attempt to divide us.

After [having] . . . disarmed us, [the British] now . . . say we are not fit to protect our country. After extinguishing our system of education, they have set in its place something which is ridiculously meagre . . . teaches us false history, and tries to educate us in the hatred of our own country and in the glorification of England. After all [this], they tell us . . . that we have not sufficient culture to be a free nation.

It is now being advertised in the English press that the Indians fight among themselves. It [should] ... be noted in this connection that [this] is extremely exaggerated. It is also the policy of the British to bring about ... disturbances, ... to sharpen them where they ...[exist] and to do everything to keep them alive. This is the policy of Britain, however much she may ... deny it. Now, what is the condition of India to-day? We are speaking of exploitation. We experience it very fully. Not a single exploitation, but often a double and [triple] exploitation.

We have a part of India—the so-called Indian States—where, under the protection of Britain, the feudal system obtains. Often the English point [these States] out to us, and [to] other countries as well, and say, "Look at these parts of India where a kind of self-government is in existence. Other parts of India are much more advanced." But the British forget to tell one thing. They forget to tell ... that these States are under their care, and they themselves have hindered progress in them. It is the British who first enslaved [these States] and [have] not [allowed] them ... to develop.

Consider the case of [the] great landowners. [Here again] you have ... the land tenure system which, in a great part of India, is a feudal system, and has been brought to us and kept up by the British. It is ... difficult to change it [so] long as the British Government is not willing to do [so]. ...

In India we must reckon ... the Indian Princes and great landowners as ... confederates [of the British Government], because a free India would lead to ... liberation [from their] exploitation. ... We [also] often [witness] harmful agreements [being made] between ... British ... and Indian capitalists. ...

A study of past history and ... of the last few years will prove that ... British world politics is in ... great measure influenced by [Britain's possession of India]. ...

Who can be deceived for a moment as to what will happen to Great Britain if she does not possess India? There would then be no British World Empire. What will take place in [the] future when India is ... free? I cannot say, but it is certain that the British World Empire will cease to exist.

From their capitalistic and imperialistic point of view, the British try to do everything in their power to retain their possession of India. The whole [of British] foreign policy is, to a great extent, influenced by this aim. Therefore, [Britain] must build up a firm overlordship in India. The result is that India has suffered and still suffers. But that is not all. [Because] of India, other lands have suffered and suffer still. You have

heard of the [most recent] instance of ... British Imperialism in India—
the sending of Indian troops to China. ... I must remind you of the
fact—even to my shame I must mention [it]—that Indian troops ...
often [have been] used to repress other people. I [shall tell] you ... of the
number of countries [to] which Indian troops have been sent by the
English for their [advantage]. In the year 1840 [our troops] went to China
for the first time, and in the year 1927 they are still going there. ... They
were in Egypt, in Abyssinia, in the Persian Gulf, in Mesopotamia, Arabia,
Syria, Tibet, Afghanistan and Burma. It is a horrifying list.

I would like you to understand that the Indian problem is not only a
national problem, but it directly affects a great number of other countries,
and ... is of world-wide interest because it [is] directly [affected by] the
greatest and ... most influential imperialism of our time. It is clear that
such a state of [affairs] is insupportable for India. We cannot tolerate it
any longer, not only because freedom is good and slavery ... bad but,
because it is a question of life and death for us and our country. You ...
who have come here from the different countries of the world, cannot
tolerate these dreadful chains which are also a great hindrance to your
own freedom. For us in India, freedom is a pressing necessity. But it is
[no] less important for you if we wish our freedom. The noble example
of Chinese Nationalists has filled us with hope and, as soon as possible,
we wish to follow in their footsteps. We want the fullest freedom for our
country, naturally ... not only [with respect to] international control,
but ... [to] making connections with our neighbours, and other lands, as
we wish. Because we believe that this ... International Congress affords
a possibility of combined work, we welcome it and greet it.[1]

["The resolution on India, drafted and moved by Nehru [at the
Brussels International Congress], declared that 'this Congress ... trusts
that the Indian national movement will base its programme on the full
emancipation of the peasants and workers of India, without which there
can be no real freedom'.

"In his report to the All-India Congress Committee, written on his
return to Switzerland ... [Jawaharlal's] acount of the conference was
most favourable and he urged the Congress to maintain a link with the
newly established League against Imperialism. It was, he wrote, a useful
channel for propaganda and it offered facilities for closer contact with
other Asian nationalist movements. '... Regarded from any point of
view, [it] was an event of first-class importance ... likely to have far-
reaching results.'"[2]]

[1] B.A.I., pp. 365–68.
[2] Quoted in M.B., pp. 111–12.

24 | Further Reflections on League Against Imperialism

The Brussels Congress, as well as the subsequent Committee meetings of the League [against Imperialism], which were held in various places from time to time, helped me to understand some of the problems of colonial and dependent countries. They gave me also an insight into the inner conflicts of the Western labor world. I knew something about them already; I had read about them, but there was no reality behind my knowledge, as there had been no personal contacts. I had some such contacts now, and sometimes had to face problems which reflected these inner conflicts. As between the labor worlds of the Second International and the Third International, my sympathies were with the latter. The whole record of the Second International from the war onward filled me with distaste, and we in India had had sufficient personal experience of the methods of one of its strongest supports—the British Labour party. . . . I did not know much about the fine points of communism, my acquaintance being limited at the time to its broad features. These attracted me, as also the tremendous changes taking place in Russia. But communists often irritated me by their dictatorial ways, their aggressive and rather vulgar methods, their habit of denouncing everybody who did not agree with them. This reaction was no doubt due, as they would say, to my own bourgeois education and up-bringing.

It was curious how, in our League against Imperialism committee meetings, I would usually be on the side of the Anglo-American members on petty matters of argument. There was a certain similarity in our outlook in regard to method at least. We would both object to declamatory and long-winded resolutions, which resembled manifestos. We preferred something simpler and shorter, but the Continental tradition was against this. There was often [a] difference of opinion between the communist elements and the non-communists. Usually we agreed on a compromise. . . .

The League [Against] Imperialism veered more toward communism in later years, though at no time, as far as I know, did it lose its individual character. . . . In 1931 . . . it grew exceedingly angry with me, and excommunicated me with bell, book, and candle—or, to be more accurate, it expelled me by some kind of . . . resolution.[1]

[1] T.F., pp. 125–27.

[From related notation.] The disadvantages [of affiliation with the League against Imperialism] . . . might be the socialist character of the League and the possibility that Russian foreign policy might influence it. [Moreover] Mr Saklatwala [a prominent Indian communist, resident in London] . . . has been criticizing the boycott of Lancashire goods in India on the ground that it injures [Communist] comrades in Lancashire. This is an example of a possible conflict between our nationalistic interests and the interests of the workers outside.[1]

[After the Brussels Conference of 1927, Motilal to Jawaharlal: "'Your participation in the Brussels Conference . . . has brought home to everybody who has read your reports the importance of our having a full-time representative in Europe and America.' Gandhi was less impressed."

Gandhi to Motilal, May 14, 1927: "'I read the public printed report of the [Brussels Conference] from beginning to end and I have now read the confidential report. Both are worthy of Jawaharlal. I appreciate the view he presents about foreign propaganda. But somehow or other, I still feel that our way lies differently.'"[2]

Gandhi to Jawaharlal, May 25, 1927: "I read most carefully your public report as also your private confidential report about the doings of the Oppressed Nations' Conference. I myself do not expect much from this league, if only because its free activity depends upon the goodwill of the very powers that are partners in the exploitation of the oppressed nations, and I feel that the members of the European nations that joined the league will not be able to sustain the last heat. For, they will not be able to accommodate themselves to what they would consider to be an injury to their self-interest. On our side there is danger of our people again looking to external forces and external aid for salvation instead of seeking to achieve it by evolving internal strength. But this is mere academic opinion. I am not at all carefully following European events. You are on the spot and you may see an altruistic improvement in the atmosphere there which I miss altogether."[3]]

[J. to G., April 23, 1927.] I fancy . . . you have got a wrong impression about my idea of the utility of the League Against Imperialism. I do not expect much from it and indeed I am quite sure that none of the members of the so-called imperialist or oppressing nations will help us in the least

---

[1] Extract from Nehru's confidential report on the *Brussels Congress* to the *Working Committee* . . . in the files of the *History of the Freedom Movement Project* in New Delhi, File I (B.19). Quoted in M.B., p. 113.

[2] T.N., p. 256.

[3] B.O.L., pp. 56–57.

whenever their interests conflict with ours. I have no illusion about their altruism. But I welcome all legitimate methods of getting into touch with other countries and peoples so that we may be able to understand their viewpoint and world politics generally. I do not think it is desirable, nor indeed is it possible, for India to plough a lonely furrow now or in the future. It is solely with a view to self-education and self-improvement that I desire external contacts. I am afraid we are terribly narrow in our outlook and the sooner we get rid of this narrowness, the better. Our salvation can of course come only from the internal strength that we may evolve, but one of the methods of evolving such strength should be study of other peoples and their ideas.[1]

["Gandhi had feared that the League Against Imperialism would not go far enough. But before long, it was the League which branded Gandhi as a 'reactionary'. In November, 1929, when the 'joint manifesto' under the signatures of several Indian leaders, including Gandhi and the Nehrus, was issued to welcome Lord Irwin's declaration on Dominion Status for India, the League Against Imperialism, without understanding the shifting complexities of Indian politics, hurled abuse in stereotyped phrases ('chronic reformism' and 'the betrayal of the cause of workers and peasants') at Gandhi and the Congress. This denunciation came, curiously enough, at a time when the Mahatma was about to launch a campaign of mass civil disobedience. Jawaharlal had no intention of dancing to the League's tune; [his] final break [with it] came in April, 1930, when he told the office of the All India Congress Committee not to correspond with it."[2]]

25 | First Visit to Russia, 1927

[During the autumn of 1927 Jawaharlal, together with his father, accepted an invitation by the Russian Government to visit the U.S.S.R. at the time of its tenth anniversary. (Lenin had died only three years before, in 1924.) The journey, made at so early a date in the development of the Soviet Union, and following, as it did, upon Jawaharlal's participation in the League Against Imperialism Congress in Brussels, as well as meetings

---

[1] T.N., pp. 256–57.
[2] Ibid., p. 257.

with such figures as Romain Rolland, Ernst Toller and Madame Sun Yat-sen, aroused his curiosity about the first "Marxist Socialist" experiment. It also fortified an already strong desire to establish further personal contacts at the international level, and a consistently fervent anti-imperialist attitude. Jawaharlal was never, however, to become a Communist, nor has he at any time favored Communism for India.

In various ways 1927 was a crucial year for Jawaharlal. Not only was his awareness of foreign affairs intensified, but his obvious ability to communicate his views forcefully and effectively had been so clearly demonstrated at Brussels that he was suddenly catapulted into being an important spokesman for India at the international level. He began to re-formulate his ideas about the need for both economic and political reforms within India. Since it was also at this juncture that Gandhi came to look upon him as the future leader of Congress—and of an eventually free India—young Nehru's influence at home mounted in quite spectacular manner after his return from Europe in the late nineteen-twenties.]

[The European sojourn of 1926–1927 gave] me time to think, to broaden my outlook, to see India from afar, to think on life itself. Until then I was so involved in Indian affairs that I had little time to think about the broad world or about life's problems in general.[1]

[Concerning his volume, *Soviet Russia*, written and published after Jawaharlal's 1927 visit to the U.S.S.R.: "This was really a series of articles which I sent mostly to the *Hindu* of Madras, articles hurriedly written. The most that can be said about them is that they conveyed some impressions fresh in my mind at the time."[2]

Among the chapters in *Soviet Russia*: The Fascination of Russia; Impressions of Moscow; The Soviet System; the U.S.S.R. Constitution; Russian Books; Lenin; The Peasantry; Criminal Law; Minority Problems; The Peasant and the Land; Women and Marriage; Russian Prison; Russia and India.]

Since my return from Europe I have frequently been asked about Russia. . . . All the world is watching her, some with fear and hatred, and others with passionate hope and the longing to follow in her path.

It is difficult to feel indifferent towards Russia, and it is still more difficult to judge of her achievements and her failures impartially. She is today too much of a live wire to be touched without a violent reaction, and those who write about her can seldom avoid superlatives of praise or denunciation. Much depends on the angle of vision and the philosophy of life of the observer; much also on the prejudices and pre-conceived

[1] Quoted in M.B., p. 29.
[2] From letter to D.N.

5+N.

notions which he brings to his task. But whichever view may be right no one can deny the fascination of this strange Eurasian country of the hammer and sickle, where workers and peasants sit on the thrones of the mighty and upset the best-laid schemes of mice and men.

For us in India the fascination is even greater, and even our self-interest compels us to understand the vast forces which have upset the old order of things and brought a new world into existence, where values have changed utterly and old standards have given place to new. We are a conservative people, not over-fond of change, always trying to forget our present misery and degradation in vague fancies of our glorious past and an immortal civilisation. But the past is dead and gone and our immortal civilisation does not help us greatly in solving the problems of today. If we desire to find a solution for these problems we shall have to venture forth along new avenues of thought and search for new methods. The world changes and the truths of yesterday and the day before may be singularly inapplicable today. We have to follow the line of life in its ever-varying curves and an attempt to adhere rigidly to an outworn creed may take us off at a tangent from this curve of life and lead us to disaster.

Russia thus interests us because it may help us to find some solution for the great problems which face the world today. It interests us specially because conditions there have not been, and are not even now, very dissimilar to conditions in India. Both are vast agricultural countries with only the beginnings of industrialisation, and both have to face poverty and illiteracy. If Russia finds a satisfactory solution for these, our work in India is made easier.

Russia again cannot be ignored by us, because she is our neighbour, a powerful neighbour, which may be friendly to us and co-operate with us, or may be a thorn in our side. In either event we have to know her and understand her and shape our policy accordingly. . . .

It is right . . . that India should be eager to learn more about Russia. So far her information has been largely derived from subsidised news agencies inimical to Russia.[1]

The Soviet system has become so much identified with Bolshevism and Russia that it is difficult to think of it apart from them. Yet it is conceivable that it may exist, or rather that its outward structure may exist, without communism. One of the fugitive ex-grand dukes of Russia, who considers himself the rightful Tsar of Russia and who still clings to a lingering hope that he might one day install himself in the Kremlin,

[1] S.R., pp. 1–4.

stated some time ago that he approved of it and would continue it, minus of course the communism. But for all practical purposes we might consider it as synonymous with the present regime in Russia.

The Soviet idea was probably first outlined in 1834, by James Smith, one of the leaders of the Grand National Consolidated Trade Union, started by Robert Owen in England. In 1847 was issued the famous Communist Manifesto of Marx and Engels, which is considered to be the parent of present day communism. Nearly a generation later, in 1871, Paris had its brief and tragic spell of the Commune. Louis Auguste Blanqui, the father of the Commune, clearly advocated a temporary dictatorship of the proletariat during a revolutionary period. Blanqui himself was put in prison the day before the Commune was declared in Paris, and largely owing to his enforced absence and the lack of efficient leadership, the Commune fell, drowned in the blood of thirty thousand Parisians, who were mercilessly slaughtered by Thiers and his generals. Today only the memory of it remains, but it is a living and a vivid memory. And the wall in the Père Lachaise cemetery in Paris—*le mur des Jederes*—where the communards who had been taken prisoners were mowed down by machine guns, has become a place of pilgrimage for the communists and socialists of the world.

During the revolution of 1905, in Russia, the Soviet system already took definite shape. It grew and developed and changed continuously, till it found itself firmly established in the seats of power in 1917. Its growth became rapid after the Bolshevik revolution, and it has since been continuously adapting itself to changing conditions.

The main characteristic of the Soviet system is its open recognition of the fact that society consists of different social groups or classes, each with different economic interests. So long as this condition lasts, every government must express the relative importance and strength of these social classes. The long course of history is interpreted as a conflict between these different social groups or classes. We thus have what is called the economic interpretation of history, or historic materialism. In each historic period, we are told, there is a dominating class, and the interests of other classes are only considered in so far as they serve to prolong or strengthen this domination. But this domination of one class over the others is seldom, if ever, clearly and openly expressed in the form of government. It is disguised in various ways to delude those who are exploited by it, and, where changes are slow, the dominating class creates an impression of eternal rights and duties, to safeguard its own interests. As society changes and newer and higher forms of the economic and social structure develop, new classes representing this development come to the front. These classes gradually get the upper hand over those older ones which had become obstacles to further development.

The dominating class controls the culture and education and the laws and customs of the people, but it always covers up its class character, specially when a new class begins to resist and to demand its own rights. Even present day "democracy," according to the communists, is a form of government based on class domination, although it seeks cleverly to cover its class character. It is not in reality a social or human democracy. Its essential characteristic is to split up society into a number of individuals with the fiction of equality, and to organise the dominating class into a formidable capitalist state against which individuals or divided groups are powerless. Its class character can be seen when efforts are made to organise other classes. Our present day democracies then ruthlessly suppress all such organisations.

The Soviets in Russia from the very beginning appeared as class organisations of workers. They were quite separate from the labour unions, although the advanced elements of the [latter] participated in the Soviets and combined with other similar elements. During the Kerensky period in 1917, the power of the Soviets increased greatly, till with Lenin's slogan, "All power to the Soviets," they became a rival and competing government.

During the earlier period before the revolution the Soviets represented the working class only. Then the soldiers and sailors came in, and later the peasants. But the peasantry were not given quite the same representation as the workers, as the latter were considered the more progressive group. Intellectuals were also allowed to participate but such as were in the service of the capitalist elements were excluded. The richer peasants were at first admitted but later most of them were excluded. Those living from the labour of others or on rent, old Tsarist officers generally and priests, were excluded, but some exceptions were made. In effect, the exclusions affected a comparatively small number of persons. . . .

The governing principle under which groups are included or excluded is said to be as follows: those groups or classes that are necessary or useful to the development of society at a certain stage should be admitted at that stage, and the most progressive element should have the opportunity to exercise influence in accordance with its energy and social significance. The power of exclusion or inclusion ultimately rests with the All Russia Congress of Soviets—the highest governing body. The principle to be followed was laid down by the Third All R. S. Congress in January 1918—

There must be no participation in the Soviet government by members of "the exploiting classes". This was embodied in the constitution as adopted by the Fifth All R. S. Congress in July 1918. The actual lists of exclusions are made by committees that supervise the elections for the different local soviets. These lists are subject to discussion and appeal to higher soviets and ultimately to the All Russia Soviet Congress or its executive committee. Communists declare that these exclusions are only necessary in the present transitional stage and that as the system develops it will embrace all useful human beings working with their hands or brains. This may be the ultimate result but for the present the system certainly helps greatly in the control of the State by a strong and well-knit minority. But the minority will not long remain in power if it has not got the support or at any rate the passive acquiescence of the masses. Hence we have what is called the "dictatorship of the proletariat" which in effect means the dictatorship of an advanced class-conscious and disciplined group claiming to represent and to possess the good-will of the masses. In defence of this dictatorship communists point out that present-day democracies are in reality also dictatorships. But the latter are dictatorships of the capitalist class or the bourgeoisie and are meant to further the interests of this class. They are the dictatorships of the ten per cent or less, whilst the dictatorship of the proletariat is supposed to be of the ninety per cent.

The characteristic feature of the Soviet system is its method of representation. It is not, as in most democratic countries, based on territorial or geographical constituencies, where the individual is the unit. The structure of the soviets is based on economic and social units, *e.g.*, factories, villages, co-operatives, trade-unions, etc. The number of delegates elected are proportional to the number of voters, small units combining for the purpose of electing representatives. There is one important deviation however from proportionality—the village, electing one delegate for ten thousand voters, the town, one delegate for two thousand voters. The town dwellers, which means chiefly the industrial workers, are considered more advanced socially and are thus given more weightage.

The village soviet is said to be the soul of the village. The word 'soviet' means *sabha* and a village soviet would correspond to a *panchayat* elected by almost all the residents of an Indian village. This soviet is elected by [a] show of hands at a kind of public meeting at which all the residents, men and women above a certain age, with certain exceptions, have the right to be present and to vote. The exceptions are rich peasants living by the labour of others, usurers, priests and such other elements as may be considered parasitical and unsocial. If there are any small industries or public institutions in the village, they will also send delegates direct to the soviet. So also the local co-operative society, the Union of peasant Labourers, women's organisations and the Young People's League.

There is generally a big non-communist majority in the village soviet, but a few communists are always present, and as these are usually the most active and intelligent members, their influence is considerable.

Most of the questions touching the daily life of the villagers are decided by the village soviet, subject to a right of appeal to higher soviets, which are also empowered to interfere when necessary. Thus the village soviet will deal with land problems and specially the distribution of land, the distribution of seeds for cultivation, wood to be cut in common forests, taxes according to general regulations, building of schools and medical halls, medical service, fire protection, mutual aid, etc. The Soviet also serves as a link between the various other organisations in the village, and there is a growing number of these co-operative mutual aid societies, women's organisations, Young People's Leagues, Pioneers (corresponding to the Boy Scouts), international aid societies, etc.

Two other important features of the Soviet system might be mentioned here. The first is the power of recall. Each constituency has the right to recall its representatives in any soviet at any time. In other countries, as is well known, representatives to the legislatures are elected for a fixed period of three or four or five years and cannot be recalled. The second feature is the combination of the legislative and executive functions in the soviets. But it is not quite clear how this is done.[1]

To understand the great drama of the Russian Revolution and the inner forces that shaped and brought the great change about, a study of cold theory is of little use. The October Revolution was undoubtedly one of the great events of world history, the greatest since the first French Revolution, and its story is more absorbing, from the human and the dramatic point of view, than any tale of phantasy.[2]

The real test of the success of the [Russian] revolution does not lie in the theory, or in the courage and enthusiasm of the people, or even in the greatness of Lenin. Nor can the revolution be said to have been a failure because the Bolsheviks ruthlessly exterminated their opponents and countered the white terror with the red. The real test of success can only be the measure of happiness of the masses of the people. It is partly a

[1] Ibid., pp. 18–25.
[2] Ibid., p. 36.

question of psychology, but partly also of material conditions, and facts and figures. It is not easy to judge the psychology of a people without the most intimate knowledge. It may be that freedom from oppression is preferable even though it results in a [diminution] of material well-being for a time; and visitors to Russia tell us that in the early years of the revolution when civil war and the blockade had brought the population to the verge of starvation, the new freedom more than compensated for the suffering and lack of food and all comforts. But leaving the realms of psychology alone, we can at least study the material conditions that have resulted from the revolution and follow their changes from year to year, and thus perhaps be able to indicate the lines of future progress or retrogression.[1]

Russia has passed through ten years since the Bolshevik Revolution. But it must be remembered that the first five of these ten years were entirely taken up in war against foreign and internal enemies and in the harder struggle against famine and blockade. A host of enemies attacked and tried to strangle her by cutting off her food supplies. For years the revolution hung in the balance and the economic life of the nation went to pieces. It is only during the past five years that she has had comparative peace and a chance to develop her resources. But even during this period she has had to contend against the hostility of most of the governments of Europe and . . . the . . . United States of America. Having little money to develop her resources she has been denied credits and capital abroad. If she has progressed then during these five years it has been despite these difficulties. And the testimony of all competent observers is that she has progressed and has already made good the losses of the War period of eight years. Today her production is greater than it was in [1914] when the German war broke out and it is said to be increasing rapidly.

The United States of America do not officially recognise the Soviet Government, but in spite of this official hostility, the progress that Russia is making is attracting numbers of American business men to her and many professors and students who go to study conditions on the spot. Indeed Russia has many foreign visitors now, not the tourists who fill every corner of Western Europe, but earnest students and enquirers; not socialists only who go to admire, but thinking capitalists who go in search of business and to find out what this strange opponent of their time-honoured ideas is like. The eastern countries are well represented in this band of enquirers—China, Persia and Afghanistan. They go to study

[1] Ibid., pp. 49–50.

specially the educational system, agriculture, co-operation and the military machine. . . .

It would be an excellent thing if our professors and students also paid visits of enquiry and studied the educational and agricultural developments in Russia. Their visits would be even more helpful to us than those of politicians. Our universities could easily arrange for a small but competent delegation for this purpose.

Our universities and others interested could also without any difficulty, unless the British Government intervenes, get into touch by means of letters with educational and cultural establishments in Russia and exchange publications with them. The Russians will welcome such co-operation and will gladly supply any information. They publish periodically pamphlets and little books in various languages, including English, showing the progress made. These will of course be entirely one-sided but they will represent the official viewpoint and they will give the latest figures.[1]

I do not claim special knowledge, and I have not considered . . . many subjects of exceeding interest. Nor have I considered the future prospects of the Soviet Union, and whether it will retain its aggressively communist character, or gradually develop a system more in harmony with that of its neighbours. Soon after the revolution Lenin wrote: "The outstanding achievement of the Revolution has been that Russia, by her political system, has in a few months overtaken the progressive countries. But this is not enough, the struggle admits of no compromise: it has either to fail, or to overtake and even to surpass the progressive countries economically as well . . . either to go under or to move forward at full steam. Thus has the question been put by History." The struggle is indeed continuing, but the period of militant communism is already over. . . . Some people say that in spite of the [communists'] desire . . . to have a classless society, new classes are gradually being formed in the Union. Whatever the future may bring, however, it may be said today that in spite of minor changes the struggle admits of no compromise. As Lenin said Russia will either go under or move forward at full steam. A middle course seems hardly likely. And ten years have shown that Russia refuses to go under. . . .

The dynamic forces released by the revolution of 1917 have not played themselves out. They have made history and they will continue to make history, and no man can afford to ignore them. . . . Indifference is out of the question.

[1] Ibid., pp. 53–55.

We have grown up in the tradition, carefully nurtured by England, of hostility to Russia. For long years past the bogey of a Russian invasion has been held up to us and has been made the excuse of vast expenditure on our armaments. . . . The Tsar has gone but the rivalry between England and Russia continues and we are now told that India is threatened by the Soviet Government.

How far is this true? There can be no doubt that there is intense antagonism between British Imperial policy and Soviet Russia, and such antagonism often leads to war. Thus the danger of war is real. But will this war be of Russia's seeking, or does England desire to precipitate an armed conflict?

Russia has only recently passed through a period of international war and civil war, of famine and blockade, and above everything she desires peace to consolidate her economic position and build up on a sure foundation her new order of society. She has already attained a large measure of success and is working at high pressure and with "full steam" to develop peacefully her vast territories. War, even successful war, must put a stop to this process of consolidation and development, and is bound to delay indefinitely the full establishment of her new social order. She cannot welcome this. And so we have seen in the past few years that she has refused to be drawn into an armed conflict in spite of great provocation and insult. . . . Russia has succeeded in avoiding war even at the cost of having to swallow her anger and resentment.[1]

[A foreshadowing in Jawaharlal's book about Russia of his later attitude toward international "pacts".] In these days of pacts and unity conferences Lenin's views on the subject may be of interest. In a letter to a friend in 1912 he wrote: "The bourgeoisie, the liberals and the social revolutionaries, who never deal with 'great problems' seriously, but trot one behind the other, make pacts and go on in the old grooves with eclecticism, are always crying out about the dissensions and discords in social democracy. That is the exact difference between all of them and social democracy; the fight between the individual social democratic groups comes from deep roots of thought whereas with them even the differences are all varnished over on the surface, while inside they are empty, petty, superficial. Never at any price would I exchange the vigorous fighting of the various tendencies in social democracy for the togged-up emptiness and poverty of the social revolutionaries and their partners."[2]

[1] Ibid., pp. 125–28.
[2] Ibid., p. 46.

5*

26

Of the Late Twenties—Development
of Interest in Socialism—Role in
Independence Movement—The Simon
Commission—Madras Congress Session,
1927—Resolutions of the Congress

Of the Late Twenties

I was returning from Europe in good physical and mental condition. . . .
I felt full of energy and vitality, and the sense of inner conflict and
frustration that had oppressed me so often previously was, for the time
being, absent. My outlook was wider, and nationalism by itself seemed to
me definitely a narrow and insufficient creed. Political freedom, independence, were no doubt essential, but they were steps only in the right
direction; without social freedom and a socialistic structure of society and
the State, neither the country nor the individual could develop much. I felt
I had a clearer perception of world affairs, more grip on the present-day
world, ever changing as it was. I had read largely, not only on current
affairs and politics, but on many other subjects that interested me, cultural
and scientific. I found the vast political, economic, and cultural changes
going on in Europe and America a fascinating study. Soviet Russia, despite certain unpleasant aspects, attracted me greatly, and seemed to hold
forth a message of hope to the world. Europe, in the middle twenties, was
trying to settle down in a way; the great depression was yet to come. But
I came back with the conviction that this settling down was superficial
only, and big eruptions and mighty changes were in store for Europe and
the world in the near future.

To train and prepare our country for these world events—to keep in
readiness for them, as far as we could—seemed to be the immediate task.
The preparation was largely an ideological one. First of all, there should
be no doubt about the objective of political independence. This should
be clearly understood as the only possible political goal for us; something
radically different from the vague and confusing talk of Dominion status.
Then there was the social goal. It would be too much, I felt, to expect the
Congress to go far in this direction just then. The Congress was a purely
political and nationalistic body, unused to thinking on other lines. But a
beginning might be made. Outside the Congress, in labor circles and

among the young, the idea could be pushed on much further. For this purpose I wanted to keep myself free from Congress office, and I had a vague idea also of spending some months in remote rural areas to study their conditions. But this was not to be, and events were to drag me again into the heart of Congress politics.[1]

Development of Interest in Socialism

[India's first Socialist weekly was founded in 1923. The first Indian Workers' and Peasants' Party was established in Bengal in 1926. Jawaharlal was invited to deliver the Presidential Address to the first All-India Socialist Youth Congress in 1928.]

I was by no means a pioneer in the socialist field in India. Indeed, I was rather backward, and I had only advanced painfully, step by step, where many others had gone ahead blazing a trail. The workers' trade-union movement was, ideologically, definitely socialist, and so were the majority of the youth leagues. A vague, confused socialism was already part of the atmosphere of India when I returned from Europe in December 1927, and even earlier than that there were many individual socialists. Mostly they thought along utopian lines, but Marxian theory was influencing them increasingly, and a few considered themselves as hundred per cent Marxists. This tendency was strengthened in India, as in Europe and America, by developments in the Soviet Union, and particularly the Five-Year Plan.

Such importance as I possessed as a socialist worker lay in the fact that I happened to be a prominent Congressman holding important Congress offices. There were many other well-known Congressmen who were beginning to think likewise. . . .

[We] even tried, as early as 1926, to draw up a mild socialist program. We declared that the existing land system must go and that there should be no intermediaries between the State and the cultivator. We had to proceed cautiously, as we were moving in an atmosphere which was, till then, unused to such ideas.[2]

Increasingly Important Role in Independence Movement

[After his return to India from Europe in December, 1927, Jawaharlal began to play an increasingly important role in Congress, despite the fact

[1] T.F., p. 128.
[2] Ibid., p. 139.

that a number of his opinions about most of the issues under consideration at the time were at variance with the attitudes of the majority of his colleagues. His stand diverged in certain significant respects even from that of his father and Gandhi.

As previously noted, during the period preceding the Madras Congress Session of 1927, Motilal Nehru had been a staunch leader of the Swaraj Party. At times, this group in Congress opposed Gandhian non-cooperation, while favoring entry into local councils and provincial and central legislatures, in order "to wreck them" from within.

Jawaharlal was out of sympathy both with the latter course of action and with the general policy of the Swaraj Party. His growing belief in Socialism also was quite decisively beginning to alter his attitude about the nature of the "independence" he felt India ultimately must achieve.

From 1927 to 1929 Jawaharlal was General Secretary of Congress. In 1928 he presided over various provincial conferences, and became President of the All-India Trades Union Congress.]

The Simon Commission

[Just before the 1927 Madras Congress Session, the Viceroy, Lord Irwin, announced the appointment by the British Parliament of a Royal Commission, headed by Sir John Simon. The duty of the Commission was to investigate the working of the 1920 Constitution for India; to inquire into "the desirability of introducing Responsible Government", and the extent to which constitutional reform might be introduced. After publication of the Commission's report, Indian public opinion was to be consulted with respect to its recommendations.

The notion that an investigation should take place to see whether India was fit to govern herself, led to serious resistance among Congress leaders. Jawaharlal was one of the principal organizers of a boycott against the Simon Commission, during a period in which there was a rising tide of nationalism throughout the country.

As a mark of protest against the Commission, Congress and various other groups decided to frame a Constitution on their own. (The draft thus prepared was incorporated in the Motilal Nehru report of 1928, to be commented upon in a later section.)]

Madras Congress Session—1927

[Jawaharlal's contribution to the Madras Congress Session of December, 1927 was to be of major significance. He moved two important resolutions extraordinary for the period: one on the existing war danger, the second on complete independence. Both resolutions, apparently, were passed without either Gandhi or Motilal Nehru—or most of the other experienced, elder statesmen within Congress—quite realizing the revolutionary nature of what Jawaharlal had proposed.]

Immediately on our arrival in Madras I was caught in the whirl. I presented a bunch of resolutions to the Working Committee—resolutions on independence, war danger, association with the League Against Imperialism, etc.—and nearly all of these were accepted and made into official Working Committee resolutions. I had to put them forward at the open session of the Congress, and, to my surprise, they were all almost unanimously adopted. The Independence resolution was supported even by Mrs Annie Besant. This all-round support was very gratifying, but I had an uncomfortable feeling that the resolutions were either not understood for what they were, or were distorted to mean something else. That this was so became apparent soon after the Congress, when a controversy arose on the meaning of the Independence resolution.

These resolutions of mine were somewhat different from the usual Congress resolutions; they represented a new outlook. Many Congressmen no doubt liked them, some had a vague dislike for them, but not enough to make them oppose. Probably the latter thought that they were academic resolutions, making little difference either way, and the best way to get rid of them was to pass them and move on to something more important. The Independence resolution thus did not represent then, as it did a year or two later, a vital and irrepressible urge on the part of the Congress; it represented a widespread and growing sentiment.

Gandhiji was in Madras, and he attended the open Congress sessions, but he did not take any part in the shaping of policy. He did not attend the meetings of the Working Committee, of which he was a member. That had been his general political attitude in the Congress since the dominance of the *Swaraj* party. But he was frequently consulted, and little of importance was done without his knowledge. I do not know how far the resolutions I put before the Congress met with his approval. I am inclined to think that he disliked them, not so much because of what they said, but because of their general trend and outlook. He did not, however, criticize them on any occasion.

The unreality of the Independence resolution came out in that very session of the Congress, when another resolution condemning the Simon Commission and appealing for its boycott was considered. As a corollary to this it was proposed to convene an All-Parties Conference, which was to draw up a constitution for India. It was manifest that the moderate groups, with whom co-operation was sought, could never think in terms of independence. The very utmost they could go to was some form of Dominion status.

I stepped back into the Congress secretaryship. . . . The real reason for my accepting office again was my fear that the Congress might, through the instrumentality of the All-Parties Conference, or because of other reasons, slide back to a more moderate and compromising position. It seemed to be in a hesitant mood, swinging alternately from one extreme to another. I wanted to prevent, as far as I could, the swing back to moderation and to hold on to the independence objective.[1]

Resolutions of the Madras Congress

I. Resolution on the War Danger:

"This congress has noted with grave concern the extraordinary and extensive war preparations which the British Government is carrying on in India and in the Eastern Seas, specially in the North-West Frontier of India. These preparations for war are not only calculated to strengthen the hold of British Imperialism in India in order to strangle all attempts at freedom, but must result in hastening a disastrous war in which an attempt will be made to make India again a tool in the hand of foreign imperialists.

"The Congress declares that the people of India have no quarrel with their neighbours and desire to live at peace with them, and asserts their right to determine whether or not they will take part in any war.

"The Congress demands that these war preparations be put an end to, and further declares that in the event of the British Government embarking on any warlike adventure and endeavouring to exploit India in it for the furtherance of their imperialist aims, it will be the duty of the people of India to refuse to take any part in such a war or to co-operate with them in any way whatsoever."[2]

[From Jawaharlal's commentary on above resolution.] Any war nowadays is an international disaster. It must result in terrible slaughter and destruction. It must let loose, as the last war let loose, the flood-gates of hatred and barbarism. When all countries and all nations are linked together and cannot be separately considered, it is inconceivable, even if a war is fought outside the frontiers of India, that it would leave India untouched. . . . Any such war . . . is likely to be fought very near our frontiers and India is very likely to be involved in it. If there is such a war, you and I will not

[1] T.F., pp. 129-30.
[2] R.I.N.C. (Ms.). Unnumbered pages.

sit peaceably holding our conferences and Congresses. Indeed, we may ourselves hear the roaring of cannons, and we may see bombshells dropping from aeroplanes upon our peaceful villages. .... Such a war may result—I hope it does not result—in strengthening British imperialism to such an extent that it may make it more difficult for us to achieve freedom. It may remove for a generation or two our hope of freedom, so that in any event we cannot ignore any preparations for war or any chance of war.

No man or woman can ignore it, least of all an Indian who desires to achieve freedom for his country. It is a well-known fact that all countries are preparing more or less for war. It is not England only; it is every country, because in Europe today there is fear. Europe is in the grip of fear, and out of fear comes hatred, and out of that comes violence and barbarism. Every country in Europe hates every other country. The most feared and hated country in Europe is England. There is talk of disarmament, there is talk of peace. But those of you who have taken the trouble to study what has been happening at Geneva and elsewhere will realize that all this talk of disarmament is mere camouflage. Today Europe is perhaps a greater powder magazine than it was in 1914 when the last great war broke out. War has not broken out yet because all nations are exhausted. But all the seeds of war are present and at present in greater number than they were thirteen years ago. When you look at the Balkans, Poland, Italy, Czecho-Slovakia, Lithuania and Russia, everywhere there is preparation for war, and there is [the possibility that there will be] war. Let us see what attitude the country with which we have [the closest relationship] has taken in these war preparations, and in this talk of peace and disarmament. We are especially interested in Britain's attitude. We have had in recent times various disarmament conferences at Geneva. There was a Naval Disarmament Conference also. But these Conferences failed largely because Britain could not agree to proposals made by other countries. Indeed, in the past, Britain has definitely refused to accept the principle of compulsory arbitration. Britain has refused even to make a treaty of compulsory arbitration with a little country like Switzerland, because it may be giving up a dangerous principle. It has [thus maintained] its right to wage war without any reference to the League of Nations, or to any other authority. At the last meeting of the Assembly of the League of Nations, Sir Austen Chamberlain made an extraordinary speech on behalf of England. He stated that he was not prepared to sacrifice the Empire for the vague ideals of peace and disarmament of the League of Nations. For him the British Commmonwealth was a greater thing than those ideals.

What is the Empire but India? It comes to this: For the sake of India, to hold India under subjection, Sir Austen Chamberlain and the British Government cannot agree to the principles of disarmament or peace. It is well recognised in Europe, especially by small nations who are always raising this question in the League of Nations, that England is the greatest obstacle today in the attainment of disarmament or world peace. I should like to indicate to you some of the war preparations which England is making. You know that preparations for war are secret preparations. Nations do not advertise when they are going to prepare for war. Nonetheless when preparations are being carried on on a most extensive scale—on the scale on which England has been [operating]—it is impossible to hide them. So some of these things have come to light. The biggest and one of the latest . . . is the Singapore base. Why is England spending millions and millions of pounds, and making this great Naval base at Singapore? Surely it can only be a challenge directed against some of the powers which have interests in the Pacific, and round about the Eastern Seas. It is primarily directed against China and Japan; also . . . France. For, if there is a war . . . then England can threaten French possessions in Indo-China from Singapore.

[The Singapore base] is also directed against the Dutch East Indies, because England can force Holland to be neutral in case of war. It is directed partly, at any rate, against America and American [domination] in the Pacific, because in case of conflict, England could sweep down on the Philippine Islands, and take possession of them. It is chiefly directed against India, because it is for the retention of India that all [of] these things are done. Imagine that [if] there is a struggle in India, then the Singapore base will facilitate the transport of troops from Australia to India, and in many other ways will help the British in taking the offensive in India. So much for the Singapore base.

Then we have another naval base which is being made at Trincomalee. We have also the great Royal Indian Navy which has recently been created with a flourish of trumpets. Whatever it may be, it is not an Indian Navy, except perhaps that the expenses for it will come out of the Indian Exchequer. This Navy is merely an adjunct of the British Navy, to help the British Government against India, although it may be at our cost. Again, I should like to draw your attention to the rapid development of the transport system in India. . . . War nowadays very largely depends on transport. That is why the transport system has been perfected. . . .

Two proposals have been made in England, and also in Anglo-Indian journals in India which, although officially denied in Parliament, persist in getting publicity in the press. These periodicals are supposed to know what the Government [does], and these proposals are of the greatest interest to us. The first [proposal] was that a part of the British Expeditionary Force should be stationed in India because there is more danger of war in Asia than in Europe. Therefore it is desirable that [such a] force should be ready in India, and should immediately start war-like preparations when necessary. The second proposal was that these highly developed mechanised forces should be used when there is any danger of war. The procedure that England should adopt was coldly stated in the English Press to be, not to wait for an attack, but to make a forward spring into Central Asia across Afghanistan in one sweep. This was proposed because just in the same way Germans are supposed, in their attack on France, to have made a forward spring across Belgium. . . . We are not in a position to stop the war, it may be. But, at any rate, we are in a position to make it clear what attitude India will [adopt]. And it is quite possible and conceivable that if India's attitude is clearly stated then England too may change hers. England might not dare to provoke war when she knows that India would not support [it], but actually hinder [its] conduct. . . . Now this resolution lays down clearly that India has no quarrel with her neighbours. As to the declaration itself, it is our right to determine whether we shall join [any] war or not. Thirdly, another declaration follows, and that is the most important. In case war comes, and an attempt is made to exploit you, you will refuse to be exploited, and to take any part in the war. I trust that if war comes, and I think war may be nearer than most of us imagine—it may come in a year, two years, or five years—this National Congress will follow up the lead given today. I also trust that the Indian people will rally round the Congress, forgetting their petty differences and generally adopt the attitude which the Congress has suggested . . . and suffer any consequences that might follow. I am convinced that if the Congress and the Indian people adopt this attitude, they will emerge from that great ordeal much better, much freer, and India will be a unified, independent Nation.[1]

II. Resolution on Independence

[The following resolution, presented by Jawaharlal at the 1927 Madras Congress Session, was the first formulation of the kind to be placed before Congress.]

"The Congress declares the goal of the Indian people to be complete national independence."

[1] Ibid.

[Commentary on above resolution.] It makes clear the goal does not change the present creed of the Congress. If you pass this resolution, you declare by a majority, I hope by an overwhelming majority, that the Congress is today for complete independence. Nonetheless you leave the doors of the Congress open to such persons as may not approve of this goal, as they perhaps are satisfied with a lesser or a smaller goal. I think that although the door of the Congress is open there should be no doubt, if you approve of this resolution, [that] then everybody must say that the majority of the Congressmen today demand complete independence for the country. Now this resolution as placed before you is a very short and simple one. . . .

I wish to make it clear to you that the adoption of this formula does not in any way change the spirit or the meaning of the resolution. It means what it says. It means complete independence. It means control of the defence forces of the country. It means control over the financial, economic policy of the country. It means control over . . . relations with . . . foreign countries. . . . Without these things independence would be a travesty and camouflage.

Thirdly I wish to point out to you lest there be any mistake that this goal, which I hope you will adopt today, is the immediate goal and not a goal of the far distant future. . . . Whether we achieve it today or to-morrow, a year hence, or ten years hence, I cannot say. That depends on your strength and the strength of the country.[1]

---

27 | Political Activity, 1928—Police Assault—Growing Appeal of Non-Violence—Effect of Brutal Lathee Charges

Growth of Indian Political Activity, 1928

The year 1928 was, politically, a full year, with plenty of activity all over the country. There seemed to be a new impulse moving the people forward, a new stir that was equally present in the most varied groups.

[1] Ibid.

Probably the change had been going on gradually during my long absence from the country; it struck me as very considerable on my return. Early in 1926, India was still quiescent, passive, perhaps not fully recovered from the effort of 1919–1922; in 1928 she seemed fresh, active, and full of suppressed energy. Everywhere there was evidence of this: among the industrial workers, the peasantry, middle-class youth, and the intelligentsia generally. The trade-union movement had grown greatly, and the All-India Trade-Union Congress, established seven or eight years previously, was already a strong and representative body. The peasantry was also astir. . . . Large gatherings of protesting tenants became common. Another very noticeable feature of the India of 1928 was the growth of the youth movement. Everywhere youth leagues were being established, youth conferences were being held.

Wherever the [Simon] Commission went it was greeted by hostile crowds and the cry of "Simon, go back," and thus vast numbers of the Indian masses became acquainted not only with Sir John Simon's name but with two words of the English language, the only two they knew. These words must have become a hated obsession for the members of the Commission. The story is related that once, when they were staying at the Western Hostel in New Delhi, the refrain seemed to come to them in the night out of the darkness. They were greatly irritated at being pursued in this way, even at night. As a matter of fact, the noise that disturbed them came from the jackals that infest the waste places of the imperial capital.[1]

Police Assault

The Simon Commission was moving about, pursued by black flags. . . . Occasionally there were minor conflicts between the police and the crowds. Lahore brought matters to a head and suddenly sent a thrill of indignation throughout the country. The anti-Simon Commission demonstration there was headed by Lala Lajpat Rai [a prominent, elderly nationalist leader from the Punjab]; and, as he stood by the roadside in front of the thousands of demonstrators, he was assaulted and beaten on his chest with a baton by a young English police officer. There had been no attempt whatever on the part of the crowd, much less on the part of Lalaji, to indulge in any methods of violence. Even so, as he stood peacefully by, he and many of his companions were severely beaten by the police. Anyone

[1] T.F., p. 131.

who takes part in street demonstrations runs the risk of a conflict with the police, and, though our demonstrations were almost always perfectly peaceful, Lalaji must have known of this risk and taken it consciously. But still, the manner of the assault, the needless brutality of it, came as a shock to vast numbers of people in India. Those were the days when we were not used to lathee charges by the police; our sensitiveness had not been blunted by repeated brutality. To find that even the greatest of our leaders, the foremost and most popular man in the Punjab, could be so treated seemed little short of monstrous, and a dull anger spread all over the country, especially in north India. How helpless we were, how despicable when we could not even protect the honor of our chosen leaders!

The physical injury to Lalaji had been serious enough, as he had been hit on the chest and he had long suffered from heart disease. Probably, in the case of a healthy young man the injury would not have been great, but Lalaji was neither young nor healthy. What effect this physical injury had on his death a few weeks later it is hardly possible to say definitely, though his doctors were of [the] opinion that it hastened the end. But I think that there can be no doubt that the mental shock which accompanied the physical injury had a tremendous effect on Lalaji. He felt angry and bitter, not so much at the personal humiliation, as at the national humiliation involved in the assault on him.

It was this sense of national humiliation that weighed on the mind of India, and when Lalaji's death came soon after, inevitably it was connected with the assault, and sorrow itself gave pride of place to anger and indignation.[1]

Growing Appeal of Non-violence

[Terrorism], in spite of occasional recrudescence, has no longer any real appeal for the youth of India. Fifteen years' stress on nonviolence has changed the whole background in India and made the masses much more indifferent to, and even hostile to, the idea of terrorism as a method of political action. Even the classes from which the terrorists are usually drawn, the lower middle-classes and intelligentsia, have been powerfully affected by the Congress propaganda against methods of violence. Their active and impatient elements, who think in terms of revolutionary action, also realize fully now that revolution does not come through terrorism, and that terrorism is an outworn and profitless method which comes in the

[1] Ibid., pp. 132–33.

way of real revolutionary action. Terrorism is a dying thing in India and elsewhere, not because of Government coercion, which can only suppress and bottle up, not eradicate, but because of basic causes and world events. Terrorism usually represents the infancy of a revolutionary urge in a country. That stage passes, and with it passes terrorism as an important phenomenon. Occasional outbursts may continue because of local causes or individual suppressions. India has undoubtedly passed that stage, and no doubt even the occasional outbursts will gradually die out. But this does not mean that all people in India have ceased to believe in methods of violence. They have, very largely, ceased to believe in individual violence and terrorism, but many, no doubt, still think that a time may come when organized, violent methods may be necessary for gaining freedom, as they have often been necessary in other countries. That is today an academic issue which time alone will put to the test; it has nothing to do with terroristic methods. . . .[1]

Effect of Brutal Lathee Charges

The assault on Lala Lajpat Rai, and his subsequent death, increased the vigor of the demonstrations against the Simon Commission in the places which it subsequently visited. It was due in Lucknow, and the local Congress committee made extensive preparations for its "reception." Huge processions, meetings, and demonstrations were organized many days in advance, both as propaganda and as rehearsals for the actual show. I went to Lucknow and was present at some of these. The success of these preliminary demonstrations, which were perfectly orderly and peaceful, evidently nettled the authorities, and they began to obstruct and issue orders against the taking out of processions in certain areas. It was in this connection that I had a new experience, and my body felt the baton and lathee blows of the police.

Processions had been prohibited, ostensibly to avoid any interference with the traffic. We decided to give no cause for complaint on this score, and arranged for small groups of sixteen, as far as I can remember, to go separately, along unfrequented routes to the meeting place. Technically, this was no doubt a breach of the order, for sixteen with a flag were a procession. I led one of the groups of sixteen and, after a big gap, came another such group. . . . My group had gone perhaps about two hundred yards—the road was a deserted one—when we heard the clatter of horses'

[1] Ibid., pp. 133-34.

hoofs behind us. We looked back to find a bunch of mounted police, probably two or three dozen in number, bearing down upon us at a rapid pace. They were soon right upon us, and the impact of the horses broke up our little column of sixteen. The mounted policemen then started belaboring our volunteers with huge batons or truncheons, and, instinctively, the volunteers sought refuge on the sidewalks, and some even entered the petty shops. They were pursued and beaten down. My own instinct had urged me to seek safety when I saw the horses charging down upon us; it was a discouraging sight. But then, I suppose, some other instinct held me to my place, and I survived the first charge, which had been checked by the volunteers behind me. Suddenly I found myself alone in the middle of the road; a few yards away from me, in various directions, were the policemen beating down our volunteers. Automatically, I began moving slowly to the side of the road to be less conspicuous, but again I stopped and had a little argument with myself, and decided that it would be unbecoming for me to move away. All this was a matter of a few seconds only, but I have the clearest recollections of that conflict within me and the decision, prompted by my pride, I suppose, which could not tolerate the idea of my behaving like a coward. Yet the line between cowardice and courage was a thin one, and I might well have been on the other side. Hardly had I so decided, when I looked round to find that a mounted policeman was trotting up to me, brandishing his long new baton. I told him to go ahead, and turned my head away—again an instinctive effort to save the head and face. He gave me two resounding blows on the back. I felt stunned, and my body quivered all over, but, to my surprise and satisfaction, I found that I was still standing. The police force was withdrawn soon after and made to block the road in front of us. Our volunteers gathered together again, many of them bleeding and with split skulls . . . and all of us sat down facing the police. So we sat for an hour or so, and it became dark. On the one side, various high officials gathered; on the other, large crowds began to assemble as the news spread. Ultimately, the officials agreed to allow us to go by our original route, and we went that way with the mounted policemen, who had charged us and belabored us, going ahead of us as a kind of escort.

I have written about this petty incident in some detail because of its effect on me. The bodily pain I felt was quite forgotten in a feeling of exhilaration that I was physically strong enough to face and bear lathee blows. And a thing that surprised me was that right through the incident, even when I was being beaten, my mind was quite clear and I was consciously analyzing my feelings. This rehearsal stood me in good stead the next morning, when a stiffer trial was in store for us. For the next morning was the time when the Simon Commission was due to arrive, and our great demonstration was going to take place.

My father was at Allahabad at the time, and I was afraid that the news of the assault on me, when he read about it in the next morning's papers, would upset him and the rest of the family. So I telephoned to him late in the evening to assure him that all was well and that he should not worry. But he did worry, and, finding it difficult to sleep over it, he decided at about midnight to come over to Lucknow. The last train had gone, and so he started by motorcar. He had some bad luck on the way, and it was nearly five in the morning by the time he had covered the journey of one hundred and forty-six miles and reached Lucknow, tired out and exhausted.

That was about the time when we were getting ready to go in procession to the station. The previous evening's incidents had the effect of rousing up Lucknow more than anything that we could have done, and, even before the sun was out, vast numbers of people made their way to the station. Innumerable little processions came from various parts of the city, and from the Congress office started the main procession, consisting of several thousands, marching in fours. We were in this main procession. We were stopped by the police as we approached the station. There was a huge open space, about half a mile square, in front of the station (this has now been built over by the new station) and we were made to line up on one side of this *maidan*, and there our procession remained, making no attempt to push our way forward. The place was full of foot and mounted police, as well as the military. The crowd of sympathetic onlookers swelled up, and many of these persons managed to spread out in twos and threes in the open space. Suddenly we saw in the far distance a moving mass. It was two or three long lines of cavalry or mounted police, covering the entire area, galloping down toward us, and striking and riding down the numerous stragglers that dotted the *maidan*. That charge of galloping horsemen was a fine sight, but for the tragedies that were being enacted on the way, as harmless and very much surprised sight-seers went under the horses' hoofs. Behind the charging lines these people lay on the ground, some still unable to move, others writhing in pain, and the whole appearance of that *maidan* was that of a battlefield. But we did not have much time for gazing on that scene or for reflections; the horsemen were soon upon us, and their front line clashed almost at a gallop with the massed ranks of our processionists. We held our ground, and, as we appeared to be unyielding, the horses had to pull up at the last moment and reared up on their hind legs with their front hoofs quivering in the air over our heads. And then began a beating of us, and battering with lathees and long batons both by the mounted and the foot police. It was a tremendous hammering, and the clearness of vision that I had had the evening before left me. All I knew was that I had to stay where I was and must not yield or go back. I felt half blinded with the blows, and sometimes a dull anger seized me and a desire to hit out. I thought how easy it would be to pull down the police officer in front of me from his horse and to mount up myself, but long training and discipline held, and I did not raise a hand, except to protect my face from a blow. Besides, I knew well enough that any aggression on our part would result in a ghastly tragedy, the shooting down of large numbers of our men.

After what seemed a tremendous length of time, but was probably only a few minutes, our line began to yield slowly, step by step, without breaking up. This left me somewhat isolated, and more exposed at the sides. More blows came, and then I was suddenly lifted off my feet from behind and carried off, to my great annoyance. Some of my younger colleagues, thinking that a dead set was being made at me, had decided to protect me in this summary fashion.

Our processionists lined up again about a hundred feet behind our original line. The police also withdrew and stood in a line, fifty feet apart from us. So we remained, when the cause of all this trouble, the Simon Commission, secretly crept away from the station in the far distance, more than half a mile away. But, even so, they did not escape the black flags or demonstrators. Soon after, we came back in full procession to the Congress office and there dispersed, and I went on to father, who was anxiously waiting for us.

Now that the excitement of the moment had passed, I felt pains all over my body and great fatigue. Almost every part of me seemed to ache, and I was covered with contused wounds and marks of blows. But fortunately I was not injured in any vital spot. . . .

The memory that endures with me, far more than that of the beating itself, is that of many of the faces of those policemen, and especially of the officers, who were attacking us. Most of the real beating and battering was done by European sergeants; the Indian rank and file were milder in their methods. And those faces, full of hate and blood-lust, almost mad, with no trace of sympathy or touch of humanity! Probably the faces on our side just then were equally hateful to look at, and the fact that we were mostly passive did not fill our minds and hearts with love for our opponents, or add to the beauty of our countenances. And yet, we had no grievance against each other; no quarrel that was personal, no ill will. We happened to represent, for the time being, strange and powerful forces which held us in thrall and cast us hither and thither, and, subtly gripping our minds and hearts, roused our desires and passions and made us their blind tools. Blindly we struggled, not knowing what we struggled for and whither we went. The excitement of action held us; but, as it passed, immediately the question arose: To what end was all this? To what end?[1]

["My dear Jawahar" [wrote Gandhi after the brutal lathee charges], "my love to you. It was all done bravely. You have braver things to do. May God spare you for many a long year to come, and make you His chosen instrument for freeing India from the yoke."[2]]

28 | From Speeches, 1928—From Letter to "Uganda Democrat", 1928

Speeches, 1928

I traveled a great deal and addressed many important gatherings. . . . The burden of my speeches was always much the same, though the form varied according to local circumstances and the stress depended on the kind of audience I happened to be addressing. Everywhere I spoke on political independence and social freedom and made the former a step toward the attainment of the latter. I wanted to spread the ideology of socialism especially among Congress workers and the intelligentsia; for these people, who were the backbone of the national movement, thought largely in terms of the narrowest nationalism.[3]

From Speech at Allahabad, April 3

To-day we see a society in which there are tremendous differences between man and man. Great riches on one side and great poverty on the other.

[1] Ibid., pp. 134–38.
[2] T.N., p. 287.
[3] T.F., p. 138.

Some people live in luxury without doing any work, whilst others work from morning to night with no rest or leisure and yet have not got the barest necessaries of life. This cannot be right. It is the negation of justice. It is not the fault of our individuals who happen to be rich. It is the fault of the system and it is up to us to change this system which permits of exploitation of man by man and produces so much misery. Our country can produce enough to permit every man and woman living in it to live in comfort and peace. Every man and woman must have the opportunity to develop to the best of his or her ability. But to do so, we shall have to forget some of our ideas of a by-gone age. Honour and merit must come from ability and hard work and not because of caste or birth or riches. Let each one of us consider the other as his brother, not higher or lower, neither to be worshipped nor despised, but treated as equal with equal rights to share this good country of ours and all it produces.

I have travelled much and I have compared with pain the condition of the peasantry in other countries with our peasants. In other countries, I have found a large measure of comfort and even luxury; here there is abject poverty, which is made worse by the evil customs which we still adhere to. We must fight and get rid of the causes of this poverty and also discard these customs which keep us from progress. We must learn what is happening in other countries and profit by their example. Our district boards often approach the Government for grants. But have you realised that the whole machinery of government is run from the rural areas? All the money spent on the army, on the huge salaries of the Viceroy and Governors and other officials—where does it largely come from except from the poverty-stricken villages of India? Even our towns live at the expense of our villages. And what do our villages get in return? There is very little education, very little sanitation or medical facilities, and absolutely no arrangements for proper housing. All your money is taken away and when you beg for doles very little is given to you by way of favour. In other countries it is the bounden and first duty of the State to give free education to every person, free medical facilities and sanitation and to build good houses for the poor. In other countries, it is felt that no nation can be strong unless its men and women are healthy and well-educated. But here it is more important to pay heavy salaries to officials and spend money on the army. No one thinks of the poor, and the country is weak and poor. We must put an end to this if we have to build up a prosperous India full of healthy and educated men and women. The future of India lies with the peasantry.[1]

[1] B.A.I., pp. 44-45.

From Presidential Address, Punjab Provincial Conference—
April 11

The world is in a ferment and strange forces are at work. The gods of yesterday are neglected and lie almost forgotten and new ideas and new myths convulse the people. Even from India with its immemorial and crushing weight of tradition and its fear of change, the challenge to the dead past has gone forth and increases in volume. Brave indeed must be the person who will don the role of prophet and point out with certainty the path to be pursued by us. . . .

The Industrial Revolution has not affected India as much as other countries. Without going into all these changes in detail, some aspects of them might be worthy of consideration here. Industrialism has resulted in greater production and greater wealth, in the concentration of wealth in a few countries and [in the hands of] a few individuals, and a more unequal distribution of wealth. It has resulted in a struggle for raw material and markets, and has thus brought into existence the imperialism of the last century. It has caused wars and has given rise to the colonial empires of to-day. It has laid the seed of future wars. And recently it has taken the shape of an economic imperialism which, without the possession of territory, is as efficient and potent in exploiting other countries as any colonial empire of yesterday. All this is well known but what is perhaps not sufficiently realised is the international character of industrialism. It has broken down national boundaries and has made each nation, however powerful it may be, dependent on other countries. The idea of nationalism is almost as strong to-day as it was, and in its holy name wars are fought and millions slaughtered. But it is a myth which is not in keeping with reality. The world has become internationalised; production is international, markets are international, and transport is international. Only men's ideas continue to be governed by a dogma which has no real meaning to-day. No nation is really independent. They are all interdependent. The world of reality has changed utterly, but our ideas continue in the old rut and thus conflicts arise, and society is ever in a ferment.

And if there is a conflict between facts and ideas in the West, how much more do we see it in India? Many of us, regardless of what is happening all around us, still live in the ancient past, and imagine that we can have it back again. Some want the Vedic age, others a reproduction of the early democratic days of Islam. . . .

We forget that our ancient civilizations, great as they [were], were meant for different ages and different conditions. We cannot have to-day in an industrial age, an early agrarian economy such as we had in Vedic times; much less can we have in our country a civilization meant for a desert country more than thirteen hundred years ago. And many of our traditions and habits and customs, our social laws, our caste system, the position we give to women, and the dogmas which religion has imposed on us, are the relics of a past, suitable in those far-off days, but utterly out of joint with modern conditions. They are shibboleths to-day, in conflict with reality. Men's ideas may lag behind, but it is not possible to arrest the course of time and the evolution of life.

But where there is conflict between the two, there is friction and stagnation, and progress is slow. Where ideas come into line with realities the fortunate country advances with a bound. Thus we have the instance of defeated, backward, disorganised and dogma-ridden Turkey changing suddenly, almost overnight, into a great and rapidly progressing country under the inspiring leadership of Kamal Pasha. We have also the instance of Russia, where a demoralised, illiterate and disunited people were changed into men of heroic mould, who faced and conquered war, famine and disease and a world of enemies. So also will India progress when she discards the myths and dogmas in favour of the reality of to-day.

We thus see that the world has now become a delicate and complicated organism, each part depending on the other, and none wholly capable of standing apart. How then can India ignore [the] rest of the world, or keep herself in splendid isolation? India must understand world forces and take her proper share in the shaping of them. India must also get her ideas in line with facts and realities. The day she does so, her progress will be stupendous.

I have referred to industrialism, and its effects on the modern world. Its evils are obvious, and many of us dislike them intensely. But whether we like them or not we must realise that the spread of industrialism cannot be checked. Even in India it is taking giant strides, and no country can stop its onward march. Must we also succumb to all the evils which come in its train or is it fruitful for us to adopt industrialism without its major evils? We must remember that industrialism means the big machine, and the machine is but a tool to be used for good or ill. Let us not blame the tool if the man who holds it misuses it and causes injuries thereby.

In the West industrialism has led to big scale capitalism and imperialism. Many of us who denounce British imperialism in India do not realise that it is not a phenomenon peculiar to the British race or to India, or that it is the necessary consequence of industrial development on capitalist lines. For capitalism necessarily leads to exploitation of one man by another, one group by another, and one country by another. Therefore we are opposed to this imperialism and exploitation. We must also be opposed to capitalism as a system, and to the domination of one country over another. The only alternative that is offered to us is some form of socialism, that is the state-ownership of the means of production and distribution. We cannot escape the choice, and if we really care for a better order of society, and for ending the exploitation of man by man, we cannot but cast our weight on the side of socialism.

And if we so decide, what consequences follow? The necessary result is that we must not only fight British dominion in India on nationalistic [grounds] but also on social and industrial grounds. This is all the more necessary as the modern form of imperial domination is not the old crude method of possession of territory, but the subtler way of economic imperialism. England may well permit us to have a larger measure of political liberty, but this will be worth little if she holds economic dominion over us. And no Indian, capitalist or socialist, if he appreciates the full significance of this new slavery, can willingly submit to it. . . .

We must remember that poverty and want are no longer economic necessities; although under the present anarchic capitalist system they may be inevitable. The world and our country produce enough or can produce enough for the masses to attain a high standard of well-being, but unhappily the good things are [had] by a few and millions live in utter want. In India, the classic land of famine, famines are not caused by want of food, but by the want of money to buy food. We have famines of money, not food.

The third consequence will affect our international contact and our international outlook. . . .

In the light of these considerations let us briefly examine the question of independence for India. Even if the National Congress had not pronounced in its favour, I am sure none of you would require to be converted to it. But some of our elders and friends suffer strangely from various complexes and delusions and the British Empire is one of them. They cannot get out of the professions and habits of a lifetime, nor can they rid themselves of the chains of their own fashioning. What is the British Empire to-day? . . . If we leave out India and the dependencies, it is like the farmer's cat in *Alice in Wonderland* whose body has entirely disappeared and only the Jin has remained. How long can this disembodied Jin remain, I leave it to you to judge. The world has judged already and few imagine that it will endure long. The Empire is fast approaching dissolution and world crisis may end it. The British people have shown extraordinary ability in adapting themselves to changing circumstances and to this they owe their strength and the long lease of power that they have enjoyed. But the world is moving too fast for them and recent events, specially in relation to India, indicate that their old skill is gone. But whether the Empire endures or not, how can India find a place in it when her national and international and economic interests conflict with it in almost every vital matter? We must recognise [the] internationalism of to-day and act internationally if we are to face realities. We cannot be independent in the narrow sense. When we talk of independence we mean the severance of the British connection. Afterwards we can develop the friendliest contact with other countries including England. The British Commonwealth, in spite of its high-sounding name, does not stand for this international co-operation, and in its world policy has consistently stood for a narrow and selfish ideal and against the peace of the world.

If independence is our only and inevitable goal, we cannot in logic, in decency, ask the British to protect us from other foreign countries. I am wholly prepared to accept the argument that if we want British help to defend our frontiers, we are not fit for independence. But I wholly deny that we cannot face the risk of foreign invasion without British aid. No country is strong enough to-day, with the possible exception of the United States of America, to withstand a group of hostile countries. England certainly is not. But no one will say that England should, therefore, be deprived of her independence and put under alien control. The security of a country depends on many factors, on its relations with its neighbours and on the world situation generally. If the problem of . . . Indian defence is examined in the light of these factors, the strength of India becomes obvious. She has no great dangers to face and in a military sense she is by no means weak. But even if there was danger, it is shameful and cowardly to seek for help from a nation which was in the past and is to-day oppressing us and preventing all growth. Whatever independence may or may not mean and whether we use that word or another, the one thing that we must keep in the forefront of our programme is the immediate withdrawal of the British army of occupation from this country. That is the real meaning of freedom. Unless that takes place, all other talk is merely moonshine.

We may demand freedom for our country on many grounds. Ultimately it is the economic problem that matters. Our educated classes have so far taken the lead in the fight for *Swaraj*. The economic pressure on them was considerable and others were only vocal elements; and so the demand has taken the form occasionally of Indianisation of services, of higher posts being thrown open to Indians. They are to blame for these demands. They have acted as every class conscious of its interests acts. But in doing so they have seldom paid heed to [needs] of the masses. Whenever vital questions affecting the masses have arisen, they have been shelved, they have been asked to stand over till *Swaraj* has been attained! Why confuse the issues now? It has been said, we can settle our problems later. Like all class-conscious groups, they have considered themselves the most vital elements in the nation and in the name of freedom have really sought to advance their own interests and many of our intellectuals have become staunchest defenders of the privileges of empire as soon as they had their share of the titles and power. What shall it profit the masses of this country—the peasantry, the landless labourers, the workers, the shopkeepers, the artisans—if everyone of the offices held by Englishmen in India is held by Indians? It may benefit them a little as they can bring more pressure to bear on their own people than on [an] alien Government. . . . But even from the narrow point of view of our intellectuals, it is now well recognised that no effective pressure can be brought to bear on the British Government without mass support. But in spite of recognition there is the fear of the masses and little is done. Mass support cannot come for [the] vague ideal of *Swaraj*. It can only come when the masses realise what *Swaraj* means for them. Therefore it is essential that we must clearly lay down an economic programme, must have an ultimate ideal in view, and must also provide for the immediate steps to be taken to bring them relief.

Our ideal thus can only be an independent democratic State, and I would add a socialistic State, and for this we must work. What can be our methods? . . . The reformer who is afraid of radical change, or of over-throwing an oppressive regime, and who seeks merely to eliminate some of its abuses, becomes in reality one of its defenders. We must, therefore, cultivate a revolutionary outlook, one that devises a radical and far-reaching change, and not merely that halting outlook of the half-hearted reformer. The way of violence not being open to us, [under] . . . present conditions, the only other course is some form of non-co-operation. . . . I use the word "revolutionary" in its proper sense without any necessary connection with violence. Indeed, violence may, and I think . . . is to-day, in India, the very reverse of revolution. Acts of terrorism . . . have counter-revolutionary effects and for this reason alone, apart from any other reasons, are injurious to the national cause. . . .

The real problem ... is how to exorcise communalism. ... There is [no] place for communalism or a dogma-ridden people. ... Communalism, of course, has to be fought [and] ruthlessly ... suppressed. But I really do not think that it is such a power as it is made out to be. It may be [a] giant to-day, but it has feet of clay. It is the outcome largely of anger and passion, and when we regain our tempers it will fade into nothingness. It is a myth with no connection with reality, and it cannot endure. It is really the creation of our educated classes in search of office and employment. How does the economic interest of a Hindu or Muslim or Sikh differ from [one another]? Certainly not [in that] they have to profess different faiths. It may be that if there is a vacancy for a judgeship of a High Court, or a like occasion, the raising of the communal issue may profit an individual. But how does it generally profit his community? What does it matter to the Muslim peasant whether a Hindu or Muslim is a judge in Lahore? Economic interests run along different lines. There is a great deal in common between the Muslim and Sikh and Hindu zamindars: and a great deal in common between the Muslim and Sikh and Hindu peasantry, [but] very little in common between a Muslim peasant and a Muslim zamindar. We must, therefore, begin to think of, and act [with respect to] ... economic issues. If we do so, the myth of communalism will automatically disappear. Conflict there may be, but it will be between different classes, and not different religions.

What communal interests are sought to be protected? I think fundamentally they are cultural. Every country in the world has cultural minorities, and it is a well-recognised principle that such minorities should have the fullest autonomy [so] far as their culture is concerned. So also, in India, every ... cultural group should be given freedom and, indeed, should be encouraged to preserve and cultivate its culture. Only thus can we build up a rich and varied ... yet common culture for India. Culture [involves] ... language, education and schools.

If [the question of] ... culture is settled satisfactorily, and sufficient safeguards are provided for the interests of minorities, and groups which may be in danger of suppression, what remains of communalism? ... It is generally recognised now, or it ought to be, that separate electorates, which are meant to protect the interests of minorities, really injure them, and reduce their effective power in the state. If anybody should be against that, it is the [minorities]. But such is the power of a myth that many of us have come to believe that separate electorates are a "valued privilege" to which we must cling. ... I think a little clear thinking will convince any person who is not a bigot on the subject, that separate electorates are not only a danger to the State, but specially to the minority community. Personally I am not in favour of territorial election at all, but if it is retained, I am wholly opposed to separate electorates.[1]

The world has become internationalized ... but our ideas continue in the old rut.[2]

From Address to Youth, All-Bengal Students Conference—Calcutta, September 22

[A typical double challenge: to India's youth to rebuild society, and to the older generation to evolve beyond a confining commitment to imperialism and the *status quo*. Although Jawaharlal was a socialist rather than a communist, his attitude toward Russia in the 1920s, was like that of many other intellectuals in countries subjected to feudalism and colonialism. He was very strongly influenced by the belief that, in contrast to the great powers of the West, the Soviet Union was virtually unique at the time in being anti-imperialist, anti-racist, "progressive", and in favor of establishing a peaceful world order.

In spite of his own criticisms of Communism, Nehru nevertheless continued to speak out against fear of the unorthodox and of change. He sought to instill in the youth of India higher ideals; to awaken them not only to the specific nationalist goals of India but to the needs of the oppressed everywhere. Internationalism, democratic socialism, political and economic equality, an end to exploitation and subjugation—these were among Jawaharlal's most ardently avowed goals. With respect to Britain, the non-violent battle for Indian freedom must be continued, but it must not be waged against the people of England as individuals, but rather against the continuing evils of Imperialism.]

It is the realisation of the common bond of humanity that has given rise to the great youth movement of to-day. Many of you may be too young to remember the despair and feeling of revolt in the minds of youth during, and specially after, the Great War. Old men sat in their comfortable cabinets and banking houses and hid their selfishness and greed and lies under a cover of fine phrases and appeals for freedom and democracy. And the young, believing in these fine phrases, went out by the millions to face death, and few returned. Seventy millions of them were mobilised, and of the fifteen millions that actually served on the front, over eight millions died, and over five-and-a-half millions were maimed for life.

[1] B.A.I., pp. 134-40.
[2] Quoted in M.B., p. 125.

6+N.

Think of these terrible figures and then remember that they were all young men with their lives stretching out in front of them, and their hopes unfulfilled! And what did this awful sacrifice bring forth? A peace of violence, and an aggravation of all the ills that the world was suffering from. You remember well that the first fruits of the peace in India were the Rowlatt Act and Martial Law. You know also how the fine principle of self-determination, which the Allies shouted from the house-tops, has been applied to India and to other countries. A new cloak for the greed of the imperialist powers was created in the shape of mandates, and in awarding mandates the "principal consideration" was to be the preference of the inhabitants. This preference was shown unaccountably by rebellion against the British in Mesopotamia, and rebellion against the French in Syria. But the aeroplane and the bomb [were] the British answer in Iraq, and the ancient and beautiful city of Damascus was reduced to ruins by the French. In Europe itself the peace created far more problems than it solved.

Is it any wonder that the youth of the world rebelled and cast out [its] old-time leaders on whom even [the] terrible lesson of the war was lost, and who still went on intriguing in the old way, and prepared for yet another and ... greater war? Youth set about organising itself, and set out to find the ways and means of establishing an order of society which would put an end to the misery and conflicts of to-day.

And so the youth of the world probed deeper into the cause of present-day misery. They studied the economic and the social conditions of the people, and they saw that although science and the changes that science had brought had in a few generations covered the track of centuries, the minds of men still lagged behind, and thought in terms of a dead past. Science had made the world international and interdependent, but national rivalries continued and resulted in war. Science had vastly increased production and there was enough for all and to spare, but poverty continued, and the contrasts between luxury and misery were more marked than ever before. But if mankind is foolish and errs, facts do not adapt themselves to errors, and the world of our imagination conflicts with the world of reality, and is it any wonder that chaos and misery result?

Facts are not to blame for this. The troubles and the difficulties lie rooted ... in our misconception of them and our misinterpretation of them. Our elders fail frequently because they are rigid in their minds, and unable to change their mental outlook, or adapt themselves to changing facts. But youth is not hidebound. Youth can think and is not afraid of the consequences of thought. Do not imagine that thought is an easy matter or that its consequences are trivial. Thought is not or should not be afraid of the wrath of heavens or the terrors of hell. It is the most revolutionary thing on earth. And it is because youth dare think and dare act that it holds out the promise of [removing] this country and this world of ours from the ruts and the mire in which they have sunk.

Are you, young men and women . . ., going to dare to think and dare to act? Are you prepared to stand shoulder to shoulder with the youth of the world, not only to free your country from an insolent and alien rule but also to establish in this unhappy world of ours a better and a happier society? That is the problem before you and if you wish to face it sincerely and fearlessly, you will have to make up your mind to rid yourselves and your country of every obstacle in your path, whether it is placed by our alien rulers or has the prestige of ancient custom.

You must have your ideal clear-cut before you. How else can you hope to build the great structure of your dream? Can you build a palace on the foundations of a mud-hut, or a fine bridge with straw? With definite ideas of your goal you will gain clearness of purpose and effectiveness of action, and each step that you take will carry you nearer to your heart's desire.

What shall this ideal be? National independence and perfect freedom to develop on the lines of our own choosing is the essential requisite of all progress. Without it there can be no political, economic or social freedom. But national independence should not mean for us merely an addition to the warring groups of nations. It should be a step towards the creation of a world commonwealth of nations in which we can assist in the fullest measure to bring about co-operation and world harmony.

But there can be no world co-operation as long as one country dominates over and exploits another, and one group or class exploits another. Therefore, we shall have to put an end to all exploitation of man by man, or woman by woman. You cannot have a purely political ideal, for politics is, after all, only a small part of life, although situated as we are under alien rule, it dominates every branch of our activity. Your ideal must be a complete whole, and must comprise life as it is today, economic, social, as well as political. . . .

Our womenfolk, in spite of the great examples of old that we are so fond of repeating, are shackled and unfree. Large classes of our countrymen have been deliberately suppressed by us in the past and denied all opportunities of growth in the name of religion and ancient practice. And, all over India, we see today millions toiling in field and factory and starving in spite of their toil. How can we rid these millions of their dire poverty and misery, and make them share in the freedom to come? We hear of the service of the poor, and sometimes even of the exaltation of the poor. And, by a little act of charity, or service, we imagine that our duty is done. Having reserved very magnanimously the kindom of heaven for [the] poor, we take good care to keep the kingdom of the earth for ourselves. Youth at least should be above this hypocrisy. Poverty is not a good thing; it is not to be exalted or praised, but [is] an evil thing which must be fought and stamped out. The poor require no petty services from us or charity. They want to cease to be poor. That can only come by your changing a system which produces poverty and misery.

In the course of the last few months you have seen the whole of India convulsed in labour troubles. Lock-outs and strikes and shootings have followed one after another. Is it amusing, do you think, to the worker to strike and starve and perhaps be shot? Surely no one does so unless his lot becomes unbearable. And indeed the lot of the Indian to-day in factory or field is past all endurance. In the jute mills of your province, the profits and reserve accumulations in ten years before 1926 amounted to nearly four hundred and forty crores of rupees. Think of this enormous figure and then see the condition of poor workers in these mills. And yet the jute workers, miserable as they are, have gone there because there was no room for them on the land, or their conditions on the land were even worse. Can you expect any peace in the land when there is so much misery and so much contrast between wealth and abject poverty?

You cannot ignore these problems or leave them to a future age for solution.

And if you are afraid of tackling them, you will find that facts can only be ignored at your peril. We are sometimes told that we must [see that] justice [is done] between landlord and tenant and capitalist and worker, and justice means the maintenance of the *status quo*. It is the kind of justice the League of Nations gives when it maintains the present *status quo*, with the imperialist powers dominating and exploiting half the earth. When the *status quo* itself is rank injustice, those who desire to maintain it must be considered as upholders of that injustice.

If your ideal is to be one of social equality and a world federation, then perforce we must work for a socialist state. The word socialism frightens many people in this country, but that matters little, for fear is their constant companion. Ignorant of everything important that has happened in the world of thought since they left their school books, they fear what they do not and will not understand.

It is for you, the youth of the country, to appreciate the new forces and ideas that are convulsing the world, and to apply them to your own country ... .It is interesting to note that during the great war, when a great crisis threatened to engulf the nations of the West, even the capitalist countries of Europe were forced to adopt socialistic measures to a large extent. This was not only done internally in each country, but also [to make it possible] to resist the pressure of events even internationally. There was co-operation in many fields and national boundaries seemed to recede into the [background]. There was economic co-operation of the closest kind [and] ultimately even the armies of many nations became one army under a single head. But the lesson of the war has been lost, and again we drift towards a greater disaster.

Socialism frightens some of our friends, but what of communism? Our elders sitting in their council chambers shake their grey heads and stroke their beards in alarm at the mere mention of the word.

And yet I doubt if any of them has the slightest knowledge of what communism is. You have read of the two new measures which are being rushed through the Assembly—one of them to throttle the Trade Union Movement, and the other to keep out people whom the Government suspects of communism. Has it struck you that it is a very curious thing that the mighty British Empire, with all its tanks and aeroplanes and dreadnaughts, should be afraid of a few individuals who come to spread a new idea? What is there in this new idea, that the British Empire should collapse like a pack of cards before this airy nothing? Surely you could not have better evidence of the weakness of this giant empire which sprawls over the fairest portions of the earth's surface. It is [a] giant with feet of clay. But if an idea is a dangerous thing, it is also a very elusive thing. It crosses frontiers and customs barriers without paying any duty, and bayonets and men of war cannot stop it. The Government of India must be strangely lacking in intelligence if they imagine that they can stop any ideas from entering India by legislation.

What is this communist idea before which the British Empire quakes? ... I wish to tell you that though, personally, I do not agree with many of the methods of the communists, and I am by no means sure to what extent communism can suit present conditions in India, I do believe in communism as an ideal of society. For essentially it is socialism, and socialism, I think, is the only way if the world is to escape disaster.

And Russia, what of her? An outcast like [ourselves] from nations, and much slandered and often erring. But in spite of her many mistakes she stands to-day as the greatest opponent of imperialism. ...

In the city of Tabriz in Persia, when the Russian ambassador first came, he called the populace together, and on behalf of the Russian nation tendered formal apology for the sins of the Tzars. Russia goes to the East as [an] equal, not as a conqueror or a race-proud superior. Is it any wonder that she is welcomed?

Some of you may go, in after years, to foreign countries for your studies. If you go to England, you will realise in full measure what race prejudice is. If you go to the Continent of Europe, you will be more welcome, whether you go to France or Germany or Italy. If any of you go to Russia, you will see how racial feeling is utterly absent, and the [Chinese] who throng the universities of Moscow are treated just like others.

I have placed before you the ideals of internationalism and socialism as the only ideals worthy of the fine temper of youth. Internationalism can of course only come to us through national independence. . . .

I have laid stress on internationalism although it may be a distant ideal for us. But the world is already largely international, although we may not realise it. And situated as we are, the reaction against foreign rule is apt to make us narrowly [nationalistic]. We talk of the greatness of India, of her special mission to the world, and we love to dwell on her past. It is well that we remember our past, for it was great and worth remembering. But it is for age to look back, youth's eyes should be turned to the future. And I have often wondered if there is any country in the world, any people, who do not fancy that they have a special mission for the world. England has her white man's burden which she insists on carrying, in spite of the ungrateful people who object and rebel; France has her mission of Civilisation; America is God's own country; Germany has Kultur; Italy has her new gospel of Fascism; and Russia her Communism. . . .

Self-admiration is always a dangerous thing in an individual. It is equally dangerous in [a] nation, for it makes it self-satisfied and indolent, and the world passes by, leaving it behind. We have little enough reason to be satisfied with our present lot, with many of our customs, with our excessive religiosity, with the sad lot of our women, and the terrible condition of the masses. What good does it do us to waste our energy and our time in chanting praises of the dead past, when the present claims our attention, and work awaits us? The world changes and is changing rapidly and if we cannot adapt our society to the new conditions, we are doomed to perish. We have seen what can be done in a brief span of years, and even months, by a Kamal Pasha, or an Amanullah, who were not afraid to break through ancient custom and prejudice. What has been done in Turkey and backward Afghanistan can be done in India. But it can only be done in the manner of Kamal Pasha or Amanullah, by fearlessly facing obstacles and removing them, and not waiting till the crack of doom for slow reform. It is not a choice for you, as it was not a choice for Turkey or Afghanistan, between slow or rapid reform. It is a choice between extinction and immediate action. Turkey and Afghanistan chose the latter path, and are reckoned to-day as great nations. What will your choice be?

The world is in a bad way, and India especially is in a perilous state, in spite of [the] glitter and superficial splendour of our great cities. There are rumours of war and awful prophecies that [the] next war may result in irretrievable disaster to civilisation. But the very excess of evil may hasten the cure.

Great men have come from age to age in this country and elsewhere to help mankind. But greater than any man is the idea which he has embodied. . . . In a changing world a custom that was good in the past may be perilous to society to-day. . . .

The great men who have come have always been rebels against the existing order. Two thousand five hundred years ago the great Buddha proclaimed his gospel of social equality, and fought against all privileges, priestly and otherwise. He was a champion of the people, against all who sought to exploit them. Then came another great rebel, Christ, and then the Prophet of Arabia, who did not hesitate to break and change almost everything he found. They were Realists who saw that the world had outgrown its ancient practices, and sought to bring it back to reality. Even so we have outgrown the creeds and rituals of yesterday, and as realists we must not hesitate to discard them wherever they clash with reality. The *avatars* of to-day are great ideas which come to reform the world. And the idea of the day is social equality. Let us listen to it and become its instruments to transform the world and make it a better place to live in.

I may be a weak instrument, capable of doing little by myself, in spite of my ardent desire to do much. And you individually may be able to do little. But you and I together can do much, and working with the awakened youth of this country we can and will achieve a great deal. For youth only can save this country and the world. . . . Our quest must be adventure, but adventure in a noble enterprise which promises to bring peace to a distracted world and security and stability to the millions who have it not.

You and I are Indians, and to India we owe much, but we are human beings also, and to humanity we also owe a debt. Let us be citizens of the commonwealth or Empire of youth. This is the only empire to which we can owe allegiance, for that is the forerunner of the future federation of the world.[1]

[1] B.A.I., pp. 62–68.

From Letter to Editor of the "Uganda Democrat"—
December 6, 1928

[The ideas expressed in the following communication, written while Jawaharlal was Secretary of the All-India Congress Committee, have remained unchanged over the years.]

I am sorry to learn that some Indians have created an impression in the minds of the natives of the country that Indians are against their aspirations. This is very unfortunate. I think it should be made perfectly clear to all concerned in East Africa that Indians have not gone there to injure the interests of the inhabitants of the country in any way. If necessary the Indians ought to be prepared to take a back place so far as the natives of the country are concerned. On no account must there be rivalry between the two. . . . This is the attitude of the Indian nationalist leaders. . . .

Indians who go to foreign countries go there not to exploit the inhabitants of those countries but to live in cooperation with them for the mutual advantage of both. We go [abroad] on these terms and we expect others to come on the same terms to India. We want no one to come to India to exploit us.

I shall be very glad if the greatest emphasis is laid on this position and every assurance is given to the native chiefs.[1]

29	Motilal Nehru Report—Calcutta Congress Session, 1928—Dominion Status under Empire vs. Complete Independence—Jawaharlal's Increasing Influence and Alleged Danger to British Government

The Motilal Nehru Report

[The boycott of the Simon Commission, which constituted a major event in India during 1928, was followed by a second significant development: appointment by an All-Parties Conference of a committee "to draw up

[1] From Photostatic copy of original letter.

some kind of a constitution for India, dealing especially with communal problems, etc".[1] Headed by Motilal Nehru the committee issued its findings, which came to be known as the Motilal Nehru Report. The Report, which aroused a certain amount of controversy, served not only to stimulate interest in the drafting of a constitution by India's leaders, but also to a series of passionate debates about whether India's goal should be dominion status or complete independence.

Although, at one point, Jawaharlal worked with Motilal on preparation of the "Nehru Report", he ultimately withdrew from the group headed by his father. One of the committee's major recommendations was acceptance of dominion status, a goal too limited at the time to satisfy Jawaharlal. Gandhi, on the other hand, agreed with the "Report", when Motilal presented it to the Calcutta Congress in 1928. It was at this juncture that Jawaharlal's political stand became increasingly far removed not only from that of the Mahatma, but also from that of his father, and various other older Congress leaders, all of whom continued to accept dominion status rather than complete independence as their ultimate aim.

John Gunther has recorded a characteristic "Jawaharlal" incident of the period. When Motilal and Gandhi strongly backed a proposal that Congress should officially adopt the "Nehru Report", Jawaharlal and his followers were opposed to such a move. Jawaharlal's side won in a close vote. Upon discovering "that there had been a technical error in the voting", Jawaharlal, "as Secretary of the Congress . . . brought this to the attention of the meeting, even though he knew that it would mean over-riding his victory and that in the next vote his group would lose."[2]

The Motilal Nehru Committee of 1928 stated in its report: "We have . . . made our recommendations on the basis (1) that we are agreed that nothing short of dominion status will satisfy India and (2) that the form of government to be established in India will be the same and not lower than that of the other self-governing dominions."[3]

It should be noted that by 1928 Muslim demands included "communal provinces", "communal electorates", guarantees of majorities in the Punjab and Bengal, "weightage" [see Glossary] for Muslim minorities in other provinces, and reservation of one-third of the seats in the Central Legislature and posts under Government.[4] (For a brief resumé of Nehru on communalism, see Appendix.)

Further, between the time of the drafting of the Nehru Report and its presentation at a conference in Calcutta, the Muslim League drew up a series of amendments, proposing that under a future Constitution a minimum of one-third of the elected representatives in both houses of the Central Legislature should be Muslims.

Disagreeing with what seemed to it to be an inequitable request by the League, the Nehru Committee ruled that whenever a reservation was to

[1] B.O.L., p. 61.
[2] G.I.A., p. 421.
[3] E.I.P., p. 229.
[4] T.N., pp. 288–89.

6*

be made for the Muslim minority, it must be in strict proportion to the Muslim population.[1]

Since the "Motilal Nehru" constitution failed to make the separatist concessions demanded by the Muslims, the rift between the Congress and League widened.]

Calcutta Congress Session, 1928

As 1928 approached its appointed end, the Calcutta Congress drew near. My father was to preside over it. He was full of the All-Parties Conference and of his report to it and wanted to push this through the Congress. To this he knew that I was not agreeable, because I was not prepared to compromise on the independence issue, and this irritated him. We did not argue about the matter much, but there was a definite feeling of mental conflict betweeen us, an attempt to pull different ways. Differences of opinion we had often had before, vital differences which had kept us in different political camps. But I do not think that at any previous or subsequent occasion the tension had been so great. Both of us were rather unhappy about it. In Calcutta matters came to this, that my father made it known that if he could not have his way in the Congress—that is, if he could not have a majority for the resolution in favor of the All-Parties Report—he would refuse to preside over the Congress. That was a perfectly reasonable and constitutional course to adopt. Nonetheless it was disconcerting to many of his opponents who did not wish to force the issue to this extent.

There were negotiations between the two groups, and a compromise formula was announced. Then this fell through. It was all rather confusing and not very edifying. The main resolution of the Congress, as it was finally adopted, accepted the All-Parties Report but intimated that if the British Government did not agree to [the recommended] constitution within a year the Congress would revert to independence. It was an offer of a year's grace and a polite ultimatum. The resolution was no doubt a come-down from the ideal of independence, for the All-Parties Report did not even ask for full Dominion status. And yet it was probably a wise resolution in the sense that it prevented a split when no one was ready for it, and kept the Congress together for the struggle that began in 1930. It was clear enough that the British Government were not going to accept the All-Parties Constitution within a year. The struggle was inevitable;

[1] Based on B.J., pp. 93-94.

and, as matters stood in the country, no such struggle could be at all effective without Gandhiji's lead.

I had opposed the [above] resolution in the open Congress, though I did so half-heartedly. And yet I was again elected general secretary. In the Congress sphere I seemed to act the part of the famous Vicar of Bray. Whatever president sat on the Congress throne, still I was secretary in charge of the organization.[1]

Dominion Status under Empire vs. Complete Independence

[The resolution dealing with dominion status introduced at the All-Parties Conference at Lucknow was discussed by Jawaharlal in the following address to the Conference on August 29, 1928.]

I am especially unable to reconcile myself to dominion status and all its implications. What is the meaning of the resolution that we are considering? The preamble tells us that it is open to us to carry on activity and propaganda for independence. But this is a mere flourish, meaning little. The second part of the resolution really commits every organisation and every individual [in] it to dominion status. The speeches in support of the motion, and specially that of the mover, made this even clearer. I wondered when I was listening to them, whether I was not attending a session of the Congress a generation ago. They embody an ideology of a past age utterly out of touch with facts and realities today. We were told of the injustice in not having Indian governors, Indians in the Service, and [on] the Railway Board. Is this what we have met here for? Is this our idea of freedom? It seems to me that we are drifting back from the twentieth century to the ways and methods of the nineteenth.

We are told that we must be practical, and being practical is taken to mean adherence to an outworn set of ideas, regardless of the changes that have happened in the world. The mover of [the] resolution told us that he had learned politics from John Stuart Mill, and Green, the author of *The Short History of the Indian People.* Eminent men they were, but may I remind him that they are dead and gone and much has happened since then? They are [as] dead as Queen Anne, as Charles I, as Louis XVI of France and as [the] last Tzar of Russia. The world has moved and changed, and if we are to be practical, let us take stock of the changes [in] the world. ... What does the British Commonwealth of Nations, as it is now called, stand for? It stands for one part [of the world] domineering over and

[1] T.F., pp. 140-41.

exploiting the other. There are England and the self-governing dominions exploiting India, parts of Africa, Malaya and other parts of the world. . . . Are we going to assist England and the other Dominions in exploiting Egypt and Africa? . . . Dominion status for India must necessarily mean the break-up of the British Empire as it is to-day.

Then again we are told that dominion status may be obtained by consent; independence only after an appeal to arms or force. I do not know if any one here imagines that dominion status is going to be achieved by sweet reasonableness and logic. If so, all I can say is that he is a very credulous individual. Dominion status or independence both require a sanction behind them, whether that is the sanction of armed force, or non-violent force. You will get dominion status the moment you make it clear to the British people that unless it is granted, they will stand to lose much more. You will get it when they feel that it will be hell for them in India unless they [agree] to it. You will not get it by logic or fine phrases. In matters of this kind justice has little place. Therefore both for independence and dominion status, a sanction and a force of some kind [are] necessary. Consent only follows . . . creation of [a] sanction. It cannot come without it. Alternatively if dominion status can be the result of agreement between India and England, I see no reason why independence . . . should not be agreed to between them. We may agree to certain safeguards, if necessary, for British interests, not because we consider that the British are entitled to any safeguards, but as the price of peace, in order to avoid bloody warfare and great suffering. Perhaps it is easier for me to co-operate with the British people than it is for many of those who talk of dominion status, but I cannot co-operate on their terms. I shall co-operate with them on equal terms only when I have some sanction and force behind me.[1]

[Emphasizing his disagreement with the older, more conservative elements within Congress, Jawaharlal favored setting a time-limit of a year for the granting of complete independence (asserting that to accept dominion status, under prevailing conditions, would be an extremely wrong and foolish act, tantamount to succumbing to the psychology of imperialism.)]

Jawaharlal's Increasing Influence and Alleged Danger to British Government

[The philosophical position Jawaharlal had been evolving in Europe matured considerably after he returned to India in 1928. During the late

[1] B.A.I., pp. 87–88.

1920s he found the Indian people themselves beginning to have a more profound awareness of the Nationalist Movement. They were more sympathetic to it, more deeply involved in it. Thus when he was asked to speak with greater frequency, not only before Congress circles, but to India's youth, workers and peasants throughout the country, the mounting interest in what he had to say served greatly to inspire the masses he addressed. Increased contact with the Indian people in turn contributed to his own growth. (He has consistently expressed his gratitude for the privilege of being so often called upon to address vast audiences in India, especially those comprising peasants and workers. His experience in doing so invariably has had the power to pour energy into him; to give him the repeated opportunity to develop his ideas through speaking them out loud.)

In precisely the same proportion as Jawaharlal's influence upon the country soared in the late 1920s, so did his "danger" to the official Government—at least in its own opinion. "His Excellency desires," Home Secretary Haig wrote on October 18, 1928, "that the utterances of Jawaharlal Nehru should be watched carefully."[1]

In an address to a Bombay Youth Conference on December 12, 1928, Jawaharlal stated, in part: "Society . . . must alternate between revolution and consolidation", adding, "it is the function of youth to supply this dynamic element".[2] As a result of this address, the Government of India suggested to the Bombay Government that there might be grounds for proceeding against him. Although the speech was pronounced seditious by the Advocate-General, the Bombay Government did not recommend a prosecution. "'The speech in question,'" wrote the . . . Government, "'does not appear to be a particularly favourable one on which to base a prosecution. With much of what is said in it, everyone must agree, for instance that the present system of society is imperfect, and that much needs to be done to improve the lot of the poor. Of the rest of the speech, a great part is abuse of imperialism and of the British and Indian Governments, which is a commonplace among the opponents of the Government today.'

"The Government of India were rather taken aback by what seemed to them the complacent reasoning of the Bombay Government, but they did not press for . . . prosecution. After a high-level review, it was decided to issue a new directive to all provincial governments to warn them of the dangers ahead."[3]]

[1] Quoted in T.N., p. 293.
[2] Quoted in M.B., p. 126.
[3] T.N., pp. 309–10.

30 | Trade Union Activities—All-India Trade Union Congress, Nagpur, 1929— Presidential Address at Nagpur— Independence League, 1928–1929— Attempts at Congress-British Government Amity

Trade Union Activities

[In 1928] the All-India Trade-Union Congress was held at Jharia, the center of the coal mine area. I attended and participated in it for the first two days. . . . It was my first trade-union congress, and I was practically an outsider, though my activities among the peasantry, and lately among the workers, had gained for me a measure of popularity with the masses. I found the old tussle going on between the reformists and the more advanced and revolutionary elements.

My own sympathies . . . were with the advanced group but, being a newcomer, I felt a little at sea in these domestic conflicts of the Trade-Union Congress, and I decided to keep aloof from them. After I had left Jharia, the annual Trade-Union Congress elections took place, and I learned at Calcutta that I had been elected president for the next year. I had been put forward by the moderate group, probably because they felt that I stood the best chance of defeating the other candidate, who was an actual worker (on the railways) and who had been put forward by the radical group. If I had been present at Jharia on the day of the election, I am sure that I would have withdrawn in favor of the worker candidate. It seemed to me positively indecent that a newcomer and nonworker should be suddenly thrust into the presidency. This was in itself a measure of the infancy and weakness of the trade-union movement in India.

In March 1929 the Government struck suddenly at organized labor by arresting some of its most prominent workers from the advanced groups. . . . Some of these were communists, others were near-communists, yet others were just trade-unionists. This was the beginning of the famous Meerut trial which lasted for four years and a half.

The Meerut Case Defense Committee (of which I was a member) did not have an easy time with the accused. There were different kinds of people among these, with different types of defenses, and often there was an utter absence of harmony among them. After some months we wound up the formal committee, but we continued to help in our individual capacities.[1]

[From letter concerning the Meerut Trial (written while Jawaharlal was President of the All-India Trade Union Congress) to Walter Citrine, Secretary of the British Trade Union Congress General Council, June 22, 1929.] I would like to point out that [the Meerut] trial cannot be isolated from the general situation and must be treated as one phase of the offensive which the Government here has started against the Labour movement. The fact is well recognized in India and the Executive Council of our Trade Union Congress has laid stress on it in their resolution on the subject. Even the Indian National Congress, which is not directly or solely concerned with labour [is] . . . constrained to admit this.

There is a lot of shouting about communists and communism in India. Undoubtedly there are some communists in India, but it is equally certain that this cry of communism is meant to cover a multitude of sins of the Government. Of the thirty-one accused in the Meerut case, now thirty-two . . . the majority knew little about communism. People connected with any kind of labour or peasant activity have been arrested and are being tried. Eight of those included in the Meerut case are members of the All-India Congress Committee—the Central Executive Committee of the National Congress. It is patently absurd to say that the Government is confining its attention to Communists.[2]

The All-India Trade Union Congress—Nagpur, 1929

[In addition to serving as President of the All-India Trade-Union Congress in 1929, Jawaharlal was to become President of the Lahore Congress during the same year.]

During [the] final weeks prior to the Lahore Congress I had to attend to important work in another field. The All-India Trade-Union Congress was meeting at Nagpur, and, as president for the year, I had to preside

[1] T.F., p. 141.
[2] E.I.P., p. 260.

over it. It was very unusual for the same person to preside over both the National Congress and the Trade-Union Congress within a few weeks of each other. I had hoped that I might be a link between the two and bring them closer to each other—the National Congress to become more socialistic, more proletarian, and organized labor to join the national struggle.

It was, perhaps, a vain hope, for nationalism can only go far in a socialistic or proletarian direction by ceasing to be nationalism. Yet I felt that, bourgeois as the outlook of the National Congress was, it did represent the only effective revolutionary force in the country. As such, labor ought to help it and co-operate with it and influence it, keeping, however, its own identity and ideology distinct and intact. And I hoped that the course of events and the participation in direct action would inevitably drive the Congress to a more radical ideology and to face social and economic issues. The development of the Congress during recent years had been in the direction of the peasant and the village. If this development continued, it might in course of time become a vast peasant organization, or, at any rate, an organization in which the peasant element predominated.

Many Congressmen took [a] prominent part in labor activities. The advanced sections of labor, however, fought shy of the National Congress. They mistrusted its leaders, and considered its ideology bourgeois and reactionary, which indeed it was, from the labor point of view. The Congress was, as its very name implied, a nationalist organization.

I played a very undistinguished role at the Nagpur Trade-Union Congress. Being a newcomer in the labor field and still feeling my way, I was a little hesitant. Generally, I expressed my views in favor of the more advanced groups, but I avoided acting with any group and played the part more of an impartial speaker than a directing president. I was thus an almost passive spectator of the breaking-up of the Trade-Union Congress and the formation of a new moderate organization. Personally, I felt that the Right groups were not justified in breaking away, and yet some of the leaders of the Left had forced the pace and given them every pretext to depart. Between the quarrels of the Right and Left, a large Center group felt a little helpless. Perhaps given a right lead, it could have curbed the two and avoided the break-up of the Trade Union Congress, and, even if the break came, it would not have had the unfortunate consequences which resulted.

I was out of all this from 1930 onward, as I was mostly in prison.[1]

[1] T.F., pp. 148-49.

From Presidential Address, Trade Union Congress—Nagpur,
November 30, 1929

[The following critical survey of the British Labour Movement is perhaps the most extensive statement on the subject made in India at the time. It seems to have been at this juncture that Jawaharlal realized how important it was for the labour movements of all countries to align themselves with one another in order to improve the condition of workers throughout the world. He was profoundly disappointed to discover that, for the majority of labour leaders, international considerations were of far less significance than were national interests. He began to see clearly, too, how such narrowness of vision served adversely to affect India's own freedom movement because of the lack of enlightened, international, mass support for its total aims.

Jawaharlal's address further reveals his independent position in relationship to both the Second and Third International, as well as his currently critical attitude toward the British Labour Party, which had come to power in June, 1929, under the leadership of Ramsay Mac-Donald. Nevertheless, within India, development of the Trade Union Movement in the 1920s gave the Congress a new source of support and, as the latter broadened its base, its policies tended to become both "more strongly nationalistic and more concerned with peasant and labor reform".[1]]

The last decade has seen strange happenings in India. New forces and ideas have arisen and have come into play even in our ancient country. They threaten not only the present political structure, under which India has suffered so long, but also the social and economic structure. In the political field we have seen the ideology and practice of direct action displace the slow and ineffective methods of an earlier generation. We have seen the growth of a great movement which convulsed the country and shook the foundations of British rule in India, and then weakened and gave place to reaction and mutual strife. We see it again gathering in strength for another and more powerful and determined move forward.

But great as has been the political achievement of the last decade no less remarkable has been the growth of the labour movement in India. None of us can call our Trade Union movement to-day strong or ready for successful battle. But, who can deny that during a few short years we have covered ground, which it took generations in other countries to traverse? In spite of the great poverty of the worker and the fear born of slavery that possesses him and makes it difficult to organise him; in spite of political difficulties which a foreign Government is ever placing in his way; in

[1] P.A. (Mar. 1940), p. 17.

spite of the preoccupation of the country as a whole with the national struggle, there has developed rapidly a class-conscious and militant and aggressive spirit in the Indian worker. This spirit has led him to numerous strikes, sometimes ill-conceived; often with failure [with regard to a] certain goal but nothing daunted he has gone on ahead. If he has weakened, it has, not unoften, been due to the weakness of his leaders.

And yet the movement is weak and the work that has been done is exceedingly little, and how much remains? The fact that I stand here to-day and address you as your president is itself a sign of your weakness. Why should I, a new-comer to the labour movement, and one, who whatever his sympathies may be is not one of you and has not suffered as you have done in field and factory, why should I preside over your deliberations? At your command I am here, and I am grateful for this honour and the confidence which it implies, but you could have given no greater sign of the infancy and [weakness] of your movement. I shall welcome the day when the worker from the mine and the factory and the field stands in this place which I occupy to-day, and when I, and those who are like me, take a secondary place in your counsels. Only then will you be able to speak with confidence and pride of your labour movement; only then will the true voice of the worker be heard from your forums and council halls.

Our country to-day is under the domination of another, and the sentiment of nationalism is strong. It is natural that the best and bravest in the country should strive for national freedom, but to how many of our workers does this make appeal? Ground down by poverty and by forces which seem to be unconquerable, with the daily struggle for wages and bread ever before us, how can we think of larger issues? And yet we cannot afford to ignore them for our future is intimately bound up with them. The lot of the worker cannot be improved much by charity nor by the goodwill of an employer or even of a Government. The trouble lies deeper as you all know. It is the system that is wrong, the system that is based on the exploitation of the few and the prostitution of labour. It is the system which is the natural outcome of capitalism and imperialism and if you would do away with this system you will have to root out both capitalism and imperialism and substitute a saner and a healthier order.

What is this ideal that you should have? It will not profit you much if there is a change in your masters and your miseries continue. You will not rejoice if a handful of Indians become high officers of the State or draw bigger dividends, and your miserable conditions remain, and your body breaks down through incessant toil and starvation and the lamp of your soul goes out. You want a living wage and not a dying wage. You want to prevent the exploitation of man and to ensure equal opportunities and fair conditions of living for all. It is certain that this cannot be done under the existing system.

We are often accused of preaching the class war and of widening the distance between the classes. The distance is wide enough, thanks to capitalism, and nothing can beat the record of capitalism in that respect. But those who accuse us are singularly unseeing and ignorant of what goes on around them. Is it the socialist or the communist who separates the classes and preaches discontent or the capitalist and imperialist who by his policy and methods has reduced the great majority of mankind into wage slaves who are worse even in many ways than the slaves of old ? The class war is none of our creation. It is the creation of capitalism and so long as capitalism endures it will endure. For those who are on the top it is easy to ignore it and to preach moderation and goodwill. But the good-will does not induce these self-proclaimed well-wishers of ours to get off our backs and shoulders. They only shout the louder from the eminence which they have acquired at our cost. The class war has existed and exists to-day. By our trying ostrich-like to ignore it, we do not get rid of it. Only by our removing the causes are we likely to bring peace.

This ideal then we must ever keep before us and we must try to get our national movement also to adopt it. It may be that before we can attain our full ideal we may be able to gain somewhat better conditions for labour and more opportunities for organising them. These will bring only some little relief but we cannot refuse anything that brings some comfort to the unhappy worker. But we cannot at the same time work for such petty relief or compromise. . . . For us the objective can only be a new order under which the worker will have true freedom and opportunity of growth.

To-day you have an immediate problem facing you and you may want me to say something about [it] on this occasion. Some of you have already decided on your lines of action. Others have not done so. Meanwhile the Labour Commission is going its way and recording evidence as is offered to it. In considering whether we should co-operate with the Commission or not we have to bear in mind many things. Some of these I shall place before you.

Let us consider the circumstances under which the Labour Commission has been appointed. The much advertised Labour Government is in office in England, and Labour everywhere should ordinarily rejoice. But its past record, specially in regard to India . . . is difficult to forget. Its present record is fresh in our memory. Having reached the promised land they seem to be content with remaining there and not . . . [doing] anything which might imperil their existence. We are told from day to day that their intentions are of the best, but what can they do with a hostile majority in Parliament? Meanwhile, like the newly rich, their chief aim appears to be to prove to the world that they are as sober and respectable as those who are the inheritors of wealth. When Prime Minister MacDonald speaks in America or in Geneva is it the socialist or the pacifist that is speaking? He speaks as the representative of Imperialist England and Sir Austen Chamberlain could be no fitter representative. Mr Snowden at the Hague forgets his socialism and stands for the prestige of John Bull and the glory of the Union Jack. The very triumphs of the Labour Government's policy, such as they are, are the triumphs of imperialist policy. Is it any wonder that Mr Stanley Baldwin has congratulated Mr MacDonald for his adoption of Conservatism? Or that Mr Winston Churchill has tauntingly promised him his "cordial co-operation in the Government's self-imposed task of carrying out the Conservatives' policy and making the world easier if not safer for capitalism"? Or that Mr Lloyd George should call Mr MacDonald the "last of the Conservatives"? We know the part played by Mr MacDonald in the appointment of the Simon Commission, in spite of the resolutions of the British Labour Party pledging itself to self-determination in India. We know also his part in the Chinese crisis when British troops were sent to Shanghai, and in the Egyptian crisis when British dreadnoughts and cruisers went to Alexandria to overawe the Egyptian Parliament into suspending a measure dealing with internal order.

Recently there has been an impression that the Labour Government has pursued a liberal policy in Egypt and elsewhere. . . . In Egypt the best judges are the Egyptian people and it appears that they do not approve of the draft Anglo-Egyptian treaty. In China extra-territoriality still continues and in Palestine we have recently seen the policy of national suppression of the Arabs.

The Labour Party in England, under Mr MacDonald's guidance, was the complacent partner of the Tory party in their Imperialist policy. Now that it is itself in the seat of authority it is taking a lead in formulating that very policy. And this policy is all the more dangerous and deceptive because it is clothed in honeyed language. Calling itself socialist, it has betrayed the principles of socialism. Calling itself the friend of freedom in other lands and of internationalism, it has acted in a rigidly national and imperialist way and has forfeited all claim to the confidence of the Indian people.

The Labour Commission is sent to India. Was it as an earnest of peace and goodwill to the suffering workers and a promise of better times to come? If so, the ways of the British Government are strange and past all understanding. We have had in India during the past year a general offensive against Labour in which the government and the employees have joined hands and co-operated together. The Trades Disputes Act and the Public Safety Ordinance were the first contributions of the Government of India. Then followed the trial of the thirty-two labour leaders and workers in Meerut and large [numbers] of individual cases against labour workers. This trial, as you know, has attracted a great deal of attention not only in India, but in foreign countries. It has now after prolonged sittings arrived at the end of the first stage, that of the magisterial enquiry. Apart from the more important considerations in the case, you will observe what vast sums the government is spending in trying to put down respected leaders of the Labour Movement. You will join with me, I have no doubt, in sending them and all other comrades of ours, who are being proceeded against or have been convicted for their labour activities, our fraternal greetings and good wishes.

These are the conditions that face us. Are they the forerunners of peace or of strife? And yet we are asked to believe in the bonafides of the Labour Government and to co-operate with [its] Commission. Some of the respected leaders of our movement are in fact so co-operating and I for one will not easily consider them wrong. But with all respect to them I do submit to you that it is utterly wrong for us to offer this co-operation. Indeed the time has come when we should make it perfectly clear that we cannot co-operate with any such Commission or with the British Government that appoints them.

The question of affiliation troubles us. If I may venture to suggest [it] it would be best for us not to be affiliated to either International. So far as the Second International is concerned the proximity and the occupancy of office in various countries has made its leaders betray their principles and . . . become the exponents of a new type of Imperialism, Labour Imperialism, which may not speak in the accents of the Tories but which is none the less thorough. The main pre-occupation of the Second International is no longer the fight against capitalism but the fight against communism. And, in particular, India and the colonial countries have been studiously ignored by it and at every vital step it has sided with the forces ranged against us. I am quite convinced that we should not affiliate ourselves with it, and to do so would be disastrous to our cause.

Should we then ally ourselves to the Third International? Recently all manner of threats have been held out to those who may do so. I hope this Congress is strong enough to ignore them and to act regardless of them.

It is obvious, however, that affiliation with the Third International is largely a gesture because under the present circumstances it is not easy for us, with various Government restrictions, to develop contact with the Communist International. There is another difficulty that I feel. Personally, I am a strong admirer of the general trend of policy in Russia. Soviet Russia to-day, in spite of heavy blunders and many sins, holds out the bright promise of a better day to the world at large and to the worker specially, more than any other country. The great experiment has already succeeded in some measure and it would be a tragedy if anything happened which interfered with it or put a stop to it. With all my sympathy for the Communist view point, however, I must confess that I do not appreciate many of their methods. The history of the past few years in China and elsewhere has shown that these methods have failed and often brought reaction in their train. To affiliate with the Third International must mean an adoption of their methods in their entirety. I do not think this is desirable for us and I would therefore respectfully recommend to this Congress not to affiliate itself to either International. This does not of course mean that we should not develop contacts with them whenever desirable.

Recently, we have had a new diversion. The Labour Government has offered some kind of a conference at some time or other, to discuss something connected with India's future constitution. In spite of the vagueness of everything in this announcement it created some excitement, which is rapidly cooling as subsequent events have revealed the true inwardness of the situation. . . . Those of us who stood by independence stand by it still. We do so not because we want isolation from other countries, but because we want the freedom to change the structure under which the worker is exploited. The Labour movement is above all international. It seeks to build society on a co-operative basis not only in the national, but also in the wider international sphere. And political freedom means nothing to it if the present exploitation is to continue. That position it cannot give up and no individuals have the right to compromise it. And by that position those who stand by independence stand to-day and nothing that has happened has made any difference to it. The time is fast approaching when our professions will be put to the test of action and suffering. And the measure of your earnestness and your desire for real freedom will be the measure of the deeds that you can do and not the strong language that you may use.

So I would beg of you to prepare yourselves for the struggle that looms ahead and not to lose yourself in mutual conflict and barren strife.[1]

[1] I.Q.R. (Vol. II, 1929), pp. 425–28.

Independence League—1928-1929

[A secret British Government report of 1929 stated that "by the end of 1928, Jawahir Lal Nehru had established his Independence League, and the ideal of independence could command such a following that amongst the younger and more ardent spirits it completely swept away the more prudent counsels of the advocates of Dominion Status"[1]. According to Jawaharlal, the Independence for India League was formed "to bring pressure on the National Congress to adopt independence as its object-ive".[2]

Although there can be but little doubt that the Government report somewhat exaggerated the League's strength, it indicates how the British themselves viewed the current state of affairs in India. Even Motilal, despite the fact that he by no means always agreed with Jawahar-lal's activities, proudly wrote to Annie Besant on September 30, 1928: "The 'complete independence' group . . . thanks to Jawahar is increasing rapidly. I have no fear from this group which have at their head an earnest patriot always willing to look at the other side of the shield as is evidenced from the fact that in spite of his raging tearing propaganda in favour of complete independence Jawahar is sparing no pains to make the All Parties decisions a complete success."[3]

The Independence League aimed "at a Social Democratic State . . . and State control of the means of production and distribution. More specifically, it called for steeply graduated income and inheritance taxes; universal, free, and compulsory primary education; adult suffrage; a minimum living wage; excess profits taxes; support for trade unions; unemployment insurance; an eight-hour work-day; the abolition of untouchability; equal status for the sexes; and far-reaching land reform—removal of intermediaries, partial annulment of debts, creation of small-holdings".[4]]

Attempts at Congress-British Government Amity

[When considered against the background of the late nineteen-twenties, it is significant to note that the Viceroy, Lord Irwin, wished sincerely "to reverse the process of estrangement of Indian opinion which had gone on unchecked since November, 1927".[5] Even before publication of the Simon Commission report, he sensed quite clearly that Indian opinion was not going to be easily placated.

[1] Quoted in M.B., p. 131.
[2] B.O.L., p. 72.
[3] Ibid., p. 67.
[4] M.B., p. 130.
[5] T.N., p. 315.

During the summer of 1929, Lord Irwin went to England, taking the opportunity while there to discuss Indian affairs with British statesmen. Although there was a change of government in Britain in June—Ramsay MacDonald having become Prime Minister—Jawaharlal remained unconvinced that the British Labour Government would be of any special benefit to the Indian Nationalist Movement.]

Events were marching, step by step, inevitably, pushed onward, so it seemed, by some motive force of their own. Individuals, for all the brave show they put up, played a very minor role. One had the feeling of being a cog in a great machine which swept on relentlessly.

Hoping perhaps to check this onward march of destiny, the British Government took a forward step, and the Viceroy, Lord Irwin, made an announcement about a forthcoming Round Table Conference. It was an ingeniously worded announcement, which could mean much or very little, and it seemed to many of us obvious that the latter was the more likely contingency. And in any event, even if there was more in the announcement, it could not be anywhere near what we wanted. Hardly had this viceregal announcement been made, when, almost with indecent haste, so it seemed, a "Leaders' Conference" was arranged at Delhi, and people from various groups were invited to it. Gandhiji was there, so was my father. . . . A joint resolution or manifesto was agreed to, accepting the Viceroy's declaration subject to some conditions, which, it was stated, were vital and must be fulfilled. If these conditions were accepted by Government, then co-operation was to be offered. These conditions were solid enough and would have made a difference. [The conditions were: (1) All discussions at the proposed conference to be on the basis of full Dominion status for India. (2) There should be a predominant representation of Congressmen at the conference. (3) A general amnesty of political prisoners. (4) The Government of India to be carried on from [then] onward, as far as . . . possible under existing conditions, on the lines of a Dominion government.[1]]

It was a triumph to get such a resolution agreed to by representatives of all the groups, moderate and advanced. For the Congress, it was a comedown; as a common measure of agreement it was high. But there was a fatal catch in it. The conditions were looked upon from at least two different viewpoints. The Congress people considered them to be essential, the *sine qua non*, without which there could be no co-operation. For them they represented the minimum required. For the Moderate groups

[1] Bracketed material, T.F., footnote, p. 146.

they were a desirable maximum which should be stated, but which could not be insisted on to the point of refusal of co-operation.

And so it happened that later on, though none of these conditions were satisfied and most of us lay in jail, together with scores of thousands of others, our Moderate friends, who had signed that manifesto with us, gave their full co-operation to our jailers.

Most of us suspected that this would happen—though hardly to the extent it did happen—but there was some hope that this joint action, whereby the Congress people had to some extent curbed themselves, would also result in curbing the propensities of the Liberals and others to indiscriminate and almost invariable co-operation with the British Government. A more powerful motive for some of us, who heartily disliked the compromising resolution, was to keep our own Congress ranks well knit together. On the eve of a big struggle we could not afford to split up the Congress. It was well known that Government was not likely to accept the conditions laid down by us, and our position would thus be stronger and we could easily carry our Right wing with us. It was only a question of a few weeks; December and the Lahore Congress were near.

And yet that joint manifesto was a bitter pill for some of us. To give up the demand for independence, even in theory and even for a short while, was wrong and dangerous; it meant that it was just a tactical affair, something to bargain with, not something which was essential and without which we could never be content. So I hesitated and refused to sign the manifesto, but, as was not unusual with me, I allowed myself to be talked into signing. Even so, I came away in great distress, and the very next day I thought of withdrawing from the Congress presidency, and wrote accordingly to Gandhiji. I do not suppose that I meant this seriously, though I was sufficiently upset. A soothing letter from Gandhiji and three days of reflection calmed me.

Just prior to the Lahore Congress, a final attempt was made to find some basis of agreement between Congress and the Government. An interview with Lord Irwin, the Viceroy, was arranged. . . . Gandhiji and my father were present . . . representing the Congress viewpoint. The interview came to nothing; there was no common ground, and the two main parties—the Government and Congress—were far apart from each other. So now nothing remained but for the Congress to go ahead. The year of grace given at Calcutta was ending; independence was to be declared once [and] for all the objective of the Congress, and the necessary steps [were to be] taken to carry on the struggle to attain it.[1]

[1] T.F., pp. 146–48.

[Gandhi's appraisal of Jawaharlal's misgivings about signing the Delhi Manifesto: "He is humble enough and practical enough not to force the pace to the breaking point." Ironically, it was precisely Nehru's act of signing that led to the attack on him by the League Against Imperialism [1] mentioned in a previous section. In Britain, on the other hand, the announcement Lord Irwin had made was widely attacked as "calculated to undermine the prestige and authority of the Simon Commission".[2]]

31 | On Gandhi—Prelude to Lahore Congress, 1929: Discussion of Congress Presidency— Jawaharlal Elected—Reception in Lahore

On Gandhi

Gandhiji was still keeping away from politics. . . . He was, however, in full touch with developments and was often consulted by the Congress leaders. His main activity for some years had been *khadi* propaganda, and with this object he had undertaken extensive tours all over India. He took each province by turn and visited every district and almost every town of any consequence, as well as remote rural areas. Everywhere he attracted enormous crowds, and it required a great deal of previous staff work to carry through this program. In this manner he has repeatedly toured India and got to know every bit of the vast country from the north to the far south, from the eastern mountains to the western sea. I do not think any other human being has ever traveled about India as much as he has done.

In the past there were great wanderers who were continually on the move, pilgrim souls with the wanderlust; but their means of locomotion were slow, and a lifetime of such wandering could hardly compete with a year by railway and motorcar. Gandhiji went by railway and automobile, but he did not confine himself to them; he tramped also. In this way he gathered his unique knowledge of India and her people, and in this

[1] M.B., p. 140.
[2] T.N., p. 317.

way also scores of millions saw him and came into personal touch with him. . . .

I accompanied him occasionally for a few days at a time and, despite previous experience, could not help marveling at the vast crowds he attracted. . . . As we motored through the rural areas, we would have gatherings of from ten thousand to twenty-five thousand every few miles, and the principal meeting of the day might even exceed a hundred thousand. There were no broadcasting facilities, except rarely in a few big cities, and it was manifestly impossible to be heard by these crowds. Probably they did not expect to hear anything; they were satisfied if they saw the Mahatma. Gandhiji usually addressed them briefly, avoiding undue strain; it would have been quite impossible to carry on otherwise in this fashion from hour to hour and day to day.

I did not accompany him throughout his United Provinces tour as I could be of no special use to him and there was no point in my adding to the number of the touring party. I had no objection to crowds, but there was not sufficient inducement to get pushed and knocked about and my feet crushed—the usual fate of people accompanying Gandhiji. I had plenty of other work to do and had no desire to confine myself to *khadi* propaganda, which seemed to me a relatively minor activity in view of the developing political situation.[1]

Prelude to Lahore Congress, 1929 : Discussion of Congress Presidency

[In the summer of 1927 there had been discussions among Congress leaders concerning the choice of a President for the ensuing Session to be held in Madras in December. It was suggested that Motilal Nehru should preside over the Madras Congress. Gandhi's support was sought for the proposal. "There are too many forces just now working against Motilalji", Gandhi had declared. "Motilal himself declined the offer, but in a letter to Gandhi suggested Jawaharlal for 'the crown' as the Congress presidency was described in Congress circles. 'Jawaharlal presiding has an irresistible appeal for me', Gandhi wrote back, 'but I wonder whether it would be proper in the present atmosphere to saddle the responsibility on him.'

"The Mahatma sounded young Nehru, who was in Switzerland."[2]

From Gandhi to Jawaharlal—1927: "There is some talk of your being chosen as President for the coming Congress. I am in correspondence

[1] T.F., pp. 142-43.
[2] T.N., pp. 273-74.

with Father about it. The outlook here is not at all happy in spite of the unanimous resolution of the A.I.C.C. on the Hindu-Muslim question. I do not know whether the process of breaking heads will in any way be checked. We have lost hold upon the masses, and it seems to me that if you become President, you will be lost for one year at any rate to the masses. That, however, does not mean that Congress work has to be neglected. Someone has got to do it; but there are many who are willing and eager to do that work, may be, due to mixed motives, even selfish motives; but they will keep the Congress going on somehow or other. The institution will always be, at their wish, at the disposal of those who may be qualified for mass work and may have gained control over the masses. The question then is how your services can be best utilised. What you yourself think, you should do. I know you are capable of taking a detached view and you will say quite unselfishly ... 'put the crown on my head', and I have no doubt that it will be so put. I do not myself see the way so clear as to make me force the crown on you and plead with you to wear it." [1]

During 1927 Jawaharlal neither felt nor displayed much enthusiasm for the proposal that he become Congress President. Both Motilal and Gandhi finally "agreed that the time had not yet come for him to take command. Gandhi wrote to Motilal, June, 19 1927: '[Jawaharlal] is too high-souled to stand the anarchy and hooliganism that seem to be growing in the Congress, and it would be cruel to expect him to evolve order all of a sudden out of chaos. I am confident, however, that the anarchy will spend itself before long and the hooligans will themselves want a disciplinarian; Jawaharlal will come in then.' ....

"If Motilal felt any embarrassment in sponsoring his son's candidature for the Congress presidency, he did not betray it. ..." Motilal to Gandhi: "You have put it very well to Jawahar to say whether he wishes the 'crown' to be put on his head. His own letters, which to my mind, breathed an unshakeable faith not only in the ultimate victory against the forces of reaction, but also in our present capacity to put up a strong fight, suggested the idea to me and I forthwith communicated it to you. His reply ... will show the extent to which he is confident himself. ... My only fear is that the habit of playing the role of the humble soldier in the presence of his great general may check the necessary assertiveness required for the occasion." [2]

From Motilal to J. M. Sen Gupta and Subhas Chandra Bose, Allahabad, July 19, 1928: "There is no question of sentiment about father and son or of the son requiring any persuasion to retire in favour of the father. The only question which weighs both with the father and the son is how to serve the country best. Jawahar never for a moment entertained the idea of wearing what Mahatmaji calls the 'Crown'. My idea of putting him in the presidential chair of the Congress is an old one and has nothing

[1] B.O.L., p. 57.
[2] T.N., pp. 274–75.

to do with the fact that he is my son. I communicated it to Mahatmaji last year. . . .

"What I said was that Vallabhbhai Patel was the hero of the hour and the first choice should go to him. Failing him however the next best choice was Jawaharlal. The reason I gave was that the type to which I belonged had had its day and that it was time that the direction of affairs in the country should be handed over to younger men. We could not last for ever and it was the latter who would sooner or later have to run the show. It was much better that they began in our presence than wait till we were dead and gone. As for myself I said that I was practically a spent force and did not feel quite up to the mark. The reason why I recommended Jawahar was that among the younger set I believed he was most likely to command the confidence of the majority. This has since been proved to be true, as is evident by the fact that he and I are being mentioned almost in the same breath. Mahatmaji wired to say that he agreed with me and was recommending Jawahar in the *Young India*. I was quite sure that Jawahar would at once retire and therefore took the precaution of sending him strict orders to Mussoorie not to be silly enough to rush to print without my permission. This is the whole story. . . .

"It is not a question between Jawahar and [me] at all. The whole question is what the situation demands. . . . My own opinion is that the occasion requires a strong go-ahead party in the country prepared to go the whole hog at all costs and that this party should have the further direction of the campaign in its own hands. A quiet climb down from independence to Dominion Status will only bring the Congress into ridicule [a quite different position from the one Motilal expressed in the 1928 Nehru Report]. What I wish to show to the world and believe to be the fact is that the country is not prepared to stand any more nonsense and unless the least common demand of all the parties is acceded to without delay those who are favouring that demand will also range themselves on the side of the stronger party. It is my belief that having regard to the temper of the country it will not be easy to pilot the so-called agreed constitution in the next Congress and if it goes through, as it is likely to, it will be due more to the personalities supporting it than the considered opinion of the younger set.

"However that may be both father and son are at the service of the country and it matters little to them who occupies the Chair. The whole question is what is best for the country.

"With all this correspondence before him I am sure Mahatmaji will come to the right decision and I am perfectly willing to abide by his decision." [1]

Motilal to Gandhi, July 13, 1929: "Your accepting the chair [as Congress President] will give additional weight, dignity and prestige to the office, though as you put it . . . there will hardly be any practical difference if you put Jawahar or Vallabhbhai in it. You are the real power, whether on the throne or behind it. . . .

[1] B.O.L., pp. 63–64.

"I have been thinking hard on the matter. It appears to me that, leaving one awkward element in the case, all reasons point to your accepting. That element was present in my case. It consists in our apparent stinginess in parting with power and keeping the younger set out of it. . . .

"The revolt of youth has become an accomplished fact. . . . It would be sheer flattery to say that you have today the same influence as you had on the youth of the country some years ago, and most of them make no secret of the fact. All this would indicate that the need of [the] hour is the head of Gandhi and the voice of Jawahar. . . . There are strong reasons for either you or Jawahar to wear the 'crown', and if you and Jawahar stand together, as to which there is no doubt in my mind, it does not really matter who it is that stands in front and who behind."

"While Motilal was pressing his son's claims for the Congress presidency, Jawaharlal himself was imploring Gandhi to leave him alone. 'I am very nervous about the matter,' he wrote to Gandhi on July 9th, 'and do not like the idea at all.' On August 21st, he telegraphed to the Mahatma: 'Beg of you not to press my name for presidentship.' A few days later he enumerated at length his limitations for the high office of the Congress president: 'I represent nobody but myself. I have not the politician's flair for forming groups and parties. My one attempt in this direction— the formation of the Independence for India League last year—was a hopeless failure so far as I was concerned . . . . Most people who put me forward for the presidentship do so because they want to keep someone else out. . . . If I have the misfortune to be president, you will see that the very people who put me there . . . will be prepared to cast me to the wolves.'

"Gandhi was not moved by these arguments." [1]

In spite of the above protests and differences of opinion, Gandhi moved to have Jawaharlal, who was General Secretary of Congress at the time, become Congress President of the 1929 Lahore Congress session, to succeed Motilal in that venerable office. Gandhi took this course of action irrespective of the great pressures brought to bear upon him to assume control of Congress himself. As noted in the foregoing correspondence, the only other serious contender for the Presidency was Vallabhbhai Patel. When Patel withdrew from the race, Jawaharlal's election was assured.

"The battle of the future", stated Gandhi to the press on July 6, 1929, "has to be fought by younger men and women. . . . And it is but meet that they [should be] led by one of themselves. . . . Responsibility will mellow and sober the youth, and prepare them for the burden they must discharge. . . . Those who know the relations that subsist between Jawaharlal and me know that his being in the chair [as a leader] is as good as my being in it. . . . A President of the Congress is not an autocrat. . . .

[1] T.N., pp. 312–14.

He can no more impose his views on the people than [can] the English King." [1]

Finally, to clarify the choice he had made, the Mahatma wrote: "I may take the reader into the secret that before recommending Pandit Jawaharlal Nehru's name for the burden [of Congress President] I had ascertained from him whether he felt himself strong enough for the weight. 'If it is thrust upon me, I hope I shall not wince,' was the characteristic reply. In bravery [Jawaharlal] is not to be surpassed. Who can excel him in . . . love of the country? 'He is rash and impetuous' say some. This quality is an additional qualification at the present moment. And if he has the dash and the rashness of a warrior, he has also the prudence of a statesman. He is undoubtedly an extremist, thinking far ahead of his surroundings. But he is humble enough and practical enough not to force the pace to the breaking point. He is pure as . . . crystal, he is truthful beyond suspicion. He is a knight *sans peur et sans reproche*. The nation is safe in his hands." [2]]

Jawaharlal Elected—Reactions and Misgivings

[As the 1929 Lahore Congress approached Jawaharlal felt tormented. His own view of his coming "presidency" was far less glowing than that of his father or Gandhi. The external situation was equally troubling.]

The 1929 Congress was going to be held in Lahore. After ten years it had come back to the Punjab. Much had happened during this decade, and India's face had changed. . . . Political tension was growing; the atmosphere of struggle was developing fast. The long shadow of the conflict to come lay over the land.

As the summer and monsoon months gradually shaded off into the autumn, the provincial Congress committees busied themselves with the election of the president for the Lahore session of the Congress. There was almost unanimity in favor of Gandhiji.

So he was recommended for the presidency by the provincial committees. But he would have none of it. His refusal, though emphatic, seemed to leave some room for argument, and it was hoped that he would reconsider it. A meeting of the All-India Congress Committee was held in Lucknow to decide finally, and almost to the last hour all of us thought that he would agree. But he would not do so, and at the last moment he pressed my name forward. The All-India Congress Committee was somewhat taken aback by his final refusal, and a little irritated at being placed

[1] Quoted in M.B., p. 137.
[2] H.I.N.C. (Vol. II), p. 9.

in a difficult and invidious position. For want of any other person, and in a spirit of resignation, they finally elected me.

I have seldom felt quite so annoyed and humiliated as I did at that election. It was not that I was not sensible of the honor, for it was a great honor, and I would have rejoiced if I had been elected in the ordinary way. But I did not come to it by the main entrance or even a side entrance; I appeared suddenly by a trap door and bewildered the audience into acceptance. They put a brave face on it and, like a necessary pill, swallowed me. My pride was hurt, and I almost felt like handing back the honor. Fortunately I restrained myself from making an exhibition of myself and stole away with a heavy heart.

Probably the person who was happiest about this decision was my father. He did not wholly like my politics, but he liked me well enough, and any good thing that came my way pleased him. Often he would criticize me and speak a little curtly to me, but no person who cared to retain his good will could run me down in his presence.

My election was indeed a great honor and a great responsibility for me; it was unique in that a son was immediately following his father in the presidential chair.[1]

[While Jawaharlal was still General Secretary of Congress, but had already been elected Congress President, a "Leaders' Conference" was held in Delhi. The Conference, according to Jawaharlal, issued a statement relating "to some kind of Dominion Status for India". After signing the statement with "much reluctance", and feeling "unhappy"[2] that he had done so, Jawaharlal wrote the following letter to Gandhi.]

I have thought well for two days. I can take, I think, a calmer view of the situation than I could two days ago but the fever in my brain has not left me.

Your appeal to me on the ground of discipline could not be ignored by me. I am myself a believer in discipline. And yet I suppose there can be too much discipline. Something seems to have snapped inside me evening before last and I am unable to piece it together. As General Secretary of the Congress I owe allegiance to it and must subject myself to its discipline. I have other capacities and other allegiances. I am President of the Indian Trade Union Congress, Secretary of the Independence for India League and am intimately connected with the Youth movement. What shall I do with the allegiance I owe to these and other movements I am

[1] T.F., p. 145.
[2] B.O.L., p. 76.

connected with? I realise now more than I have ever done before that it is not possible to ride a number of horses at the same time. Indeed it is hard enough to ride one. In the conflict of responsibilities and allegiances what is one to do except to rely on one's own instincts and reason?

I have therefore considered the position apart from all outside connections and allegiances and the conviction has grown stronger that I acted wrongly day before yesterday. I shall not enter into the merits of the statement or the policy underlying it. I am afraid we differ fundamentally on that issue and I am not likely to convert you. I shall only say that I believe the statement to have been injurious and a wholly inadequate reply to the Labour Government's declaration. I believe that in our attempts to soothe and retain a few estimable gentlemen we have ruffled and practically turned out of our camp many others who were far more worth having. I believe that we have fallen into a dangerous trap out of which it will be no easy matter to escape. . . .

I do not know what the British Government will do. . . . In any event it is . . . clear to me that my position in . . . Congress will become daily more . . . difficult. I accepted the presidentship of . . . Congress with . . . misgivings but in the hope that we shall fight on a clear issue next year. That issue is already clouded and the only reason for my acceptance has gone. What am I to do with these "Leaders' Conferences"? I feel an interloper and am ill at ease. I cannot have my say because I am afraid of upsetting the conference. I repress myself and sometimes the repression is too much for me and I break out and even say things which I do not wholly mean.

I feel I must resign from the Secretaryship of the A.I.C.C. I have sent a formal letter to Father, a copy of which I enclose.

The question of the presidentship is a far more difficult one. At this late hour I do not know what I can do. But I am convinced that I was a wrong choice. You were the only possible president for the occasion and the year. . . . Even now if you agree there is a possible course which does not necessitate a meeting of the A.I.C.C. A circular might be sent round to A.I.C.C. members saying that you are agreeable to accepting the presidentship. I would beg of them to excuse me. This would be a formal matter as of course all the members, or nearly all, would welcome your decision with joy.

An alternative course is that I should declare that in view of the circumstances, and also in view of the difficulty of choosing another president now, I shall not retire now but immediately after the Congress is over, I shall act as the chairman and the Congress can decide what it likes regardless of me.

7+N.

One of these two courses seems to me to be necessary if I am to retain my physical and mental health.

As I wrote to you from Delhi I am not issuing any public statement. What others say or do not say does not worry me very much. But I must be at peace with myself. . . .

I am sending a copy of this letter to Father. I feel a little lighter after writing this letter. I am afraid it will trouble you a little and I do not want to do so. I feel half inclined not to send it to you just yet but to wait for your arrival here. Ten days more will no doubt lessen my agitation and give me a better perspective. But it is better that you should know how my mind has been working.[1]

[Gandhi to Jawaharlal, Brindaban, November 8, 1929: "I have your letter. You must have got my wire. You must not resign just now. I have not the time to argue out my point. All I know is that it will affect the national cause. There is no hurry and no principle at stake. About the crown, no one else can wear it. It never was to be a crown of roses. Let it be all thorns now. If I could have persuaded myself to wear it, I would have done so at Lucknow. The contingency I had in mind when I would be forced to wear it was not of this type. One of them was your arrest and increased repression. But let us reserve the whole of this for calm and detached discussion when we meet.

"Meanwhile may God give you peace."[2]]

Reception in Lahore

["The momentous decision that Jawaharlal should be elected President of the 1929 Session of the Congress at Lahore was taken at a meeting of the A.I.C.C. held at Lucknow. The proposal was not acceptable to certain sections, but because of Gandhiji's whole-hearted support the decision was almost unanimous. It was generally welcomed by the people; [Jawaharlal's] friends and admirers were jubilant; he . . . was not nervous as a little while before his election, he had told me, 'if it came I [would] not flinch". But the far-sighted father became somewhat anxious, for he was concerned not merely with getting [his] son into that august office. He wanted him to fill the place with dignity, and function effectively. 'Well begun is half done', he used to say; and so in every important matter the first impression counted for the most. A good start for the son would be impossible unless the Session was held in a peaceful atmosphere. Popular feelings, particularly amongst the youth, ran high because of the 'Meerut and Lahore Conspiracy Cases', which portended heavy repression on the part of [the]

---

[1] Ibid., pp. 76–78.
[2] Ibid., p. 80.

Government. The youth were restive, exasperated and ready to take up the challenge. Pandit Motilal reflected pensively in a letter to Gandhiji. 'What form the repression will take, it is difficult to say; but I have no doubt in my mind that it is coming. . . .'

"The President-elect—young Jawahar—was accorded a rousing reception at the station and was taken out in a grand procession through the decorated and crowded bazars of the city, amidst shouts. . . . It was for the first time in the history of the Congress that the President-elect rode on horse-back, even as it was the first time that a son took over from the father as President. Thousands upon thousands of people thronged the long route, showered flowers and demonstrated their enthusiasm. The father and the mother watched the Presidential procession . . . visibly moved, their eyes laved with tears. The father was in a happy frame of mind. He had feelings of supreme satisfaction, of having done his job well. He had put his son in the saddle with Mahatma Gandhi behind him as friend, philosopher and guide to conduct the national struggle from the place he himself had left." [1]]

32 | Before Lahore Congress Session, 1929— From Presidential Address, Lahore

Before Lahore Congress Session, 1929

[Shortly before the Lahore Congress Session was to convene, an already tense situation in India was heightened by an attempt to assassinate the Viceroy on December 22, 1929, as his train approached New Delhi. A conference with Indian leaders was nevertheless held as scheduled the following day, but to no avail. [2] No more definite assurances about India's future status were forthcoming than had been given by British officials in the past.]

From Presidential Address, Lahore Congress—December 29, 1929

For four and forty years this National Congress has laboured for the freedom of India. During this period it has somewhat slowly, but surely

[1] C.M.N., pp. 173–76. (Saksena, Mohanlal: "A Divine Quality".)
[2] M.B., p. 141.

awakened national consciousness from its long stupor and built up the national movement. If to-day we are gathered here at a crisis of our destiny, conscious of our strength as well as of our weakness and looking with hope and apprehension to the future, it is well that we give first thought to those who have gone before us and who spent out their lives with little hope of reward so that those that followed them may have the joy of achievement. Many of the giants of old are not with us and we of a later day standing on an eminence of their creation may often decry their efforts. That is the way of the world. But none of you can forget them, or the great work they did in laying the foundations of a free India. And none of us can ever forget that glorious band of men and women who without reckoning the consequences have laid down their young lives or spent their bright youth in suffering and torment in utter protest against a foreign domination. Many of their names even are not known to us. They laboured and suffered in silence without any expectation of public applause and by their heart's blood they nursed the tender plant of India's freedom. While many of us temporised and compromised, they stood up and proclaimed a people's right to freedom and declared to the world that India even in her degradation had the spark of life in her, because she refused to submit to tyranny and serfdom. Brick by brick has our national movement been built up, and often on the prostrate bodies of her martyred sons has India advanced. The giants of old may not be with us but the courage of old is with us still.

This is the glorious heritage that we have inherited and you wish to put me in charge of it. I know well that I occupy this honoured place by chance more than by your deliberate design. Your desire was to choose another—one who towers above all others, in the present day world of ours—and there could have been no wiser choice. But fate and he conspired together and thrust me against your will and mine into the terrible seat of responsibility. Should I express my gratitude to you for having placed me in this dilemma? But I am grateful indeed for your confidence in one who strangely lacks it himself.

You will discuss many vital national problems that face us to-day and your decisions may change the course of Indian history. But you are not the only people that are faced with problems. The whole world to-day is one vast question-mark and every country and every people is in the melting pot. The age of faith, with the comfort and stability it brings, is past, and there is questioning about everything, however permanent or sacred it might have appeared to our forefathers. Everywhere there is doubt and restlessness and the foundations of the state and society are in process of transformation. Old established ideas of liberty, justice, property and even family are being attacked and the outcome hangs in the balance. We appear to be in a dissolving period of history when the world is in labour and out of her travail will give birth to a new order.

No one can say what the future will bring, but we may assert with some confidence that Asia and even India will play a determining part in future world policy.

The brief day of European domination is already approaching its end. Europe has ceased to be the centre of activity and interest. The future is with America and Asia. Owing to false and incomplete history many of us have been led to think that Europe has always dominated over the rest of the world and Asia has always let the legions of the West thunder past. . . . We have forgotten that for millennia the legions of Asia overran Europe and modern Europe itself largely consists of the descendants of those invaders from Asia. We have forgotten that it was India that finally broke the military power of Alexander. Thought has undoubtedly been the glory of Asia and specially of India, but in the field of action the record of Asia has been equally great. But none of us desires that the legions of Asia or Europe should overrun continents again. We have all had enough of them.

India to-day is a part of a world movement. Not only China, Turkey, Persia and Egypt, but also Russia and the countries of the West are taking part in this movement, and India cannot isolate herself from it. We have our own problems, difficult and intricate, and we cannot run away from them and take shelter in the wider problems that affect the world. But if we ignore the world we do so at our peril.

Civilisation to-day, such as it is, is not the creation or the monopoly of one people or nation. It is a complete fabric to which all countries have contributed and then have adapted to suit their particular needs. And if India has a message to give to the world, as I hope she has, she has also to receive and learn much from the messages of other peoples.

When everything is changing it is well to remember the long course of Indian history. Few things in history are more amazing than the wonderful stability of social structure in India which withstood the impact of numerous alien influences and thousands of years of change and conflict. It withstood them because it always sought to absorb them and tolerate them. Its aim was not to exterminate but to establish an equilibrium between different cultures. Aryans and non-Aryans settled down together recognising each other's right to their culture, and outsiders who came like the Parsis found a welcome and a place in the social order. With the coming of the Moslems the equilibrium was disturbed, but India sought to restore it and largely succeeded. Unhappily for us, before we could adjust our differences, the political structure broke down, the British came and we fell.

Great as was the success of India in evolving a stable society she failed in a vital particular and because she failed in this she fell and remains fallen. No solution was found for the problem of equality. India deliberately ignored this and built up her social structure on inequality and we have the tragic consequences of this in the millions of our people who till yesterday were suppressed and had little opportunity for growth.

And yet when Europe fought her wars of religion and Christians massacred each other in the name of their Saviour, India was tolerant, although, alas, there is little of this toleration to-day. Having attained some measure of religious liberty, Europe sought after political liberty and political and legal equality. Having attained these also she finds that they mean very little without economic liberty and equality. And so to-day politics have ceased to have much meaning and the most vital question is that of social and economic equality.

India also will have to find a solution to this problem and until she does so her political and social structure cannot have stability. That solution need not necessarily follow the example of any other country. It must, if it has to endure, be based on the genius of her people and be an outcome of her thought and culture. And when it is found, the unhappy differences between various communities, which trouble us to-day . . . will automatically disappear.

Indeed the real differences have already largely gone, but fear of each other and distrust and suspicion remain and sow seeds of discord. The problem before us is not one of removing differences. They can well remain side by side and enrich our many sided culture. The problem is how to remove fear and suspicion and being intangible they are hard to get at. An earnest attempt was made last year by the All Parties Conference and much progress was made towards the goal. But we must admit with sorrow that success has not wholly crowned its efforts. Many of our Muslim and Sikh friends have strenuously opposed the solutions suggested and passions have been roused over mathematical figures and percentages. Logic and cold reason are poor weapons to fight fear and distrust. Only faith and generosity can overcome them. I can only hope that the leaders of various communities will have this faith and generosity in ample measure. What shall we gain for ourselves or for our community if all of us are slaves in a slave country? And what can we lose if once we remove the shackles from India and can breathe the air of freedom ? Do we want outsiders who are not of us and who have kept us in bondage to be the protectors of our little rights and privileges, when they deny us the very right to freedom! No majority can crush a determined minority and no minority can be sufficiently protected by a little addition to its seats in a legislature. Let us remember that in the world to-day almost everywhere a very small minority holds wealth and power and dominates over the great majority.

I have no love for bigotry and dogmatism in religion and I am glad that they are weakening. Nor do I love communalism in any shape or form. I find it difficult to appreciate why political or economic rights should depend on the membership of a religious group or community. I can fully understand the right to freedom in religion and the right to one's own culture, and in India specially, which has always acknowledged and granted these rights, it should be no difficult matter to ensure their continuance. We have only to find out some way whereby we may root out the fear and distrust that darken our horizon to-day. The politics of a subject race are largely based on fear and we have been too long under subjection to get rid of them easily.

I was born a Hindu, but I do not know how far I am justified in calling myself one or in speaking on behalf of Hindus. But birth still counts in this country and by right of birth I shall venture to submit to the leaders of the Hindus that it should be their privilege to take the lead in generosity. Generosity is not only good morals but is often good politics and sound expediency. And it is inconceivable to me that in a free India the Hindus can ever be powerless. So far as I am concerned I would gladly ask our Moslem and Sikh friends to take what they will without protest or argument from me. I know that the time is coming soon when these labels and appellations will have little meaning and when our struggle will be on an economic basis. Meanwhile it matters little what our mutual arrangements are, provided only that we do not build up barriers which will come in the way of our future progress.

The time has indeed already come when the All Parties Report has to be put aside and we march forward unfettered to our goal. You will remember the resolution of the last Congress which fixed a year of grace for the adoption of the All Parties scheme. That year is nearly over and the natural issue of that decision is for this Congress to declare in favour of independence and devise sanctions to achieve it.

That year has not brought Dominion Status of the All Parties Constitution. It has brought instead suffering and greater repression of our national and labour movements and how many of our comrades are to-day forcibly kept away from us by the alien power! How many of them suffer exile in foreign countries and are refused facilities to return to the Motherland! The army of occupation holds our country in its iron grip and the whip of the master is ever ready to come down on the best of us who dare to raise their heads. The answer to the Calcutta resolution has been clear and definite.

Recently there has been a seeming offer of peace. The Viceroy has stated on behalf of the British Government that the leaders of Indian opinion will be invited to confer with the Government on the subject of India's future constitution. The Viceroy means well and his language was the language of peace. But even the Viceroy's goodwill and courteous phrases are poor substitutes for the hard facts that confront us.

We have sufficient experience of the devious ways of ... British diplomacy to beware of it. The offer that the British Government made was vague and there was no commitment or promise of performance. Only by the greatest stretch of imagination could it be interpreted as a possible response to the Calcutta resolution. Many leaders of various political parties met together soon after and considered it. They gave it the most favourable interpretation for they desired peace and were willing to go half way to meet it. But in courteous language they made it clear what the vital conditions for its acceptance were.

Many of us who believed in independence and were convinced that the offer was only a device to lead us astray and create division in our ranks suffered bitter anguish and were torn with doubt. Were we justified in precipitating a terrible national struggle with all its inevitable consequences of suffering for many when there was even an outside chance of honourable peace?

With much searching of heart we signed that manifesto and I know not to-day if we did right or wrong. Later came the explanations and amplifications in the British Parliament and elsewhere and all doubt, if doubt there was, was removed as to the true significance of the offer. Even so your Working Committee chose to keep open the door of negotiation and left it to this Congress to take the final decision.

During the last few days there has been another discussion of this subject in the British House of Commons and the Secretary of State for India has endeavoured to point out that successive British Governments have tried to prove not only by words but by deed also the sincerity of their faith in regard to India. We must recognise Mr Wedgwood Benn's desire to do something for India and his anxiety to secure the goodwill of the

Indian people. But his speech and the other speeches made in Parliament carry us no further. "Dominion Status in action" to which he draws attention has been a snare for us and has certainly not reduced the exploitation of India. The burdens on the Indian masses are even greater to-day because of this "Dominion Status in action" and the so-called constitutional reforms of ten years ago. High Commissioners in London ... representatives on the League of Nations ... and Indian Governors and high officials are no parts of our demand. We want to ... end ... exploitation of India's poor and [achieve] the reality of power and not merely the livery of office. Mr Wedgwood Benn has given us a record of the achievements of the past decade. He could have added to it by referring to martial law in the Punjab, and the Jallianwala Bagh shooting and the repression and exploitation that have gone [on] continually during this period of "Dominion Status in action". He has given us some insight into what more of Dominion Status may mean for us. It means the shadow of authority to a handful of Indians and more repression and exploitation of the masses.

What will this Congress do? The conditions for co-operation remain unfulfilled. Can we co-operate so long as there are [no] guarantees that real freedom will come to us? Can we co-operate when our comrades lie in prison and repression continues? Can we co-operate until we are assured that real peace is sought after and not merely a tactical advantage over us? Peace cannot come at the point of the bayonet and if we are to continue to be dominated over by an alien people let us at least be no consenting parties to it.

If the [1928] Calcutta resolution holds we have but one goal to-day ... independence. Independence is not a happy word in the world to-day for it means exclusiveness and isolation. Civilization has had enough of narrow nationalism and gropes towards a wider co-operation and interdependence. And if we use the word independence we do so [not] in [a] sense hostile to the larger ideals. Independence for us means complete freedom from British domination and British imperialism. Having attained our freedom I have no doubt that India will welcome all attempts at world co-operation and federation and will even agree to give up part of her own independence to a larger group of which she is an equal member.

The British Empire to-day is not such a group and cannot be so long as it dominates over millions of people and holds large areas of the world's surface despite the will of their inhabitants. It cannot be a true commonwealth so long as imperialism is its basis and the exploitation of other

7*

races its chief means of sustenance. The British Empire to-day is indeed gradually undergoing a process of political dissolution, it is in a state of unstable equilibrium. The Union of South Africa is not a very happy member of the family nor is the Irish Free State a willing one. Egypt drifts away. India could never be an equal member of the commonwealth unless imperialism and all it implies is discarded. So long as this is not done India's position in the Empire must be one of subservience and her exploitation will continue. The embrace of the British Empire is a dangerous thing. It is not and cannot be the life-giving embrace of affection freely given and returned. And if it is not that it will be what it has been in the past, the embrace of death.

There is talk of world peace and pacts have been signed by the nations of the world. But despite pacts armaments grow and beautiful language is the only homage that is paid to the Goddess of Peace. Peace can only come when the causes of war are removed. So long as there is the domination of one country over another there will always be attempts to subvert the existing order and no stable equilibrium can endure. Out of imperialism and capitalism peace can never come. And it is because the British Empire stands for these and bases itself on the exploitation of the masses that we can find no willing place in it. No gain that may come to us is worth anything unless it helps in removing the grievous burdens on our masses. The weight of a great empire is heavy to carry and long our people have endured it. Their backs are bent down and their spirit has almost broken. How will they share in the commonwealth partnership if the burden of exploitation continues? Many of the problems we have to face are the problems of vested interests, mostly created or encouraged by the British Government. The interests of Rulers of Indian States, of British officials and British capital and Indian capital and of the owners of big zamindaris are ever thrust before us and they clamour for protection. The unhappy millions who really need protection are almost voiceless and have few advocates. So long as the British Empire continues in India, in whatever shape it may do so, it will strengthen these vested interests and create more. And each one of them will be [a] fresh obstacle in our way. Of necessity the Government has to rely on opposition and the symbol of its rule is the secret service with its despicable and contemptible train of provocateurs, informers and approvers.

We have had much controversy about independence and Dominion Status and we have quarrelled about words. But the real thing is the conquest of power by whatever name it may be called. I do not think that any form of Dominion Status applicable to India will give us real power.

A test of this power would be the entire withdrawal of the alien army of occupation and economic control. Let us therefore concentrate on these and the rest will follow easily.

We stand, therefore, to-day for the fullest freedom of India. This Congress has not acknowledged and will not acknowledge the right of the British Parliament to dictate to us in any way. To it we make no appeal. But we do appeal to the Parliament and conscience of the world and to them we shall demonstrate, I hope that India submits no longer to any foreign domination. To-day or to-morrow we may not be strong enough to assert our will.

We are very conscious of our weakness and there is no boasting in us or pride of strength. But let no one, least of all England, mistake or underrate the meaning or strength of our resolve. Solemnly, with full knowledge of consequences I hope, we shall take it and there will be no turning back. A great nation cannot be thwarted for long when once its mind is clear and resolved. If to-day we fail and to-morrow brings no success, the day after will follow and bring achievement.

We are weary of strife and hunger for peace and opportunity to work constructively for our country. Do we enjoy the breaking up of our homes and the sight of our brave young men going on strike and losing even [their] miserable pittance and starving? [They do] so by sheer compulsion when there is no other way. . . .

And we who take this perilous path of national strife do so because there is no other way to an honourable peace. But we long for peace and the hand of fellowship will always be stretched out to all who may care to grasp it. But behind the hand will be a body which will not bend to injustice and a mind that will not surrender on any vital point.

With the struggle before us the time for determining our future constitution is not yet. For two years or more we have drawn up constitutions and finally the All Parties Committee put a crown to these efforts by drawing up a scheme of its own which the Congress adopted for a year. The labour that went to the making of this scheme was not wasted and India has profited by it. But the year is past and we have to face new circumstances which require action rather than constitution making. Yet we cannot ignore the problems that beset us and that will make or mar our struggle and our future constitution. We have to aim at social adjustment and equilibrium and to overcome the forces of disruption that have been the bane of India.

I must frankly confess that I am a socialist and a republican and am no believer in kings and princes or in the order which produces the modern kings of industry, who have greater power over the lives and fortunes of men than even the kings of old, and whose methods are as predatory as those of old feudal aristocracy. I recognise, however, that it may not be possible for a body constituted as is this National Congress and in the present circumstances of the country to adopt a full socialistic programme. But we must realise that the philosophy of socialism has gradually permeated the entire structure of society the world over and almost . . . the only point in dispute is the pace and the methods of advance to its full realisation. India will have to go that way too if she seeks to end her poverty and inequality though she may evolve her own methods and may adopt the ideal to the genius of her race.

We have three major problems—the minorities, the Indian States, and labour and peasantry. I have dealt already with the question of minorities. I shall only repeat that we must give the fullest assurance by our words and our deeds that their culture and traditions will be safe.

The Indian States, even for India, are the most curious relics of a bygone age. Many of their rulers apparently still believe in the divine right of kings—puppet kings though they be—and consider the state and all it contains to be their personal property, which they can squander at will. A few of them have a sense of responsibility and have endeavoured to serve their people, but many of them have hardly any redeeming feature.

It is perhaps unjust to blame them, for they are but the products of a vicious system and it is the system that will ultimately have to go. One of the rulers has told us frankly that even in case of war between India and England he will stand for England and fight his mother country. That is the measure of his patriotism. It is not surprising then that they claim, and their claim finds acceptance with the British Government, that they alone can represent their subjects at any conference and no one even of their subjects may have any say. The Indian States cannot live apart from the rest of India and their rulers must, unless they accept their inevitable limitations, go the way of others who thought like them. And the only people who have a right to determine the future of the States must be the people of those States including the rulers. This Congress which claims self-determination cannot deny it to the people of the States. Meanwhile the Congress is perfectly willing to confer with such rulers as are prepared to do so and to devise means whereby the transition may not be too sudden. But in no event can the people of the States be ignored.

Our third major problem is the biggest of all. For India means the peasantry and labour and to the extent that we raise them and satisfy their wants will we succeed in our task. And the measure of the strength of our national movement will be the measure of their adherence to it. We can only gain them to our side by our espousing their cause which is really the country's cause. The Congress has often expressed its good-will towards them but beyond that it has not gone. The Congress it is said must hold the balance fairly between capital and labour and zamindar and tenant. But the balance has been and is terribly [weighted] on one side . . . to maintain injustice and exploitation. The only way to right it is to do away with the domination of any one class over another. The All-India Congress Committee accepted this ideal of social and economic change in a resolution it passed some months ago in Bombay. I hope the Congress will also set its seal on it and will further draw up a programme of such changes as can be immediately put in operation.

In this programme perhaps the Congress as a whole cannot go very far to-day. But it must keep the ultimate ideal in view and work for it. The question is not merely of wages and charity doled out by an employer or landlord. Paternalism in industry or [on] the land is but a form of charity with all its sting and its utter incapacity to root out the evil. The new theory of trusteeship, which some advocate, is equally barren. For trusteeship means that the power for good or evil remains with the self-appointed trustee and he may exercise it as he wills. The sole trusteeship that can be fair is the trusteeship of the nation and not of one individual or a group. Many Englishmen honestly consider themselves the trustees for India, and yet to what a condition they have reduced our country!

We have to decide for whose benefit industry must be run and the land produce food. To-day the abundance that the land produces is not for the peasant or the labourer who work on it; and industry's chief function is supposed to be to produce millionaires. However golden the harvest and heavy the dividends, the mud huts and hovels and nakedness of our people testify to the glory of the British Empire and of our present social system.

Our economic programme must therefore be based on a human outlook and must not sacrifice man to money. If an industry cannot be run without starving its workers then the industry must close down. If the workers on the land have not enough to eat then the intermediaries who deprive them of their full share must go. The least that every worker in field or factory is entitled to is a minimum wage which will enable him to live in moderate comfort, and human hours of labour which do not break his strength and spirit. The All-Parties Committee accepted the principle and included it in their recommendations. I hope the Congress will also do [so] and will in addition be prepared to accept its natural consequences. Further that it will adopt the well-known demands of labour for a better life, and will give every assistance to it to organise itself and prepare itself for the day when it can control industry on a co-operative basis.

But industrial labour is only a small part of India although it is rapidly becoming a force that cannot be ignored. It is the peasantry that cry loudly, piteously for relief and our programme must deal with their present condition. Real relief can only come by a great change in the land laws and the basis of the present system of land tenure. We have among us many big landowners and we welcome them. But they must realise that the ownership of large estates by individuals, which is the outcome of a state resembling the old feudalism of Europe, is a rapidly disappearing phenomenon all over the world. Even in countries which are the strongholds of capitalism the large estates are being split up and given to the peasantry who work on them. In India also we have large areas where the system of peasant proprietorship prevails and we shall have to extend this all over the country. I hope that in doing so we may have the co-operation of some at least of the big landowners.

It is not possible for this Congress at its annual session to draw up any detailed economic programme. It can only lay down some general principles and call upon the All-India Congress Committee to fill in the details in cooperation with the representatives of the Trade Union Congress and other organisations which are vitally interested in this matter. Indeed I hope that the cooperation between this Congress and the Trade Union Congress will grow and the two organisations will fight side by side in future struggles.

All these are pious hopes till we gain power and the real problem therefore before us is the conquest of power. We shall not [succeed] by subtle reasoning or argument or lawyers' quibbles, but by the forging of sanctions to enforce the nation's will. To that end this Congress must address itself.

The past year has been one of preparation for us and we have made every effort to reorganise and strengthen the Congress organisation. The results have been considerable and our organisation is in a better state to-day than at any time since the reaction which followed the non-co-operation movement. But our weaknesses are many and are apparent enough. Mutual strife even within Congress Committees, is unhappily too common and election squabbles drain all our strength and energy. How can we fight a great fight if we cannot get over this ancient weakness of ours and rise above our petty selves? I earnestly hope that with a strong programme of action before the country our perspective will improve and we will not tolerate this barren and demoralising strife.

What can this programme be? Our choice is limited, not by our own constitution which we can change at our will, but by facts and circumstances. Article One of our constitution lays down that our methods must be legitimate and peaceful. Legitimate I hope they will always be, for we must not sully the great cause for which we stand by any deed that will bring dishonour to it and that we may ourselves regret later. Peaceful I should like them to be for the methods of peace are more desirable and more enduring than those of violence. Violence too often brings reaction and demoralisation in its train, and in our country specially it may lead to disruption. It is perfectly true that organised violence rules the world to-day and it may be that we could profit by its use. But we have not the material or the training for organised violence and individual or sporadic violence is a confession of despair. The great majority of us, I take it, judge the issue not on moral but on practical grounds, and if we reject the way of violence it is because it promises no substantial results. But if this Congress or the nation at any future time comes to the conclusion that methods of violence will rid us of slavery then I have no doubt that it will adopt them. Violence is bad but slavery is far worse. Let us also remember that the great apostle of non-violence has himself told us that it is better to fight than to refuse to fight out of cowardice.

Any great movement for liberation to-day must necessarily be a mass movement and mass [movements] must essentially be peaceful, except in times of organised revolt. Whether we have the non-cooperation of a decade ago or the modern industrial weapon of the general strike, the basis is peaceful organisation and peaceful action. And if the principal movement is a peaceful one contemporaneous attempts at sporadic violence can only distract attention and weaken it. It is not possible to carry on at one and the same time the two movements side by side. We have to choose and strictly to abide by our choice. What the choice of this Congress is likely to be I have no doubt. It can only choose a peaceful mass movement.

Should we repeat the programme and tactics of the non-cooperation movement? Not necessarily, but the basic idea must remain. Programmes and tactics must be made to fit in with circumstances and it is neither easy nor desirable for this Congress at this stage to determine them in detail. That should be the work of its executive, the All-India Congress Committee. But the principles have to be fixed.

The old programme was one of the three boycotts—Councils, Law Courts and Schools—leading up to refusal of service in the army and non-payment of taxes. When the national struggle is at its height I fail to see how it will be possible for any person engaged in it to continue in the courts or the schools. But still I think that it will be unwise to declare a boycott of the courts and schools at this stage.

The boycott of the legislative councils has led to much heated debate in the past and this Congress itself has been rent in twain over it. We need not revive that controversy for the circumstances to-day are entirely different. I feel that the step the Congress took some years ago to permit Congressmen to enter the councils was an inevitable step and I am not prepared to say that some good has not resulted from it. But we have exhausted that good and there is no middle course left to-day between boycott and full co-operation. All of us know the demoralisation that these sham legislatures have brought in our ranks and how many of our good men their committees and commissions lure away. Our workers are limited in number and we can have no mass movement unless they concentrate on it and turn [their] backs to the palatial council chambers of our legislatures. And if we declare for independence how can we enter the councils and carry on our humdrum and profitless activities there? No programme or policy can be laid down for ever, nor can this Congress bind the country or even itself to pursue one line of action indefinitely. But to-day I would respectfully urge the Congress that the only policy in regard to the councils is a complete boycott of them. The All-India Congress Committee recommended this course . . . and the time has come to give effect to it.

This boycott will only be a means to an end. It will release energy and divert attention to the real struggle which must take the shape of non-payment of taxes and, where possible, with the cooperation of the labour movement, general strikes. But non-payment of taxes must be well organised in specific areas, and for this purpose the Congress should authorise the All-India Congress Committee to take the necessary action wherever and whenever it considers desirable.

I have not so far referred to the demonstrative programme of the Congress. This should certainly continue but the experience of the last few years shows us that by itself it does not carry us swiftly enough. It prepares the ground for future action and ten years' silent work is bearing fruit to-day. In particular we shall, I hope, continue our boycott of foreign cloth and the boycott of British goods.

Our programme must therefore be one of political and economic boycott. It is not possible for us, so long as we are not actually independent, and not even then completely, to boycott another country wholly or to sever all connection with it. But our endeavour must be to reduce all

points of contact with [the] British Government and to rely on ourselves.

We must also make it clear that India will not accept responsibility for all
the debts that England has piled on her. The . . . Congress[has]repudiated
liability to pay these debts and we must repeat this repudiation and stand
by it. Such of India's public debt as has been used for purposes beneficial
to India we are prepared to admit and pay back. But we wholly deny all
liability to pay back the vast sums which have been raised so that India
may be held in subjection and her burdens may be increased. In particular
the poverty-stricken people of India cannot agree to shoulder the burden
of the wars fought by England to extend her domain and consolidate her
position in India. Nor can they accept the many concessions lavishly
bestowed without even proper compensation on foreign exploiters.

I have not referred so far to the Indians overseas and I do not propose
to say much about them. This is not from any want of fellow-feeling with
our brethren in East Africa or South Africa or Fiji or elsewhere, who are
bravely struggling against great odds. But their fate will be decided in the
plains of India and the struggle we are launching into is as much for them
as for ourselves.

For this struggle we want efficient machinery. Our Congress constitution and organisation have become too archaic and slow moving and are
ill suited to times of crisis. The times of great demonstrations are past.
We want quiet and irresistible action now and this can only be brought
about by the strictest discipline in our ranks. Our resolution must be
passed in order to be acted upon. The Congress will gain in strength,
however small its actual membership may become, if it acts in a disciplined way. Small determined minorities have changed the fate of nations.
Mobs and crowds can do little. Freedom itself involves restraint and discipline, and each one of us will have to subordinate himself to the larger good.

The Congress represents no small minority in the country, and though
many may be too weak to join it or to work for it, they look to it with hope
longing to bring them deliverance. Ever since the Calcutta resolution the
country has waited with anxious expectation for this great day when this
Congress meets. None of us can say what and when we can achieve. We
cannot command success. But success often comes to those who dare and
act; it seldom goes to the timid who are ever afraid of the consequences.
We play for high stakes; and if we seek to achieve great things it can only
be through great dangers. Whether we succeed soon or late, none but
ourselves can stop us from high endeavour and from writing a noble page
in our country's long and splendid history.

We have conspiracy cases going on in various parts of the country. They are ever with us. But the time has gone for secret conspiracy. We have now an open conspiracy to free this country from foreign rule, and you, comrades, and all our countrymen and countrywomen are invited to join it. But the rewards that are in store for you are suffering and prison and it may be death. But you shall also have the satisfaction that you have done your little bit for India, the ancient, but ever young, and have helped a little in the liberation of humanity from its present bondage.[1]

[Irked that Britain had failed to respond to even its mild demands of the recent past, the Lahore Congress Session of December, 1929 decided that there could be no purpose in Congress leaders attending the forthcoming 1930 Round Table Conference in London. It was resolved that "Purna Swaraj" (complete independence) must be attained by legitimate and peaceful means. Non-payment of taxes was deemed fit. The legislatures were to be boycotted. Various other planks in Jawaharlal's earlier Independence League platform were approved.

Despite his swift rise to power, Jawaharlal was nevertheless faced by strong opposition from both the Left and the Right. "We have got a stiff time ahead of us . . ." he wrote. Of at least one possible hazard, he observed: "Probably the [British] Labour Government will have the honour of sending some of us to prison before long."[2]]

[1] I.Q.R. (II, 1929), pp. 288–97.
[2] Quoted in M.B., p. 146.

PART TWO

1930–1933

Nationalism was and is inevitable in the India of my day; it is a natural and healthy growth. For any subject country national freedom must be the first and dominant urge; for India with her intense sense of individuality and ... past heritage, it [is] doubly so.[1]

*

The promised land may yet be far from us and we may have to march wearily through the deserts, but who will take away from us that deathless hope which has survived the scaffold and immeasurable suffering and sorrow; who will dare to crush the spirit of India which has found rebirth again and again after so many crucifixions? ...

Danger seems terrible from a distance; it is not so bad if you have a close look at it. And often it is a pleasant companion, adding to the zest and delight of life.[2]

*

Socialism cannot thrive in a society based on acquisitiveness. It becomes necessary to change the basis of the acquisitive society and remove the profit motive.[3]

*

The people ... will go as far as you can take them. It is only vested interests which block the path of progress. These, and confused, selfish thinking.[4]

[1] D.I., pp. 40–41.
[2] M.H.I., pp. 7–8.
[3] Ibid., p. 25.
[4] M.J.N., p. 257.

I | A Troubled Decade

[The thirties, so anguished for the world at large, were especially difficult for Jawaharlal. During that tormenting decade he lost his father, mother and wife in heart-breaking and rapid succession. Jail sentences, as well as other related indignities, occurred with alarming regularity. Inconclusive Round Table Conferences, at which British and Indian leaders unsuccessfully attempted to come to some agreement about an acceptable Constitution for India, further intensified the general mood of frustration. Independence seemed distressingly remote, yet the struggle to attain it was to continue unabated.

Nehru's passionate belief in a democratic form of Socialism as the most desirable solution for India's economic problems, like the majority of his other attitudes, continued to be shared by relatively few of his Congress colleagues. Even Gandhi continued to hold an almost diametrically opposed view about what the very word Socialism properly should signify, and how it should be brought into being.

Jawaharlal became increasingly disturbed by poverty, inequality and suppression at home, by the widespread economic depression abroad, by the rise of totalitarianism and the mounting threat of war. His was the first effective outcry—and it was a resounding one—to be raised in India on behalf of the victims and opponents of Fascism and Nazism. He passionately protested against Japan's aggression in China, Fascist Italy's invasion of Abyssinia, the Nazi rape of Czechoslovakia, the war against the Loyalists in Spain. He was greatly disturbed by Britain's initial appeasement of Hitler, as by her continued oppression of India.

There were formidable foreign policy dilemmas to be resolved at home. Nehru's general attitude toward the international situation might readily lead one to assume that he was an ardent proponent of collective security against potential aggression in the nineteen thirties. He nevertheless pondered how a subjugated India could be expected to align herself militarily with Britain, even if the latter finally did decide to oppose Nazi Germany. For what of India's own freedom? On the other hand, how was it possible to make common cause with those Indians holding a merely hollowly theoretical pacifist position, in view of the inevitable results of a Nazi-Fascist victory, both for the rest of the world and for India herself? It was equally difficult to co-operate with such an Indian leader as Subhas Bose who, despite his allegedly progressive ideas, was willing to aid the Japanese and the Germans, purportedly to fight

Imperialism. (Details relating to Bose's activities are to be found in Sections dealing with the late 1930s and the 1940s.)

Virtually from the time of the 1927 Brussels Conference (described in Part One), Nehru was singularly alone in Congress, with regard to his preoccupation with international affairs. Yet it was he, above all others, beginning at even so early a date, who was to become largely responsible for formulating Congress—and subsequently India's—foreign policy.

Throughout the thirties Nehru feared that India's communalists, with their divisive tactics and destructive fanaticism, would further jeopardize the winning of independence, as well as pose a continuing threat to the internal peace of the country.

Even in the nineteenth century, suggestions had been made concerning territorial separation of India's Muslims. It was not, however, until after 1930, when the well-known Muslim, Sir Muhammed Iqbal, put forward a precise demand for an autonomous Muslim area, that Muslim League leaders began to place primary emphasis upon creation of an independent entity, namely Pakistan. It remained impossible for Nehru to favor a separate Muslim state. He continued, instead, consistently to advocate attainment of a free, democratic, united and secular India.]

2 | The Call to Action—Declaration of Independence, 1930—Independence Day: Approach of Civil Disobedience

The Call to Action

[The Lahore Congress, which Nehru had addressed on December 29, 1929, continued into early 1930.]

The Lahore Congress remains fresh in my memory—a vivid patch. . . . The whole atmosphere was electric and surcharged with the gravity of the occasion. Our decisions were not going to be mere criticisms or protests or expressions of opinion, but a call to action which was bound to convulse the country and affect the lives of millions.

What the distant future held for us and our country, none dared prophesy; the immediate future was clear enough, and it held the promise of strife and suffering for us and those who were dear to us. This thought sobered our enthusiasms and made us very conscious of our responsibility. Every vote that we gave became a message of farewell to ease, comfort, domestic happiness, and the intercourse of friends, and an invitation to lonely days and nights and physical and mental distress.

The main resolution on independence, and the action to be taken in furtherance of our freedom struggle, was passed almost unanimously, barely a score of persons, out of many thousands, voting against it. The All-India Congress Committee had been authorized to plan and carry out our campaign, but all knew that the real decision lay with Gandhiji. . . .

In spite of the enthusiasm shown at the Congress session, no one knew what the response of the country would be to a program of action. We had burned our boats and could not go back, but the country ahead of us was an almost strange and uncharted land. To give a start to our campaign, and partly also to judge the temper of the country, January 26 was fixed as Independence Day, when a pledge of independence was to be taken all over the country.

And so, full of doubt about our program, but pushed on by enthusiasm and the desire to do something effective, we waited for the march of events.[1]

[Henceforth, January 26 was to be observed annually in India as Independence Day. It was on this date that the free Republic of India was to be formally inaugurated in 1950.]

India's Declaration of Independence—Adopted at Lahore Congress Session under Jawaharlal's Presidency, 1930

"We believe that it is the inalienable right of the Indian people, as of any other people, to have freedom and to enjoy the fruits of their toil and have the necessities of life, so that they may have full opportunities of growth. We believe also that if any government deprives a people of these rights and oppresses them the people have a further right to alter it or to abolish it. The British government in India has not only deprived the Indian people of their freedom but has based itself on the exploitation of the masses, and has ruined India economically, politically, culturally, and spiritually. We believe, therefore, that India must sever

[1] T.F., pp. 149–50.

the British connection and attain *Purna Swaraj* or complete independence.

"India has been ruined economically. The revenue derived from our people is out of all proportion to our income. Our average income is seven pice (less than twopence) per day, and of the heavy taxes we pay, twenty per cent are raised from the land revenue derived from the peasantry and three per cent from the salt tax, which falls most heavily on the poor.

"Village industries, such as hand-spinning, have been destroyed, leaving the peasantry idle for at least four months in the year, and dulling their intellect for want of handicrafts, and nothing has been substituted, as in other countries, for the crafts thus destroyed.

"Customs and currency have been so manipulated as to heap further burdens on the peasantry. The British manufactured goods constitute the bulk of our imports. Customs duties betray clear partiality for British manufactures, and revenue from them is used not to lessen the burden on the masses but for sustaining a highly extravagant administration. Still more arbitrary has been the manipulation of the exchange ratio, which has resulted in millions being drained away from the country.

"Politically, India's status has never been so reduced as under the British regime. No reforms have given real political power to the people. The tallest of us have to bend before foreign authority. The rights of free expression of opinion and free association have been denied to us, and many of our countrymen are compelled to live in exile abroad and cannot return to their homes. All administrative talent is killed, and the masses have to be satisfied with petty village offices and clerkships.

"Culturally, the system of education has torn us from our moorings, and our training has made us hug the very chains that bind us.

"Spiritually, compulsory disarmament has made us unmanly, and the presence of an alien army of occupation, employed with deadly effect to crush in us the spirit of resistance, has made us think that we cannot look after ourselves or put up a defense against foreign aggression, or even defend our homes and families from the attacks of thieves, robbers and miscreants.

"We hold it to be a crime against man and God to submit any longer to a rule that has caused this fourfold disaster to our country. We recognize, however, that the most effective way of gaining our freedom is not through violence. We will therefore prepare ourselves by withdrawing, so far as we can, all voluntary association from the British Government, and will prepare for civil disobedience, including nonpayment of taxes. We are convinced that if we can but withdraw our voluntary help and stop payment of taxes without doing violence, even under provocation, the end of this inhuman rule is assured. We therefore hereby solemnly resolve to carry out the Congress instructions issued from time to time for the purpose of establishing *Purna Swaraj*."[1]

---

[1] Ibid., pp. 388-89.

Independence Day, January 26, 1930 : Approach of Civil Disobedience

Independence Day came, January 26, 1930, and it revealed to us, as in a flash, the earnest and enthusiastic mood of the country. There was something vastly impressive about the great gatherings everywhere, peacefully and solemnly taking the pledge of independence without any speeches or exhortation. This celebration gave the necessary impetus to Gandhiji, and he felt, with his sure touch on the pulse of the people, that the time was ripe for action. Events followed then in quick succession, like a drama working up to its climax.

[Civil] disobedience approached and electrified the atmosphere. . . . The technique was understood to some extent, but more important still from Gandhiji's point of view, it was fully realized by everyone that he was terribly in earnest about nonviolence. There could be no doubt about that now, as there probably was in the minds of some people ten years before. Despite all this, how could we possibly be certain that an outbreak of violence might not occur in some locality either spontaneously or as the result of an intrigue? And, if such an incident occurred, what would be its effect on our civil disobedience movement? Would it be suddenly wound up as before? The prospect was most disconcerting.

Gandhiji probably thought over this question also in his own way, though the problem that seemed to trouble him, as far as I could gather from scraps of conversation, was put differently.

The nonviolent method of action to bring about a change for the better was to him the only right method and, if rightly pursued, an infallible method. Must it be said that this method required a specially favorable atmosphere for its functioning and success, and that it should not be tried if outward conditions were not suited to it? That led to the conclusion that the nonviolent method was not meant for all contingencies, and was thus neither a universal nor an infallible method. This conclusion was intolerable for Gandhiji, for he firmly believed that it was a universal and infallible method. Therefore, necessarily, it must function even though . . . external conditions were unfavorable, and even in the midst of strife and violence. The way of its functioning might be varied to suit varying circumstances, but to stop it would be a confession of failure of the method itself.

Perhaps his mind worked in some such way, but I cannot be sure of his thoughts. He did give us the impression that there was a slightly different orientation to his thinking, and that civil disobedience, when it came, need not be stopped because of a sporadic act of violence. If, however, the violence became in any way part of the movement itself, then it ceased to be a peaceful civil disobedience movement, and its activities had to be curtailed or varied. This assurance went a long way in satisfying many of us. The great question that hung in the air now was—how? How were we to begin? What form of civil disobedience should we take up that would be effective, suited to the circumstances, and popular with the masses? And then the Mahatma gave the hint.

Salt suddenly became a mysterious word, a word of power. The salt tax was to be attacked, the salt laws were to be broken. We were bewildered and could not quite fit in a national struggle with common salt.[1]

3 | Gandhi's Salt March—Gandhi's Influence—Civil Disobedience— Resistance and Arrests

Gandhi's Salt March

[Among the various reforms Gandhi demanded in the early 1930s were such measures as reduction of the land tax, the military budget, the salaries of high officials; an amnesty for political prisoners, and termination of colonial rule in India. He declared that if his requests were not met, civil disobedience would be initiated by way of a pilgrimage, in defiance of the salt tax.

"On March 2, 1930, Gandhi addressed a letter to the Viceroy, enumerating, in brief, the evils of British rule, and intimating his programme of breaking the salt laws . . .: 'The British system seems to be designed to crush the very life out of the *ryot*. Even the salt he must use to live is so taxed as to make the burden fall heaviest on him, if only because of the heartless impartiality of its incidence. The tax shows itself still more burdensome on the poor man, when it is remembered that salt is the one thing he must eat more than the rich man, both individually and collectively.'"[2]]

[1] Ibid., pp. 156–57.
[2] T.T.N., p. 38.

[After] Gandhiji's correspondence with the Viceroy . . . the Dandi Salt March [was undertaken]. . . . As people followed the fortunes of this marching column of pilgrims from day to day, the temperature of the country went up. A meeting of the All-India Congress Committee was held . . . to make final arrangements for the struggle that was now almost upon us. The leader in the struggle was not present, for he was already tramping . . . to the sea, and he refused to return. The All-India Congress Committee planned what should be done in case of arrests, and large powers were given to the president to act on behalf of the Committee, in case it could not meet. . . .

I went to see Gandhiji. He was . . . with his pilgrim band, and we spent a few hours with him . . . and then saw him stride away with his party to the next stage in the journey to the salt sea. That was my last glimpse of him then as I saw him, staff in hand, marching along at the head of his followers, with firm step and a peaceful but undaunted look. It was a moving sight.

April came, and Gandhiji drew near to the sea, and we waited for the word to begin civil disobedience by an attack on the salt laws. For months past we had been drilling our volunteers. . . .

The volunteers had, of course, no arms or even sticks. The object of training them was to make them more efficient in their work and capable of dealing with large crowds. The 6th of April was the first day of the National Week, which is celebrated annually in memory of the happenings in 1919. [See Amritsar Section, Part One]. . . . On that day Gandhiji began the breach of the salt laws at Dandi beach, and three or four days later permission was given to all Congress organizations to do likewise and begin civil disobedience in their own areas.

It seemed as though a spring had been suddenly released; all over the country, in town and village, salt manufacture was the topic of the day, and many curious expedients were adopted to produce salt. We knew precious little about it, and so we read it up where we could and issued leaflets giving directions; we collected pots and pans and ultimately succeeded in producing some unwholesome stuff, which we waved about in triumph and often auctioned for fancy prices. It was really immaterial whether the stuff was good or bad; the main thing was to commit a breach of the obnoxious salt law, and we were successful in that, even though the quality of our salt was poor. As we saw the abounding enthusiasm of the people and the way salt-making was spreading like a prairie fire, we felt a little abashed and ashamed for having questioned the efficacy of this method when it was first proposed by Gandhiji. And we marveled at the amazing knack of the man to impress the multitude and make it act in an organized way.[1]

Gandhi's Influence

How came we to associate ourselves with Gandhiji politically, and to become, in many instances, his devoted followers? The question is hard to answer, and to one who does not know Gandhiji, no answer is likely to satisfy. Personality is an indefinable thing, a strange force that has power over the souls of men, and he possesses this in ample measure, and to all who come to him he often appears in a different aspect. He attracted people, but it was ultimately intellectual conviction that brought them to him and kept them there. They did not agree with his philosophy of life, or even with many of his ideals. Often they did not understand him. But the action that he proposed was something tangible which could be understood and appreciated intellectually. Any action would have been welcome after the long tradition of inaction which our spineless politics had nurtured; brave and effective action with an ethical halo about it had an irresistible appeal, both to the intellect and the emotions. Step by step he convinced us of the rightness of the action, and we went with him, although we did not accept his philosophy. To divorce action from the thought underlying it was not perhaps a proper procedure and was bound to lead to mental conflict and trouble later. Vaguely we hoped that Gandhiji, being essentially a man of action and very sensitive to changing conditions, would advance along the line that seemed to us to be right. And in any event the road he was following was the right one thus far; and, if the future meant a parting, it would be folly to anticipate it.

All this shows that we were by no means clear or certain in our minds. Always we had the feeling that, while we might be more logical, Gandhiji knew India far better than we did, and a man who could command such tremendous devotion and loyalty must have something in him that corresponded to the needs and aspirations of the masses. If we could convince him, we felt that we could also convert these masses. And it seemed possible to convince him; for, in spite of his peasant outlook, he was the born rebel, a revolutionary out for big changes, whom no fear of consequences could stop.

How he disciplined our lazy and demoralized people and made them

[1] T.F., pp. 157, 159–60.

work—not by force or any material inducement, but by a gentle look and a soft word and, above all, by personal example![1]

We felt that through action and self-imposed suffering and sacrifice, through voluntarily facing risk and danger, through refusal to submit to what we considered evil and wrong, we would recharge the battery of India's spirit and waken her from her long slumber. Though we came into conflict continually with the British Government in India, our eyes were always turned toward our own people. Political advantage had value only in so far as it helped in that fundamental purpose of ours. Because of this governing motive, frequently we acted as no politician moving in the narrow sphere of politics, only, would have done, and foreign and Indian critics expressed surprise at the folly and intransigence of our ways. Whether we were foolish or not the historians of the future will judge. We aimed high and looked far. Probably we were often foolish, from the point of view of opportunist politics, but at no time did we forget that our main purpose was to raise the whole level of the Indian people, psychologically and spiritually and also, of course, politically and economically. It was the building up of that real inner strength of the people that we were after, knowing that the rest would inevitably follow. We had to wipe out the evil aftermath from some generations of shameful subservience and timid submission to an arrogant alien authority.[2]

Nineteen-thirty [was] indeed . . . a wonder year for us, and Gandhiji seemed to have changed the face of our country with his magic touch. No one was foolish enough to think that we had triumphed finally over the British Government. Our feeling of elation had little to do with the Government. We were proud of our people, of our womenfolk, of our youth, of our children for the part they had played in the movement. It was a spiritual gain, valuable at any time and to any people, but doubly so to us, a subject and downtrodden people. And we were anxious that nothing should happen to take this away from us.[3]

Civil Disobedience

The civil disobedience movement of 1930 happened to fit in unbeknown to its own leaders at first, with the great world slump in industry and agriculture. The rural masses were powerfully affected by this slump, and

[1] Ibid., p. 191.
[2] D.I., p. 45.
[3] T.F., p. 192.

they turned to the Congress and civil disobedience. For them it was not a matter of a fine constitution drawn up in London or elsewhere, but of a basic change in the land system, especially in the zamindari areas. The zamindari system, indeed, seemed to have outlived its day and had no stability left in it. But the British Government, situated as it was, could not venture to undertake a radical change of this land system. Even when it had appointed the Royal Agricultural Commission, the terms of reference to it barred a discussion of the question of ownership of land or the system of land tenure.

The British Government, like most governments I suppose, has an idea that much of the trouble in India is due to "agitators". It is a singularly inept notion. India has had a great leader during the past fifteen years who has won the affection and even adoration of her millions and has seemed to impose his will on her in many ways. He has played a vitally important part in her recent history, and yet more important than he were the people themselves who seemed to follow blindly his behests. The people were the principal actors, and behind them, pushing them on, were great historical urges which prepared them and made them ready to listen to their leader's piping. But for that historical setting and political and social urges, no leaders or agitators could have inspired them to action. It was Gandhiji's chief virtue as a leader that he could instinctively feel the pulse of the people and know when conditions were ripe for growth and action.

In 1930 the national movement in India fitted in for a while with the growing social forces of the country, and because of this a great power came to it, a sense of reality, as if it were indeed marching step by step with history. The Congress represented that national movement, and this power and strength were reflected in the growth of Congress prestige. This was something vague, incalculable, indefinable, but nevertheless very much present. The peasantry, of course, turned to the Congress and gave it its real strength; the lower middle-class formed the backbone of its fighting ranks. Even the upper *bourgeoisie*, troubled by this new atmosphere, thought it safer to be friendly with the Congress. The great majority of the textile mills in India signed undertakings prescribed by the Congress and were afraid of doing things which might bring on them the displeasure of the Congress. . . .

This vague sense of a dual authority growing in the country was naturally most irritating to the Government. The sense of conflict grew, and we could feel the hardening on the side of Government.[1]

[1] Ibid., pp. 205–06.

Resistance and Arrests

The breach of the Salt Act soon became just one activity, and civil resistance spread to other fields. This was facilitated by the promulgation of various ordinances by the Viceroy prohibiting a number of activities. As these ordinances and prohibitions grew, the opportunities for breaking them also grew, and civil resistance took the form of doing the very thing that the ordinance was intended to stop. The initiative definitely remained with the Congress and the people; and, as each ordinance law failed to control the situation from the point of view of government, fresh ordinances were issued by the Viceroy. Many of the Congress Working Committee members had been arrested, but it continued to function with new members added on to it, and each official ordinance was countered by a resolution of the Working Committee giving directions as to how to meet it. These directions were carried out with surprising uniformity all over [India]—with one exception, the one relating to the publication of newspapers.

When an ordinance was issued for the further control of the press and the demand of security from newspapers, the Working Committee called upon the nationalist press to refuse to give any security, and to stop publication instead. This was a hard pill to swallow for the newspapermen, for just then the public demand for news was very great. Still the great majority of newspapers—some Moderate papers excepted—stopped publication, with the result that all manner of rumors began to spread. But they could not hold out for long; the temptation was too great, and the sight of their Moderate rivals picking up their business too irritating. So most of them drifted back to publication.

Gandhiji [was] arrested on May 5. After his arrest big raids on the salt pans and depots were organized on the west coast. There were very painful incidents of police brutality during these raids.[1]

During the second civil disobedience movement of 1930 the response from the Moslems was very considerable, though less than in 1920–23.[2]

[Typical of the directives Nehru issued during the Salt March campaign, was one on "Defence in Political Cases", which fell into the hands of the authorities.] If volunteers are arrested for civil disobedience, it is clear that there can be no question of offering defence. . . . [They] should

[1] Ibid., p. 162.
[2] D.I., p. 385.

take up a dignified attitude in court ... [and] give no information. ...
Our very creed at present is sedition and there can be no denial of this.[1]

4 | Fourth Arrest—Observations on Civil Liberties, from Prison—From Introspective Reveries in Jail— Sapru-Jayakar Proposals—Further Observations on Events of 1930

Fourth Arrest

[At a meeting of the All-India Congress Committee held during the
third week of March, 1930, Jawaharlal was empowered, as Congress
President, to act on its behalf to nominate his successor, and to fill
vacancies in the Working Committee. As the "most exposed person" in
Congress, and as one of the most energetic coordinators of the Salt
March Campaign, he was arrested on April 14 for violating the Salt Law
while on his way to attend a conference. Tried the same day in jail, he
was sentenced to six months' confinement in Central Prison, Naini.
Jawaharlal nominated Motilal to be "acting president" of Congress in
his absence.]

Those were days of stirring news—processions and lathee charges and
firing, frequent *hartals* to celebrate noted arrests, and special obser-
vances. ... For the time being the boycott of foreign cloth and all British
goods was almost complete.[2]

[During the court proceedings against Jawaharlal, in conjunction with
the Salt March of 1930, the magistrate asked him whether he wished to
plead guilty or not guilty. J.N.: "May I know what [this] is, a public ...
or a private trial?"
    Magistrate: "All the members of your family have been permitted to

[1] Quoted in M.B., p. 151.
[2] T.F., p. 160.

attend the court, and the representatives of the press, but not the public in general."

J.N.: "I do not propose to take part in the trial at any time. But quite apart from the trial, I have stated on many occasions and I am prepared to state for your information that I have deliberately broken the salt law."

The Magistrate later questioned a witness. "[Did Pandit Nehru himself make salt on a piece of paper or did] somebody else [give] it to him in a packet?"

Witness: "Pandit Nehru had himself made pieces of paper for making packets of salt. This process was repeated three times."

Magistrate: "What did Pandit Nehru do?"

Witness: "He helped the volunteers by telling them if the salt was ready . . . and also scraped the salt. . . ."

Referring to the material with which salt was prepared, the magistrate asked the witness, "What was this deposit?"

Witness: "This deposit was a saline substance composed of earth, saltpetre and salt."

Magistrate: "Did you see this deposit in your hand and examine it? How do you say that it was a combination of these three things?"

Witness: "I saw the deposit and from its colour I thought that it was composed of these three things."

"The Magistrate was satisfied that a case for conviction under [a] section . . . of the Salt Act had been made out."[1]

"Early in June the Viceroy [Lord Irwin] informed the Secretary of State in London: 'All thinking Indians deeply resent [what they regard as our assumption of racial superiority], and they passionately want substantial advance which will give them power to manage their own affairs. . . . I think every European and Indian would tell you that he was surprised at the dimensions the [Salt March—Civil Disobedience] Movement . . . assumed. I certainly am myself—and we should delude ourselves if we sought to underrate it.'"[2]

Observations on Civil Liberties, from Prison

[It was at Jawaharlal's insistence that a Civil Liberties Union was founded in India in the thirties.]

When the most ordinary civil liberties have been curtailed in India, it is hardly pertinent to talk of a prisoner's rights. And yet the subject is worthy of consideration. If a court of law sentences a person to imprisonment, does it follow that not only his body but also his mind should be

[1] T.T.N., pp. 40–41.
[2] Quoted in M.B., p. 153.

8+N.

incarcerated? Why should not the minds of prisoners be free even if their bodies are not? Those in charge of the prison administrations in India will no doubt be horrified at such a question, for their capacity for new ideas and sustained thought is usually limited. Censorship is bad enough at any time and is partisan and stupid. In India it deprives us of a great deal of modern literature and advanced journals and newspapers. The list of proscribed books is extensive and is frequently added to. To add to all this, the prisoner has to suffer a second and separate censorship, and thus many books and newspapers that can be legally purchased and read outside the prison may not reach him. . . .

It is a little absurd to discuss this question of freedom of mind in prison in India when, as it happens, the vast majority of the prisoners are not allowed any newspapers or writing materials. It is not a question of censorship but of total denial. Only A-Class prisoners are allowed writing materials as a matter of course, and not even all these are allowed daily newspapers. The daily newspaper allowed is of the Government's choice. For the rest, the nine hundred and ninety-nine in every thousand, two or three books are permitted at a time, but conditions are such that they cannot always take advantage of this privilege. Writing or the taking of notes on books read are dangerous pastimes in which they must not indulge. This deliberate discouragement of intellectual development is curious and revealing. From the point of view of reclaiming a prisoner and of making him a fit citizen, his mind should be approached and diverted, and he should be made literate and taught some craft. But this point of view has perhaps not struck the prison authorities in India.[1]

As I watched the working of an Indian prison, it struck me that it was not unlike the British government of India. There is great efficiency in the apparatus of government, which goes to strengthen the hold of the Government on the country, and little or no care for the human material of the country. Outwardly the prison must appear efficiently run, and to some extent this was true. But no one seemed to think that the main purpose of the prison must be to improve and help the unhappy individuals who come to it. Break them!—that is the idea, so that by the time they go out, they may not have the least bit of spirit left in them. And how is the prison controlled, and the convicts kept in check and punished? Very largely with the help of the convicts themselves, some of whom are made convict warders (C.W.'s) or convict overseers (C.O.'s), and are induced to co-operate with the authorities because of fear, and

[1] T.F., pp. 7–8.

in the hope of rewards and special remissions. There are relatively few paid non-convict warders; most of the guarding inside the prison is done by convict warders and C.O.'s. A widespread system of spying pervades the prison, convicts being encouraged to become stool pigeons and to spy on one another; and no combination or joint action is, of course, permitted among the prisoners. This is easy to understand, for only by keeping them divided up could they be kept in check.

Outside, in the government of our country, we see much the same, on a larger, though less obvious, scale. But there the C.W.'s or C.O.'s are known differently. They have impressive titles, and their liveries of office are more gorgeous. And behind them, as in prison, stands the armed guard with weapons ever ready to enforce conformity.

How important and essential is a prison to the modern State! The prisoner at least begins to think so, and the numerous administrative and other functions of the Government appear almost superficial before the basic functions of the prison, the police, the army.[1]

From time to time the prisoner's body is weighed and measured. But how is one to weigh the mind and the spirit which wilt and stunt themselves and wither away in this terrible atmosphere of oppression?[2]

[During his imprisonment in 1930, Jawaharlal "begged his father not to send him fruit or ice; he could not, he wrote, 'hold high festival in gaol, when imprisonment, floggings, firings and martial law are the lot of those outside'".[3]]

From Introspective Reveries in Jail

[The] shouting crowds, the dull and wearying public functions, the interminable arguments, and the dust and tumble of politics [have] touched me on the surface only, though sometimes the touch was sharp and pointed. My real conflict lay within me, a conflict of ideas, desires, and loyalties, of subconscious depths struggling with outer circumstances, of an inner hunger unsatisfied. I became a battleground, where various forces struggled for mastery. I sought an escape from this; I tried to find harmony and equilibrium, and in this attempt I rushed into action. That gave me some peace; outer conflict relieved the strain of the inner struggle.

[1] Ibid., pp. 170–71.
[2] Quoted in C.D.N., p. 9.
[3] T.N., p. 331.

Why am I writing all this sitting here in prison? The quest is still the same, in prison or outside, and I write down my past feelings and experiences in the hope that this may bring me some peace and psychic satisfaction.[1]

I have been fortunate in . . . the possession of family members . . . friends . . . comrades, who have helped me to retain a proper perspective and not to lose my mental equilibrium. Public functions, addresses by municipalities, local boards, and other public bodies, processions, and the like, used to be a great strain on my nerves and my sense of humor and reality. The most extravagant and pompous language would be used, and everybody would look so solemn and pious that I felt an almost uncontrollable desire to laugh, or to stick out my tongue, or stand on my head, just for the pleasure of shocking and watching the reactions on the faces at that august assembly! Fortunately for my reputation and for the sober respectability of public life in India, I have suppressed this mad desire and usually behaved with due propriety. But not always. Sometimes there has been an exhibition on my part in a crowded meeting, or more often in processions, which I find extraordinarily trying. I have suddenly left a procession, arranged in our honor, and disappeared in the crowd, leaving my wife or some other person to carry on, perched up in a car or carriage, with that procession.

This continuous effort to suppress one's feelings and behave in public is a bit of a strain, and the usual result is that one puts on a glum and solid look on public occasions.[2]

Sapru-Jayakar Proposals: Attempt to Restore Peaceful Conditions in India

[The following letter refers to Jawaharlal's objections to an attempt made by two distinguished but, for him, too moderate, nationalist leaders—Sir Tej Bahadur Sapru and Mr M. R. Jayakar—to restore "peaceful conditions in the country" during 1930. Jawaharlal considered their recommendations toward this end far too conciliatory, hence potentially damaging to the freedom movement.

On July 27 and 28, Sir Tej and Mr Jayakar visited Motilal (who also was imprisoned during 1930) and Jawaharlal in Naini Jail, to discuss their proposal. Gandhi was in Yeravda Jail, Poona, at the time.]

[1] T.F., p. 155.
[2] Ibid., p. 154.

[Jawaharlal to Gandhi, from Central Prison, Naini—July 28, 1930.] Father and I entirely agree with you that we can be "no parties to any truce which would undo the position at which we have arrived today". It is because of this that fullest consideration is essential before any final decision is arrived at. I must confess I do not see an appreciable advance yet from the other side and I greatly fear a false or weak move on our part. I am expressing myself moderately. For myself I delight in warfare. It makes me feel that I am alive. Events of the last four months in India have gladdened my heart and have made me prouder of Indian men, women and even children [than] I have ever been, but I realize that most people are not warlike and like peace and so I try hard to suppress myself and take a peaceful view. May I congratulate you on the new India you have created by your magic touch! What the future will bring I know not but the past has made life worth living and our prosaic existence has developed something of epic greatness in it. Sitting here in Naini Jail, I have pondered on the wonderful efficacy of non-violence as a weapon and have become a greater convert with [a greater convert's response] than ever before. I hope you are not dissatisfied with the response of the country to the non-violence creed. Despite occasional lapses, the country has stuck to it wonderfully, certainly far more grimly than I had expected.[1]

Further Observations on Events of 1930

[The] year 1930 was full of dramatic situations and inspiring happenings. . . . Peaceful civil disobedience as a technique of action for achieving great national ends seemed to have justified itself, and a quiet confidence grew in the country, shared by friend and opponent alike, that we were marching toward victory. A strange excitement filled those who were active in the movement, and some of this even crept inside the jail. "*Swaraj* is coming!" said the ordinary convicts; and they waited impatiently for it, in the selfish hope that it might do them some good. The warders, coming in contact with the gossip of the bazaars, also expected that *Swaraj* was near; the petty jail official grew a little more nervous.

We had no daily newspapers in prison, but a Hindi weekly brought us some news, and often this news would set our imaginations afire. Daily lathee charges, sometimes firing, martial law . . . with sentences of ten

[1] H.I.N.C. (Vol. I), First Edition, Appendix, p. xxx.

years for carrying the national flag. We felt proud of our people, and especially of our womenfolk, all over the country.

The thought that I was having a relatively easy time in prison, at a time when others were facing danger and suffering outside, began to oppress me. I longed to go out; and, as I could not do that, I made my life in prison a hard one, full of work. I used to spin daily for nearly three hours on my own *charkha*; for another two or three hours I did *newar* weaving, which I had especially asked for from the jail authorities. I liked these activities. They kept me occupied without undue strain or requiring too much attention, and they soothed the fever of my mind. I read a great deal, and otherwise busied myself with cleaning up, washing my clothes, etc. The manual labor I did was of my own choice, as my imprisonment was "simple." [1]

[During 1930, Motilal's health began steadily to fail while he was confined in jail. When he was finally released on the advice of doctors in September, his end was near.]

| 5 | Release from Jail and Fresh Conviction—
No Tax Campaign and Fifth
Imprisonment—
Statements at Time of Trial, 1930 |

Release from Jail and Fresh Conviction

[To Jawaharlal from his wife, Kamala, September, 1930: "The day of your release is approaching, but I am doubtful if you would be set free. And even if you are, you will again be put behind . . . bars. But I am prepared for everything. . . . How I wish I were arrested before you come out!" [2]

[1] T.F., pp. 169–70.
[2] T.N., p. 336.

During the last week of September 1930, the Director of the Intelligence Bureau penned the following note: "'I suggest that the Home Department should at once consult the U.P. [United Provinces, where Jawaharlal lived] as to the desirability of allowing this irreconcilable [fellow] at large to stir up mischief all over again.' The Secretary of the Home Department agreed to suggest that a letter be written to the Governor of the U.P., 'expressing the hope that the first opportunity will be taken to put Jawahar Lal out of harm's way.'" [1]

Nehru was released from prison on October 11, 1930, at the end of his six months' sentence, whereupon he was almost immediately convicted for a speech made on October 12 in Allahabad, in favor of a no-tax campaign. "On the very day I was discharged one or two more ordinances were announced. I was glad to be out [of jail] and eager to do something effective during my short spell of freedom." [2]

Jawaharlal's subsequent prosecution was initiated on October 19, barely a week after he had left jail. His sentence rendered, he found himself in Naini Prison once more, where he was confined until January 26, 1931. Together with other nationalists, he was purportedly to be released on the latter date so that consultation might be facilitated among Congress leaders, in order to work out an accord with the British.]

No Tax Campaign and Fifth Imprisonment

The great question before us [at the time of my fifth imprisonment] . . . was whether a no-tax campaign in the rural areas should be started or not. The time for rent collection and payment of revenue was close at hand, and, in any event, collections were going to be difficult because of the tremendous fall in the prices of agricultural produce. The world slump was now very evident in India.

It seemed an ideal opportunity for a no-tax campaign, both as a part of the general civil disobedience movement and, independently, on its own merits. It was manifestly impossible both for landlords and tenants to pay up the full demand out of that year's produce. They had to fall back on old reserves, if they had any, or borrow. The zamindars usually had something to fall back upon, or could borrow more easily. The average tenant, always on the verge of destitution and starvation, had nothing to fall back upon. In any democratic country, or where the agriculturists were properly organized and had influence, it would have been quite impossible, under those circumstances, to make them pay much. In India their influence was negligible, except in so far as the Congress, in some parts of the country, stood for them; and except, of

[1] Quoted in M.B., p. 160.
[2] T.F., p. 174.

course, for the ever-present fear of peasant risings when the situation
became intolerable for them. But they had become accustomed for
generations past to stand almost anything without much murmuring.

When I came out of jail in October, both political and economic conditions seemed to me to be crying out for a no-tax campaign in rural
areas. The economic difficulties of the agriculturists were obvious enough.
Politically, our civil disobedience activities, though still flourishing everywhere, were getting a bit stale. People went on going to jail in small
numbers, and sometimes in large groups, but the sting had gone from
the atmosphere. The cities and the middle classes were a bit tired of the
hartals and processions. Obviously something was needed to liven things
up, a fresh infusion of blood was necessary. Where could this come from
except from the peasantry?—and the reserve stocks there were enormous.
It would again become a mass movement touching the vital interests of the
masses and, what was to me very important, would raise social issues. . . .

We decided to convene a representative *kisan* or peasants' conference
of the district a week later, to give the new campaign a push. I felt that
I had done a good first day's work after release from jail. I added to it a
big mass meeting in Allahabad city, where I spoke at length. It was for
this speech that I was subsequently convicted again. . . .

I was tried in prison on a number of charges, all based on various parts
of that one speech I had delivered at Allahabad, the day after my discharge. As usual with us, I did not defend myself, but made a brief statement in court. I was sentenced for sedition under Section 124A to eighteen
months' rigorous imprisonment and a fine of five hundred rupees; under
the Salt Act of 1882 to six months and a fine of one hundred rupees; . . .
under Ordinance VI of 1930 (I forget what this ordinance was about)
also to six months and a fine of one hundred rupees. As the last two were
concurrent, the total sentence was two years' rigorous imprisonment and,
in addition, five months in default of fines. This was my fifth term.[1]

Statements at Time of Trial, 1930

[From statement before trial in Naini Central Prison—October 24,
1930.] The honour of arrest has again been accorded to me. I am about
to stand my trial and have no doubt that I shall be convicted for the fifth
time. That honour is always welcome. . . .

[1] T.F., pp. 175–77.

I have been arrested principally for my part in inaugurating a no-tax campaign in my province. I trust that the United Provinces will answer the challenge and I will carry this campaign from village to village and town to town. . . . I trust also that other provinces will do likewise. The freedom we seek is the freedom from all exploitation of the peasant and the worker. Let this message of freedom be carried to field and factory, and together let all of us face and overthrow the imperialism which dominates over us and exploits us.

Be of good cheer, comrades, for the day of our deliverance approaches. And if in the great struggle we lose our property and our belongings, why, then we shall be the lighter and more unencumbered and can march the more swiftly to our goal. In a long and difficult journey often one has to leave one's baggage behind.

Keep smiling! Let the enemy lose his temper and his composure. He has reason to, for defeat approaches him. But we know that we are in the right and we are going to win. Why should we not smile even though the fight rages fiercely and clouds occasionally darken the horizon? Behind the clouds lies the sun of freedom and presently it will break through the mists and vapours and rejuvenate us with its life-giving energy.

[From statement at time of trial—Naini Central Jail, October 24, 1930.] For the fifth time I have been arrested and charged with various crimes by the officials of the British Government. For the fifth time, I have no doubt I shall be convicted. I have so far taken no part in this trial and I desire to take none. But I wish to say a few words so that those who are trying me today, and my own people, who have honoured me beyond measure, may have a glimpse of what [is] . . . in my heart.

I am charged with sedition and with the spreading of disaffection against the British Government. Eight and a half years ago I was charged with a similar offence and I stated then that sedition against the present Government in India had become the creed of the Indian people, and to preach and practise disaffection against the evil which it represents had become their chief occupation. For the Indian people had come to realize that there could be no freedom for them, no lessening of the terrible exploitation which has crushed the life out of millions, till British rule was removed from India. Since this realisation came upon me in all its tragic intensity, I have had no other profession, no other business, no other aim than to fight British imperialism and to drive it from India.

On the first day of this year the . . . Congress finally resolved to achieve the independence of India, and on the 26th of January the Indian people

8*

pledged themselves in their millions to put an end to British rule in India. They declared the age-long right of a people to subvert any government which had mis-governed and crushed them, and they charged the British Government with having exploited them ruthlessly and done . . . almost irreparable injury politically, economically, culturally and spiritually. Since that pledge was taken, there can be no willing submission of any Indian to British authority, no recognition by him of British rule. . . . If a few . . . side with the enemy or parley with him while the fight is in progress, it is a terrible measure of the spiritual injury caused by British rule, making [such individuals] kiss the rod that smites them and hug the very chains that bind [them]. Some . . . misguided and erring countrymen of ours have chosen to desert the motherland in her hour of need and talk of compromises with British imperialism. But the country has chosen another path under the guidance and inspiration of our great leader, and that path it will pursue till success comes to it. There can be no compromise between freedom and slavery, and between truth and falsehood. We realise that the price of freedom is blood and suffering—the blood of our own countrymen and the suffering of the noblest in the land—and that price we shall pay in full measure.

Already the world is witness to the sacrifice and suffering of our people at the altar of freedom, to the wonderful courage of our women, and to the indomitable spirit of our brave peasantry. Strong in the faith with which our leader has inspired them, with confidence in themselves and in their great cause, they have willingly set aside their material pleasures and belongings, and written a stirring and . . . shining chapter in India's long history. And the world has also seen how our peaceful struggle is sought to be crushed by frightfulness, and methods of barbarism which have earned for the British Government in India a comparison with the Huns of old. Unlike the Huns, however, they have added insult to deep injury and have sought, after the manner of their kind, to cover their deeds of frightfulness with a cloak of piety and [sanctity]. Fearful of exposure, they have sought to suppress truth in every way. Those whom the gods [wish] to destroy, they first drive mad, and all the mad deeds which the British Government has done in India during the last seven months—desperate devices of a tottering empire—are visible emblems of the crash to come.

We have no quarrel with [the] English people, much less with the English worker. Like us, [they have themselves] been the [victims] of imperialism, and it is against this imperialism that we fight. With it there can be no compromise. To this imperialism, or to England, we owe no allegiance, and the flag of England in India is an insult to every Indian. The British Government today is an enemy for us, a foreign usurping power holding on to India with the help of their army of occupation. My allegiance is to the Indian people, and to no king [or] foreign government. I am a servant of the Indian people, and I recognise no other master.

The end of our struggle approaches and the British Empire will soon go the way of all the Empires of . . . old. The strangling and the degradation of India has gone on long enough. It will be tolerated no longer, and let England and the world take notice that the people of India are prepared to be friends with all who meet them frankly as equals and do not interfere with their freedom. But they will be no friends with such as seek to interfere with their liberties or to exploit the peasant or the worker. Nor will they tolerate in future the humbug and hypocrisy which has been doled out to them in such ample measure [in] England.

To the Indian people I cannot express my gratitude sufficiently for their confidence and affection. It has been the greatest joy in my life to serve in this glorious struggle and to do my little bit for this cause. I pray that my countrymen and countrywomen will carry on the good fight unceasingly till success crowns their effort and we realise the India of our dreams.[1]

[When Jawaharlal was brought before the magistrate for trial on October 24, 1930, one of his speeches, for which he had been arrested, "as transcribed by a reporter of the intelligence department from his shorthand notes, was read out to him. The speech . . . made in Hindustani . . . was rendered into English by court officials. . . . When the reading was over, the magistrate interrogated Nehru: 'Did you . . . deliver the speech read out to you?'

"A. 'I am not taking any particular part in these proceedings. I do not congratulate this gentleman (witness) on his power of reporting. Probably the speech was above him. I consider myself a far better speaker than he makes me out to be.'"[2]

"The reimprisonment of Jawaharlal so soon after his release angered his father and infused the flagging civil disobedience campaign with new vigour. Despite his grave illness, Motilal rose from his sick-bed, determined to 'avenge' this action of the *Raj*. Aside from providing leadership to his colleagues, he organized 'Jawahar Day' on 14 November, [1930] the date of his son's forty-first birthday. All over India the Congress held public meetings at which were read those portions of [Jawaharlal's]

[1] B.S.W.J.N., pp. 31–34.
[2] T.T.N., p. 50.

original speech which had caused his rearrest. To [Jawaharlal himself] it
was a 'unique birthday celebration', for about five thousand persons
were arrested. . . . Another source of pride was the news of Kamala's
arrest on 1 January, 1931. 'It was a pleasant New Year's gift for me', he
wrote. . . . Although concerned about his wife's health, he was delighted
that Kamala had attained the goal of all *satyagrahis*—imprisonment. He
was especially touched by her parting message to nationalist women: 'I
am happy beyond measure and proud to follow in the footsteps of my
husband. I hope the people will keep the flag flying.'" [1]]

	1930 Round Table Conference—
6	Release From Jail—Independence Day,
	1931—Death of Motilal Nehru

1930 Round Table Conference

["British officialdom, realizing the futility of a further approach through
an all-British parliamentary commission, assembled the leading Indian
princes and political leaders in London in 1930–1932 for three round-
table conferences after publication of the report of the Simon Commission." [2]

Jawaharlal was in jail when the first Round Table Conference met in
London on November 12, 1930, to discuss possible changes in the manner
in which India was to be governed in the future. Since the recent Simon
Commission Report had concerned itself merely with changes at the
provincial, rather than the central level, and Jawaharlal felt that subsequent deliberations of the London Conference would have but little more
significance than the Simon Report, he had virtually no interest in its
proceedings. In his view the composition of the group conferring in
Britain left much to be desired. It seemed odd and inconsistent to him
also that the British should hold its London conference while simultaneously adopting repressive measures within India, including promulgation of drastic ordinances to suppress the Civil Disobedience
Movement.]

[The] last days of the first [London] Round Table Conference . . . we

[1] Quoted in M.B., p. 162.
[2] I.P.C., p. 170.

were a little amused—and I am afraid our amusement had a touch of disdain in it. In the hour of our country's sorest trial, and when our men and women had behaved so wonderfully, there were some of our country-men who were prepared to ignore our struggle and give their moral support to the other side. It became clearer to us than it had been before how, under the deceptive cover of nationalism, conflicting economic interests were at work, and how these with vested interests were trying to preserve them for the future in the name of this very nationalism. The Round Table Conference was an obvious collection of these vested interests.

We did not really mind or care what the Round Table Conference did. It was far away, unreal and shadowy, and the struggle lay [in India] in our towns and villages. We had no illusions about the speedy termination of our struggle or about the dangers ahead, and yet the events of 1930 had given us a certain confidence in our national strength and stamina, and with that confidence we faced the future.

What filled our minds most was the approach of January 26, the first anniversary of Independence Day, and we wondered how this would be celebrated. It was observed, as we learned subsequently, all over the country by the holding of mass meetings which confirmed the resolution of independence, and passed an identical resolution called the "Resolution of Remembrance". The organization of this celebration was a remarkable feat, for newspapers and printing presses were not available, nor could the post or telegraph be utilized. And yet an identical resolution, in the particular language of the province concerned, was passed at large gatherings held at more or less the same times at innumerable places, urban and rural, throughout the country. Most of these gatherings were held in defiance of the law and were forcibly dispersed by the police.[1]

While people argued fine legal points in London . . . the reality of power seemed to be slowly and imperceptibly flowing toward the Congress as representing the people.[2]

Release from Jail

["At first no progress was made [at the 1930 Round Table Conference], particularly on the vexed issue of communal representation, as the Hindu Mahasabha and Muslim parties clung to their fixed positions. It seemed

[1] T.F., pp. 182–83.
[2] Ibid., pp. 205–06.

as if the search for a suitable basis of constitutional reform was doomed to failure. However, at the beginning of January 1931, the deadlock was broken by Sir Tej Bahadur Sapru's proposal for responsible self-government in an All-India Federation with appropriate safeguards in the transition period. To the surprise of most, the [Indian] Princes indicated a willingness to join such a federation, and British Liberal and Labour spokesmen approved the scheme.

"The communal representation had not been resolved, but enough progress had been made to adjourn the proceedings—in the hope that the Congress could be induced to abandon civil disobedience and cooperate in the plan. Thus, on 19 January 1931, Prime Minister Ramsay MacDonald declared that the British Government was prepared to recognize the all-important principle of Executive responsibility to the Legislature, except for the safeguards, notably defence, external affairs, the maintenance of tranquility in the realm, and the guarantee of financial stability. Exactly one week later, ironically on the first anniversary of the Congress 'Independence Day', the Viceroy passed the burden of decision to the Congress by releasing Gandhi and nineteen members of the Working Committee [from jail, including Jawaharlal]." [1]

Independence Day, 1931

[On the first anniversary of Independence Day, a Resolution of Remembrance was adopted—January 26, 1931.] "We ... record our proud and grateful appreciation of the sons and daughters of India who have taken part in the great struggle for independence and have suffered and sacrificed so that the motherland may be free; of our great and beloved leader, Mahatma Gandhi, who has been a constant inspiration for us, ever pointing to the path of high purpose and noble endeavour; of the hundreds of our brave youths who have laid down their lives at the altar of freedom ... of the scores of thousands who have faced and suffered barbarous lathi attacks from the forces of the enemy; of ... Indians in the military and the police ranks of the Government, who have refused, at the peril of their own lives, to fire or take other action against their own countrymen; of ... the brave and long-suffering peasantry ... of India, which has taken full part in the struggle despite every effort to suppress it; of the merchants and other members of the commercial community, who have helped, at great loss to themselves, in the national struggle and especially in the boycotts of foreign cloth and British goods; of the one hundred thousand men and women who have gone to the prisons and suffered all manner of privation and sometimes assaults and beatings even inside the gaol walls; and especially of the ordinary volunteer who, like a true soldier of India, without care of fame or reward, thinking only of the great cause he served, has laboured unceasingly and peacefully through suffering and hardship.

[1] M.B., p. 167.

"And we record our homage and deep admiration for the womanhood of India. . . .

"Further, we record our grateful appreciation of the fact that all the major and minor communities and classes in India have joined together in the great struggle and given of their best to the cause; of, particularly, the minority communities—the Muslims, Sikhs, Parsis, Christians and others who, by their valour and loyal devotion to the cause of the common motherland, have helped in building up a united and indissoluble nation, certain of victory, and resolved to achieve and maintain the independence of India, and to use this new freedom to raise the shackles from, and to remove the inequalities among, all classes of the people of India, and thus also to serve the larger cause of humanity. And with this splendid and inspiring example of sacrifice and suffering in India's cause before us, we repeat our Pledge of Independence, and resolve to carry on the fight till India is completely free." [1]

Death of Motilal Nehru

[From the time of Jawaharlal's fifth arrest in October, 1930, Motilal's health had begun steadily to deteriorate.]

On the 12th of January [1931, my father] came to see me in Naini [jail]. I saw him after nearly two months, and I had a shock which I could conceal with difficulty. He seemed to be unaware of the dismay that his appearance had produced in me, and told me that he was much better than he had lately been. . . . His face was swollen, and he seemed to think that this was due to some temporary cause.

That face of his haunted me. It was so utterly unlike him. For the first time a fear began to creep in my mind that there was real danger for him ahead. I had always associated him with strength and health, and I could not think of death in connection with him. He had always laughed at the idea of death, made fun of it, and told us that he proposed to live for a further long term of years. Latterly I had noticed that whenever an old friend of his youth died, he had a sense of loneliness, of being left by himself in strange company, and even a hint of an approaching end. But generally this mood passed, and his overflowing vitality asserted itself; we of his family had grown so used to his rich personality and the all-embracing warmth of his affection that it was difficult for us to think of the world without him.

I was troubled by that look of his, and my mind was full of forebodings. Yet I did not think that any danger to him lay in the near future. . . .

[1] J.N.A., pp. 615–16.

[On] January 26, [1931] . . . I was told suddenly that . . . father's condition was serious and that I must go home immediately. On inquiry, I was informed that I was being discharged [from jail]. . . .

That [same] evening, many other persons were discharged from various prisons throughout India. These were the original and substitute members of the Congress Working Committee. The Government was giving us a chance to meet and consider the [current] situation. So, in any event, I would have been discharged that evening. Father's condition hastened my release by a few hours. . . .

On January 26, the same day that I was discharged, Gandhiji was also discharged from Yeravda Prison. I was anxious to have him in Allahabad, and, when I mentioned his release to father, I found that he was eager to see him. The very next day Gandhiji started from Bombay after a stupendous . . . meeting of welcome . . . such as even Bombay had not seen before. He arrived at Allahabad late at night, but father was lying awake, waiting for him, and his presence and the few words he uttered had a markedly soothing effect on father. To my mother also his coming brought solace and relief. . . .

As I watched [my father, when many of his colleagues came to visit him] I wondered what thoughts passed through his head, or whether he was past taking interest in our activities. He was evidently often struggling with himself, trying to keep a grip of things which threatened to slip away from his grasp. To the end this struggle continued, and he did not give in, occasionally speaking to us with extreme clarity. Even when a constriction in his throat made it difficult for him to make himself understood, he took to writing on slips of paper what he wanted to say. . . .

[On] February 6, I was watching by his bedside. He had had a troublesome and restless night; suddenly I noticed that his face grew calm and the sense of struggle vanished from it. I thought that he had fallen asleep, and I was glad of it. But my mother's perceptions were keener, and she uttered a cry. I turned to her and begged her not to disturb him as he had fallen asleep. But that sleep was his last long sleep, and from it there was no awakening. . . .

I was dazed all that day, hardly realizing what had happened, and a succession of events and large crowds kept me from thinking. . . . As evening fell on the river bank on that winter day, the great flames leaped up and consumed that body which had meant so much to us who were close to him as well as to millions in India. Gandhiji said a few moving words to the multitude, and then all of us crept silently home. The stars were out and shining brightly when we returned, lonely and desolate.[1]

[After Motilal's death, when asked to describe his greatest quality, Gandhi declared: "'Love of his son.' 'Was it not love of India?' the Mahatma was asked. 'No', he replied, 'Motilal's love for India was derived from his love for Jawaharlal.'"[2]]

7 | The Delhi Pact

[After the failure of the 1930 Round Table Conference to come to decisions of any consequence; after the Civil Disobedience Movement was in jeopardy, and a truce with the *Raj* had been effected (the latter a major defeat in the eyes of Jawaharlal), Gandhi conferred with the Viceroy, Lord Irwin, during February and March, 1931. (Nehru: "The civil disobedience movement was still going on, though it had toned down because there was much talk of *pourparlers* with Government".[3])

As a result of the Gandhi-Irwin talks, an agreement was reached to be known as the Delhi Pact. According to the pact, civil disobedience was to be called off, prisoners released, and salt manufacture permitted on the coast. Congress would attend the next Round Table Conference in London, but neither independence nor dominion status was assured.[4]

The Delhi Pact, ratified at the Karachi Congress session of March, 1931, initially dismayed Nehru: "We should not have agreed [to suspension of civil disobedience]. It will demoralize our Movement."[5] Clause 2 (described below) especially disturbed him. Finally, however, he consented to move the resolution accepting the Pact.]

Gandhi had frequent interviews with [the Viceroy] Lord Irwin, but sometimes there was a gap of three or four days [between their talks] probably because the Government of India was communicating with the India Office in London. Sometimes apparently small matters or even certain

[1] T.F., pp. 181–85.
[2] T.N., p. 343.
[3] T.F., p. 187.
[4] L.M.G., p. 283.
[5] M.B., p. 173.

words would hold up progress. One such word was "suspension" of civil disobedience. Gandhiji had all along made it clear that civil disobedience could not be finally stopped or given up, as it was the only weapon in the hands of the people. It could, however, be suspended. Lord Irwin objected to this word and wanted finality about [it], to which Gandhiji would not agree. Ultimately the word "discontinued" was used.[1]

[Later—of the Delhi Pact.] Two matters interested me above all others. One was that our objective of independence should in no way be toned down, and the second was the effect of the [Delhi] settlement on our United Provinces agrarian situation. . . . The peasants were unable to pay the taxes demanded by the Government. . . .

I saw in . . . Clause 2 of the settlement [dated March 5, 1931] that [independence] . . . seemed to be jeopardized. Was it for this that our people had behaved so gallantly for a year? Were all our brave words and deeds to end in this? The independence resolution of the Congress, the pledge of January 26, so often repeated? . . .[2]

[Clause 2 of the Delhi Pact stated: "As regards constitutional questions, the scope of future discussion is stated, with the assent of His Majesty's Government, to be with the object of considering further the scheme for the constitutional Government of India discussed at the Round Table Conference. Of the scheme there outlined, Federation is an essential part; so also are Indian responsibility and reservations or safeguards in the interests of India, for such matters as, for instance, defense; external affairs; the position of minorities; the financial credit of India; and the discharge of obligations."[3]]

I was wholly unprepared for [Clause 2]. I said nothing then. . . . There was nothing more to be said. The thing had been done, our leader had committed himself; and, even if we disagreed with him, what could we do? Throw him over? Break from him? Announce our disagreement? That might bring about some personal satisfaction to an individual, but it made no difference to the final decision. The civil disobedience movement was ended for the time being at least, and not even the Working Committee could push it on now, when the Government could declare that Mr Gandhi had already agreed to a settlement. I was perfectly willing, as were our other colleagues, to suspend civil disobedience and to come to a temporary settlement with the Government. It was not an

[1] T.F., p. 187.
[2] Ibid., p. 193.
[3] Ibid., p. 192.

easy matter for any of us to send our comrades back to jail, or to be instrumental in keeping many thousands in prison who were already there. Prison is not a pleasant place to spend our days and nights, though many of us may train ourselves for it and talk light-heartedly of its crushing routine. Besides, three weeks or more of conversations between Gandhiji and Lord Irwin had led the country to expect that a settlement was coming, and a final break would have been a disappointment. So all of us in the Working Committee were decidedly in favor of a provisional settlement (for obviously it could be nothing more), provided that thereby we did not surrender any vital position. . . .

Gandhiji learned indirectly of my distress, and . . . asked me to accompany him in his usual walk. We had a long talk, and he tried to convince me that nothing vital had been lost, no surrender of principle made. He interpreted Clause 2 of the [Delhi] agreement in a particular way so as to make it fit in with our demand for independence, relying chiefly on the words in it: "in the interests of India". The interpretation seemed to me to be a forced one, and I was not convinced, but I was somewhat soothed by his talk. The merits of the agreement apart, I told him that his way of springing surprises upon us frightened me; there was something unknown about him which, in spite of the closest association for fourteen years, I could not understand at all and which filled me with apprehension. He admitted the presence of this unknown element in him, and said that he himself could not answer for it or foretell what it might lead to. . . .

There was no question of opposing or preventing that agreement then. That stage was past, and all I could do was to dissociate myself theoretically from it, though accepting it as a matter of fact. That would have soothed my personal vanity, but how did it help the larger issue? Would it not be better to accept gracefully what had been done, and put the most favourable interpretation upon it, as Gandhiji had done? In an interview to the press immediately after the agreement he had stressed that interpretation and that we stood completely by independence. He went to Lord Irwin and made this point quite clear, so that there might be no misapprehension then or in the future. In the event of the Congress sending any representative to the Round Table Conference, he told him, it could only be on this basis and to advance this claim. Lord Irwin could not, of course, admit the claim, but he recognized the right of the Congress to advance it.

So I decided, not without great mental conflict and physical distress, to accept the agreement and work for it wholeheartedly. There appeared to me to be no middle way.

In the course of Gandhiji's interviews with Lord Irwin prior to the agreement, as well as after, he had pleaded for the release of political prisoners other than the civil disobedience prisoners. The latter were going to be discharged as part of the agreement itself. But there were thousands of others, both those convicted after trial and *détenus* kept without any charge, trial or conviction. Many of these *détenus* had been kept so for years, and there had always been a great deal of resentment all over India, and especially in Bengal, which was most affected, at this method of imprisonment without trial. Gandhiji had pleaded for their release, not necessarily as part of the agreement, but as eminently desirable in order to relieve political tension and establish a more normal atmosphere in Bengal. But the Government was not agreeable to this.

I left Delhi soon after the provisional settlement was arrived at and went to Lucknow. We had taken immediate steps to stop civil disobedience all over the country, and the whole Congress organization had responded to our new instructions with remarkable discipline. We had many people in our ranks who were dissatisfied, many firebrands; and we had no means of compelling them to desist from the old activities. But without a single exception known to me, the huge organization accepted in practice the new role, though many criticized it. Our first job was to see that the civil disobedience prisoners were discharged. Thousands of these were discharged from day to day, and after some time only a number of disputed cases were left in prison; apart, of course, from the thousands of *détenus* and those convicted for violent activities, who were not released.

These discharged prisoners, when they went home to their towns or villages, were naturally welcomed back by their people. There were often decorations and buntings, and processions, and meetings, and speeches and addresses of welcome. It was all very natural and to be expected, but the change was sudden from the time when the police lathee was always in evidence, and meetings and processions were forcibly dispersed. The police felt rather uncomfortable, and probably there was a feeling of triumph among many of our people who came out of jail. There was little enough reason to be triumphant, but a coming out of jail always brings a feeling of elation (unless the spirit has been crushed in jail), and mass jail deliveries add very much to this exhilaration.

I mention this fact here, because in later months great exception was taken by the Government to this "air of triumph," and it was made a charge against us! Brought up and living always in an authoritarian atmosphere, with a military notion of government and with no roots or supports in the people, nothing is more painful to them than a weakening of what they consider their prestige. None of us, so far as I know, had given the least thought to the matter, and it was with great surprise that we learned later that Government officials, from the heights of Simla to the plains below, were simmering with anger and wounded pride at this impudence of the people. These outbursts on the part of the Government and its friends in the press came as a revelation to us. They showed what a state of nerves they had been in, what suppressions they had put up with, resulting in all manner of complexes. It was extraordinary that a few processions and a few speeches of our rank-and-file men should so upset them.

As a matter of fact there was in Congress ranks then, and even less in the leadership, no idea of having "defeated" the British Government. But there was a feeling of triumph among us at our own people's sacrifices and courage.[1]

[In view of the uncompromising attitude of Lord Irwin regarding more crucial issues, it was small comfort to Congress leaders that the humanitarian clause of the Gandhi-Irwin Pact should permit individuals and families to produce salt without payment of tax, for local use, provided it was carried by headloads and no transport was used.

It was at the time of Gandhi's talks with the Viceroy in 1931 that Winston Churchill referred contemptuously to "the nauseating and humiliating spectacle of this one-time Inner Temple lawyer, now seditious fakir, striding half-naked up the steps of the Viceroy's Palace, there to negotiate and to parley on equal terms with the representative of the King-Emperor".[2]

On December 3, 1931, Churchill stated further: "Most of the leading public men—of whom I was one . . . —made speeches—I certainly did —about . . . Dominion Status, but I did not contemplate India having the same constitutional rights and system as Canada in any period which we could foresee."

Again, on January 26, 1931: "Of course, we have always contemplated [Dominion Status for India] as an ultimate goal, but no one has supposed that, except in a purely ceremonial sense in the way in which representatives of India attended conferences during the war, that principle and policy for India would be carried into effect in any time which it is reasonable or useful to foresee."

On February 23 of the same year: "The Indian Congress and other

---

[1] Ibid., pp. 192–96.
[2] Quoted in M.B., p. 171.

elements in this agitation represent neither the numbers, the strength
nor the virtue of the Indian people. They merely represent those Indians
who have acquired a veneer of Western civilization, and have read all
those books about democracy which Europe is now beginning increasingly
to discard. It would be wrong to entrust India to her political classes. . . .
To transfer that responsibility to this highly artificial and restricted
oligarchy of Indian politicians would be a retrograde act. It would be a
shameful act. It would be an act of cowardice, desertion and dishonor.
It would bring upon Great Britain a moral shame which would challenge
forever the reputation of the British Empire as a valiant and benignant
force in the history of mankind." [1]]

Soon after the Delhi Pact, Lord Irwin . . . left India, and Lord Willing-
don [came] in his place as Viceroy. A legend grew up that the new Viceroy was a hard and stern person and not so amenable to compromise as
his predecessor. Many of our politicians have inherited a "liberal" habit
of thinking of politics in terms of persons rather than of principles. They
do not realize that the broad imperial policy of the British Government
does not depend on the personal views of the Viceroys. The change of
Viceroys, therefore, did not and could not make any difference, but, as it
happened, the policy of Government gradually changed owing to the
development of the situation. The Civil Service hierarchy had not
approved of pacts and dealings with the Congress; all their training and
authoritarian conceptions of government were opposed to this. They had
an idea that they had added to the Congress influence and Gandhiji's
prestige by dealing with him almost as an equal and it was about time
that he was brought down a peg or two. The notion was a very foolish
one, but then the Indian Civil Service [was] not known for the originality
of its conceptions. Whatever the reason, the Government stiffened its
back and tightened its hold.[2]

[1] F.E.S. (Mar. 22, 1943), pp. 61–62.
[2] T.F., p. 206.

8 | The Karachi Congress, 1931—Resolution on Fundamental Rights and Economic Policy—Tagore's Nationalism— Stand on China

The Karachi Congress, 1931

[The Karachi Resolution on Fundamental Rights, Economic and Social Changes, adopted at the 1931 Karachi Congress Session, helped to lay the groundwork for significant future reforms in India. Such advances— for which Nehru deserves major credit, and which stemmed primarily from his own earlier efforts—were, in the long run, to be of far greater importance for the development of free India, than was the temporary set-back to the Civil Disobedience Movement resulting from the Delhi Pact.]

The Karachi Congress was an even greater personal triumph for Gandhiji than any previous Congress had been. The president, Sardar Vallabhbhai Patel, was one of the most popular and forceful men in India with the prestige of victorious leadership in Gujrat, but it was the Mahatma who dominated the scene.

The principal resolution dealt with the Delhi Pact and the Round Table Conference. I accepted it, of course, as it emerged from the Working Committee; but, when I was asked by Gandhiji to move it in the open Congress, I hesitated. It went against the grain, and I refused at first, and then this seemed a weak and unsatisfactory position to take up. Either I was for it or against it, and it was not proper to prevaricate or leave the people guessing in the matter. Almost at the last moment, a few minutes before the resolution was taken up in the open Congress, I decided to sponsor it. In my speech I tried to lay before the great gathering quite frankly what my feelings were and why I had whole-heartedly accepted that resolution and pleaded with them to accept it. That speech, made on the spur of the moment and coming from the heart, and with little of ornament or fine phrasing in it, was probably a greater success than many of my other efforts which had followed a more careful preparation.

I spoke on other resolutions, too ... [including] ... one on funda-mental rights and economic policy. The latter resolution interested me especially, partly because of what it contained, and even more so because it represented a new outlook in the Congress. So far the Congress had thought along purely nationalist lines, and had avoided facing economic issues, except in so far as it encouraged cottage industries and Swadeshi generally. In the Karachi resolution it took a step, a very short step, in a socialist direction by advocating nationalization of key industries and services, and various other measures to lessen the burden on the poor and increase it on the rich. This was not socialism at all, and a capitalist state could easily accept almost everything contained in that resolution.

This very mild and prosaic resolution evidently made the big people of the Government of India [think] furiously.... Perhaps they even pictured, with their usual perspicacity, the red gold of the Bolsheviks stealing its way into Karachi and corrupting the Congress leaders. Living in a kind of political harem, cut off from the outer world, and surrounded by an atmosphere of secrecy, their receptive minds love to hear tales of mystery and imagination. And then these stories are given out in little bits in a mysterious manner, through favored newspapers, with a hint that much more could be seen if only the veil were lifted. In this approved and well-practiced manner, frequent references have been made to the Karachi resolution on Fundamental Rights, etc., and I can only conclude that they represent the Government view of [the] resolution. The story goes that a certain mysterious individual with communist affiliations drew up this resolution, or the greater part of it, and thrust it down upon me at Karachi; that thereupon I issued an ultimatum to Mr Gandhi to accept this or to face my opposition on the Delhi Pact issue, and Mr Gandhi accepted it as a sop to me and forced it down on a tired Subjects Committee and Congress on the concluding day.

So far as Mr Gandhi is concerned, I have had the privilege of knowing him pretty intimately for the last twenty-one years, and the idea of my presenting ultimatums to him or bargaining with him seems to me monstrous. We may accommodate ourselves to each other; or we may, on a particular issue, part company; but the methods of the market place can never affect our mutual dealings.[1]

1931 Indian National Congress Resolution on Fundamental Rights and Economic Policy, passed at Karachi, as amended by All-India Congress Committee—August 6–8, 1931

"This Congress is of [the] opinion that to enable the masses to appreciate what 'Swaraj', as conceived by the Congress, will mean to them, it is

[1] T.F., pp. 196–97.

desirable to state the position of the Congress in a manner easily understood by them. In order to end the exploitation of the masses, political
freedom must include real economic freedom of the starving millions.
The Congress, therefore, declares that any Constitution which may be
agreed to on its behalf should provide, or enable the Swaraj Government
to provide, for the following:

Fundamental Rights and Duties

1. (i) Every citizen of India has the right of free expression of opinion,
the right of free association and combination, and the right to assemble
peacefully and without arms, for purposes not opposed to law or morality.

(ii) Every citizen shall enjoy freedom of conscience and the right
freely to profess and practise his religion, subject to public order and
morality.

(iii) The culture, language and script of the Minorities and of the
different linguistic areas shall be protected.

(iv) All citizens are equal before the law, irrespective of religion,
caste, creed or sex.

(v) No disability attaches to any citizen, by reason of his or her
religion, caste, creed or sex, in regard to public employment, office of
power or honour, and in the exercise of any trade or calling.

(vi) All citizens have equal rights and duties in regard to wells, tanks,
roads, schools and places of public resort, maintained out of State or
local funds, or dedicated by private persons for the use of the general
public.

(vii) Every citizen has the right to keep and bear arms, in accordance
with regulations and reservations made in that behalf.

(viii) No person shall be deprived of his liberty nor shall his dwelling
or property be entered, sequestered, or confiscated, save in accordance
with law.

(ix) The State shall observe neutrality in regard to all religions.

(x) The franchise shall be on the basis of universal adult suffrage.

(xi) The State shall provide for free and compulsory primary education.

(xii) The State shall confer no titles.

(xiii) There shall be no capital punishment.

(xiv) Every citizen is free to move throughout India and to stay and
settle in any part thereof, to acquire property and to follow any trade or
calling, and to be treated equally with regard to legal prosecution or
protection in all parts of India.

Labour

2. (a) The organization of economic life must conform to the principle
of justice, to the end that it may secure a decent standard of living.

(b) The State shall safeguard the interests of industrial workers
and shall secure for them, by suitable legislation and in other ways, a
living wage, healthy conditions of work, limited hours of labour, suitable

machinery for the settlement of disputes between employers and work-
men, and protection against the economic consequences of old age, sick-
ness, and unemployment.

3. Labour to be freed from serfdom and conditions bordering on
serfdom.

4. Protection of women workers, and specially adequate provision for
leave during maternity period.

5. Children of school-going age shall not be employed in mines and
factories.

6. Peasants and workers shall have the right to form unions to protect
their interests.

Taxation and Expenditure

7. The system of land tenure and revenue and rent shall be reformed
and an equitable adjustment made of the burden on agricultural land,
immediately giving relief to the smaller peasantry, by a substantial reduction of agricultural rent and revenue now paid by them, and in case of
uneconomic holdings, exempting them from rent so long as necessary,
with such relief as may be just and necessary to holders of small estates
affected by such exemption or reduction in rent, and to the same end,
imposing a graded tax on net incomes from land above a reasonable
minimum.

8. Death duties on a graduated scale shall be levied on property above
a fixed minimum.

9. There shall be a drastic reduction of military expenditure so as to
bring it down to at least one half of the present scale.

10. Expenditure and salaries in civil departments shall be largely
reduced. No servant of the State, other than specially employed experts
and the like, shall be paid above a certain fixed figure, which should not
ordinarily exceed five hundred rupees per month.

11. No duty shall be levied on salt manufactured in India.

Economic and Social Programme

12. The State shall protect indigenous cloth; and for this purpose
pursue the policy of exclusion of foreign cloth and foreign yarn from the
country and adopt such other measures as may be found necessary. The
State shall also protect other indigenous industries, when necessary,
against foreign competition.

13. Intoxicating drinks and drugs shall be totally prohibited, except
for medicinal purposes.

14. Currency and exchange shall be regulated in the national interest.

15. The State shall own or control key industries and services, mineral
resources, railways, waterways, shipping and other means of public
transport.

16. Relief [of] agricultural indebtedness and control of usury, direct
and indirect.

17. The State shall provide for the military training of citizens so as

to organize a means of national defence apart from the regular military forces."[1]

Tagore's Nationalism

[Rabindranath Tagore's philosophy was beginning to have increasing significance for Nehru.]

Nationalism, especially when it urges us to fight for freedom, is noble and life-giving. But often it becomes a narrow creed, and limits and encompasses its votaries and makes them forget the many-sidedness of life. . . . Rabindranath Tagore has given to our nationalism the outlook of internationalism and has enriched it with art and music and the magic of his words, so that it has become the full-blooded emblem of India's awakened spirit.[2]

Stand on China

[From the very beginning of Sino–Japanese hostilities (Japan invaded Manchuria on September 18, 1931), Nehru and other leading Indian nationalists vigorously supported the Chinese fight for independence. Statements were made on the subject by outstanding Congress leaders, resolutions were passed by Congress and help was given to China in the form of financial aid and an ambulance corps. An anti-Japanese boycott was adopted, Japanese propaganda was to be rejected. Throughout the thirties Jawaharlal was "the leading defender in India of the Chinese cause. In India and in Europe . . . both in and out of [Congress] office, he . . . consistently maintained this stand."[3] At a later period, because of his sympathetic attitude, he was to pay a visit to Chungking, as described in Part V.]

<table>
<tr><td>9</td><td>Of Gandhi and Congress—
Second Round Table Conference</td></tr>
</table>

Of Gandhi and Congress

Often . . . I used to accompany Gandhiji in his early morning walks in New Delhi. That was usually the only time one had a chance of talking

[1] S.D.I.C. (Vol. I), pp. 248–50.
[2] T.R., p. 386.
[3] P.A. (Mar. 1940), p. 24.

to him, for the rest of the day was cut up into little bits, each minute allotted to somebody or something. Even the early morning walk was sometimes given over to an interviewer, usually from abroad, or to a friend, come for a personal consultation. We talked of many matters, of the past, of the present, and especially of the future. I remember how he surprised me with one of his ideas about the future of the Congress. I had imagined that the Congress, as such, would automatically cease to exist with the coming of freedom. He thought that the Congress should continue, but on one condition: that it [pass] a self-denying ordinance, laying it down that none of its members could accept a pay job under the State, and, if anyone wanted such a post of authority in the State, he would have to leave the Congress. I do not at present remember how he worked this out, but the whole idea underlying it was that the Congress, by its detachment and having no [axe] to grind, could exercise tremendous moral pressure on the Executive as well as other departments of the Government, and thus keep them on the right track.

Now this is an extraordinary idea which I find difficult to grasp, and innumerable difficulties present themselves. It seems to me that such an assembly, if it could be conceived, would be exploited by some vested interest. But, practicality apart, it does help one to understand a little the background of Gandhiji's thought.

Gandhiji's conception of democracy has nothing to do with numbers or majority or representation in the ordinary sense. It is based on service and sacrifice, and it uses moral pressure. He claims to be "a born democrat". "I make that claim, if complete identification with the poorest of mankind, longing to live no better than they, and a corresponding conscious effort to approach that level to the best of one's ability, can entitle one to make it." This is his definition of a democrat. . . .

Whether Gandhiji is a democrat or not, he does represent the peasant masses of India; he is the quintessence of the conscious and subconscious will of those millions. It is perhaps something more than representation; for he is the idealized personification of those vast millions. Of course, he is not the average peasant. A man of the keenest intellect, of fine feeling and good taste, wide vision; very human, and yet essentially the ascetic who has suppressed his passions and emotions, sublimated them and directed them in spiritual channels; a tremendous personality, drawing people to himself like a magnet, and calling out fierce loyalties and attachments—all this so utterly unlike and beyond a peasant. And yet withal he is the greatest peasant, with a peasant's outlook on affairs, and with a peasant's blindness to some aspects of life. But India is peasant

India, and so he knows his India well, reacts to her slightest tremors, gauges a situation accurately and almost instinctively, and has a knack of acting at the psychological moment.

What a problem and a puzzle he has been not only to the British Government but to his own people and his closest associates! Perhaps in every other country he would be out of place today, but India still seems to understand, or at least appreciate, the prophetic-religious type of man, talking of sin and salvation and nonviolence. Indian mythology is full of stories of great ascetics, who, by the rigor of their sacrifices and self-imposed penance, built up a "mountain of merit" which threatened the dominion of some of the lesser gods and upset the established order. These myths have often come to my mind when I have watched the amazing energy and inner power of Gandhiji, coming out of some in-exhaustible spiritual reservoir. He was obviously not of the world's ordinary coinage; he was minted of a different and rare variety, and often the unknown stared at us through his eyes.

India, even urban India, even the new industrial India, had the impress of the peasant upon her; and it was natural enough for her to make this son of hers, so like her and yet so unlike, an idol and a beloved leader. He revived ancient and half-forgotten memories, and gave her glimpses of her own soul. Crushed in the dark misery of the present, she had tried to find relief in helpless muttering and in vague dreams of the past and the future, but he came and gave hope to her mind and strength to her much-battered body, and the future became an alluring vision. Two-faced like Janus, she looked both backward into the past and forward into the future, and tried to combine the two.

Many of us had cut adrift from this peasant outlook, and the old ways of thought and custom and religion had become alien to us. We called ourselves moderns and thought in terms of "progress," and industrialization and a higher standard of living and collectivization. We considered the peasant's viewpoint reactionary; and some, a growing number, looked with favor toward socialism and communism.[1]

Second Round Table Conference

We were told repeatedly, on behalf of the British Government and their friends, that the first Round Table Conference had already laid down the framework of the constitution, that the principal lines of the picture

[1] T.F., pp. 188–91.

had been drawn, and all that remained was the filling in of this picture. But the Congress did not think so; so far as it was concerned, the picture had to be drawn or painted from the very beginning on an almost blank canvas. It was true that by the Delhi agreement the federal basis had been approved and the idea of safeguards accepted. But a federation had long seemed to many of us the best solution of the Indian constitutional problem, and our approval of this idea did not mean our acceptance of the particular type of federation envisaged by the first Round Table Conference.

The gulf between the Congress viewpoint and that of the British Government was immense, and it seemed exceedingly unlikely that it could be bridged at that stage.

Very few Congressmen expected any measure of agreement between the Congress and the Government at the second Round Table Conference, and even Gandhiji, optimistic as . . . always . . . could not look forward to much. And yet he was never hopeless and was determined to try to the very end. All of us felt that, whether success came or not, the effort had to be made. . . . But there were two vital considerations which might have barred our participation in the second Round Table Conference. We could only go if we had full freedom to place our viewpoint in its entirety before the Round Table Conference, and were not prevented from doing so by being told that the matter had already been decided, or for any other reason. We could also be prevented from being represented at the Round Table Conference by conditions in India. A situation might have developed here which precipitated a conflict with the Government, or in which we had to face severe repression. If this took place in India and our very house was on fire, it would have been singularly out of place for any representative of ours to ignore the fire and talk academically of constitutions and the like in London.

The situation was developing swiftly in India. In Bengal . . . tension continued and grew worse. Some civil disobedience prisoners were discharged, but thousands of politicals, who were technically not civil disobedience prisoners, remained in prison. The *détenus* also continued in jail or detention camps. Fresh arrests were frequently made for "seditious" speeches or other political activities, and generally it was felt that the Government offensive had continued without any abatement.[1]

[1] Ibid., pp. 201–02.

Gandhiji went to London as the sole representative of the Congress to the [Second] Round Table Conference. We had decided, after long debate, not to have additional representatives. Partly this was due to our desire to have our best men in India at a very critical time, when the most tactful handling of the situation was necessary. We felt that, in spite of the Round Table Conference meeting in London, the center of gravity lay in India, and developments in India would inevitably have their reactions in London. We wanted to check untoward developments, and to keep our organization in proper condition. This was, however, not the real reason for our sending only one representative.

We were not joining the Round Table Conference to talk interminably about the petty details of a constitution. We were not interested in those details at that stage, and they could only be considered when some agreement on fundamental matters had been arrived at with the British Government. The real question was how much power was to be transferred to a democratic India. If by a strange chance a basis of agreement was found on those fundamentals, the rest followed easily enough. It had been settled between us that, in case of such an agreement, Gandhiji would immediately summon to London some or even all the members of the Working Committee, so that we could then share the work of detailed negotiation.

The British Government had, however, no intention of falling in with our wishes in the matter. Their policy was to postpone the consideration of fundamental questions and to make the Conference exhaust itself, more or less, on minor and immaterial matters. Even when major matters were considered, the Government held its hand, refused to commit itself, and promised to express its opinion after mature consideration later on. Their trump card was, of course, the communal issue, and they played it for all it was worth. It dominated the Conference.

The great majority of the Indian members of the Conference fell in, most of them willingly, some unwillingly, with this official maneuvering. They were a motley assembly. Few of them represented any but themselves. Some were able and respected; of many others this could not be said. As a whole they represented, politically and socially, the most reactionary elements in India. So backward and reactionary were they that the Indian Liberals, so very moderate and cautious in India, shone as progressives in their company.

It was fitting that in this assembly of vested interests—imperialist, feudal, financial, industrial, religious, communal—the leadership of the British Indian delegation should usually fall to the Aga Khan, who in his own person happened to combine all these interests in some degree. Closely associated as he has been with British imperialism and the British ruling class for over a generation, he could thoroughly appreciate and represent our rulers' interests and viewpoint. He was an able representative of Imperialist England at that Round Table Conference. The irony of it was that he was supposed to represent India.

The scales were terribly loaded against us at that Conference, and, little as we expected from it, we watched its proceedings with amazement and ever-growing disgust. We saw the pitiful and absurdly inadequate attempts to scratch the surface of national and economic problems, the pacts and intrigues and maneuvers, the joining of hands of some of our own countrymen with the most reactionary elements of the British Conservative party, the endless talk over petty issues, the deliberate shelving of all that really mattered, the continuous playing into the hands of the big vested interests and especially British imperialism, the mutual squabbles, varied by feasting and mutual admiration. It was all jobbery—big jobs, little jobs, jobs and seats for the Hindus, for the Moslems, for the Sikhs, for the Anglo-Indians, for the Europeans; but all jobs for the upper classes—the masses had no look-in. Opportunism was rampant, and different groups seemed to prowl about like hungry wolves waiting for their prey—the spoils under the new constitution. The very conception of freedom had taken the form of large-scale jobbery—"Indianization" it was called—more jobs for Indians in the army, in the civil services, etc. No one thought in terms of independence, of real freedom, of a transfer of power to a democratic India, of the solution of any of the vital and urgent economic problems facing the Indian people. Was it for this that India had struggled so manfully? Must we exchange this murky air for the rare atmosphere of fine idealism and sacrifice?

Gandhiji was in an extraordinarily difficult position in that Conference, and we wondered from afar how he could tolerate it. But with amazing patience he carried on and made attempt after attempt to find some basis of agreement. One characteristic gesture he made, which suddenly showed up how communalism really covered political reaction. He did not like many of the communal demands put forward on behalf of the Moslem delegates to the Conference; he thought, and his own Moslem nationalist colleagues thought so, that some of these demands were a bar to freedom and democracy. But still he offered to accept the whole lot of them, without question or argument, if the Moslem delegates there joined forces with him and the Congress on the political issue, that is, on independence.

The offer, however, was not accepted, and indeed it is a little difficult to imagine the Aga Khan standing for Indian independence. This demonstrated that the real trouble was not communal, although the communal issue loomed large before the Conference. It was political reaction that barred all progress and sheltered itself behind the communal issue. By careful selection of its nominees for the Conference, the British Government had collected these reactionary elements, and, by controlling the procedure, they had made the communal issue the major issue, and an issue on which no agreement was possible between the irreconcilables gathered there.

The British Government succeeded in its endeavor, and thereby demonstrated that it still has, not only the physical strength to uphold its Empire, but also the cunning and statecraft to carry on the imperial tradition for a while longer.

The Conference itself, with all its scheming and opportunism and futile meandering, was no failure for India. It was constituted so as to fail, and the people of India could hardly be made responsible for its failing. But it succeeded in diverting world attention from real issues in India, and, in India itself, it produced disillusion and depression and a sense of humiliation. It gave a handle to reactionary forces to raise their heads again.

Success or failure was to come to the people of the country by events in India itself. The powerful nationalist movement could not fade away, because of distant maneuvering in London. Nationalism represented a real and immediate need of the middle classes and peasantry, and by its means they sought to solve their problems. The movement could thus either succeed, fulfil its function, and give place to some other movement, which would carry the people further on the road to progress and freedom, or else it could be forcibly suppressed for the time being. That struggle was to come in India soon after and was to result in temporary disablement. The second Round Table Conference could not affect this struggle much, but it did create an atmosphere somewhat unfavorable to it.[1]

[1] Ibid., pp. 207–10.

	No-Rent Campaign: Sixth Arrest—
10	Interchange Before Court, and
	Imprisonment—*Glimpses of World History*

No-Rent Campaign : Sixth Arrest

[On December 26, 1931, Nehru was again arrested, this time for a breach of an internment order prohibiting him from departing from the municipal limits of Allahabad, from participating in or organizing hartals and public meetings, and from engaging in any writing. He was arrested while going to Bombay from Allahabad to meet Gandhi, who was returning from the Second London Round Table Conference.

"On October 16, Nehru [had] cabled to Gandhi in London that tenants were being harassed, and that a representative peasant meeting was to be called . . . at Allahabad to decide the question of non-payment of rent. Gandhi cabled back . . . that Nehru should take necessary steps to meet the situation. On October 23, a peasants' conference, held at Allahabad, adopted [the following] resolution. . . . 'This conference places on record the view that in case Government does not adopt suitable measures for meeting the condition, the tenants of the whole district will oppose Government by resorting to a no-rent campaign. . . .'

"From Allahabad, the spirit of the no-rent campaign spread to other parts of the province. . . . The [United Provinces] Government was perturbed, and on its request, the Governor-General promulgated on December 15, 1931 an ordinance 'to provide against instigation to the illegal refusal of payment of certain liabilities and to confer special powers on the Government of the United Provinces and its officers for the purpose of maintaining law and order. . . .'

"It was for failure to comply with an order under Section 5 of this Ordinance that Nehru was arrested, and it was under [Section] 13 that he was sentenced." [1] (All such ordinances, as Nehru has noted, were meant to crush the nationalist movement, before Gandhi returned from London.) [2]

Although a technical charge was brought against Jawaharlal on January 4, 1932, for having disobeyed a prohibition to leave the municipal limits of Allahabad, it is generally acknowledged that he was prosecuted for championing the United Provinces Agrarian Movement.]

[1] T.T.N., p. 64.
[2] Based on B.O.L., p. 106.

Interchange Before Court, January 4, 1932, and Imprisonment

[Nehru stated: "'I am not particularly interested in the present proceedings against me, but I should like to express my deep gratitude to the peasants in these provinces who have given me this fresh opportunity of service, and I [would] also like to say that I am proud of my *kisan* brethren in these provinces, especially in my district of Allahabad.'

"Hardly had [Nehru] finished the first sentence [when] he was interrupted by the magistrate who said that he had had [a] foretaste of the statement which Nehru was going to make: it referred to *kisans*, and he would not permit it.

"How could the *kisans* be irrelevant to the present proceedings, Nehru suggested, and asked if all the proceedings of the trial and the Ordinance under which they were being held, had not 'the question of the *kisans* in the background or the foreground.'

"Magistrate: 'The proceedings are concerned with only a part of the Ordinance which relates to the disobedience of the order of the district magistrate. As you are going into "basic things", my only course is to clear the court of the audience before I hear you.'

"Nehru: 'I wish to lay before the court in a few sentences my motive for what I did, and I think that it is necessary for the magistrate, as the presiding officer, to understand what I did. It will help you to decide about the sentence.'

"Magistrate: 'I say I shall hear you, but after clearing the court room of the audience.'

"Nehru declined to submit to this procedure, and sat down saying, 'This Government will be reduced to ashes.'

"But, as had been his principle in the previous trials, he filed a written statement. (It was not read out, and the request of the press to have a copy of it was turned down.)"][1]

[Statement Before Court—January, 1932.] I wish to say nothing about the present proceedings against me. I should like to express my deep gratitude to the peasantry of these provinces for the fresh opportunity of service that they have given me. And I should like to say how proud I am of my *kisan* brethren of my province and especially of my district of Allahabad. They have lighted a fire which will spread and burn brightly till it has consumed and reduced to ashes the British domination and exploitation of this country, which has sucked the life-blood out of them, and till it has put an end finally to the system which has ground them down and deprived them of the fruits of their toil, and reduced them almost to the level of . . . beasts of the field. For long years I have laboured to this end, and so long as any strength is left in me, I will carry on this

[1] T.T.N., p. 69.

fight. Inside prison walls I shall think of many things, but most frequently
my mind will dwell on the villages and fields where my *kisan* brethren
live and labour and suffer, and my good wishes will go out to them and
I shall pray that success may come to them in this great struggle, so that
their present sufferings and misery may become an evil dream of the
past. Till such success comes there can be no compromise and no peace. [1]

[Nehru was sentenced to two years' rigorous imprisonment, and a fine
was imposed upon him, in default of which he was to be sentenced to
six months' further rigorous imprisonment. When "the fine was not
paid . . . the magistrate and the police proceeded to recover it by attachment of property. A motor car, belonging to a member of the Nehru
family, was seized, and an advertisement announcing the date of its
auction, was inserted in the two English dailies of Allahabad. . . . The
'auction' was a quiet affair and 'confidential'. . . . The sum realized was
in excess of the fine but the balance was not returned to the owner of the
car, and was withheld to be 'utilized in paying off the income tax and
other charges incurred on account of the printing and publication of the
advertisement, etc.'"[2]
As a result of Nehru's prolonged imprisonment, he was forced to be
politically inactive for another protracted period.]

[Note relating to jail sentences of early 1930s.] Our policy in prison was
to observe the jail rules unless we considered them humiliating or otherwise improper. Nevertheless, incidents occurred from time to time. On
one occasion when I was in Naini Central Prison, some of us undertook
a full three-day (seventy-two hour) fast as a protest. We were normally
allowed interviews in prison. At one time these interviews were once in
three months, then once a month . . . [then] I was permitted to have fort-
nightly interviews. As I was kept in Dehra Dun District Jail, my mother
and wife had to undertake a long journey from Allahabad for the interview. After their arrival in Dehra Dun, they were told that they could
not interview me. As a consequence of this incident I gave up all interviews for several months. At that time I was in more or less solitary
confinement and had no companion.[3]

"Glimpses of World History"

[*Glimpses of World History*: In 1928, Nehru had begun to write a
series of letters to his daughter, Indira, who was barely a dozen years old

[1] Ibid., pp. 69–70.
[2] Ibid., p. 71.
[3] B.O.L., p. 107.

at the time. The series contained "a brief and simple account of the early days of the world". After the communications had been published in book form, and were warmly received, "the idea of continuing them hovered" in Nehru's mind. Although "a busy life full of political activity prevented" the idea "from taking shape . . . prison gave me the chance I needed" at a later date, "and I seized it".[1] The result was the volume, *Glimpses of World History*, composed of letters written to Indira from various Indian prisons between October 1930 and August 1933. The writing of this book stemmed also from an "attempt to discover the past in its relation to the present".[2]]

[Letter, from Jawaharlal to his sister, Krishna Hutheesing—from Ahmednagar Fort Prison, June 22, 1943.] I have always found it difficult to revise a book I have written. Having finished it, I am reluctant to go back to it. My *Glimpses of World History* was never revised after the first writing and I saw it again in print. . . . It was only some years later, when a second edition was coming out, that I revised it carefully and pruned it down a bit. But this is a bad habit. . . . It has led to . . . errors and loose sentences creeping into my writings. As a matter of fact I could not easily help this, situated as I was. . . . It is odd how the success of a book ultimately depends on certain immaterial and insubstantial factors which one cannot easily measure. Good writing and presentation are of course important, the content is even more important, but over and above these comes a certain sincerity in writing, combined with restraint, which colours a book and makes it liked.[3]

[From letters to Indira written in jail (from *Glimpses of World History*).]

I. [March 26, 1932.] All roads in India in these days sooner or later lead to one destination; all journeys, dream ones or real, end in prison! And so here I am back again behind my old familiar walls, with plenty of time to think of or write to you, though my letters may not reach you. Again the fight is on and our people, men and women, boys and girls, go forth to battle for freedom and to rid this country of the curse of poverty. But freedom is a goddess hard to win; she demands, as of old, human sacrifice from her votaries.[4]

II. [March 28, 1932.] People boast of our enlightened and progressive age, and of the wonders of our modern civilization and of our great

[1] G.W.H., Preface, p. vii.
[2] D.I., p. 11.
[3] N.L.H.S., p. 125.
[4] G.W.H., p. 56.

culture and science; and yet the poor remain poor and miserable, and great nations fight each other and slaughter millions; and great countries like our own are ruled by an alien people. What is the good of civilization to us if we cannot even have freedom in our own households? But now we are up and doing.

How fortunate we are to live in these stirring times, when each one of us can take part in the great adventure and see not only India but the whole world in process of change! You are a lucky girl... You are... witness to a revolution in your own country, and soon you may be an actor in it. All over the world there is trouble and change. In the Far East, Japan is at the throat of China; in the West, and indeed all over the world, the old system totters and threatens to collapse. Countries talk of disarmament, but look suspiciously at each other and keep armed to the teeth. It is the twilight of Capitalism, which has lorded it for so long over the world. And when it goes, as go it must, it will take many an evil thing with it.[1]

III. [Brief Historical Resumé—August 8, 1933.] The whole past tendency has been towards greater interdependence between nations, a greater internationalism. Even though separate independent national States remained, an enormous and intricate structure of international relations and trade grew up. This process went so far as to conflict with the national States and with nationalism itself. The next natural step was a socialized international structure. Capitalism, having had its day, had reached the stage when it was time for it to retire in favour of socialism. But unhappily such a voluntary retirement never takes place. Because crisis and collapse threatened it, it has withdrawn into its shell and tried to reverse the past tendency towards interdependence. Hence economic nationalism. The question is if this can succeed, and even if it does so, for how long?

The whole world is a strange mix-up, a terrible tangle of conflicts and jealousies, and the new tendencies but increase the field of these conflicts. In every continent, in every country, the weak and the oppressed want to share in the good things of life which they themselves help to produce. They claim payment of their debt, long overdue to them. In some places they are doing so loudly and harshly and aggressively; in other places more quietly. Can we blame them if, angry and bitter at the treatment and exploitation they have been subjected to for so long, they act in a manner we do not like? They were ignored and looked down upon; no one took the trouble to teach them drawing-room manners.

[1] Ibid., p. 59.

This upheaval of the weak and the oppressed frightens the possessing classes everywhere, and they band themselves together to suppress it. And thus fascism grows and imperialism crushes all opposition. The fine phrases about democracy and the people's good and trusteeship retire into the background, and the naked rule of the possessing classes and vested interests becomes more obvious, and in many places it seems to meet with triumph. A harsher age appears, an age of iron and aggressive violence, for everywhere the fight is one of life and death between the old order and the new. Everywhere, whether it is in Europe or America or India, the stakes are high and the fate of the old régime hangs in the balance, even though for the moment it may be strongly entrenched. Partial reform does not meet or solve the problems of the day when the whole imperialist-capitalist system is shaken to its foundation and cannot even meet its liabilities or the demands made upon it.

All these innumerable conflicts, political, economic, racial, darken the world today, and carry the shadow of war with them. It is said that the greatest of these conflicts, the most fundamental of them, is the one between imperialism and fascism on the one side and communism on the other. These face each other all over the world. . . .

Feudalism, capitalism, socialism, syndicalism, anarchism, communism —so many isms! And behind . . . all stalks opportunism! But . . . also idealism for those who care to have it; not the idealism of empty fancies and an imagination run riot, but the idealism of working for a great human purpose, a great ideal which we seek to make real. . . .

The world has indeed become one single inseparable whole, each part influencing, and being influenced by, the other. It is quite impossible now to have a separate history of nations. We have outgrown that stage, and only a single world history, connecting the different threads from all the nations, and seeking to find the real forces that move them, can now be written with any useful purpose.

Even in past times, when nations were cut off from each other by many physical and other barriers, we have seen how common international and inter-continental forces shaped them. Great individuals have always counted in history, for the human factor is important in every crisis of destiny; but greater than any individual are the mighty forces at work which, almost blindly and sometimes cruelly, forge ahead, pushing us hither and thither.

So it is today with us. Mighty forces are at work moving the hundreds of millions of human beings, and they go ahead like an earthquake or some other upheaval of Nature. We cannot stop them, however much we may try, and yet we may, in our own little corner of the world, make some slight difference to them in speed or direction. According to our different temperaments we meet them—some frightened by them, others welcoming them, some trying to combat them, others submitting helplessly to the heavy hand of fate, while still others try to ride the tempest and control it a little and direct it, willingly facing the perils that this involves for the joy of helping actively in a mighty process. . . .

All of us, or at any rate those who think, are looking forward expectantly to the future as it unrolls itself and becomes the present. Some await the outcome with hope, others with fear. Will it be a fairer and happier world, where the good things of life will not be reserved for a few, but are freely enjoyed by the masses. Or a harsher world than even today, from which many of the amenities of present-day civilization have gone after fierce and destructive wars? These are two extremes. Either may occur, it seems improbable that a middle course will prevail.

While we wait and watch, we work for the kind of world we would like to have. Man has not progressed from his brute stage by helpless submission to the ways of Nature, but often by a defiance of them and a desire to dominate them for human advantage.

Such is Today. The making of Tomorrow lies with you and your generation, the millions of girls and boys all over the world who are growing up and training themselves to take part in this Tomorrow.[1]

IV. [From last letter to Indira—*Glimpses of World History*—August 9, 1933.] Benjamin Disraeli, the great English statesman of the nineteenth century, has written: "Other men condemned to exile and captivity, if they survive, despair; the man of letters may reckon those days as the sweetest of his life." He was writing about Hugo Grotius, a famous Dutch jurist and philosopher of the seventeenth century, who was condemned to imprisonment for life, but managed to escape after two years. He spent these two years in prison in philosophic and literary work. There have been many famous literary gaolbirds, the two best known perhaps being the Spaniard, Cervantes, who wrote *Don Quixote*, and the Englishman, John Bunyan, the author of *The Pilgrim's Progress*.

I am not a man of letters, and I am not prepared to say that the many years I have spent in gaol have been the sweetest of my life, but I must say that reading and writing have helped me wonderfully to get through them. I am not a literary man, and I am not a historian; what, indeed, am I? I find it difficult to answer that question. . . . I began with science

[1] Ibid., pp. 946-48.

at college, and then took to the law, and, after developing various other interests in life, finally adopted the popular and widely practised profession of gaol-going in India!

You must not take what I have written in these letters as the final authority on any subject. A politician wants to have a say on every subject, and he always pretends to know much more than he actually does. He has to be watched carefully! . . .

My likes and dislikes are pretty obvious, and so also sometimes are my moods in gaol. . . . There may, indeed, be many errors in my accounts. A prison, with no libraries or reference books at hand, is not the most suitable place in which to write on historical subjects. I have had to rely very largely on the many note-books which I have accumulated since I began my visits to gaol twelve years ago. Many books have also come to me here; they have come and gone, for I could not collect a library here. . . .

If history interests you, if you feel some of the fascination of history, you will find your way to many books which will help you to unravel the threads of past ages. But reading books alone will not help. If you would know the past you must look upon it with sympathy and with understanding. To understand a person who lived long ago, you will have to understand his environment, the conditions under which he lived, the ideas that filled his mind. It is absurd for us to judge of past people as if they lived now and thought as we do. . . . We cannot judge the past from [present] standards. . . . Every one will willingly admit this. But every one will not admit the equally absurd habit of judging the present by the standards of the past. The various religions have especially helped in petrifying old beliefs and faiths and customs, which may have had some use in the age and country of their birth, but which are singularly unsuitable in our present age.

If, then, you look upon past history with the eye of sympathy, the dry bones will fill up with flesh and blood, and you will see a mighty procession of living men and women and children in every age and every clime, different from us and yet very like us, with much the same human virtues and human failings. History is not a magic show, but there is plenty of magic in it for those who have eyes to see. . . .

The past brings us many gifts; indeed, all that we have today of culture, civilization, science, or knowledge of some aspects of the truth, is a gift of the distant or recent past to us. It is right that we acknowledge our obligation to the past. But the past does not exhaust our duty or obligation. We owe a duty to the future also, and perhaps that obligation is even greater than the one we owe to the past. For the past is past and

9*

done with, we cannot change it; the future is yet to come, and perhaps we may be able to shape it a little. If the past has given us some part of the truth, the future also hides many aspects of the truth, and invites us to search for them. But often the past is jealous of the future and holds us in a terrible grip, and we have to struggle with it to get free to face and advance towards the future.

History, it is said, has many lessons to teach us; and there is another saying that history never repeats itself. Both are true, for we cannot learn anything from it by slavishly trying to copy it, or by expecting it to repeat itself or remain stagnant; but we can learn something from it by prying behind it and trying to discover the forces that move it. Even so, what we get is seldom a straight answer. "History," says Karl Marx, "has no other way of answering old questions than by putting new ones."

The old days were days of faith, blind, unquestioning faith. The wonderful temples and mosques and cathedrals of past centuries could never have been built but for the overpowering faith of the architects and builders and people generally. The very stones that they reverently put one on top of the other, or carved into beautiful designs, tell us of this faith. The old temple spire, the mosque with its slender minarets, the Gothic cathedral—all of them pointing upward with an amazing intensity of devotion, as if offering a prayer in stone or marble to the sky above—thrill us even now, though we may be lacking in that faith of old of which they are the embodiments. But the days of that faith are gone, and gone with them is that magic touch in stone. Thousands of temples and mosques and cathedrals continue to be built, but they lack the spirit that made them live during the Middle Ages. There is little difference between them and the commercial offices which are so representative of our age.

Our age is a different one; it is an age of disillusion, of doubt and uncertainty and questioning. We can no longer accept many of the ancient beliefs and customs; we have no more faith in them, in Asia or in Europe or America. So we search for new ways, new aspects of the truth more in harmony with our environment. And we question each other and debate and quarrel and evolve any number of "isms" and philosophies. As in the days of Socrates, we live in an age of questioning, but that questioning is not confined to a city like Athens; it is world-wide.

Sometimes the injustice, the unhappiness, the brutality of the world oppress us and darken our minds, and we see no way out. . . .

And yet if we take such a dismal view we have not learnt aright the lesson of life or of history. For history teaches us of growth and progress and the possibility of an infinite advance for man. And life is rich and varied, and though it has many swamps and marshes and muddy places, it has also the great sea, and the mountains, and snow, and glaciers, and wonderful starlit nights (especially in gaol!), and the love of family and friends, and the comradeship of workers in a common cause, and music, and books and the empire of ideas. . . .

It is easy to admire the beauties of the universe and to live in a world of thought and imagination. But to try to escape in this way from the unhappiness of others, caring little what happens to them, is no sign of courage or fellow-feeling. Thought, in order to justify itself, must lead to action. "Action is the end of thought", says our friend Romain Rolland. "All thought which does not look towards action is an abortion and a treachery. If then we are the servants of thought we must be the servants of action."

People avoid action often because they are afraid of the consequences, for action means risk and danger. Danger seems terrible from a distance; it is not so bad if you have a close look at it. And often it is a pleasant companion, adding to the zest and delight of life. The ordinary course of life becomes dull at times, and we take too many things for granted and have no joy in them. And yet how we appreciate these common things of life when we have lived without them for a while! Many people go up high mountains and risk life and limb for the joy of the climb and the exhilaration that comes from a difficulty surmounted, a danger overcome; and because of the danger that hovers all around them, their perceptions get keener, their joy of the life which hangs by a thread, the more intense.

All of us have our choice of living in the valleys below, with their unhealthy mists and fogs, but giving a measure of bodily security; or of climbing the high mountains, with risk and danger for companions, to breathe the pure air above, and take joy in the distant views, and welcome the rising sun.[1]

[1] Ibid., pp. 949-53.

II | Civil Disobedience—Early 1932—The Communal Award: A Gandhi Fast: The Poona Pact

Civil Disobedience

[The Civil Disobedience Movement of 1932–1934 was undertaken because Congress demands continued to be ignored by the British Government. The "movement was precipitated . . . by the arrest of . . . Gandhi on his return from London to India after the Second Round Table Conference. It passed the peak of its strength towards the end of 1932. Mr Gandhi then called on his followers to devote themselves to the removal of untouchability. There followed a period during which civil disobedience was still the policy but no resistance was offered. By stages it was withdrawn."[1]]

[At first during the early 1930s] civil disobedience functioned strongly and aggressively, and then there was a gradual decline with occasional bursts. A direct action struggle can only remain at a revolutionary pitch for a very short time. It cannot remain static; it has to go up or down. Civil disobedience, after the first flush, went down slowly, but it could carry on at a lower level for long periods. In spite of outlawry, the All-India Congress organization continued to function with a fair measure of success. It kept in touch with its provincial workers, sent instructions, received reports, occasionally gave financial assistance.

The provincial organizations also continued with more or less success. . . .

Our experience of 1930 and 1932 showed that it was easily possible for us to organize a secret network of information all over India. Without much effort, and in spite of some opposition, good results were produced. But many of us had the feeling that secrecy did not fit in with the spirit of civil disobedience, and produced a damping effect on the mass consciousness. As a small part of a big open mass-movement it was useful, but there was always the danger, especially when the movement was declining, of a few more or less ineffective secret activities taking the place of the mass-movement. Gandhiji condemned all secrecy in July 1933.[2]

[1] U.I., footnote, p. 95.
[2] P.H., pp. 53–55.

Early 1932

[The] early months of 1932 were remarkable, among other things, for an extraordinary exhibition of ballyhoo on the part of the British authorities. Officials, high and low, shouted out how virtuous and peaceful they were, and how sinful and pugnacious was the Congress. They stood for democracy while the Congress favored dictatorships. Was not its president called a dictator? In their enthusiasm for a righteous cause they forgot trifles like ordinances, and suppression of all liberties, and muzzling of newspapers and presses, imprisonment of people without trial, seizure of properties and moneys, and the many other odd things that were happening from day to day. They forgot also the basic character of British rule in India. Ministers of Government (our own countrymen) grew eloquent on how Congressmen were "grinding their axes"—in prison—while they labored for the public good on paltry salaries of a few thousand rupees per month. The lower magistracy not only sentenced us to heavy terms but lectured to us in the process, and sometimes abused the Congress and individuals connected with it. . . .

It was all very natural, I suppose, this exhibition of a hysterical war mentality; and no one could expect truth or restraint under the circumstances. But it did seem to go beyond expectation and was surprising in its intensity and abandon. It was some indication of the state of nerves of the ruling group in India, and of how they had been repressing themselves in the past. Probably the anger was not caused by anything we had done or said, but by the realization of their own previous fear of losing their empire. Rulers who are confident of their own strength do not give way in this manner.

It was evident that the Government had long prepared its blow, and it wanted it to be as thorough and staggering as possible [in 1930]. . . . The 1932 methods were different, and Government began with an offensive all along the line. Every conceivable power was given and taken under a batch of all-India and provincial ordinances; organizations were outlawed; buildings, property, automobiles, bank accounts were seized; public gatherings and processions forbidden; and newspapers and printing presses fully controlled. India lived practically under martial law, and Congress never really got back the initiative or any freedom of action. The first blows stunned it and most of its bourgeois sympathizers who had been its principal supporters in the past. Their pockets were hit, and it became obvious that those who joined the civil disobedience movement, or were known to help it in any way, stood to lose not only their liberty, but perhaps all their property.

I do not think any Congressman has a right to object to the procedure adopted by the Government, although the violence and coercion used . . . against an overwhelmingly nonviolent movement was certainly most objectionable from any civilized standards. If we choose to adopt revolutionary direct-action methods, however nonviolent they might be, we must expect every resistance. We cannot play at revolution in a drawing room, but many people want to have the advantage of both. For a person to dabble in revolutionary methods, he must be prepared to lose everything he possesses. The prosperous and the well-to-do are therefore seldom revolutionaries, though individuals may play the fool in the eyes of the worldly wise and be dubbed traitors to their own class.

The new environment in India tolerated no neutral hues, and so some of our countrymen appeared in the brightest of approved colors, and, with song and feasting, they declared their love and admiration for our rulers. They had nothing to fear from the ordinances and the numerous prohibitions and inhibitions and curfew orders and sunset laws; for had it not been officially stated that all this was meant for the disloyal and the seditious, and the loyal need have no cause for alarm? [1]

The Communal Award : A Gandhi Fast : The Poona Pact

[In August, 1932 the British introduced constitutional changes in India entitled the Communal Award, which provided, in part, for a separate electorate for untouchables in the Legislative Councils.

Gandhi, profoundly dedicated to ameliorating the condition of the Harijans, or Children of God (his name for India's untouchables), considered creation of such an electorate intolerable. Numerous other Congress leaders were equally outraged by the Award's provisions.]

If there is one thing more than another that Gandhiji has stood for and stands for today, it is that the depressed classes should cease to be depressed or exploited or handicapped in any way, and that they should be on a perfect level with every other group. It was because he felt that if they were placed in a separate compartment by themselves they would have a stigma attached to them and fusion with others would become more difficult, that he opposed their separation. It is well-known that a certain alliance was formed in London during the second Round Table Conference between the delegates of some minority groups and British Conservatives. Gandhiji evidently wanted the Muslim delegates not to

[1] T.F., pp. 218-19.

support the demand for the separation of the depressed classes into a distinct group. So far as I know, he has never opposed the grant of special and additional representation to the depressed classes. Indeed, he holds that every facility must be given them to advance and catch up to the more advanced groups and communities. Subsequent events have demonstrated how far he is prepared to go in this direction. Socialist as I am, I fail to see any flaw or any impropriety in this reasoning. . . .

It is because [Gandhiji] feels that untouchability is a degrading and disgusting accretion that he fights against it.[1]

Our peaceful and monotonous routine in jail was suddenly upset in the middle of September 1932 by a bombshell. News came that Gandhiji had decided to "fast unto death" in disapproval of the separate electorates given by Mr Ramsay MacDonald's communal award to the depressed classes.[2] What a capacity he had to give shocks to people! Suddenly all manner of ideas rushed into my head; all kinds of possibilities and contingencies rose up before me and upset my equilibrium completely. For two days I was in darkness with no light to show the way out, my heart sinking when I thought of some results of Gandhiji's action. The personal aspect was powerful enough, and I thought with anguish that I might not see him again. It was over a year ago that I had seen him last on board ship on the way to England. Was that going to be my last sight of him?

And then I felt annoyed with him for choosing a side issue for his final sacrifice. What would be the [effect] on our freedom movement? Would not the larger issues fade into the background, for the time being at least? And, if he attained his immediate object and got a joint electorate for the depressed classes, would not that result in a reaction and a feeling that something had been achieved and nothing more need be done for a while? And was not his action a recognition, and in part an acceptance, of the communal award and the general scheme of things as sponsored by the Government? Was this consistent with nonco-operation and civil disobedience? After so much sacrifice and brave endeavor, was our movement to tail off into something insignificant?

I felt angry with him at his religious and sentimental approach to a political question, and his frequent references to God in connection with it. He even seemed to suggest that God had indicated the very date of the fast. What a terrible example to set!

[1] R.E.W., pp. 61–62.
[2] Although it has been claimed that Mr MacDonald authorized the Award against his own will, its repercussions in India were nevertheless "shocking", as indicated above.

If Bapu died! What would India be like then? And how would her politics run? There seemed to be a dreary and dismal future ahead, and despair seized my heart when I thought of it.

So I thought and thought, while confusion reigned in my head, with anger and hopelessness, and love for him who was the cause of this upheaval. I hardly knew what to do, and I was irritable and short-tempered with everybody, most of all with myself.

And then a strange thing happened to me. I had quite an emotional crisis, and at the end of it I felt calmer, and the future seemed not so dark. Bapu had a curious knack of doing the right thing at the psychological moment, and it might be that his action—impossible to justify as it was from my point of view—would lead to great results, not only in the narrow field in which it was confined, but in the wider aspects of our national struggle. And, even if Bapu died, our struggle for freedom would go on. So whatever happened, one had to keep ready and fit for it. Having made up my mind to face even Gandhiji's death without flinching, I felt calm and collected and ready to face the world and all it might offer.

Then came news of the tremendous upheaval all over the country, a magic wave of enthusiasm running through Hindu society, and untouchability appeared to be doomed. What a magician, I thought, was this little man sitting in Yeravda Prison, and how well he knew how to pull the strings that move people's hearts!

A telegram from him reached me. It was the first message I had received from him since my conviction, and it did me good to hear from him after that long interval. In this telegram he said:

During all these days of agony you have been before mind's eye. I am most anxious to know your opinion. You know how I value your opinion....

News also came to me just then that some settlement had been reached over the electorate issue. The superintendent of the jail was good enough to allow me to send an answer to Gandhiji, and I sent him the following telegram:

Your telegram and brief news that some settlement reached filled me with relief and joy. First news of your decision to fast caused mental agony and confusion, but ultimately optimism triumphed and I regained peace of mind. No sacrifice too great for suppressed downtrodden classes. Freedom must be judged by freedom of lowest but feel danger of other issues obscuring only goal. Am unable to judge from religious viewpoint.

Danger your methods being exploited by others but how can I presume to advise a magician. Love.

A "pact" was signed by various people gathered in Poona; with unusual speed the British Prime Minister accepted it and varied his previous award accordingly, and the fast was broken. I disliked such pacts and agreements greatly, but I welcomed the Poona Pact apart from its contents. The excitement was over, and we reverted to our jail routine. News of the Harijan movement and of Gandhiji's activities from prison came to us, and I was not very happy about it. There was no doubt that a tremendous push had been given to the movement to end untouchability and raise the unhappy depressed classes, not so much by the pact as by the crusading enthusiasm created all over the country. That was to be welcomed. But it was equally obvious that civil disobedience had suffered. The country's attention had been diverted to other issues, and many Congress workers had turned to the Harijan cause. Probably most of these people wanted an excuse to revert to safer activities which did not involve the risk of jail-going or, worse still, lathee blows and confiscations of property. That was natural, and it was not fair to expect all the thousands of our workers to keep always ready for intense suffering and the break-up and destruction of their homes. But still it was painful to watch this slow decay of our great movement. Civil disobedience was, however, still going on, and occasionally there were mass demonstrations. . . . Gandhiji was in Yeravda Prison, but he had been given certain privileges to meet people and issue directions for the Harijan movements. Somehow this took away from the sting of his being in prison. All this depressed me.[1]

[Among additional Communal Award provisions objectionable to Congress leaders were the following: Separate communal groups were to vote for seats allotted to Muslim, European and Sikh constituencies. Such voting, as well as other similar arrangements, could be altered only after ten years, with the assent of the communities affected. Only qualified electors not included in a Muslim, Sikh, Indian Christian, Anglo-Indian or European constituency, were to be entitled to vote in a general constituency. In other words, the Communal Award went counter to the democratic, secular ideals of Congress in multiple fashion.

Nehru described the Communal Award as "merely a problem created by the middle or upper classes for the sake of a few seats in the Legislature or appointments in Government service or for Ministerial positions".[2]

[1] T.F., pp. 236-39.
[2] S.D.I.C. (Vol. I), p. 407.

The Poona Pact was soon substituted for the Communal Award.
As described by Sitaramayya, leaders of the untouchables had every
reason to be grateful, since the "Pact secured them double the number
of the seats granted in . . . Prime Minister [MacDonald's previous
Award] . . . and a measure of representation somewhat in excess of the
proportion of their population. The question of a referendum at the end
of ten years became the subject of a last moment controversy but Gandhi
fixed five years instead of ten if there should be a referendum. . . .
Ultimately it was decided to leave the whole question to be decided by
mutual agreement in the future—a formula . . . approved of as 'excellent'
by Gandhi. . . . Simultaneous statements were [made] in England and India
. . . announcing . . . acceptance of the Poona Agreement." Whereupon
Gandhi decided to break his fast. Although his life had been saved for
the moment, "almost in the same breath in which he had agreed to
break [his] fast, he foreshadowed the certainty of its resumption if the
reform of the removal of untouchability was not faithfully achieved
within a measurable period".[1]

A minor victory had been won, but one by no means gratifying to
Jawaharlal.]

12 | Third Round Table Conference—Life in Jail—Indo–British Relations, 1931–1933

Third Round Table Conference

While fire raged all over India, and men's and women's souls were put
to the test, far away in London the chosen ones foregathered to draw up
a constitution for India at the third Round Table Conference in 1932.

It was surprising to find how far these people had alienated themselves,
not only in their day-to-day lives, but morally and mentally, from the
Indian masses. Reality for these distinguished statesmen consisted of one
thing—British imperial power, which could not be successfully challenged
and therefore should be accepted with good or bad grace. It did not seem
to strike them that it was quite impossible for them to solve India's
problem or draw up a real live constitution without the good will of the
masses.

[1] H.I.N.C. (Vol. I), pp. 534–35.

In India there was an amazing growth of the spirit of violence in official circles. An inspector-general of prisons went to the length of issuing a circular to all the prisons, pointing out that civil disobedience prisoners must be "dealt with grimly". [This circular was dated June 30, 1932, and it contained the following: "The Inspector-General impresses upon superintendents and jail subordinates the fact that there is no justification for preferential treatment in favor of civil disobedience movement prisoners as such. This class require to be kept in their places and dealt with grimly." [1]]

Life in Jail

Whipping became a frequent jail punishment. On April 27, 1933, the Under-Secretary for India stated in the House of Commons "that Sir Samuel Hoare was aware that over five hundred persons in India were whipped during 1932 for offences in connection with the civil disobedience movement". It is not clear if this figure includes the many whippings in prisons for breaches of jail discipline. As news of frequent whippings came to us in prison in 1932, I remembered our protest and our three-day fast in December 1930 against one or two odd instances of whipping. I had felt shocked then at the brutality of it; now I was still shocked, and there was a dull pain inside me, but it did not strike me that I should protest and fast again. I felt much more helpless in the matter. The mind gets blunted to brutality after a while.

The hardest of labor was given to our men in prison—mills, oil presses, etc.—and their lot was made as unbearable as possible in order to induce them to apologize and be released on an undertaking being given to the Government. That was considered a great triumph for the jail authorities.

Most of these jail punishments fell to the lot of boys and young men, who resented coercion and humiliation. A fine and spirited lot of boys they were, full of self-respect and "pep" and the spirit of adventure, the kind that in an English public school or university would have received every encouragement and praise. Here in India their youthful idealism and pride led them to fetters and solitary confinement and whipping.

The lot of our womenfolk in prison was especially hard and painful to contemplate. They were mostly middle-class women, accustomed to a

[1] T.F., pp. 225–26. (Section in brackets above from footnote, p. 226.)

sheltered life, and suffering chiefly from the many repressions and customs produced by a society dominated to his own advantage by man. The call of freedom had always a double meaning for them, and the enthusiasm and energy with which they threw themselves into the struggle had no doubt their springs in the vague and hardly conscious, but nevertheless intense, desire to rid themselves of domestic slavery also. Excepting a very few, they were classed as ordinary prisoners and placed with the most degraded of companions, and often under horrid conditions. I was once lodged in a barrack next to a female enclosure, a wall separating us. In that enclosure there were, besides other convicts, some women political prisoners, including one who had been my hostess and in whose house I had once stayed. A high wall separated us, but it did not prevent me from listening in horror to the language and curses which our friends had to put up with from the women convict warders.

It was very noticeable that the treatment of political prisoners in 1932 and 1933 was worse than it had been two years earlier, in 1930. This could not have been due merely to the whims of individual officers, and the only reasonable inference seems to be that this was the deliberate policy of the Government.[1]

At Anuradhapura [Ceylon, where Nehru went briefly in 1931] I [had] liked greatly an old seated statue of the Buddha. A year later, when I was in Dehra Dun Jail, a friend in Ceylon sent me a picture of this statue, and I kept it on my little table in my cell. It became a precious companion for me, and the strong, calm features of Buddha's statue soothed me and gave me strength and helped me to overcome many a period of depression.

Buddha has always had a great appeal for me. It is difficult for me to analyze this appeal, but it is not a religious appeal, and I am not interested in the dogmas that have grown up round Buddhism. It is the personality that has drawn me. So also the personality of Christ has attracted me greatly.

I saw many Buddhist *bhikkus* (monks) in their monasteries and on the highways, meeting with respect wherever they went. The dominant expression of almost all of them was one of peace and calm, a strange detachment from the cares of the world. They did not have intellectual faces, as a rule, and there was no trace of the fierce conflicts of the mind on their countenances. Life seemed to be for them a smooth-flowing river moving slowly to the great ocean. I looked at them with some envy, with just a faint yearning for a haven; but I knew well enough that my

[1] Ibid., pp. 226-27.

lot was a different one, cast in storms and tempests. There was to be no haven for me, for the tempests within me were as stormy as those outside. And if perchance I found myself in a safe harbor, protected from the fury of the winds, would I be contented or happy there?[1]

Indo–British Relations—1931–1933

[Between the time of Nehru's arrest on December 31, 1931, and his release on August 30, 1933, he was confined at different periods in Naini Central Prison, Bareilly District Jail and Dehra Dun Jail. From thoughts during a mid-night drive, while being transferred from Bareilly District Jail to Dehra Dun Jail, during the 1931–1933 prison sentence.] I mused over the relations of Englishmen and Indians, of ruler and ruled, of official and nonofficial, of those in authority and those who have to obey. What a great gulf divided the two races, and how they distrusted and disliked each other! But more than the distrust and the dislike was the ignorance of each other, and, because of this, each side was a little afraid of the other and was constantly on its guard in the other's presence. To each, the other appeared as a sour-looking, unamiable creature, and neither realized that there was decency and kindliness behind the mask. As the rulers of the land, with enormous patronage at their command, the English had attracted to themselves crowds of cringing place hunters and opportunists, and they judged of India from these unsavory specimens. The Indian saw the Englishman function only as an official with all the inhumanity of the machine and with all the passion of a vested interest trying to preserve itself. How different was the behavior of a person acting as an individual and obeying his own impulses from his behavior as an official or a unit in an army! The soldier, stiffening to attention, drops his humanity and, acting as an automaton, shoots and kills inoffensive and harmless persons who have done him no ill. So also, I thought, the police officer who would hesitate to do an unkindness to an individual would, the day after, direct a lathee charge on innocent people. He will not think of himself as an individual then, nor will he consider as individuals those crowds whom he beats down or shoots.

As soon as one begins to think of the other side as a mass or a crowd, the human link seems to go. We forget that crowds also consist of individuals, of men and women and children, who love and hate and suffer. An average Englishman, if he were frank, would probably confess that he knows some quite decent Indians but they are exceptions and as a

[1] Ibid., pp. 198–99.

whole Indians are a detestable crowd. The average Indian would admit that some Englishmen whom he knows are admirable, but, apart from these few, the English are an overbearing, brutal, and thoroughly bad lot. Curious how each person judges of the other race, not from the individual with whom he has come in contact, but from others about whom he knows very little or nothing at all.

Personally, I have been very fortunate and, almost invariably, I have received courtesy from my own countrymen as well as from the English. Even my jailers and the policemen who have arrested me or escorted me as a prisoner from place to place, have been kind to me, and much of the bitterness of conflict and the sting of jail life has been toned down because of this human touch. . . .

Even for Englishmen I was an individual and not merely one of the mass, and, I imagine, the fact that I had received my education in England, and especially my having been to an English public school, brought me nearer to them. Because of this, they could not help considering me as more or less civilized after their own pattern, however perverted my public activities appeared to be.[1]

13 | Reactions to Events Abroad and at Home, 1933

As our struggle toned down and stabilized itself at a low level, there was little of excitement in it, except at long intervals. My thoughts traveled more to other countries, and I watched and studied, as far as I could in jail, the world situation in the grip of the great depression. I read as many books as I could find on the subject, and the more I read the more fascinated I grew. India with her problems and struggles became just a part of this mighty world drama, of the great struggle of political and economic forces that was going on everywhere, nationally and inter-nationally. . . .

The great world crisis and slump seemed to justify the Marxist analysis. While all other systems and theories were groping about in the dark,

[1] Ibid., pp. 3–4.

Marxism alone explained it more or less satisfactorily and offered a real solution.

As this conviction grew upon me, I was filled with a new excitement, and my depression at the nonsuccess of civil disobedience grew much less. Was not the world marching rapidly toward the desired consummation? There were grave dangers of wars and catastrophes, but at any rate we were moving. There was no stagnation. Our national struggle became a stage in the longer journey, and it was as well that repression and suffering were tempering our people for future struggles and forcing them to consider the new ideas that were stirring the world. We would be the stronger and the more disciplined and hardened by the elimination of the weaker elements. Time was in our favor.

And so I studied carefully what was happening in Russia, Germany, England, America, Japan, China, France, Spain, Italy, and Central Europe, and tried to understand the tangled web of current affairs. I followed with interest the attempts of each country separately, and of all of them together, to weather the storm. The repeated failures of international conferences to find a solution for political and economic ills and the problem of disarmament reminded me forcibly of a little, but sufficiently troublesome, problem of our own—the communal problem. With all the good will in the world, we have so far not solved the problem; and, in spite of a widespread belief that failure would lead to world catastrophe, the great statesmen of Europe and America have failed to pull together. In either case the approach was wrong, and the people concerned did not dare to go the right way.

In thinking over the troubles and conflicts of the world, I forgot to some extent my own personal and national troubles. I would even feel buoyant occasionally at the fact that I was alive at this great revolutionary period of the world's history. Perhaps I might also have to play some little part in my own corner of the world in the great changes that were to come. At other times I would find the atmosphere of conflict and violence all over the world very depressing. Worse still was the sight of intelligent men and women who had become so accustomed to human degradation and slavery that their minds were too coarsened to resent suffering and poverty and inhumanity. Noisy vulgarity and organized humbug flourished in this stifling moral atmosphere, and good men were silent. The triumph of Hitler and the Brown Terror that followed was a great shock, though I consoled myself that it could only be temporary. Almost one had the feeling of the futility of human endeavor. The machine went on blindly; what could a little cog in it do? . . .

We had not solved yet the problem of political freedom [in India] and the nationalistic outlook filled our minds. Were we to jump to economic freedom at the same time or take them in turn, however short the interval might be? World events as well as happenings in India were forcing the social issue to the front, and it seemed that political freedom could no longer be separated from it.

The policy of the British Government in India had resulted in ranging the socially reactionary classes in opposition to political independence. That was inevitable, and I welcomed the clearer demarcation of the various classes and groups in India. But was this fact appreciated by others? Apparently not by many. It was true that there were a handful of orthodox communists in some of the big cities, and they were hostile to, and bitterly critical of, the national movement. The organized labor movement, especially in Bombay and, to a lesser extent, in Calcutta, was also socialistic in a loose kind of way, but it was broken up into bits and suffering from the depression. Vague communistic and socialistic ideas had spread among the intelligentsia, even among intelligent Government officials. The younger men and women of the Congress, who used to read Bryce on democracies and Morley and Keith and Mazzini, were now reading, when they could get them, books on socialism and communism and Russia. . . . Everywhere there was in evidence a new spirit of inquiry, a questioning and a challenge to existing institutions. The general direction of the mental wind was obvious, but still it was a gentle breeze, unsure of itself. Some people flirted with fascist ideas. A clear and definite ideology was lacking. Nationalism still was the dominating thought.

It seemed clear to me that nationalism would remain the outstanding urge, till some measure of political freedom was attained. Because of this the Congress had been, and was still (apart from certain labor circles), the most advanced organization in India, as it was far the most powerful. During the past thirteen years, under Gandhiji's leadership, it had produced a wonderful awakening of the masses, and, in spite of its vague bourgeois ideology, it had served a revolutionary purpose. It had not exhausted its utility yet and was not likely to do so till the nationalist urge gave place to a social one. Future progress, both ideological and in action, must therefore be largely associated with the Congress, though other avenues could also be used.

To desert the Congress seemed to me thus to cut oneself adrift from the vital urge of the nation, to blunt the most powerful weapon we had, and perhaps to waste energy in ineffective adventurism. And yet, was the

Congress, constituted as it was, ever likely to adopt a really radical social solution? If such an issue were placed before it, the result was bound to be to split it into two or more parts, or at least to drive away large sections from it. That in itself was not undesirable or unwelcome if the issues became clearer and a strongly knit group, either a majority or minority in the Congress, stood for a radical social program.

But Congress at present meant Gandhiji. What would he do? Ideologically he was sometimes amazingly backward, and yet in action he had been the greatest revolutionary of recent times in India. He was a unique personality, and it was impossible to judge him by the usual standards, or even to apply the ordinary canons of logic to him. But, because he was a revolutionary at bottom and was pledged to political independence for India, he was bound to play an uncompromising role till that independence was achieved. And in this very process he would release tremendous mass energies and would himself, I half hoped, advance step by step toward the social goal.

The orthodox communists in India and outside have for many years past attacked Gandhiji and the Congress bitterly, and imputed all manner of base motives to the Congress leaders. Many of their theoretical criticisms of Congress ideology were able and pointed, and subsequent events partly justified them. Some of the earlier communist analyses of the general Indian political situation turned out to be remarkably correct. But, as soon as they leave their general principles and enter into details, and especially when they consider the role of the Congress, they go hopelessly astray. One of the reasons for the weakness in numbers as well as influence of the communists in India is that, instead of spreading a scientific knowledge of communism and trying to convert people's minds to it, they have largely concentrated on abuse of others. This has reacted on them and done them great injury. Most of them are used to working in labor areas, where a few slogans are usually enough to win over the workers. But mere slogans are not enough for the intellectual, and they have not realized that in India today the middle-class intellectual is the most revolutionary force. Almost in spite of the orthodox communists, many intellectuals have been drawn to communism, but even so there is a gulf between them.

According to the communists, the objective of the Congress leaders has been to bring mass pressure on the Government in order to obtain industrial and commercial concessions in the interests of Indian capitalists and zamindars. The task of the Congress is "to harness the economic and political discontent of the peasantry, the lower middle class, and the industrial working class to the chariot of the mill owners and financiers of Bombay, Ahmedabad, and Calcutta." The Indian capitalists are supposed to sit behind the scenes and issue orders to the Congress Working Committee first to organize a mass movement and, when it becomes too vast and dangerous, to suspend it or sidetrack it. Further . . . the Congress leaders really do not want the British to go away, as they are required to control and exploit a starving population, and the Indian middle class do not feel themselves equal to this.

It is surprising that able communists should believe this fantastic analysis, but, believing this as they apparently do, it is not surprising that they should fail so remarkably in India. Their basic error seems to be that they judge the Indian national movement from European labor standards; and, used as they are to the repeated betrayals of the labor movement by the labor leaders, they apply the analogy to India. The Indian national movement is obviously not a labor or proletarian movement. It is a bourgeois movement, as its very name implies, and its objective so far has been, not a change of the social order, but political independence. This objective may be criticized as not far-reaching enough, and nationalism itself may be condemned as out of date. But, accepting the fundamental basis of the movement, it is absurd to say that the leaders betray the masses because they do not try to upset the land system or the capitalist system. They never claimed to do so. Some people in the Congress, and they are a growing number, want to change the land system and the capitalist system, but they cannot speak in the name of the Congress.

It is true that the Indian capitalist classes (not the big zamindars and talukdars) have profited greatly by the national movement because of British and other foreign boycotts, and the push given to Swadeshi. This was inevitable, as every national movement encourages home industries and preaches boycotts. As a matter of fact, the Bombay mill industry in a body, during the continuance of civil disobedience and when we were preaching the boycott of British goods, had the temerity to conclude a pact with Lancashire. From the point of view of the Congress, this was a gross betrayal of the national cause, and it was characterized as such. The representative of the Bombay mill owners in the Assembly also consistently ran down the Congress and "extremists" while most of us were in jail.

The part that many capitalist elements have played in India during the past few years has been scandalous, even from the Congress and nationalist viewpoint. As for the big zamindars and talukdars, they ranged

themselves completely against the Congress in the Round Table Conference, and they openly and aggressively declared themselves on the
side of the Government right through civil disobedience. It was with
their help that Government passed repressive legislation in various
provinces embodying the ordinances. . . .

Communists in India have associated with the industrial workers of
the big towns. They have little knowledge of, or contact with, the rural
areas. The industrial workers, important as they are, and likely to be
more so in the future, must take second place before the peasants, for the
problem of today in India is the problem of the peasantry. Congress
workers, on the other hand, have spread all over these rural areas, and,
in the ordinary course, the Congress must develop into a vast peasant
organization. Peasants are seldom revolutionary after their immediate
objective is attained, and it is likely that sometime in the future the usual
problem of city versus village and industrial worker versus peasant will
rise in India also.

It has been my privilege to be associated very closely with a large
number of Congress leaders and workers, and I could not wish for a
finer set of men and women. And yet I have differed from them on vital
issues, and often I have felt a little weary at finding that they do not
appreciate or understand something that seems to me quite obvious. It
was not due to want of intelligence; somehow we moved in different
ideological grooves. I realize how difficult it is to cross these boundaries
suddenly. They constitute different philosophies of life, and we grow
into them gradually and unconsciously. It is futile to blame the other
party. Socialism involves a certain psychological outlook on life and its
problems. It is more than mere logic. So also are the other outlooks based
on heredity, upbringing, the unseen influences of the past, and our
present environments. Only life itself with its bitter lessons forces us
along new paths and ultimately, which is far harder, makes us think
differently. Perhaps we may help a little in this process. And perhaps

> *On recontre sa destinée*
> *Souvent par les chemins q'on prend pour l'éviter.*[1]

In our own country the fight for freedom goes on, and yet many of
our countrymen pay little heed to it and argue and quarrel among themselves, and think in terms of a sect or a religious group or narrow class,
and forget the larger good. And some, blind to the vision of freedom,

[1] T.F., pp. 228-36.

"... *took truce with tyrants and grew tame,*
And gathered up cast crowns and creeds to wear,
And rags and shards regilded."

In the name of law and order, tyranny flourishes and tries to crush those who will not submit to it. Strange that the very thing that should be a refuge of the weak and the oppressed should become a weapon in the hand of the oppressors.[1]

What has been the record of British rule in India? Who are we to complain of its deficiencies when they were but the consequences of our own failings? If we lose touch with the river of change and enter a backwater, become self-centered and self-satisfied, and, ostrichlike, ignore what happens elsewhere, we do so at our peril. The British came to us on the crest of a wave of new impulse in the world, and represented mighty historic forces which they themselves hardly realized. Are we to complain of the cyclone that uproots us and hurls us about, or the cold wind that makes us shiver? Let us have done with the past and its bickering and face the future. To the British we must be grateful for one splendid gift of which they were the bearers, the gift of science and its rich offspring. It is difficult, however, to forget or view with equanimity the efforts of the British Government in India to encourage the disruptive obscurantist, reactionary, sectarian, and opportunist elements in the country. Perhaps that too is a needed test and challenge for us, and, before India is reborn, it will have to go through again and again the fire that cleanses and tempers and burns up the weak, the impure, and the corrupt.[2]

[1] G.W.H., pp. 476–77.
[2] T.F., p. 285.

14 | A Gandhi Fast—Need for Social Reform in India: Repressions—Rise of Nazism—Cultural Poverty and Renaissance—Decline of Civil Disobedience Movement—Congress Resolutions, 1933—Gandhi's 1933 Imprisonment: Political Developments

Gandhi's Fast of May, 1933

[In July, 1933, soon after his release from jail, and completion of an extraordinary twenty-one-day fast in May, Gandhi decided to call off the Civil Disobedience Movement. He had undertaken his fast as a "self-purificatory process for inducing in the workers connected with the Harijan [untouchable] movement a purer spirit of service".[1]

Initially Gandhi had decided not to terminate the Mass C.D. Movement, in the hope of having an interview with the Viceroy, at which he might discuss the precarious political situation of the moment. When a meeting was refused, the Mahatma had advocated individual C.D., as an alternative to mass civil disobedience. Deprecating what he termed the "secret ways" in which those who had carried on the Mass C.D. Movement had betrayed the spirit of what he felt should be done, he pleaded that it was the quality, rather than the quantity, of individual civil disobedience that was of paramount importance. Nehru was as deeply perturbed by Gandhi's fast, as by his calling off of the Mass C.D. Movement.]

Early in May 1933, Gandhiji began his twenty-one-day fast. The first news of this had again come as a shock to me, but I accepted it as an inevitable occurrence and schooled myself to it. Indeed I was irritated that people should urge him to give it up, after he had made up his mind and declared it to the public. For me the fast was an incomprehensible thing, and, if I had been asked before the decision had been taken, I would certainly have spoken strongly against it. But I attached great value to Gandhiji's word, and it seemed to me wrong for anyone to try to make him break it, in a personal matter which, to him, was of supreme importance. So, unhappy as I was, I put up with it.

[1] R.H.C., p. 162.

A few days before beginning his fast he wrote to me, a typical letter which moved me very much. As he asked for a reply I sent him the following telegram:

> Your letter. What can I say about matters I do not understand?
> I feel lost in strange country where you are the only familiar land-
> mark and I try to grope my way in dark but I stumble. Whatever
> happens my love and thoughts will be with you.

I had struggled against my utter disapproval of his act and my desire not to hurt him. I felt, however, that I had not sent him a cheerful message, and now that he was bent on undergoing his terrible ordeal, which might even end in his death, I ought to cheer him up as much as I could. Little things make a difference psychologically, and he would have to strain every nerve to survive. I felt also that we should accept whatever happened, even his death, if unhappily it should occur, with a stout heart. So I sent him another telegram:

> Now that you are launched on your great enterprise may I send
> you again love and greetings and assure you that I feel more clearly
> now that whatever happens it is well and whatever happens you
> win.

He survived the fast. . . . On his advice civil disobedience was suspended for six weeks.

Again I watched the emotional upheaval of the country during [Gandhiji's] fast, and I wondered more and more if this was the right method in politics. It seemed to be sheer revivalism, and clear thinking had not a ghost of a chance against it. All India, or most of it, stared reverently at the Mahatma and expected him to perform miracle after miracle and put an end to untouchability and get *Swaraj* and so on— and did precious little itself! And Gandhiji did not encourage others to think; his insistence was only on purity and sacrifice. I felt that I was drifting further and further away from him mentally, in spite of my strong emotional attachment to him. Often enough he was guided in his political activities by an unerring instinct. He had the flair for action, but was the way of faith the right way to train a nation? It might pay for a short while, but in the long run? And I could not understand how he could accept, as he seemed to do, the present social order, which was based on violence and conflict. Within me also conflict raged, and I was torn between rival loyalties. I knew that there was trouble ahead for me, when the enforced protection of jail was removed. I felt lonely and homeless; and India, to whom I had given my love and for whom I had labored, seemed a strange and bewildering land to me. Was it my fault that I could not enter into the spirit and ways of thinking of my countrymen? Even with my closest associates I felt that an invisible barrier came between us, and, unhappy at being unable to overcome it, I shrank back into my shell. The old world seemed to envelop them, the old world of past ideologies, hopes, and desires. The new world was yet far distant.

> *Wandering between two worlds, one dead,*
> *The other powerless to be born,*
> *With nowhere yet to rest his head.*

India is supposed to be a religious country above everything else; Hindu, Moslem, Sikh, and others take pride in their faiths and testify to their truth by breaking heads. The spectacle of what is called religion, or at any rate organized religion, in India and elsewhere has filled me with horror, and I have frequently condemned it and wished to make a clean sweep of it. Almost always it seems to stand for blind belief and reaction, dogma and bigotry, superstition and exploitation, and the preservation of vested interests. And yet I knew well that there was something else in it, something which supplied a deep inner craving of human beings. How else could it have been the tremendous power it has been and brought peace and comfort to innumerable tortured souls? Was that peace merely the shelter of blind belief and absence of questioning, the calm that comes from being safe in harbor, protected from the storms of the open sea, or was it something more? In some cases certainly it was something more.[1]

Need for Social Reform in India : Repressions

[The] real reason why the Congress and other nonofficial organizations cannot do much for social reform . . .[:] We suffer from the disease of nationalism; [it] absorbs our attention, and it will continue to do so till we get political freedom.

[1] T.F., pp. 239-41.

Past experience shows us that we can make little social progress under present conditions, in spite of apparent transfers of subjects to elected ministers. I am sure that if the Congress started a nationwide propaganda for the greater use of soap it would come in conflict with Government in many places.

I do not think it is very difficult to convert the masses to social reform if the State takes the matter in hand. But alien rulers are always suspect, and they cannot go far in the process of conversion. If the alien element were removed and economic changes were given precedence, an energetic administration could easily introduce far-reaching social reforms.[1]

Brave men and women defied peacefully a powerful and entrenched government, though they knew that it was not for them to achieve what they wanted in the present or the near future. And repression without break and with ever-increasing intensity demonstrated the basis of British rule in India. There was no camouflage about it now, and this at least was some satisfaction to us. Bayonets were triumphant, but a great warrior had once said that "you can do everything with bayonets save sit on them". It was better that we should be governed thus, we thought, than that we should sell our souls and submit to spiritual prostitution. We were physically helpless in prison, but we felt we served our cause even there and served it better than many outside.

Should we, because of our weakness, sacrifice the future of India to save ourselves? It was true that the limits of human vitality and human strength were narrow, and many an individual was physically disabled, or died, or fell out of the ranks, or even betrayed the cause. But the cause went on despite setbacks; there could be no failure if ideals remained undimmed and spirits undaunted. Real failure was a desertion of principle, a denial of our right, and an ignoble submission to wrong. Self-made wounds always took longer to heal than those caused by an adversary.

There was often a weariness at our weaknesses and at a world gone awry, and yet there was a measure of pride for our achievement. For our people had indeed behaved splendidly, and it was good to feel oneself to be a member of a gallant band.[2]

Naked coercion . . . is an expensive affair for the rulers. Even for them it is a painful and nerve-shaking ordeal, and they know well that ultimately it weakens their foundations. It exposes continually the real

[1] Ibid., pp. 245–46.
[2] Ibid., pp. 227–28.

character of their rule, both to the people coerced and the world at large. They infinitely prefer to put on the velvet glove to hide the iron fist. Nothing is more irritating and, in the final analysis, harmful to a Government than to have to deal with people who will not bend to its will, whatever the consequences. So even sporadic defiance of the repressive measures had value; it strengthened the people and sapped the morale of Government.

The moral consideration was even more important to us. In a famous passage Thoreau has said: "At a time when men and women are unjustly imprisoned the place for just men and women is also in prison." Many of us often feel that a moral life under existing conditions is intolerable, when, even apart from civil disobedience, many of our colleagues are always in prison and the coercive apparatus of the State is continually repressing us and humiliating us, as well as helping in the exploitation of our people. In our own country we move about as suspects, shadowed and watched, our words recorded lest they infringe the all-pervading law of sedition, our correspondence opened, the possibility of some executive prohibition or arrest always facing us. For us the choice is: abject submission to the power of the State, spiritual degradation, the denial of the truth that is in us, and our moral prostitution for purposes that we consider base—or opposition with all the consequences thereof. No one likes to go to jail or to invite trouble. But often jail is preferable to the other alternative.[1]

Rise of Nazism

Politically, India was more or less quiet; public activities were largely controlled and suppressed by the Government, and arrests occasionally took place. But the silence of India . . . was full of significance. It was the ominous silence which follows exhaustion after experiencing a period of fierce repression, a silence which is often very eloquent, but is beyond the ken of governments that repress. India was the ideal police state, and the police mentality pervaded all spheres of government. Outwardly all nonconformity was suppressed, and a vast army of spies and secret agents covered the land. There was an atmosphere of demoralization and an all-pervading fear among the people. Any political activity, especially in the rural areas, was immediately suppressed, and the various provincial governments were trying to hound out Congressmen from the service of

[1] Ibid., p. 249-50.
10+N.

municipalities and local boards. Every person who had been to prison as a civil resister was unfit, according to Government, for teaching in a municipal school or serving the municipality in any other way. Great pressure was brought to bear on municipalities, etc., and threats were held out that Government grants would be stopped if the offending Congressmen were not dismissed. . . .

Reports of Nazi excesses in Germany had a curious effect on British officials and their press in India. They gave them a justification for all they had done in India, and it was pointed out to us, with a glow of conscious virtue, how much worse our lot would have been if the Nazis had had anything to do with us. New standards and records had been set up by the Nazis, and it was certainly not an easy matter to rival them. Perhaps our lot would have been worse; it is difficult for me to judge, for I have not all the facts of the occurrences that have taken place in various parts of India during the past five years. The British Government in India believes in the charity that its right hand should not know what its left hand does, and so it has turned down every suggestion for an impartial enquiry, although such inquiries are always weighted on the official side. I think it is true that the average Englishman hates brutality, and I cannot conceive English people openly glorying in and repeating lovingly the word *Brutalität* (or its English equivalent), as the Nazis do. Even when they indulge in the deed, they are a little ashamed of it. But whether we are Germans or English or Indians, I am afraid our veneer of civilized conduct is thin enough, and, when passions are aroused, it rubs off and reveals something that is not good to look at.[1]

Cultural Poverty and Renaissance

Recently there has been an artistic awakening, led by the brilliant Tagore family, and its influence is already apparent all over India. But how can any art flourish widely when the people of the country are hampered and restricted and suppressed at every turn and live in an atmosphere of fear?[2]

A great deal of our cultural poverty in India during the last few generations is due to our people's excessive poverty. It is an insult to talk of culture to people who have nothing to eat. This blight of poverty

[1] Ibid., pp. 253-54.
[2] Ibid., p. 257.

affects even those few who happen to be relatively well-to-do, and so unhappily even these classes in India are today singularly uncultured. What a host of evils foreign rule and social backwardness have to answer for. But even in this general poverty and drabness, India can still produce splendid men and magnificent exemplars of culture like Gandhi and Rabindranath Tagore.[1]

Decline of Civil Disobedience Movement

Gradually, the Civil Disobedience Movement declined; but still it carried on, not without distinction. Progressively it ceased to be a mass movement. ... Civil Disobedience was finally killed for all practical purposes by the suspension of it in May 1933. It continued after that more in theory than in practice. It is no doubt true that, even without that suspension, it would have gradually petered out. India was numbed by the violence and harshness of repression. The nervous energy of the nation as a whole was for the moment exhausted, and it was not being re-charged. Individually there were still many who could carry on civil resistance, but they functioned in a somewhat artificial atmosphere.

It was not pleasant for us in prison to learn of this slow decay of a great movement. And yet very few of us had expected a flashing success. There was always an odd chance that something flashing might happen if there was an irrepressible upheaval of the masses. But that was not to be counted upon, and so we looked forward to a long struggle with ups and downs and many a stalemate in between, and a progressive strengthening of the masses in discipline and united action and ideology. Sometimes ... I almost feared a quick and spectacular success, for this seemed to lead inevitably to a compromise leaving the "Governmentarians" and opportunists at the top.

[Nehru began to be especially disturbed by what he felt to be the lack of clarity and vigor of India's Liberal Party, or her Gradualists.]

In the Congress itself there was a great deal of loose thinking and no clear [idea] as to what system of government or society we were driving at. Some Congressmen, indeed, did not think of changing the existing system of Government much, but simply of replacing the British alien element in it by the *swadeshi* brand.

[1] G.W.H., p. 519.

The "Governmentarians" of the pure variety did not matter much, for their first article of faith was subservience to the State authority whatever it was. But even the Liberals and Responsivists accepted the ideology of the British Government almost completely; and their occasional criticism, such as it was, was thus wholly ineffective and valueless. It was well known that they were legalists at any price, and as such they could not welcome civil resistance. But they went much further, and more or less ranged themselves on the side of the Government. They were almost silent and rather frightened spectators of the complete suppression of civil liberties of all kinds. It was not merely a question of civil disobedience being countered and suppressed by the Government, but of all political life and public activity being stopped, and hardly a voice was raised against this. Those who usually stood for these liberties were involved in the struggle itself, and they took the penalties for refusing to submit to the State's coercion. Others were cowed into abject submission, and hardly raised their voices in criticism. Mild criticism, when it was indulged in, was apologetic in tone and was accompanied by strong denunciation of the Congress and those who were carrying on the struggle.

In Western countries a strong public opinion had been built up in favour of civil liberties, and any limitation of them is resented and opposed. . . . There are large numbers of people who, though not prepared to participate in strong and direct action themselves care enough for the liberty of speech and writing, assembly and organization, person and press, to agitate for them ceaselessly and thus help to check the tendency of the State to encroach upon them. The Indian Liberals claim to some extent to carry on the traditions of British Liberalism (although they have nothing in common with them except the name), and might have been expected to put up some intellectual opposition to the suppression of these liberties for they suffered from this also. But they played no such part. It was not for them to say with Voltaire: "I disagree absolutely with what you say, but I will defend to the death your right to say it."

It is not perhaps fair to blame them for this, for they have never stood out as the champions of democracy or liberty, and they had to face a situation in which a loose word might have got them into trouble. It is more pertinent to observe the reactions of those ancient lovers of liberty, the British Liberals, and the new socialists of the British Labour Party to repression in India. They managed to contemplate the Indian scene with a certain measure of equanimity, painful as it was, and sometimes their satisfaction at the success of the "scientific application of repression," as a correspondent of the *Manchester Guardian* put it, was evident. Recently the National Government of Great Britain has sought to pass a Sedition Bill, and a great deal of criticism has been directed to it, especially from Liberals and Labourites on the ground, *inter alia*, that it restricts free speech and gives magistrates the right of issuing warrants for searches. Whenever I read this criticism I sympathised with it, and I had at the same time the picture of India before me, where the actual laws in force today are approximately a hundred times worse than the British Sedition Bill seeks to enact. I wondered how it was that Britishers who strain at a gnat in England could swallow a camel in India without turning a hair. Indeed I have always wondered at and admired the astonishing knack of the British people of making their moral standards correspond with their material interests, and of seeing virtue in everything that advances their imperial designs. Mussolini and Hitler are condemned by them in perfect good faith and with righteous indignation for their attacks on liberty and democracy; and in equal good faith, similar attacks and deprivation of liberty in India seem to them as necessary, and the highest moral reasons are advanced to show that true disinterested behaviour on their part demands them.[1]

Congress Resolutions—1933

[After the Third Round Table Conference of 1932, the British Government drafted a provisional Constitution for India, issued as a White Paper in 1933. Nehru, however, was passionately committed to the idea that Indians should draft their own Constitution.

Developments within Congress, 1933: A resolution passed at the Calcutta Session of March 21 reaffirmed previous stands adopted on independence, as well as civil disobedience as a legitimate means for attaining the "national goal". Congress further urged: (1) strengthening of the Nationalist Movement; (2) that there be a firm boycott of foreign cloth and British goods; (3) increased use of khadi; (4) that any consideration of a constitution framed for India while its people were victims of barbarous repression should be refused; (5) that Indians should not be duped by Britain's White Paper Constitutional scheme. Congress also reasserted its approval of the resolution on Fundamental Rights passed by the 1931 Karachi Congress Session.[2]]

[1] P.H., pp. 57–63.
[2] Based on R.H.C., p. 161.

Gandhi's 1933 Imprisonment : Political Developments

Gandhiji has again been arrested [August, 1933] and sentenced and is back in Yeravda Prison. Civil disobedience has been resumed, though in restricted form, and our comrades go to gaol again.

Life merges into death, but the great work to make life worth living for the people of India goes on. Many thousands of India's sons and daughters, the most spirited and often the most gifted, lie in prison or internment camps, spending their youth and energy in conflict against the existing system which enslaves India. All this life and energy might have gone in a building up, in construction; there is so much to be done in this world. But before the construction must come destruction, so that the ground may be cleared for the new structure. We cannot put up a fine building on top of the mud walls of a hovel. The state of India to-day can best be appreciated by the fact that in certain parts of India in Bengal even the manner of dress is regulated by government order, and to dress otherwise means prison. And in Chittagong even little boys (and presumably little girls also) of twelve and upwards have to carry about identity cards with them wherever they go. I do not know if such an extraordinary order has ever been enforced elsewhere, even . . . a war area occupied by enemy troops. We are indeed a ticket-of-leave nation to-day under British rule. And across our north-west frontier our neighbours are being bombed by British aeroplanes.[1]

[The *Indian Annual Register* of 1933 stated that, despite Congress activities and Gandhi's "fast", the Viceroy had made pronouncements which had indicated that he had not been stampeded away from dominion status as the natural and inevitable goal of the British policy in India. He had not been frightened, apparently, into abjuring the forbidden phrase.

The *Register* stated further of this period: "During the first week of September [1933] and for some time [thereafter], there was a discussion going on among some of the Congress leaders about fresh developments of the political situation incidental to Mahatmaji's last fast and unconditional release and some other events. . . . Some Congressmen had again passed through the jail gates into their wonted prison cells. But the example had not proved 'infectious', and the number of individual civil resisters had not swelled into 'millions'. Individual civil disobedience had been sporadic rather than epidemic, and the Government had practically but little trouble with it. . . . Jawaharlal Nehru was one of

[1] G.W.H., p. 937.

those who had felt dissatisfied with some aspects of the matter of this
latter-day Congress policy and practice, and he was invited by Gandhiji
to [talk] the matter over with him. . . . Jawaharlal's main idea was [that]
India's problem, though peculiar in one sense, was also, in another
sense, the problem common to the whole world. So that there could be
no solution for an India in isolation. . . . The common problem of the
world was primarily economic and not political. 'We agitators [stated
Nehru] are accused of upsetting the State. But [the] truth is that no
agitator has such superhuman powers as to be able to do that. The agitator, though he may temporarily direct the events, merely gives expression to the existing grievances. In India those grievances are agrarian.'
He characterised the zamindari system as both anachronism and autocracy, and his plain meaning was that what the world, including India,
needed primarily and fundamentally was a plan of social and political
foundations laid upon economic justice. The test and the only test of a
just and workable constitution in India is that it reduces the cost of
administration and brings relief to the masses. So-called political good
is no good if it is not accompanied or followed by economic relief and
well-being."[1]

Because the British became more blatantly repressive than at any
previous time during 1933, Nehru has described Congress policy of that
period as having been mainly one of defiance, which inevitably led to
jail. "Congress and the nation," he stated, "were exhausted after [their]
long struggle and could not bring any effective pressure on the Government."[2]]

15

Release from Jail and Meeting with Gandhi—From Gandhi–Nehru Correspondence, September, 1933— Further Developments, Autumn, 1933

Release from Jail and Meeting with Gandhi

[Due to his mother's ill-health, Nehru finally was released from prison
on August 30, 1933, a few days before his sentence was to expire. After

[1] I.A.R. (1933, Vol. II), p. 52.
[2] T.F., p. 249.

his mother's condition had somewhat improved, he went to Poona to see Gandhi, who was also ill. In their first meeting since 1931, the discussion between the two men led to an exchange of letters containing a statement of their views, published in September, 1933.]

[From September 14, 1933 statement, after term in jail.] For over twenty months I had been cut off from activity; for over two years I had not met Gandhiji and much had happened during this period. I sought to find out how matters stood from some of my colleagues . . . but above all, I desired to meet Gandhiji after my long separation from him. . . . I have now had the privilege of long and intimate conversations with him and placed my viewpoint before him and listened to his advice. . . .

I find that considerable public interest has been taken in our conversations and there seems to be an expectation that some public statement should be made in regard to them. It has been thought that a convenient way of placing some of the important points before the public would be by an exchange of letters between Gandhiji and myself. It is proposed to exchange and issue these letters to the press in due course.

It has been my privilege in common with the vast numbers of my countrymen and countrywomen to take part in the struggle for India's freedom during the last memorable thirteen years under the leadership and inspiration of Gandhiji. My own view-point has always been political and economic and I have seldom been influenced by religious or other like considerations though the moral and practical aspect of Satyagraha has always appealed to me. Gandhiji, as is well known, is essentially a man of religion and his outlook is governed by this. In spite of this difference in outlook, many of us have found numerous points of agreement with him and have most willingly and joyously followed his lead in action. India knows and the world knows how great a leader in action he is and how he has infused the breath of life and hope in our suffering and toiling masses. Politically and to some extent economically, the objective he had in view appealed to us and we worked to the best of our ability to achieve it. I feel that the methods he has taught us to follow are fundamentally right for us and we must continue to pursue them till we gain that objective and that for these methods his leadership is essential. Freedom can have no real meaning for us unless it is . . . freedom of the most exploited in the land. Gandhiji has always laid stress on this and it is from these down-trodden classes that he has drawn his strength. I feel however that it would be desirable to define our objective more clearly so that there may be no misapprehensions in India and abroad. In particular, I feel that in these days of economic breakdown of the capitalist order, it is essential for us to lay down a clear economic policy for the national movement.[1]

From Gandhi-Nehru Correspondence—September, 1933

[From the *Indian Annual Register*: On September 15, 1933, correspondence between Gandhi and Nehru "was released for publication. Lengthy letters had passed between them. The central idea running through the letters of both was that the economic programme of the Congress, particularly as expressed in the enunciation of . . . Fundamental Rights in the Karachi Congress, should be stressed. Thus Mahatmaji wrote to Panditji—'I have no doubt in my mind that our goal can be no less than complete independence. I am also in whole-hearted agreement with you when you say that without a material revision of the vested interests the condition of the masses can never be improved.' As regards the position of the ruling princes, Gandhiji was not prepared to go as far as Panditji would like to go; still he thought that they would have to part with much of their power and become popular representatives of the people over [whom] they were ruling. He was also in agreement with Panditji that India must not live in isolation but range herself with the progressive forces of the world. 'But I know that though there is such an agreement between you and me in the enunciation of . . . ideals, there are temperamental differences between [us].' Then Gandhiji proceeded to outline those temperamental differences. As regards the definition of the goal [sought] he said: 'I have concerned myself more with the conservation of the means and their progressive use. I know if we can take care of them the attainment of the goal is assured. I feel too that our progress towards the goal will be in exact proportion to the purity of our means.'"[2]]

[Letter to Gandhi, Poona—September 13, 1933.] [Our national] objective of political independence has been finally laid down by the Congress and there is nothing to add to or take away from it. We stand for complete independence. Sometimes a little confusion arises because of vague phraseology and misleading propaganda and it is therefore as well to remove this confusion by a reiteration of our political demand. Even the word independence is used with a variety of meanings. Obviously, it must include, as the Congress has clearly and definitely laid down, full control of the army and of foreign relations, as well as financial and economic control. . . .

It seems to me that if we are to improve the condition of the masses, to raise them economically and give them freedom, it is inevitable that

[1] B.S.W.J.N., pp. 185-86.
[2] I.A.R. (1933, Vol. II), pp. 52-53.
10*

vested interests in India will have to give up their special position and
many of their privileges. It is inconceivable to me how else the masses
can rise. Therefore, the problem of achieving freedom [becomes] one of
revising vested interests in favour of the masses. To the extent this is
done, to that extent only will freedom come. The biggest vested interest in
India is that of the British Government; next come the Indian princes;
and others follow. We do not wish to injure any class or group, and the
[divesting] should be done as gently as possible and with every effort to
avoid injury. But it is obvious that the [divesting] is bound to cause loss
to the classes or groups which enjoy special privileges at the expense of
the masses. It is also obvious that the process of [divesting] must be as
speedy as possible to bring relief to the masses whose condition . . . is as
bad as it can well be. Indeed economic forces themselves are acting with
amazing rapidity today and breaking up the old order. The big zamindari
and taluqadari system in the United Provinces has largely collapsed,
though it may be kept up for sometime longer by outside agencies. Even
the condition of the zamindars is very bad and the peasantry of course is
in a far worse position.

We are all agreed that the Round Table Conference and its various
productions are utterly useless to solve even one of India's many problems. As I conceive it, the Round Table Conference was an effort to
consolidate the vested interests of India behind the British Government
so as to face the rising and powerful national and economic movements
in the country which threaten these interests. Essentially, in international
parlance, it was a fascist grouping of vested and possessing interests, and
fascist methods were adopted in India to suppress the national movement. And because the mere preservation of all these vested interests in
India cannot possibly solve our economic ills—whether those of the
masses or even of the middle classes—the effort is foredoomed to inevitable failure. Even from the point of view of a democratic nationalism,
as you yourself stated at the Round Table Conference, democracy and
autocracy can ill go together.

Another aspect has to be borne in mind. The problem of Indian freedom cannot be separated from the vital international problems of the
world. The present crisis in the world's affairs is having its repercussions
in India. At any moment it may result in a complete breakdown or in a
violent international conflagration. Everywhere there is a conflict and a
contest between the forces of progress and betterment of the masses and
the forces of reaction and vested interests. We cannot remain silent
witnesses to this titanic struggle, for it affects us intimately. Both on the

narrower ground of [our] own interests and the wider ground of international welfare and human progress, we must, I feel, range ourselves with the progressive forces of the world. This ranging ourselves at present can of course be ideological only.

These are some of the larger issues that fill my mind and I am convinced, not only that we ignore them at our peril, but that a true appreciation of them will vitalize and give new meaning to our struggle for freedom which we must continue till the full objective is achieved.[1]

[The gulf between Gandhi and Nehru seemed very great at the time, yet essentially the bond between them was of far greater significance.]

Further Developments—Autumn, 1933

[Out of jail.] In Bombay I met many friends and comrades, some only recently out of prison. The socialistic element was strong ... and there was much resentment at recent happenings in the upper ranks of the Congress. Gandhiji was severely criticized for his metaphysical outlook applied to politics. With much of the criticism I was in agreement, but I was quite clear that, situated as we were, we had little choice in the matter and had to carry on. ... Our national movement had arrived at a stage when it had to be suppressed by Government, or it would impose its will on the British Government. This meant that it had arrived at a stage when it was always likely to be declared illegal, and, as a movement, it could not go back. ... The continuance of disobedience made little difference in practice, but it was an act of moral defiance which had value. It was easier to spread new ideas during a struggle than it would be when the struggle was wound up for the time being, and demoralization ensued. The only alternative to the struggle was a compromising attitude to the British authority and constitutional action in the councils.

It was a difficult position, and the choice was not an easy one. I appreciated the mental conflicts of my colleagues, for I had myself had to face them. But I found ... as I have found elsewhere in India, some people who wanted to make high socialistic doctrine a refuge for inaction. It was a little irritating to find people who did little themselves criticizing others who had shouldered the burden in the heat and dust of the fray, as reactionaries. These parlor socialists are especially hard on Gandhiji as the archreactionary, and advance arguments which in logic leave little to be desired. But the little fact remains that this "reactionary" knows

[1] B.S.W.J.N., pp. 186–88.

India, understands India, almost *is* peasant India, and has shaken up India as no so-called revolutionary has done. Even his latest Harijan activities have gently but irresistibly undermined orthodox Hinduism and shaken it to its foundations. The whole tribe of the Orthodox have ranged themselves against him and consider him their most dangerous enemy, although he continues to treat them with all gentleness and courtesy. In his own peculiar way he has a knack of releasing powerful forces which spread out, like ripples on the water's surface, and affect millions. Reactionary or revolutionary, he has changed the face of India, given pride and character to a cringing and demoralized people, built up strength and consciousness in the masses, and made the Indian problem a world problem. Quite apart from the objectives aimed at and its meta-physical implications, the method of nonviolent nonco-operation or civil resistance is a unique and powerful contribution of his to India and the world, and there can be no doubt that it has been peculiarly suited to Indian conditions.

I think it is right that we should encourage honest criticism and have as much public discussion of our problems as possible. It is unfortunate that Gandhiji's dominating position has to some extent prevented this discussion. There was always a tendency to rely on him and to leave the decision to him. This is obviously wrong, and the nation can only advance by reasoned acceptance of objectives and methods, and a co-operation and discipline based on them and not on blind obedience. No one, how-ever great he may be, should be above criticism. But, when criticism becomes a mere refuge for inaction, there is something wrong with it. For socialists to indulge in this kind of thing is to invite condemnation from the public, for the masses judge by acts. . . .

Socialists and communists in India are largely nurtured on literature dealing with the industrial proletariat. In some selected areas, like Bombay or near Calcutta, large numbers of factory workers abound, but for the rest India remains agricultural, and the Indian problem cannot be disposed of, or treated effectively, in terms of the industrial workers. Nationalism and rural economy are the dominating considerations, and European socialism seldom deals with these. Prewar conditions in Russia were a much nearer approach to India, but there again the most extra-ordinary and unusual occurrences took place, and it is absurd to expect a repetition of these anywhere else. I do believe that the philosophy of communism helps us to understand and analyze existing conditions in any country. . . . But it is doing violence and injustice to that philosophy to apply it blindfold and without due regard to facts and conditions.

Life is anyhow a complex affair . . . [Its] conflicts and contradictions . . .
sometimes make one despair a little. It is not surprising that people
should differ, or even that comrades with a common approach to problems should draw different conclusions. But a person who tries to hide
his own weakness in high-sounding phrases and noble principles is apt
to be suspect. A person who tries to save himself from prison by giving
undertakings and assurances to the Government, or by other dubious
conduct, and then has the temerity to criticize others, is likely to injure
the cause he espouses.[1]

	A Backward Look at Development
16	of British Policy, and Observations
	on Communalism and Language

It is interesting to trace British policy since the Rising of 1857 in its
relation to the communal question. Fundamentally and inevitably it has
been one of preventing the Hindu and Moslem from acting together, and
of playing off one community against another. After 1857 the heavy
hand of the British fell more on the Moslems than on the Hindus. They
considered the Moslems more aggressive and militant, possessing
memories of recent rule in India, and therefore, more dangerous. The
Moslems had also kept away from the new education and had few jobs
under the Government.

The new nationalism then grew up from above—the upper-class,
English-speaking intelligentsia—and this was naturally confined to the
Hindus, for the Moslems were educationally very backward. The
Government encouraged the Moslems more to keep them away from the
new nationalist platform. In this task they were helped by an outstanding
personality—Sir Syed Ahmad Khan. Like many of his contemporaries,
he was a great admirer of the British, and a visit to Europe seems to have
had a most powerful effect on him. Visiting England in 1869, he wrote
letters home giving his impressions. In one of these he stated: "All good

[1] T.F., pp. 257-60.

things, spiritual and worldly, which should be found in man, have been bestowed by the Almighty on Europe, and especially on England. . . ." [1]

Sir Valentine Chirol wrote in 1910 in his *Indian Unrest*: "It may be confidently asserted that never before have the Mohammedans of India as a whole identified their interests and their aspirations so closely as at the present day with the consolidation and performance of British rule." Political prophecies are dangerous. Within five years after Sir Valentine wrote, the Moslem intelligentsia was trying hard to break through from the fetters that kept it back and to range itself beside the Congress. Within a decade the Indian Moslems seemed to have outstripped the Congress and were actually giving the lead to it. But these ten years were momentous years, and the Great War had come and gone and left a broken-down world as a legacy.

And yet Sir Valentine had superficially every reason to come to the conclusion he did. The Aga Khan had emerged as the leader of the Moslems, and that fact alone showed that they still clung to their feudal traditions, for the Aga Khan was no bourgeois leader. He was an exceedingly wealthy prince and the religious head of a sect, and from the British point of view he was very much a *persona grata* because of his close association with the British ruling classes. Sir Valentine Chirol tells us that the Aga Khan impressed upon Lord Minto, the Viceroy, "the Mohammedan view of the political situation created by the partition of Bengal, lest political concessions should be hastily made to the Hindus which would pave the way for the ascendency of a Hindu majority equally dangerous to the stability of British rule and to the interests of the Mohammedan minority whose loyalty was beyond dispute."

But behind this superficial lining up with the British Government other forces were working. Inevitably the new Moslem *bourgeoisie* was feeling more and more dissatisfied with existing conditions and was being drawn toward the nationalist movement. The Aga Khan himself had to take notice of this and to warn the British in characteristic language. He wrote in the *Edinburgh Review* of January 1914 (that is, long before the war) advising the Government to abandon the policy of separating Hindus from Moslems, and to rally the moderate of both creeds in a common camp so as to provide a counterpoise to the radical nationalist tendencies of young India—both Hindu and Moslem.

But the Aga Khan or the British Government could not stop the inevitable drift of the Moslem *bourgeoisie* toward nationalism. The World

[1] Quotation from Hans Kohn, *History of Nationalism in the East*, 1929. Harcourt, New York.

War hastened the process, and, as new leaders arose, the Aga Khan seemed to retire into the background. Gandhiji swept most of these leaders and the Moslems generally into his nonco-operation movement, and they played a leading part in the events of 1919–23.

Then came the reaction, and communal and backward elements, both among the Hindus and the Moslems, began to emerge from their enforced retirement. The outstanding fact seems to me how, on both sides, the communal leaders represent a small upper-class reactionary group, and how these people exploit and take advantage of the religious passions of the masses for their own ends.

Latterly there has been an interesting development in the speeches and statements of some of the Moslem communal leaders. This has no real importance, and I doubt if many people think so; nevertheless it is significant of the mentality of communalism, and a great deal of prominence has been given to it. Stress has been laid on the "Moslem nation" in India, on "Moslem culture," on the utter incompatibility of Hindu and Moslem "cultures." The inevitable deduction from this is (although it is not put baldly) that the British must remain in India for ever and ever to hold the scales and mediate between the two "cultures".

A few Hindu communal leaders think exactly on the same lines, with this difference, however, that they hope that, being a majority, their brand of "culture" will ultimately prevail.

Hindu and Moslem "cultures" and the "Moslem nation"—how these words open out fascinating vistas of past history and present and future speculation! The Moslem nation in India—a nation within a nation, and not even compact, but vague, spread out, indeterminate. Politically, the idea is absurd; economically it is fantastic; it is hardly worth considering. To talk of a "Moslem nation", therefore, means that there is no nation at all but a religious bond; it means that no nation in the modern sense must be allowed to grow; it means that modern civilization should be discarded and we should go back to . . . medieval ways; it means either autocratic government or a foreign government; it means, finally, just nothing at all except an emotional state of mind and a conscious or unconscious desire not to face realities, especially economic realities. Emotions have a way of upsetting logic, and we may ignore them simply because they seem so unreasonable. But this idea of a Moslem nation is the figment of a few imaginations only, and, but for the publicity given to it by the press, few people would have heard of it. And, even if many people believed in it, it would still vanish at the touch of reality.

But what is this "Moslem culture"? Is it a kind of racial memory of

the great deeds of the Arabs, Persians, Turks, etc.? Or language? Or art
and music? Or customs? I do not remember any one referring to present-
day Moslem art or Moslem music. The two languages which have
influenced Moslem thought in India are Arabic and Persian, especially
the latter. But the influence of Persian has no element of religion about
it. The Persian language and many Persian customs and traditions came
to India in the course of thousands of years and impressed themselves
powerfully all over north India. Persia was the France of the East,
sending its language and culture to all its neighbours. That is a common
and precious heritage for all of us in India.

I have tried hard to understand what this "Moslem culture" is, but I
confess that I have not succeeded. I find a tiny handful of middle-class
Moslems as well as Hindus in north India influenced by the Persian
language and traditions. The Moslem peasantry and industrial workers
are hardly distinguishable from the Hindu.

I must say that those Hindus and Moslems who are always looking
backward, always clutching at things which are slipping away from their
grasp, are a singularly pathetic sight. I do not wish to damn the past or
to reject it, for there is much that is singularly beautiful in our past. That
will endure, I have no doubt. But it is not the beautiful that these people
clutch at, but something that is seldom worth while and is often harmful.

If progress consists in the individual's taking a broader view of what
constitutes politics, our communalists as well as our Government have
deliberately and consistently aimed at the opposite of this—the narrowing of this view.[1]

In India we are told that our communal divisions come in the way of
our democratic progress, and, therefore, with incontrovertible logic,
those divisions are perpetuated. We are further told that we are not
united enough. In Egypt there are no communal divisions, and it appears
that . . . political unity prevails. And yet, this very unity becomes an
obstacle in the way of democracy and freedom! Truly the path of democracy is straight and narrow. Democracy for an Eastern country seems to
mean only one thing: to carry out the behests of the imperialist ruling
power and not to touch any of its interests. Subject to that proviso,
democratic freedom can flourish unchecked.[2]

[On Language.] I have no doubt whatever that Hindustani is going to
be the common language of India. Indeed it is largely so today for ordinary
purposes. Its progress has been hampered by foolish controversies about

[1] T.F., pp. 289-93.
[2] Ibid., p. 309.

the script. An effort must be made to discourage the extreme tendencies and develop a middle literary language, on the lines of the spoken language in common use. With mass education this will inevitably take place.

Some people imagine that English is likely to become the *lingua franca* of India. That seems to me a fantastic conception, except in respect of a handful of upper-class intelligentsia. It has no relation to the problem of mass education and culture. It may be, as it is partly today, that English will become increasingly a language used for technical, scientific, and business communications, and especially for international contacts. It is essential for many of us to know foreign languages in order to keep in touch with world thought and activities, and I should like our universities to encourage the learning of other languages besides English— French, German, Russian, Spanish, Italian. This does not mean that English should be neglected, but, if we are to have a balanced view of the world, we must not confine ourselves to English spectacles. We have already become sufficiently lopsided in our mental outlook because of this concentration on one aspect and ideology, and even the most rabid of our nationalists hardly realize how much they are cribbed and confined by the British outlook in relation to India.[1]

17 | Whither India, 1933: Social, Economic, Political Factors in Nationalist Struggle

Never in the long range of history has the world been in such a state of flux as it is to-day. Never has there been so much anxious questioning, so much doubt and bewilderment, so much examining of old institutions, existing ills, and suggested remedies. There is a continuous process of change and revolution going on all over the world, and everywhere anxious statesmen are almost at their wits' end and grope about in the dark. It is obvious that we are a part of this great world problem, and must be affected by world events. And yet, judging from the attention

[1] Ibid., p. 287.

paid to these events in India, one would not think so. Major events are recorded in the news columns of papers, but little attempt is made to see behind and beneath them, to understand the forces that are shaking and reforming the world before our eyes, to comprehend the essential nature of social, economic, and political reality. History, whether past or present, becomes just a magic show with little rhyme or reason, and with no lesson for us which might guide our future path. On the gaily-decked official stage of India or England phantom figures come and go, posing for a while as great statesmen; Round Tablers flit about like pale shadows of those who created them, engaged in pitiful and interminable talk which interests few and affects an even smaller number. Their main concern is how to save the vested interests of various classes or groups; their main diversion, apart from feasting, is self-praise. Others, blissfully ignorant of all that has happened in the last half-century, still talk the jargon of the Victorian Age and are surprised and resentful that nobody listens to them. Even the Nasmyth [see Glossary] hammer of war and revolution and world change has failed to produce the slightest dent on their remarkably hard heads. Yet others hide vested interests under cover of communalism or even nationalism. And then there is the vague but passionate nationalism of many who find present conditions intolerable and hunger for national freedom without clearly realizing what form that freedom will take. And there are also here, as in many other countries, the usual accompaniments of a growing nationalism—an idealism, a mysticism, a feeling of exaltation, a belief in the mission of one's country, and something of the nature of religious revivalism. Essentially all these are middle class phenomena.

Our politics must either be those of magic or of science. The former of course requires no argument or logic; the latter is in theory at least entirely based on clarity of thought and reasoning, and has no room for vague idealistic or religious or sentimental processes which confuse and befog the mind. Personally I have no faith in or use for the ways of magic and religion, and I can only consider the question on scientific grounds.

What, then, are we driving at? Freedom? Swaraj? Independence? Dominion Status? Words which may mean much or little or nothing at all. Egypt is "independent," and yet, as everybody knows, it is at present little better than an Indian State, an autocracy imposed upon an unwilling people and propped up by the British. Economically, Egypt is a colony of some of the European imperialist Powers, notably the British. Ever since the World War there has been continuous conflict between Egyptian nationalism and the ruling authorities, and this continues to-day. So in spite of a so-called "independence" Egypt is very far from even national freedom.

Again, whose freedom are we particularly striving for, for nationalism covers many sins and includes many conflicting elements? There is the feudal India of the princes, the India of the big zamindars, of small zamindars, of the professional classes, of the agriculturists, of the industrialists, of the bankers, of the lower middle class, of the workers. There are the interests of foreign capital and those of home capital, of foreign services and home services. The nationalist answer is to prefer home interests to foreign interests, but beyond that it does not go. It tries to avoid disturbing the class divisions or the social *status quo*. It imagines that the various interests will somehow be accommodated when the country is free. Being essentially a middle-class movement, nationalism works chiefly in the interests of that class. It is obvious that there are serious conflicts between various interests in the country, and every law, every policy which is good for one interest may be harmful for another. What is good for the Indian prince may be thoroughly bad for the people of his State, what is profitable for the zamindar may ruin many of his tenants, what is demanded by foreign capital may crush the rising industries of the country.

Nothing is more absurd than to imagine that all the interests in the nation can be fitted in without injury to any. At every step some have to be sacrificed for others. A currency policy may be good for creditors or debtors, not for both at the same time. Inflation, resulting in a reduction or even wiping off of debts, will be welcomed by all debtors and by industry as a rule, but cursed by bankers and those who have fixed incomes. Early in the nineteenth century England deliberately sacrificed her agriculture for her rising industry. A few years ago, in 1925, by insisting on keeping the value of the pound sterling at par she sacrificed, to some extent, her industry to her banking and financial system, and faced industrial troubles and a huge general strike.

Any number of such instances can be given; they deal with the rival claims of different groups of the possessing classes. A more vital conflict of interests arises between these possessing classes as a whole and the others; between the Haves and Have-Nots. All this is obvious enough, but every effort is made to confuse the real issue by the holders of power, whether political or economic. The British Government is continually declaring before high heaven that they are trustees for our masses and India and England have common interests and can march hand in hand to a common destiny. Few people are taken in by this because nationalism makes us realize the inherent conflict between the two national interests. But nationalism does not make us realize the equally inherent and fundamental conflict between economic interests within the nation. There is an attempt to cover this up and avoid it on the ground that the national issue must be settled first. Appeals are issued for unity between different classes and groups to face the common national foe, and those who point out the inherent conflict between landlord and tenant, or capitalist and wage labourer, are criticized.

We may take it that the average person does not like conflict and continuous tension; he prefers peace and quiet, and is even prepared to sacrifice much for it. But the ostrich-like policy of refusing to see a conflict and a disorder which not only exist but are eating into society's vitals, to blind oneself to reality, will not end the conflict and the disorder, or suddenly change reality into unreality; for a politician or a man of action such a policy can only end in disaster. It is therefore essential that we keep this in mind and fashion our idea of freedom accordingly. We cannot escape having to answer the question, now or later, for the freedom of which class or classes in India are we especially striving? Do we place the masses, the peasantry and workers, first, or some other small class at the head of our list? Let us give the benefits of freedom to as many, groups and classes as possible, but essentially whom do we stand for, and when a conflict arises whose side must we take? To say that we shall not answer that question now is itself an answer and taking of sides, for it means that we stand by the existing order, the *status quo*.

The form of government is after all a means to an end; even freedom itself is a means, the end being human well-being, human growth, the ending of poverty and disease and suffering, and the opportunity for every one to live the "good life," physically and mentally. What the "good life" is is a matter we cannot go into here, but most people will agree that freedom is essential to it—national freedom so far as the nation is concerned, personal freedom so far as the individual is concerned. For every restriction and inhibition stops growth and development, and produces, apart from economic disorders, complexes and perversions in the nation and individual. So freedom is necessary. Equally necessary is the will and the capacity for co-operation. Modern life grows so complex, there is so much interdependence, that co-operation is the very breath that keeps it functioning.

The long course of history shows us a succession of different forms of government and changing economic forms of production and organization. The two fit in and shape and influence each other. When economic change goes ahead too fast and the forms of government remain more or less static, a hiatus occurs, which is usually bridged over by a sudden change called revolution. The tremendous importance of economic events in shaping history and forms of government is now almost universally admitted.

We are often told that there is a world of difference between the East and the West. The West is said to be materialistic, the East spiritual, religious, etc. What exactly the East signifies is seldom indicated, for the East includes the Bedouins of the Arabian deserts, the Hindus of India, the nomads of the Siberian Steppes, the pastoral tribes of Mongolia, the typically irreligious Confucians of China, and the Samurai of Japan. There are tremendous national and cultural differences between the different countries of Asia as well as of Europe; but there is no such thing as East and West except in the minds of those who wish to make this an excuse for imperialist domination, or those who have inherited such myths and fictions from a confused metaphysical past. Differences there are but they are chiefly due to different stages of economic growth.

We see, in north-western Europe, autocracy and feudalism giving place to the present capitalist order involving competition and large-scale production. The old small holdings disappear; the feudal checks on the serfs and cultivators go, and these agriculturists are also deprived of the little land they had. Large numbers of landless people are thrown out of employment and they have no land to fall back upon. A landless, property-less proletariat is thus created. At the same time the checks and the controlled prices of the limited markets of feudal times disappear, and the open market appears. Ultimately this leads to the world market, the characteristic feature of capitalism.

Capitalism builds up on the basis of the landless proletariat, which could be employed as wage labourers in the factories, and the open market, where ... machine-made goods could be sold. It grows rapidly and spreads all over the world. In the producing countries it [has been] an active and living capitalism; in the colonial and consuming countries ... just a passive consumption of goods made by machine industry in the West. North-western Europe, and a little later North America [have exploited] the resources of the world ... Asia, Africa, East Europe, and South America. They add vastly to the wealth of the world, but this wealth is largely concentrated in a few nations and a few hands.

In this growth of capitalism, dominion over India [has been] of vital importance to England. India's gold, in the early stages, helped in the further industrialization of England. And then India became a great

producer of raw material to feed the factories of England and a huge
market to consume the goods made in these factories. England, in her
passionate desire to accumulate wealth, sacrificed her agriculture to her
industry. England became almost a kind of vast city, and India the rural
area attached to her.

The concentration of wealth in fewer hands [has gone] on. But the
exploitation of India and other countries brought so much wealth to
England that some of it trickled down to the working class and their
standards of living rose. Working-class agitations were controlled and
soothed by concessions from the capitalist owners, which they could well
afford from the profits of imperialist exploitation. Wages rose; hours of
work went down; there were insurance and other welfare schemes for
the workers. A general prosperity in England took the edge off working-
class discontent.

In India, passive industrialization meant an ever-growing burden on
the land. She became just a consumer of foreign machine-made goods.
Her own cottage industries were partly destroyed forcibly, and partly by
economic forces, and nothing took their place. All the ingredients and
conditions for industrialization were present, but England did not
encourage this, and indeed tried to prevent it by taxing machinery. And
so the burden on the land grew and with it unemployment and poverty,
and there was a progressive ruralization of India.

But the processes of history and economics cannot be stopped for long.
Although general poverty [increased], small groups accumulated some
capital and wanted fields for investment. And so machine industry grew
in India, partly with Indian capital, very much more so with foreign
capital. Indian capital was largely dependent on foreign capital, and, in
particular, could be controlled by the foreign banking system. It is well
known that the World War gave a great push to Indian industry and
afterwards, for reasons of imperial policy, England changed her policy
towards Indian industry and began to encourage it, but mostly with
foreign capital. The growth of so-called swadeshi industries in India thus
represented to a very great extent the increasing hold of British capital
on India.

The growth of industries and nationalist movements in all the countries
of the East checked Western exploitation, and the profits of Western
capitalism began to go down. War debts and other consequences of the
war were a tremendous burden for all the countries concerned. There
was not so much money or profits of industry to be distributed to the
working class in the West, and the discontent and pressure of the workers

grew. There was also the living incentive and inspiration of the Russian Revolution for the workers.

Meanwhile two other processes were working silently but with great rapidity. One was the concentration of wealth and industrial power in fewer hands by the formation of huge trusts, cartels, and combines. The other was a continuous improvement in technique in the methods of production, leading to greater mechanization, far greater production, and more unemployment as workers were replaced by machinery. And this led to a curious result. Just when industry was producing goods on the biggest mass scale in history, there were few people to buy them, as the great majority were too poor to be able to afford them. The armies of the unemployed were not earning anything, so how could they spend? [And] even the majority of those earning had little to spare. A new truth suddenly dawned on the perplexed minds of the great captains of industry (this dawning has not yet taken place among the leaders of industry in India), and the truth was this: that mass production necessitates mass consumption. But if the masses have no money how are they to buy or consume? And what of production then? So production is stopped or restricted and the wheels of industry slow down till they barely move. Unemployment grows all the more, and this again makes consumption diminish.

This is the crisis of capitalism which has had the world by the throat for over four years. Essentially it is due to the ill distribution of the world's wealth; to its concentration in a few hands. And the disease seems to be of the essence of capitalism and grows with it till it eats and destroys the very system which created it. There is no lack of money in the world, no lack of foodstuffs, or the many other things that man requires. The world is richer to-day than it has ever been, and holds promise of untold advance in the near future. And yet the system breaks down, and while millions starve and endure privation huge quantities of foodstuffs and other articles are destroyed, insect pests are let loose on the fields to destroy crops, harvests are not gathered, and nations meet together to confer how to restrict future crops of wheat and cotton and tea and coffee and many other articles. From the beginning of history man has fought with nature to get the barest necessities of life, and now that nature's wealth is poured out before him, enough to remove poverty forever from the world, his only way of dealing with it is to burn and destroy it, and become poorer and more destitute in the process.

History has never offered a more amazing paradox.... Technical advance has gone far ahead of the existing social structure, and, as in the past, this hiatus causes most of our present-day disorders. Till that lag is made up and a new system in keeping with the new technique is adopted, the disorders are likely to continue. The change over to the new system is of course opposed by those who have vested interests in the old system, and though this old system is dying before their eyes they prefer to hold on to their little rather than share a lot with others.

It is not, fundamentally, a moral issue, as some people imagine, although there is a moral side to it. It is not a question of blaming capitalism or cursing capitalists and the like. Capitalism has been of the greatest service to the world, and individual capitalists are but tiny wheels in the big machine. The question now is whether the capitalist system has not outlived its day and must now give place to a better and a saner ordering of human affairs, which is more in keeping with the progress of science and human knowledge.

In India, during this period, the tremendous burden on land continued and even increased, despite the growth of industry in certain areas. Economic discontent increased. The middle class grew up and, finding no sufficient scope for self-development, demanded political changes and took to agitation. More or less similar causes worked all over the colonial and dependent East. Especially after the war, national movements grew rapidly in Egypt and most of the countries of Asia. These movements were essentially due to the distress of the masses and the lower middle classes. There was a strange similarity even in the methods employed by these movements—non-co-operation, boycotts of legislatures, boycotts of goods, *hartals*, strikes, etc. Occasionally there were violent outbreaks, as in Egypt and Syria, but stress was laid far more on peaceful methods. In India, of course, non-violence was made a basic principle by the Congress at the suggestion of Gandhiji. All these national struggles for freedom have continued till now, and they are bound to continue till a solution of the basic problem is found. Fundamentally, this solution is not merely a question of satisfying the natural desire for self-rule, but one of filling hungry stomachs.

The great revolutionary nationalist urge in Asia of the after-war years gradually exhausted itself for the time being and conditions stabilized themselves. In India this took the form of the Swarajist entry into the Assembly and the Councils. In Europe also the middle nineteen-twenties was a period of settling down and adaptation to the new conditions created by the World War. The revolution that had hovered all over Europe in 1919 and 1920 failed to come off and receded into the background. American gold poured into Europe and revived to some extent the war-weary and disillusioned peoples of that continent, and created a false appearance of prosperity. But this prosperity had no real basis and the crash came in 1929, when the United States of America stopped lending money to Europe and South America. Many factors, and especially the inherent conflicts of a declining capitalism, contributed to this crash, and the house of cards of after-war capitalist prosperity began to tumble down. That process of tumbling down has been going on at a tremendous pace for four years, and there is no end to it yet. It is called the slump, trade depression, the crisis, etc., but it is really the evening of the capitalist system, and the world is being compelled by circumstances to recognize this. International trade is reaching [a] vanishing point, international co-operation has failed, the world-market which was the essential basis of capitalism is disappearing, and each nation is trying frantically to shift for itself at the cost of others. Whatever the future may bring, one thing is certain: that the old order has gone and all the king's horses and all the king's men will not set it up again.

As the old capitalist order has tottered the challenge to it by the growing forces of labour has grown more intense. This challenge, when it has become dangerous, has induced the possessing classes to sink their petty differences and band themselves together to fight the common foe. This has led to Fascism and, in its milder forms, to the formation of so-called national governments. Essentially, these are the last ditch efforts of the possessing classes, or the "kept classes" as they have been called by an American economist, to hold on to what they have. The struggle becomes more intense and the forms of nineteenth-century democracy are discarded. But Fascism or national governments offer no solution of the fundamental economic inconsistencies of the present-day capitalist system, and so long as they do not remove the inequalities of wealth and solve the problem of distribution they are doomed to fail. Of the major capitalist countries the United States of America is the only place where some attempt is being made to-day towards lessening to a slight extent inequalities in wealth by State action. . . . England, as is her habit, is grimly muddling through and waiting for something to happen. Meanwhile she has derived considerable help from India's gold and resources. But all this is temporary relief only and the nations slide downhill and approach the brink.

Thus, if we survey the world to-day, we find that capitalism, having solved the problem of production, helplessly faces the allied problem of distribution and is unable to solve it. It was not in the nature of the capitalist system to deal satisfactorily with distribution, and production alone makes the world top-heavy and unbalanced. To find a solution for distributing wealth and purchasing power evenly is to put an end to the basic inequalities of the capitalist system and to replace capitalism itself by a more scientific system.

Capitalism has led to imperialism and to the conflicts of imperialist powers in search for colonial areas for exploitation, for areas of raw produce and for markets for manufactured goods. It has led to ever-increasing conflicts with the rising nationalism of colonial countries, and to social conflicts with powerful movements of the exploited working class. It has resulted in recurrent crises, political and economic, leading to economic and tariff wars as well as political wars on an enormous scale. Every subsequent crisis is on a bigger scale than the previous one, and now we live in a perpetual state of crisis and slump and the shadow of war darkens the horizon.

And yet it is well to remember that the world to-day has a surfeit of food and the other good things of life. Terrible want exists because the present system does not know how to distribute them. Repeated international conferences have failed to find a way out because they represented the claims of vested interests and dared not touch the system itself. They grope blindly in the dark in their stuffy rooms while the foundations of the house they built are being sapped by the advance of science and economic events. Everywhere thinkers have recognized the utter inadequacy of the existing system, though they have differed as to the remedies. . . .

Asia is the main field of conflict between nationalism and imperialism. Asia is still undeveloped as compared to Europe and North America. It has a vast population which can consume goods if [it] had the necessary purchasing power to do so. To the hard-pressed imperialist Powers seeking frantically for areas of economic expansion, Asia still offers a field, though nationalism offers many obstructions. Hence the talk of a "push to Asia" to find an outlet for the surplus goods of the West and thus stabilize Western capitalism for another period. Capitalism is a young and growing force in the East; it has not, as in India, wholly overthrown feudalism yet. But even before capitalism had established itself other forces, inimical to it, have risen to challenge it. And it is obvious that if capitalism collapses in Europe and America it cannot survive in Asia.

Nationalism is still the strongest force in Asia (we can ignore for our present purpose the Soviet territories of Asia). This is natural as a country under alien domination must inevitably think first in terms of nationalism.

But the powerful economic forces working for change in the world to-day have influenced this nationalism to an ever-increasing extent, and everywhere it is appearing in Socialistic garb. Gradually the nationalist struggle for political freedom is becoming a social struggle also for economic freedom. Independence and the Socialist State become the objectives, with varying degrees of stress being laid on the two aspects of the problem. As political freedom is delayed, the other aspect assumes greater importance, and it now seems probable, especially because of world conditions, that political and social emancipation will come together to some at least of the countries of Asia. . . .

In India, as in other Asiatic colonial countries, we find a struggle to-day between the old nationalist ideology and the new economic ideology. Most of us have grown up under the nationalist tradition, and it is hard to give up the mental habits of a lifetime. And yet we realize that this outlook is inadequate; it does not fit in with existing conditions in our country or in the world; there is a hiatus, a lag. We try to bridge this hiatus, but the process of crossing over to a new ideology is always a painful one. Many of us are confused and perplexed to-day because of this. But the crossing has to be made, unless we are to remain in a stagnant backwater, overwhelmed from time to time by the wash of the boats that move down the river of progress. We must realize that the nineteenth century cannot solve the problems of the twentieth. . . .

Having glanced at the general background of Asia and the world we can have a clearer view of our own national problem. India's freedom affects each one of us intimately, and we are apt to look upon it as a thing apart and unconnected with world events. But the Indian problem is a part of the Asiatic problem and is tied up with the problems of the world. We cannot, even if we will it, separate it from the rest. What happens in India will affect the world and world events will change India's future. Indeed it may be said that the three great world problems to-day are: the fate of capitalism, which means the fate of Europe and America, the future of India, and the future of China, and all these are interrelated.

India's struggle to-day is part of the great struggle which is going on all over the world for the emancipation of the oppressed. Essentially, this is an economic struggle, with hunger and want as its driving forces, although it puts on nationalist and other dresses.

Indian freedom is necessary because the burden on the Indian masses as well as the middle classes is too heavy to be borne, and must be lightened or done away with. The measure of freedom is the extent to which this burden is removed. This burden is due to the vested interests of a foreign government as well as those of certain groups and classes in India and abroad. The achievement of freedom thus becomes a question, as Gandhiji said recently, of divesting vested interests. If an indigenous government took the place of the foreign government and kept all the vested interests intact, this would not even be the shadow of freedom.

We have got into an extraordinary habit of thinking of freedom in terms of paper constitutions. Nothing could be more absurd than this lawyer's mentality which ignores life and the vital economic issues and can only proceed on the basis of the *status quo* and precedents. . . .

The [recent] Round Table scheme is almost as dead as Queen Anne and hardly deserves notice. It was not meant to give an iota of freedom to the Indian people; it sought to win over certain Indian vested interests to the British side and in this it succeeded. It answered, to the satisfaction of its votaries, the question I had formulated at the beginning of this essay: whose freedom are we striving for? It gave greater protection and assurance and freedom to the British vested interests in India. It was Home Rule for the Viceroy. . . . It confirmed the interests of British capital and British services and, in some cases, gave them even more than they have now. It tried to perpetuate the alien military occupation of India. Further, it gave greater freedom and importance to the vested interests of the princes and the semi-feudal magnates. In brief, the whole scheme was meant for the protection and perpetuation of the numerous vested interests that exploit the Indian masses. Having done this useful and, to themselves, profitable piece of work, the originators of the scheme told us that autonomy was a costly affair and would mean the expenditure of many extra millions for each province! Thus not only were all the old burdens on the masses to be continued, but many new ones were to be added. This was the ingenious solution discovered by the wise and learned men who foregathered at the Round Table Conference. Intent on protecting their class privileges they happened to forget an odd three hundred and fifty million people in India.

Even a child in politics can point out the folly of this procedure. The whole basis and urge of the national movement came from a desire for economic betterment, to throw off the burdens that crushed the masses, and to end the exploitation of the Indian people. If these burdens continue and are actually added to, it does not require a powerful mind to realize that the fight must not only continue but grow more intense. Leaders and individuals may come and go; they may get tired and slacken off; they may compromise or betray; but the exploited and suffering masses must carry on the struggle, for their drill-sergeant is hunger. Swaraj or freedom from exploitation for them is not a fine paper constitution or a problem of the hereafter. It is a question of the here and now, of immediate relief. Roast lamb and mint sauce may be a tasty dish for those who eat it, but the poor lamb is not likely to appreciate the force of the best of arguments which point out the beauty of sacrifice for the good of the elect and the joys of close communion, even though dead, with mint sauce.

India's immediate goal can therefore only be considered in terms of the ending of the exploitation of her people. Politically, it must mean independence and the severance of the British connection, which means imperialist dominion; economically and socially it must mean the ending of all special class privileges and vested interests. The whole world is struggling to this end; India can do no less, and in this way the Indian struggle for freedom lines up with the world struggle. Is our aim human welfare or the preservation of class privileges and the vested interests of pampered groups? The question must be answered clearly and unequivocally by each one of us. There is no room for quibbling when the fate of nations and millions of human beings is at stake. The day for palace intrigues and parlour politics and pacts and compromises passes when the masses enter politics. Their manners are not those of the drawing-room; we never took the trouble to teach them any manners. Their school is the school of events and suffering is their teacher. They learn their politics from great movements which bring out the true nature of individuals and classes, and the civil disobedience movement has taught the Indian masses many a lesson which they will never forget.

Independence is a much-abused word and it hardly connotes what we are driving at. And yet there is no other suitable word and, for want of a better, we must use it. National isolation is neither a desirable nor a possible ideal in a world which is daily becoming more of a unit. International and intranational activities dominate the world and nations are growing more and more interdependent. Our ideal and objective cannot go against this historical tendency, and we must be prepared to discard a narrow nationalism in favour of world co-operation and real internationalism. Independence therefore cannot mean for us isolation but freedom from all imperialist control, and because Britain to-day represents imperialism, our freedom can only come after the British connection is severed. We have no quarrel with the British people, but between British imperialism and Indian freedom there is no meeting ground and there can be no peace. If imperialism goes from Britain we shall

gladly co-operate with her in the wider international field; not otherwise.

British statesmen of the Liberal and Labour variety often point out to
us the ills of a narrow nationalism and dwell on the virtues of what used
to be known as the British Empire and is now euphemistically called the
British Commonwealth of Nations. Under cover of fine and radical
words and phrases they seek to hide the ugly and brutal face of imperialism
and try to keep us in its embrace of death. Some Indian public men,
who ought to know better, also praise the virtues of internationalism,
meaning thereby the British Empire, and tell us in sorrow how narrow-
minded we are in demanding independence, in place of that wonderful
thing (which nobody offers us) Dominion Status. The British, it is well
known, have a remarkable capacity for combining their moral instincts
with their self-interest. That is perhaps not unnatural, but it is remarkable
how some of our own countrymen are taken in by this unctuous and
hypocritical attitude. Even the light of day is wasted on those who keep
their eyes shut. It is worth noting, however, that the foreign policy of
England has been the greatest stumbling-block to international co-
operation through the League of Nations or otherwise. All the European
and American world knows this, but most of us, who look at foreign
politics through English spectacles, have not grasped this fact yet. Disarmament, air-bombing, the attitude to the Manchurian question, are
some of the recent witnesses to England's attitude. Even the Kellogg-
Briand Pact of Paris, which was to have outlawed war, was only accepted
by England subject to certain qualifications and reservations regarding
her empire, which effectively nullified the Pact. The British Empire and
real internationalism are as the poles apart, and it is not through that
empire that we can march to internationalism.

The real question before us, and before the whole world, is one of
fundamental change of regime politically, economically, socially. Only
thus can we put India on the road to progress and stop the progressive
deterioration of our country. In a revolutionary period, such as exists in
the world to-day, it is [a] foolish waste of energy to think and act in
terms of carrying on the existing regime and trying to reform it and
improve it. To do so is to waste the opportunity which history offers
once in a while. . . .

Whither India? Surely to the great human goal of social and economic
equality, to the ending of an exploitation of nation by nation and class by
class, to national freedom within the framework of an international co-
operative Socialist world federation. This is not such an empty idealist

dream as some people imagine. It is within the range of the practical politics of to-day and the near future. We may not have it within our grasp, but those with vision can see it emerging on the horizon. And even if there be delay in the realization of our goal, what does it matter if our steps march in the right direction and our eyes look steadily in front? For in the pursuit itself of a mighty purpose there is joy and happiness and a measure of achievement.[1]

18 | A Fresh Look at India— Her Strengths and Weaknesses

If there had only been a long and unrelieved period of frigidity and stagnation, this might well have resulted in a complete break with the past, the death of an era, and the erection of something new on its ruins. There has not been such a break and there is a definite continuity. Also from time to time vivid flashes of renascence have occurred, and some of them have been long and brilliant. Always there is visible an attempt to understand and adapt the new and harmonize it with the old, or at any rate with parts of the old which were considered worth preserving. Often that old retains an external form only, as a kind of symbol, and changes its inner content. But something vital and living continued, some urge driving the people in a direction not wholly realized, always a desire for synthesis between the old and the new. It was this urge and desire that kept them going and enabled them to absorb new ideas while retaining much of the old. Whether there was such a thing as an Indian dream through the ages, vivid and full of life or sometimes reduced to the murmurings of troubled sleep, I do not know. Every people and every nation has some such belief or myth of national destiny, and perhaps it is partly true in each case. Being an Indian, I am myself influenced by this reality or myth about India, and I feel that anything that had the power to mold hundreds of generations, without a break, must have drawn its enduring vitality from some deep well of strength, and have had the capacity to renew that vitality from age to age.

[1] I.T.W., pp. 39–63.

Was there some such well of strength? And if so, did it dry up, or did it have hidden springs to replenish it? What of today? Are there any springs still functioning from which we can refresh and strengthen ourselves? We are an old race, or rather an odd mixture of many races, and our racial memories go back to the dawn of history. Have we had our day and are we now living in the later afternoon or evening of our existence, just carrying on after the manner of the aged, quiescent, devitalized, uncreative, desiring peace and sleep above all else?

No people, no race continues unchanged. Continually it is mixing with others and slowly changing; it may appear to die almost and then rise again as a new people or just a variation of the old. There may be a definite break between the old people and the new, or vital links of thought and ideals may join them.

History has numerous instances of old and well-established civilizations fading away or being ended suddenly, and vigorous new cultures taking their place. Is it some vital energy, some inner source of strength that gives life to a civilization or a people, without it all effort being ineffective, like the vain attempt of an aged person to play the part of a youth?

Among the peoples of the world today I have sensed this vital energy chiefly in three—Americans, Russians, and the Chinese: a queer combination! Americans, in spite of having their roots in the old world, are a new people, uninhibited and without the burdens and complexes of old races, and it is easy to understand their abounding vitality. So also are the Canadians, Australians, and New Zealanders, all of them largely cut off from the old world and facing life in all its newness.

Russians are not a new people, and yet there has been a complete break from the old, like that of death, and they have been reincarnated anew, in a manner for which there is no example in history. They have become youthful again.... They are searching for some of their old roots again, but for all practical purposes they are a new people, a new race and a new civilization.

The Russian example shows how a people can revitalize itself, become youthful again, if it is prepared to pay the price for it, and tap the springs of suppressed strength and energy among the masses....

The Chinese stand apart from all these. They are not a new race, nor have they gone through that shock of change, from top to bottom, which came to Russia. [But] the vitality of the Chinese people astonishes me. I cannot imagine a people endowed with such bedrock strength going under.

Something of that vitality which I saw in China, I have sensed at times in the Indian people also. Not always, and anyway it is difficult for me to take an objective view. Perhaps my wishes distort my thinking. But always I was in search for this in my wanderings among the Indian people. If they had this vitality, then it was well with them and they would make good. If they lacked it completely, then our political efforts and shouting were all make-believe and would not carry us far. I was not interested in making some political arrangement which would enable our people to carry on more or less as before, only a little better. I felt they had vast stores of suppressed energy and ability, and I wanted to release these and make them feel young and vital again. India, constituted as she is, cannot play a secondary part in the world. She will either count for a great deal or not count at all. No middle position attracted me. Nor did I think any intermediate position feasible.

Behind the vast quarter of a century's struggle for India's independence, and all our conflicts with British authority, lay in my mind and that of many others the desire to revitalize India.[1]

During the thirties, in the intervals of my life out of prison . . . I traveled more extensively throughout India, in towns and cities and villages. . . . Except for rural Bengal, which unhappily I have only rarely visited, I toured in every province and went deep into villages. I spoke of political and economic issues. . . . But all this while, in a corner of my mind, lay something deeper and more vivid. . . . Another and a major excitement had seized me, and I was again on a great voyage of discovery and the land of India and the people of India lay spread out before me. India with all her infinite charm and variety began to grow upon me more and more, and yet the more I saw of her, the more I realized how very difficult it was for me or for anyone else to grasp the ideas she had embodied. It was not her wide spaces that eluded me, or even her diversity, but some depth of soul which I could not fathom, though I had occasional glimpses of it. She was like some ancient palimpsest on which layer upon layer of thought and revery had been inscribed, and yet no succeeding layer had completely hidden or erased what had been written previously. All of these existed together in our conscious or subconscious selves, though we might not be aware of them, and they had gone to build up the complex and mysterious personality of India. That sphinxlike face with its elusive and sometimes mocking smile was to be seen throughout the length and breadth of the land. Though outwardly there was diversity

[1] D.I., pp. 42–45.

and infinite variety among our people, everywhere there was that tremendous impress of oneness, which had held all of us together for ages past, whatever political fate or misfortune had befallen us. The unity of India was no longer merely an intellectual conception for me: it was an emotional experience which overpowered me. That essential unity had been so powerful that no political division, no disaster or catastrophe had been able to overcome it.

It was absurd, of course, to think of India or any country as a kind of anthropomorphic entity. I did not do so. I was also fully aware of the diversities and divisions of Indian life, of classes, castes, religions, races, different degrees of cultural development. Yet I think that a country with a long cultural background and a common outlook on life develops a spirit that is peculiar to it and that is impressed on all its children, however much they may differ among themselves. Can anyone fail to see this in China, whether he meets an old-fashioned mandarin or a Communist who has apparently broken with the past? It was this spirit of India that I was after, not through idle curiosity, though I was curious enough, but because I felt that it might give me some key to the understanding of my country and people, some guidance to thought and action. Politics and elections were day-to-day affairs when we grew excited over trumpery matters. But if we were going to build the house of India's future, strong and secure and beautiful, we would have to dig deep for the foundations. . . .

The diversity of India is tremendous; it is obvious; it lies on the surface and anybody can see it. It concerns itself with physical appearances as well as with certain mental habits and traits. There is little in common, to outward seeming, between the Pathan of the northwest and the Tamil in the far south. Their racial stocks are not the same, though there may be common strands running through them; they differ in face and figure, food and clothing, and, of course, language. In the North-Western Frontier Province there is already the breath of central Asia, and many a custom there, as in Kashmir, reminds one of the countries on the other side of the Himalayas. Pathan popular dances are singularly like Russian Cossack dancing. Yet with all these differences, there is no mistaking the impress of India on the Pathan, as this is obvious on the Tamil. It is not surprising, for these border lands, and indeed Afghanistan also, were united with India for thousands of years. The old Turkish and other races who inhabited Afghanistan and parts of central Asia before the advent of Islam were largely Buddhists, and earlier still, during the period of the

Epics, Hindus. The frontier area was one of the principal centers of old Indian culture, and it abounds still with ruins of monuments and monasteries and especially of the great university of Taxila, which was at the height of its fame two thousand years ago, attracting students from all over India as well as different parts of Asia. Changes of religion made a difference but could not change entirely the mental backgrounds which the people of those areas had developed.

The Pathan and the Tamil are two extreme examples; the others lie somewhere in between. All of them have their distinctive features, all of them have still more the distinguishing mark of India. It is fascinating to find how the Bengalese, the Marathas, the Gujratis, the Tamils, the Andhras, the Oriyas, the Assamese, the Canarese, the Malayalis, the Sindhis, the Punjabis, the Pathans, the Kashmiris, the Rajputs, and the great central bloc comprising the Hindustani-speaking people, have retained their peculiar characteristics for hundreds of years, have still more or less the same virtues and failings of which old tradition or record tells us, and yet have been throughout these ages distinctively Indian, with the same national heritage and the same set of moral and mental qualities. There was something living and dynamic about this heritage which showed itself in ways of living and a philosophical attitude to life and its problems. Ancient India, like ancient China, was a world in itself, a culture and a civilisation which gave shape to all things. Foreign influences poured in and often influenced that culture and were absorbed. Disruptive tendencies gave rise immediately to an attempt to find a synthesis. Some kind of a dream of unity has occupied the mind of India since the dawn of civilization. That unity was not conceived as something imposed from outside, a standardization of externals or even of beliefs. It was something deeper, and within its fold the widest tolerance of belief and custom was practiced and every variety acknowledged and even encouraged.

Differences, big or small, can always be noticed even within a national group, however closely bound together it may be. The essential unity of that group becomes apparent when it is compared to another national group, though often the differences between two adjoining groups fade out or intermingle near the frontiers, and modern developments are tending to produce a certain uniformity everywhere. In ancient and medieval times the idea of the modern nation was nonexistent, and feudal, religious, racial or cultural bonds had more importance. Yet I think that at almost any time in recorded history an Indian would have felt more or less at home in any part of India, and would have felt as a

stranger and alien in any other country. He would certainly have felt less
of a stranger in countries which had partly adopted his culture or
religion. Those who professed a religion of non-Indian origin and coming
to India settled down there, became distinctively Indian in the course of
a few generations, such as Christians, Jews, Parsees, Moslems. Indian
converts to some of these religions never ceased to be Indians in spite of
a change of faith. All these were looked upon in other countries as
Indians and foreigners, even though there might have been a community
of faith between them.

Today, when the conception of nationalism has developed much more,
Indians in foreign countries inevitably form a national group and hang
together for various purposes, in spite of their internal differences. An
Indian Christian is looked upon as an Indian wherever he may go. An
Indian Moslem is considered an Indian in Turkey or Arabia or Iran or
any other country where Islam is the dominant religion.

All of us, I suppose, have varying pictures of our native land and no
two persons will think exactly alike. When I think of India, I think of
many things: of broad fields dotted with innumerable small villages; of
towns and cities I have visited; of the magic of the rainy season which
pours life into the dry, parched-up land and converts it suddenly into a
glistening expanse of beauty and greenery, of great rivers and flowing
water; of the Khyber Pass in all its bleak surroundings; of the southern
tip of India; of people, individually and in the mass; and above all, of
the Himalayas, snow-capped, or some mountain valley in Kashmir in the
spring, covered with new flowers, and with a brook bubbling and gurgling
through it. We make and preserve the pictures of our choice, and so I
have chosen this mountain background rather than the more normal
picture of a hot, subtropical country. Both pictures would be correct,
for India stretches from the tropics right up to the temperate regions,
from the near equator to the cold heart of Asia.[1]

I [have seen] the moving drama of the Indian people in the present,
and could often trace the threads which bound their lives to the past,
even while their eyes were turned toward the future. Everywhere I found
a cultural background which had exerted a powerful influence on their
lives. This background was a mixture of popular philosophy, tradition,
history, myth and legend, and it was not possible to draw a line between
any of these. Even the entirely uneducated and illiterate shared this
background. The old epics of India, the *Ramayana* and the *Mahabharata*

[1] Ibid., pp. 47-51.

and other books, in popular translations and paraphrases, were widely known among the masses, and every incident and story and moral in them was engraved on the popular mind and gave a richness and content to it. Illiterate villagers would know hundreds of verses by heart, and their conversation would be full of references to them or to some story with a moral, enshrined in some old classic. Often I was surprised by some such literary turn given by a group of villagers to a simple talk about present-day affairs. If my mind was full of pictures from recorded history and more-or-less ascertained fact, I realized that even the illiterate peasant had a picture gallery in his mind, though this was largely drawn from myth and tradition and epic heroes and heroines, and only very little from history. Nevertheless it was vivid enough.

I looked at their faces and their figures and watched their movements. There was many a sensitive face and many a sturdy body, straight and clean-limbed; and among the women there was grace and suppleness and dignity and poise and, very often, a look that was full of melancholy. Usually the finer physical types were among the upper castes, who were just a little better off in the economic sense. Sometimes, as I was passing along a country road or through a village, I would start with surprise on seeing a fine type of a man, or a beautiful woman who reminded me of some fresco of ancient times. And I wondered how the type endured and continued through ages, in spite of all the horror and misery that India had gone through. What could we not do with these people under better conditions and with greater opportunities opening out to them?[1]

19 | Possibility of Rearrest, 1933–1934—
Further Thoughts on Communalism—
Impact of Domestic and International
Developments

Possibility of Rearrest, 1933–1934

The possibility of my rearrest and conviction always hung over me. It was, indeed, more than a possibility when the land was ruled by ordinances

[1] Ibid., p. 56.

... and Congress itself was an illegal organization. Constituted as the British Government was, and constituted as I was, my suppression seemed inevitable. This ever-present prospect influenced my work. I could not settle down to anything, and I was in a hurry to get through as much as possible.

Yet I had no desire to invite arrest, and to a large extent I avoided activities which might lead to it. Invitations came to me from many places ... to undertake a tour. I refused them, for any such speaking tour could only be a raging campaign which would be abruptly ended. There was no halfway house for me then. When I visited any place for some other object—to confer with Gandhiji and the Working Committee members—I addressed public meetings and spoke freely. . . . Indeed, the very success of these meetings made it clear that the Government would not tolerate their frequent repetition. In Delhi, soon after [a] meeting, there was a strong rumour of my impending arrest, but I survived and returned to Allahabad. . . .

Twice ... the members of the Working Committee met together to consider the all-India situation. The Committee itself was not functioning, not so much because it was an illegal body but because, at Gandhiji's [insistence] . . . all Congress committees and offices had been suspended. I happened to occupy a peculiar position as, on coming out of jail [in August, 1933] I refused to join this self-denying ordinance and insisted on calling myself the general secretary of the Congress. But I functioned in the air. There was no proper office, no staff, no acting president. . . .

There was an impasse, and no way out of it agreeable to everybody. . . .

Meanwhile I continued sending articles and statements to the press. To some extent I had to tone down my writings, for they were written with a view to publication, and there was the censor and various laws whose octopuslike tentacles reached far. Even if I was prepared to take risks, the printers, publishers, and editors were not. On the whole the newspapers were good to me and stretched many a point in my favor. But not always. Sometimes statements and passages were suppressed, and once a whole long article, over which I had taken some pains, never saw the light of day. When I was in Calcutta in January 1934, the editor of one of the leading dailies came to see me. He told me that he had sent one of my statements to the editor-in-chief of all Calcutta newspapers for his opinion, and, as the editor-in-chief had disapproved of it, it had not been published. The "editor-in-chief" was the Government press censor for Calcutta.

In some of my press interviews and statements I ventured to criticize forcibly some groups and individuals. This was resented, partly because of the idea, which Gandhiji had helped to spread, that Congress could be attacked without any danger of its hitting back.

The effect of my socialist propaganda upset even some of my colleagues of the Working Committee. They would have put up with me without complaint, as they had done for several years during which I had been carrying on this propaganda, but I was now frightening to some extent the vested interests in the country, and my activities could no longer be called innocuous. I knew that some of my colleagues were no socialists, but I had always thought that, as a member of the Congress Executive, I had perfect freedom to carry on socialist propaganda without committing the Congress to it. The realization that some members of the Working Committee did not think that I had that freedom came as a surprise. I was putting them in a false position, and they resented it. But what was I to do? I was not going to give up what I considered the most important part of my work. I would much rather resign from the Working Committee if there was a conflict between the two. But how could I resign when the Committee was illegal and was not even functioning properly?

This difficulty faced me again later . . . when Gandhiji wrote to me from Madras. He sent me a cutting from the *Madras Mail* containing an interview he had given. The interviewer had asked him about me, and he had replied almost apologizing for my activities and expressing his faith in my rectitude: I would not commit the Congress to these novel ways. I did not particularly fancy this reference to me, but what upset me much more was Gandhiji's defense, further on in the interview, of the big zamindari system. He seemed to think that this was a very desirable part of rural and national economy. This was a great surprise to me, for the big zamindaris and talukas have very few defenders today. All over the world they have been broken up, and even in India most people recognize that they cannot last long. Even talukdars and zamindars would welcome an end of the system, provided, of course, they got sufficient compensation therefor. The system is indeed sinking of its own weight. And yet Gandhiji was in favor of it and talked of trusteeship and the like. How very different was his outlook from mine, I thought again, and I wondered how far I could co-operate with him in future. Must I continue to remain in the Working Committee? There was no way out just then, and a few weeks later the question became irrelevant because of my return to prison.[1]

[1] T.F., pp. 293–95.

Further Thoughts on Communalism

[Nehru continued to find it incomprehensible that the various religious groups in India should not be able to live together in harmony.]

Personally I think that it is generally possible to cooperate with communalists provided the political objective is the same. But between progress and reaction, between those who struggle for freedom and those who are content with servitude, and even wish to prolong it, there is no meeting ground. And it is this political reaction which has stalked the land under cover of communalism and taken advantage of the fear of each community of the other. It is the fear complex that we have to deal with in these communal problems. Honest communalism is fear; false communalism is political reaction. . . .

It [is] natural for the British government to support and push on the reactionary leaders of the Muslims and to try to ignore the nationalist ones. It . . . also [has been] natural . . . to accede to most of [the former's] demands . . . to strengthen their position in their own community and weaken the national struggle. A very little knowledge of history will show that this has always been done by ruling powers. The Muslim demands [have] not in any way [lessened] the control of the British in India. To some extent they helped the British to add to their proposed special powers and to show to the world how necessary their continued presence in India [is].[1]

I am convinced that nationalism can only come out of the ideological fusion of Hindu, Muslim, Sikh and other groups in India. That does not and need not mean the extinction of any real culture of any group, but it does mean a common national outlook, to which other matters are subordinated. I do not think that Hindu-Muslim or other unity will come merely by reciting it like a *mantra*. That it will come, I have no doubt, but it will come from below, not above, for many of those above are too much interested in British domination, and hope to preserve their special privileges through it. Social and economic forces will inevitably bring other problems to the front. They will create cleavages along different lines, but the communal cleavage will go.[2]

I do not think that the Muslim communal organisations, chief among whom are the Muslim All Parties Conference and the Muslim League,

[1] R.E.W., pp. 48–49.
[2] Ibid., p. 58.

represent any large group of Muslims in India except in the sense that they exploit the prevailing communal sentiment. But the fact remains that they claim to speak for Muslims and no other organization has so far arisen which can successfully challenge that claim. Their aggressively communal character gives them a pull over the large number of nationalist Muslims who merge themselves in the Congress. The leaders of these organisations are patently and intensely communal. That, from the very nature of things, one can understand. But it is equally obvious that most of them are definitely anti-national and political reactionaries of the worst kind. Apparently they do not even look forward to any common nation developing in India.[1]

How do ... communal demands meet the needs of the masses? What is the programme of the Hindu Mahasabha or the Muslim League for the workers, the peasants, and the lower middle classes, which form the great bulk of the nation? They have no programme except a negative one.... The Muslim communalists tell us a great deal about the democracy of Islam but are afraid of democracy in practice; the Hindu communalists talk of nationalism and think in terms of a 'Hindu nationalism'.[2]

The chief Hindu communal organization is the Hindu Mahasabha, the counterpart of the Moslem League, but relatively less important. It is as aggressively communal as the League, but it tries to cover up its extreme narrowness of outlook by using some kind of vague national terminology, though its outlook is more revivalist than progressive. It is peculiarly unfortunate in some of its leaders who indulge in irresponsible and violent diatribes, as indeed some of the Moslem League leaders also do. This verbal warfare, indulged in on both sides, is a constant irritant. It takes the place of action.

The Moslem League's communal attitude was often difficult and unreasonable in the past, but no less unreasonable [than] the attitude of the Hindu Mahasabha.... British policy [has been] to encourage and emphasize ... differences and to give importance to communal organizations as against the Congress.[3]

Much as I dislike communalism I realise that it does not disappear by suppression but by a removal of the feeling of fear, or by a diversion of interests. We should therefore remove this fear complex and make the

[1] Ibid., p. 47.
[2] Ibid., pp. 57–58.
[3] D.I., p. 391.

Muslim masses realise that they can have any protection that they really desire. I feel that this realisation will go a long way in toning down the feeling of communalism. . . .

Communalism is essentially a hunt for favours from a third party— the ruling power. The communalist can think only in terms of a continuation of foreign domination and he tries to make the best of it for his own particular group. Delete the foreign power and communal arguments and demands fall to the ground. Both the foreign power and the communalists, as representing some upper class groups, want no essential change of the political and economic structure; both are interested in the preservation and augmentation of their vested interests. Because of this, both cannot tackle the real economic problems which confront the country, for a solution of these would upset the present social structure and divest the vested interests. For both, this ostrich-like policy of ignoring real issues is bound to end in disaster. Facts and economic forces are more powerful than governments and empires and can only be ignored at peril.

Communalism thus becomes another name for political and social reaction and the British Government, being the citadel of this reaction in India, naturally throws its sheltering wings over a useful ally. Many a false trail is drawn to confuse the issue; we are told of Islamic culture and Hindu culture, of religion and old custom, of ancient glories and the like. But behind all this lies political and social reaction, and communalism must therefore be fought on all fronts and given no quarter. Because the inward nature of communalism has not been sufficiently realized, it has often sailed under false colours and taken in many an unwary person. It is an undoubted fact that many a Congressman has almost unconsciously partly succumbed to it and tried to reconcile his nationalism with this narrow and reactionary creed. . . . It is time that Congressmen and others who have flirted with Hindu or Muslim or Sikh or any other communalism should understand [its true nature] and make their choice. No one can have it both ways, and the choice lies between political progress [on the one hand] . . . [and] a blind ignoring of world forces and events [on the other].

What are communal organizations? They are not religious although they confine themselves to religious groups and exploit the name of religion. They are not cultural and have done nothing for culture although they talk bravely of a past culture. They are not ethical or moral groups for their teachings are singularly devoid of all ethics and morality. They are certainly not economic groupings for there is no economic link binding their members and they have no shadow of an economic programme. Some of them claim not [even] to be political. . . . What then are they?

As a matter of fact they function politically and their demands are political, but calling themselves non-political, they avoid the real issues and only succeed in obstructing the path of others. If they are political organizations then we are entitled to know exactly how they stand. Do they stand for the complete freedom of India or a partial freedom, if such a thing exists? Do they stand for independence or what is called dominion status? The best of words are apt to be misleading and many people still think that dominion status [under empire] is something next door to independence. As a matter of fact they are . . . different . . . entirely, two roads going in opposite directions.[1]

Whether socialism or communism is the right answer or some other, one thing is certain—that the answer must be in terms of economics and not merely politics. For India and the world are oppressed by economic problems and there is no escaping them. So long as the fullest economic freedom does not come to us, there can be no freedom whatever the political structure may be. Economic freedom must of course include political freedom. That is the reality today; all else is myth and delusion, and there is no greater myth than the communal myth. . . . If a really popular Assembly met with freedom to face and decide the real issues, immediately these real economic problems would occupy attention. The so-called communal problem will fade into the background for the masses will be far more interested in filling their hungry stomachs than in questions of percentages. [Such an] Assembly will release the vital forces in the country which are at present suppressed by our foreign rulers as well as by Indian vested interests. The lead will go to the masses and the masses, when free, though they may sometimes err, think in terms of reality and have no use for myths. The workers and the peasantry will dominate the situation, and their decisions, imperfect though they be, will take us a long way to freedom. . . . I am sure that the communal problem will cease to exist when it is put to the hard test of real mass opinion. It has been a hot house growth nurtured in the heated atmosphere of conference rooms and so-called All Parties' Conferences. It will not find a solution in that artificial environment, but it will wilt and die in the fresh air and the sunlight.[2]

[1] R.E.W., pp. 72–75.
[2] Ibid., pp. 78–79.

Impact of Domestic and International Developments

Are we to prepare for some distant future struggle for a problematic freedom in the hereafter, or do we consider that objective conditions in the country and the world are such that the struggle is here and now, or in the near future, and we have to face it. If we adopt the latter answer, as I think we must, then we must carry on the struggle and try to shape it and try to develop a new ideology through it and in the course of it.

World events of the past decade or more have many lessons to teach us. There is the pitiful and miserable failure of social democracy in England, Germany and other countries. There is also the failure to make good or to rouse the masses, in spite of suitable economic conditions, of the communist parties of various countries (excluding the Soviet Union). In most countries communism is represented by three or four different groups or parties, each cursing and slandering the other, wholly incapable of united action, and often forgetting the common foe in their mutual hatreds. It is perfectly clear that however correct the ideology of the Communist International may have been, their tactics have failed.

In India we see, during the past thirteen years, a subservient and demoralised people, incapable of any action and much less united action, suddenly develop backbone and [the] power of resistance and an amazing capacity for united action, [also the power to] challenge the might of a great and entrenched empire. Is this a little thing that we have achieved? Or is it not one of the most remarkable examples of mass regeneration? And are we not entitled to claim that the methods that brought about this great change are worthy and desirable methods? Those who criticise these methods might well compare the achievement of India during these years with that of any other colonial and semi-colonial country. They might also compare the achievement of others in India trying to work differently. . . .

It would be a good thing if some of our critics made a grand tour of India from the Khyber Pass in the north to the south and east and west and studied the situation for themselves. They would find that the Congress is not only not defunct but is very much alive and functioning in many areas, and is going to function despite anything that might happen. They would discover the strange ferment in the peasantry and the new temper of the army. One is a little apt to misjudge India by conditions prevailing in a city, especially when our newspapers do not even publish the news. . . . The mere fact that . . . amazing methods of repression are being resorted to still is proof enough of the strength of our movement and the nervous and fearful state of Government. Why should it resort to these extraordinary methods if it felt that there was no life left in our movement?

I have been told that I stand for a federation with the princes and feudal lords without in any way questioning their despotism. This is a somewhat remarkable interpretation of what I have said. Certainly I think that a federation is likely to be established in the India that is to be, but I cannot conceive of any stable federation, certainly not one to which I can agree, to which the feudal chiefs are parties. I believe that the whole Indian State system must go root and branch.

It might be as well to remember that I am not the Congress and the Congress is not Jawaharlal Nehru. It has been my great privilege to work in the Congress for the best years of my life and perhaps sometimes I have had a little influence over its decisions. But I am not presumptuous enough to imagine that I can carry the Congress with me wherever I will. I have long felt that the Congress is [by] far the most effective radical organisation in the country and it is easier to work great changes in the mass mentality through it rather than through any other means. So long as I feel that I shall gladly and most willingly work with this great organisation, which has done so much for the country, even though it may not go far enough from my point of view. And so long as that is the case no question can arise of my thinking of another organisation.

People forget sometimes that we are functioning abnormally. They discuss the constitutional issue in terms of normality or they criticise the Congress for its seeming inactivity, forgetting that the Congress has arrived at a certain stage of historical growth. It is not at present a constitutional or legal body and many of the safe and brave deeds that are performed on public platforms are no longer in its line. Constitutionalists naturally dislike this; they cannot function in an illegal atmosphere. But why should those who think in terms of revolutionary change object to this inevitable and desirable development?[1]

[1]Ibid., pp. 39-42.

PART THREE

1934–1936

[Socialism] can only follow independence if India is ripe for it and the great majority of the people desire it. But the socialistic outlook helps in the political struggle. It clears the issues before us and makes us realise what the real political content (apart from the social content) of freedom must be. . . .

Further the socialist outlook stresses (what the Congress has been emphasizing in varying degrees during these past fifteen years) that we must stand for the masses and that our struggle should be of the masses. Freedom should mean the ending of the exploitation of the masses.[1]

*

I shall gladly welcome the election of any of my colleagues and cooperate with him in another capacity in the great enterprise we have undertaken. Should the choice of my countrymen fall on me, I dare not say "no" to it. I shall submit to their pleasure. But before they so decide they must fully realize what I stand for, what thoughts move me, and what the springs of action are for me. In speech and writing I have given enough indication of this and from this I want to be judged.[2]

*

As an active politician, having to face day to day problems, I have sometimes had to make compromises with life and the conditions that I found existing at a particular moment. But even so I am not aware of any betrayal of the ideal that drew me on or the principles I held.[3]

*

It is perfectly true that I have felt puzzled and perplexed. This perplexity is not due to any doubt in my own mind as to what should be done but rather to the difficulty of inducing any considerable numbers of others to act in a particular way. . . . The larger good is often forgotten, politics, seldom pleasant, become singularly unpleasant then. . . .

When I cannot act effectively I try at any rate to preserve a certain integrity of mind and I wait for the time when I can act more effectively. It is a cheerless task.[4]

[1] E.M.I., p. 36.
[2] T.D.G. (Vol. IV), p. 108.
[3] R.E.W., pp. 25–26.
[4] C.D.N., p. 15.

I | Earthquake of 1934, and Seventh Arrest— Trial: Prison Once More—Alipore Jail

Earthquake of January 1934, and Seventh Arrest

Arrests of our workers continued in the villages of the Allahabad district. January 26—Independence Day—was coming and it could not be ignored. But who was to give the lead? And what was the lead to be? There was no one besides me who was functioning, even in theory, as an official of the All-India Congress. I consulted some friends, and almost all agreed that something should be done, but there was no agreement as to what this something should be. I found a general tendency to avoid any action which might lead to arrests on a large scale. Eventually I issued a brief appeal for the appropriate celebration of Independence Day, the manner of doing so to be decided by each local area for itself. In Allahabad we planned a fairly widespread celebration all over the district.[1]

[The afternoon of January 15, 1934] I was standing in the veranda of our house in Allahabad addressing a group of peasants. The annual *Magh Mela* had begun, and we had crowds of visitors all day. Suddenly I became unsteady on my feet and could hardly keep my balance. I clung on to a column near by. Doors started banging, and a rumbling noise came from the adjoining Swaraj Bhawan, where many of the tiles were sliding down the roof. Being unaccustomed to earthquakes, I did not know at first what was happening, but I soon realized it. I was rather amused and interested at this novel experience, and I continued my talk to the peasants and began telling them about the earthquake. My old aunt shouted to me from some distance to run out of the building. The idea struck me as absurd. I did not take the earthquake seriously, and in any event I was not going to leave my bedridden mother upstairs, and my wife, who was probably packing, also upstairs and seek safety for myself. For what seemed quite an appreciable time the shocks continued and then passed

[1] T.F., p. 296.

off. They provided a few minutes' conversation and soon were almost forgotten. We did not know then, nor could we guess, what those two or
three minutes had meant to millions in Behar and elsewhere. . . .

I left for Calcutta, and, all unknowing, we were carried by our train
that night through the southern earthquake area. The next day there was
little news in Calcutta about the disaster. The day after bits of news began
to come in. On the third day we began to have a faint notion of the
calamity.

We spent three and a half days in Calcutta, and during this period I
addressed three public meetings. As I had done before in Calcutta, I
condemned and argued against terroristic acts, and then I passed on to the
methods that the Government had adopted in Bengal. I spoke from a full
heart, for I had been greatly moved by accounts of occurrences in the
province. What pained me most was the manner in which human dignity
had been outraged by indiscriminate suppression of whole populations.
The political problem, urgent as it was, took second place before this human
problem. These three speeches of mine formed the three counts in the
charge against me in my subsequent trial in Calcutta. I was . . . sentenced
[February 16] on that charge [to two years' imprisonment]. . . .

Seven days after the earthquake . . . little had so far been done to
remove the debris, except from some of the main streets. As these streets
were cleaned, corpses were being discovered, some in curiously expressive
attitudes, as if trying to ward off a falling wall or roof. The ruins were an
impressive and terrifying sight. The survivors were thoroughly shaken up
and cowed by their nerve-racking experiences.

We returned to Allahabad, and collections of funds and materials were
immediately organized, and all of us, of the Congress or out of it, took
this up in earnest. Some of my colleagues were of [the] opinion that
because of the earthquake the Independence Day celebrations should be
called off. But other colleagues and I saw no reason why even an earthquake should interfere with our program. So on January 26 we had a
large number of meetings in the villages of Allahabad district and a
meeting in the city, and we met with greater success than we had antici-
pated.

Soon after returning from Behar I issued a statement about the earthquake, ending up with an appeal for funds. In this statement I criticized
the inactivity of the Behar Government during the first few days after the
earthquake. Thousands of people were killed in Monghyr city alone, and
three weeks later I saw a vast quantity of debris still lying untouched,
although a few miles away . . . there was a large colony of many thousands

of railway workers, who could have been [used to clear everything] within a few hours of the catastrophe. Living people were unearthed even twelve days after the earthquake. The Government had taken immediate steps to protect property, but they had not been so expeditious in trying to rescue people who lay buried.

My criticism was resented, and soon afterward a few people in Behar came out with a general testimonial in favor of the Government as a kind of counterblast. The earthquake and its demands became almost a secondary matter. More important was the fact that the Government had been criticized, and it had to be defended by its loyal subjects. This was an interesting instance of a widespread phenomenon in India—the dislike of criticism of the Government, which is a commonplace in Western countries. It is the military mentality which cannot tolerate criticism. Like the King, the British Government in India and all of its superior officials can do no wrong. To hint at any such thing is *lèse majesté*.

The curious part of it is that a charge of inefficiency and incompetence is resented far more than an accusation of harsh government or tyranny. The latter might indeed land the person making it in prison, but the Government is used to it and does not really mind it. After all, in a way, it might almost be considered a compliment to an imperial race. But to be called inefficient and wanting in nerve hurts, for this strikes at the root of their self-esteem; it disturbs the messianic delusions of the English officials in India.

There is a general belief among Englishmen, frequently asserted as if it was an incontrovertible maxim, that a change of government in India, involving a reduction or elimination of British influence, would result in a much worse and more inefficient government. I believe that self-government is good for any country. But I am not prepared to accept even self-government at the cost of really good government. Self-government, if it is to justify itself, must stand ultimately for better government for the masses. It is because I believe that the British Government in India, whatever its claims in the past may have been, is incapable of providing good government and rising standards for the masses today, that I feel that it has outlived its utility, such as it was, in India. The only real justification for Indian freedom is the promise of better government, of a higher standard for the masses, of industrial and cultural growth, and of the removal of the atmosphere of fear and suppression that foreign imperialist rule invariably brings in its train.

The Allahabad Earthquake Relief Committee deputed me to visit the areas affected by the earthquake and to report on the methods of relief work adopted there. I went immediately, alone, and for ten days I wandered about those torn and ruined territories. It was a very strenuous tour, and I had little sleep during those days. From five in the morning till almost midnight we were up and about, motoring over the cracked and crumpled-up roads, or going by little boats where the bridges had collapsed and the roads were under water owing to a change in level. The towns were impressive enough with their extensive ruins, and their roads torn up and twisted sometimes as by a giant hand, or raised high above the plinth of the houses on either side. Out of huge cracks in these roads water and sand had gushed out and swept away men and cattle. More even than these towns, the plains of north Behar—the garden of Behar, they used to be called—had desolation and destruction stamped upon them. Mile upon mile of sand, and large sheets of water, and huge cracks and vast numbers of little craters out of which this sand and water had come. Some British officers who flew over this area said that it bore some resemblance to the battlefields of northern France in wartime and soon after. . . .

During my tour in the earthquake areas, or just before going there, I read with a great shock Gandhiji's statement to the effect that the earthquake had been a punishment for the sin of untouchability. This was a staggering remark. . . .

I got back home in Allahabad on February 11, dead tired after my tour. . . . We were standing in the veranda when a car drove up and a police officer alighted. I knew immediately that my time had come. I went up to him and said: "Bahut dinōn se āpkā intazār thā"—"I have been waiting for you for a long time." He was a little apologetic and said that he was not to blame. The warrant was from Calcutta.[1]

[Just before Nehru's arrival in the state of Bengal, and his appearances at public meetings there in mid-January 1934: "There was a . . . march of . . . troops . . . and . . . an outcry against the excesses committed by them on the civil population. When . . . reports of the incidents reached Calcutta, a public meeting was called to express protest."[2] It was at this meeting—on January 17—that Nehru made his first speech during his visit to Calcutta. He supported a suggestion that there should be country-wide agitation against the brutality that had occurred.

Although Nehru delivered three provocative speeches in protest against the current policies of the British Raj during his brief stay in Calcutta, he was not apprehended immediately, much time being "required to determine whether or not his speeches were seditious. He [also] had made an outspoken anti-British speech in Delhi a month earlier". On December

[1] Ibid., pp. 297-301.
[5] T.T.N., p. 75.

23, 1933, before the All-India Trades Union Congress, he uttered a further sharp attack on the British Raj. But, despite his alleged "danger", and the fact that machinery already had been set in motion to prosecute him, his speeches in Calcutta seemed to offer a stronger case for his arrest. "Word was passed from the Home Department in New Delhi to the Government of the United Provinces: 'The Government of India regard [Nehru] as by far the most dangerous element at large in India and . . . are definitely of the opinion that the opportunity afforded . . . [in Calcutta] should not be lost and that it is desirable to institute a prosecution at once.[1]'" Thus it was that Jawaharlal was arrested for his January 17 speech, as well as for two others delivered in rapid succession after his tour of Behar. During a period of almost four years—from the end of 1931 to early September, 1935—he was to be out of jail for only six months.[2]]

Trial, February, 1934 : Prison Once More

Five months and thirteen days I had been out [of prison] and now I went back again to seclusion and loneliness. But the real burden was not mine; it had to be shouldered, as always, by the womenfolk—by my ailing mother, my wife, my sister. . . .

That very night I was taken to Calcutta. From Howrah station a huge Black Maria carried me to Lal Bazaar Police Station. I had read much of this famous headquarters of the Calcutta police, and I looked round with interest. There were large numbers of European sergeants and inspectors to be seen, far more than would have been in evidence in any police headquarters in northern India. The constables seemed to be almost all from Behar or the eastern districts of the United Provinces. During the many journeys I made in the big prison lorry, to court and back or from one prison to another, a number of these constables used to accompany me inside. They looked thoroughly unhappy, disliking their job, and obviously full of sympathy for me. Sometimes their eyes glistened with tears.

I was kept in the Presidency Jail to begin with, and from there I was taken for my trial to the Chief Presidency Magistrate's court. This was a novel experience. The courtroom and building had more the appearance of a besieged fortress than of an open court. Except for a few newspapermen and the usual lawyers, no outsiders were allowed anywhere in the neighborhood. The police were present in some force. These arrangements

[1] M.B., pp. 198–99.
[2] Ibid., p. 200.

apparently had not been made especially for me; that was the daily routine. When I was taken to the courtroom I had to march through a long passage (inside the room) which was closely wired on top and at the side. It was like going through a cage. The dock was far from the magistrate's seat. The courtroom was crowded with policemen and blackcoated and -gowned lawyers.

I was used enough to court trials. Many of my previous trials had taken place in jail precincts. But there had always been some friends, relatives, familiar faces about, and the whole atmosphere had been a little easier. The police had usually kept in the background, and there had never been any cagelike structures about. Here it was very different, and I gazed at strange, unfamiliar faces between whom and me there was nothing in common. It was not an attractive crowd. I am afraid gowned lawyers en masse are not beautiful to look at, and police-court lawyers seem to develop a peculiarly unlovely look. At last I managed to spot one familiar lawyer's face in that black array, but he was lost in the crowd.

I felt very lonely and isolated even when I sat on the balcony outside before the trial began. My pulse must have quickened a little, and inwardly I was not quite so composed as I usually had been during my previous trials. It struck me then that if even I, with so much experience of trials and convictions, could react abnormally to that situation, how much more must young and inexperienced people feel the tension? ... The next day, February 16, I was sentenced to two years. My seventh term of imprisonment had begun.[1]

[At his Calcutta trial Nehru began by "congratulating the reporters for the very good transcriptions, they had done of his English speeches, and by criticising those who reported his Urdu speech, which was 'scrappy and incomprehensible'. 'This report of my speech,' he added, 'does less than justice to me.'

"Then he congratulated Government: 'I should like to express my gratitude to the Government of Bengal for the opportunity they have accorded me by taking these proceedings against me to associate myself in a small measure with the past and present lot of the people of Bengal. This is a privilege I shall long treasure.'"

Nehru stated proudly that not only in his Bengal "speeches but for many years before ... his activities had been seditious, if by sedition was meant the desire to achieve the independence of India and to put an end to foreign domination. ... The public prosecutor, looking into the eyes of the magistrate, interjected ... 'Is the accused entitled to make another seditious speech here?' The magistrate ... as if ... shaken to a

[1] T.F., pp. 302–03.

sense of duty of which he had become oblivious . . . asked Nehru not to proceed further." [1]]

Individuals sometimes misbehave; officials also sometimes misbehave; crowds and mobs get excited and misbehave; all that is very regrettable. But it is a terrible thing when brutality becomes a method of behaviour.[2]

Alipore Jail

Again the Black Maria carried me back to prison. On our way we passed plenty of troops on the march with machine guns, armored cars, etc. I peeped at them through the tiny openings of our prison van. How ugly an armored car is, I thought, and a tank. They reminded me of prehistoric monsters—dinosaurs and the like.

I was transferred from the Presidency Jail to the Alipore Central Jail, and there I was given a little cell, about ten feet by nine. In front of it were a veranda and a small open yard. The wall enclosing the yard was a low one, about seven feet, and looking over it I was confronted by a strange sight. All manner of odd buildings—single-story, double-story, round, rectangular, curious roofings—rose all round, some over-topping the others. It seemed that the structures had grown one by one, being fitted in anyhow to take advantage of all the available space. Almost it looked like a jigsaw puzzle or a futurist attempt at the fantastic. And yet I was told that all the buildings had been arranged very methodically with a tower in the center (which was a church for the Christian prisoners) and radiating lines. Being a city jail, the area was limited, and every little bit of it had to be utilized.

I had hardly recovered from my first view of the seemingly fantastic structures around me when a terrifying sight greeted me. Two chimneys, right in front of my cell and yard, were belching forth dense volumes of black smoke, and sometimes the wind blew this smoke in my direction, almost suffocating me. They were the chimneys of the jail kitchens. I suggested to the superintendent later that gas masks might be provided to meet this offensive. . . .

There were vast numbers of warders and guards and officers and clerks in the Alipore Jail, as also in the Presidency. Both these prisons housed a population about equal to that of Naini Prison—twenty-two hundred to twenty-three hundred—but the staff in each must have been more than double that of Naini. There were many European warders and retired

[1] T.T.N., p. 78.
[2] Quoted in M.B., p. 200.

Indian army officers. It was evident that the British Empire functioned more intensively and more expensively in Calcutta than in the United Provinces. A sign and a perpetual reminder of the might of the Empire was the cry that prisoners had to shout out when high officials approached them, "*Sarkar salaam*" was the cry, lengthened out, and it was accompanied by certain physical movements of the body. The voices of the prisoners shouting out this cry came to me many times a day over my yard wall, and especially when the superintendent passed by daily. I could just see over my seven-foot wall the top of the huge State umbrella under which the superintendent marched.

Was this extraordinary cry—*sarkar salaam*—and the movements that went with it relics of old times, I wondered; or were they the invention of some inspired English official? I do not know, but I imagine that it was an English invention. It has a typical Anglo-Indian sound about it. Fortunately this cry does not prevail in the United Provinces jails or probably in any other province besides Bengal and Assam. The way this enforced salutation to the might of the *sarkar* is shouted out seemed to me very degrading.[1]

	Upheaval in Europe—Gandhi's Withdrawal of the Civil Disobedience Movement—Thoughts about Religion— Letters from Jail—Further Observations in Prison—On Britain and India— India's Liberals—Temporary Release From Jail, and Correspondence with Gandhi
2	

Upheaval in Europe

My arrest and trial in February [1934] coincided with upheavals and bitter conflicts in Europe. There was the ferment in France resulting in fascist

[1] T.F., pp. 304–06.

riots and the formation of a "National" Government. . . . Far worse, in Austria, Chancellor Dollfuss was shooting down workers and putting an end to the great edifice of social democracy there. The news of the Austrian bloodshed depressed me greatly. What an awful and bloody place this world was, and how barbarous was man when he wanted to protect his vested interests! All over Europe . . . fascism seemed to be advancing. When Hitler came into power in Germany [he became Chancellor in January 1933], I had imagined that his regime could not possibly last long, as he was offering no solution of Germany's economic troubles. So also, as fascism spread elsewhere, I consoled myself that it represented the last ditch of reaction. After it must come the breaking of the shackles. But I began to wonder if my wish was not father to my thought. Was it so obvious that this fascist wave would retire so easily or so quickly? And, even if conditions became intolerable for the fascist dictatorships, would they not rather hurl their countries into devastating war rather than give in? What would be the result of such a conflict?

Meanwhile, fascism of various kinds and shapes spread. Spain, that new "Republic of Honest Men"—*los hombres honrados*—the very *Manchester Guardian* of governments, as someone called it, had gone far back and deep into reaction. All the fine phrases of its honest Liberal leaders had not kept it from sliding down. Everywhere Liberalism showed its utter ineffectiveness to face modern conditions. It clung to words and phrases, and thought that they could take the place of action. When a crisis came, it simply faded off like the end of a film that is over.

I read the leading articles of the *Manchester Guardian* on the Austrian tragedy with deep interest and appreciation.

"Austrian democracy has been destroyed, although to its everlasting glory it went down fighting and so created a legend that may rekindle the spirit of European freedom some day in years to come."

"The Europe that is unfree has ceased to breathe; there is no flow or counterflow of healthy spirits; a gradual suffocation has set in, and only some violent convulsion or inner paroxysm and a striking out to the right and left can avert the mental coma that is approaching. . . . Europe from the Rhine to the Urals is one great prison."

Moving passages which found an echo in my heart. But I wondered: what of India? How can it be that the *Manchester Guardian* or the many lovers of freedom who undoubtedly exist in England should be so oblivious to our fate? How can they miss seeing here what they condemn with such fervor elsewhere? It was a great English Liberal leader, trained in the nineteenth-century tradition, cautious by temperament, restrained in his language, who said twenty years ago, on the eve of the Great War: "Sooner than be a silent witness of the tragic triumph of force over law, I would see this country of ours blotted out of the page of history." A brave thought eloquently put, and the gallant youth of England went in their millions to vindicate it. But if an Indian ventures to make a statement similar to Mr Asquith's, what fate is his?

The British are an insular race, and long success and prosperity have made them look down on almost all others. For them, as some one has said, "*les nègres commencent à Calais.*" But that is too general a statement. Perhaps the British upper-class division of the world would be somewhat as follows: (1) Britain—a long gap, and then (2) the British Dominions (white populations only) and America (Anglo-Saxons only, and not dagoes, wops, etc.), (3) Western Europe, (4) Rest of Europe, (5) South America (Latin races), a long lag, and then (6) the brown, yellow, and black races of Asia and Africa.

How far we of the last of these classes are from the heights where our rulers live! Is it any wonder that their vision grows dim when they look toward us, and that we should irritate them when we talk of democracy and liberty? These words were not coined for our use. Was it not a great Liberal statesman, John Morley, who declared that he could not conceive of democratic institutions in India even in the far, dim future? Democracy for India was, like Canada's fur coat, unsuited to her climate. And, later on, Britain's Labour party, the standard-bearers of socialism, the champions of the underdog, presented us, in the flush of their triumph, with a revival of the Bengal Ordinance in 1924, and during their second government our fate was even worse. I am quite sure that none of them mean us ill, and, when they address us in their best pulpit manner— "Dearly beloved brethren"—they feel a glow of conscious virtue. But, to them, we are not as they are and must be judged by other standards. It is difficult enough for an Englishman and a Frenchman to think alike because of linguistic and cultural differences; how much vaster must be the difference between an Englishman and an Asiatic?[1]

Gandhi's Withdrawal of the Civil Disobedience Movement

April [1934] came. Rumours reached me in my cell in Alipore of happenings outside, rumors that were unpleasant and disturbing. The superintendent of the jail informed me casually one day that Mr Gandhi had

[1] T.F., pp. 306–08.

withdrawn civil disobedience. I knew no more. The news was not welcome, and I felt sad at this winding up of something that had meant so much to me for many years. And yet I reasoned with myself that the end was bound to come. I knew in my heart that sometime or other civil disobedience would have to be wound up, for the time being at least. Individuals may hold out almost indefinitely, regardless of the consequences, but national organizations do not behave in this manner. I had no doubt that Gandhiji had interpreted correctly the mind of the country and of the great majority of Congressmen, and I tried to reconcile myself to the new development, unpleasant as it was.

Some days later the weekly *Statesman* came to me, and I read in it the statement which Gandhiji had issued when withdrawing civil disobedience. I read it with amazement and sinking of heart. Again and again I read it; civil disobedience and much else vanished from my mind, and other doubts and conflicts filled it. "This statement," wrote Gandhiji, "owes its inspiration to a personal chat with the inmates and associates of the *Satyagraha Ashrama.* . . . More especially is it due to revealing information I got in the course of a conversation about a valued companion of long standing who was found reluctant to perform the full prison task, preferring his private studies to the allotted task. This was undoubtedly contrary to the rules of *Satyagraha.* More than the imperfection of the friend whom I love, more than ever it brought home to me my own imperfections. The friend said he had thought that I was aware of his weakness. I was blind. Blindness in a leader is unpardonable. I saw at once that I must for the time being remain the sole representative of civil resistance in action."

The imperfection or fault, if such it was, of the "friend" was a very trivial affair. I confess that I have often been guilty of it, and I am wholly unrepentant. But, even if it was a serious matter, was a vast national movement involving scores of thousands directly and millions indirectly to be thrown out of gear because an individual had erred? This seemed to me a monstrous proposition and an immoral one. I cannot presume to speak of what is and what is not *Satyagraha*, but in my own little way I have endeavored to follow certain standards of conduct, and all those standards were shocked and upset by this statement of Gandhiji's. I knew that Gandhiji usually acts on instinct (I prefer to call it that than the "inner voice" or an answer to prayer), and very often that instinct is right. He has repeatedly shown what a wonderful knack he has of sensing the mass mind and of acting at the psychological moment. The reasons which he afterward adduces to justify his action are usually afterthoughts and seldom carry one very far. A leader or a man of action in a crisis almost acts subconsciously and then thinks of the reasons for his action. I felt also that Gandhiji had acted rightly in suspending civil resistance. But the reason he had given seemed to me an insult to intelligence and an amazing performance for a leader of a national movement. He was perfectly entitled to treat his *ashrama* inmates in any manner he liked; they had taken all kinds of pledges and accepted a certain regime. But the Congress had not done so; I had not done so. Why should we be tossed hither and thither for, what seemed to me, metaphysical and mystical reasons in which I was not interested? Was it conceivable to have any political movement on this basis? I had willingly accepted the moral aspect of *Satyagraha* as I understood it (within certain limits, I admit). That basic aspect appealed to me, and it seemed to raise politics to a higher and nobler level. I was prepared to agree that the end does not justify all kinds of means. But this new development or interpretation was something much more far-reaching, and it held forth some possibilities which frightened me.

The whole statement frightened and oppressed me tremendously. And then finally the advice he gave to Congressmen was that "they must learn the art and beauty of self-denial and voluntary poverty. They must engage themselves in nation-building activities, the spread of *khadi* through personal hand-spinning and hand-weaving, the spread of communal unity of hearts by irreproachable personal conduct toward one another in every walk of life, the banishing of untouchability in every shape or form in one's own person, the spread of total abstinence from intoxicating drinks and drugs by personal contact with individual addicts and generally by cultivating personal purity. These are services which provide maintenance on the poor man's scale. Those for whom the poor man's scale is not feasible should find a place in small unorganized industries of national importance which give a better wage."

This was the political program that we were to follow. A vast distance seemed to separate him from me. With a stab of pain I felt that the cords of allegiance that had bound me to him for many years had snapped. For long a mental tussle had been going on within me. I had not understood or appreciated much that Gandhiji had done. His fasts and his concentration on other issues during the continuance of civil disobedience, when his comrades were in the grip of the struggle, his personal and self-created entanglements, which led him to the extraordinary position that, while out of prison, he was yet pledged to himself not to take part in the political movement, his new loyalties and pledges which put in the shade the old loyalty and pledge and job, undertaken together with many colleagues, while yet that job was unfinished, had all oppressed me. During my short period out of prison I had felt these and other differences more than ever. Gandhiji had stated that there were temperamental differences between us. They were perhaps more than temperamental, and I realized that I held clear and definite views about many matters which were opposed to his. And yet in the past I had tried to subordinate them, as far as I could, to what I conceived to be the larger loyalty—the cause of national freedom for which the Congress seemed to be working. I tried to be loyal and faithful to my leader and my colleagues, for in my spiritual make-up loyalty to a cause and to one's colleagues holds a high place. I fought many a battle within myself when I felt that I was being dragged away from the anchor of my spiritual faith. Somehow I managed to compromise. Perhaps I did wrong, for it can never be right for anyone to let go of that anchor. But in the conflict of ideals I clung to my loyalty to my colleagues, and hoped that the rush of events and the development of our struggle might dissolve the difficulties that troubled me and bring my colleagues nearer to my viewpoint.[1]

Thoughts about Religion

Suddenly I felt very lonely in that cell of Alipore Jail. Life seemed to be a dreary affair, a very wilderness of desolation. Of the many hard lessons that I had learned, the hardest and the most painful now faced me: that it is not possible in any vital matter to rely on anyone. One must journey through life alone; to rely on others is to invite heartbreak.

Some of my accumulated irritation directed itself against religion and the religious outlook. What an enemy this was to clearness of thought and fixity of purpose, I thought; for was it not based on emotion and passion? Presuming to be spiritual, how far removed it was from real spirituality and things of the spirit. Thinking in terms of some other world, it had little conception of human values and social values and social justice. With its preconceived notions it deliberately shut its eyes to reality for fear that this might not fit in with them. It based itself on truth, and yet so sure was it of having discovered it, and the whole of it, that it did not take the trouble to search for it; all that concerned it was to tell others of it. The will to truth was not the same thing as the will to believe. It talked of peace and yet supported systems and organizations that could not exist but for

[1] Ibid., pp. 309–12.

violence. It condemned the violence of the sword, but what of the violence that comes quietly and often in peaceful garb and starves and kills; or, worse still, without doing any outward physical injury, outrages the mind and crushes the spirit and breaks the heart?[1]

Letters from Jail

[To Krishna Hutheesing, from Alipore Central Jail—Calcutta, March 1, 1934.] I shall read a lot here for indeed there is little else to do—just to read and think and go through the day's routine. And so when I come out—and that is a long way off—I may be a little wiser than I am. Perhaps and perhaps not. Wisdom is a very elusive thing and difficult to seize. And yet sometimes it comes suddenly and unawares. Meanwhile, I shall be a faithful votary and seek her goodwill. Someday she may show me favour. Anyway jail is not an unsuitable place to woo her. The hurly-burly of life seems far off and does not distract and it is good to see the life of every day from a little distance, detached.[2]

[To Krishna Hutheesing, from Dehra Dun Jail—June 1, 1934.] So far as I am concerned I am likely to be a fixture here in Dehra for a long time, as I was in 1932–1933. Indeed, nowhere else in India or outside, have I spent quite such a long time without a change.[3]

Further Observations in Prison

The years I have spent in prison! Sitting alone, wrapped in my thoughts, how many seasons I have seen go by, following one another into oblivion! How many moons I have watched wax and wane, and the pageant of the stars moving along inexorably and majestically! How many yesterdays of my youth lie buried here! Sometimes I see the ghosts of these dead yesterdays rise up, bringing poignant memories, and whispering to me: "Was it worth while?" There is no hesitation about the answer. If I were given the chance to go through my life again, with my present knowledge and experience added, I would no doubt try to make many changes in my personal life; I would endeavor to improve in many ways on what I had previously done, but my major decisions in public affairs would remain

[1] Ibid., p. 312.
[2] N.L.H.S., p. 41.
[3] Ibid., p. 43.

untouched. Indeed, I could not vary them, for they were stronger than myself, and a force beyond my control drove me to them.[1]

All activity seems to be far away in prison. One becomes the object of events, not the subject of action. And one waits and waits for something to happen. I write of political and social problems of India and the world, but what are they to this little self-contained world of jail which has long been my home? Prisoners have only one major interest: the date of their release.[2]

I have become a queer mixture of the East and the West, out of place everywhere, at home nowhere. Perhaps my thoughts and approach to life are more akin to what is called Western than Eastern, but India clings to me, as she does to all her children, in innumerable ways; and behind me lie, somewhere in the subconscious, racial memories of a hundred, or whatever the number may be, generations of [Brahmins]. I cannot get rid of either that past inheritance or my recent acquisitions. They are both part of me, and, though they help me in both the East and the West, they also create in me a feeling of spiritual loneliness not only in public activities but in life itself. I am a stranger and alien in the West. I cannot be of it. But in my own country also, sometimes, I have an exile's feeling.[3]

[Although the above description is doubtless as valid as when originally penned, Nehru later made an additional statement that is perhaps equally true: "India is big enough or small enough for me, and I am at home everywhere."[4]]

On Britain and India

For many generations the British treated India as a kind of enormous country house (after the old English fashion) that they owned. They were the gentry owning the house and occupying the desirable parts of it, while the Indians were consigned to the servants' hall, the pantry, and the kitchen. As in every proper country house, there was a fixed hierarchy in those lower regions—butler, housekeeper, cook, valet, maid, footman, etc.—and strict precedence was observed among them. But between the

[1] T.F., p. 353.
[2] Ibid., p. 351.
[3] Ibid., p. 353.
[4] T.I. (Oct. 3, 1953).

upper and lower regions of the house there was, socially and politically, an impassable barrier. The fact that the British Government should have imposed this arrangement upon us was not surprising; but what does seem surprising is that we, or most of us, accepted it as the natural and inevitable ordering of our lives and destiny. We developed the mentality of a good country-house servant. Sometimes we were treated to a rare honor—we were given a cup of tea in the drawing room. The height of our ambition was to become respectable and to be promoted individually to the upper regions. Greater than any victory of arms or diplomacy was this psychological triumph of the British in India. The slave began to think as a slave, as the wise men of old had said.

Times have changed, and the country-house type of civilization is not accepted willingly now, either in England or India. But still there remain people among us who desire to stick to the servants' hall and take pride in the gold braid and livery of their service. Others, like the Liberals, accept that country house in its entirety, admire its architecture and the whole edifice, but look forward to replacing the owners, one by one, by themselves. They call this Indianization. For them the problem is one of changing the color of the administration, or at most having a new administration. They never think in terms of a new State.

For them *Swaraj* means that everything continues as before, only with a darker shade. They can only conceive of a future in which they, or people like them, will play the principal role and take the place of the English high officials; in which there are the same types of services, government departments, legislatures, trade, industry—with the Indian Civil Service at their jobs; the princes in their palaces, occasionally appearing in fancy dress or carnival attire with all their jewels glittering to impress their subjects; the landlords claiming special protection, and meanwhile harassing their tenants; the moneylender, with his moneybags, harassing both zamindar and tenant; the lawyer with his fees; and God in His heaven.

Essentially their outlook is based on the maintenance of the *status quo*, and the changes they desire can almost be termed personal changes. And they seek to achieve these changes by a slow infiltration with the good will of the British. The whole foundation of their politics and economics rests on the continuance and stability of the British Empire. Looking on this Empire as unshakable, at least for a considerable time, they adapt themselves to it and accept not only its political and economic ideology but also, to a large extent, its moral standards, which have all been framed to secure the continuance of British dominance.

The Congress attitude differs fundamentally from this because it seeks a new State and not just a different administration. What that new State is going to be may not be quite clear to the average Congressman, and opinions may differ about it. But it is common ground in the Congress (except perhaps for a moderate fringe) that present conditions and methods cannot and must not continue, and basic changes are essential. Herein lies the difference between Dominion status and independence. The former envisages the same old structure, with many bonds visible and invisible tying us to the British economic system; the latter gives us, or ought to give us, freedom to erect a new structure to suit our circumstances.

It is not a question of an implacable and irreconcilable antagonism to England and the English people, or the desire to break from them at all costs. It would be natural enough if there were bad blood between India and England after what has happened. "The clumsiness of power spoils the key and uses the pickax," says Tagore; the key to our hearts was destroyed long ago, and the abundant use of the pickax on us has not made us partial to the British. But, if we claim to serve the larger cause of India and humanity, we cannot afford to be carried away by our momentary passions. And, even if we were so inclined, the hard training which Gandhiji had given us for the last fifteen years would prevent us. I write this sitting in a British prison, and for months past my mind has been full of anxiety, and I have perhaps suffered more during this solitary imprisonment than I have done in jail before. Anger and resentment have often filled my mind at various happenings, and yet, as I sit here and look deep into my mind and heart, I do not find any anger against England or the English people. I dislike British imperialism, and I resent its imposition on India; I dislike the capitalist system; I dislike exceedingly and resent the way India is exploited by the ruling classes of Britain. But I do not hold England or the English people as a whole responsible for this; and, even if I did, I do not think it would make much difference, for it is a little foolish to lose one's temper at or to condemn a whole people. They are as much the victims of circumstances as we are.

Personally, I owe too much to England in my mental make-up ever to feel wholly alien to her. And, do what I will, I cannot get rid of the habits of mind, and the standards and ways of judging other countries as well as life generally, which I acquired at school and college in England. My predilections (apart from the political ones) are in favor of England and the English people, and, if I have become what is called an uncompromising opponent of British rule in India, it is almost in spite of these.

It is their rule, their domination, to which we object, and with which

12+N.

we cannot compromise willingly—not the English people. Let us by all means have the closest contacts with the English and other foreign peoples. We want fresh air in India, fresh and vital ideas, healthy co-operation; we have grown too musty with age. But, if the English come in the role of a tiger they can expect no friendship or co-operation. To the tiger of imperialism there will be only the fiercest opposition, and today our country has to deal with that ferocious animal. It may be possible to tame the wild tiger of the forest and to charm away his native ferocity, but there is no such possibility of taming capitalism and imperialism when they combine and swoop down on an unhappy land.

For anyone to say that he or his country will not compromise is, in a sense, a foolish remark, for life is always forcing us to compromise. When applied to another country or people, it is completely foolish. But there is truth in it when it is applied to a system or a particular set of circumstances, and then it becomes something beyond human power to accomplish. Indian freedom and British imperialism are two incompatibles, and neither martial law nor all the sugar coating in the world can make them compatible or bring them together. Only with the elimination of British imperialism from India will conditions be created which permit of real Indo-British co-operation.

We are told that independence is a narrow creed in the modern world, which is increasingly becoming interdependent, and therefore in demanding independence we are trying to put the clock back. Liberals and pacifists and even so-called socialists in Britain advance this plea and chide us for our narrow nationalism, and incidentally suggest to us that the way to a fuller national life is through the "British Commonwealth of Nations". It is curious how all roads in England—liberalism, pacifism, socialism, etc.—lead to the maintenance of the Empire.

I do not know what India will be like or what she will do when she is politically free. But I do know that those of her people who stand for national independence today stand also for the widest internationalism. For a socialist, nationalism can have no meaning; but even many of the nonsocialists in the advanced ranks of the Congress are confirmed internationalists. If we claim independence today, it is with no desire for isolation. On the contrary, we are perfectly willing to surrender part of that independence, in common with other countries, to a real international order. Any imperial system, by whatever high-sounding name it may be called, is an enemy of such an order, and it is not through such a system that world co-operation or world peace can be reached.

Recent developments have shown all over the world how the various imperialist systems are isolating themselves more and more by autarchy and economic imperialism. Instead of the growth of internationalism we see a reversal of the process. The reasons for this are not difficult to discover, and they indicate the growing weakness of the present economic order. One of the results of this policy is that, while it produces greater co-operation within the area of autarchy, it also means isolation from the rest of the world. For India . . . it has meant a progressive lessening of our ties and contacts with other countries. We have become, even more than we were, the hangers-on of British industry; and the dangers of this policy, apart from the immediate harm it has done in various ways, are obvious. Thus Dominion status seems to lead to isolation and not to wider international contacts.[1]

India's Liberals

[Critical references to India's "Liberals" recur in Nehru's writings over the years. He was impatient with what he considered their excessive moderation, their vagueness, their opposition to dynamic social and political reforms, their remoteness from both Gandhi and the problems of India's masses.]

The Indian Liberals are not liberal at all in any sense of the word, or at most they are liberal only in spots and patches. What they exactly are it is difficult to say, for they have no firm positive basis of ideas and, though small in numbers, differ from one another. They are strong only in negation. They see error everywhere and attempt to avoid it, and hope that in doing so they will find the truth. Truth for them, indeed, always lies between two extremes. By criticizing everything they consider extreme, they experience the feeling of being virtuous and moderate and good. This method helps them in avoiding painful and difficult processes of thought and in having to put forward constructive ideas.

Moderation and conservatism and a desire to avoid risks and sudden changes are often the inevitable accompaniments of old age. They do not seem quite so appropriate in the young, but ours is an ancient land, and sometimes its children seem to be born tired and weary, with all the lack-luster and marks of age upon them. But even this old country is now convulsed by the forces of change, and the moderate outlook is bewildered. The old world is passing, and all the sweet reasonableness of which the

[1] T.F., pp. 264–68.

Liberals are capable does not make any difference; they might as well argue with the hurricane or the flood or the earthquake.

We are all moderates or extremists in varying degrees, and for various objects. If we care enough for anything, we are likely to feel strongly about it, to be extremist about it. Otherwise we can afford a gracious tolerance, a philosophical moderation, which really hides to some extent our indifference. I have known the mildest of Moderates to grow very aggressive and extremist when a suggestion was made for the sweeping away of certain vested interests in land. Our liberal friends represent to some extent the prosperous and well-to-do. They can afford to wait for *Swaraj* and need not excite themselves about it. But any proposal for radical social change disturbs them greatly, and they are no longer moderate or sweetly reasonable about it. Thus their moderation is really confined to their attitude toward the British Government, and they nurse the hope that if they are sufficiently respectful and compromising perhaps, as a reward for this behavior, they might be listened to. Inevitably they have to accept the British viewpoint.

I write of Liberals, but what I write applies to many of us also in the Congress. . . . There is a great deal of difference between the average Liberal and the average Congressman, and yet the dividing line is not clear and definite. Ideologically there is little to choose between the advanced Liberal and the moderate Congressman. But, thanks to Gandhiji, every Congressman has kept some touch with the soil and the people of the country and has dabbled in action; because of this he has escaped some of the consequences of a vague and defective ideology. Not so the Liberals: they have lost touch with both the old and the new. As a group they represent a vanishing species. . . .

Most of those who have shaped Congress policy during the last seventeen years have come from the middle classes. Liberal or Congressmen, they have come from the same class and have grown up in the same environment. Their social life and contacts and friendships have been similar, and there was little difference to begin with between the two varieties of bourgeois ideals that they professed. Temperamental and psychological differences began to separate them, and they began to look in different directions—one group more toward the Government and the rich, upper middle class, the other toward the lower middle classes. The ideology still remained the same, the objectives did not differ, but behind the second group there was now the push of larger numbers from the market place and the humbler professions as well as the unemployed intelligentsia.

The tone changed; it was no longer respectful and polite, but strident and aggressive. Lacking strength to act effectively, some relief was found in strong language. Frightened by this new development, the moderate elements dropped out and sought safety in seclusion. Even so, the upper middle class was strongly represented in the Congress, though in numbers the lower *bourgeoisie* was predominant. They were drawn not only by the desire for success in their national struggle, but because they sought an inner satisfaction in that struggle. They sought thereby to recover their lost pride and self-respect, and to rehabilitate their shattered dignity. It was the usual nationalist urge and, though this was common to all, it was here that the temperamental differences between the Moderate and the Extremist became evident. Gradually the lower middle class began to dominate the Congress, and later the peasantry made their influence felt.

As the Congress became more and more the representative of the rural masses, the gulf that separated it from the Liberals widened, and it became almost impossible for the Liberal to understand or appreciate the Congress viewpoint. It is not easy for the upper-class drawing room to understand the humble cottage or the mud hut. Yet, in spite of these differences, both the ideologies were nationalist and bourgeois; the variation was one of degree, not of kind. In the Congress many people remained to the last who would have been quite at home in the Liberal group.[1]

Temporary Release from Jail, August, 1934, and Correspondence with Gandhi

[Because of his wife's serious illness, Nehru was permitted to leave jail temporarily on August 11, 1934. In less than two weeks the anti-Government speeches he made resulted in his re-imprisonment. First he was confined in Naini Central Jail, subsequently in Almora District Jail. He was released on September 4, 1935 because his wife's condition again had become critical.

A note on the Swaraj Bhawan Trust mentioned in the following letter to Gandhi: In 1930 Motilal Nehru had given his family residence, Anand Bhawan (Abode of Happiness), to Congress as a gift. It was thereafter named Swaraj Bhawan (Abode of Freedom, or Independence). The Swaraj Bhawan Trust was created by Jawaharlal, according to his father's wishes.

When Anand Bhawan was presented to, and was used by, Congress prior to independence, the Nehru family moved into a smaller home,

[1] Ibid., 261-64.

also called Anand Bhawan, constructed within the compound of the family's original estate.

Motilal's decision to give, rather than to sell, the Nehru family home "was prompted by his resolve to throw his all into the battle which Gandhi had begun". The formal ceremony of presentation to Congress had taken place on April 6, 1930, the day on which the Salt Satyagraha was launched. As Congress President, Jawaharlal had accepted the gift from his father.[1] Swaraj Bhawan remained the official headquarters of the All-India Congress Committee until independence was achieved.

A later reference, from Jawaharlal's letter to Krishna Hutheesing, October, 1941: "Do not think . . . in terms of . . . losing Anand Bhawan. . . . Our lives have become part of the larger life of the nation and we go up and down with it. If that is so, why not share the house also?"[2]]

[Letter to Gandhi, written immediately after release from prison— Allahabad, August 13, 1934.] After just six months of absolute seclusion and little exercise I have felt rather lost in the anxiety, excitement and activity of the past twenty-seven hours. I feel very tired. I am writing this letter to you at midnight. All day there have been crowds of people coming. If I have the chance I shall write to you again, but I doubt if I shall be able to do so for some months. I am, therefore, going to indicate to you briefly how I have reacted to the various major Congress decisions of the last five months or so. My sources of information have naturally been strictly limited but I think that they were sufficient to enable me to form a fairly correct idea of the general trend of events.

When I heard that you had called off the C.D. [Civil Disobedience] movement I felt unhappy. Only the brief announcement reached me at first. Much later I read your statement and this gave me one of the biggest shocks I have ever had. I was prepared to reconcile myself to the withdrawal of C.D. But the reasons you gave for doing so and the suggestions you made for future work astounded me. I had a sudden and intense feeling, that something broke inside me, a bond that I had valued very greatly had snapped. I felt terribly lonely in this wide world. I have always felt a little lonely almost from childhood up. But a few bonds strengthened me, a few strong supports held me up. That loneliness never went, but it was lessened. But now I felt absolutely alone, left high and dry on a desert island.

Human beings have an enormous capacity for adapting themselves and so I too adapted myself to some extent to the new conditions. The keenness of my feelings on the subject, which amounted almost to physical

[1] T.N., pp. 328–29.
[2] N.L.H.S., p. 81.

pain, passed off; the edge was dulled. But shock after shock, a succession of events sharpened that edge to a fine point, and allowed my mind or feelings no peace or rest. Again I felt that sensation of spiritual isolation, of being a perfect stranger out of harmony, not only with the crowds that passed me, but also with those whom I had valued as dear and close comrades. My stay in prison this time became a greater ordeal for my nerves than any previous visit had been. I almost wished that all newspapers might be kept away from me so that I might be spared these repeated shocks.

Physically I kept fairly well. I always do in prison. My body has served me well and can stand a great deal of ill-treatment and strain. And being vain enough to imagine that perhaps I might yet do some effective work in this land to which fate had tied me, I looked after it well.

But I wondered often enough if I was not a square peg in a round hole, or a bubble of conceit thrown about hither and thither on an ocean which spurned me. But vanity and conceit triumphed and the intellectual apparatus that functions within me refused to admit defeat. If the ideals that had spurred me to action and had kept me buoyed up through stormy weather were right—and the conviction of their rightness ever grew within me—they were bound to triumph though my generation might not live to witness that triumph.

But what had happened to those ideals during these long and weary months of this year when I was a silent and distant witness, fretting at my helplessness? Setbacks and temporary defeats are common enough in all great struggles. [One grieves] but one recovers soon enough. One recovers soon if the light of those ideals is not allowed to grow dim and the anchor of principles holds fast. But what I saw was not setback and defeat but that spiritual defeat which is the most terrible of all. Do not imagine that I am referring to the council entry question. I do not attatch vital importance to it. Under certain circumstances I can even imagine entering a legislature myself. But whether I function inside or outside the legislature I function as a revolutionary, meaning thereby a person working for . . . fundamental and revolutionary changes, political and social, for I am convinced that no other changes can bring peace or satisfaction to India and the world.

So I thought. Not so evidently the leaders who were functioning outside. They began to talk the language of an age gone by before the heady wine of N.C.O. [Non-Co-Operation] and C.D. had fired our heads. Sometimes they used the same words and phrases but they were dead words without life or real meaning. The leading figures of . . . Congress suddenly became ... people who had obstructed us, held us back, kept aloof from the struggle and even cooperated with the opposite party in the time of our direst need. They became the high priests in our temple of freedom and many a brave soldier who had shouldered the burden in the heat and dust of the fray was not even allowed inside the temple precincts. He and many like him had become untouchables and unapproachables. And if he ventured to raise his voice and criticise the new high priests, he was shouted down and told that he was a traitor to the cause because he spoilt the harmony of the sacred precincts.

And so the flag of Indian freedom was entrusted with all pomp and circumstance to those who had actually hauled it down at the height of our national struggle at the bidding of the enemy; to those who had proclaimed from the house-tops that they had given up politics—for politics were unsafe then—but who emerged with a jump to the front ranks when politics became safe.

And what of the ideals they set forth before them, speaking as they did on behalf of the Congress and the nation? A pitiful hotch-potch, avoiding real issues, toning down, as far as they dared, even the political objective of the Congress, expressing a tender solicitude for every vested interest, bowing down to many a declared enemy of freedom, but showing great truculence and courage in facing the advanced and fighting elements in the congress ranks. ...

I am referring especially to the political objectives which are the special province of the Congress. I feel that the time is overdue for the Congress to think clearly on social and economic issues but I recognise that education on these issues takes time and the Congress as a whole may not be able to go as far at present as I would like it to. But it appears that whether the Working Committee knows anything about the subject or not it is perfectly willing to denounce and to excommunicate people who happen to have made a special study of the subject and hold certain views. No attempt is made to understand those views, which it is notorious are held by a very large number of the ablest and most self-sacrificing people in the world. Those views may be right or wrong but they deserve at least some understanding before the Working Committee sets out to denounce them. It is hardly becoming for a reasoned argument to be answered by sentimental appeals or by the cheap remark that the conditions in India are different and the economic laws that apply elsewhere do not function here. The resolution of the Working Committee on the subject showed such an astounding ignorance of the elements of socialism that it was painful to read it and to realise that it might be read outside India. It seemed that the overmastering desire of the committee was somehow to assure various vested interests even at the risk of talking nonsense.

A strange way of dealing with the subject of socialism is to use the word, which has a clearly defined meaning in the English language, in a totally different sense. For individuals to use words in a sense peculiar to themselves is not helpful in the commerce of ideas. A person who declares himself to be an engine-driver and then adds that his engine is of wood and is drawn by bullocks is misusing the word engine-driver.

This letter has become a much longer one than I expected and the night is already far spent. Probably I have written in a confused and scrappy way for my brain is tired. But still it will convey some picture of my mind. The last few months have been very painful ones for me and I take it for many others. I have felt sometimes that in the modern world, and perhaps in the ancient world also, it is oft preferred to break some people's hearts rather than touch others' pockets. Pockets are indeed more valuable and more cherished than hearts and brains and bodies and human justice and dignity . . . .

There is one other subject I should like to mention. That is the Swaraj Bhawan Trust. I understand that the Working Committee recently considered the question of the upkeep of the Swaraj Bhawan and came to the conclusion that it was not responsible for it. As however it had already made a grant about three years ago and this had not been paid yet, although expenses were incurred on the strength of it, a fresh grant was sanctioned. This will probably be enough for some months. In regard to the future, the Working Committee was evidently anxious not to be saddled with the burden of maintaining the house and grounds. This burden amounts to Rs. 100 a month, which includes taxes, etc. The trustees, I understand, were also a little frightened of the burden and suggested that parts of the house might be let in the ordinary way to raise money for the maintenance. Another suggestion was made that part of the grounds might be sold off for this purpose. I was surprised to learn of these suggestions, as some of them seemed to me to be contrary to the letter of the trust and all of them against its spirit. As an individual trustee I have only one voice in the matter but I should like to say that I have the strongest possible objection to any such misuse of the trust property. The very idea of the wishes of my father being flouted in this way is intolerable to me. The trust represented not only his wishes but also in a small way a memorial to him and his wishes and his memory is dearer to me than a hundred rupees a month. I should, therefore, like to assure the Working Committee and the trustees that they need have no anxiety on the score

12*

of the money required for maintenance of the property. As soon as the funds, now granted by the Working Committee for some months, are exhausted, I shall make myself personally responsible for the maintenance and no further grant need be made by the Working Committee. I would also beg the trustees to respect my feelings in this matter and not to break up the property or to hire it for the sake of hiring it out. I shall endeavour to maintain the Swaraj Bhawan property till such time as it is put to some worthy use.

I have not the figures by me but I believe that even thus far the Swaraj Bhawan has not been, in any sense, a financial burden on the Working Committee. The grants that have been paid to it will probably not be much in excess of reasonable rent for the quarters occupied by the office of the A.I.C.C. [All-India Congress Committee]. This rent could have been reduced by occupying smaller and cheaper quarters. At the same time in the past the A.I.C.C. has paid as much as Rs. 150 a month for rent of an upper floor only in Madras.

Perhaps some parts of this letter might pain you. But you would not have me hide my heart from you.[1]

[Gandhi reply (August 17, 1934) to Nehru letter of August 13, 1934: "I understand your deep sorrow. You are quite right in giving full and free expression to your feelings. But I am quite sure that from our common standpoint a closer study of the written word will show you that there is not enough reason for all the grief and disappointment you have felt. Let me assure you that you have not lost a comrade in me. I am the same as you knew me in 1917 and after. I have the same passion that you knew me to possess for the common goal. I want complete independence for the country in the full English sense of the term. And every resolution that has pained you has been framed with that end in view. I must take full responsibility for the resolutions and the whole conception surrounding them.

"But I fancy that I have the knack for knowing [the] need of the time. And the resolutions are a response thereto. Of course here comes in the difference of our emphasis on the method or the means which to me are just as important as the goal and in a sense more important in that we have some control over them whereas we have none over the goal if we lose control over the means.

"Do read the resolution about 'loose talk' dispassionately. There is not a word in it about socialism. Greatest consideration has been paid to the socialists some of whom I know so intimately. Do I not know their sacrifice? But I have found them as a body to be in a hurry. Why should they not be? Only if I cannot march quite as quick, I must ask them to halt and take me along with them. That is literally my attitude. I have looked

[1] B.O.L., pp. 115-20.

up the dictionary meaning of socialism. It takes me no further than where I was before I read the definition. What will you have me to read to know its full content? . . .

"You are hard on the members of the Working Committee. They are our colleagues such as they are. After all we are a free institution. They must be displaced, if they do not deserve confidence. But it is wrong to blame them for their inability to undergo the sufferings that some others have gone through."[1]]

3 | 1935 Government of India Act— Bombay Congress: Constituent Assembly Proposed—Of Continued Battle against Government of India Act Federal Structure—After Bombay Congress— Reflections on Social and Political Change—Statements by British Statesmen—Gandhi's Continued Preference for Nehru as Congress "Helmsman"

1935 Government of India Act

[After the Third Round Table Conference of 1932, the British Government drafted a provisional Constitution for India, issued as a White Paper in 1933. Subsequently, a Joint Committee on Indian Constitutional Reform was set up. Its report, made public in 1934, formed the basis of the India Bill, introduced in the British Parliament in January, 1935. It was not until August 1935, after six years of discussions, that the Bill finally became law. It was thereafter referred to as the Government of India Act of 1935. The Act remained in effect until India became a Republic in January, 1950. It outlined a constitution for India, approved by the British Parliament, which by no means found favor in India, despite the fact that it expanded the provincial electorates to cover approximately thirty-three million voters.

[1] Ibid., pp. 120-21.

The proposed constitution provided for "a measure of provincial autonomy, with numerous safeguards and federation between the provinces and the Indian states. . . . The safeguards and special powers in the hands of the Governors and the Viceroy were especially objected to [by Congress] as taking the substance out of . . . provincial autonomy".[1] The plan for federation of all of India, which "rested on the assumptions that the chief political parties would work the constitution and that the main units would enter the Federation,"[2] was opposed because it would perpetuate the autocratic regimes of the Indian states, and foster "an unnatural union between the feudal units and semi-democratic provinces. A communal arrangement was also made a part of the new constitution, which created numerous separate electorates."[3]

India's princes, at first willing to accede to the federation proposed in the 1935 Act, "shied off in such numbers that the federal part of the act remained a dead letter. The Congress Party, which had always inveighed against the scheme as being too heavily weighted in the princes' favor, was not loath to see it die. The Moslem League, with its fears of a Hindu raj, was also not displeased with the result. Thenceforth, the political struggle shifted to the provinces, where, under the act . . . autonomy was to be tested for the first time [in 1937]."[4]

Nehru continued to be convinced that Indians should be permitted to work out their own future political destiny. His proposal that this might be accomplished by means of a Constituent Assembly was adopted by Congress in 1934.]

Bombay Congress: Adoption of Proposal for Constituent Assembly

I followed from the newspapers supplied to me [in jail] the proceedings of the [1934] Bombay session of the Congress. . . .

Gandhiji's retirement from the Congress was a striking feature of the session, and outwardly it marked the end of a great chapter in Congress and Indian history. But, essentially, its significance was not great, for he cannot rid himself, even if he wanted to, of his dominating position.

I was glad that the Congress had adopted the idea of a Constituent Assembly for settling the constitution of the country. It seemed to me that there was no other way of solving the problem, and I am sure that sometime or other some such assembly will have to meet. Manifestly it cannot do so without the consent of the British Government, unless there has been a successful revolution. It is equally manifest that this consent is not

[1] T.D.G. (Vol. IV), p. 39.
[2] E.I.P., p. 202.
[3] T.D.G. (Vol. IV), p. 39.
[4] I.P.C., p. 170.

likely to be forthcoming under present circumstances. A real assembly can therefore not meet till enough strength has been evolved in the country to force the pace. This inevitably means that even the political problem will remain unsolved till then.[1]

I am personally prepared to have elections for this Assembly by separate electorates for those minorities who so desire it. The representatives of these minorities, so elected, will have every right to speak for them and no one can say that the majority community has influenced their election.[2]

[The] Assembly would also deal with the communal problem, and I have suggested that, in order to remove all suspicion from the minds of a minority, it may even, if it so chooses, have its representatives elected by separate electorates. These separate electorates would only be for the Constituent Assembly. The future method of election, as well as all other matters connected with the constitution, would be settled by the Assembly itself.[3]

Of Continued Battle against Government of India Act Federal Structure (written in 1938)

The new Constitution of India, though giving a certain leverage in the provinces owing to the extension of the electorate, is essentially designed to protect these special interests and keep British imperialism in India intact. Even in the provinces real power rests with the Governors and the revenues are largely mortgaged to these interests. Such strength as there is behind the provincial governments comes far more from the organized national movement than from the Constitution Act. Fear of conflict with this movement, resulting possibly in the suspension of the Constitution, prevents too much interference with the provincial governments. But the position is essentially unstable; conflicts are inherent in it. Besides, under the financial provisions and reservations really big schemes of social reform simply cannot be undertaken. . . .

By far the worst part of the Constitution is the proposed Federal structure, for it makes the feudal Indian States permanent and, in addition, gives them some power to interfere in the affairs of the rest of India.

[1] T.F., p. 342.
[2] R.E.W., p. 68.
[3] Ibid., p. 72.

The whole conception of a union of imperialism, feudalism and democracy is incapable of realization and can only mean the entrenchment of all the reactionary elements. It must be remembered that the Indian State system is over a hundred years old and that during this century it has continued more or less unchanged. In this period Europe and the world have altered past recognition, and it is a monstrous imposition on us that we should be saddled permanently with feudal relics which prevent all growth. Hence the fierce opposition to the Federal structure and the Constitution Act as a whole. [The Federal structure was never to become operative.]

The National Congress stands for independence and a democratic state. It has proposed that the constitution of a free India must be framed, without outside interference, by a Constituent Assembly elected on the basis of an adult franchise. That is the democratic way and there is no other way short of revolution which can bring the needed result. An Assembly so elected will represent the people as a whole and will be far more interested in the economic and social problems of the masses than in the petty communal issues which affect small groups. Thus it will solve without much difficulty the communal and other like problems. It will not solve so easily the economic problems, but the clash of interest there is similar to that found all over the world.[1]

[In October, 1934 the Congress met in Bombay. Among the results of the meeting Congress "endorsed the policy of entering the Legislatures and laid down a . . . programme including revival of and encouragement to hand-spinning and hand-weaving, promotion of useful village and small industries, reconstruction of village life in its economic, educational, social and hygienic aspects, removal of untouchability, promotion of inter-communal unity, total abstinence, national education, spread of useful knowledge among the adult population, organisation of industrial labour and peasants and strengthening of the Congress organisation. Under a revised [Congress] Constitution it reduced the number of delegates and made it proportionate to the number of primary members on the Congress roll and insisted on manual labour and habitual wearing of Khadi on all elected members and office-bearers of Congress Committees."[2]]

After the Bombay Congress

Soon after the Bombay Congress came the [Legislative] Assembly elections. With all my lack of enthusiasm for the Congress parliamentary

[1] U.I., pp. 22–23.
[2] H.I.N.C. (Vol. I), Prasad Introduction, fourth and fifth pages, unnumbered.

program, I was greatly interested, and I wished the Congress candidates success, or to put it more correctly, I hoped for the defeat of their opponents. Among these opponents was a curious assortment of careerists, communalists, renegades, and people who had [staunchly] supported the Government in its policy of repression. The Congress met with remarkable success, and I was pleased that a good number of undesirables had been kept out.

The Assembly elections threw a revealing light on the people at the back of the reactionary communal bodies. They were the big landlords, the feudal elements and the banker class.

Soon after the Assembly elections the Report of the Joint Parliamentary Committee on Indian Constitutional Reform was issued. Among the varied and widespread criticisms to which it was subjected, stress was often laid on the fact that it showed "distrust" and "suspicion" of the Indian people. This seemed to me a very strange way of looking at our national and social problems. Were there no vital conflicts of interest between British imperial policy and our national interests? The question was which was to prevail. Did we want freedom merely to continue that imperial policy? Apparently that was the British Government's notion, for we were informed that the "safeguards" would not be used so long as we behaved and demonstrated our fitness for self-rule by doing just what British policy required. If British policy was to be continued in India, why all this shouting about getting the reins in our own hands?

The measure of liberty that this proposed gift of Britain offers to India can be taken from the fact that even the most moderate and politically backward groups in India have condemned it as reactionary. The habitual and persistent supporters of Government have had to combine criticisms of it with their usual genuflections. Others have been more vehement.

In view of these proposals the Liberals found it difficult to retain in full measure their abiding faith in the inscrutable wisdom of Providence in placing India under British dominion.

A certain hopeful reliance is placed by Liberal leaders, and probably by many others including some Congressmen, on the victory of the Labour party in Britain and the formation of a Labour Government there. There is absolutely no reason why India should not endeavor to go ahead with the co-operation of advanced groups in Britain, or should not try to profit by the advent of a Labour Government. But to rely helplessly on a change in fortune's wheel in England is hardly dignified or in consonance with national honor. Dignity apart, it is not good common sense. Why should we expect much from the British Labour party? We have had two Labour Governments already, and we are not likely to forget their gifts to India. . . .

It is perfectly clear that in matters of imperial policy there is little to choose between Tory or Labour in England. It is true that the Labour rank and file is far more advanced, but it has little influence on its very conservative leadership. It may be that the Labour Left wing will gather strength, for conditions change rapidly nowadays; but do national or social movements curl themselves up and go to sleep, waiting for problematical changes elsewhere?[1]

Reflections on Social and Political Change

I have tried to follow [the] superficial developments in the Indian political scene, but I cannot help feeling that they are unreal, and the background in India oppresses me. The background is one of continual repression of every kind of freedom, of enormous suffering and frustration, of distortion of good will, and encouragement of many evil tendencies. Large numbers lie in prison and spend their young lives, year after year, eating their hearts out. Their families and friends and connections and thousands of others grow bitter, and a nauseating sense of humiliation and powerlessness before brute strength takes possession of them. Numerous organizations are outlawed even in normal times, while "Emergency Powers" and "Tranquillity Acts" make for themselves almost a permanent home in the Government's armory. Exceptions in the matter of restrictions of liberties rapidly become the general rule. Large numbers of books and periodicals are proscribed or prevented entry by a "Sea Customs Act," and the possession of "dangerous" literature may lead to a long term of imprisonment. A frank expression of opinion on the political or economic problems of the day, or a favorable report of social and cultural conditions in Russia meets with the strong disapproval of the censor. The *Modern Review* was warned by the Bengal Government because it published an article by Dr Rabindranath Tagore on Russia, an article written after a personal visit to that country. We are informed by the Under-Secretary for India in Parliament that "the article gave a distorted view of the achievements of British rule in India", and hence action was taken against it [November 12, 1934]. The judge of these achievements is the censor, and we may not have a contrary opinion or give expression to it. Objection

[1] T.F., pp. 343–44.

was also taken by Government to the publication of a brief message from Rabindranath Tagore to the Dublin Society of Friends. This is a strange background for the introduction of reforms and responsible government and the like.

Far-reaching changes are taking place before our eyes, and the future, whatever shape it might take, is not a remote, far-off thing which arouses a purely academic interest in the detached minds of philosophers, sociologists, and economists. It is a matter which affects every human being for better or for worse, and surely it is every citizen's duty to try to understand the various forces at play and decide on his own course of action. A world is coming to an end, and a new world is taking shape. To find an answer to a problem it is necessary to know what it is.[1]

As these pages will show, I am very far from being a communist. My roots are still perhaps partly in the nineteenth century, and I have been too much influenced by the humanist liberal tradition to get out of it completely. This bourgeois background follows me about and is naturally a source of irritation to many communists. I dislike dogmatism, and the treatment of Karl Marx's writings or any other books as revealed scripture which cannot be challenged, and the regimentation and heresy hunts which seem to be a feature of modern communism. I dislike also much that has happened in Russia, and especially the excessive use of violence in normal times. . . .

Marx may be wrong in some of his statements, or his theory of value; this I am not competent to judge. But he seems to me to have possessed quite an extraordinary degree of insight into social phenomena, and this insight was apparently due to the scientific method he adopted. This method, applied to past history as well as current events, helps us in understanding them far more than any other method of approach, and it is because of this that the most revealing and keen analysis of the changes that are taking place in the world today come from Marxist writers. It is easy to point out that Marx ignored or underrated certain subsequent tendencies, like the rise of a revolutionary element in the middle class, which is so notable today. But the whole value of Marxism seems to me to lie in its absence of dogmatism, in its stress on a certain outlook and mode of approach, and in its attitude to action. That outlook helps us in understanding the social phenomena of our own times and points out the way of action and escape. . . .

[1] Ibid., pp. 345-46.

Coming back to India, communism and socialism seem a far cry, unless the rush of external events forces the pace here.[1]

[The Congress Socialist Party of India (whose policies Nehru greatly influenced, but which he did not join), was founded in 1934. The Indian Communist Party, formed during the 1920s, was outlawed by the British in 1934 and remained so until the early 1940s.]

Statements by British Statesmen

[Of Lord Lytton.] Lord Lytton, a former governor of an Indian province, who acted as Viceroy for a while, often referred to as a liberal and sympathetic governor, is reported to have said [in the House of Lords, December 17, 1934] that "the Government of India was far more representative of India as a whole than the Congress politicians. The Government of India was able to speak in the name of officials, the Army, the Police, the Princes, the fighting regiments and both Moslems and Hindus, whereas the Congress politicians could not even speak on behalf of one of the great Indian communities." He went on to make his meaning quite clear: "When I speak of Indian opinion, I am thinking of those on whose co-operation I had to rely and on whose co-operation the future Governors and Viceroys will have to rely."

Two interesting points emerge from his speech: the India that counts means those who help the British; and the British Government of India is the most representative and, therefore, democratic body in the country. That this argument should be advanced seriously shows that English words seem to change their meanings when they cross the Suez Canal. The next and obvious step in reasoning would be, that autocratic government is the most representative and democratic form because the King represents everybody. We get back to the divine right of kings and "*l'état, c'est moi!*"[2]

[Two other statements of the period deserve equal attention. From Winston Churchill's speech on second reading of Government of India Bill, already described—February 11, 1935: "We have as good a right to be in India as anyone there except, perhaps, the Depressed Classes, who are the original stock. Our Government is not an irresponsible Government. It is a Government responsible to the Crown and to Parliament. It is incomparably the best Government that India has ever seen or will see. It is not true to say that the Indians, whatever their creed, would not rather have their affairs dealt with in many cases by British courts and

[1] Ibid., pp. 348–50.
[2] Ibid., pp. 308–09.

British officers than by their own people, especially their own people of the opposite religion."

By way of contrast with the above, it is of interest to note the following excerpt from Clement Attlee's speech relating to the same Bill, delivered on June 4, 1935: "The question that we should put is this: Does this Constitutional scheme provide a medium through which the living forces of India can operate, because what we have to deal with are the forces of modern India, a living India, and not the dead India of the past. If we are to do anything with India, we have to bring modern forces into play. . . . For good or ill, the Congress party is one of the dominating factors in the situation. It is no use ignoring it, and it is useless and futile merely to abuse it. We may disagree with it, but within it are very many of the forces that are going to make for modern India."[1]]

Gandhi's Continued Preference for Nehru as Congress "Helmsman"

[Even after Gandhi had resigned from Congress, he continued to favor Nehru as its "rightful helmsman". In September, 1934, Gandhi wrote to Sardar Patel: "I miss at this juncture the association and advice of Jawaharlal who is bound to be the rightful helmsman of the organization in the near future." (This was the first indication that Gandhi favoured Nehru for the presidency upon his release from prison, a preference that came to fruition at the Lucknow Congress session in 1936.) "I feel that I am in no sense deserting one who is much more than a comrade and whom no amount of political differences will ever separate from me. . . . He is courage personified. He has an indomitable faith in his mission. . . ." The reasons for Gandhi's own formal resignation from Congress were his feeling that "I am a dead weight on the Congress now", that there was a growing and vital difference between him and the intelligentsia, and that the socialists, recently organized into the Congress Socialist Party, must have free right to expression.[2]]

4 | ## On Gandhi's Social Theories: Autumn, 1935

[In spite of their many differences, Nehru continued to support the Mahatma publicly, once Gandhi had gained majority support for a

[1] E.I.P., pp. 315, 318.
[2] T.D.G. (Vol. III), pp. 317-18.

particular measure in Congress—a prime objective of Jawaharlal's being to help maintain party unity. He knew also that, ultimately, there would be further occasions upon which he could champion his own beliefs, never ceasing to write and speak in independent fashion, in spite of subjecting himself to a certain discipline within Congress.

The following commentary about Gandhi, like all else contained in *Toward Freedom*—except its "postscript and minor changes"—was written in prison between June, 1934 and February, 1935.]

"India's salvation consists," [Gandhi] wrote in 1909, "in unlearning what she has learned during the last fifty years. The railways, telegraphs, hospitals, lawyers, doctors, and suchlike have all to go; and the so-called upper classes have to learn consciously, religiously, and deliberately the simple peasant life, knowing it to be a life giving true happiness." And again: "Every time I get into a railway car or use a motor bus I know that I am doing violence to my sense of what is right"; "to attempt to reform the world by means of highly artificial and speedy locomotion is to attempt the impossible."

All this seems to me utterly wrong and harmful doctrine, and impossible of achievement. Behind it lies Gandhiji's love and praise of poverty and suffering and the ascetic life. For him progress and civilization consist not in the multiplication of wants, of higher standards of living, "but in the deliberate and voluntary restriction of wants, which promotes real happiness and contentment, and increases the capacity for service". If these premises are once accepted, it becomes easy to follow the rest of Gandhiji's thought and to have a better understanding of his activities. But most of us do not accept those premises, and yet we complain later on when we find that his activities are not to our liking.

Personally I dislike the praise of poverty and suffering. I do not think they are at all desirable, and they ought to be abolished. Nor do I appreciate the ascetic life as a social ideal, though it may suit individuals. I understand and appreciate simplicity, equality, self-control; but not the mortification of the flesh. Just as an athlete requires to train his body, I believe that the mind and habits have also to be trained and brought under control. It would be absurd to expect that a person who is given to too much self-indulgence can endure much suffering or show unusual self-control or behave like a hero when the crisis comes. To be in good moral condition requires at least as much training as to be in good physical condition. But that certainly does not mean asceticism or self-mortification.

Nor do I appreciate in the least the idealization of the "simple peasant life". I have almost a horror of it, and instead of submitting to it myself I want to drag out even the peasantry from it, not to urbanization, but to the spread of urban cultural facilities to rural areas. Far from this life's giving me true happiness, it would be almost as bad as imprisonment for me. . . .

This desire to get away from the mind of man to primitive conditions where mind does not count, seems to me quite incomprehensible. The very thing that is the glory and triumph of man is decried and discouraged, and a physical environment which will oppress the mind and prevent its growth is considered desirable. Present-day civilization is full of evils, but it is also full of good; and it has the capacity in it to rid itself of those evils. To destroy it root and branch is to remove that capacity from it and revert to a dull, sunless, and miserable existence. But even if that were desirable it is an impossible undertaking. We cannot stop the river of change or cut ourselves adrift from it, and psychologically we who have eaten of the apple of Eden cannot forget that taste and go back to primitiveness.

It is difficult to argue this, for the two standpoints are utterly different. Gandhiji is always thinking in terms of personal salvation and of sin, while most of us have society's welfare uppermost in our minds. I find it difficult to grasp the idea of sin, and perhaps it is because of this that I cannot appreciate Gandhiji's general outlook. He is not out to change society or the social structure; he devotes himself to the eradication of sin from individuals. "The follower of Swadeshi," he has written, "never takes upon himself the vain task of trying to reform the world, for he believes that the world is moved and always will be moved according to the rules set by God." And yet he is aggressive enough in his attempts to reform the world; but the reform he aims at is individual reform, the conquest over the senses and the desire to indulge them, which is sin. Probably he will agree with the definition of liberty which an able Roman Catholic writer on fascism has given: "Liberty is no more than freedom from the bondage of sin." How almost identical this is with the words of the Bishop of London written two hundred years ago: "The Freedom which Christianity gives is Freedom from the Bondage of sin and Satan and from the Dominion of Men's Lusts and Passions and inordinate Desires."

If this standpoint is once appreciated, then one begins to understand a little Gandhiji's attitude to sex, extraordinary as that seems to the average person today. For him "any union is a crime when the desire for progeny is absent", and "the adoption of artificial methods must result in imbecility and nervous prostration". "It is wrong and immoral to seek to escape the consequences of one's act. . . . It is bad for [one] to indulge [one's] appetite and then escape the consequences by taking tonics or other medicines. It is still worse for a person to indulge his animal passions and escape the consequences of his acts."

Personally I find this attitude unnatural and shocking, and if he is right, then I am a criminal on the verge of imbecility and nervous prostration. The Roman Catholics have also vigorously opposed birth control, but they have not carried their argument to the logical limit, as Gandhiji has done. They have temporized and compromised with what they consider to be human nature. But Gandhiji has gone to the extreme limit of his argument and does not recognize the validity or necessity of the sexual act at any time except for the sake of children; he refuses to recognize any natural sex attraction between man and woman. "But I am told," he says, "that this is an impossible ideal, that I do not take account of the natural attraction between man and woman. I refuse to believe that the sensual affinity, referred to here, can be at all regarded as natural; in that case the deluge would soon be over us. The natural affinity between man and woman is the attraction between brother and sister, mother and son, or father and daughter. It is this natural attraction that sustains the world." And more emphatically still: "No, I must declare with all the power I can command that sensual attraction, even between husband and wife, is unnatural."

One can accept it as an act of faith or reject it. There is no halfway house, for it is a question of faith, not of reason. For my part I think Gandhiji is absolutely wrong in this matter. His advice may fit in with some cases, but as a general policy it can only lead to frustration, inhibition, neurosis, and all manner of physical and nervous ills. Sexual restraint is certainly desirable, but I doubt if Gandhiji's doctrine is likely to result in this to any widespread extent. It is too extreme, and most people decide that it is beyond their capacity and go their usual ways, or there is friction between husband and wife. Evidently Gandhiji thinks that birth-control methods necessarily mean inordinate indulgence in the sex act, and that if the sexual affinity between man and woman is admitted every man will run after every woman, and vice versa. Neither inference is justified, and I do not know why he is so obsessed by this problem of sex, important as it is. For him it is a "soot or whitewash" question; there are no intermediate shades. At either end he takes up an extreme position which seems to me most abnormal and unnatural. Perhaps this is a reaction from the deluge of literature on sexology that is descending on us in these days. I presume I am a normal individual and sex has played its part in my life, but it has not obsessed me or diverted me from my other activities. . . .

People who do not know Gandhiji personally and have only read his writings are apt to think that he is a priestly type, extremely puritanical, long-faced, Calvinistic, and a kill-joy, something like the "priests in black gowns walking their rounds". But his writings do him an injustice; he is far greater than what he writes, and it is not quite fair to quote what he has written and criticize it. He is the very opposite of the Calvinistic priestly type. His smile is delightful, his laughter infectious, and he radiates light-heartedness. There is something childlike about him which is full of charm. When he enters a room, he brings a breath of fresh air with him which lightens the atmosphere.

He is an extraordinary paradox. I suppose all outstanding men are so to some extent. For years I have puzzled over this problem: why with all his love and solicitude for the underdog he yet supports a system which inevitably produces it and crushes it; why with all his passion for non-violence he is in favor of a political and social structure which is wholly based on violence and coercion? Perhaps it is not correct to say that he is in favor of such a system; he is more or less of a philosophical anarchist. But, as the ideal anarchist state is too far off still and cannot easily be conceived, he accepts the present order. It is not, I think, a question of means, that he objects, as he does, to the use of violence in bringing about a change. Quite apart from the methods to be adopted for changing the existing order, an ideal objective can be envisaged, something that is possible of achievement in the not-distant future.

Sometimes he calls himself a socialist, but he uses the word in a sense peculiar to himself which has little or nothing to do with the economic framework of society which usually goes by the name of socialism. Following his lead, a number of prominent Congressmen have taken to the use of that word, meaning thereby a kind of muddled humanitarianism. I know that Gandhiji is not ignorant of the subject, for he has read many books on economics and socialism and even Marxism, and has discussed it with others. But I am becoming more and more convinced that in vital matters the mind by itself does not carry us far.

Gandhiji underwent a tremendous conversion during his early days in South Africa, and this shook him up greatly and altered his whole outlook on life. Since then he has had a fixed basis for all his ideas, and his mind is hardly an open mind. He listens with the greatest patience and attention to people who make new suggestions to him, but behind all his courteous interest one has the impression that one is addressing a closed door. He is so firmly anchored to some ideas that everything else seems unimportant. To insist on other and secondary matters would be a distraction and a distortion of the larger scheme. To hold on to that anchor would necessarily result in a proper adjustment of these other matters. If the means are right, the end is bound to be right.

That, I think, is the main background of his thought. He suspects also socialism, and more particularly Marxism, because of their association with violence. The very words "class war" breathe conflict and violence and are thus repugnant to him. He has also no desire to raise the standards of the masses beyond a certain very modest competence, for higher standards and leisure may lead to self-indulgence and sin. It is bad enough that the handful of the well-to-do are self-indulgent; it would be much worse if their numbers were added to.

That outlook is as far removed from the socialistic, or for that matter the capitalistic, as anything can be. To say that science and industrial technique today can demonstrably feed, clothe, and house everybody and raise their standards of living very greatly, if vested interests did not intervene, does not interest him much, for he is not keen on those results, beyond a certain limit. The promise of socialism therefore holds no attraction for him, and capitalism is only partly tolerable because it circumscribes the evil. He dislikes both, but puts up with the latter for the present as a lesser evil and as something which exists and of which he has to take cognizance.

I may be wrong perhaps in imputing these ideas to him, but I do feel that he tends to think in this manner, and the paradoxes and confusions in his utterances that trouble us are really due to entirely different premises from which he starts. He does not want people to make an ideal of ever-increasing comfort and leisure, but to think of the moral life, give up their bad habits, to indulge themselves less and less, and thus to develop themselves individually and spiritually. And those who wish to serve the masses have not so much to raise them materially as to go down themselves to their level and mix with them on equal terms. In so doing inevitably they will help in raising them somewhat. That, according to him, is true democracy. "Many have despaired of resisting me," he writes in a statement he issued on September 17, 1934. "This is a humiliating revelation to me, a born democrat. I make that claim, if complete identification with the poorest of mankind, longing to live no better than they, and a corresponding conscious effort to approach that level to the best of one's ability, can entitle one to make it."

Gandhiji is always laying stress on the idea of the trusteeship of the feudal prince, of the big landlord, of the capitalist. He follows a long succession of men of religion. The Pope has declared that "the rich must consider themselves the servants of the Almighty as well as the guardians and the distributors of his wealth, to whom Jesus Christ himself entrusted the fate of the poor". Popular Hinduism and Islam repeat this idea and are always calling upon the rich to be charitable, and they respond by building temples or mosques or *dharamshalas*, or giving, out of their abundance, coppers or silver to the poor and feeling very virtuous in consequence.

This religious attitude is bound up with the world of long ago, when the only possible escape from present misery was in the hope of a world to come. But, though conditions changed and raised the human level in material prosperity beyond the wildest dreams of the past, the stranglehold of that past continued, the stress now being laid on certain vague, unmeasurable spiritual values.

Gandhiji wants to improve the individual internally, morally and spiritually, and thereby to change the external environment. He wants people to give up bad habits and indulgences and to become pure. He lays stress on sexual abstinence, on the giving up of drink, smoking, etc. Opinions may differ about the relative wickedness of these indulgences, but can there be any doubt that even from the individual point of view, and much more so from the social, these personal failings are less harmful than covetousness, selfishness, acquisitiveness, the fierce conflicts of individuals for personal gain, the ruthless struggles of groups and classes, the inhuman suppression and exploitation of one group by another, the terrible wars between nations? Of course he detests all this violence and degrading conflict. But are they not inherent in the acquisitive society of today with its law that the strong must prey on the weak, and its motto, that, as of old, "they shall take who have the power and they shall keep who can"? The profit motive today inevitably leads to conflict. The whole system protects and gives every scope to man's predatory instincts; it encourages some finer instincts, no doubt, but much more the baser instincts of man. Success means the knocking down of others and mounting on their vanquished selves. If these motives and ambitions are encouraged by society and attract the best of our people, does Gandhiji think that he can achieve his ideal—the moral man—in this environment? He wants to develop the spirit of service; he will succeed in the case of some individuals, but, so long as society puts forward as exemplars the victors of an acquisitive society and the chief urge as the personal profit motive, the vast majority will follow this course.

But the problem is no longer merely a moral or an ethical one. It is a practical and urgent problem of today, for the world is in a hopeless muddle, and some way out must be found. We cannot wait, Micawber-like, for something to turn up. Nor can we live by negation alone, criticizing the evil aspects of capitalism, socialism, communism, etc., and hoping vaguely for the golden mean, which will produce a happy compromise combining the best features of all systems, old and new. The malady has to be diagnosed and the cure suggested and worked for. It is quite certain that we cannot stand where we are, nationally and internationally; we may try to go back or we may push forward. Probably there is no choice in the matter, for going back seems inconceivable.

And yet many of Gandhiji's activities might lead one to think that he wants to go back to the narrowest autarchy, not only a self-sufficient nation, but almost a self-sufficient village. In primitive communities the village was more or less self-sufficient and fed and clothed itself and otherwise provided for its needs. Of necessity that means an extremely low standard of living. I do not think Gandhiji is permanently aiming at this, for it is an impossible objective. The huge populations of today would not be able even to subsist in some countries; they would not tolerate this reversion to scarcity and starvation. It is possible, I think, that in an agricultural country like India, so very low is our present standard, that there might be a slight improvement for the masses with the development of village industries. But we are tied up, as every country is tied up, with the rest of the world, and it seems to me quite impossible for us to cut adrift. We must think, therefore, in terms of the world, and in these terms a narrow autarchy is out of the question. Personally I consider it undesirable from every point of view.

Inevitably we are led to the only possible solution—the establishment of a socialist order, first within national boundaries, and eventually in the world as a whole, with a controlled production and distribution of wealth for the public good. How this is to be brought about is another matter, but it is clear that the good of a nation or of mankind must not be held up because some people who profit by the existing order object to the change. If political or social institutions stand in the way of such a change, they have to be removed. To compromise with them at the cost of that desirable and practical ideal would be a gross betrayal. Such a change may partly be forced or expedited by world conditions, but it can hardly take place without the willing consent or acquiescence of the great majority of the people concerned. They have therefore to be converted and won over to it. Conspiratorial violence of a small group will not help. Naturally efforts must be made to win over even those who profit by the existing system, but it is highly unlikely that any large percentage of them will be converted.

The *khadi* movement, hand-spinning and hand-weaving, which is Gandhiji's special favorite, is an intensification of individualism in production, and is thus a throwback to the preindustrial age. As a solution of any vital present-day problem it cannot be taken seriously, and it produces a mentality which may become an obstacle to growth in the right direction. Nevertheless, as a temporary measure I am convinced that it has served a useful purpose, and it is likely to be helpful for some time to come, so long as the State itself does not undertake the rightful solution of agrarian and industrial problems on a countrywide scale.

Again I think of the paradox that is Gandhiji. With all his keen intellect and passion for bettering the downtrodden and oppressed, why does he support a system, and a system which is obviously decaying, which creates this misery and waste? He seeks a way out, it is true, but is not that way to the past barred and bolted? And meanwhile he blesses all the relics of the old order which stand as obstacles in the way of advance— the feudal states, the big zamindaris and talukdaris, the present capitalist system. Is it reasonable to believe in the theory of trusteeship—to give unchecked power and wealth to an individual and to expect him to use it entirely for the public good? Are the best of us so perfect as to be trusted in this way? Even Plato's philosopher-kings could hardly have borne this burden worthily. And is it good for the others to have even these benevolent supermen over them? But there are no supermen or philosopher-kings; there are only frail human beings who cannot help thinking that their own personal good or the advancement of their own ideas is identical with the public good. The snobbery of birth, position, and economic power is perpetuated, and the consequences in many ways are disastrous.

Again, I would repeat that I am not at present considering the question of how to effect the change, of how to get rid of the obstacles in the way, by compulsion or conversion, violence or nonviolence. . . . But the necessity for the change must be recognized and clearly stated. If leaders and thinkers do not clearly envisage this and state it, how can they expect ever to convert anybody to their way of thinking, or develop the necessary ideology in the people? Events are undoubtedly the most powerful educators, but events have to be properly understood and interpreted if their significance is to be realized and properly directed action is to result from them.

I have often been asked by friends and colleagues who have occasionally been exasperated by my utterances: Have you not come across good and benevolent princes, charitable landlords, well-meaning and amiable capitalists? Indeed I have. I myself belong to a class which mixes with these lords of the land and owners of wealth. I am a typical bourgeois, brought up in bourgeois surroundings, with all the early prejudices that this training has given me. Communists have called me a petty bourgeois with perfect justification. Perhaps they might label me now one of the "repentant *bourgeoisie*." But whatever I may be is beside the point. It is absurd to consider national, international, economic, and social problems in terms of isolated individuals. Those very friends who question me are never tired of repeating that our quarrel is with the sin and not the sinner. I would not even go so far. I would say that my quarrel is with a system and not with individuals. A system is certainly embodied to a great extent in individuals and groups, and these individuals and groups have to be converted or combated. But, if a system has ceased to be of value and is a drag, it has to go, and the classes or groups that cling to it will also have to undergo a transformation. That process of change should involve as little suffering as possible, but unhappily suffering and dislocation are inevitable. We cannot put up with a major evil for fear of a far lesser one, which in any event is beyond our power to remedy.

Every type of human association—political, social, or economic—has some philosophy at the back of it. When these associations change, this philosophical foundation must also change in order to fit in with it and to utilize it to the best advantage. Usually the philosophy lags behind the course of events, and this lag creates all the trouble. Democracy and capitalism grew up together in the nineteenth century, but they were not mutually compatible. There was a basic contradiction between them, for democracy laid stress on the power of the many, while capitalism gave real power to the few. This ill-assorted pair carried on somehow because political parliamentary democracy was in itself a very limited kind of democracy and did not interfere much with the growth of monopoly and power concentration.

Even so, as the spirit of democracy grew, a divorce became inevitable, and the time for that has come now. Parliamentary democracy is in disrepute today, and as a reaction from it all manner of new slogans fill the air. Because of this, the British Government in India becomes more reactionary still and makes it an excuse for withholding from us even the outer forms of political freedom. The Indian princes, strangely enough, make this a justification for their unchecked autocracy and stoutly declare their intention of maintaining medieval conditions in their domains such as exist nowhere else in the world. But the failure of parliamentary democracy is not that it has gone too far, but that it has not gone far enough. It was not democratic enough because it did not provide for economic democracy, and its methods were slow and cumbrous and unsuited to a period of rapid change.

The Indian states represent today probably the extremest type of autocracy existing in the world. They are, of course, subject to British suzerainty, but the British Government interferes only for the protection or advancement of British interests. A veil of mystery surrounds these states. Newspapers are not encouraged there, and at the most a literary or semiofficial weekly might flourish. Outside newspapers are often barred. Literacy is very low, except in some of the southern states—Travancore, Cochin, etc.—where it is far higher than in British India. The principal news that comes from the states is of a viceregal visit, with all its pomp and ceremonial and mutually complimentary speeches, or of an extravagantly celebrated marriage or birthday of the ruler, or an agrarian rising. Special laws protect the princes from criticism, even in British India, and within the states the mildest criticism is rigorously suppressed. Public meetings are almost unknown, and even meetings for social purposes are often banned. Leading public men from outside are frequently prevented from entering the states.

When such conditions prevail in the states, it would have been natural for the Congress to stand up for the elementary rights of the people of the states and to criticize their wholesale suppression. But Gandhiji fathered a novel policy on the Congress in regard to the states—the "policy of noninterference in the internal administration of the states." This hush-hush policy has been adhered to by him in spite of the most extraordinary and painful occurrences in the states, and in spite of wholly unprovoked attacks by the states' governments on the Congress. Apparently the fear is that Congress criticism might offend the rulers and make it more difficult to "convert" them.

More or less the same considerations apply to the talukdari and big zamindari system. It hardly seems a matter for argument that this semifeudal system is out of date and is a great hindrance to production and general progress. It conflicts even with a developing capitalism, and almost all over the world large landed estates have gradually vanished and given place to peasant proprietors. I had always imagined that the only possible question that could arise in India was one of compensation. But to my surprise I have discovered during the last year or so (1934–5) that Gandhiji approves of the talukdari system as such and wants it to continue. He said in July 1934 at Cawnpore that "better relations between landlords and tenants could be brought about by a change of hearts on both sides. If that was done, both could live in peace and harmony." He was "never in favor of abolition of the talukdari or zamindari system, and those who thought that it should be abolished did not know their own minds." (This last charge is rather unkind.)

He is further reported to have said: "I shall be no party to dispossessing propertied classes of their private property without just cause. My objective is to reach your hearts and convert you [he was addressing a deputation of big zamindars] so that you may hold all your private property in trust for your tenants and use it primarily for their welfare. ... But supposing that there is an attempt unjustly to deprive you of your property, you will find me fighting on your side. ... The socialism and communism of the West is based on certain conceptions which are fundamentally different from ours. One such conception is their belief in the essential selfishness of human nature. ... Our socialism and communism should therefore be based on nonviolence and on the harmonious co-operation of labor and capital, landlord and tenant."

I do not know if there are any such differences in the basic conceptions of the East and West. Perhaps there are. But an obvious difference in the recent past has been that the Indian capitalist and landlord have ignored far more the interests of their workers and tenants than their Western prototypes. There has been practically no attempt on the part of the Indian landlord to interest himself in any social service for the tenants' welfare. Many landlords have been deprived of their lands by moneylenders, and the smaller ones have sunk to the position of tenants on the land they once owned. These moneylenders from the city advanced money on mortgages and foreclosed, thus blossoming out into zamindars; according to Gandhiji, they are now the trustees for the unhappy people whom they have themselves dispossessed of their lands, and are expected to devote their income primarily to the welfare of their tenantry.

If the talukdari system is good, why should it not be introduced all over India? Large tracts of India have peasant proprietors. I wonder if Gandhiji would be agreeable to the creation of large zamindaris and talukas in Gujrat? I imagine not. But then why is one land system good for the United Provinces or Behar or Bengal, and another for Gujrat and the Punjab? Presumably there is not any vital difference between the people of the north and east and west and south of India, and their basic conceptions are the same. It comes to this, then, that whatever is should continue, the *status quo* should be maintained. There should be no economic inquiry as to what is most desirable or beneficial for the people, no attempts to change present conditions; all that is necessary is to change the people's hearts. That is the pure religious attitude to life and its problems. It has nothing to do with politics or economics or sociology. And yet Gandhiji goes beyond this in the political, national sphere.

Such are some of the paradoxes that face India today. We have managed to tie ourselves up into a number of knots, and it is difficult to get on till we untie them. That release will not come emotionally. What is better, Spinoza asked long ago, "freedom through knowledge and understanding, or emotional bondage?" He preferred the former.[1]

[Gandhi] had always listened patiently to whatever I had to say and had made every effort to meet my wishes. This had, indeed, led me to think that perhaps some colleagues and I could influence him continuously in a socialist direction, and he had himself said that he was prepared to go step by step as he saw his way to do so. It seemed to me almost inevitable then that he would accept the fundamental socialist position, as I saw no other way out from the violence and injustice and waste and misery of the existing order. He might disagree about the methods but not about the ideal. So I thought . . . [in the early 30's], but I realize now that there are basic differences between Gandhiji's ideals and the socialist objective.[2]

---

5 | Illness and Death of Kamala—Europe, Autumn, 1935—Letters from Europe

Illness and Death of Kamala

Owing to the rapid deterioration in my wife's health [in the spring of 1935], it was decided to send her to Europe for treatment. I was then in

[1] T.F., pp. 314–26.
[2] Ibid., p. 192.

Almora Jail and I continued to remain there, though I was allowed out for a day to visit Bhawali Sanatorium to bid her good-bye. My daughter, Indira, who was [then] at Santiniketan [the college founded by Rabindranath Tagore] accompanied her mother to Europe.[1]

[Because of the further deterioration of Kamala's health, Nehru suddenly was discharged from jail on September 4. Immediately upon his release, he hurried to Kamala's side in Europe. (To add to his anguish, his mother had suffered from a paralytic stroke earlier in 1935.) Kamala, who grew steadily weaker, died in Switzerland, on February 28, 1936. Great as was his stoicism, Nehru's grief was overwhelming.]

Europe, Autumn 1935

[While abroad, Nehru went briefly to England, France and Germany. The dangers inherent in the European political situation became increasingly apparent and distressing at close range; the complexity of the obstacles to be overcome before India's freedom might be attained seemed even more formidable at a distance.]

[Of the situation in Europe, autumn, 1935.] Europe in turmoil, fearful of war and tumult and with economic crises always on the horizon; Abyssinia invaded and her people bombed; various imperialist systems in conflict and threatening each other; and England, the greatest of the imperialist Powers, standing up for peace and the League Covenant while it bombs and ruthlessly oppresses its subject peoples.[2]

[Ethiopia appealed to the League of Nations upon being invaded by Italy on October 2-4, 1935.]

Letters from Europe—1935-1936

[The following letters were written in reply to communications from Lord Lothian, who had headed one of the Committees formed to discuss the new constitution for India. Whereas Lord Lothian believed that Congress members should enter elections for provincial legislatures, in accordance with provisions of the proposed new constitution for India, Nehru's point of view was quite the reverse at the time, as noted in his second letter that follows. Despite this fact, the dialogue between the two men on this, as on other issues, proved obviously stimulating to Nehru.]

[1] B.O.L., p. 122.
[2] T.F., p. 355.

[To Lord Lothian, from Badenweiler—December 9, 1935.] I have been considerably interested in various writings of yours that have come my way. Often I could not agree with your approach to a question or to your conclusion, but invariably I found them provoking me to think and there was also sometimes a measure of agreement. It is always a pleasure to meet people who open out new avenues of thought and help one to see a little more than the tiny corner of the world which is the average person's mental beat. As you say, few people see more than this little corner, and the agonising conflicts of today are certainly made worse by this narrowness of approach. This would be unfortunate at any time; in the present revolutionary epoch it is far more so. I do not think it is possible to charm away the conflicts merely by friendly contacts between well-intentioned persons. The conflicts are obviously deeper and the best of individuals seem to me to play a relatively unimportant role when vast elemental forces are at play against each other. We can try to understand the root causes of these conflicts, as far as we can, and then seek to remove them. But it is so very, very difficult to consider them apart from our own prejudices and sectional interests. The pleasantest of smiles does not get over these ingrained prejudices and the varying world-outlooks that they produce. Still, the attempt must be made to cultivate friendly contacts for without them the world would be a drearier place even than it is. They do certainly help, to a certain extent, in creating an atmosphere which makes understanding possible later on; they lessen the bitterness of individuals and groups; they widen the individual's horizon; and it is one of the chief delights of life to meet worthwhile persons.

All this, surely, is very much worth having and so I am all in favour of developing such contacts. Personally, in spite of my strong convictions, I am not devoid of the student's approach to life and its problems. Dogmas irritate me, whether they are religious or political or economic, and my mind is always searching for the path I should follow. I try not to close it. This makes me welcome all the more personal contacts. Books help, and they have been an unfailing solace to me for many years; but personal touch with the people behind books and ideas and actions has something vital about it which even books do not have.

I should have liked to meet you. Your friendly and welcome letter has increased my desire to do so. I like the beautiful houses and countryside of England and your superlative description of Blickling attracts me, but it is really the man whom I want to see, not the house he owns. I should have liked to meet Lord Halifax also, though I must confess to you that I feel a certain hesitation in meeting people who have been officially

13+N.

associated with the government of India during the past nightmare years. That period is full of horror to us and it is very difficult for me to understand how any sensitive person could tolerate it, much less give his approval to it. It is not so much the repression and suppression of much that was best in India that I refer to, but the manner of it. There was, and is, in it an indecency and vulgarity that I could hardly have conceived. And the wonder of it is that hardly anyone in England realizes this or has any idea of what is happening in India's mind and heart.

I suppose ultimately this will pass. But with this overpowering background it is a little difficult to think in terms of personal contacts. It is not easy to shake hands with a person who is endeavouring to strangle you. In spite of this, I am sure the time will come when we will shake hands and it is up to us to hasten that time.[1]

[Second letter to Lord Lothian, from Badenweiler—January 17, 1936.] I entirely agree with you that we are in the midst of one of the most creative and changing epochs in human history. It does seem that we have reached the end of an era and are on the threshold of another. I also agree that the two ideals which are moving most intelligent and sensitive persons are: the ending of the present anarchy of sovereign states, with their hatreds, fears and conflicts, and the creation of a world order; and the socialistic ideal, aiming at "a system whereby the earth and its fruits will be exploited for the benefit of all members of the community in proportion to the services they render to it and not according to the accident of property ownership." The League of Nations, you say, represents the former ideal. I think this is true insofar as it represents a widespread sentiment. In actual practice, however, it hardly functions that way, and it represents the policies of certain great Powers who have no intention of giving up their privileged positions or their absolute sovereignty and who endeavour to utilise the League to make the world safe for themselves.

Another question arises. Even if the people behind the League honestly desired the ending of the anarchy of sovereign states, or were pushed by popular opinion in that direction, could they succeed in that objective without changing fundamentally the social order—without, in other words, accepting socialism? Of course they would have to shed their imperialism. The League today does not look beyond the present capitalistic system; indeed it does not contemplate even an ending of imperialism. It is essentially based on the *status quo* and its chief function is to preserve it. In practice, therefore, it is actually a hindrance to the realisation of the

[1] B.O.L., pp. 130-32.

very ideal which many people think it represents. If it is true, as I believe it is, that imperialism and the anarchy of sovereign states are inevitable developments of the present phase of capitalism, then it follows that you cannot get rid of the former without also getting rid of the latter. Thus in practice the League has little to do with its supposed ideals and even puts difficulties in the way of their realisation; but even its ideals, by themselves, are such that they lead to a blind alley. It is not surprising that it finds it-self frequently involved in hopeless contradictions. It simply cannot go ahead on the basis of the *status quo* because the root of the trouble is that *status quo* both in its imperialist and social aspects. It is right and proper that the League should condemn Italian aggression in Abyssinia and try to curb it, but the very system which it protects and seeks to perpetuate inevitably leads to that aggression. There is no valid answer for an im-perialist to Mussolini's taunt that he is doing what other imperialist Powers have done before, and are doing now, though not in his particularly blatant way. It does seem rather illogical to condemn Italian bombing in East Africa and maintain a dignified silence about British bombing in the North West Frontier of India.

You yourself are of [the] opinion that . . . achievement of the end is not likely to be by the methods of the Covenant of the League. The League, therefore, offers little hope except insofar as it represents a vague and widespread sentiment in favour of world order and peace. It helps some-times in mobilising that sentiment and in postponing conflict.

The two ideals you have mentioned run into each other and I do not think they can be separated. The second ideal, of Socialism, indeed in-cludes the first, and it may be said that real world order and peace will only come when socialism is realised on a world scale. It is perfectly true, as you say, that real socialism involves a profound transformation of the deeper habits of opinion and of character and this inevitably takes time. Under favourable circumstances and with the goodwill of a large number of people concerned, these changes may be brought about within a gener-ation. But as things are, instead of that goodwill, we have the fiercest opposition and illwill, and it is therefore likely that the period will be a much longer one. The main question for us to consider is how to create an environment and circumstances under which these deeper changes can take place. Only that will be a real step in the right direction. Under present conditions the environment is against us and instead of lessening our mutual hatreds and selfishness and acquisitiveness, which lead to conflict, actually encourage all these evil traits. It is true that in spite of this grave disadvantage some progress is made and some of us at least begin to challenge our old habits and opinions. But the process is very slow and it is almost counterbalanced by the growth of contrary tendencies.

Capitalism stimulated acquisitiveness and these deeper instincts which we want to get rid of now. It did much good also in its earlier stages and by raising production greatly increased the standard of living. In other ways too it served a useful purpose and it was certainly an improvement on the stage that preceded it. But it seems to have outlived its utility and today it not only bars all progress in a socialistic direction but encourages many undesirable habits and instincts in us. I do not see how we can move along socialistic lines in a society which is based on acquisitiveness and in which the profit motive is the dominant urge. It thus becomes necessary to change the basis of this acquisitive society and to remove the profit motive, as far as we can, in order to develop new and more desirable habits and ways of thinking. That involves a complete change over from the capitalist system.

It is true, as you state it, that the capitalist system has not created international anarchy; it merely succeeded to it. It has in the past removed or lessened actual civil war within the state, but it has intensified the conflict of classes, which has grown to such an extent as to threaten civil war in the future. In the international sphere it has perpetuated anarchy on a bigger scale and, instead of petty local wars, it has brought about vast and terrible national conflicts. And so, though it does not create this anarchy, it inevitably increases it and cannot put an end to it unless it puts an end to itself. It has produced the modern imperialisms which not only crush and exploit large parts of the earth's surface and vast numbers of people, but also come into continual conflict with each other.

It may be that Marx overstates the case for the materialist or economic interpretation of history. Perhaps he did so for the simple reason that it had been largely ignored, or at any rate very much understated till then. But Marx never denied the influence of other factors on the shaping of events. He laid the greatest stress on one—the economic factor. Whether that stress was a little overdone does not make much difference. . . .

How will socialism come? You say that it is not likely to be achieved by the universal nationalisation of the instruments of production and distribution. Must it not involve the ending of the profit and acquisitive motive and the replacement of it by a communal and cooperative motive? And does it not involve the building up of a new civilisation on a different basis from that of the present? It may be that a great deal of private initiative is left; in some matters, cultural etc., it must be left. But in all that counts, in a material sense, nationalisation of the instruments of production and distribution seems to be inevitable. There may be half-way houses to it, but one can hardly have two contradictory and conflicting processes going on side by side. The choice must be made and for one who aims at socialism there can be only one choice.

I think it is possible, in theory, to establish socialism by democratic means, provided of course the full democratic process is available. In practice, however, there are likely to be very great difficulties, because the opponents of socialism will reject the democratic method when they see their power threatened. The rejection of democracy does not or should not come from the socialist side but from the other. That of course is Fascism. How is this to be avoided? The democratic method has many triumphs to its credit, but I do not know that it has yet succeeded in resolving a conflict about the very basic structure of the state or of society. When this question arises, the group or class which controls the state-power does not voluntarily give it up because the majority demands it. We have seen enough examples of this in post-war Europe and in the decline of democracy itself. Obviously no socialist transformation can be brought about without the goodwill, or at least the passive acquiescence, of the great majority.

Coming to Britain and India, I find a large number of assumptions in your letter which I think have little justification. As I do not agree with many of your premises, I also find myself in disagreement with some of your conclusions. You say that "Britain is shedding the old imperialism and is actively concerned with trying to find the way to prevent the anarchy involved in universal national self-determination from ending in fresh wars or in a new deluge of imperialism". I am afraid I fail to see entirely that Britain is acting in this role. I do not see any shedding of the old imperialism, but only repeated and strenuous attempts to hold on to it, and to strengthen it, though a new façade is presented to the public view in some instances. Britain certainly does not want fresh wars. She is a satisfied and surfeited Power. Why should she risk what she has got? She wants to maintain the *status quo* which is eminently to her advantage. She dislikes new imperialisms because they conflict with her old imperialism and not because of any dislike of imperialism itself.

You refer also to the "constitutional road" in India. What exactly is this constitutional road? I can understand constitutional activities where there is a democratic constitution, but where there is no such thing, constitutional methods have no meaning. The word constitutional then simply means legal, and legal simply means in accordance with the wishes of an autocratic executive which can make laws and issue decrees and ordinances regardless of public opinion. What is the constitutional method in Germany or Italy today? What was this method in the India of the nineteenth century or of the early twentieth century or even now? There was no possibility of bringing about a change in India then (or now) through any constitutional apparatus which the people of India could sufficiently influence. They could only beg or revolt. The mere fact that it is impossible for the great majority of the people of India to make their will effective shows that they have no constitutional way open to them. They can either submit to something they dislike intensely or adopt other than so-called constitutional methods. Such methods may be wise or unwise, under the particular circumstances, but the question of their being constitutional or not does not arise.

Most of us, I suppose, are unable to get rid of our particular national bias and often ignore the beam in our own eyes. I realise that I must be subject to this, especially when I consider the relation of Britain and India. You will allow for that. Nevertheless I must say that nothing astonishes me so much as the way the British people manage to combine their material interests with their moral fervour; how they proceed on the irrebuttable presumption that they are always doing good to the world and acting from the highest motives, and trouble and conflict and difficulty are caused by the obstinacy and evil-mindedness of others. That presumption, as you know, is not universally accepted, and in Europe and America and Asia it is the subject of humorous comment. In India especially we may be forgiven if we reject it utterly after our experience of British rule in the past and present. To talk of democracy and constitutionalism in India, in the face of what has happened and is happening there, seems to me to distort utterly the significance of these terms. Ruling powers and ruling classes have not been known in history to abdicate willingly. And if the teaching of history was not enough, we in India have had enough experience of hard fact.

It is true, I think, that the British ruling classes possess a certain instinct for adaptability, but when the very basis of their power is challenged there is little room for superficial adaptation. For any one to imagine that the British Government or Parliament are kindly trustees for Indian freedom and are beneficently presiding over its development seems to me one of the most extraordinary of delusions. I believe there are many Britishers who feel kindly towards India and her people and would like to see India free, but they count for little in the shaping of policy, and even they, or most of them, think in terms of Indian freedom fitting in with British desires and interests. More freedom, greater responsibility, will come to us, we are told, as we show our fitness for it, and the test of this is how far we fit in with the British scheme of things. One almost feels like suggesting to our mentors and well-wishers in England to renew their acquaintance with Æsop's fables and especially to read afresh the story of the wolf and the lamb.

It is perfectly true that in politics, as in most other things, we cannot start with a clean slate. It is also true that life is often too complex for human logic. We have to take things as they are, whether we like them or not, and to reconcile our idealism with them. But we must move in the right direction. This means, according to you, first of all the preservation of the unity of India, and then the elimination of communalism, the control and gradual devesting of vested interests and the raising of the standard of living of the people, the development of a true Indian Army, and the training of the youth of India in constructive practical work required in a democratic state. Beyond all this lies the socialistic ideal, and the general background must be such as to develop those deeper instincts and habits which are necessary for the real working of this ideal.

I suppose many of us would agree with that statement, so far as it goes, though we may word it differently and add to it, and stress some points more than others. I agree with you also that the political phase comes first; indeed without that phase there is no other phase. It may be accompanied by social changes or followed soon after by them. Personally I am perfectly prepared to accept political democracy only in the hope that this will lead to social democracy. Political democracy is only the way to the goal and is not the final objective. The real demand for it comes from a desire, sometimes unconscious, for economic changes. If these changes do not follow soon enough the political structure is likely to be unstable. I am inclined to think that in India, circumstanced as she is today, the need for economic change is urgent and a vital political change will be inevitably accompanied or followed by substantial economic changes. In any event the political change should be such as to facilitate these social changes. If it becomes a barrier to them then it is not a desirable change or one worth having.

I am not aware of any responsible Indian who thinks in terms other than those of the unity of India. That is an essential article of our political faith and everything that we do has that for its goal. That unity, I agree, is likely to be a federal unity, but that does not mean of course anything like the federation of the new Act. That unity also is not the unity of subjection under a common yoke. It is possible that a period of chaos might result in disunity and the formation of separate states in India, but that danger seems to me very unreal. The tendency to unity is too strong all over the country.

The disruptive factors are according to you: religion, race and language. I do not see the importance of race. Race in India became intertwined with religion and partly took the shape of caste. Hindus and Moslems do not form different races; they are essentially the same amalgam of races. Thus though there are various races, they run into one another and on the whole form a definite unit, racially and culturally. The so-called hundreds of languages of India are a favourite subject for our critics, who usually have little acquaintance with a single one of them. As a matter of fact India is linguistically singularly well-knit and it is only due to the absence of popular education that numerous dialects have grown. There are ten major languages of India which cover the entire country, except for some small tracts. These belong to the two groups—Indo-Aryan and Dravidian—and between the two there is the common background of Sanskrit. Of the Indo-Aryan languages, I suppose you know that Hindustani with its various dialects accounts for over one hundred and twenty millions of people, and it is spreading. The other Indo-Aryan languages— Bengali, Gujerati, Marathi—are very closely allied to it. I am sure that whatever other difficulties we may have to face in the way of Indian unity, the language question will not be a major difficulty.

You compare the state of religion in India with that of Europe at the time of the Renaissance and the Reformation. It is true that the people of India have a definite religious outlook on life which is comparable to the outlook in Europe during the Middle Ages. Still your comparison does not go below the surface. India has never known in the whole course of her long history the religious strife that has soaked Europe in blood. The whole background of Indian religion, culture and philosophy was one of tolerance, and even encouragement of other beliefs. Some conflict arose when Islam came, but even that was far more political than religious, although stress is always laid on the religious side. It was the conflict between the conquerors and the conquered. In spite of recent developments, I cannot easily envisage religious conflict in India on any substantial scale. The communalism of today is essentially political, economic and middle class. I imagine (but I say so without personal knowledge) that the religious bitterness in Ulster today is far more deep-seated than anywhere in India. It is a fact that one must never forget that communalism in India is a latter-day phenomenon which has grown up before our eyes. That does not lessen its significance and we may not ignore it, for it is at present a tremendous obstacle in our way and is likely to interfere with our future progress. And yet I think it is over-rated and over-emphasised; it does not fundamentally affect the masses although sometimes their passions are roused. With the coming of social issues to the forefront it is bound to recede into the background. Examine the communal demands of the extreme communalists and you will find that not a single one of them has the slightest reference to the masses. The communal leaders of all groups are terribly afraid of social and economic questions and it is interesting to find them joining hands in their opposition to social progress.

British rule in India has inevitably helped in creating political unity in the country. The mere fact of common subjection was bound to result in a common desire to be rid of it. It must be remembered—a fact that is not sufficiently realised—that throughout history there has been a quite extraordinary sense of cultural and geographical unity in India, and the desire for political unity was bound to grow under modern conditions of transport and communication. Throughout the British period, however, there has been an attempt on the part of the ruling power, partly conscious and deliberate, partly unconscious, to retard this unity. That of course was only to be expected for that has been the invariable policy of all empires and ruling groups. It is interesting to read the frank expressions of opinion of high officers in India during the nineteenth century. The problem was then not very urgent but with the growth of the nationalist movement, and especially during the last thirty years, it became acute. The reaction of the British Government was to devise new methods for creating and, if possible, perpetuating these divisions. Obviously no one can say that there was not an inherent tendency towards division in India, and with the prospect of the approach of political power, this was likely to grow. It was possible to adopt a policy to tone down this tendency; it was also possible to accentuate it. The Government adopted the latter policy and encouraged in every way every fissiparous tendency in the country. It is not possible for them or for anyone to stop the historical growth of the people, but they can and they have put checks and obstructions in the way. And the latest and most important of these are in the new Act. You commend this Act because it symbolises the unity of India. As a matter of fact it is the very reverse; it is the prelude (if it is not combated) of greater disunity. It divides up India into religious and numerous other compartments, preserves large parts of it as feudal enclaves which cannot be touched but which can influence other parts, and checks the growth of healthy political parties on social and economic

13*

issues, which you consider "the most important urgent need in India today".

The policy of the British Government on social issues is equally marked. Far from looking towards any form of socialism or control or devesting of vested interests, it has deliberately protected numerous vested interests, created fresh ones and invariably sided with the political, social and religious reactionaries in India. The new Act is again a culmination of this policy and at no time before have these vested interests and obscurantists and reactionaries had so much power as they will have under the new federal India. The Act legally bars the door to that social progress which, according to you, should be our goal, by protecting and entrenching these vested interests, foreign and Indian. Even small measures of social reform are hardly within reach as a very great part of the financial resources of the state is mortgaged and earmarked for the maintenance of the vested interests.

Every country today has to put up a stiff fight against the forces of reaction and evil. India is no exception to the rule. The tragedy of the situation is that the British people, without being conscious of it, stand today through their Parliament and Officials entirely on the side of the forces of evil in India. What they would not tolerate for an instant in their own country, they encourage in India. You mention the great name of Abraham Lincoln and remind me of the vital importance he attached to the Union. Presumably you think that the British Government, in trying to suppress the Congress movement, was actuated by the same noble motive of maintaining the unity of India in the face of disruptive forces. I do not quite see how the unity of India was threatened by that movement—indeed I think that that movement or some similar movement alone can bring about an organic unity in the country, and the British Government's activities push us in a contrary direction. But apart from this, do you not think that the comparison of Lincoln with the attempt of an imperialist Power to crush the freedom movement in a country subject to it, is very far-fetched?

You want to eradicate undesirable and selfish habits and instincts in the people. Do you think that the British in India are helping in this direction? Quite apart from their support of the reactionary elements, the background of British rule is worth considering. It is of course based on an extreme form of widespread violence and the only sanction is fear. It suppresses the usual liberties which are supposed to be essential to the growth of a people; it crushes the adventurous, the brave, the sensitive types, and encourages the timid, the opportunist and time-serving, the sneak and the bully. It surrounds itself with a vast army of spies and informers and *agents provocateurs*. Is this the atmosphere in which the more desirable virtues grow or democratic institutions flourish?

You ask me whether the Congress could at any time have established a liberal constitution for all India by consent, except by making in fundamentals the same kind of concessions to communalism . . . the Princes and . . . property. That presumes that the present Act establishes a liberal constitution by consent. If this constitution is a liberal one it is difficult for me to imagine what an illiberal constitution can be like, and as for consent, I doubt if anything that the British Government have ever done in India has been quite so much resented and disapproved of as the new Act. Incidentally, the measures to obtain the necessary consent involved the fiercest repression all over the country, and even now, as a prelude to the enforcement of the Act, all-India and provincial laws suppressing all kinds of civil liberty have been passed. To talk of consent under these circumstances does seem most extraordinary. There is an amazing amount of misconception about this in England. If the problem has to be faced the dominant facts cannot be ignored.

It is true that the Government has succeeded in making some arrangement with the Princes and with various minority groups, but even these groups are highly dissatisfied except, to some extent, with the minor arrangements affecting their representation. Take the principal minority, the Moslems. No one can say that the aristocratic, semi-feudal and other hand-picked Moslem members of the Round Table Conference represented the Moslem masses. You may be surprised to know that the Congress has still considerable Moslem backing.

Could the Congress have done better? I have no doubt that the nationalist movement, of which the Congress is the symbol and the principal standard bearer, could have done infinitely better. The Congress is of course a bourgeois organisation (I wish it was more socialistic) and therefore the property question would not have arisen in any acute form at that stage. The communal question would have had to be faced and, I think, solved for the time being at least by a large measure of consent. Probably some degree of communalism would have remained to begin with, but far less than what we are presented with under the new Act. What is more important—circumstances would have been created for the elimination of communalism in the near future and for growth along social lines; the land problem would have been tackled. The real difficulties would have been two: the vested interests of the British Government and the City of London, and the Princes. The former represent the crux of the question, all else is really secondary. The Princes would, under the circumstances, have adapted themselves to a considerable extent to the new situation, and the Congress, constituted as it is today, would have given them a long enough rope. The pressure of public opinion, including that of their own subjects, would have been too great for them to resist. Probably some temporary arrangement might have been made with the Indian States to begin with to enable this public opinion to come into play and shape developments. Presuming of course that the British Government is not there to back up the undiluted autocracy of the Princes, there is little doubt that the States would gradually fall into line. No question of civil conflict need have arisen.

All this would have been very far from what I desire but it would at least have been a definite political and democratic step in the right direction. In the framing of a constitution or a political structure it is manifestly impossible to get everyone concerned to agree. One tries to have the maximum agreement and the others, who do not agree, either fall into line according to democratic procedure, or have to be pressed or coerced into doing so. The British Government, representing the autocratic and authoritarian tradition, and chiefly bent on preserving their own interests, tried to win the consent of the Princes and some other reactionary elements, and coerced the vast majority of the people. The Congress would inevitably have functioned differently.

All this is of course airy talk without substance for it ignores the principal factor—the British Government and British financial interests.

There is another consideration which deserves notice. The Congress, under Mr Gandhi's leadership, had laid great stress on non-violence and the conversion of the adversary rather than his coercion. Quite apart from the metaphysical aspects of this doctrine and its feasibility or otherwise in the final sense, there can be no doubt that this has created a powerful feeling against civil conflict and in favour of attempting to win over various groups in India. That is a factor of great value to us in preserving the unity of India and in toning down opposition.

People discuss the non-cooperation and civil disobedience movements in terms of constitutional action or otherwise. I have referred to this aspect earlier. May I put to you how they have always impressed themselves on me? Of course these movements exercised tremendous pressure on the British Government and shook the government machinery. But the real importance, to my mind, lay in the effect they had on our own people, and especially the village masses. Poverty and a long period of autocratic rule, with its inevitable atmosphere of fear and coercion, had thoroughly demoralised and degraded them. They had hardly any of the virtues that are necessary for citizenship, they were cuffed and bullied by every petty official, tax-collector, policeman, landlord's agent; they were utterly lacking in courage or the capacity for united action or resistance to oppression; they sneaked and told tales against each other; and when life became too hard they sought an escape from it in death. It was all very depressing and deplorable and yet one could hardly blame them for it; they were the victims of all-powerful circumstances. Non-cooperation dragged them out of this mire and gave them self-respect and self-reliance; they developed the habit of cooperative action; they acted courageously and did not submit so easily to unjust oppression; their outlook widened and they began to think a little in terms of India as a whole; they discussed political and economic questions (crudely no doubt) in their bazaars and meeting places. The lower middle classes were affected in the same way but the change in the masses was the most significant. It was a remarkable transformation and the Congress, under Gandhi's leadership, must have the credit for it. It was something far more important than constitutions and the structure of government. It was the foundation on which only a stable structure or constitution could be built up.

All this of course involved a cataclysmic upheaval of Indian life. Usually in other countries this has involved a vast amount of hatred and violence. And yet in India, thanks to Mahatma Gandhi, there was, relatively speaking, exceedingly little of this. We developed many of the virtues of war without its terrible evils. And the real organic unity of India was brought far nearer than it had ever been. Even the religious and communal differences toned down. You know that the most vital question which affects rural India, which means eighty-five per cent of India, is the land question. Any such upheaval in another country, together with the terrible economic depression, would have resulted there in *jacqueries*. It is extraordinary that India escaped them. That was not because of government repression but because of Gandhi's teaching and the message of the Congress.

Congress thus released all the live forces in the country and suppressed the evil and disruptive tendencies. It did so in a peaceful, disciplined and as civilised a way as was possible under the circumstances, though inevitably there were risks in such a mass release. How did the Government react? You know that well enough. By trying to crush those live and virile forces and encouraging all the evil and disruptive tendencies, and doing so in the most uncivilised way. The British Government has functioned in a purely Fascist way in India during the past six years, and the only difference has been that it did not take open pride in this fact as the Fascist countries do.

This letter has become terribly long and I do not want now to consider the new Constitution Act in detail. That is hardly necessary for the Act has been analysed and criticised by a host of persons in India holding all sorts of opinions, but agreeing in one thing—their utter disapproval of the Act. Very recently one of the most eminent leaders of the Indian Liberals described the new constitution privately as "the quintessence of the most venomous opposition to all our national aspirations". Is it not remarkable that even our moderate politicians should think so and yet you, with all your broad sympathy for Indian aspirations, should approve of it and say that it "involves the transfer of the citadel of power in India to Indian hands"? Is the gulf between our ways of thinking so vast? Why is it so? It almost becomes more of a problem in psychology than in politics or economics.

The psychological aspect is after all very important. Is it realised in England what the past few years have meant to India? How the attempt to crush human dignity and decency, the injuries to the soul more even than to the body, have left a lasting impress on the Indian people? Never have I realised so well how a tyrannical use of power degrades those who use it as well as those who suffer from it. How can we forget it without forgetting everything that is decent and honourable? How can we forget it when it continues from day to day? Is this the prelude to freedom and the transfer of the citadel of power?

People react in different ways to oppression. Some are broken, others harden. We have both kinds in India as elsewhere. Many of us cannot desert our colleagues, who suffer in prison or otherwise, whatever the consequences might be to our individual selves. Many of us cannot tolerate an insult to Gandhi, whether we differ from him or not, for Gandhi represents to us the honour of India. No one in his senses likes conflict and suffering and the way of catastrophe. The Indian national movement has done all in its power to avoid this way, without at the same time giving up the very basis of its existence. But it is the British Government that has proceeded along that path and made a peaceful solution more and more difficult. If it imagines that by merely persisting in this direction it will succeed, it seems to have strangely misread both the lesson of history and the present temper of the Indian people. If catastrophe is to be avoided, it will have to be for the British Government to retrace its steps.[1]

[1] Ibid., pp. 141–54.

6 | Further Statements from Europe, 1936

[Lord Linlithgow was Indian Viceroy from 1936 to 1943.]

["The Way to Peace."]

In a recent speech in the House of Commons, Mr Lloyd George pleaded for the "Have-nots" amongst the great imperialist Powers—"Have-nots" in the sense that they do not possess colonies to supply them with raw materials and provide sheltered markets for their manufactured goods. From a strictly imperialist point of view, perhaps there was some force in his argument; bribery on a big enough scale might lessen the war-hunger of these "Have-not" Powers for a while and relieve the immediate tension in Europe. It might also of course whet the appetite and increase the demand and convince the peoples and the Governments concerned that threat of and preparation for war pays. Whatever the immediate result might be, the ultimate result could hardly be doubted—the increase in rivalry between these Powers and inevitable conflicts. That has been the history of the growth of modern imperialism, and as fresh colonial areas have come under its domination, these conflicts have increased. The fact that science can provide food and leisure and an ever-increasing standard for all does not, under the peculiar system we live in, lessen these conflicts but only creates more unemployment and international friction.

As I listened to Mr Lloyd George, it struck me as very odd that he should feel so keenly for the unhappy state of the "Have-not" Powers and yet ignore completely the colonial countries and their peoples. Have they no rights in the matter or no say in it? But even apart from the rights and the moralities, is it imagined that peace will be ensured and entrenched by a sharing of the booty by the imperialist Powers?

So long as there are "haves" and "have-nots" friction and conflict will continue, and it is desirable to put an end to this state of affairs. But it seems a mockery to call powerful nations "Have-nots" and ignore the real "Have-not" countries and classes which are being dominated over and exploited. If Mr Lloyd George's argument is to be carried to its logical conclusion, the first thing to be done is to equalize from below upwards, put an end to the exploitation of one country or people or class by another, and thus remove the causes of conflict. But that of course would mean an ending of capitalist-imperialism.

Many pacifists and others who desire ardently to prevent war imagine that the way to bring this about is by satisfying the greed of certain European nations and generally preaching goodwill to all, but otherwise maintaining the *status quo*. It does not seem to be realized by them that it is this very *status quo* that produces ill will and conflict, and is bound to lead to war. Africa may still be a helpless victim of aggression, but it is not likely to remain so for ever. India and China and several other colonial and semi-colonial countries are even now not so weak and helpless, in spite of their present condition. They can never tolerate willingly their subjection and exploitation, and they will struggle against it with all their strength. So also, as we see all around us, the classes that are exploited for the benefit of the upper strata. The *status quo* has to go throughout the world before war goes and the causes of war.

Ultimately of course this involves something more than a political or even social change; it involves a change in our habits and beliefs and instincts, and that is a terribly difficult process. But even this change in our beliefs and instincts is not likely to come till a suitable environment for it has been created. . . .

Few people will deny the importance of the psychological approach and the attempt to convert others. Facts are with us, science, reason, decency, "spirit of the Age", enlightened self-interest, all help us. And in no event, can we get a move on unless we have converted a sufficient number of people.

Granting all that, an insuperable barrier remains. It is perfectly true that the world would be a much better place to live in for all of us if we could change it to fit in with the latest developments of science and provide full scope for growth to all countries and individuals. But it is equally true that certain groups and classes which dominate to-day will lose that privileged position and, especially, the period of transition will be hard for them. They will not be convinced of the beauty of the new order or willing to accept the change. It is possible to convert individuals and even induce them to put up with loss and suffering for a larger cause, but such a conversion is not known to take place in groups and classes as a whole. They move in their own rigid ideologies and refuse to open their minds to anything which injures their group interests. Being in the seats of power they use that advantageous position to influence mass opinion in their own favour in a variety of ways and the psychological approach is thwarted by them and often neutralized.

It is hard enough to get over this difficulty in approaching even others than the groups whose self-interest is affected. But what of these groups themselves? Are we to wait indefinitely till each group and each individual concerned is converted to our ideals and objectives? And are we likely to succeed in this endeavour even after a long lapse of time? Meanwhile danger grows, and the crisis might overwhelm us while we wait and pray.

To take an instance. Must we in India convert the class or order of Indian Princes to democracy and Socialism before we can set our house in order? Granting (though it is a difficult supposition) that some individuals among them might be so converted, it is an inconceivable notion that the group will agree to give up its feudal, autocratic position. To-day most of them treat their States as their private domains where they can do what they will and can draw upon the entire State revenue for their private needs and pleasures. They will inevitably have to give all this up in any new order.... Similar considerations apply to imperialist Powers and their subject countries....

The psychological approach, though admirable and worth stressing, does not thus seem to be quite enough. Something more is necessary to induce the recalcitrant groups to accept or submit to ... change. That something is pressure or some kind of coercion, and the bringing about of circumstances which make it more worth while for the vested interests to accept change than to suffer greater loss in an attempt to avoid it.

The application of coercion immediately conflicts with the psychological approach. We are back again where we were. Is there no way out? Cannot that coercion be applied in such a way as to minimize the fear and hatred and greed which accompany conflict and neutralize even the results of victory? Is it possible to have that psychological approach and yet have the coercion?

That, I take it, is the real problem. Pacifists, as a rule, seem to avoid it and move in an ineffective sphere. Inevitably they become upholders of an unjust system and support the very causes that lead to war. An ardent apostle of peace, a champion of sanctions against Italy, who has received the Nobel Peace Prize, tells us in India that we are narrow-minded and perverted because we do not see the beauty of the British Empire and seek to walk out of it....

So far, I have failed to discover any practical or effective steps in the proposals of the pacifists. I can hardly imagine that the proposal to hold a world peace conference will, under present conditions, lead to anything.

The only practical solution of the problem came from Gandhi. Whether that was a final solution or not remains to be seen, but it did combine the Sermon on the Mount with effective action. In considering his methods one should not be diverted by a discussion of his views on science, or modern industry, or asceticism, or birth control. The technique and the method of approach stand quite apart from those particular views though they might sometimes be coloured by them. That approach is the psychological approach, the refusal to subordinate means to an end, the constant endeavour to lessen ill will and fear, the continuous willingness to make friends of his opponents, and yet at the same time effective and dynamic action. For it must be remembered that in spite of the abundance of "nons" in his movement (non-violence, non-cooperation, etc.), it was not a negative, passive affair. It was an active, dynamic, energizing drive which lifted a whole nation out of a morass of demoralization and helplessness. . . .

Of course there were lapses and bitterness and hatred, but the surprising thing is that they were so few and that within a short term of years [Gandhiji] could have worked this astounding change.

The effect on the Indian people was very marked, and that in itself was success enough. Equally interesting, though very different, was the effect on the British people. Individuals apart, this reaction was one of increasing hostility. Partly this was due to the suppression and distortion of Indian news in England. Fleet Street declared a ban on India, except when the antics of a Maharaja were prominently figured. While millions in India were living through a nightmare of horror, most people in England no doubt imagined that all was well in this bright jewel of the British crown. But news did occasionally trickle through and, in any event, informed people always had a fair notion of what was happening. Even so, these informed and intelligent people, generous and liberal in their ideas, freedom-loving when remote people and other interests were concerned, became more and more hostile to India and her people and tolerated conditions there, of their own Government's making, which shocked them nearer home. It was a very striking example of one's own interests perverting one's sense of values and suppressing the moral sense.

In India the same reaction took place among British officials. But they were in the thick of events and could not ignore them or pass academical judgments. So they went from one brutality to another, progressively deteriorated, and what had been an abnormality, hesitatingly indulged in, became a normal daily occurrence.

Thus we see that the psychological approach did not have a very marked effect on the opposite party. It was smothered by those in power and places of authority and not allowed to reach wider groups, and even when it did so reach, the real or imaginary interests of the group prevented it from producing its expected result. Indeed the idea that the group was being placed morally in the wrong produced the strongest irritation and anger and led to the conviction that there must be something deep and diabolical about this seemingly moral approach.

Perhaps it is too soon to judge. But meanwhile all over the world the clouds gather and pacifists talk vaguely of goodwill and refuse to face realities. They will have to do something more if they wish to be effective.[1]

[In answer to questions concerning fundamental problems of Indian politics—at meeting in London, February, 1936, held under auspices of Indian Conciliation Group.] (With regard to the question—"Will you outline what is meant by the term 'Complete independence for India'?"—the query presumably referred to a phrase to be found in the first Article of the Congress Constitution). Therein it refers, I take it, to the political side only and not the economic side. Of course, the Congress as a whole is beginning to think on economic lines also and otherwise develop its economic policy, and some of us, including myself, think much more on the lines of economic freedom than on the line of political freedom. Obviously economic freedom includes political freedom. But, defining this phrase simply in its political sense, as it occurs in the Congress Constitution, it means national freedom, not only domestic but foreign, financial, military, i.e. control of foreign affairs; in other words, whatever national freedom usually signifies. That does not mean necessarily that we lay stress on an isolation of India or a breaking away of India from such associations as might exist with England or with other countries, but it does mean—the word "independence" is used specially to lay stress on the fact—that we want to break the imperialist connection with Britain. If imperialism survives in England, we must part from England, because so long as imperialism survives in England, the only connection between England and India is likely to be the connection of an imperialist domination in India in some form or other. It may become vaguer and vaguer; it may become less obvious than it is; it may even not be obvious on the political side and yet be very powerful on the economic side. Therefore, in terms of imperialist Britain, the independence of

[1] I.T.W., pp. 218–25.

India means the separation of India from England. Personally I can conceive and welcome the idea of a close association between India and England on terms other than those of imperialism.

The second question is — "Do you recognize the need for an intermediate period of transition, and, if so, does the India Act in any way meet this? If not, what are the next steps to be taken?" Whenever any change comes about, inevitably there are all manner of intermediate and transitional phases, but often it so happens that the structure of government becomes rather petrified and does not change rapidly enough, while economic and other changes are inevitably going on, because economic changes do not wait for laws and enactments; they go on while the structure does not change. The result is that in extreme cases there are big upheavals which forcibly change the structure, and those are called revolutions, but even in that case there are transition periods. I take [it that] this question refers more to the structure of government than to any intermediate period and it is therefore difficult to answer, because [it] depends on so many factors. It depends partly on us but largely on the British Government and largely on various forces, national and international. Obviously if there was a mutual arrangement between Britain and the people of India there would inevitably be transitional stages in the process of reaching [a] goal. It might take a long time, but there would have to be some steps in the process; one cannot suddenly and all at once bring about a big change. On the other hand if there is no possibility of a change being brought about by mutual agreement, then there are likely to be upheavals, and it is difficult to say what the result of an upheaval will be. It depends on the size of the upheaval; it depends on the great economic forces that cause the upheaval, and anything might happen, because, as I conceive it, the fundamental problem of India really is economic in its various aspects. The chief problem is the land problem, with its enormous amount of unemployment and over-pressure on land, and connected with that is the industrial problem, because probably if one tries to solve the land problem one will have to consider the question of industry. There are also many other problems, such as unemployment in the middle classes, and they will really have to be tackled all together so that they may fit into each other, and not [be permitted to exist] individually and separately.

All these problems have to be tackled for many reasons, but the fundamental reason is that the economic situation is growing worse and the condition of the vast masses is going further and further down. They cannot be tackled by merely changing the political structure at the top.

The political structure might be such as to help us in tackling the problems, and the real test of the political structure is this: Does it help us and will it make [it] easier for us to tackle these problems and solve them?

With regard to an intermediate period, therefore, all one can say is that there is bound to be some intermediate period. We are passing through an intermediate period now, but whether the development is going to be by arrangement or agreement or by sudden jumps or big jumps, the future alone can show.

In India the Congress and some groups outside the Congress have suggested that the proper and democratic way to deal with the political aspect of the problem is by means of a Constituent Assembly, that is to say, fundamentally the people of India should [create] the Constitution of India; they do not admit that the people of India should remain merely passive agents of a foreign authority in regard to the drawing up of such a Constitution. The only way in which the desires of the people of India can take shape is through [a possible] Constituent Assembly. To-day that is not a feasible proposition, simply because it cannot be put into effect unless the British Government itself decides to put an end to its domination in India and leave the Indian people to develop their own Constitution, or, whether the British Government so decides or not, the pressure of events brings it about, because a real Constituent Assembly involves ultimately or, in fact, in the near future after it is formed, the end of British domination in India. A Constituent Assembly does not mean merely a group of so-called leaders coming together and drawing up a Constitution. The whole idea behind the Constituent Assembly is this: that it should be elected by means of an adult franchise, men and women together, so that there should be really mass representation, in order to give effect to the economic urges of the masses. The present difficulty is that a number of upper middle-class people sit down and, instead of talking in terms of economics, they discuss the question of offices in the new Constitution and who will be appointed to them; there is a desire to share in the spoils of office, in patronage, and so forth, which the new Constitution might bring, and that partly gives rise to the communal problem. If the mass elements take part in the election of the Constituent Assembly, obviously they will not be interested in getting jobs in the new Constitution; they are interested in their own economic troubles and attention will immediately be given to social and economic issues, whilst some of the other problems, which appear to loom large but are fundamentally not important, will recede into the background, like the communal problem.

The second part of the question is: Does the India Act in any way meet the need for an intermediate period of transition? I have just said the test of a Constitution is this: Whether it helps us to solve the economic problems which face us and which are the real problems. The India Act, as you perhaps know, has been criticized from almost every possible angle by almost every possible group in India, moderate or advanced. I doubt if it has any friends at all in India. If there are a few persons who are prepared to tolerate it, either they belong to the big vested interests in India or they are people who by sheer habit tolerate everything that the British Government does. Apart from these people, almost every political group in India has taken the strongest exception to the India Act. They all object to it and have criticized it in very great detail, and the general feeling is that, far from helping us, it really takes us back and it binds our hands and feet so tightly that we cannot get a move on. All the vested interests in Britain and in India have found such a permanent place in this Act that any substantial, social or economic change or political change becomes almost impossible, short of revolution. On the one hand, under the India Act we cannot even endeavour to make substantial economic changes; on the other hand, we cannot change the India Act itself. You must not think that in the India Act we are getting some democratic instrument which can be developed into something better. That is not so. You must not apply the analogy of the various steps taken in the Dominions—in Canada and in Australia—in the early stages of the development of self-government in those countries. The problems there were simple; there were simple communities to be dealt with, and, whatever the steps taken . . . there was room for inevitable development, and that development did take place. That does not apply to India at all. To-day India has not to face a simple problem; it has to face a very complicated economic problem and the decision to be taken on that problem cannot be postponed. Secondly, the India Act is such that it cannot be developed. Of course, there can be development from time to time if the British Government itself changes the India Act, but, as it is even if 99 or 100 per cent. of the people of India want to change it they cannot do so. It has no seeds of change in it; it is a permanent fixing of chains of the vested interest on the Indian people. The only choice that is offered to the Indian people is to submit to it or, if they want to change it, to revolt against it in some form or other. Therefore the India Act does not in any way meet the need for an intermediate period of transition. Under the Act a wider electorate is created, and that is a desirable thing, but it is the only desirable thing in the Act.

The third question is — "What is the [relationship] of the Indian problem ... to ... world problems? Does the League of Nations help in this connection?" I think that nearly all the major problems that we have to face in the world to-day—in Europe or India or China or America—are intimately connected together, and it is really difficult to understand any one of them or ultimately to solve any one of them without thinking of the other problems. The different parts of the world to-day are becoming extraordinarily inter-related with each other, and events which happen in one part of the world immediately react and interact upon the other parts of the world. If there is a big thing such as an international war, obviously the whole world is upset. If there is an economic crisis—we have had a very big one in the last few years—that affects the whole world. These big waves and movements affect the whole world, [and] obviously the Indian problem is intimately connected with other problems. Anything big that happens in India obviously affects the whole British group of nations—British imperialism. Anything that affects British imperialism makes a great difference in the world, because British imperialism to-day is a very important factor in world politics. So far as India is concerned, it is a well-known fact that India has had the greatest influence on British foreign policy in the last hundred years or so. During the Napoleonic period India loomed large; although perhaps when you read about the Napoleonic campaigns, you find that India is seldom mentioned, it was in the background all the time. Whether it was the Crimean War or the occupation of Egypt, always there was the question of India in the background and the routes to India. The routes to India have often been before British statesmen. Perhaps some of you may remember that even after the Great War there was [the] idea, fostered by Mr Winston Churchill and some of the leading figures in British public life, of having an enormous Middle Eastern Empire from the borders of India to Constantinople, but it did not take shape. It sounds rather curious now, but at that time, after the war, all that area was in British occupation; Persia was in British occupation, and so were Mesopotamia, Palestine, parts of Arabia, and Constantinople. Therefore the idea was not such a fanciful one as it seems to be now, but various things happened to prevent its taking shape; there was the Soviet Government and there were events in Turkey and Persia and so forth, and the whole thing was upset by various developments. Even so, the object of the British Government was to control the land route to India, because the land route was becoming important, owing to the development of aeroplanes and motor traffic. The question of Mosul nearly brought about conflict between Turkey and England, chiefly because Mosul dominates the land route to India.

Therefore from many points of view, the question of India affects world problems very greatly. Anything that happens to India inevitably affects other countries.

With regard to the League of Nations in this connection, the League of Nations might perhaps help India if the Indian viewpoint was put before it properly and pressed before it, but so far the position has been that India has really nothing to do with the League of Nations except that it is represented on the league. The so-called Indian representatives on the League of Nations are nominated by the Government of India in consultation with the British Government so that they really represent on the League the viewpoint of the British Government; they do not represent in the slightest Indian public opinion. Therefore you might say that India is not represented at all on the League of Nations, but that the British Government gets an extra representative. If India could be properly represented, I suppose the League of Nations would do some good, although fundamentally the League of Nations, of course, is an organization for the maintenance of the *status quo* in the world, and obviously the Indian people desire to change their *status quo*. Therefore, if they laid any fundamental proposition before the League of Nations, it would probably be barred under some section of the Covenant or of the rules under which the League functions, on the ground that it would interfere with the domestic policy of the British Empire.

With regard to the fourth question: "How far is the communal problem due to economic causes?" This question perhaps is not properly framed (I am partly responsible for that), in the sense that the communal question is not fundamentally due to economic causes. It has an economic back-ground which often influences it, but it is due much more to political causes. It is not due to religious causes; I should like you to remember that. Religious hostility or antagonism has very little to do with [the] communal question. It has something to do with the communal question in that there is a slight background of religious hostility which has in the past sometimes given rise to conflict and sometimes to broken heads, in the case of processions and so forth, but the present communal question is not a religious one, although sometimes it exploits religious sentiment and there is trouble. It is [a] political question of the upper middle classes which has arisen partly because of the attempts of the British Government to weaken the national movement or to create rifts in it, and partly because of the prospect of political power coming into India and the upper classes desiring to share in the spoils of office. It is to this extent economic, that the Mohammadans, the Muslims, are on the whole the poorer community as compared with the Hindus. Sometimes you find that the creditors are the Hindus and the debtors the Mohammadans; sometimes the landlords are Hindus and the tenants are Mohammadans. Of course the Hindus are tenants also, and they form the majority of the population. It sometimes happens that a conflict is really between a money-lender and his debtors or between a landlord and tenants, but it is reported in the Press and it assumes importance as a communal conflict between Hindus and Mohammadans. Fundamentally this communal problem is a problem of the conflict between the members of the upper middle-class Hindus and Muslims for jobs and power under the new Constitution. It does not affect the masses at all. Not a single communal demand has the least reference to any economic issue in India or has the least reference to the masses. If you examine the communal demands you will see they refer only to seats in the Legislature or to various kinds of jobs which might be available in the future.[1]

[Further questions and answers—London, February 4, 1936.]

Q : "We sometimes meet with the objection or the criticism that if the British withdrew from India it would only open the way for Japan. It used to be Russia, but now it is Japan that is mentioned in that connection. Might we hear Mr Nehru's opinion on that?"

N: "It seems to me that the people who say [that] do not know very much about the present position or the probable future position of Japan with regard to India. The question can be considered in many ways but I would put it to you briefly thus: How do you expect Japan to come to India, by sea or by land? Do you expect Japan to come to India after having subjugated the whole of China or before it has done so?

"You must realize that it takes a little longer to go from India to Japan than it takes to go from India to England by sea. By the land route, by air, it takes a very little time to go from England to India, but it takes a very long time to go to Japan. One cannot too easily cross over the Himalayan mountains and the various deserts and other tracts of China. Therefore you must realize that India is not very easily accessible to Japan if Japan goes through China, so Japan has to come by a fairly intricate route through the Singapore Straits, and any hostile fleet could make it difficult for the Japanese to approach India. Even so, of course, Japan might come, but the real point is this, that Japan can never think in terms of the conquest of India so long as it has not completely subjugated China and made it part of its Empire. The conquest of China is a very difficult

[1] B.A.I., pp. 297–302.

matter. At the moment Japan has overrun North China and it may perhaps extend further south, but I do not think that anyone acquainted with the history of China or the present position of China or the international position, imagines that Japan is likely to succeed in consolidating her Empire in the whole of China. China is a tremendous problem for Japan, and even if it is conquered, it will continue to be a problem and something which will really absorb the energies of Japan and probably bring about its downfall. Look at Japan as it stands to-day as a world power. It seems very strong. Nobody interferes with Japan's territorial instincts and activities. It does what it likes in North China and Manchuria. Yet fundamentally the position of Japan in the world is [a] very unhappy position. It is isolated from the rest of the world; it has no friends in the world. On the one side there is a tremendous power, America, and there is not much love lost between Japan and the United States of America. On the other side [there is] China, which, although weak in one sense is very strong in many ways. . . . But even apart from . . . the weakness of China today [there is] the fact that some . . . Chinese leaders are false to China, they are betraying China. It is not so much the weakness of China as the weakness of her leaders, Chiang Kai-shek, and others. . . . This may lead to the overthrow of Chiang Kai-shek, and some kind of a combined and powerful resistance later on. Therefore, in any event, Japan would have a hostile China to deal with, whether it was [itself] subjugated or not. With America on one side . . . China on the other, and the Soviet Republic in the north, which is always likely to be hostile, [the notion] that Japan should embark on an adventure in India [which is] three weeks' journey away, is to me inconceivable. Then, of course, India presumably would not sit idle. It may not be a strong country, but obviously it would do its utmost to defend itself against any aggression."

Q : "We do not want to talk about only this aspect of the question. . . . We need not go [as] far as China and Japan and the Far East to consider . . . [the North-West Frontier question and the] very immediate and close danger of Russian aggression. There we come up against that imperialistic policy which has dominated the whole . . . history of the North-West Frontier, and that imperialism which Mr Nehru says must be got rid of before [India] can come to any terms at all with Great Britain. What will be the position on the [North-West] Frontier if that imperialism is . . . discarded? What will be the position as regards the security of India if that imperialism, which means constant jealousy and suspicion between the two great powers—Soviet Russia and Great Britain—is finally abolished? What will be the position with regard to the defence policy of

India, and what will then be the [nature of] the organization and ...
cost of the Indian army?

N: "The result of the allaying of ... suspicion would be peace and
contentment on the frontier" [with respect to the defense of India against
Soviet aggression.]

Q: "And Afghanistan. . . . That is also an element."

N: "Yes, an element. Afghanistan is an unadvanced, industrially backward country, and as an effective military force it is strong only within its
own [territory]. It is a difficult country to invade, because it is a moun-
tainous country, and the people are good fighters. But, as an invading
country, it has no strength at all. So we can leave Afghanistan out of
consideration.

"With regard to Soviet Russia, the first proposition is that there is no
power in the world today which is more peaceful, and less inclined to
aggression than Soviet Russia. I think that is admitted by everybody; it is
publicly admitted by the British Foreign Office; in fact the Foreign
Secretary, Mr Eden, said so the other day."

Q: "The Government of India does not say that, it says the. . .
opposite."

N: "For various reasons, you can [assume] that Soviet Russia, from an
economic point of view, does not require India in the least, as Japan might.
. . . India is a source of raw materials for England. Raw materials exist in
sufficient quantities in Soviet territories. . . . Fundamentally Soviet
Russia does not require India; it has not that economic urge. At the
present moment it is absolutely full of its own economic problems of
development, and it wants to take no risk at all of war or adventure.
Obviously an invasion of India is a very big risk, not so much because of
the strength of India, but because any such thing [today] involves
international complications, whether the invader is Japan or Russia. If
Japan comes to India, it is not a question merely of defeating the people
of India, but there is the risk of having to fight on various fronts. Other
powers step in and international complications are introduced. So that
Russian policy to-day (nobody can say what will happen thirty years hence)
is bound to be an [extraordinarily] peaceful policy; there is no doubt about
that. If it were not, Russia would immediately be afraid of trouble from
Japan in the East, and from Germany in the West. We know that many
European countries fear Russia to-day. The biggest factor at work is a
great fear complex of being attacked, and so the countries go on increasing
their military machines. So that there is no question of expecting, in the
ordinary course, an invasion from Russia. . . . I think we ought to be

the most friendly of neighbours, instead of being in conflict with each other. But, apart from that, obviously India, whatever its system of government is, whether socialist or not, will have to take steps to guard her frontiers."

Q : "Against whom?"

N: "It does not matter. The steps taken may not be very extensive, but [we] will have to take some steps. If the world continues to be divided into various capitalist states, armies will have to be kept. It is relatively easy, I think, to protect India on the North-West Frontier. You have probably read histories of various invasions of India from the north-west, but those histories exaggerate a little. There have been invasions, but if you spread them out over a period of two or three thousand years, they have not been so frequent as some people seem to think. Those invasions took place not because of the strength of the attacking force but because, at the time, there was internal trouble in India, and the attacking force simply walked in. An attacking force can always be stopped on the North-West Frontier by an efficient army, without any great numbers being employed. An efficient defence force must be built up to defend India from invasion; one has to face the risk of these things. One of the countries suffering most from a terrible fear of invasion is also at the same time one of the most powerful countries in the military sense, that is, France, [which] is terribly afraid of a Nazi invasion, and yet it has one of the biggest military machines in the world."

Q : "The question has not actually arisen in the course of Mr Nehru's addresses, but it might be of interest to know what is [his] view with regard to the contributions that may be expected from Indian women in the regeneration of India."

N: "Those contributions have been considerable. Indian women in the last fifteen or sixteen years have played a tremendous part in our national movement. You may remember that in 1930 Mr Gandhi started the Civil Disobedience Movement in connection with the Salt Tax, and I think the most important and significant feature of that movement was the tremendous part that the women of India took in it. It was astonishing. Most of us were astounded [at] what we saw. It was not as if we had to push [the women] out; they simply came out and took charge of the situation when most of their menfolk were in prison, and they functioned in an extraordinarily efficient way. The surprising thing was that, although many of them had had no experience of public activity, yet they became good organizers, and they ran the whole movement practically without any men for a long time. They ran it not only very well, but in a much more uncompromising way than the men might have done; they did become much more uncompromising about it in every way. That was such [an] eye-opener that I do not think [that] after that any person in India [will dare to] say [that Indian women] are going to play a subordinate part in the public life of India in the future. Of course, as you know, they have suffered in the past, and they still suffer from a large number of social and semi-religious disabilities. They are trying to remove [these disabilities], and to some extent they have to fight the inevitable reactions of men in that process. Certain orthodox elements in the community are trying to prevent [Indian women] from removing these disabilities, but I think they are sufficiently alive to their task, and I do not think anyone can really stop them from carrying it out. So far as the national movement is concerned, the mere fact that such large numbers of women have taken such a large part in it makes it absolutely impossible for any nationalist to conceive of keeping them down in any political or social sense. The Fundamental Rights Resolution which the Congress passed some years ago, laid down as a fundamental right in the Constitution, the removal of all disabilities, and the absolute equality of women with men, in the eyes of the Constitution."

Q : "Regarding the communal problem, you suggested, I think, that the religious element was a small part of it, and that it was not primarily economic, but ... resolved itself into political jealousy and political ambitions. How do you see [the problem resolving itself] in the light of the national movement? Do you feel that the central national aim would be so big that it would bring all the parties together?"

N: "No, first of all I said that the communal movement was not religious, but that does not mean, of course, that there is not a religious background [to it] in India, and sometimes that is exploited. It is political mainly. It is also economic in the sense that the political problem largely arises because of the problem of unemployment in the middle classes, and it is the unemployment among the middle classes that helps the communal movement to gain importance. It is there that the jobs come in. To some extent the growth of nationalism, and the nationalist spirit, suppressed the communal idea, but fundamentally it will go when economic issues and social issues come to the forefront, and divert the attention of the masses, and even of the lower middle classes, because these issues really affect them, and inevitably then the communal leaders would have to sink into the background. That happened in 1921, at the time of the first Non-co-operation Movement, when no communal leaders in India dared to come out into the open. There was no meeting held, and there was no reference to them in the papers. They disappeared absolutely because there was such a big movement [relating to] other issues. . . . [Communal leaders] are always being pushed to the front by the British Government in India. Therefore the right way to deal with the communal question is to allow economic questions affecting the masses to be discussed. One of the chief objections to the India Act is that, because it divides India into seven or eight—I am not sure how many—separate religious compartments, it makes it difficult for economic and social questions to be brought up. Of course they will come up, because there is the economic urge behind them, but still it [is] . . . difficult."

Q: "Do [you not] think caste comes into the communal question at all? [Brahmin] against [non-Brahmin]? That is a matter we know so well, in Madras."

N: "I do not think the communal question is affected much by caste. In South India, of course, the question of caste comes in, and it has given rise to great bitterness. I was thinking more of Hindu *versus* Muslim. . . . In the South, in recent years . . . it used to be . . . a question of [non-Brahmin] versus the vested [interests. As for] the depressed classes, they really are the proletariat in the economic sense; the others are the better-off people. All these matters can be converted into economic terms, and then one can understand the position better. I do not think the [Brahmin] and the [non-Brahmin] question, as such, is very important now. There [are] a very large number of [non-Brahmins] in . . . Congress. In the Congress the question does not arise. It has some importance in local areas in the South, because of various local factors, but I do not think the question of [Brahmin] and [non-Brahmin] comes into the communal question at all. . . ."

Q: "Could Mr Nehru tell us what, in his opinion, is the way that India should develop in regard to economic arrangements and systems?"

N: "Whatever I say on this subject will be my own personal view, because I cannot say that India as a whole desires what I desire.

"Fundamentally we have to face the land problem chiefly, and the problem of unemployment, which is connected with it. I think that nothing short of large-scale collectivist or co-operative farming will deal effectively with the land question. [Our] wretched small holdings will then disappear. Production will greatly increase, and many other benefits will follow, but unemployment would not be affected thereby. In fact, by scientific farming, it is possible that unemployment might even increase a little, as far as direct employment on the land is concerned, though indirectly other avenues of employment would be opened up. In order to provide employment we must absorb people in industrial development, in cottage industries, in big machine industries, and in the enormous development of the social services, such as education, hygiene and sanitation. There are practically no social services in India to-day. The development of industry and the land would have to be planned as a whole; it cannot be dealt with in sections. If one tries to tackle one part, one finds something left over which one cannot provide for. The whole basis should be, in my opinion, not the profit motive, but producing for consumption, because if we produce for profit, the result is that we simply glut the market; we cannot sell the goods, because people have no money with which to buy them, and so we get over-production while, at the same time, many people have nothing at all. We should organise on the Socialist basis, and have large-scale agriculture, co-operative or collectivist; big machine industries and cottage industries. The cottage industries must not be such as would be likely to conflict with big industries, because then they would collapse, but I think there will be plenty of room for the growth of cottage industries for a long time to come, simultaneously with the growth of big industries. If big industries are not developed on a capitalist basis, they will deal with the essentials which are required, and there will be no needless waste of energy. If all these things are taken together, [I] imagine we might go a little way towards the solution of the various problems that confront us. I do not see any movement in that direction under present conditions."

Q: "You mean something similar to the Soviet system of the organization of industry and agriculture?"

N: "I personally should like to have something similar to that, but I was really envisaging something much less for the moment. I do not want India to be drilled and forced into [a] certain position, because the costs of such drilling are too great; it is not worth while; it is not desirable from many points of view. I want to go in the direction I have indicated. I may not be able to go far, but that [is] the direction in which I want to go. I have expressed my personal view. . . . I do not speak for India."[1]

[1] Ibid., pp. 308-14.

	Publication of Autobiography—On Not
7	Meeting Mussolini—Statement Calling
	for Observance of Abyssinia Day

Publication of Autobiography on Return to India, 1936

[Nehru returned to India from Europe in April, 1936. He had been elected President of the 1936 Lucknow Congress while he was still abroad. During the same month the first edition of his autobiography, virtually all of which had been written in jail during 1934–1935, was published. The volume was entitled *An Autobiography* when first issued in England in 1936. Various additions were written for the American edition, published in 1941, under the title *Toward Freedom*.]

I wrote my autobiography entirely in prison, cut off from outside activity. I suffered from various humors in prison, as every prisoner does; but gradually I developed a mood of introspection and some peace of mind.[1]

The primary object in writing these pages was to occupy myself with a definite task, so necessary in the long solitudes of jail life, as well as to review past events in India, with which I had been connected, to enable myself to think clearly about them. I began the task in a mood of self-questioning, and, to a large extent, this persisted throughout. I was not writing deliberately for an audience, but, if I thought of an audience, it was one of my own countrymen and countrywomen. For foreign readers I would probably have written differently, or with a different emphasis, stressing certain aspects which have been slurred over in the narrative and passing over lightly certain other aspects which I have treated at some length. . . .

The reader will, I hope, remember that the book was written during a particularly distressful period of my existence. It bears obvious traces of this. If the writing had been done under more normal conditions, it would have been different and perhaps occasionally more restrained. Yet I have decided to leave it as it is, for it may have some interest for others in so far as it represents what I felt at the time of writing.[2]

[1] T.F., p. 356.
[2] Ibid., p. xi.

What is my Autobiography? It is not meant to be a record of all the important events of the past few years. It is a record of my own thoughts and moods and how they were affected by external happenings. I endeavoured to make this a truthful record of my own mental development. How far I succeeded in doing so, it is not for me to say. But the important thing is not what happened, but how it struck me and what impression it produced on me. That is the test of the truth or otherwise of the book.[1]

[On his way home to India, after his wife's death, Nehru sent a cable to his English publisher, requesting that his autobiography be dedicated "To Kamala who is no more."[2]]

On Not Meeting Mussolini

[A significant incident occurred while Nehru was on his way back to India from Europe in 1936.]

A friend in Rome had written to me [while I was in Europe] to say that Signor Mussolini would like to meet me. There was no question of my going to Rome then and I said so. Later, when I was thinking of returning to India by air, that message was repeated and there was a touch of eagerness and insistence about it. I wanted to avoid this interview, and yet I had no desire to be discourteous. Normally I might have got over my distaste for meeting [Mussolini], for I was curious also to know what kind of man the Duce was. But the Abyssinian campaign was being carried on then, and my meeting him would inevitably lead to all manner of inferences and was bound to be used for fascist propaganda. No denial from me would go far. I knew of several recent instances when Indian students and others visiting Italy had been utilized, against their wishes and sometimes even without their knowledge, for fascist propaganda. And then there had been the bogus interview with Mr Gandhi which the *Giornale d'Italia* had published in 1931.

I conveyed my regrets therefore to my friend, and later wrote again and telephoned to him to avoid any possibility of misunderstanding. . . . After [my wife's] death I sent another message pointing out that, even apart from other reasons, I was in no mood then for an interview with anyone.

All this insistence on my part became necessary as I was passing through

[1] E.M.I., p. 16.
[2] D.I., p. 36.

14+N.

Rome by the K.L.M. and would have to spend an evening and night there. I could not avoid this passing visit and brief stay.

After a few days at Montreux I proceeded to Geneva and Marseilles where I boarded the K.L.M. air liner for the East. On arrival in Rome in the late afternoon, I was met by a high official who handed me a letter from the *chef de cabinet* of Signor Mussolini. The Duce, it stated, would be glad to meet me and he had fixed six o'clock that evening for the interview. I was surprised and reminded him of my previous messages. But he insisted that it had now all been fixed up and the arrangement could not be upset. Indeed if the interview did not take place there was every likelihood of his being dismissed from his office. I was assured that nothing would appear in the press, and that I need only see the Duce for a few minutes. All that he wanted to do was to shake hands with me and to convey personally his condolences at my wife's death. So we argued for a full hour with all courtesy on both sides but with an increasing strain; it was a most exhausting hour for me and probably more so for the other party. The time fixed for the interview was at last upon us and I had my way. A telephone message was sent to the Duce's palace that I could not come.

That evening I sent a letter to Signor Mussolini expressing my regret that I could not take advantage of his kind invitation to me to see him and thanking him for his message of sympathy.[1]

Statement Calling for Observance of "Abyssinia Day"— *May 5, 1936*

Addis Ababa lies at the foot of the conqueror. Ethiopia in spite of her gallant defence of her independence, lies helpless and prostrate before the brutal might of fascist imperialism. Poison gas and liquid fire and all the modern engines of destruction have triumphed and in their triumph have not only exposed afresh the true nature of imperialism, but have also shown us the hypocrisy and duplicity of the Great Powers and the utter futility of that body which is known as the League of Nations.

For the moment imperialism triumphs again in the long world struggle for freedom, but that struggle will go on in Ethiopia as elsewhere till freedom comes and puts an end to imperialism everywhere. We, in India, can do nothing to help our brethren in distress in Ethiopia for we also are the victims of imperialism. But we can at least send them our

[1] Ibid., pp. 35–36.

deep sympathy in this hour of their trial. We stand with them today in their sorrow as we hope to stand together when better days come.

I appeal to the Indian people therefore to give countrywide expression to our sympathy and solidarity with the Ethiopian people and our resolve not to submit to the fascist imperialist menace.[1]

8 | Responsibility and Frustration, 1936—Lucknow Congress—From Presidential Address and Congress Resolutions—Conflict and Controversies (Concerning Political Attitudes) after Lucknow Congress—Further Thoughts about Socialism and Democracy—Further Repercussions after Lucknow Congress—From Letters Relating to Disagreements

Responsibility and Frustration, 1936

My wife's death in Switzerland ended a chapter of my existence and took away much from my life that had been part of my being. It was difficult for me to realize that she was no more, and I could not adjust myself easily. I threw myself into my work, seeking some satisfaction in it, and rushed about from end to end of India. Even more than in my earlier days, my life became an alternation of huge crowds and intensive activity and loneliness. My mother's death later broke a final link with the past. My daughter was away studying at Oxford. . . .

But there was no peace in my work or my mind, and the responsibility that I had to shoulder often oppressed me very greatly. I could not align myself with various parties and groups; I did not even fit in with my

[1] I.A.A., pp. 59-60.

closest colleagues. I could not function as I wanted to, and at the same time I prevented others from functioning as they wanted to. A sense of suppression and frustration grew, and I became a solitary figure in public life, though vast crowds came to hear me and enthusiasm surrounded me.

I was affected more than others by the development of events in Europe and the Far East. Munich was a shock hard to bear, and the tragedy of Spain became a personal sorrow to me. As these years of horror succeeded one another, the sense of impending catastrophe overwhelmed me, and my faith in a bright future for the world became dim.[1]

Lucknow Congress Session

Within a few days of my return [to India] I had to preside over the annual session of the [Lucknow] National Congress. For some years, which I had spent mainly in prison, I had been out of touch with [Congress] developments. I found many changes, new alignments, a hardening on party lines within ... Congress. There was an atmosphere of suspicion ... bitterness and conflict. I treated this lightly, having confidence in my own capacity to deal with the situation. For a short while I seemed to carry the Congress in the direction I wanted it to go. But I realized soon that the conflict was deep-rooted, and it was not so easy to charm away the suspicion of each other and the bitterness that had grown in our ranks. I thought seriously of resigning from the presidency, but, realizing that this would only make matters worse, I refrained.[2]

[In March, 1936, Rabindranath Tagore stated in conjunction with Nehru's having been elected Congress President: "Jawaharlal has his undoubted right to the throne of Young India. His is a majestic character. Unflinching is his patient determination and indomitable his courage, but what raises him far above his fellows is his unwavering adherence to moral integrity and intellectual honesty. He has kept unusually high the standard of purity in the midst of political turmoils, where deceptions of all kinds, including that of one's self, run rampant. He has never fought shy of truth when it was dangerous, nor made alliance with falsehood when it would be convenient. His brilliant intellect has ever turned away in outspoken disgust from the dishonourable path of policies where success is as easy as it is mean. This lofty ideal of truth is Jawaharlal's greatest contribution in his fight for freedom."[3]

Other reactions—within Congress—were far less clear-cut. There was,

[1] T.F., p. 356.
[2] Ibid., pp. 357–58.
[3] B.O.L., p. 179.

to begin with, "a sharp ideological cleavage between the conservatives, led by Patel and Prasad, and the recently formed Congress Socialists ... who looked to Nehru for leadership. It was the old pro-changer-no-changer controversy [see Part One] in a different guise."[1]

Dr Ansari, for example, an outstanding Congress leader, had written to Nehru, while the latter was still in Europe: "I have felt all along that all those who are responsible for your election this year are very thoughtless and unkind to you. ... I do not think that in the present condition of things even your dynamic personality would be able to do much during your year of Presidentship."

As Brecher has noted, more ominous portents were contained in a letter to Nehru, written by "Dr Rajendra Prasad, later President of India, on 19 December 1935: 'I know that there is a certain difference between your outlook and that of men like Vallabhbhai [Patel] ... and myself and it is even of a fundamental character. ... I believe that *unless a radical change comes to be made in the programme and methods of our work it will be still possible for all of us to continue to work together*. ... The difficulties [facing the party] are inherent in the situation and it seems to us it is not possible to force the pace or cause any wholesale change.' Nehru was assured he would have a free hand to form a Working Committee of his own choice and 'to shape things as you would like'; 'none of us will create any difficulty'. But the implied warning could not have been lost on Nehru—do not attempt any fundamental revision of the *status quo*, or else. ... And he was aware of the fact that the Old Guard controlled the party organization. Prasad's letter is noteworthy because it foreshadowed the constant friction between Nehru and the right-wing Congress leaders during the next few years and, in particular, because it gave advance notice of the major crisis to follow in the summer of 1936.

"It was Gandhi who had pressed Nehru to accept 'the crown of thorns'. 'If you are elected [a foregone conclusion because of Gandhi's support], you will be elected for the policy and principles you stand for', the Mahatma assured him."

Nevertheless Nehru was "reminded that 'in the huge organisation the Congress has become, no one man can hope to run the show'. And Gandhi's ultimate control of the party was reaffirmed: 'As to the present policy of the Congress, whilst I can in no way be responsible for the detailed working of it, it is in the main of my shaping.' About the likely response of the Old Guard, he was far from encouraging: 'So far as I know they will not resist you, even though they may not be able to follow you.'

"Why then was Gandhi anxious to have Nehru as formal head of the Congress at that stage? There were various reasons, both personal and political. For one thing, the Mahatma admired him much more than any other party leader. ... He was also concerned about his protégé's drift to the Left. As in 1929, when Nehru showed signs of discontent, Gandhi hoped that responsibility would moderate his views.

"The basic motive, however, arose from the rift between conservatives

[1] M.B., p. 212.

and radicals which threatened to wreck the party. Gandhi knew that Nehru was the one person who could bridge the growing gap between Socialism and Gandhism. As the godfather of the Congress Socialist Party Nehru was entirely acceptable to the Left. As Gandhi's favourite son he was tolerated by the Old Guard, most of whom were colleagues of at least fifteen years' standing. Thus he was uniquely suited to the task of reconciliation.

"Nehru himself frankly admitted this special quality and seemed to relish the role of mediation—then as later. 'In a way I represented a link between various sets of ideas and so I helped somewhat in toning down the differences and emphasizing the essential unity of our struggle against imperialism.' Indeed, this was one of the main reasons why he succumbed to the temptation of party leadership. . . .

"[His] sense of urgency was strengthened by disquieting conditions at home. Communal tension showed no signs of abating. The will to direct action had gone out of the Congress. But most important from Nehru's point of view was the challenge posed by the latest instalment of constitutional reform, embodied in the 1935 Government of India Act. In essence [the Government of India Act] provided virtually complete responsible government in the provinces of British India and the framework for a loose All-India Federation of the provinces and as many of the six hundred-odd princely States as wished to join.

"It had taken eight years to produce the Act, from the Simon Commission through the three Round Table Conferences, the White Paper, the Report of the Joint Select Committee of the British Parliament, to the final document itself. Much care had been taken to ensure the ultimate authority of Great Britain in the affairs of India, through an array of special powers vested in the Viceroy and, to a lesser extent, in the Governors of the provinces. Over ninety articles conferred 'discretionary powers' on the Viceroy. There were, as well, 'reserve powers' which gave him exclusive control over defence, external affairs, ecclesiastical affairs and certain frontier areas. Finally came the 'safeguards' or 'special responsibilities' which were all-embracing, for example 'the prevention of any grave menace to the peace or tranquillity of India or any part thereof', the prevention of discrimination against British imports, corporations or individuals, protection of the rights of Princes, etc. Moreover, representation in the federal legislature was to be heavily weighted in favour of the Princes—forty per cent. in the Council of States and thirty-three and a third per cent. in the Federal Assembly, whereas the population of the princely States was only twenty-four per cent. of the total population of India at the time. The States' representatives were to be *appointed* by the Princes. . . . In its original form the *federal* part of the Act was hedged by so many 'safeguards' as to deny complete self-government to *India as a whole*. . . .

"By contrast, the *provincial* part of the Act was a far-reaching concession to self-government. Apart from some general safe-guards, which were not intended to be used except in rare circumstances, daily administration was to be entrusted to a Cabinet selected from the legislature, all of whose members were to be elected by a much larger proportion of the population than at any time previously.

"It was this temptation of power, however limited it might be, which attracted many Congress moderates. For Nehru it was precisely this possibility of 'co-operation' with the *Raj* which had to be severely condemned as a grave danger to the nationalist movement. He had no strong objections in principle to contesting the elections but he was vehemently opposed to the idea of taking office under what he termed the 'slave' constitution. If he [had] refused Gandhi's offer of the presidency, the Congress would certainly [have adopted] this 'reformist' line. (It ultimately did so anyway.) And if the Congress were determined to wage an electoral campaign, unity was an absolute precondition to success. Nehru's actions in earlier party crises, notably in 1922–3 and 1928–9, revealed his emphasis on unity. Now, in the shadow of international tension and Congress strife, this concern asserted itself once more.

"Beyond these specific factors was his desire to push the Congress to the Left. Conditions, he felt, were ripe for an injection of socialism into the party programme. In this he proved to be prescient, for beneath the surface of Indian politics new social forces were fermenting. The peasants had been galvanized into action during the civil disobedience campaign of the early 'thirties and were becoming aware of their power for the first time. The economic hardships imposed by the Great Depression had made them susceptible to socialist propaganda, spread in many parts of the country by radical young nationalists and individual Communists. . . . [At the time *Kisan sabhas*, or peasant leagues, were being organized.] The cry of land reform had . . . become too loud to be ignored. Similarly, urban workers began to demand greater recognition from the nationalist movement. And even that oft-forgotten segment of Indian society, the women, had been aroused by the years of political struggle.

"Much of this ferment found expression in the Congress Socialist Party (C.S.P.), created in the spring of 1934 by a group of left-nationalists headed by Jaya Prakash Narayan. Nehru was in prison at the time, but his influence among them was great. His clear enunciation of socialist ideas . . . was a model for many of them. Politically, he was their main hope to 'capture' the Congress machine".[1]

"[Nehru's] role at this time was to give direction to the growing body of leftist opinion within the Congress, to channel the new social forces into the nationalist movement, and to act as the supreme spokesman of radical ideas in the late 'thirties. With this background and in this frame of mind Nehru took up the reins of office at Lucknow.

"From the outset a clash with the Old Guard seemed inevitable. Nehru realized that his election to the presidency did not mean the party's conversion to socialism. But he did assume that it reflected a growing desire for change among sections of the rank and file. Acting on this belief he sponsored a number of radical resolutions at a meeting of the Working

[1] M.B., pp. 213–17.

Committee on the eve of the Lucknow session. The right-wing leaders played their cards skilfully. They did not object at that stage, partly because, in theory at least, they were about to make way for a new Working Committee of the President's own choosing, and partly because it was more convenient to place the onus of rejection on the Congress organization as a whole. [Nehru's] proposals were approved by the High Command. But when they came before the All-India Congress Committee some of the controversial ones were either rejected or drastically modified. At the open session the changes were confirmed.

"On the peripheral issue of 'foreign policy', so dear to Nehru's heart, the Old Guard could afford to be generous. His request for a Foreign Department to act as a liaison with the outside world was granted. There were expressions of sympathy for Ethiopia and for Indians abroad. And the Congress reaffirmed its refusal to participate in an 'Imperialist War'. But on the key resolutions of substance the Right wing triumphed.

"Nehru's proposal to permit the collective affiliation of trade unions and peasant leagues with the Congress was rejected, almost certainly because it would have shifted the balance of power in favour of the Left wing. Instead, a Mass Contacts Committee was formed, leaving control over this crucial sphere of activity in the hands of the High Command. Similarly Nehru's attempt to associate the Congress more directly with the struggle for political reform in the princely States was turned down and Gandhi's policy of passive support was reiterated. The resolution on agrarian reform was as moderate as conditions permitted; there was no frontal attack on the land problem. On the vital issue of the moment, the party's attitude to the 1935 Government of India Act, Nehru also suffered a defeat. The Congress rejected the Act 'in its entirety' and renewed the demand for a Constituent Assembly. But at the same time it agreed to contest the elections and, most important, it shelved the question of 'office acceptance'. Critics on the Left endorsed Nehru's views and called for an unequivocal rejection of office in advance, but the lure of power and prestige was too great for the majority.

"Nehru was bitterly disappointed by this turn of events. Confronted with formidable opposition to his views, despite the assurance of a 'free hand' by Prasad, he decided to resign, the first of three such 'decisions' in the next few months. 'After much mental conflict' he changed his mind because 'our whole organization might have been shaken up by it'. The fixation on party unity had come to the fore again." [1]]

From Presidential Address at Lucknow Congress Session— April, 1936

[Nehru's Lucknow Address was unique and daring, when viewed in relationship to prevailing Congress attitudes of the period.]

[1] Ibid., pp. 219-20.

After many years I face you again from this tribune—many weary years of strife and turmoil and common suffering. It is good for us to meet again; it is good for me to see this great host of old comrades and friends, linked together by strong bonds that cannot break, to sense the old brave spirit yet again, to feel your overwhelming kindness and good will to one whose greatest privilege it is to have been a comrade and a soldier with all of you in a mighty struggle for freedom. I am heartened and strengthened by you, though even in this great gathering I feel a little lonely. Many a dear comrade and friend has left us, worn out, long before the normal length of our earthly days, by the stress and strain of conflict. One by one they go, leaving a void in our hearts and a dull misery in our minds. They find peace from this turmoil perhaps, and it is well, for they deserved it. They rest after their labors.

But what of us who remain behind with a heavier burden to carry? There is no rest for us or for those who languish in prison or in detention camp. We cannot rest, for rest is betrayal of those who have gone and in going handed the torch of freedom to us to keep alight; it is betrayal of the cause we have espoused and the pledge we have taken; it is betrayal of the millions who never rest.

I am weary and I have come back like a tired child yearning for solace in the bosom of our common mother, India. That solace has come to me in overflowing measure; thousands of hands have been stretched out to me in love and sympathy; millions of silent voices have carried their message of affection to my heart. How can I thank you, men and women of India? How can I express in words feelings that are too deep for utterance?

For many years now I have been a distant looker-on on this Indian scene where once I was an actor, and many a thing has happened that has filled me with distress and anguish. I do not wish to survey this recent past of ours, which must be fresh in your memory, and which has left a sorry trail behind and many knots which are difficult to unravel. But we may not ignore it, for out of that past as well as the present, we have to build our future. We have followed high ideals, and we have taken pride in the fact that our means are worthy of those ideals. We have been witnesses of many a miracle in this old and battered land of ours, and yet our very success has been followed by failure and disillusion. Temporary failure has little significance when the aim is high and the struggle bound to be a long one; it is but the incentive to further effort. Often it teaches us more than a victory easily won and becomes a prelude to a greater success. But we profit by it only if we learn its lesson and search our minds for an explanation of that failure. Only by constant self-questioning, individual

14*

and national, can we keep on the right path. An easy and unthinking confidence is almost as bad as a weak submission to helpless dejection. Real failure comes only when we forget our ideals and objectives and principles and begin to wander away from the road which leads to their realization.

In this crisis of our history, therefore, let us look into ourselves and examine, without pity or prejudice, what we have done and what others have done to us, and seek to find out where we stand today. We dare not delude ourselves or evade real issues for fear of offending others, even though some of these others are comrades whom we respect. That is the way of self-deception which none who seek great and vital changes can follow except at their peril.

Sixteen years ago, under the inspiration of our leader, we took a new and long step converting this Congress from an ineffective body, feebly functioning among the upper classes, into a powerful democratic organization with its roots in the Indian soil and the vast masses who live on it. A handful of our old friends, representing an age and a class which had had its day, left us, fearful of this democratic upsurge, and preferring the shelter and protection of British imperialism to joining hands with the new vital forces which convulsed the country and struggled for freedom. Historically, they lapsed into the past. But we heard the rumbling of those forces and, for the moment, lined up with them and played a not unworthy part in current history. We sensed the new spirit of mass release, of psychological escape from the cramping effects of long subjection; we gloried in the breaking of the mental bonds that encompassed us. And, because our minds became free, we felt that political freedom could not be far, for it is often harder to break ... bonds of the spirit than physical bonds and chains of iron and steel. We represented the Spirit of the Age and were marching step by step with countless others in our country and outside. The exhilaration of being in tune with the masses and with the world forces came upon us and the feeling that we were the agents of historic destiny.

We were engrossed in our national struggle, and the turn it took bore the powerful impress of our great leader and of our national genius. We were hardly conscious then of what was happening outside. And yet our struggle was but part of a far wider struggle for freedom, and the forces that moved us were moving millions of people all over the world and driving them into action. ... There were great differences in the many aspects of this freedom struggle all over the world, and we were misled by them and did not see the common background. Yet, if we are to understand these varied phenomena and derive a lesson from them for our own national struggle, we must try to see and understand the whole picture. And, if we do so, we cannot fail to observe an organic connection between them which endures through changing situations. If once we grasp this organic bond, the world situation becomes easier to understand, and our own national problems take their proper places in the wider picture. . . .

During the troubled aftermath of the Great War came revolutionary changes in Europe and Asia, and the intensification of the struggle for social freedom in Europe, and a new aggressive nationalism in the countries of Asia. There were ups and downs, and sometimes it appeared as if the revolutionary urge had exhausted itself and things were settling down. But economic and political conditions were such that there could be no settling down, the existing structure could no longer cope with these new conditions, and all its efforts to do so were vain and fruitless. . . .

Capitalism, in its difficulties, took to fascism with all its brutal suppression of what Western civilization had apparently stood for; it became, even in some of its homelands, what its imperialist counterpart had long been in the subject colonial countries. Fascism and imperialism thus stood out as the two faces of the now decaying capitalism, and, though they varied in different countries according to national characteristics and economic and political conditions, they represented the same forces of reaction and supported each other, and at the same time came into conflict with each other, for such conflict was inherent in their very nature. Socialism in the west and the rising nationalisms of the Eastern and other dependent countries opposed this combination of fascism and imperialism. Nationalism in the East, it must be remembered, was essentially different from the new and terribly narrow nationalism of fascist countries; the former was the historical urge to freedom, the latter the last refuge of reaction.

Thus we see the world divided up into two vast groups today—the imperialist and fascist on one side, the socialist and nationalist on the other. There is some overlapping of the two, and the line between them is difficult to draw, for there is mutual conflict between the fascist and imperialist Powers, and the nationalism of subject countries has sometimes a tendency to fascism. But the main division holds, and, if we keep it in mind, it will be easier for us to understand world conditions and our own place in them.

Where do we stand then, we who labor for a free India? Inevitably we take our stand with the progressive forces of the world which are ranged against fascism and imperialism. We have to deal with one imperialism in particular, the oldest and the most far-reaching of the modern world; but, powerful as it is, it is but one aspect of world imperialism. And that is the final argument for Indian independence and for the severance of our connection with the British Empire. Between Indian nationalism, Indian freedom, and British imperialism there can be no common ground, and, if we remain within the imperialist fold, whatever our name or status, whatever outward semblance of political power we might have, we remain cribbed and confined and allied to and dominated by the reactionary forces and the great financial vested interests of the capitalist world. The exploitation of our masses will still continue, and all the vital social problems that face us will remain unsolved. Even real political freedom will be out of our reach, much more so radical social changes.

With the development of this great struggle all over the world we have seen the progressive deterioration of many of the capitalist-imperialist countries and an attempt at consolidation of the reactionary forces under fascism or Nazi-ism or so-called "national" governments. In India the same process has been evident to us during these past years, and the stronger the nationalist movement has grown, the more have efforts been made by our imperialist rulers to break our ranks and to gather together under their banner the reactionary elements in the country. The Round Table Conferences were such attempts, and, though they helped our rulers in some measure, they served a useful purpose by showing us clearly the division between the imperialist and the anti-imperialist forces in the country. Unhappily we did not fully profit by this lesson, and we still imagine that we can win over some of these imperialist groups to the side of Indian freedom and anti-imperialism, and in a vain attempt to do so we suppress our ideals, blush for our objectives, and tone down our activities.

Meanwhile the decay of British imperialism in India becomes ever more apparent. . . .It is astonishing to find to what depths of vulgarity our rulers have descended in their ardent desire to hold on to what they have got, and it is depressing, though perhaps inevitable, that some of our own countrymen, more interested in British imperialism than the British themselves, should excel at this deplorable game. So wanting in mental equilibrium are they, so obsessed by fear of the Congress and the national movement it represents, that their wishes become thoughts, their thoughts inferences, and their inferences facts, solemnly stated in official publications, and on which the majesty of the British Government rests in India, and people are kept in prison and detention camp without charge or trial. Being interested in psychology, I have watched this process of moral and intellectual decay and realized, even more than I did previously, how autocratic power corrupts and degrades and vulgarizes. I have read sometimes the reports of the recent Assembly meetings and noted the great difference in tone and content between them and the Assembly of ten years ago. . . .

[The] psychological aspect interests me even more than the more aggressive manifestations of British authority in India, for it throws light on much that has happened. It shows us how a clear and definite fascist mentality has developed among our rulers and how closely allied is imperialism to fascism. How this fascist mentality has functioned in the recent past and is functioning today, I shall not go into now. You know well the horror of these years and of the nightmare that we have all experienced. We shall not easily forget it, and, if there are some who have been cowed by it, there are others who have steeled themselves to a greater resolve to end this infamy in India.

But of one thing I must say a few words, for to me it is one of the most vital things that I value. That is the tremendous deprivation of civil liberties in India. A government that has to rely on the Criminal Law Amendment Act and similar laws, that suppress the press and literature, that ban hundreds of organizations, that keep people in prison without trial, and that do so many other things that are happening in India today, is a government that has ceased to have even a shadow of a justification for its existence. I can never adjust myself to these conditions; I find them intolerable. And yet I find many of my own countrymen complacent about them, some even supporting them, some, who have made the practice of sitting on a fence into a fine art, being neutral when such questions are discussed. And I have wondered what there was in common between them and me and those who think as I do. We in the Congress welcome all co-operation in the struggle for Indian freedom; our doors are ever open to all who stand for that freedom and are against imperialism. But they are not open to the allies of imperialism and the supporters of repression and those who stand by the British Government in its suppression of civil liberty. We belong to opposite camps. . . .

Terrorism is always a sign of political immaturity in a people, just as so-called constitutionalism, where there is no democratic constitution, is a sign of political senility. Our national movement has long outgrown that immature stage, and even the odd individuals who have in the past indulged in terrorist acts have apparently given up that tragic and futile philosophy. The Congress, by its stress on peaceful and effective action, has drawn the youth of the country into its fold, and all traces of terroristic activity would long have vanished but for the policy of the Government, which feeds the roots out of which a helpless violence grows. . . .

I have found a spirit of disunion spreading over the land, a strange malaise, and petty conflicts among old comrades growing ever bigger and interfering with all activity. We have forgotten for the moment the larger ideals we stood for, and we quarrel over petty issues. We have largely lost touch with the masses, and, deprived of the life-giving energy that flows from them, we dry up and weaken, and our organization shrinks and loses the power it had. First things must always come first, and, because we have forgotten this and argue and dispute over secondary matters, we are in danger of losing our bearings.

Every great struggle has its ups and downs and temporary failures. When such a setback occurs, there is a reaction when the fund of national energy is exhausted and has to be recharged. That happens again and again, and yet that is not an adequate explanation of all that has taken place. Our direct-action struggles in the past were based on the masses, and especially the peasantry, but the backbone and leadership were always supplied by the middle classes, and this, under the circumstances, was inevitable. The middle classes are a vague group or groups; at the top, a handful of them are closely allied to British imperialism; at the bottom are the dispossessed and other groups who have been progressively crushed by economic circumstances and out of whose ranks come the advanced political workers and revolutionaries; in between are the center groups, which tend often to side with the advanced elements, but which also have alliances with the upper groups and live in the hope of joining their superior ranks. A middle-class leadership is thus often a distracted leadership, looking in two directions at the same time. In times of crisis and struggle, when unity of aim and activity is essential, this two-faced leadership is bound to injure the cause and to hold back when a forward move is called for. Being too much tied up with property and the goods of this world, it is fearful of losing them, and it is easier to bring pressure on it and to exhaust its stamina. And yet, paradoxically, it is only from the middle-class intellectuals that revolutionary leadership comes, and we in India know that our bravest leaders and our stoutest comrades have come from the ranks of the middle classes. But by the very nature of our struggle, these front-rank leaders are taken away, and the others who take their places tire and are influenced more by the static element of their class. That has been very evident during our recent struggle, when our propertied classes were hit hard by the Government's drastic policy of seizure and confiscation of moneys and properties, and were thus induced to bring pressure for the suspension of the struggle.

How is this problem to be solved, then? Inevitably, we must have middle-class leadership, but this must look more and more toward the masses and draw strength and inspiration from them. The Congress must be not only *for* the masses, as it claims to be, but *of* the masses; only then will it really be for the masses. I have a feeling that our relative weakness today is due to a certain decay of our middle-class elements and our divorce from the people at large. Our policies and ideas are governed far more by this middle-class outlook than by a consideration of the needs of the great majority of the population. Even the problems that trouble us are essentially middle-class problems, like the communal problem, which have no significance for the masses.

This is partly due, I think, to a certain historical growth during the last fifteen years to which we have failed to adapt ourselves, to a growing urgency of economic problems affecting the masses, and to a rising mass consciousness which does not find sufficient outlet through the Congress. This was not so in 1920 and later when there was an organic link between Congress and the masses, and their needs and desires, vague as they were, found expression in the Congress. But, as those needs and desires have taken more definite shape, they have not been so welcome to other elements in the Congress, and that organic connection has gone. That, though regrettable, is really a sign of growth, and, instead of lamenting it, we must find a new link and a new connection on a fresh basis which allows for growth of mass consciousness within the Congress. The middle-class claim to represent the masses had some justification in 1920; it has much less today, though the lower middle classes have still a great deal in common with the masses.

Partly also our divorce from the people at large is due to a certain narrowness of our Congress constitution. The radical changes made in it fifteen years ago brought it in line with existing conditions then, and it drew in large numbers and became an effective instrument of national activity. Though the control and background were essentially middle-class and city, it reached the remotest village and brought with it political and economic consciousness to the masses, and there was widespread discussion of national issues in city and village alike. One could feel the new life pulsating through this vast land of ours, and, as we were in harmony with it, we drew strength from it. The intense repression by the Government during later years broke many of our physical and outward bonds with our countryside. But something more than that happened. The vague appeal of earlier days no longer sufficed, and on the new economic issues that were forcing themselves on us we hesitated to give a definite opinion. Worse even than the physical divorce, there was a mental divorce between the middle-class elements and the mass elements. Our constitution no longer fitted in with changing conditions; it lost its roots in the soil and became a matter of small committees functioning in the air. It still had the mighty prestige of the Congress name behind it, and this carried it a long way, but it had lost the living democratic touch. It became a prey to authoritarianism and a battleground for rival cliques fighting for control, and, in doing so, stooping to the lowest and most objectionable of tactics. Idealism disappeared, and in its place there came opportunism and corruption. The constitutional structure of the Congress was unequal to facing the new situation; it could be shaken up anywhere almost by a handful of unscrupulous individuals. Only a broad democratic basis could have saved it, and this was lacking.

Last year an attempt was made to revise the constitution in order to get rid of some of these evils. How far that attempt has succeeded or not I am not competent to judge. Perhaps it has made the organization more efficient, but efficiency means little if it has no strength behind it, and strength, for us, can come only from the masses. The present constitution stresses still further the authoritarian side of the organization, and in spite of stressing rural representation does not provide effective links with the masses.

The real problem for us is, how in our struggle for independence we can join together all the anti-imperialist forces in the country, how we can make a broad front of our mass elements with the great majority of the middle classes which stands for independence. There has been some talk of a joint front, but, so far as I can gather, this refers to some alliance among the upper classes, probably at the expense of the masses. That surely can never be the idea of the Congress, and, if it favors it, it betrays the interests it has claimed to represent and loses the very reason for its existence. The essence of a joint popular front must be uncompromising opposition to imperialism, and the strength of it must inevitably come from the active participation of the peasantry and workers.

Perhaps you have wondered at the way I have dealt at some length with the background of international and national affairs and not touched so far the immediate problems that fill your minds. You may have grown impatient. But I am convinced that the only right way of looking at our own problems is to see them in their proper place in a world setting. I am convinced that there is intimate connection beween world events, and our national problem is but a part of the world problem of capitalist imperialism. To look at each event apart from the others and without understanding the connection between them must lead us to the formation of erratic and erroneous views. Look at the vast panorama of world change today, where mighty forces are at grips with each other and dreadful war darkens the horizon. Subject peoples struggling for freedom and imperialism crushing them down; exploited classes facing their exploiters and seeking freedom and equality. Italian imperialism bombing and killing the brave Ethiopians; Japanese imperialism continuing its aggression in north China and Mongolia; British imperialism piously objecting to other countries misbehaving, yet carrying on in much the same way in India and the Frontier; and behind it all a decaying economic order which intensifies all these conflicts. Can we not see an organic connection in all these various phenomena? Let us try to develop the historic sense so that we can view current events in proper perspective and understand their real significance. Only then can we appreciate the march of history and keep step with it.

I realize that in this address I am going a little beyond the usual beat of the Congress president. But I do not want you to have me under any false pretenses, and we must have perfect frankness with each other. Most of you must know my views on social and economic matters, for I have often given expression to them. Yet you chose me as president. I do not take that choice to mean an endorsement by you all, or by a majority, of those views, but I take it that this does mean that those views are spreading in India and that most of you will be indulgent in considering them at least.

I am convinced that the only key to the solution of the world's problems and of India's problems lies in socialism, and, when I use this word, I do so not in a vague humanitarian way but in the scientific, economic sense. Socialism is, however, something even more than an economic doctrine; it is a philosophy of life, and as such also it appeals to me. I see no way of ending the poverty, the vast unemployment, the degradation and the subjection of the Indian people except through socialism. That involves vast and revolutionary changes in our political and social structure, the ending of vested interests in land and industry, as well as the feudal and autocratic Indian states system. That means the ending of private property, except in a restricted sense, and the replacement of the present profit system by a higher ideal of co-operative service. It means ultimately a change in our instincts and habits and desires. In short, it means a new civilization, radically different from the present capitalist order. . . .

I do not know how or when this new order will come to India. I imagine that every country will fashion it after its own way and fit it in with its national genius. But the essential basis of that order must remain and be a link in the world order that will emerge out of the present chaos.

Socialism is thus for me not merely an economic doctrine which I favor; it is a vital creed which I hold with all my head and heart. I work for Indian independence because the nationalist in me cannot tolerate alien domination; I work for it even more because for me it is the inevitable step to social and economic change. I should like the Congress to become a socialist organization and to join hands with the other forces in the world who are working for the new civilization. But I realize that the majority in the Congress, as it is constituted today, may not be prepared to go thus far. We are a nationalist organization, and we think and work on the nationalist plane. It is evident enough now that this is too narrow even for the limited objective of political independence, and so we talk of the masses and their economic needs. But still most of us hesitate, because of our nationalist backgrounds, to take a step which might frighten away some vested interests. Most of those interests are already ranged against us, and we can expect little from them except opposition even in the political struggle.

Much as I wish for the advancement of socialism in this country, I have no desire to force the issue in the Congress and thereby create difficulties in the way of our struggle for independence. I shall co-operate gladly and with all the strength in me with all those who work for independence even though they do not agree with the socialist solution. But I shall do so stating my position frankly and hoping in course of time to convert the Congress and the country to it, for only thus can I see it achieving independence. It should surely be possible for all of us who believe in independence to join our ranks together even though we might differ on the social issue. The Congress has been in the past a broad front representing various opinions joined together by that common bond. It must continue as such even though the difference of those opinions becomes more marked.

How does socialism fit in with the present ideology of the Congress? I do not think it does. I believe in the rapid industrialization of the country; and only thus, I think, will the standards of the people rise substantially and poverty be combated. Yet I have co-operated whole-heartedly in the past with the *khadi* program, and I hope to do so in the future because I believe that *khadi* and village industries have a definite place in our present economy. They have a social, a political, and an economic value which is difficult to measure but which is apparent enough to those who have studied their effects. But I look upon them more as temporary expedients of a transition stage than as solutions of our vital problems. That transition stage might be a long one, and, in a country like India, village industries might well play an important, though subsidiary, role even after the development of industrialism. But, though I co-operate in the village-industries program, my ideological approach to it differs considerably from that of many others in the Congress who are opposed to industrialization and socialism.

The problem of untouchability and the Harijans again can be approached in different ways. For a socialist it presents no difficulty, for under socialism there can be no such differentiation or victimization. Economically speaking, the Harijans have constituted the landless proletariat, and an economic solution removes the social barriers that custom and tradition have raised.

I come now to a question which is probably occupying your minds—the new [Government of India] Act passed by the British Parliament and our policy in regard to it. This Act has come into being since the last Congress met, but even at that time we had had a foretaste of it in the shape of the White Paper. . . .

The Congress rejected [the] proposed constitution and resolved to have nothing to do with it. The new Act, as is well known, is an even more retrograde measure and has been condemned by even the most moderate and cautious of our politicians. If we rejected the White Paper, what then are we to do with this new charter of slavery to strengthen the bonds of imperialist domination and to intensify the exploitation of our masses? And, even if we forget its content for a while, can we forget the insult and injury that have accompanied it, the contemptuous defiance of our wishes, the suppression of civil liberties, and the widespread repression that has been our normal lot? If they had offered to us the crown of heaven with this accompaniment and with dishonor, would we not have spurned it as inconsistent with our national honor and self-respect? What then of this?

A charter of slavery is no law for the slave, and, though we may perforce submit for a while to it and to the humiliation of ordinances and the like, inherent in that enforced submission are the right and the desire to rebel against it and to end it.

Our lawyers have examined this new constitution and have condemned it. But constitutions are something much more than legal documents. "The real constitution," said Ferdinand Lassalle, consists of "the actual relationships of power", and the working of this power we see even today, after the Act has been passed. That is the constitution we have to face, not the fine phrases which are sometimes presented to us, and we can only deal with it with the strength and power generated by the people of the country.

To this Act our attitude can only be one of uncompromising hostility and a constant endeavor to end it. How can we do this?

Since my return from Europe I have had the advantage of full and frank discussion with my colleagues of the Working Committee. All of us have agreed that the Act has to be rejected and combated, but all of us have not been able to agree to the manner of doing so. We have pulled together in the past, and I earnestly hope that we shall do so in the future, but in order to do so effectively we must recognize that there are marked differences in our outlooks. I do not yet know, as I write, what the final recommendation of the Working Committee will be on this issue. I can only, therefore, venture to put before you my own personal views on the subject, not knowing how far they represent the views of Congressmen. I should like to make it clear, however, in fairness to my old colleagues of the Working Committee, that the majority of them do not agree with all the views I am going to express. But, whether we agree or disagree, or whether we agree to differ, there is a strong desire on our part to continue to cooperate together, laying stress on our many points of agreement rather than on the differences. That is the right course for us, and, as a democratic organization, that is the only course open to us.

I think that, under the circumstances, we have no choice but to contest the election to the new provincial legislatures, in the event of their taking place. We should seek election on the basis of a detailed political and economic program, with our demand for a Constituent Assembly in the forefront. I am convinced that the only solution of our political and communal problems will come through such an assembly, provided it is elected on an adult franchise and a mass basis. That Assembly will not come into existence till at least a semirevolutionary situation has been created in this country and the actual relationships of power, apart from paper constitutions, are such that the people of India can make their will felt. When that will happen, I cannot say, but the world is too much in the grip of dynamic forces today to admit of static conditions in India or elsewhere for long. We may thus have to face this issue sooner than we might expect. But, obviously, a Constituent Assembly will not come through the new Act or the new legislatures. Yet we must press this demand and keep it before our country and the world, so that when the time comes we may be ripe for it.

A Constituent Assembly is the only proper and democratic method for the framing of our constitution, and for its delegates then to negotiate a treaty with the representatives of the British Government. But we cannot go to it with blank minds in the hope that something good will emerge out of it. Such an assembly, in order to be fruitful, must have previous thought behind it and a definite scheme put forward by an organized group. The actual details, as to how the Assembly is to be convened, must depend on the circumstances then existing and need not trouble us now. But it will be our function as the Congress to know exactly what we are after, to place this clearly and definitely before the Assembly, and to press for its acceptance.

One of the principal reasons for our seeking election will be to carry the message of the Congress to the millions of voters and to the scores of millions of the disfranchised, to acquaint them with our future program and policy, to make the masses realize that we not only stand for them but that we are of them and seek to co-operate with them in removing their social and economic burdens. Our appeal and message will not be limited to the voters, for we must remember that hundreds of millions are disfranchised and they need our help most, for they are at the bottom of the social ladder and suffer most from exploitation. We have seen in the past widespread official interference in the elections; we shall have to face that, as well as the serried and moneyed ranks of the reactionaries. But the real danger will come from our toning down our program and policy in order to win over the hesitating and compromising groups and individuals. If we compromise on principles, we shall fall between two stools and deserve our fall. The only right way and the only safe way is to stand foursquare on our own program and to compromise with no one who has opposed the national struggle for freedom in the past, or who is in any way giving support to British imperialism.

When we have survived the election, what then are we to do? Office or no office? A secondary matter perhaps, and yet behind that issue lie deep questions of principle and vital differences of outlook, and a decision on that, either way, has far-reaching consequences. Behind it lies, somewhat hidden, the question of independence itself and whether we seek revolutionary changes in India or are working for petty reforms under the aegis of British imperialism. We go back again in thought to the clash of ideas which preceded the changes in the Congress in 1920. We made a choice then deliberately and with determination discarded the old sterile creed of reformism. Are we to go back again to that blind and suffocating lane, after all these years of brave endeavor, and to wipe out the memory of what we have done and achieved and suffered? That is the issue, and let none of us forget it when we have to give our decision. In this India, crying aloud for radical and fundamental change, in this world pregnant with revolutionary and dynamic possibility, are we to forget our mission and our historic destiny, and slide back to static futility? And, if some of us feel tired and hunger for rest and quiet, do we imagine that India's masses will follow our lead, when elemental forces and economic necessity are driving them to their inevitable goal? If we enter the backwaters, others will take our place on the bosom of the flowing stream and will dare to take the rapids and ride the torrent.

How has this question arisen? If we express our hostility to the Act and reject the entire scheme, does it not follow logically that we should have nothing to do with the working of it and should prevent its functioning, in so far as we can? To accept office and ministry under the conditions of the Act is to negate our rejection of it and to stand self-condemned. National honor and self-respect cannot accept this position, for it would inevitably mean our co-operation in some measure with the repressive apparatus of imperialism, and we would become partners in this repression and in the exploitation of our people. Of course we would try to champion the rights of the people and would protest against repression, but as ministers under the Act we could do very little to give relief, and we would have to share responsibility for the administration with the apparatus of imperialism, for the deficit budgets, for the suppression of labor and the peasantry. It is always dangerous to assume responsibility without power, even in democratic countries; it will be far worse with this undemocratic constitution, hedged in with safeguards and reserved powers and mortgaged funds, where we have to follow the rules and regulations of our opponents' making. Imperialism sometimes talks of co-operation, but the kind of co-operation it wants is usually known as surrender, and the ministers who accept office will have to do so at the price of surrender of much that they might have stood for in public. That is a humiliating position which self-respect itself should prevent one from accepting. For our great national organization to be party to it is to give up the very basis and background of our existence.

Self-respect apart, common sense tells us that we can lose much and gain little by acceptance of office in terms of the Act. We cannot get much out of it, or else our criticism of the Act itself is wrong, and we know that it is not so. The big things for which we stand will fade into the background, and petty issues will absorb our attention, and we shall lose ourselves in compromises and communal tangles, and disillusion with us will spread over the land. If we have a majority, and only then can the question of acceptance of office arise, we shall be in a position to dominate the situation and to prevent reactionaries and imperialists from profiting by it. Office will not add to our real strength; it will only weaken us by making us responsible for many things that we utterly dislike.

Again, if we are in a minority, the question of office does not arise. It may be, however, that we are on the verge of a majority and with the co-operation of other individuals and groups we can obtain office. There is nothing inherently wrong in our acting together with others on specific issues of civil liberty or economic or other demands, provided we do not compromise on any principle. But I can imagine few things more dangerous and more likely to injure us than the acceptance of office on the sufferance of others. That would be an intolerable position.

It is said that our chances at the elections would increase if we announced that we were prepared to accept offices and ministries. Perhaps that might be so, for all manner of other people, eager for the spoils and patronage that office gives, would then hurry to join us. Does any Congressman imagine that this would be a desirable development or that we would gain strength thereby? Again, it is said more voters would vote for us if they knew that we were going to form ministries. That might happen if we deluded them with false promises of what we might do for them within the Act, but a quick nemesis would follow our failure to give effect to those promises, and failure would be inevitable if the promises were worth while.

There is only one straight course open to us: to go to the people with our program and make it clear to them that we cannot give effect to the major items in it under present conditions, and therefore, while we use the platform of the legislatures to press that program, we seek to end these imperialist bodies by creating deadlocks in them whenever we are in a position to do so. Those deadlocks should preferably take place on those programs so that the masses might learn how ineffective for their purposes are these legislatures.

One fact is sometimes forgotten—the provision for second chambers in many of the provinces. These chambers will be reactionary and will be exploited by the Governor to check any forward tendencies in the lower house. They will make the position of a minister who seeks advance even more difficult and unenviable.

Some people have suggested, though their voices are hushed now, that provincial autonomy might be given on this office issue and each Provincial Congress Committee should be empowered to decide it for its own province. An astonishing and fatal suggestion playing into the hands of our imperialist rulers. We who have labored for Indian unity can never be parties to any proposal which tends to lessen that unity. That way lies disaster and a disruption of the forces working for freedom. If we agree to this, why then should we also not agree to the communal issue being decided provincially, or many other issues where individual provinces might think differently? First issues will sink into the background, independence itself will fade away, and the narrowest provincialism raise its ugly head. Our policy must be uniform for the whole of India, and it must place first things first, and independence is the first thing of all.

So that I am convinced that for the Congress to favor the acceptance of office, or even to hesitate and waver about it, would be a vital error. It will be a pit from which it would be difficult for us to come out. Practical statesmanship is against it, as well as the traditions of the Congress and the mentality we have sought to develop in the people. Psychologically, any such lead might have disastrous consequences. If we stand for revolutionary changes, as we do, we have to cultivate a revolutionary mentality among our people, and anything that goes against it is harmful to our cause.

This psychological aspect is important. For we must never forget, and never delude our masses into imagining, that we can get any real power or real freedom through working these legislatures. We may use them certainly to advance our cause to some extent, but the burden of the struggle for freedom must fall on the masses, and primarily, therefore, our effective work must lie outside these legislatures. Strength will come from the masses and from our work among them and our organization of them.

Of secondary importance though the work in the legislatures is, we may not treat it casually and allow it to become a hindrance to our other work. Therefore it is necessary for the Congress, through its executive to have direct control over the elections and the program placed before the country, as well as the activity in the legislatures. Such control will inevitably be exercised through committees and boards appointed for the purpose, but the continued existence of semi-autonomous parliamentary boards seems to be undesirable. Provision should also be made for a periodical review of all such activities so that Congressmen in general and the country should keep in touch with them and should influence them.

We have considered the provincial elections which, it is said, may take place early next year. The time is far off yet, and it is by no means impossible that these elections may not take place for a much longer time, or may not take place at all, and the new Act may take its rightful place in oblivion. Much may happen in the course of the next year, and war is ever on the horizon, to upset the schemes and timetables of our rulers. But we cannot speculate on this, and we have to make provision for contingencies. That decision might even have been delayed, but dangerous and compromising tendencies seek to influence Congress policy, and the Congress cannot remain silent when the issue is raised and its whole future is in the balance.

The provincial legislatures may come, but few persons, I imagine, are confident about the coming of the federal part of this unholy structure. So far as we are concerned, we shall fight against it to our utmost strength, and the primary object of our creating deadlocks in the provinces and making the new Act difficult of functioning, is to kill the federation. With the federation dead, the provincial end of the Act will also go and leave the slate clean for the people of India to write on. That writing, whatever it be, can never admit the right of the Indian states to continue as feudal and autocratic monarchies. They have long survived their day, propped up by an alien Power, and have become the strangest anomalies in a changing world. The future has no place for autocracy or feudalism; a free India cannot tolerate the subjection of many of her children and their deprivation of human rights, nor can it ever agree to a dissection of its body and a cutting up of its limbs. If we stand for any human, political, social, or economic rights for ourselves, we stand for those identical rights for the people of the states.

I have referred to the terrible suppression of civil liberties by the British Government in India. But in the states matters are even worse, and, though we know that the real power behind those states is that of British imperialism, this tragic suppression of our brothers by their own countrymen is of painful significance. Indian rulers and their ministers have spoken and acted increasingly in the approved fascist manner, and their record during the past few years especially has been one of aggressive opposition to our national demands. States which are considered advanced ban the Congress organization and offer insult to our national flag and decree new laws to suppress the press. What shall we say of the more backward and primitive states?

There is one more matter concerning the Constitution Act which has given rise to much controversy. This is the communal decision. Many people have condemned it strongly and, I think, rightly; few have a good word for it. My own viewpoint is, however, somewhat different from that of others. I am not concerned so much with what it gives to this group or that but more so with the basic idea behind it. It seeks to divide India into numerous separate compartments, chiefly on a religious basis, and thus makes the development of democracy and economic policy very difficult. Indeed, the communal decision and democracy can never go together. We have to admit that, under present circumstances, and so long as our politics are dominated by middle-class elements, we cannot do away with communalism altogether. But to make a necessary exception in favor of our Moslem or Sikh friends is one thing, to spread this evil principle to numerous other groups and thus to divide up the electoral machinery and the legislature into many compartments is a far more dangerous proposition. If we wish to function democratically, the proposed communal arrangement will have to go, and I have no doubt that it will go. But it will not go by the methods adopted by the aggressive opponents of the decision. These methods result inevitably in perpetuating the decision, for they help in continuing a situation which prevents any reconsideration.

I have not been enamored of the past Congress policy in regard to the communal question and its attempts to make pacts and compromises. Yet essentially I think it was based on a sound instinct. First of all, the Congress always put independence first and other questions, including the communal one, second, and refused to allow any of those other questions to take pride of place. Secondly, it argued that the communal problem had arisen from a certain set of circumstances which enabled the third party to exploit the other two. In order to solve it, one had either to get rid of the third party (and that meant independence), or get rid of that set of circumstances, which meant a friendly approach by the parties concerned and an attempt to soften the prejudice and fear that filled them. Thirdly, that the majority community must show generosity in the matter to allay the fear and suspicion that minorities, even though unreasonably, might have.

That analysis, is, I think, perfectly sound. I would add that, in my opinion, a real solution of the problem will only come when economic issues, affecting all religious groups and cutting across communal boundaries, arise. . . .

I am afraid I cannot get excited over [the] communal issue, important as it is temporarily. It is, after all, a side issue, and it can have no real importance in the larger scheme of things. Those who think of it as the major issue think in terms of British imperialism continuing permanently in this country. Without that basis of thought, they would not attach so much importance to one of its inevitable offshoots. I have no such fear, and so my vision of a future India contains neither imperialism nor communalism.

Yet the present difficulty remains and has to be faced. Especially our sympathy must go to the people of Bengal, who have suffered most from these communal decisions, as well as from the heavy hand of the Government. Whenever opportunity offers to improve their situation in a friendly way, we must seize it. But always the background of our action must be the national struggle for independence and the social freedom of the masses.

I have referred previously to the growing divorce between our organization and the masses. Individually many of us still have influence with the masses and our word carries weight with them, and who can measure the love and reverence of India's millions for our leader, Gandhiji? And yet organizationally we have lost that intimate touch that we had. The social reform activities of the *khadi* and village industries and Harijan organizations keep large numbers of our comrades in touch with the masses, and those contacts bear fruit. But they are essentially nonpolitical, and so, politically, we have largely lost touch. There are many reasons for this, and some are beyond our control. Our present Congress constitution is, I feel, not helpful in developing these contacts or in encouraging enough the democratic spirit in its primary committees. These committees are practically rolls of voters who meet only to elect delegates or representatives, and take no part in discussion or the formation of policy. . . .

But we can . . . try in our own limited way to develop democracy on the lowest rungs of the Congress ladder and make the primary committee a living organization.

An additional method for us to increase our contacts with the masses is to organize them as producers and then affiliate such organizations to the Congress or have full co-operation between the two. Such organizations of producers as exist today, such as trade-unions and peasant unions, as well as other anti-imperialist organizations, could be brought within this sphere of mutual co-operation for the good of the masses and the struggle for national freedom. Thus Congress could have an individual as well as a corporate membership and, retaining its individual character, could influence, and be influenced by, other mass elements.

These are big changes that I have hinted at, and I am by no means sure how they can be brought about, or whether it is possible to go far in this direction in the near future. Still, we must move to some extent at least if we are to have our roots in the soil of India and draw life and strength from its millions. The subject is fascinating but complicated and can only be tackled by an expert committee, which I trust will be appointed on behalf of the Congress. The report of that committee must be freely discussed so as to get the widest backing for it.

All this will take us to the next Congress. Meanwhile perhaps some urgent changes are needed in our constitution to remove anomalies and avoid difficulties. Owing to my absence, I have had little experience of the working of the new constitution and cannot make any concrete suggestions. The reduction in the numbers of delegates and All-India Congress Committee members would be, to some extent, desirable if there was a background of widespread activity in the primary and secondary committees. Without it, it makes us even less responsive to mass opinion, and, therefore, an increase seems desirable. But the real solution is to increase the interest and day-to-day activity of the lower committees. . . .

The Congress is an all-inclusive body and represents many interests, but essentially it is a political organization with various subsidiary and allied organizations, like the Spinners' Association and the Village Industries Association. These allied organizations work in the economic field, but they do not seek directly to remove the burdens of the peasantry under the present system of land tenure. Nor can the Congress, situated as it is, wholly function as a peasant organization, although in many provinces it has espoused the cause of the peasantry and brought them much relief. It seems to me necessary that the Congress should encourage the formation of peasant unions as well as workers' unions, and co-operate with such as already exist, so that the day-to-day struggle of the masses might be continued on the basis of their economic demands and other grievances. This identification of the Congress with the economic struggle of the masses will bring us nearer to them and nearer to freedom than anything else. I would welcome also the organization of other special interests, like those of the women, in the general framework of our national struggle for freedom. The Congress would be in a position to co-ordinate all these vital activities and thus to base itself on the widest possible mass foundation.

There has been some talk of a militant program and militant action. I do not know what exactly is meant, but, if direct action on a national scale or civil disobedience are meant, then I would say that I see no near prospect of them. Let us not indulge in tall talk before we are ready for big action. Our business today is to put our house in order, to sweep away the defeatist mentality of some people, and to build up our organization with its mass affiliations, as well as to work among the masses. The time may come, and that sooner perhaps than we expect, when we might be put to the test. Let us get ready for that test. Civil disobedience and the like cannot be switched on and off when we feel like doing so. It depends on many things, some of which are beyond our control, but in these days of revolutionary change and constantly recurring crises in the world, events often move faster than we do. We shall not lack for opportunities.

The major problem of India today is that of the land—of rural poverty and unemployment and a thoroughly out-of-date land system. A curious combination of circumstances has held back India during the past few generations, and the political and economic garments it wears no longer fit it and are torn and tattered. In some ways our agrarian conditions are not unlike those of France a hundred and fifty years ago, prior to the great revolution. They cannot continue so for long. At the same time we have become parts of international capitalism, and we suffer the pains and crises which afflict this decaying system. As a result of these elemental urges and conflicts of world forces, what will emerge in India none can say. But we can say with confidence that the present order has reached the evening of its day, and it is up to us to try to mold the future as we would like it to be.

The world is filled with rumors and alarms of war. In Abyssinia bloody and cruel war has already gone on for many months, and we have watched anew how hungry and predatory imperialism behaves in its mad search for colonial domains. We have watched also with admiration the brave fight of the Ethiopians for their freedom against heavy odds. You will permit me, I feel sure, to greet them on your behalf and express our deep sympathy for them. Their struggle is something more than a local struggle. It is one of the first effective checks by an African people on an advancing imperialism, and already it has had far-reaching consequences.

In the Far East also war hovers on the horizon, and we see an Eastern imperialism advancing methodically and pitilessly over ancient China and dreaming of world empire. Imperialism shows its claws wherever it may be, in the West or in the East.

In Europe an aggressive fascism or Nazi-ism steps continuously on the brink of war, and vast armed camps arise in preparation for what seems to be the inevitable end of all this. Nations join hands to fight other nations, and progressive forces in each country ally themselves to fight the fascist menace.

Where do we come in in this awful game? What part shall we play in this approaching tragedy? It is difficult to say. But we must not permit ourselves to be passive tools exploited for imperialist ends. It must be our right to say whether we join a war or not, and without that consent there should be no co-operation from us. When the time comes, we may have little say in the matter, and so it becomes necessary for the Congress to declare clearly now its opposition to India's participation in any imperialist war, and every war that will be waged by imperialist Powers will be an imperialist war, whatever the excuses put forward might be. Therefore we must keep out of it and not allow Indian lives and Indian money to be sacrificed.

To the progressive forces of the world, to those who stand for human freedom and the breaking of political and social bonds, we offer our full co-operation in their struggle against imperialism and fascist reaction, for we realize that our struggle is a common one. Our grievance is not against any people or any country as such, and we know that even in imperialist England, which throttles us, there are many who do not love imperialism and who stand for freedom.

During this period of difficulty and storm and stress, inevitably our minds and hearts turn to our great leader who has guided us and inspired us by his dynamic personality these many years. Physical ill-health prevents him now from taking his full share in public activities. Our good wishes go ... to him for his rapid and complete recovery, and with those wishes is the selfish desire to have him back again among us. We have differed with him in the past, and we shall differ with him in the future about many things, and it is right that each one of us should act up to his convictions. But the bonds that hold us together are stronger and more vital than our differences, and the pledges we took together still ring in our ears. How many of us have that passionate desire for Indian independence and the raising of our poverty-stricken masses which consumes him? Many things he taught us long years ago, it seems now—fearlessness and discipline and the will to sacrifice ourselves for the larger cause. That lesson may have grown dim, but we have not forgotten it, nor can we ever forget him who has made us what we are and raised India again from the depths. The pledge of independence that we took together still remains to be redeemed, and we await again for him to guide us with his wise counsel.

But no leader, however great he be, can shoulder the burden single-handed; we must all share it to the best of our ability and not seek helplessly to rely on others to perform miracles. Leaders come and go; many of our best-loved captains and comrades have left us all too soon, but India goes on, and so does India's struggle for freedom. It may be that many of us must suffer still and die so that India may live and be free. The promised land may yet be far from us, and we may have to march wearily through the deserts, but who will take away from us that deathless hope which has survived the scaffold and immeasurable suffering and sorrow;

who will dare to crush the spirit of India which has found rebirth again and again after so many crucifixions?[1]

From Lucknow Congress Resolutions

[The following statements further reflect Nehru's growing concern about international events in 1936.]

I. The Congress at its session held in Madras in 1927, had drawn India's attention "to the danger of an imperialist war and the possibility of India being made a tool in such a conflict for imperialist purposes, and declared the right of the Indian people to refuse to participate in any such war without their express permission.

"That danger has become more evident and urgent since then with the growth of Fascist dictatorships, the Italian attack on Abyssinia, the continuing Japanese aggression in North China and Mongolia, the rivalries and conflicts of the great imperialist Powers, and the feverish growth of armaments. . . . A vast and terrible war threatens the world.

"In such a war an attempt will inevitably be made to drag in and exploit India to her manifest disadvantage and for the benefit of British imperialism. The Congress therefore reiterates its old resolve and warns the people of the country against this danger, and declares its opposition to the participation of India in any imperialist war."

II. "The Congress expresses the sympathy of the Indian nation for the Ethiopian people who are so heroically defending their country against imperialist aggression, and considers Abyssinia's fight as part of the fight of all exploited nations for freedom. . . .

"The Congress, as representing the will of the Indian people for national freedom and a democratic state, declares that no constitution imposed by outside authority and no constitution which curtails the sovereignty of the people of India and does not recognise their right to shape and control fully their political and economic future can be accepted. In the opinion of the Congress such a constitution must be based on the independence of India as a nation and it can only be framed by a Constituent Assembly elected on adult franchise, or a franchise which approximates to it as nearly as possible.

"The Congress therefore reiterates and stresses the demand for a Constituent Assembly in the name of the Indian people and calls upon its representatives and members in legislatures and outside to work for the fulfilment of this demand."[2]

---

[1] T.F., pp. 389–416.
[2] I.A.A., pp. 116–17.

Conflict and Controversies (Concerning Political Attitudes) after Lucknow Congress

[There was neither unanimous approval of Nehru's socialist ideas at the 1936 Lucknow Congress Session, nor substantial agreement about various other important political issues. Controversy raged to such an extent that there was even talk of a "split" within Congress ranks.]

Again and again . . . I considered [the] question of resignation. I found it difficult to work smoothly with my own colleagues in the Congress executive, and it became clear to me that they viewed my activities with apprehension. It was not so much that they objected to any specific act, but they disliked the general trend and direction. They had justification for this, as my outlook was different. I was completely loyal to Congress decisions, but I emphasized certain aspects of them, while my colleagues emphasized other aspects. I decided finally to resign, and I informed Gandhiji of my decision. . . .

Soon afterward a far-away occurrence, unconnected with India, affected me greatly and made me change my decision. This was the news of General Franco's revolt in Spain [during July, 1936]. I saw this rising, with its background of German and Italian assistance, developing into a European or even a world conflict. India was bound to be drawn into this, and I could not afford to weaken our organization and create an internal crisis by resigning just when it was essential for us to pull together. I was not wholly wrong in my analysis of the situation, though I was premature and my mind rushed to conclusions which took some years to materialize.

The reaction of the Spanish War on me indicates how, in my mind, the problem of India was tied up with other world problems. More and more I came to think that these separate problems, political or economic, in China, Abyssinia, Spain, Central Europe, India, or elsewhere, were facets of one and the same world problem. There could be no final solution of any one of them till this basic problem was solved. And in all probability there would be upheaval and disaster before the final solution was reached. As peace was said to be indivisible in the present-day world, so also freedom was indivisible, and the world could not continue for long part free, part unfree. The challenge of fascism and Nazi-ism was in essence the challenge of imperialism. They were twin brothers, with this variation, that imperialism functioned abroad in colonies and dependencies while fascism and Nazi-ism functioned in the same way in the home country also. If freedom was to be established in the world, not only fascism and Nazi-ism had to go, but imperialism had to be completely liquidated.

This reaction to foreign events was not confined to me. Many others in India began, to some extent, to feel that way, and even the public was interested. This public interest was kept up by thousands of meetings and demonstrations that the Congress organized all over the country in sympathy with the people of China, Abyssinia, Palestine, and Spain. Some attempts were also made by us to send aid, in the shape of medical supplies and food, to China and Spain. This wider interest in international affairs helped to raise our own national struggle to a higher level and to lessen somewhat the narrowness which is always a feature of nationalism.

But, inevitably, foreign affairs did not touch the life of the average person, who was absorbed in his own troubles. The peasant was full of his growing difficulties, his appalling poverty, and of the many burdens that crushed him. The agrarian problem was, after all, the major problem of India, and the Congress had gradually evolved an agrarian program which, though going far, yet accepted the present structure. The industrial worker was little better off, and there were frequent strikes.[1]

[From a communication to "Friends and Critics"—Spring, 1936.] I believe ... I have been frank enough at Lucknow and later about the anomalous position which I occupy in the Congress executive. That curious and somewhat embarrassing position has, however, nothing to do with my socialist faith. It was entirely a political difference which saw the light of day at Lucknow. None of us made a secret of it for we felt that about vital matters we had all to be perfectly open and above board and frank with the public whose suffrages we seek and who will be arbiter of India's destiny. So we agreed to differ and differ openly. But having done so we also agreed to cooperate and pull together. Not only because of the large cause of Indian independence which we all had at heart but also because our points of agreement were far more numerous than our points of disagreement. There was inevitably a difference in outlook in various things. All this was political not social, except in so far as socialism produced this difference in outlook and stress. Nothing that could be called socialistic appeared in any of the resolutions at Lucknow. Even the socialists realised that the primary issue was political, that of independence and on that they concentrated. To talk of splits and the like is an absurdity. There can be no division in our ranks [since] the call of independence came to all of us and tingles the blood in our veins. We may agree or disagree.

[1] T.F., pp. 358–59.

15+N.

We may even part company sometimes. But we still march together to the tune of that call. [1]

Further Thoughts about Socialism and Democracy— June 5, 1936

Socialism is an economic doctrine. It is a way of organizing the production and distribution and other activities of society. It is, according to its votaries, a solution of the ills from which society suffers today. And yet, in considering this economic policy, we are continually having God and religion hurled at us, and Russia, like King Charles' head, is always cropping up. I am perfectly prepared to discuss the Almighty or the strange and mysterious ways in which He is worshipped, and I am equally willing to talk of Russia, for Russia is a fascinating country today. But I do object to being side-tracked from the main issue. That can only be caused by confusion or a deliberate avoidance of the real question.

About religion I am quite convinced that there must be the most perfect freedom of faiths and observance. People can worship God in any of the thousand ways they like. But I also claim [the] freedom not to worship God if I so choose, and I also claim freedom to draw people away from what I consider superstition and unsocial practices. But when religion comes in the garb of vested interest and exploits people, it is not religion and it must be countered.

I believe in the basic economic theory which underlies the social structure of Russia. I think also that Russia has made the most remarkable progress culturally, educationally and industrially, and even spiritually, if I may use the word in its real sense. But nevertheless I do not accept or approve of everything that has taken place in Russia and I do not therefore propose to follow blindfold the example of Russia. Therefore I prefer to use the word socialism rather than communism, because the latter has come to signify Soviet Russia. Some captains of industry in Bombay take great exception to my use of the word socialism instead of communism, apparently thinking that thereby I seek to delude our people. They need not excite themselves over this matter. . . . Constituted as I am, all my sympathies go to the under-dog and to him who is persecuted most. . . . Others move in a different way and naturally and gracefully incline to an alliance with power and the top dog. That power in India is British Imperialism.

[1] H.I.N.C. (Vol. II), p. 26.

But words and labels confuse. What I seek is an elimination of the profit motive in society and its replacement by a spirit of social service, co-operation taking the place of competition, production for consumption instead of for profit. Because I hate violence and consider it an abomination I cannot tolerate willingly our present system which is based on violence. I seek therefore a more enduring and peaceful system from which the roots of violence have been removed, and where hatred shrivels up and yields place to nobler feelings. All this I call socialism.

How this will come to India I cannot say, what intermediate steps there will be, what crises to overcome. But I know this, that without some such effort we shall not solve our problems of poverty and unemployment. If there are other ways why do not my critics place them before the country, instead of getting angry at something which they do not like or perhaps do not understand?

But before socialism comes, or can even be attempted, there must be the power to shape our destiny; there must be political independence. That remains the big and all-absorbing issue before us, and whether we believe in socialism or not, if we are serious about independence, we must join forces to wrest it from unwilling hands.

I believe in full democracy, political and economic. For the moment I work for political democracy but I hope that this will enlarge itself into social democracy also. . . .

Do we stand for a democratic solution of our problems? That is a question I should like to ask my critics. If so then why all this shouting and trembling and wrathful utterance when I place these problems before our people and try to make them think of them? I have hardly mentioned socialism to them except incidentally, but I have laid stress on the amazing poverty of our people, on the vast unemployment of our peasants and workers and middle classes, on the progressive deterioration of all classes except the handful at the top. That has been my sin in the eyes of that handful. But that is the only picture that comes before my eyes when I think of India. I cannot rid myself of it, try as I may. It is not a pleasant picture. I do not like it, and, as I see it, sometimes my blood freezes within me, and sometimes it boils with indignation that such things should be.[1]

Further Repercussions, after Lucknow Congress

The [1936] Lucknow Congress was over and a Working Committee was announced. I had decided, after much mental conflict, not to resign, as the

[1] E.M.I., pp. 12-15.

consequences of resignation were serious and our whole organization might have been shaken up by it. I threw myself into the work before me and drew up schemes for developing the A.I.C.C. office and opening various departments in it. With these plans in my head I went to the first meeting of the Working Committee. No questions of principle or high policy were involved, and yet I was surprised to find that my proposals were viewed with suspicion by many of my colleagues. It was not that they objected to them, but they did not know where these developments might lead to. After long and exhausting arguments, certain more or less routine proposals were agreed to which should not have taken more than a few minutes.

I undertook some tours and visited, among other places, Bombay. Everywhere I spoke about the Congress programme, as decided at Lucknow, and emphasized the need for strengthening the organization. In the course of my speeches I laid stress on the poverty and unemployment in India, and said that a true solution could only come through Socialism. But there could be no Socialism without independence, and all of us had therefore to concentrate on the latter. I met with an enthusiastic and overwhelming response everywhere.

Early in July, 1936, there was another meeting of the Working Committee and I went to it heartened by the enthusiasm I had met with. To my surprise and dismay I found that some of my colleagues did not share this and they were full of apprehension at the developments that were taking place. They offered their resignations from the Working Committee. . . . I was stunned. It appeared that they were deeply hurt at what they considered was a regular and continuous campaign against them, treating them as persons whose time was over, who represented ideas that were worn out, and who were obstructing the progress of the country. I was of course not said to be a party to such a campaign, but my ideological sympathy with some of those who indulged in it was taken as passive support of it.

All this surprised me greatly. There had been some foolish and objectionable speeches and statements by odd individuals, but that was no sufficient reason for the offer to resign. Perhaps it was the long background of bitterness and conflict which influenced my colleagues, although this was improving rapidly. To some extent there was a feeling that the Congress Socialist party was not playing fair. Three of their number were in the Working Committee and yet the party continued in a sense to play the part of an opposition. But the dominating reason at the time was, I think, a feeling that my speeches might scare away voters and thus affect adversely the general elections that were coming. Later it was realized that I was a fairly efficient election winner.[1]

[Among other "developments" that had caused consternation at Lucknow was a Resolution favoring a broader Agrarian Program. The Resolution had stated: "[The] Congress is of [the] opinion that the most important and urgent problem of the country is the appalling poverty, unemployment and indebtedness of the peasantry, fundamentally due to antiquated and repressive land tenure and revenue systems, and intensified in recent years by the great slump in prices of agricultural produce. The final solution of this problem inevitably involves the removal of British imperialistic exploitation, a thorough change of . . . land tenure and revenue systems and a recognition by the State of its duty to provide work for the rural unemployed masses. . . ."

The Provincial Congress Committees were asked to make recommendations on such matters as: (1) Freedom of organization of agricultural labourers and peasants; (2) safeguarding of the interests of peasants where there were intermediaries between the State and themselves; (3) just and fair relief of agricultural indebtedness, including arrears of rent and revenue; (4) emancipation of the peasants from feudal and semi-feudal levies; (5) substantial reduction in respect of rent and revenue demands; (6) a just allotment of the State expenditure for the social, economic and cultural amenities of villages; (7) protection against harassing restrictions on the utilization of local natural facilities for their domestic and agricultural needs; (8) freedom from oppression and harassment at the hands of Government officials and landlords; (9) fostering industries for relieving rural unemployment.[2]]

From Letters Relating to Disagreements
Following the 1936 Lucknow Congress Session

[I. Gandhi to Agatha Harrison[3]—Wardha, April 30, 1936.

"Jawaharlal's way is not my way. I accept his ideal about land etc. But I do not accept practically any of his methods. I would strain every nerve to prevent a class war. So would he, I expect. But he does not believe it to be possible to avoid it. I believe it to be perfectly possible if my method is accepted. But though Jawaharlal is extreme in his presentation of his methods, he is sober in action. So far as I know him, he will not precipitate a conflict. Nor will he shirk it, if it is forced on him. But there perhaps the whole Congress is not of one mind. A difference there certainly is. My method is designed to avoid conflict. His is not so designed. My own

[1] U.I., pp. 99–100.
[2] Ibid., pp. 408–09.
[3] Miss Harrison was an English Quaker, deeply attached to Gandhi and India.

feeling is that Jawaharlal will accept the decisions of the majority of his
colleagues. For a man of his temperament, this is most difficult. He is
finding it so already. Whatever he does, he will do it nobly. Though the
gulf between us as to [our] outlook upon life has undoubtedly widened, we
have never been so near each other in [our] hearts as perhaps we are
today." [1]

II. Rajendra Prasad and Others to Nehru—Wardha, June 29, 1936.

"When you appointed us members of the Working Committee after
the Lucknow Congress in spite of known differences of opinion and outlooks, we hoped it would be possible to evolve a common line of action and
to work jointly keeping in the background the differences and concentrating on the point of agreement. We have been trying our best to accommodate ourselves but unfortunately we find that it has not been possible
to secure an adjustment that can enable the two differing elements to
work harmoniously or speak with one voice. We feel that the preaching
and emphasising of socialism particularly at this stage by the President and
other socialist members of the Working Committee while the Congress has
not adopted it is prejudicial to the best interests of the country and to the
success of the national struggle for freedom which we all hold to be the
first and paramount concern of the country. You also appear to feel and
have even expressed that the Working Committee as it is constituted is not
of your choice but forced on you and that you accepted it against your own
better judgment. Our own impression of the events at Lucknow is contrary to yours. We are wholly unaware of the slightest pressure being put
upon [you] by any of us. Anyway the position created by your declarations
is highly unsatisfactory and we think we should give you the fullest latitude to work without feeling hampered in any way by the presence of
colleagues in the Working Committee whom you regard as a drag. We feel
on the other hand that the Congress should still follow the ideals, and the
line of action and policy which it has been following since 1920 and which
we consider to be best suited to our country particularly in the present
conditions and which have already shown great results. We are of [the]
opinion that through your speeches and those of . . . other socialist colleagues and the acts of other socialists who have been emboldened by the
speeches we have referred to the Congress organisation has been weakened
throughout the country without any compensating gain. The effect of your
propaganda on the political work immediately before the nation, particularly the programme of election has been very harmful and we feel that
in the situation created we cannot shoulder the responsibility of organising and fighting the coming elections.

"It is not without much reluctance that we have, therefore, decided to
tender our resignation from the Working Committee. We think that the
step we have decided upon after much deliberation is just to you and to

[1] B.O.L., p. 182.

ourselves and in the best interest of the country as we see it.

"Yours sincerely,

RAJENDRA PRASAD	VALLABHBHAI PATEL
C. RAJAGOPALACHARI	J. B. KRIPALANI
JAIRAMDAS DOULATRAM	S. D. DEV"[1]
JAMNALAL BAJAJ	

III. Rajendra Prasad to Nehru—Wardha, July 1, 1936.

"Since we parted yesterday we have had a long conversation with Mahatmaji and a prolonged consultation among ourselves. We understand that you have felt much hurt by the course of action taken by us and particularly the tone of our letter has caused you much pain. It was never our intention either to embarrass you or to hurt you and if you had suggested or indicated that it hurt you we would have without the least hesitation amended or altered the letter. But we have decided to withdraw it and our resignation on a reconsideration of the whole situation.

"Since we are withdrawing the resignation you will permit us to make it clear in this private communication with a somewhat greater elaboration our feelings than could be done in a letter which was bound to find publication. In doing so there is nothing further from our mind than to hurt you.

"We have felt that in all your utterances as published in the Press you have been speaking not so much on the general Congress programme as on a topic which has not been accepted by the Congress and in doing so you have been acting more as the mouthpiece of the minority of our colleagues on the Working Committee as also on the Congress than as the mouthpiece of the majority which we expected you as Congress President to do. It may be, as you tell us, that only that portion of your speeches is published which deals with socialism and the rest is not given prominence in the Press as it is supposed to have less news value. We must however remember that for one person who actually listens to your spoken word there are hundreds who read only the published report in the Press and you may not ignore the effect on this larger audience of your speeches.

"There is a regular continuous campaign against us treating us as persons whose time is over, who represent and stand for ideas that are worn out and that have no present value, who are only obstructing the progress of the country and who deserve to be cast out of the position which they undeservedly hold. The very ideals, methods of work and tactics which we have learnt in company with Gandhiji forbid any scramble for power in any organisation and we have felt that a great injustice has been and is being done to us by others, and we are not receiving the protection we are entitled to from you as our colleague and as our President. When elaborate preparations are being made to oust us and declarations to that effect are made in your presence and it is stated that your sympathies are with such groups as was done at the Trade Union Congress we feel that what is stated represents the feeling not only of those who speak in those

[1] Ibid., pp. 188, 191.

terms but also to some extent your own opinion. This hurts us as we have not the least desire to stick to any position. We have been led step by step to think that as colleagues we do not enjoy your confidence to the extent we ought to and that you have no respect left for us or our views. We have naturally felt from all this that you regard us as a drag and it serves no useful purpose to occupy such a position.

"Your speech at the Women's meeting in Bombay touched many of us to the quick and we thought that your feeling was that we had forced ourselves on you and that you had to accept the Working Committee against your better judgment. Had we understood this to be your feeling at Lucknow, things would certainly have taken a different course.

"We also think that your handling of the situation in the country is doing damage to the constructive programme which we consider to be an essential and vital part of the Congress programme.

"Apart from all personal considerations we have also strongly felt that the ideals and the policy for which we have stood all these sixteen or seventeen years and which we believe to be the only right ones for the country are being most assiduously undermined and that your own views and sympathies are with those who are engaged in that game. We have felt that our association gives a false impression and that we are in a way contributing unwillingly and unconsciously to that process. It is this kind of activity which is gradually injuring the Congress organisation and the Congress prestige in the country, as the country as a whole still holds to those ideals and that policy. This results in a weakening of the Congress and encourages fissiparous tendencies among workers. This naturally lessens the chances of Congress success at the next elections. You hold a different opinion on this point. The results of elections are after all a matter of speculation and there may well be differences of opinion on that score. We have recognised the force of the argument that we should not take the drastic step we had proposed to take unless we felt sure that our resignation and its consequences will on the whole not injure the chances of success at the elections if not improve them. Some of us feel that it is possible that this action of ours may result in a course of events which may cause a further deterioration in the position as regards elections and we do not consider it proper to take any chance. At the same time the apprehension in our minds regarding a general weakening of the Congress organisation and discipline is based on our personal experience of the state of things in the Provinces and we deem it our duty to bring it to your notice so that you may deal with it in the best manner that suggests itself to you.

"As we repeatedly told you all this impression has been created in our minds not by any single act or speech but as a result of the totality of activities and we feel we owe it to you to tell all this in frankness so that you may be in full cognisance of what is passing in our minds and if you feel that anything needs to be done you may do it as you deem best. We are sorry for having hurt your feelings and I only hope that this letter will help to smooth matters and not make them worse as nothing is further from our mind. I am writing this as a result of consultation and on behalf of all of us. So far as we are concerned this is an episode for which in the best interest of the country as we conceive it we were responsible and you may treat the letter of resignation as never having been tendered by us. Please therefore return it." [1]]

Owing to the intervention of Gandhiji the resignations [from Congress] were withdrawn, but I . . . [was] in a depressed frame of mind. I felt . . . I should resign and place the whole matter before the A.I.C.C. so that suitable arrangements could be made for future work. I sent a long letter to Gandhiji. [2]

[From letter to Gandhi, July 5, 1936.] I have been feeling weak in body and troubled in mind. Partly this is no doubt due to physical causes—a chill which has aggravated my throat trouble. But partly also it is due to other causes which touch the mind and the spirit directly. Since my return from Europe, I have found that meetings of the Working Committee exhaust me greatly; they have a devitalizing effect on me and I have almost the feeling of being older in years after every fresh experience. I should not be surprised if this feeling was also experienced by my colleagues of the Committee. It is an unhealthy experience and it comes in the way of effective work.

I was told, when I returned from Europe, that the country was demoralised and hence we had to go slow. My own little experience during the past four months has not confirmed this impression. Indeed I have found a bubbling vitality wherever I have gone and I have been surprised at the public response. What this is due to I cannot say definitely. I can only make various guesses. This public response has naturally heartened me and filled me with fresh energy. But this energy seems to ooze out of me at every meeting of the Working Committee and I return feeling very much like a discharged battery. The reaction has been greatest on this occasion because of my being physically in a low condition.

But it was not about my physical or mental condition that I wished to write to you. There are more important matters which worry me and so far I have seen no clear way out. I do not wish to act in a hurry or without giving the fullest thought to the matter. But even before my own mind is decided I want to tell you which way I am looking.

I am grateful to you for all the trouble you took in smoothing over matters and in helping to avoid a crisis. I was convinced then and I am convinced now that a break of the kind suggested would have had serious consequences for all our work, including the elections. And yet, where are

[1] Ibid., pp. 192–94.   [2] U.I., p. 101.
15*

we now and what does the future hold for us? I read again Rajendra
Babu's [Prasad] letter to me (the second one) and his formidable indictment of me. That indictment, though formidable, is not specific, except
for my speech at the women's meeting, which, as a matter of fact, has
nothing to do with any wider issue. The main thing is that my activities
are harmful to the Congress cause. They are doing damage to the Congress
and are lessening its chances of success at the elections. If I continue in
this way there is likely to be further deterioration and my colleagues do
not wish to take any chances in this vital matter.

Now, obviously, if there is any truth in this charge it must be faced.
The matter is too serious to be glossed over. There are no black and white
shades, no delicate balancing of the resultant good or evil; it is all black
and that really makes it easier to decide. For however tenderly the fact
may be stated, it amounts to this: that I am an intolerable nuisance and
the very qualities I possess—a measure of ability, energy, earnestness,
some personality which has a vague appeal—become dangerous for they
are harnessed to a wrong chariot. The conclusion from all this is obvious.

My own impression before Lucknow, and to some extent even at Lucknow, was that it should not be difficult for all of us to pull together this
year. It is evident now that I was mistaken, though there has been no lack
of trying on either side. Perhaps the fault may lie with me; I am not
aware of it; but one can seldom see the beam in one's own eye. The fact
remains, and today there is no loyalty of the spirit which binds our group
together. It is a mechanical group and on either side there is a dull resentment and a sense of suppression, and that, as every student of psychology
knows, results in all manner of undesirable complexes, both individual and
social.

When I reached Bombay this time many people stared hard at me
finding it difficult to believe how I had survived. It seemed to be common
knowledge there (as reported in the *Times of India* previously) that a
peaceful end awaited me—politically of course. All had been fixed up
except the cremation. Hence the surprise. It struck me as curious that I
should be wholly ignorant of all these confident rumours when many
people in the street were full of them. But though I had been ignorant of
them, the rumours had the strongest justification. That in itself is a
measure of my present isolation.

I have written at length, both in my book [*Autobiography—Toward
Freedom*] and subsequently, about my present ideas. There is no lack of
material for me to be judged. Those views are not casual. They are part
of me, and though I might change them or vary them in future, so long

as I hold them I must give expression to them. Because I attached importance to a larger unity I tried to express them in the mildest way possible and more as an invitation to thought than as fixed conclusions. I saw no conflict in this approach and in anything that the Congress was doing. So far as the elections were concerned I felt definitely that my approach was a definite asset to us as it enthused the masses. But my approach, mild and vague as it was, is considered dangerous and harmful by my colleagues. I was even told that my laying stress always on the poverty and unemployment in India was unwise, or at any rate the way I did it was wrong.

You will remember that both in Delhi and in Lucknow I made it clear that I must have freedom to express my views on social matters. I understood you and the members of the Committee to agree to this. The question now becomes one more of this freedom of expression than of the views themselves. Even more so it is a question of values in life, and if we value anything greatly we may not sacrifice it.

There is this undeniable conflict. Who is right and who is wrong it is futile to argue. But after last week's incidents I am beginning to doubt if we are really following the correct course. I am inclined to think that the right thing for us to do will be to put the matter briefly before the A.I.C.C. at its next meeting and take its direction in the matter. How best to do this I am not clear yet but it should be done as simply as possible and without much argument. So far as I am concerned there will be little argument.

Presumably the result of this will be that I shall retire and a more homogeneous Committee will be formed.

You told me that you intended issuing some kind of a statement. I shall welcome this for I believe in every viewpoint being placed clearly before the country.[1]

[From Gandhi letter to Nehru, July 8, 1936: "I have just received your letter. I was seeking time to be able to write to you. . . . Your letter makes it difficult. I would however just like to say that the letter of withdrawal does not bear the meaning you put upon it when it was given to you. It was sent to you after I had seen it. The sending of such a letter in . . . place of resignation was my suggestion. I wish that you could take a juster view of that letter. In any case I am firmly of [the] opinion that during the remainder of the year, all wrangling should cease and no resignations should take place. A.I.C.C. will be paralysed and powerless to deal with the crisis. It will be torn between two emotions. It would be most unfair to spring upon it a crisis, in the name of democracy, which it has never

[1] B.O.L., pp. 194–97.

been called upon to face. You are exaggerating the implications of the letter. I must not argue. But I would urge you to consider the situation calmly and not succumb to it in a moment of depression so unworthy of you. Why should you not allow your humour to play upon the meetings of the W.C.? Why should it be so difficult for you to get on with those with whom you have worked without a jar for years? If they are guilty of intolerance, you have more than your share of it. The country should not be made to suffer for your mutual intolerance."[1]

Despite such altercations, Gandhi firmly denied press reports of a widening gulf between Nehru and himself, in an article "Are We Rivals?" published in *Harijan*, July 25: "'I have had two typical cuttings sent to me giving altogether false news about relations between Pandit Jawaharlal Nehru and myself. Remarks said to have been made by me have been reproduced in quotation marks. Thus I am reported to have said, "My life-work is ruined (that is, by Jawaharlal's programme); not even the firmness and repression of the British Government have harmed my work as much as the policy outlined by Nehru."

"'I have never said anything of the kind, nor uttered one single remark attributed to me in the two articles sent to me. What is more I have not even entertained the opinions contained in those articles. So far as I am aware, Jawaharlal has come to the conclusion that India's freedom cannot be gained by violent means and that it can be gained by non-violent means. And I know for a fact that he did not in Lucknow "come out for the use of violence in the struggle for independence".

"'No doubt, there are differences of opinion between us. They were clearly set forth in the letters we exchanged some years ago. But they do not affect our personal relations in any way whatsoever. We remain the same adherents to the Congress goal that we have ever been. My life-work is not, cannot be ruined by Jawaharlal's programme, nor have I ever believed for that matter that it has been harmed even by "the firmness and repression of the British Government". My philosophy, if I can be said to have any, excludes the possibility of harm to one's cause by outside agencies. The harm comes deservedly and only when the cause itself is bad, or being good its champions are untrue, faint-hearted, or unclean. The article in question refers to "Gandhi's secret plans". If I know Gandhi at all, I can vouchsafe for it that he never had any secret plans in his life. And if beyond what the readers of *Harijan* know there is no plan that I can disclose, it is because I know none myself. Then one of the articles presents Jawaharlal and me as rivals. I cannot think of myself as a rival to Jawaharlal or him to me. Or, if we are, we are rivals in making love to each other in the pursuit of the common goal. And if in the joint work for reaching the goal we at times seem to be taking different routes, I hope the world will find that we had lost sight of each other only for the moment and only to meet again with greater mutual attraction and affection.'"[2]

[1] Ibid., p. 198.
[2] As quoted in T.D.G (Vol. IV), pp. 86-87.

	Bombay Election Manifesto—Before
9	Faizpur Congress Session—Presidential Address, Faizpur, December, 1936— From Faizpur Congress Resolution

Bombay Election Manifesto—August, 1936

A new atmosphere of co-operation surrounded us and the tension seemed to lessen. As a colleague remarked with pleasure, it was like old times again.

As the elections approached, all of us plunged into the campaign and our internal conflicts vanished for the moment. For many months I wandered about India and millions of faces passed before my eyes. I saw a thousand facets of this country of mine in all their rich diversity, and yet always with the unifying impress of India upon them. I sought to understand what lay behind those millions of eyes that stared at me, what hopes and desires, what untold sorrow and misery unexpressed. Glimpses came to me that illumined my vision and made me realize the immensity of the problems of the hundreds of millions of our people.[1]

[From Bombay Election Manifesto of August, 1936.]

"In view of the present situation and in order to prevent the operation of forces calculated to strengthen alien domination and exploitation, the Congress decided to contest seats in the coming elections for the provincial legislatures. But the purpose of sending congressmen to the legislatures under the new [Government of India] Act is not to co-operate in any way with the Act but to combat it and seek to end it. It is to carry out, in so far as is possible, the Congress policy of rejection of the Act, and to resist British imperialism in its attempts to strengthen its hold on India and its exploitation of the Indian people. In the opinion of the Congress, activity in the legislatures should be such as to help in the work outside, in the strengthening of the people, and in the development of the sanctions which are essential to freedom.

"The new legislatures, hedged and circumscribed by safeguards and special powers for the protection of British and other vested interests, cannot yield substantial benefits, and they are totally incapable of solving

[1] U.I., p. 102.

the vital problems of poverty and unemployment. But they may well be used by British imperialism for its own purposes to the disadvantage and injury of the Indian people. The Congress representatives will seek to resist this, and to take all possible steps to end the various regulations, Ordinances and Acts which oppress the Indian people and smother their will to freedom. They will work for the establishment of civil liberty, for the release of political prisoners and detenus, and to repair the wrongs done to the peasantry and to public institutions in the course of the national struggle.

"The Congress realizes that independence cannot be achieved through these legislatures, nor can the problems of poverty and unemployment be effectively tackled by them. Nevertheless the Congress places its general programme before the people of India so that they may know what it stands for and what it will try to achieve, whenever it has the power to do so."[1]

[The general aims of the Bombay Manifesto: "(a) Rejection of the 1935 Constitution; (b) the demand for a Constituent Assembly; (c) the establishment of national independence; (d) relief of the burdens of the peasantry; (e) the abolition of untouchability."[2]]

Before Faizpur Congress Session

[September 16, 1936.] Every few miles along the road-side crowds gather together and wait for hours. It is ungracious to ignore them and pass them by without stopping. So one has to stop [for] them . . . thank them for their affectionate welcome and say a few words to them. Often enough the villages on the route are decorated and elaborate arches are put up. At the entrance to the village or town half the population turns out and waits patiently for hours. What is one to do with all this love and affection? It is overpowering and one has to bow to it.

For various reasons I attract enormous crowds and I evoke an astonishing amount of enthusiasm. Partly this may be due to a certain personal popularity, but largely, I think it is due to the great prestige and influence of the Congress. Whatever the reasons may be, the fact of these vast gatherings of human beings, full of enthusiasm and excitement, must be taken into account and they must be dealt with fairly and squarely.[3]

[October 18, 1936.] Only one thing mattered—the independence of India—and we were all comrades struggling shoulder to shoulder to

[1] Ibid., p. 402.
[2] Ibid., p. 102, footnote.
[3] E.M.I., p. 49.

realise this desire of our hearts. The love of India filled us and we looked forward, eagerly and anxiously, to the promise of freedom.

And everywhere with this love of independence was a passion for social freedom, a desire to end the exploitation of our people and establish a [more just] order which would put an end to the cause of poverty and the vast and growing unemployment which strangles us. The great crowds that gathered to hear me were largely naked poverty-stricken people, hungering for relief from their terrible burdens. And in their minds and ours political freedom and social freedom were mixed together and were two facets of the future we worked for.

But all this wonderful enthusiasm and overpowering affection have to be disciplined and organised lest they waste themselves on trivial objects. The Congress has endeavoured with much success to do this, but we must go further still, and harness this energy and vitality to the cause of the Congress and of India's freedom. For this, the Congress must spread its organisation, just as it has already done its appeal, to every village, and function throughout on a democratic basis. Leadership is essential, but authoritarianism is bad, and already we suffer from it sufficiently under British domination.[1]

[Nehru became President of the 1936 Faizpur Congress Session. His intensive campaigning for Congress candidates entering the forthcoming elections proved to be extremely effective.]

As I was travelling from Allahabad to Bareilly I drafted a statement in [the] train about the coming Congress Presidential election [for the Faizpur Congress Session]. I was in somewhat of a quandary and not knowing what to do, decided to take [the] public into my confidence. That statement seems to have given rise to some controversy in the Press. As I have been incessantly touring in the interior, I have not been able to see most of the Press comments and do not know what they are. Such as I have seen have surprised me for they seem to raise issues which I had not intended to raise.

I did not wish to enter into [a] controversy, for I am placed in a peculiar position. I had no desire to be re-elected President and I had stated I would welcome the election of another and would gladly co-operate with him. Eminent and respected colleagues have been suggested for the Presidentship and election of any one of them would be in the fitness of things. Yet under the circumstances, as I pointed out previously I could

[1] E.M.I., p. 59.

not say "no". I have, however, just received a telegram to the following effect from two close colleagues of mine: "Newspapers interpret your statement treating your election as a vote for Socialism and anti-office acceptance. We think it reiterates your own views on Socialism and at the same time treating political independence as of paramount importance and pleading for joint action and your election as no vote for Socialism or anti-office acceptance. Misunderstanding needs clearing. . . ."

It would be absurd for me to treat this presidential election as [a] vote for Socialism or anti-office acceptance. I have expressed my views on Socialism and pointed out how this colours all my outlook and my activity. I have further expressed myself often enough against office acceptance and, whenever opportunity occurs, I shall press this viewpoint before the Congress, but it is for the Congress to decide this issue directly and on full consideration of it and not as it were by casual and indirect vote. I do believe political independence is the paramount issue before the country and necessity for joint, united action on this is incumbent on all of us. I say this to remove any misunderstanding and not [to] suggest even indirectly that I should be elected. If in spite of this I am . . . it can only mean my general line of activity during [the] last eight months is approved by [a] majority of Congressmen and not my particular views on any issue. Considerations that have led me to act in that way hold and in so far as I can, I shall continue to act in the same way whether I am President or not.[1]

From Presidential Address—Faizpur Congress Session, December, 1936

The problem of maintaining peace cannot be isolated by us, in our present condition, from war resistance. The Congress has already declared that we can be no parties to an imperialist war, and we will not allow the exploitation of India's man power and resources for such a war. Any such attempt will be resisted by us.

The League of Nations has fallen very low, and there are few who take it seriously as an instrument for the preservation of peace. India has no enthusiasm for it whatever, and the Indian membership of the League is a farce, for the selection of delegates is made by the British Government. We must work for a real League of Nations, democratically constructed,

[1] H.I.N.C. (Vol. II), pp. 32–33.

which would in effect be a League of Peoples. If even the present League, ineffective and powerless as it is, can be used in favor of peace, we shall welcome it.

With this international background in view, let us consider our national problems. The Government of India Act of 1935, the new Constitution, stares at us offensively, this new charter of bondage which has been imposed upon us despite our utter rejection of it; and we are preparing to fight elections under it. Why we have entered into this election contest and how we propose to follow it up has been fully stated in the Election Manifesto of the All-India Congress Committee, and I commend this manifesto for your adoption. We go to the legislatures not to cooperate with the apparatus of British imperialism, but to combat the Act and seek to end it, and to resist in every way British imperialism in its attempt to strengthen its hold on India and its exploitation of the Indian people. That is the basic policy of the Congress, and no Congressman, no candidate for election, must forget this. Whatever we do must be within the four corners of this policy. We are not going to the legislatures to pursue the path of constitutionalism or a barren reformism.

There is a certain tendency to compromise over these elections, to seek a majority at any cost. This is a dangerous drift and must be stopped. The elections must be used to rally the masses to the Congress standard, to carry the message of the Congress to the millions of voters and nonvoters alike, to press forward the mass struggle. The biggest majority in a legislature will be of little use to us if we have not got this mass movement behind us, and a majority built on compromises with reactionary groups or individuals will defeat the very purpose of the Congress.

With the effort to fight the Act, and as a corollary to it, we have to stress our positive demand for a Constituent Assembly elected under adult suffrage. That is the very cornerstone of Congress policy today, and our election campaign must be based on it. This Assembly must not be conceived as something emanating from the British Government or as a compromise with British imperialism. If it is to have any reality, it must have the will of the people behind it and the organized strength of the masses to support it, and the power to draw up the constitution of a free India. We have to create that mass support for it through these elections and later through our other activities. . . .

We are not against the conception of a federation. It is likely that a free India may be a federal India, though in any event there must be a great deal of unitary control. But the present federation that is being thrust upon us is a federation in bondage and under the control, politically and socially, of the most backward elements in the country. The present Indian states took shape early in the nineteenth century in the unsettled conditions of early British rule. The treaties with their autocratic rulers, which are held up to us so often now as sacred documents which may not be touched, date from that period.

It is worth while comparing the state of Europe then with that of India. In Europe then there were numerous tiny kingdoms and princedoms; kings were autocratic, holy alliances and royal prerogatives flourished. Slavery was legal. During these hundred years and more Europe has changed out of recognition. As a result of numerous revolutions and changes the princedoms have gone and very few kings remain. Slavery has gone. Modern industry has spread, and democratic institutions have grown up with an ever-widening franchise. These in their turn have given place in some countries to fascist dictatorships. Backward Russia, with one mighty jump, has established a Soviet Socialist state and an economic order which has resulted in tremendous progress in all directions. The world has gone on changing and hovers on the brink of yet another vast change. But not so the Indian states; they remain static in this ever-changing panorama, staring at us with the eyes of the early nineteenth century. The old treaties are sacrosanct, treaties made not with the people or their representatives but with their autocratic rulers.

This is a state of affairs which no nation, no people can tolerate. We cannot recognize these old settlements of more than a hundred years ago as permanent and unchanging. The Indian states will have to fit into the scheme of a free India, and their peoples must have, as the Congress has declared, the same personal, civil, and democratic liberties as those of the rest of India.

Till recent years little was heard of the treaties of the states or of paramountcy. The rulers knew their proper places in the imperial scheme of things, and the heavy hand of the British Government was always in evidence. But the growth of the national movement in India gave them a fictitious importance, for the British Government began to rely upon them more and more to help it in combating this nationalism. The rulers and their ministers were quick to notice the change in the angle of vision and to profit by it. They tried to play, not without success, the British Government and the Indian people against each other and to gain advantages from both. They have succeeded to a remarkable degree and have gained extraordinary power under the federal scheme. Having preserved themselves as autocratic units, which are wholly outside the control of the rest of India, they have gained power over other parts of India. Today we find them talking as if they were independent and laying down conditions for their adherence to the federation. There is talk even of the abolition of the viceregal paramountcy, so that these states may remain, alone in the whole world, naked and unchecked autocracies, which cannot be tampered with by any constitutional means. A sinister development is the building up of the armies of some of the bigger states on an efficient basis.

Thus our opposition to the federal part of the Constitution Act is not merely a theoretical one, but a vital matter which affects our freedom struggle and our future destiny. We have got to make it a central pivot of our struggle against the Act. We have got to break this federation.

Our policy is to put an end to the Act and have a clean slate to write afresh. We are told by people who can think only in terms of action taken in the legislatures, that it is not possible to wreck it and there are ample provisions and safeguards to enable the Government to carry on despite a hostile majority. We are well aware of these safeguards; they are one of the principal reasons why we reject the Act. We know also that there are second chambers to obstruct us. We can create constitutional crises inside the legislatures, we can have deadlocks, we can obstruct the imperialist machine, but always there is a way out. The Constitution cannot be wrecked by action inside the legislatures only. For that, mass action outside is necessary, and that is why we must always remember that the essence of our freedom struggle lies in mass organization and mass action.

The policy of the Congress in regard to the legislatures is perfectly clear; only in one matter it still remains undecided—the question of acceptance or not of office. Probably the decision of this question will be postponed till after the elections. At Lucknow I ventured to tell you that, in my opinion, acceptance of office was a negation of our policy of rejection of the Act; it was further a reversal of the policy we had adopted in 1920 and followed since then. Since Lucknow the Congress has further clarified its position in the Election Manifesto and declared that we are not going to the legislatures to co-operate in any way with the Act but to combat it. That limits the field of our decision in regard to offices, and those who incline to acceptance of them must demonstrate that this is the way to nonco-operate with the Act, and to end it.

It seems to me that the only logical consequence of the Congress policy, as defined in our resolutions and in the Election Manifesto, is to have nothing to do with office and ministry. Any deviation from this would mean a reversal of that policy. It would inevitably mean a kind of partnership with British imperialism in the exploitation of the Indian people, an acquiescence, even though under protest and subject to reservations, in the basic ideas underlying the Act, an association to some extent with British imperialism in the hateful task of the repression of our advanced elements. Office accepted on any other basis is hardly possible, and, if it is possible, it will lead almost immediately to deadlock and conflict. That deadlock and impasse does not frighten us; we welcome it. But then we must think in terms of deadlocks and not in terms of carrying on with the office.

There seems to be a fear that if we do not accept office others will do so and they will put obstacles in the way of our freedom movement. But, if we are in a majority, we can prevent others from misbehaving; we can even prevent the formation of any ministry. If our majority is a doubtful one, then office for us depends on compromises with non-Congress elements, a policy full of danger for our cause and one which would inevitably lead to our acting in direct opposition to the Congress mandate of rejection of the Act. Whether we are in a majority or in a minority, the real thing will always be the organized mass backing behind us. A majority without that backing can do little in the legislatures; even a militant minority with conscious and organized mass support can make the functioning of the Act very difficult.

We have put the Constituent Assembly in the forefront of our program, as well as the fight against the federal structure. With what force can we press these two vital points and build up a mass agitation around them if we wobble over the question of office and get entangled in its web?

We have great tasks ahead, great problems to solve both in India and in the international sphere. Who can face and solve these problems in India but this great organization of ours, which has, through fifty years' effort and sacrifice, established its unchallengeable right to speak for the millions of India? Has it not become the mirror of their hopes and desires, their urge to freedom, and the strong arm that will wrest this freedom from unwilling and resisting hands? It started in a small way with a gallant band of pioneers, but even then it represented a historic force, and it drew to itself the good will of the Indian people. From year to year it grew, faced inner conflicts whenever it wanted to advance and was held back by some of its members. But the urge to go ahead was too great, the push from below increased; and, though a few left us, unable to adjust themselves to changing conditions, vast numbers of others joined the Congress. It became a great propaganda machine dominating the public platform of India. But it was an amorphous mass; its organizational side was weak, and effective action on a large scale was beyond its powers. The coming of Gandhiji brought the peasant masses to the Congress, and the new constitution that was adopted at his instance in Nagpur in 1920 tightened up the organization, limited the number of delegates according to population, and gave it strength and capacity for joint and effective action. That action followed soon after on a countrywide scale and was repeated in later years. But the very success and prestige of the Congress often drew undesirable elements to its fold and accentuated the defects of the constitution. The organization was becoming unwieldy and slow of movement and capable of being exploited in local areas by particular groups. Two years ago radical changes were made in the constitution again at Gandhiji's instance. One of these was the fixation of the number of delegates according to membership, a change which has given a greater reality to our elections and strengthened us organizationally. But still our organizational side lags far behind the great prestige of the Congress, and there is a tendency for our committees to function in the air, cut off from the rank and file.

It was partly to remedy this that the Mass Contacts resolution was passed by the Lucknow Congress, but unhappily the committee that was in charge of this matter has not reported yet. The problem is a wider one than was comprised in that resolution, for it includes an overhauling of the Congress constitution with the object of making it a closer-knit body, capable of disciplined and effective action. That action to be effective must be mass action, and the essence of the strength of . . . Congress has been this mass basis and mass response to its calls. But, though that mass basis is there, it is not reflected in the organizational side . . . hence [there is] an inherent weakness in our activities. We have seen the gradual transformation of the Congress from a small upper-class body to one representing the great body of the lower middle classes, and later the masses of this country. As this drift to the masses continued, the political role of the organization changed and is changing, for this political role is largely determined by the economic roots of the organization.

We are already and inevitably committed to this mass basis, for without it there is no power or strength in us. We have now to bring that into line with the organization, so as to give our primary members greater powers of initiative and control and opportunities for day-to-day activities. We have, in other words, to democratize the Congress still further.

Another aspect of this problem that has been debated during the past year has been the desirability of affiliating other organizations, of peasants, workers, and others, which also aim at the freedom of the Indian people, and thus to make . . . Congress the widest possible joint front of all . . . anti-imperialist forces in the country. As it is . . . Congress has an extensive direct membership among these groups; probably seventy-five per cent of its members come from the peasantry. But, it is argued, that functional representation will give far greater reality to the peasants and workers in the Congress. This proposal has been resisted because of a fear that the Congress might be swamped by new elements, sometimes even politically backward elements. As a matter of fact, although this question is an important one for us, any decision of it will make little difference at present; its chief significance will be as a gesture of good will. For there are few well-organized workers' or peasants' unions in the country which are likely to profit by Congress affiliation. There is not the least possibility of any swamping, and, in any event, this can easily be avoided. I think that now or later some kind of functional representation in the Congress is inevitable and desirable. It is easy for the Congress to lay down conditions for such affiliation, so as to prevent bogus and mushroom growths or undesirable organizations from profiting by it. . . .

The real object before us is to build up a powerful joint front of all the anti-imperialist forces in the country. The Congress has indeed been in the past, and is today, such a united popular front, and inevitably the Congress must be the basis and pivot of united action. The active participation of the organized workers and peasants in such a front would add to its strength and must be welcomed. Co-operation between them and the Congress organization has been growing and has been a marked feature of the past year. This tendency must be encouraged. The most urgent and vital need of India today is this united national front of all forces and elements that are ranged against imperialism. Within the Congress itself most of these forces are represented, and in spite of their diversity and difference in outlook, they have co-operated and worked together for the common good. That is a healthy sign both of the vitality of our great movement and the unity that binds it together. The basis of it is anti-imperialism and independence. Its immediate demand is for a Constituent Assembly leading to a democratic state where political power has been transferred to the mass of the people. An inevitable consequence of this is the withdrawal of the alien army of occupation.

These are the objectives before us, but we cannot ignore the present-day realities and the day-to-day problems of our people. These ever-present realities are the poverty and unemployment of our millions, appalling poverty and an unemployment which has even the middle classes in its grip and grows like a creeping paralysis. The world is full of painful contrasts today, but surely nowhere else are these contrasts so astounding as in India. Imperial Delhi stands, visible symbol of British power, with all its pomp and circumstance and vulgar ostentation and wasteful extravagance; and within a few miles of it are the mud huts of India's starving peasantry, out of whose meager earnings these great palaces have been built, huge salaries and allowances paid. The ruler of a state flaunts his palaces and his luxury before his wretched and miserable subjects, and talks of his treaties and his inherent right to autocracy. And the new Act and Constitution have come to us to preserve and perpetuate these contrasts, to make India safe for autocracy and imperialist exploitation. . . .

The workers in our country have yet to gain elementary rights; they have yet to have an eight-hour day and unemployment insurance and a guaranteed living wage.

But a vaster and more pressing problem is that of the peasantry, for India is essentially a land of the peasants. In recognition of this fact, and to bring the Congress nearer to the peasant masses, we are meeting here today at the village of Faizpur and not, as of old, in some great city. The Lucknow Congress laid stress on this land problem and called on the provincial committees to frame agrarian programs. This work is still incomplete, for the vastness and intricacy of it has demanded full investigation. But the urgency of the problem calls for immediate solution. Demands for radical reforms in the rent and revenue and the abolition of feudal levies have been made from most of the provinces. The crushing burden of debt on the agricultural classes has led to a widespread cry for a moratorium and a substantial liquidation of debt. . . .

Vast gatherings of peasants testify to their inability to carry their present burdens. Yet it is highly doubtful if this problem can be solved piecemeal and without changing completely the land system. That land system cannot endure, and an obvious step is to remove the intermediaries between the cultivator and the State. Co-operative or collective farming must follow.

The reform of the land system is tied up with the development of industry, both large-scale and cottage, in order to give work to our scores of millions of unemployed and raise the pitiful standards of our people. That again is connected with so many other things—education, housing, roads and transport, sanitation, medical relief, social services, etc. Industry cannot expand properly because of the economic and financial policy of the Government, which, in the name of Imperial Preference, encourages British manufactures in India, and works for the profit of Big Finance in the City of London. The currency ratio continues in spite of persistent Indian protest; gold has been pouring out of India continuously now for five years at a prodigious rate, though all India vehemently opposes this outflow. And the new Act tells us that we may do nothing which the Viceroy or the Governor might consider as an unfair discrimination against British trade or commercial interests. The old order may yield place to the new, but British interests are safe and secure.

And so one problem runs into another, and all together form that vast complex that is India today. Are we going to solve this by petty tinkering and patchwork with all manner of vested interests obstructing us and preventing advance? Only a great planned system for the whole land and dealing with all these various national activities, co-ordinating them, making each serve the larger whole and the interests of the mass of our people—only such a planned system, with vision and courage to back it, can find a solution. But planned systems do not flourish under the shadow of monopolies and vested interests and imperialist exploitation. They require the air and soil of political and social freedom.

These are distant goals for us today though the rapid march of events may bring us face to face with them sooner than we imagine. The immediate goal—independence—is nearer and more definite, and that is why perhaps we escape, to a large extent, that tragic disillusion and hopelessness which affect so many in Europe.

We are apparently weak, not really so. We grow in strength, the Empire of Britain fades away. Because we are politically and economically crushed, our civil liberties taken away, hundreds of our organizations made illegal, thousands of our young men and women always kept in prison or in detention camp, our movements continually watched by hordes of secret service men and informers, our spoken word taken down, lest it offend the law of sedition—because of all this and more we are not weaker but stronger, for all this intense repression is the measure of our growing national strength. War and revolution dominate the world, and nations arm desperately. If war comes or other great crisis, India's attitude will make a difference. We hold the keys of success in our hands if we but turn them rightly. And it is the increasing realization of this that has swept away the defeatist mentality of our people.[1]

From Resolution—Faizpur Congress Session, December, 1936

"The Congress has followed with deepest sympathy and anxiety the struggle that is going on in Spain between the people of Spain and a

[1] T.F., pp. 422–31.

military group aided by foreign mercenary troops and Fascist Powers in Europe. The Congress realizes that this struggle between democratic progress and Fascism is of great consequence to the future of the world and will affect the future of imperialism and India.

"The Congress has noted without surprise in this struggle the policy of non-intervention followed by the British Government has been such as to hamper in many ways the Spanish people fighting the Fascist rebels and has thus, in effect, aided these rebels who are being openly backed and helped by the Fascists.

"The Congress, on behalf of the people of India, sends greetings to the Spanish people and the assurance of their solidarity with them in the great struggle for liberty.

"The Congress has drawn repeated attention in the past to the danger of imperialism and has declared that India can be no party to it. Since the last session of the Congress the crisis has deepened and Fascist aggression has increased, the Fascist Powers forming alliances and grouping themselves together for war with the intention of dominating Europe and the world and crushing political and social freedom.

"The Congress is fully conscious of the necessity of facing this world menace in cooperation with the progressive nations and peoples of the world, and especially with those peoples who are dominated and exploited by imperialism and Fascism. In the event of such a world war taking place, there is grave danger of Indian manpower and resources being utilised for the purposes of British Imperialism and it is, therefore, necessary for the Congress to warn the country again against this and prepare it and resist such an exploitation of India and her peoples.

"No credits must be voted for such a war and voluntary subscriptions and war loans must not be supported and all other war preparations resisted." [1]

[1] I.A.A., pp. 118–19.

PART FOUR
1937–1938

I like to be at the storm centre of life.[1]

*

[Of the Hindi–Urdu (Hindu–Muslim) controversy.]
Open the way to both scripts everywhere.[2]

*

We worked for the dawn, but the long night has
continued, and it may continue . . . how long I do
not know. Many of us now in the vanguard of the
nation's fight may not live to see the dawn. But the
dawn will come. Meanwhile, the torch has got to be
kept burning to light the path.[3]

[1] Quoted in M.J.N., p. 257.
[2] Quoted in G.I.A., p. 420.
[3] B.I.S.J.N. (Vol. I), unnumbered page.

General Elections—Presidential Address, All-India Convention of Congress Members of Provincial Legislatures— Congress Decision to Enter Legislatures— New Situation Created Thereby

General Elections

[Beginning in April, 1936, Nehru toured India, covering forty-five thousand miles, talking to over ten million people. He spoke on behalf of Congress candidates who subsequently met with great success at the polls.]

[The] general election was a memorable affair for me. I was not a candidate myself, but I toured all over India on behalf of Congress candidates, and I imagine that I created some kind of a record in the way of election campaigns. In the course of about four months I traveled about fifty thousand miles, using every kind of convenience for this purpose, and often going into remote rural areas where there were no proper means of transport. I traveled by airplane, railway, automobile, motor truck, horse carriages of various kinds, bullock cart, bicycle, elephant, camel, horse, steamer, paddle-boat, canoe, and on foot.

I carried about with me microphones and loud-speakers and addressed a dozen meetings a day, apart from impromptu gatherings by the roadside. Some mammoth gatherings approached a hundred thousand; the average audience was usually twenty thousand. The daily total of persons attending was frequently a hundred thousand, and sometimes it was much greater. On a rough estimate it can be said that ten million persons actually attended the meetings I addressed, and probably several million more were brought into some kind of touch with me during my journeying by road.

I rushed about from place to place, from the northern frontiers of India to the southern seas, taking little rest, kept up by the excitement of the moment and the enormous enthusiasm that met me. It was an extraordinary feat of physical endurance which surprised me. This election campaign, in which large numbers of people took part on our behalf, stirred up the whole countryside, and a new life was visible everywhere. For us it was something much more than an election campaign. . . .

The Congress triumphed in the general election, and there was a great argument as to whether we should accept ministries in the provinces. Ultimately it was decided that we should do so but on the understanding that there would be no interference from the Viceroy or the governors.[1]

Acceptance of office does not mean by an iota acceptance of the slave constitution. It means a fight against the coming of federation [which denied complete self-government to India as a whole] by all means in our power, inside as well as outside the legislatures. We have taken a new step involving new responsibilities and some risk. But if we are true to our objectives and are ever vigilant, we shall overcome these risks and gain strength and power from this step also. Eternal vigilance is the price of liberty.[2]

From Presidential Address, All-India Convention
  of Congress Members of Provincial Legislatures—
New Delhi, March, 1937

The Congress policy and programme are clear and fixed for us by repeated resolutions of the Congress itself and by our Election Manifesto. We must move within that orbit and any attempt to go out of it would be a betrayal of that policy and of the larger interests for which the Congress has stood. Those of you who have been elected to the new legislatures have asked the suffrage of the people on the basis of the Congress Election Manifesto, and you must inevitably take your stand on this. The very greatness of your success at the polls is striking testimony of the response of the masses to this policy and programme. Millions have testified to their faith and confidence in this; they have given it the final seal of the approval of the Indian people.

The electorate was confined to a bare ten per cent of our people, but everybody knows that the lower down the scale we go, the greater is the

[1] T.F., pp. 360–61.
[2] Quoted in T.D.G. (Vol. IV), p. 152.

Congress strength. The remaining ninety per cent are even more solidly for the Congress than the ten per cent who have supported us. Though our success has been overwhelming and has confounded our opponents, and swept away the representatives of the big vested interests who opposed us, it should be remembered that the whole machinery of election was so designed as to weaken us. The pressure of an autocratic and entrenched Government was exercised against us, and behind it were ranged all the reactionaries and obscurantists who always flourish under the shadow of imperialism. Yet we won in resounding manner.

Only in regard to the Muslim seats did we lack success. But our very failure on this occasion has demonstrated that success is easily in our grasp and the Muslim masses are increasingly turning to the Congress. We failed because we had long neglected working among the Muslim masses and we could not reach them in time. But where we reached [them], especially in the rural areas, we found almost the same response, the same anti-imperialist spirit, as in others. The communal problem, of which we hear so much, seemed to be utterly non-existent, when we talked to the peasant, whether Hindu, Muslim or Sikh. We failed also among the Muslims because of their much smaller electorate which could be easily manipulated and coerced by authority and vested interests. But I am convinced that, even so, we would have had a much larger measure of success if we had paid more attention to the Muslim masses. They have been too long neglected and misled and they deserve special consideration. I have no manner of doubt that they are turning to the Congress to seek relief from their innumerable burdens and their future cooperation is assured, provided we approach them rightly and on the basis of economic questions.

We have too long thought in terms of pacts and compromises between communal leaders and neglected the people behind them. That is a discredited policy and I trust that we shall not revert to it. And yet some people still talk of the Muslims as a group dealing with the Hindus or others as a group, a medieval conception which has no place in the modern world. We deal with economic groups today and the problems of poverty and unemployment and national freedom are common for the Hindu, the Muslim, the Sikh, and the Christian. As soon as we leave the top fringe, which is continually talking of percentages of seats in the legislatures and State jobs, and reach the masses, we come up against these problems. This way lies the ending of what has long been known as the communal problem.

One of the most remarkable signs of the times is the ferment amongst the Muslims in India, both the intelligentsia and the masses. Without any

effective leadership, they have drifted aimlessly, and they resent this helpless position and feel that the communal leadership they have had has
weakened them politically, in spite of the trivial and superficial gains
which they are supposed to have got from an imperialism which seeks to
wean them away from the national movement. Muslim young men and
old, and the Muslim press, are full of this self-analysis, and the desire to
get out of the communal rut and line up with the forces of freedom and
progress is strong within them. They see how the Congress has swept
away Hindu communal organisations, how it has captured the imagination
of the masses, and they feel a little desolate and left out. They want to
share in the triumphs of today and tomorrow, and are prepared to take
their share of the burdens also. And so this election and our campaign,
though they resulted in the loss of Muslim seats as a rule, have been a
triumph for us even in regard to the Muslims. They have gone some way
to lay the ghost of communalism. It is for us now to go ahead and welcome
the Muslim masses and intelligentsia in our great organisation and rid
this country of communalism in every shape and form.

The elections have many lessons to teach us but the outstanding fact is
this: Where we went to the masses direct we won overwhelmingly. Our
partial lack of success in some provinces was clearly due to the Congress
organisation there being confined to the cities and having little contact
with the peasantry. We must remedy these failings and speak more and
more the language of the masses and fashion our policy to meet their
needs. We must carry the Congress organisation to every village, the Congress message to every mud hut.

I have referred to some of our failings and some of our failures. It is
well to remember these and not to allow ourselves to be swept away by
success into forgetting them. We build for the future and our foundations
must be well and truly laid. To win an election is a small matter for us;
we are out to win the freedom of our people.

Having disposed of these failures let me refer to the success that has
come to us, for it is this tremendous success, not surprising for us who
know our people, but astounding and upsetting to others, that is the outstanding feature of these elections. How carefully and lovingly the Government had nursed the great vested interests of India, encouraged the big
landlords and communalists, helped them to organise themselves to
oppose us, and looked confidently for success in its evil venture! Where
are they now, these pillars of imperialism in India and exploiters of the
Indian people? Sunk almost without trace, overwhelmed by the sea of
Indian humanity, swept away by the big broom of the masses from the

political scene. Like a house of cards, they have fallen at the touch of reality; even so will others go who oppose India's freedom, and a day will come when British imperialism throttles and crushes our people no more and is a dream of the past for us.

We went to our people and spoke to them of freedom and the ending of their exploitation; we went to that forgotten creature, the Indian peasant, and remembered that his poverty was the basic problem of India: we identified ourselves with him in his suffering and talked to him of how to get rid of it through political and social freedom. We told him of imperialism and of this new [1935 Government of India] Act and Constitution which bind us still further and which we were out to end and replace by *panchayati raj*, fashioned by a Constituent Assembly, a grand *panchayat* of the nation, elected by all our people. We read out to him our Election Manifesto and explained its significance. He and his kind gathered in vast numbers to hear us and, listening to the Congress message, his sunken eyes glistened and his shrunken starved body rose up in enthusiasm and the wine of hope filled his veins. Who that saw that vision can forget it, or that subsequent sight of thousands marching to the polling booths in disciplined array, ignoring pressure and threat, disdaining the free conveyances and free food offered to them by our opponents? It was a pilgrimage for them to give their allegiance to the Congress, to vote for the ending of the new Constitution, for the establishment of *panchayati raj* when they would themselves have power to liquidate the poverty that consumed them.

That is the significance of this election. If there is any meaning in democracy, if this complicated and expensive apparatus of elections and voting has any sense behind it and is not an impertinent farce, then the Indian people have spoken, so that even the deaf might hear, and proclaimed that they will not have this Constitution. They have given notice to quit British imperialism. This Constitution must therefore go, lock, stock and barrel, and leave the field clear for our Constituent Assembly.

We talk of and discuss our policy in the legislatures, but all this is vain and profitless parleying before the fundamental and dominant fact of the situation that this Constitution must go. So the people of India have decided and we shall be false and unfaithful representatives of our people if we allow ourselves to forget this fact contrary to that emphatic direction.

I know that there are elements amongst us who are too fond of slurring over these fundamentals, who look longingly to office, and who have even compromised the dignity of our great cause and of the Congress by discussing the personnel of ministries long before the question of acceptance

16+N.

or non-acceptance of ministerial office has been decided by the All-India Congress Committee. Whatever their views may be on this issue, whatever the decision of the A.I.C.C. might be, I would have them remember, now and for the future, that no Congressman, worthy of his name, no Congress member of a legislature, can act except with the dignity and discipline that our cause and organisation demand. I would have them remember the Election Manifesto and the Congress resolutions on the basis of which they sought the suffrage of the people. Let no one forget that we have entered the legislatures not to cooperate in any way with British imperialism but to fight and end this Act which enslaves and binds us. Let no one forget that we fight for independence. . . .

It is said, and I believe Gandhiji holds this view, that if we achieved national freedom, this would mean the end of British imperialism in India, and a necessary result of this would be the winding up of British imperialism itself. Under such conditions there is no reason why we should not continue our connection with Britain. There is force in the argument for our quarrel is not with Britain or the British people, but with British imperialism. But when we think in these terms, a larger and a different world comes into our ken. . . . That larger world does not think of a British group of nations, but of a world group based on political and social freedom. . . .

And so our pledge must hold and we must labour for the severance of the British connection. But let us repeat again that we favor no policy of isolation or aggressive nationalism, as the word is understood in the Central European countries today. We shall have the closest of contacts, we hope, with all progressive countries, including England, if she has shed her imperialism.[1]

More Detailed Summary of Congress Decision to Enter Legislatures and Form Ministries—1937

On April 1, 1937, Part III of the Act of 1935 was put into operation, and Provincial Autonomy as envisaged in the new Constitution was inaugurated. The parties or groups controlling a majority in the Provincial Assemblies were then entitled to shoulder the responsibilities of government, in terms of the Act, in all the provinces. In six provinces the Congress Assembly Parties were in a clear majority over all other parties; in some provinces they were the largest single party. . . . The Congress was

[1] E.M.I., pp. 105–13.

thus in a position to undertake, if it so chose, the formation of Ministries in these six provinces. In most of the remaining provinces it could have done so by forming an alliance or coalition with another group.

The question of office acceptance and formation of Ministries had agitated the Congress for the past two years and a final decision had been repeatedly postponed. After the General Elections had brought striking success to the Congress and the inauguration of the new Constitution was imminent, the decision could no longer be delayed. The All-India Congress Committee therefore met for this purpose in Delhi in the third week of March, 1937, and finally decided to permit acceptance of office in the provinces where the Congress commanded a majority in the Legislature, but they made this subject to a condition. Ministries were only to be formed by Congressmen if the leader of the Congress Party in the provincial Legislature was satisfied, and was in a position to declare publicly, that the Governor would not use his special powers of interference, or set aside the advice of Ministers in regard to their constitutional activities. The All-India Convention, consisting of Congress members of the various Provincial Assemblies and members of the All-India Congress Committee, accepted this decision of the All-India Congress Committee.

In accordance with this direction the leaders of Congress Parties who were invited by Governors to form Ministries asked for the necessary assurances, and these not having been given, the leaders expressed their inability to undertake the formation of Ministries.

The majority party having refused office, a deadlock ensued in these six provinces, and the Governors appointed *ad interim* Ministers who had no backing in the Legislatures. The Legislatures themselves were not summoned, as this would have inevitably led to the defeat of the *ad interim* ministries and a sharpening of the conflict.

During the three months that followed many statements were issued on behalf of the Congress as well as of the British Government, defending and justifying the position taken up by each. The controversy was often carried on in legal and constitutional terms, but, in essence, the conflict went deeper and represented the antagonism between British Imperialism and the desire of the Indian people to be free. By asking for assurances from Governors not to use their special powers of interference, the Congress wanted to develop a convention that the Ministers' advice would prevail even as regards these special powers. It wanted a free hand in the provincial Government within the limits of the Act.

The Governors' executive powers and functions, according to the Act, are of three kinds:

(i) Those to be exercised in the Governor's sole discretion;
(ii) those in which he is to exercise his individual judgment; and
(iii) those in which he must act upon the advice of his Ministers.

The assurances demanded by the Congress referred to the first two classes. In the first of these the Governor need not even refer to his Ministers, if he so chooses, and can take decisions entirely on his own responsibility. In the second class fall certain obligations imposed upon the Governor in which he must exercise his individual judgment, but, before he does so, he is to consult his Ministers. Should the advice of the Ministers not be acceptable to him, he can disregard it. The list of matters in which the Governor is entitled to exercise his own judgment is formidable and imposing, and it was an appreciation of this fact that led the Congress to ask for assurances to avoid obstruction and continual deadlocks in the government of the province.

It was stated on behalf of the British Government that such assurances could not be given without doing violence to the Act. The Congress leaders stated that, while they were entirely opposed to the Act as a whole, they did not contemplate amendments to the Act by demanding assurances. Such assurances could be given even within the terms of the Act. Where discretion was given to the Governor he could certainly exercise it in favour of the advice of the Ministers, and he could give an assurance to this effect. The Governor was nowhere prohibited by the Act from exercising his discretion in accordance with his Ministers' advice.

As the controversy took a legal turn, as to whether the assurances demanded could or could not be given under the Act, Mahatma Gandhi, on behalf of the Congress, proposed that the matter be referred to an impartial tribunal for decision. This offer was not accepted by the British Government. Nor was recourse had to [the] Section . . . of the Act . . . framed especially to meet possible difficulties during the transitional period.

As the controversy proceeded there was a slight toning down by interpretations of the original demand for assurances on behalf of the Congress. The British Government also changed their ground by slow degrees and finally took up the position that, though a definite assurance in terms of the Congress resolution could not be given, the essence of Provincial Autonomy, as envisaged in the new Constitution, was the co-operation of the Governor with his Ministers.

The position of the *ad interim* Ministries was becoming more and more difficult. They were highly unpopular and they had no sanction behind them except the will of the Governor. As they could not face the Legislature, the Legislature was not summoned in spite of repeated demands from the elected members. Provincial Autonomy seemed to be reduced to a farce. It was obvious that these conditions could not last much longer, as the Legislatures had to be summoned within six months and the Budget had to be passed. It was this deepening crisis which led to the largest advance on the part of the British Government, but this advance was accompanied by a broad hint from the Viceroy that if the Congress majorities persisted in their refusal to accept office, the Constitution would have to be suspended under [a particular] Section . . . of the Act in those provinces where the Congress commanded a majority.

It was to consider this situation that the Working Committee of the Indian National Congress met, and on July 7, 1937, it decided to permit acceptance of Cabinet responsibilities. It declared that while the declarations on behalf of the British Government exhibit a desire to make an approach to the Congress demand, they fall short of the assurances asked for in terms of the A.I.C.C. resolution. It stated further that it was unable to subscribe to the doctrine of partnership propounded in the aforesaid declarations, and that the proper description of the existing relationship between the British Government and the people of India is that of exploiter and exploited, and hence they have a different outlook upon almost everything of vital importance. Nevertheless the Committee felt that the situation created as a result of the circumstances and events that had occurred since the Congress demand was put forward, warranted the belief that it will not be easy for the Governors to use their special powers. The Committee therefore resolved that Congressmen be permitted to accept office where they may be invited thereto. But it added that it wished to make it clear that office was to be accepted and utilised for the purpose of working in accordance with the lines laid down in the Congress election manifesto and to further in every way the Congress policy of combating the new Act on the one hand, and of prosecuting the constructive programme of the Congress on the other.

Within a few days of this resolution of the Working Committee, the leaders of Congress Parties in the six provinces were invited to form Cabinets, and they accepted the invitation. The constitutional deadlock thus ended.[1]

---

[1] From Joint Note for *National Publications Society*, by Narendra Dev. K. T. Shah and Jawaharlal Nehru. Quoted in U.I., pp. 55–59.

New Political Situation Created by Decision to Accept Office— July 20, 1937

The resolution of the Working Committee giving permission to accept office and the consequent formation of Congress Ministries in six provinces has created a new situation. Many Congressmen view this with a measure of apprehension, many others expect great things out of this change. Both these reactions are natural. We have swerved off to some extent from the path we have followed for so long, and a feeling of hesitation in treading over strange ground is inevitable. Some fear unknown pitfalls, others look forward to an easy march. But all of us, who have deemed it a privilege to serve our country and our people through the Congress, have loyally accepted the Working Committee decision, and in accordance with the traditions of our great organization kept faith with each other.

If tried Congressmen feel hesitant on new ground, what of the masses? What do they think of this new orientation of our policy? What do they expect from the Congress now? Do any of them imagine that our struggle for freedom has ended because Congressmen occupy high offices? Do they think foolishly that Swaraj is at hand? They must be puzzled to see some of their old comrades who were in prison with them but yesterday, sitting in the seats of the mighty in those imposing structures which have been the citadels of British Imperialism. Red-liveried chaprasis hover about them and the enervating perfume of power surrounds them. What has happened to these comrades of ours? they must wonder. What strange sea-change has transformed the convict of yesterday into the Minister of today? Is it that they have forgotten and deserted us poor starving folk, we who looked to them so hopefully for relief from misery? Or are they going to lead us to a land overflowing with milk and honey, the happy land of our dreams, so different from our present lot?

Both these pictures would be wrong. We have not left them and we are their comrades as of old. Though some of us may sit on chairs of state, the same khadi covers our bodies, the same thoughts fill our minds, the same goal calls to us insistently and drives us to action. But we are yet far from that goal and the power to mould our country's destiny is not ours yet. There is no Swaraj or Congress raj, though Congressmen may be ministers. And yet we have a new opportunity for serving and strengthening the masses and perhaps easing their many burdens a little. But even that service will depend on the attitude of the masses, on their organized strength and on their intelligent appreciation of what is happening.

It is incumbent on us, therefore, to go to the masses and explain to them what has happened. The Working Committee resolution must be read out to them and all its implications fully explained. They must understand that while there is this great apparent change on the surface, the old conflict between imperialism and nationalism continues, and in this conflict strength comes to us from them and not from high office. And those of our comrades who are in office today, and who deserve every help and sympathy from us in the arduous and responsible work they have undertaken, will only work effectively if the masses are vigilant and press forward the Congress demands.

I suggest, therefore, that meetings for this purpose be held all over India, in town and village, on ... August 1, when the Working Committee resolution should be read out and explained and, while offering comradely greeting to the Congress Ministers, we should pledge ourselves anew to independence and the removal of the poverty of our people. On that day also the Flag salutation ceremony should be solemnly performed everywhere. August 1 is a special and significant day for us, a day long dedicated to India's freedom. On that day seventeen years ago the great Lokamanya [Tilak, Extremist Congress leader of the early twentieth century] passed away, and on that very day India launched the non-co-operation movement and began wielding that weapon which has strengthened and vitalized our people so greatly. It is fitting, therefore, that this day be suitably celebrated, and we should remember the past and we should look to the future with the same determination which has held us for so long.

A change has come over our provincial governments, and though this change does not vitally affect the relation of Britain to India, it is right that it should affect all our own countrymen whether they are in Government service or not. It is time that every Indian came out on India's side and co-operated with the Congress in the high tasks that it has undertaken. I trust that as an earnest of this sympathy and goodwill every Indian, who stands for India's freedom, will wear khadi, the emblem of our freedom, and will display and honour the National Flag. I trust also that the police force, which has so long been hostile to our people, will think in terms of India now and not of alien masters, and will seek the co-operation and goodwill of the masses. The Congress ministers, if they mean anything at all, mean that the interests of these masses will be dominant.[1]

[1] U.I., pp. 62–64.

2 | India's Princes and Federation

The constitutional deadlock that has arisen in India, immediately on the introduction of the new Constitution, has brought home to many the real significance of that constitution more than any amount of explanation and analysis. The Act may remain on the statute book yet awhile and shadow ministries function, backed by the British power. But . . . [the] Act has no place in the picture and so it is collapsing at the first touch. . . . [We] must remember that the Federal part of it still raises its ugly head in the mists of the future. The Congress has directed us to fight this Federal structure and to prevent its introduction, for nothing is so bad in the Act as this Federal part.

What of the Princes? We hear vague rumours of some agreeing and some doubting. These Princes, or nearly all of them, have acted during the past years of national struggle as the close allies of British Imperialism. Consistently they have been unfriendly to the national movement. Are they going to register another unfriendly act by joining the Federation despite the unanimous opposition of political India to this structure? This will be a grave decision for them and they will thus align themselves even more than before in opposition to the people of India. There is a great deal of talk of the independence of the States and of the special treaties and the like. But the thing that is going to count in the future is the treaty that the people of India make with others. The Act will go inevitably with all its hundreds of sections and its special powers and its Federation. And so I would ask the Princes to consider this matter from this point of view and not rush in where wiser people fear to tread.[1]

The solicitude of the Tory die-hards for [the Princes] and their "independence" has put new life into them. Never before have they had so much importance thrust on them. Previously they had dared not say no to a hint from the British Resident, and the Government of India's attitude to the numerous highnesses was openly disdainful. There was continual interference in their internal affairs, and often this was justified. Even today a large number of the states are directly or indirectly being governed by British officers "lent" to the states. But . . . the Government

[1] E.M.I., pp. 201-02.

of India . . . has grown cautious about interfering with their decisions. The Princes also now talk in a much more superior way.[1]

	Trip to Burma and Malaya—Of Period Following Congress Elections—Congress and Political Prisoners—Further Commentary on 1937 Elections and Congress Problems—Congress Attitude on Minorities and Fundamental Rights— Boycott of Japanese Goods
3	

Trip to Burma and Malaya

In the summer of 1937 I visited Burma and Malaya. It was no holiday, as crowds and engagements pursued me everywhere, but the change was pleasant, and I loved to see and meet the flowery and youthful people of Burma, so unlike in many ways the people of India with the stamp of long ages past upon them.

New problems faced us in India. In most of the provinces Congress governments were in power, and many of the ministers had spent years in prison previously.[2]

Of Period Following Congress Elections

[After Congress candidates had entered, and achieved a certain success in, elections for provincial legislatures in 1937—and then did a creditable job in governing—Congress prestige temporarily increased. The Congress gained in membership, and was responsible for introducing at least a limited number of social and economic reforms. Concurrently the progressive Nehru wing of Congress, which began to grow in substantial

[1] T.F., pp. 344-45.
[2] Ibid., p. 361.
16*

manner, believed that the new ministries were behaving in far too conservative a manner; too much in the fashion of the very officials they had replaced. Nehru was keenly aware of the many problems that existed.

In reply to a later criticism that Congress should have achieved greater agreement with the Muslim League in Uttar Pradesh, in 1937, he stated that he was anxious that the Congress Ministries should take up the question of land reform and the abolition of landlordism as soon as they took office; that he felt the Muslim League in the U.P. was largely representative of the large zamindars and hence might prevent the reforms he wished to see carried out.[1]

By March 1938, the Council of the All-India Muslim League protested about what it termed Congress injustices, requesting that a special committee inquire into the matter and rectify the situation. When Nehru agreed to accompany a leading Muslim League member to investigate the truth of such allegations, the appointment to do so was not kept by the League member.]

The Congress ministers worked hard and made others work hard also. But they had to work with the old apparatus of government, which was wholly alien to them and often hostile. Even the services were not under their control. Twice there was a conflict with the governors, and the ministers offered their resignations. Thereupon the governors accepted the viewpoint of the ministers, and the crisis ended. But the power and influence of the old services—the civil service, the police, and others—backed by the governor and buttressed by the constitution itself, were great and could make themselves felt in a hundred ways. Progress was slow, and dissatisfaction arose.

The dissatisfaction found expression in the Congress itself, and the more advanced elements grew restive. I was myself unhappy at the trend of events as I noticed that our fine fighting organization was being converted gradually into just an electioneering organization. A struggle for independence seemed to be inevitable, and this phase of provincial autonomy was just a passing one. In April 1938 I wrote to Gandhiji expressing my dissatisfaction at the work of the Congress ministries. "They are trying to adapt themselves far too much to the old order and trying to justify it. But all this, bad as it is, might be tolerated. What is far worse is that we are losing the high position that we have built up, with so much labor, in the hearts of the people. We are sinking to the level of ordinary politicians."

I was perhaps unnecessarily hard on the Congress ministers; the fault lay much more in the situation itself and in the circumstances. The record of these ministries was in fact a formidable one in numerous fields of

[1] I.G.M., No. 27 (Feb. 10, 1959), p. 1.

national activity. But they had to function within certain limits, and our problems required going outside these limits. Among the many good things that they did were the agrarian legislation they passed, giving considerable relief to the peasantry, and the introduction of what is called basic education. This basic education is intended to be made free and compulsory for every child in the country for seven years, from the age of seven to fourteen. It is based on the modern method of teaching through a craft, and it has been so evolved as to reduce the capital and recurring cost very greatly, without in any way impairing the efficiency of education. For a poor country like India, with scores of millions of children to educate, the question of cost is important. This system has already revolutionized education in India and is full of promise.

Higher education was also tackled vigorously, and so also public health, but the efforts of the Congress governments had not borne much fruit when they finally resigned. Adult literacy, however, was pushed with enthusiasm and yielded good results. Rural reconstruction also had a great deal of attention paid to it.

The record of the Congress governments was impressive, but all this good work could not solve the fundamental problems of India. That required deeper and more basic changes and an ending of the imperialistic structure which preserved all manner of vested interests.

So conflict grew within the Congress between the more moderate and the more advanced sections.[1]

The working of provincial autonomy, restricted as it was, had many dangers for us. It tended to emphasize, as it was no doubt meant to, provincialism and diverted our anti-imperialist struggle into narrower channels. Because of this, internal conflicts grew—communal, social, and organizational. The major problems of poverty, unemployment, the land, industry, clamoured for solution, and yet they could not be solved within the framework of the existing constitution and economic structure. The only course open to us was to go as far as we could towards this solution—it was not very far—and to relieve somewhat the burdens on the masses, and at the same time to prepare ourselves to change that constitution and structure. A time was bound to come when we would have exhausted the potentialities of this constitution, and have to choose between a tame submission to it and a challenge to it. Both involved a crisis. For if we submitted, the major problems, finding no solution or outlet, would overwhelm us. If we did not—and we had no intention of doing so—a conflict

[1] T.F., pp. 361–62.

with British Imperialism was inevitable unless the latter surrendered, which it was not likely to do. There was an odd possibility, however, that if the national movement grew powerful enough, and in view of the critical situation, we might gain our objective without a major struggle.

Our strength had certainly increased greatly, and in spite of internal conflicts and sometimes bogus membership, there is no doubt that the Congress is a more powerful organization today than at any previous period of its history. The masses are more politically awake than ever before. Yet these very signs of strength may turn against us if they are not organized and directed into right channels. For the moment I am not considering the communal problem, in spite of its obvious importance and its repercussions on our national struggle.

We had to deal with, both in the Organization and in the provincial governments, the co-ordination of the political struggle with the social and economic problems of the masses. Failure to integrate the two meant weakness and a growing paralysis. On the one hand, we had to keep our struggle predominantly political and anti-imperialistic; on the other, we had to go as far as we possibly could in the direction of social advance. Above all, it was essential that the Congress must continue to be a disciplined, well-knit organization, keeping the various aspects of the struggle well under control. If the Congress weakened there was no possibility of effective struggle for us. . . .

I was dissatisfied with the progress made by the Congress Ministries. It is true that they had done good work, their record of achievement was impressive, the Ministers were working terribly hard and yet had to put up with all manner of attacks and criticisms, often based on ignorance. Theirs was a thankless job. Still, I felt that progress was slow and their outlook was not what it should be. Nor was I satisfied with the approach of the Congress leadership to the problems that faced us. It was not so much a question of difference of opinion as of emphasis, though there was difference of opinion also sometimes. What alarmed me was a tendency to put down certain vital elements which were considered too advanced or which did not quite fit in with the prevailing outlook. This was a dangerous drift, though it had not gone far, and it reminded me of the fate of the German Social Democrats and the British Labour Party.

It is true that some of the so-called Leftist elements in the Congress had not behaved with responsibility and had deliberately encouraged tendencies which could only lead to internal conflict and the weakening of the Congress. Their idea of a joint front was to have the full protection of the Congress, the advantage of its prestige, and yet to attack it and criticize it from outside. The Red Flag, perfectly justified in its own sphere, became often a challenge to the National Flag. The Kisan Sabha [Peasant Organization] frequently functioned as a permanent opposition to the local Congress Committee and sometimes demonstrations were organized which could only lead to friction and irritation. Much of this took place in the lower ranks, but even the Kisan Sabha leadership was quite astonishingly irresponsible. In the villages, all manner of undesirables who had found no place in the local Congress, or were otherwise disgruntled elements, found shelter in a local Kisan Sabha. Even politically reactionary elements sometimes utilized the Kisan Sabha ... to weaken the Congress.

All this led to petty conflicts, and what was worse, a growing spirit of indiscipline in the Congress. If this had represented the growth of an organized and disciplined Left, it would have been a healthy sign, whether one agreed with it or not. In effect it represented a healthy awakening of the masses which was being exploited by numerous mutually differing groups among those who called themselves the Leftists. For a considerable time the conflict among the Leftist groups themselves absorbed most of their energy.

Gandhiji was not interested in these ideological conflicts, but, with his extraordinary capacity to sense a situation, he felt that indiscipline was growing rapidly and chaotic forces were being let loose. He was thinking more and more in terms of a great struggle with British Imperialism, and indiscipline could not be the prelude to this. I was myself distressed by this development. It reminded me of various unfortunate stages of the Chinese Revolution, and I had no desire to see India go through that chaotic process.[1]

Congress and Political Prisoners

[An important problem to be faced, after Congress Ministries had accepted power in provincial legislatures in 1937, was what to do about political prisoners who previously had been jailed for their violent opposition to British policy. On the one hand, Congress was accused of favoring "violence" because it released such prisoners; on the other, British provincial governors quite naturally objected to their liberation.]

[August 30, 1937.] A number of political prisoners, convicted for

[1] U.I., pp. 107–09.

violent activities, have recently been released by the Congress Ministries after long terms in prison. They have been welcomed by the public and by Congressmen, and we have been asked if this welcome did not signify an approval of violence. That question reveals an ignorance of public psychology and of the minds of Congressmen. The public and Congressmen alike welcomed them because of the mantle of long suffering that they bore. How many of them had spent their entire youth in prison, how many had faced death without flinching? They had erred and pursued a wrong path, they had followed a policy injurious to the very cause they sought to serve, but they had paid for it in pain and torment and by long years in solitary cells. They had come to realise that the old policy of theirs was utterly wrong. And so the public welcomed them and friendly faces greeted them wherever they went. Has this not got a lesson for governments who imagine that by suppressing a number of individuals they solve a problem? They succeed thereby in intensifying that very problem, and public sympathy, which might well have been against the individual's deeds, turns to him because of his suffering.

The problem of the political prisoners . . . is with us today and we see the amazing folly of Government in pursuing a policy which is creating a frenzy of excitement among the public. Thus they intensify the very atmosphere which they seek to remove.

The Congress Ministries have rightly followed a contrary policy because they try to move with public approval, and seek to win over these brave young men, and create an atmosphere favourable to the working of the Congress programme. In that favourable atmosphere even wrong tendencies will wilt and wither away. Everybody of any consequence in Indian politics knows that terrorism is a thing of the past in India. It would have vanished even earlier but for the policy of the British Government. . . . Violence is not killed by violence, but by a different approach and by removing the causes which lead to it.

On those comrades of ours, who have been released after one or two decades of prison life, rests a special responsibility to be loyal to Congress policy and to work for the fulfilment of the Congress programme. The foundation of that policy is non-violence and the noble structure of the Congress has been built on that firm foundation. It is necessary that this should be remembered by all Congressmen, for it is even more important today than it has so far been. Loose talk encouraging violence and communal conflict is especially harmful at the present juncture and it might do grave injury to the Congress cause as well as embarrass the Congress Ministries. We are children no longer in politics; we have grown to man's estate and we have big work ahead, big conflicts to face, difficulties to overcome. Let us face them like men with courage and dignity and discipline. Only through a great organisation, deriving its sanctions from the masses, can we face our problems, and great mass organisations are built up through peaceful methods.[1]

Further Commentary on 1937 Elections and Congress Problems

One test of the importance of a group or party, or at any rate of its hold on the people, is an election. During the general elections in India in 1937 the Hindu Mahasabha failed completely; it was nowhere in the picture. The Moslem League did better, but on the whole its showing was poor, especially in the predominantly Moslem provinces. In the Punjab and Sind it failed completely, in Bengal it met with only partial success. In the North-West Frontier Province, Congress formed a ministry later. In the Moslem minority provinces the League met with greater success on the whole, but there were also independent Moslem groups as well as Moslems elected as Congressmen.

Then began a remarkable campaign on behalf of the Moslem League against the Congress governments in the provinces and the Congress organization itself. Day after day it was repeated that these governments were committing "atrocities" on the Moslems. Those governments contained Moslem ministers also, but they were not members of the Moslem League. What these "atrocities" were it was not usually stated; or some petty local incidents, which had nothing to do with the government, were distorted and magnified. Some minor errors of some departments, which were soon rectified, became "atrocities". Sometimes entirely false and baseless charges were made.... [A] report was issued, fantastic in its contents and having little to do with any facts. Congress governments invited those who made the charges to supply particulars for investigation or to come and inquire themselves with government help. No one took advantage of these offers. But the campaign continued unchecked.[2]

[On Congress problems, November 4, 1937.] Our past history has been an agitational history and we have developed as a semi-revolutionary organisation. By our day to day activities and especially through the great mass movements that the Congress has undertaken, we have released an

[1] E.M.I., pp. 290–92.
[2] D.I., pp. 391–92.

enormous amount of energy among our people. That energy represents the strength of the nation, provided it is not frittered away, but is directed in a disciplined way to consciously held objectives. To some extent it was directed in the past to constructive activity but the background was largely agitational. That background has still to remain as our struggle for freedom is likely to bring in the future severe conflicts with British imperialism. Nevertheless the acceptance of office and responsibility and the formation of Congress Ministries have changed considerably the aspect of our work. Our general attitude to these Ministries cannot be agitational in the old sense of the word; we cannot agitate against ourselves. We may and should, when necessity arises, criticise them or press them to further the Congress programme, but that criticism must be friendly and co-operative criticism. Any unfriendly or hostile attitude to them must inevitably react on the Congress organisation and weaken it. Hostile criticism must logically lead to the changing or the ending of [a] Ministry. Circumstances might arise when this is necessary, and when this happens we shall take the step deliberately and after full consideration, realising the consequences which will flow from our action. To indulge in any action on the spur of sentiment and without thought of the consequences is likely to lead us to trouble, out of which it may be difficult to extricate ourselves.

It is not an easy matter for the Congress organisation, with its vast membership and past traditions, to adapt itself to new conditions. Contradictions and conflicts are inherent in the situation, yet perhaps we may tone them down to some extent with some more experience and adjust ourselves to the new scheme of things. But that scheme has no permanence in it for our very acceptance of office is limited and circumscribed by our pledge to combat and end the new Constitution, and to produce the conditions and the strength in the nation for a Constituent Assembly to meet and frame the constitution for an independent India.[1]

The Congress Reiterates Its Attitude Toward Minorities and Fundamental Rights in Working Committee Resolution— October, 1937

"The Congress has solemnly and repeatedly declared its policy in regard to the rights of the minorities in India and has stated that it considers it its duty to protect these rights and ensure the widest possible scope for

[1] I.A.R. (Vol. 11, 1937), pp. 334–35.

the development of these minorities and their participation in the fullest measure in the political, economic and cultural life of the nation.

"The objective of the Congress is an independent and united India where no class or group or majority or minority may exploit another to its own advantage, and where all the elements in the nation may co-operate together for the common good and the advancement of the people of India.

"This objective of unity and mutual co-operation in a common freedom does not mean the suppression in any way of the rich variety and cultural diversity of Indian life, which have to be preserved in order to give freedom and opportunity to the individual as well as to each group to develop unhindered according to its capacity and inclination." [1]

Boycott of Japanese Goods : Resolution Passed by All-India Congress Committee—Calcutta, October, 1937

"The All-India Congress Committee view with grave concern and horror the imperialist aggression of Japan in China attended with wanton cruelty and the bombing of the civil population.

"The Committee express their deep admiration for the brave and heroic struggle which the Chinese people are conducting against heavy odds for maintaining the integrity and the independence of their country and congratulate them on achieving internal unity in the face of national danger.

"The Committee offer their heartfelt sympathy to the Chinese people in their national calamity and, on behalf of the people of India, assure them of their solidarity with them in their struggle for maintaining their freedom.

"The Committee, further, call upon the Indian people to refrain from the use of Japanese goods as a mark of their sympathy with the people of China." [2]

4 | 1937—An Anonymous Article

I felt that I could no longer carry on as a responsible member of the Executive [Committee of Congress] but I decided not to do anything to

[1] I.A.A., p. 120.
[2] Ibid., p. 119.

precipitate a crisis. My term of office as Congress president was drawing to an end, and I could drop out quietly. . . . I had been president for two successive years and three times in all. There was some talk of my being elected for another term, but I was quite clear in my own mind that I should not stand. About this time I played a little trick which amused me greatly. I wrote an article, which was published anonymously in the *Modern Review* of Calcutta, in which I opposed my own re-election. No one, not even the editor, knew who had written it, and I watched with great interest its reaction on my colleagues and others.[1]

[Nehru wrote the following "Anonymous Article", published in the *Modern Review* in November, 1937. It was entitled "The Rashtrapati", and was signed with the pseudonym "Chanakya".]

"Rashtrapati Jawaharlal ki Jai!" The Rashtrapati looked up as he passed swiftly through the waiting crowds, his hands went up and were joined together in salute and his pale hard face was lit up by a smile. It was a warm personal smile and the people who saw it responded to it immediately and smiled and cheered in return.

The smile passed away and again the face became stern and sad, impassive in the midst of the emotion that it had roused in the multitude. Almost it seemed that the smile and the gesture accompanying it had little reality behind them; they were just tricks of the trade to gain the goodwill of the crowds whose darling he had become. Was it so?

Watch him again. There is a great procession and tens of thousands of persons surround his car and cheer him in an ecstasy of abandonment. He stands on the seat of the car balancing himself rather well, straight and seemingly tall, like a god, serene and unmoved by the seething multitude. Suddenly there is that smile again, or even a merry laugh, and the tension seems to break and the crowd laughs with him not knowing what it is laughing at. He is godlike no longer but a human being claiming kinship and comradeship with the thousands who surround him, and the crowd feels happy and friendly and takes him to its heart. But the smile is gone and the pale stern face is there again.

Is all this natural or the carefully thought out trickery of the public man? Perhaps it is both and long habit has become second nature now. The most effective pose is one in which there seems to be least of posing, and Jawaharlal has learnt well to act without the paint and powder of the actor. With his seeming carelessness and insouciance, he performs on the

[1] T.F., pp. 362–63.

public stage with consummate artistry. Whither is this going to lead him and the country? What is he aiming at with all his apparent want of aim? What lies behind that mask of his, what desires, what will to power, what insatiate longings?

These questions would be interesting in any event; for Jawaharlal is a personality which compels interest and attention. But they have a vital significance for us, for he is bound up with the present in India, and probably the future, and he has the power in him to do great good to India or great injury. We must therefore seek answers to these questions.

For nearly two years now he has been President of the Congress and some people imagine that he is just a camp-follower in the Working Committee of the Congress, suppressed or kept in check by others. And yet steadily and persistently he goes on increasing his personal prestige and influence both with the masses and with all manner of groups and people. He goes to the peasant and the worker, to the zamindar and the capitalist, to the merchant and the peddler, to the Brahmin and the untouchable, to the Muslim, the Sikh, the Parsi, the Christian and the Jew—to all those who make up the great variety of Indian life. To all these he speaks in a slightly different language, ever seeking to win them over to his side. With an energy that is astonishing at his age, he has rushed about across this vast land of India, and everywhere he has received the most extraordinary of popular welcomes. From the far North to Cape Comorin he has gone like some triumphant Caesar passing by, leaving a trail of glory and a legend behind him. Is all this for him just a passing fancy which amuses him, or some deep design or the play of some force which he himself does not know? Is it his will to power of which he speaks in his autobiography that is driving him from crowd to crowd and making him whisper to himself:

I drew these tides of men into my hands and wrote my will across the sky in stars.

What if the fancy turn? Men like Jawaharlal with all their capacity for great and good work are unsafe in [a] democracy. He calls himself a democrat and a socialist, and no doubt he does so in all earnestness, but every psychologist knows that the mind is ultimately a slave to the heart and that logic can always be made to fit in with the desires and irrepressible urges of man. A little twist and Jawaharlal might turn a dictator sweeping aside the paraphernalia of a slow-moving democracy. He might still use the language and slogans of democracy and socialism, but we all know how fascism has fattened on this language and then cast it away as useless lumber.

Jawaharlal is certainly not a fascist either by conviction or by temperament. He is far too much of an aristocrat for the crudity and vulgarity of fascism. His very face and voice tell us that:

> "*Private faces in public places*
> *are better and nicer than*
> *Public faces in private places.*"

The fascist face is a public face and it is not a pleasant face in public or private. Jawaharlal's face as well as his voice are definitely private. There is no mistaking that even in a crowd, and his voice at public meetings is an intimate voice which seems to speak to individuals separately in a matter-of-fact homely way. One wonders as one hears it or sees that sensitive face what lies behind them, what thoughts and desires, what strange complexes and repressions, what passions suppressed and turned to energy, what longings which he dare not acknowledge even to himself. The train of thought holds him in public speech, but at other times his looks betray him for his mind wanders away to strange fields and fancies and he forgets for a moment his companion and holds inaudible converse with the creatures of his brain. Does he think of the human contacts he has missed on his life's journey, hard and tempestuous as it has been; does he long for them? Or does he dream of the future of his fashioning and of the conflicts and triumphs that he would fain have? He must know well that there is no resting by the wayside on the path he has chosen, and that even triumph itself means greater burdens. As Lawrence said to the Arabs:

> "*There can be no rest houses for revolt, no dividend of joy paid out.*"

Joy may not be for him, but something greater than joy may be his if fate and fortune are kind—the fulfilment of a life purpose.

Jawaharlal cannot become a fascist. And yet he has all the makings of a dictator in him—vast popularity, a strong will directed to a well-defined purpose, energy, pride, organizational capacity, ability, hardness, and, with all his love of the crowd, an intolerance of others and a certain contempt for the weak and inefficient. His flashes of temper are well-known and even when they are controlled, the curling of the lips betrays him. His overmastering desire to get things done, to sweep away what he dislikes and build anew, will hardly brook for long the slow processes of democracy. He may keep the husk but he will see to it that it bends to his will. In normal times he would just be an efficient and successful executive, but in this revolutionary epoch Caesarism is always at the door, and is it not possible that Jawaharlal might fancy himself as a Caesar?

Therein lies danger for Jawaharlal and for India. For it is not through Caesarism that India will attain freedom, and though she may prosper a little under a benevolent and efficient despotism she will remain stunted and the day of the emancipation of her people will be delayed.

For two consecutive years Jawaharlal has been President of the Congress and in some ways he has made himself so indispensable that there are many who suggest that he should be elected for a third term. But a greater disservice to India and to Jawaharlal himself can hardly be done. By electing him a third time we shall exalt one man at the cost of the Congress and make the people think in terms of Caesarism. We shall encourage in Jawaharlal the wrong tendencies and increase his conceit and pride. He will become convinced that he alone can bear this burden or tackle India's problems. Let us remember that in spite of his apparent indifference to office he has managed to hold important offices in the Congress for the last seventeen years. He must imagine that he is indispensable, and no man must be allowed to think so. India cannot afford to have him as President of the Congress for a third year in succession.

There is a personal reason also for this. In spite of his brave talk Jawaharlal is obviously tired and stale and he will progressively deteriorate if he continues as President. He cannot rest, for he who rides a tiger cannot dismount. But we can at least prevent him from going astray and from mental deterioration under too heavy burdens and responsibilities. We have a right to expect good work from him in the future. Let us not spoil that and spoil him by too much adulation and praise. His conceit, if any, is already formidable. It must be checked. We want no Caesars.[1]

[According to Nehru, no one except his daughter, Indira, suspected that it was he who had written the above article about himself. Although it had no effect whatever on the forthcoming Congress Presidential election (Nehru was not standing for election), it did, temporarily, at least, serve as an outlet for his own pent-up emotions.]

[1] M.R. (Nov. 1937), pp. 546-47.

5	Statement on Congress Position in Event of War, 1938—Haripura Congress Session— Calcutta Congress Resolution

Statement on Congress Position in Event of War—January, 1938

[Nehru continued to be plagued by the problem of how to reconcile his desire simultaneously to combat totalitarianism and imperialism.]

In the world-wide conflict of ideas and politics, India stands for democracy and against Fascism and the totalitarian state. She stands for peace and cooperation between nations and ultimately the building up of a world order.

Will an independent India be strong enough to protect herself from outside aggression and invasion? If India is strong enough to gain her freedom from British imperialism, which has so long been entrenched on her soil, it seems to follow that she will also be strong enough to resist fresh aggression. The strength of a nation is a relative affair, depending on a host of internal and external factors. Most independent countries today are not strong enough to stop by themselves the aggression of a Great Power. Even a Great Power might succumb to a combination of other Great Powers. Probably the United States is the only country so fortunately situated and so strong in every way as to be able to hope to resist successfully almost any hostile combination. The others rely for their independence partly on their own strength, but more so on a combination of circumstances.

India will, of course, take all necessary steps to strengthen her defences. For this she has the industrial and other necessary resources. Her policy will be one of friendship to her neighbours and others, and she will rigorously avoid conflict. The National Congress has already declared that in the event of Britain being involved in an imperialist war, India will not be a party to it. There is no doubt that India can build up a strong defence apparatus. Her army today, though lacking in Indian officers, is considered an efficient force.[1]

[1] U.I., pp. 23–24.

From Haripura Congress Resolution on "Foreign Policy and War Danger"—February, 1938

"The people of India desire to live in peace and friendship with their neighbours and with all other countries, and for this purpose wish to remove all causes of conflict between them. Striving for their own freedom and independence as a nation, they desire to respect the freedom of others and to build up their strength on the basis of international cooperation and goodwill. Such cooperation must be founded on a world order, and a free India will gladly associate itself with such an order and stand for disarmament and collective security. But world cooperation is impossible of achievement so long as the roots of international conflict remain and one nation dominates over another and imperialism holds sway. In order, therefore, to establish world peace on an enduring basis, imperialism and exploitation of one people by another must end.

"During the past few years there has been a rapid and deplorable deterioration in international relations, Fascist aggression has increased and unabashed defiance of international obligations has become the avowed policy of the Fascist Powers. British foreign policy, in spite of its evasions and indecisions, has consistently supported the Fascist Powers in Germany, Spain and the Far East, and must, therefore, largely shoulder the responsibility for progressive deterioration of the world situation. That policy still seeks an arrangement with Nazi Germany, and has developed closer relations with rebel Spain. It is helping in the drift towards an imperialist world war."[1]

"India can be no party to such an imperialist war, and will not permit her man-power and resources to be exploited in the interests of British imperialism. Nor can India join any war without the express consent of her people. The Congress, therefore, entirely disapproves of the war preparations being made in India and large-scale manoeuvres and air-raid precautions by which it has been sought to spread an atmosphere of approaching war in India. In the event of an attempt being made to involve India in war, this will be resisted."[2]

[Congress reiterated its concern about the brutal invasion of China, and its previous calls upon "the people of India to refrain from purchasing Japanese goods".[3]]

From Speech, Haripura Congress Session

[Although Nehru was not Congress President in 1938, he nevertheless addressed the February Haripura Congress Session.]

[1] I.A.A., p. 123-24.
[2] P.A.I., pp. 27-28.
[3] I.A.A., p. 123.

Obviously for an Indian [collective security has no meaning if it] involves the subjection of India. Similarly, for any person who is a subject, he is not very much interested in assisting to maintain a *status quo* which involves his subjection. Yet . . . conditions may arise when it may be to our advantage to get rid of that subjection and support collective security at the same time. I cannot lay down a hard and fast rule. No practical politician can do that long beforehand, and in speaking to you I am not prepared to do that. I have functioned for many years as what might be called an agitator. At the same time the time has come in India when, though we have still to function as agitators, we have to think in terms of a free India and advise accordingly. Now to-day, suppose I go and put a certain thing before Congress and it adopts it, it will mean that millions of people will follow that advice. It is no light burden that the Congress has to carry when it shoulders this tremendous responsibility. Therefore I am not prepared to say exactly how under a certain set of circumstances we shall certainly act, but I am prepared to tell you that we are prepared to act only with one [objective] before us—the independence of India. But also, because we do believe and we are convinced that this isolated national independence is out of date and cannot exist for long in future, we cannot always consider problems in terms of isolated national independence. We have to consider them in a larger way. If we think only in terms of national independence I feel that we will act narrowly and ineffectively. The Indian National Congress must think in larger terms, must think of the greater perils that are overshadowing the world and try to avert those perils.[1]

Resolution—Congress Working Committee— Calcutta, April 2, 1938

"Resolved that in view of the critical international situation and the possibilities of crises which must involve India's interests, a foreign affairs committee, consisting of the Congress President, the general Secretary and Mr Jawaharlal Nehru be appointed . . . [to] keep in touch with the international situation . . . advise the Working Committee thereon, and take such steps as it might deem necessary to make clear to the people of foreign countries the Congress viewpoint and policy in regard to international affairs."[2]

[1] P.A.I., pp. 16–17.
[2] I.A.A., p. 127.

6 | Of Congress and the Muslims— Nehru–Jinnah, Muslim League–Congress Relationship—The Muslim League— Question of Language—Nehru–Jinnah Correspondence, 1938—Resumé of Attitude Toward Muslim League

Of Congress and the Muslims

[Although Jinnah appeared to favor more friendly relations with Congress —once he felt reassured by what he considered to be safeguards in the 1935 Government of India Act—communal strife and tensions between the Muslim League and Congress nevertheless increased after establishment of provincial self-government in 1937. During the same year Jinnah termed the 1935 Act a failure.

Since Nehru considered Jinnah's continuing request that the Muslim League be recognized as the sole representative of India's Muslims an untenable demand, and the two men disagreed about numerous other points as well, the schism between them continued to widen in the late 1930s.]

I. [January 10, 1937.] Mr Jinnah has in a recent utterance taken exception to my saying that essentially there were only two parties in the country— the Government and the Congress—and he has reminded me that there was a third party and that was the Indian Muslims. In the course of this speech he has made some remarkable statements. . . .

Mr Jinnah, it seems to me, has said something which surely is communalism raised to the nth power. . . . Carried to a logical conclusion [his] statement means that in no department of public activity must non-Muslims have anything to do with Muslim affairs. In politics and social and economic matters Muslims must function separately as a group and deal with other groups as one nation deals with another. So also in trade unions, peasant unions, business, Chambers of Commerce and like organisations and activities. Muslims in India are indeed a nation apart and those who forget this fact commit a sin against the Holy Ghost and offend Mr Jinnah.

Again, who are the Muslims? Apparently only those who follow Mr

Jinnah and the Muslim League. When Maulana Mohammad Ali [a Muslim leader] joined the Congress, Mr Jinnah tells us that he fought against the Muslims. It was a small matter that scores of thousands of Muslims were members of the Congress then and millions sympathised and cooperated with it. Being outside the fold of the Muslim League and not following Mr Jinnah's lead, they can be presumed to be other than Muslims. Presumably, according to Mr Jinnah, [other] powerful Muslim organisations in the Punjab and in Bengal . . . being outside the fold of the Muslim League, are not really Muslim. We have a new test of orthodoxy.

What exactly Mr Jinnah would like us of the Congress to do with the large numbers of Muslims in the Congress I do not know. Would he like us to ask them to resign and go on bended knee to him? And what shall I say to the great crowds of Muslim peasants and workers who come to listen to me?

All this seems to me extraordinary and harmful doctrine and most unjust to the Muslims. . . .

I am totally unable to think along these or any other communal lines, and with all deference to Mr Jinnah, may I suggest that such ideas are medieval and out of date. They bear no relation whatever to modern conditions and modern problems, which are essentially economic and political. Religion is both a personal matter and a bond of faith, but to stress religion in matters political and economic is obscurantism and leads to the avoidance of real issues. In what way are the interests of the Muslim peasant different from those of a Hindu peasant? Or those of a Muslim labourer or artisan or merchant or landlord or manufacturer different from those of his Hindu prototype? The ties that bind people are common economic interests, and, in the case of a subject country especially, a common national interest. Religious questions may arise and religious conflicts may take place, and they should be faced and settled. But the right way to deal with them is to limit their sphere of action and influence, and to prevent them from encroaching on politics and economics. To encourage a communal consideration of political and economic problems is to encourage reaction and go back to the Middle Ages. It is an impossible attempt for it ignores realities.

The realities of today are poverty and hunger and unemployment and the conflict between British imperialism and Indian nationalism. How are these to be considered communally?

There are of course many groups and parties and odd individuals in the country today. But, historically speaking, the present contest lies between imperialism and nationalism. All "third parties," middle and undecided groups, etc., have no real importance in this historic sense. They have consequently no great strength and they function only in elections and the like and fade away at other times. The Congress represents Indian nationalism and is thus charged with a historic destiny. Because of this, it is the only organisation which has developed a vast prestige in India and the strength and will to stand up against British imperialism. Thus, in the final analysis, there are only two forces in India today—British imperialism and the Congress representing Indian nationalism. There are other vital forces in the country, representing a new social outlook, but they are allied to the Congress. The communal groupings have no such real importance in spite of occasional importance being thrust upon them.

Mr Jinnah leads a party in the Legislative Assembly. The members of that party have shown the most remarkable independence of each other and of the party. Why is that so? Because no common principle or policy binds them and at the touch of any real problem they break apart. That must also be the inevitable fate of communal parties.

There is no question of dictators and camp followers. The Congress is a democratic organisation with its roots deep down in the Indian soil. Its doors are open to every Indian who believes in independence. For it the dominant issue is that of independence to enable us to get rid of poverty and the exploitation of the people. It may make mistakes but it tries always to think in terms of the nation and in terms of national freedom, and deliberately to avoid a narrower or a communal outlook.

What does the Muslim League stand for? Does it stand for the independence of India, for anti-imperialism? I believe not. It represents a group of Muslims, no doubt highly estimable persons but functioning in the higher regions of the upper middle classes and having no contacts with the Muslim masses and few even with the Muslim lower middle class. May I suggest to Mr Jinnah that I come into greater touch with the Muslim masses than most of the members of the Muslim League? I know more about their hunger and poverty and misery than those who talk in terms of percentages and seats in the Councils and places in the State service. I have had vast Muslim audiences in the Punjab and elsewhere. They did not ask me about the communal problem or percentages or separate electorates. They were intensely interested in the burden of land revenue or rent, of debt, of water rates, of unemployment, and the many other burdens they carry.

As President of the Congress I have [had] the honour and privilege to represent the innumerable Muslims throughout the country who have taken a valiant part in the struggle for freedom, who have suffered for the great cause of independence and who have stood shoulder to shoulder with others in our historic fight under the banner of the Congress. I represent the many brave Muslim comrades who still stand in the front ranks of our forces and who have been true to the Congress through the strain and stress of past years. I represent the hunger and poverty of the masses, Muslim as well as Hindu; the demand for bread and land and work and relief from innumerable burdens which crush them; the urge to freedom from an intolerable oppression. I represent all this because the Congress represents it, and I have been charged by the Congress to hold aloft its principles and the torch that it has lighted to bring hope and strength and brightness to the dark corners of our land and to the suffering hearts of our people.

The Congress welcomes all cooperation; it has repeatedly stressed the need for a joint front against imperialism. It will cooperate with pleasure with the Muslim League as with other organisations, but the basis of this cooperation must be anti-imperialism and the good of the masses. In its opinion no pacts and compromises between handfuls of upper class people, and ignoring the interests of the masses, have any real or permanent value. It is with the masses that it deals for it is concerned above all with their interests. But it knows that the masses, Hindu and Muslim, care little for communal questions. They demand urgently and insistently economic relief and, in order to obtain this, political freedom. On this broad basis there can be the fullest cooperation between all elements in the country who seek the good of the people as a whole and their freedom from imperialism.[1]

II. [April 4, 1937.] For various reasons the problem of increasing the Muslim element in the Congress has recently received considerable attention. This has been so both on the side of prominent Congressmen, Hindu and Muslim alike, and on the part of others who, though sympathetic, have hesitated to join the Congress. There is no doubt about it that Muslim India is in a state of ferment today. The Muslim masses inevitably think more and more in terms of common economic problems and common burdens together with others. As a reaction to these new currents certain prominent Muslims, connected with communal organisations, have tried to dissuade Muslims from joining the Congress and

[1] E.M.I., pp. 143-48.

have even hinted at dire consequences and catastrophes if this should happen. I have no desire to enter into these controversies which tend to become personal and in which irrelevant issues are often raised. It is not therefore with a view to controversy that I issue this statement, but I do feel that clarity of ideas is desirable and the Congress position should be clearly understood. I find that even Congressmen sometimes fail to appreciate this and talk in terms of pacts and compromises with Muslims or other religious groups.

The Congress is a political organisation dealing also inevitably with economic problems, for these problems affect the masses of India more than anything else. The objective of the Congress is political independence, that is, the capture of power by the people of India, irrespective of their religion. Every Indian of the hundreds of millions who inhabit this country must be a sharer in this power and must benefit by the new order that we strive for. For ultimately it is this order, which removes our crushing poverty and unemployment, which we work for. Subjection and poverty are the common lot of Indians whatever their religion might be; freedom and economic and cultural betterment must also be the common lot of all of us. In the struggle to obtain this the Congress offers a common platform to all, and because it thinks in terms of the masses and their betterment, it goes to them, organises them, advises them, seeks strength and guidance from them.

The Congress, being a political organisation, does not concern itself with religion or connected matters. But religion and culture being important matters in the life of many individuals, it is right that they should want to know how these are viewed by the Congress. Therefore the Congress declared at Karachi and subsequently in the clearest language, that the fundamental and basic rights of all Indians must contain provisions for the free exercise of religion, for freedom of conscience, for the protection of the culture, language and script of minorities, and further that all citizens whatever their religion or caste or sex, were equal before the law and in regard to public employment, office, trade or calling. The franchise must be on the basis of universal adult suffrage.

This assurance has been repeated in the Congress election manifesto and is the basis of all Congress policy. It applies to all majorities and minorities alike and it is unthinkable that the Congress will ever vary it.

Having given this solemn assurance, the Congress has nothing further to do with religious or cultural matters and it pursues its political struggle. In this political struggle it has gained great power because millions of people have sided with it, approved of its programme, and looked to it for deliverance from their thraldom and misery. That programme was a common programme for all Indians whatever their religious persuasions may be. The development of the nationalist movement has crystallised power in two opposing ranks and we have in India today two dominating forces: Congress India, representing Indian nationalism, and British Imperialism. I have often been made to say in the public press, owing to a mistranslation, that there were only two parties in India. That is manifestly wrong for there may be, and are, any number of parties, big or small, important or confined to a handful. But what I have said, and what I think is true, is that there are two principal forces in India today, that of the Congress and that of imperialism. Others incline during a crisis towards the one or the other, or are mere lookers-on and do not count. We have had big crises and conflicts in the past and, as is the way with nations and communities, we have gained strength and self-reliance thereby. Out of the fiery furnace of a nation's suffering and conflict, the Congress has steeled itself and risen higher and higher, strong in the love and strength of our millions. Those who kept out of it and relied on the feeble prop of an alien and vanishing government, remain themselves feeble, without self-reliance or strength, unable to charge themselves with the energy of a nation on the move.

Strength does not come to a nation or a community from mere numbers, or special seats in the legislatures, or protection given by outsiders. It comes from within and from the cooperation and goodwill of comrades in a common cause. The minorities in India will not flourish by being spoon-fed from above but by their own merits and strength. Can anyone imagine that any majority in India can crush the brave Sikhs, small as they are in numbers? Only a lunatic can think that the Muslims can be dominated and coerced by any religious majority in India. . . .

To think in terms of communal groups functioning politically is to think in terms of medievalism. And this is the reason why communal groups in India fail so dismally in the political field; they have and can have no common political or economic policy; they split up and are usually dominated by reactionaries. Having no inner strength they look inevitably to favours from the imperialist masters. And what are those favours? A few State jobs, a few seats in the legislatures. How does this affect the hunger of the millions or the unemployment of vast numbers? . . .

We talk of approaching the Muslim masses. That is no new programme for us although the stress may be new. That is part of our principal programme of developing increasing contacts with the masses, whether they are Hindu or Muslim, Sikh or Christian or any others. . . . We think of them not as religious units but as suffering units of the hungry Indian masses who cry loudly for succour.

It must be remembered that the Congress has always had large numbers of Muslims in its fold, and larger numbers have sympathised with its activities. Some of the most eminent of our national leaders have been and are Muslims. But it is true that the Muslim masses have been largely neglected by us in recent years. We want to repair that omission and carry the message of the Congress to them. Why do others object to this? If they disagree with the political or economic policy of the Congress, they are at perfect liberty to place their policy before the masses. But it is to the masses that the appeal must be made.

This is important, the appeal to the masses. Our problems cannot be solved, we hold, by a few people at the top. And that is why we have lost faith in the old style All Parties Conferences, in a few persons, representing communal organisations with no common political background, meeting together and discussing and quarrelling. We have had enough experience of these in the past and that experience does not call for repetition. We are of course always willing to discuss our problems with all who earnestly desire their solution, whether they agree with us or not.

Those who talk of the Congress entering into a pact or alliance with Muslims or others fail to understand the Congress or the new forces that are moving our people. We have already made a great pact amongst ourselves, amongst all who desire national and economic freedom, to work together to this common end. The Muslims are in this pact just as the Hindus and Sikhs and so many Christians. They are there as Indians, and if they have problems *inter se*, as they must have occasionally, they will discuss them and decide them democratically within the great organisation which has come to represent to such a remarkable degree the will of the Indian people. Is it not better and more dignified to do this than to seek favours from and take deputations to, our alien rulers who dominate over us, and seek to play off one against the other?

When we have gained our freedom, that is the only possible and democratic way for us. And even now, in the course of our struggle for freedom that is the only way.

Some people suggest that semi-communal nationalist parties should be formed, like a Muslim Congress Party. That seems to me a wrong course and one which will encourage communalism and injure the larger cause. . . . Such half-way groupings confuse the issue and the masses are perplexed. Those who disagree with the Congress will of course form their groups and parties. But those who agree should not stand on the doorstep; they should enter the nation's chamber and take full share in shaping the nation's policy. There are many today who talk vaguely of being Congressmen and of being in favour of independence. But they work through other and communal organisations and waste their strength thereby.

The crisis deepens and the people of India will soon have to make many fateful decisions. Already these petty and unreal problems, communal and the like, shade off into the background, and the real issues, pregnant with destiny, overshadow India and the world. What will our answer be, whether we are Hindus or Muslims or Sikhs or Christians? Shall we stick to our little ways, lost in a wilderness of pettiness? Or will we, united and firm of purpose, take the shaping of events in our strong hands and make the history of our choice?[1]

III. [May 2, 1937.] I agree with [Jinnah] that the Muslim League is a political organisation and often acts on the political plane. But because it is confined to a religious group it is like others of its kind, essentially a religious or communal organisation. I can fully understand and appreciate a religious or cultural organisation acting on a religious or cultural plane only. I can also understand a political organisation acting politically, whatever its views might be. But to mix the two is to create confusion and prevent the proper decision of any issue. Mr Jinnah tells us that the Muslim League is a political organisation and its policy and programme differ in vital respects from that of the Congress. The mere fact that a person is born to or professes the faith of Islam does not surely mean that he must also conform to the political policy and programme of the Muslim League. If he disagrees with that policy, as large numbers of Muslims do, he must inevitably seek some other political organisation whose policy and programme appeal to him. If he agrees with the Congress policy he will join it and function through it politically. That does not mean that he wants the disruption of Muslims. He is merely acting as politically thinking people act. Obviously there are great differences of political opinion *inter se* among Muslims, Hindus, Sikhs, Christians, Parsees, etc. Among each of these religious groups one may find Congressmen, socialists, anti-socialists, communists, liberals, direct actionists, revolutionaries, moderates, extremists, believers in different kinds of economic theory. . . . These cleavages of political and economic opinion are rightly represented by political and economic parties in the public life of the country. But to

[1] Ibid., pp. 149–55.

form a religious or communal party, which also dabbles in political and economic matters, cuts across these real cleavages of opinion on live issues and thus is an unreal party in the political sense. Or else it partly represents, as the Muslim League or Hindu Sabha or Sikh League may claim to represent, a certain section of a religious group which holds by certain political and economic theories. But even this it does not do with clarity and precision as it is always talking in terms of a religious group which, by its very nature, is a politically mixed one.

I do not agree with the policy of the Liberal Party but I can understand it. It is a political party which bases its appeal on a certain political theory and its doors are open to all, Hindus or Muslims or others, who agree with that theory. Not so the Muslim League or the Hindu Sabha.

Mr Jinnah has failed to understand me if he thinks that I am out to destroy other parties. But, because I believe in the Congress policy and programme, I try my hardest to push that forward and to convert all others, Muslims, Hindus, Christians, Sikhs, etc., to that viewpoint. Mr Jinnah, or the Liberals, or any other individual or group, are perfectly entitled to push their policy forward in the same way. Why then does Mr Jinnah object to my working amongst the Muslims for the spread of Congress ideals? The objection is not political, it is communal, and hence the confusion of thought and action. When Mr Jinnah talks of the Musalmans, or warns them to do this or that, he is not speaking politically but communally. He is presuming that all Musalmans must inevitably think on the same political lines and these should be in accordance with the policy laid down by him and the Muslim League. Surely that is a large presumption.

Mr Jinnah thinks that the Congress policy is wrong and harmful. I think likewise of his policy. We differ. Let us agree to differ and work democratically for the spread of our respective viewpoints. I would gladly welcome Mr Jinnah as the leader of a purely political party open to all denominations and with a defined policy. Political and economic issues will then be placed clearly before the country and the people of the country, who will ultimately decide these issues, will be enabled to think about them on right lines. . . .

When Mr Jinnah says, quite rightly, that the Muslim League differs in vital respects from the Congress in political matters, does he expect the Congress, including the Muslims who agree with the Congress, to give up its policy, in deference to the Muslim League, a policy which has been a beacon-light to us and to millions in this country these many years, and for which so many of us have gone repeatedly through the valley of the shadow? Mr Jinnah knows that in the hour of our trial when we faced the might of a proud empire, many prominent leaders of the Muslim League sought alliance with the die-hard leaders of the Conservative Party in England, than whom there are no greater enemies of Indian freedom. Are we to submit to them now, we who have refused to submit to the embattled power of that Empire, and who prepare afresh for fresh trials and tribulations in the struggle for independence which has become the life-blood of all our activities?

Mr Jinnah refers apparently to my faith in socialism. It is true that I desire to put an end to imperialism all over the world and I look forward to the establishment of a socialist State not only in India but elsewhere also. I believe in a world order based on the principles of socialism, and I am convinced that only thus will the distempers and miseries that afflict us find final burial. But the Congress is not committed to this creed or policy. Nevertheless the Congress thinks and acts in terms of the masses, Hindu or Muslim or other, seeks strength from them, and determines its policy with reference to them. Therefore it considers that even political adjustments with minorities will have a surer and more real basis if the masses are enabled to have their say in the matter.

Do I talk like a dictator or a sovereign authority? It is for others to judge. But may I venture to say that Mr Jinnah when he objects to our carrying on our ordinary political work amongst Muslims, or issues mandates and warnings to Musalmans as a whole, regardless of their political opinions or affiliations, adopts an attitude which may, without impropriety, be called dictatorial?[1]

Nehru–Jinnah, Congress–Muslim League Relationship of the Period

When I was Congress president [in 1936, 1937], I wrote to Mr Jinnah on several occasions and requested him to tell us exactly what he would like us to do. I asked him what the League wanted and what its definite objectives were. I also wanted to know what the grievances of the League were against the Congress governments. The idea was that we might clarify matters by correspondence and then discuss personally the important points that had arisen in it. Mr Jinnah sent me long replies but failed to enlighten me. It was extraordinary how he avoided telling me, or anyone else, exactly what he wanted or what the grievances of the

[1] Ibid., pp. 155-60.

League were. Repeatedly we exchanged letters, and yet always there was the same vagueness and inconclusiveness and I could get nothing definite. This surprised me very much and made me feel a little helpless. It seemed as if Mr Jinnah did not want to commit himself in any way and was not at all eager for a settlement.

Subsequently Gandhiji and others among us met Mr Jinnah several times. They talked for hours but never got beyond a preliminary stage. Our proposal was that representatives of the Congress and the League should meet and discuss all their mutual problems. Mr Jinnah said that this could only be done after we recognized publicly that the Moslem League was the sole representative organization of the Moslems of India, and the Congress should consider itself a purely Hindu organization. This created an obvious difficulty. We recognized, of course, the importance of the League, and because of that we had approached it. But how could we ignore many other Moslem organizations in the country, some closely associated with us? Also there were large numbers of Moslems in the Congress itself and among our highest executives. To admit Mr Jinnah's claim meant in effect to push out our old Moslem colleagues from the Congress and declare that the Congress was not open to them. It was to change the fundamental character of the Congress, and from a national organization, open to all, convert it into a communal body. That was inconceivable for us. If the Congress had not already been there, we would have had to build up a new national organization open to every Indian.

We could not understand Mr Jinnah's insistence on this and refusing to discuss any other matter. Again we could only conclude that he did not want any settlement, nor did he want to commit himself in any way. He was satisfied in letting matters drift and in expecting that he could get more out of the British government this way.

Mr Jinnah's demand was based on a new theory he had recently propounded—that India consisted of two nations, Hindu and Moslem. Why only two I do not know, for if nationality was based on religion, then there were many nations in India. Of two brothers one may be a Hindu, another a Moslem; they would belong to two different nations. These two nations existed in varying proportions in most of the villages of India. They were nations which had no boundaries; they overlapped. A Bengali Moslem and a Bengali Hindu, living together, speaking the same language and having much the same traditions and customs, belonged to different nations. All this was very difficult to grasp; it seemed a reversion to some medieval theory. What a nation is it is difficult to define. Possibly the essential characteristic of national consciousness is a sense of belonging together and of together facing the rest of mankind. How far that is present in India as a whole may be a debatable point. It may even be said that India developed in the past as a multinational state and gradually acquired a national consciousness. But all these are theoretical abstractions which hardly concern us. Today the most powerful states are multinational, but at the same time developing a national consciousness, like the U.S.A. or the U.S.S.R.

From Mr Jinnah's two-nation theory developed the conception of Pakistan, or splitting up of India. That of course did not solve the problem of the "two nations", for they were all over the place. But that gave body to a metaphysical conception. This again gave rise to a passionate reaction among many in favor of the unity of India. Ordinarily national unity is taken for granted. Only when it is challenged or attacked or attempts are made to disrupt it, is unity really appreciated, and a positive reaction to maintain it takes place. Thus sometimes attempts at disruption actually help to weld that unity.

There was a fundamental difference between the outlook of the Congress and that of the religious-communal organizations. Of the latter the chief were the Moslem League and its Hindu counterpart, the Hindu Mahasabha. These communal organizations, while in theory standing for India's independence, were more interested in claiming protection and special privileges for their respective groups. They had inevitably to look to the British government for such privileges, and this led them to avoid conflict with it. The Congress outlook was so tied up with India's freedom as a united nation that everything else was secondary, and this meant ceaseless conflict or friction with the British power. Indian nationalism, as represented by the Congress, opposed British imperialism. The Congress had further developed agrarian, economic, and social programs. Neither the Moslem League nor the Hindu Mahasabha had ever considered any such question or attempted to frame a program. Socialists and Communists were of course intensely interested in such matters and had their own programs which they tried to push in the Congress as well as outside.

There was yet another marked difference between Congress policy and work and those of the religious-communal organizations. Quite apart from its agitational side and its legislative activity, when such existed, the Congress laid the greatest stress on certain constructive activities among the masses. These activities consisted in organizing and developing cottage industries, in raising the depressed classes, and later in the spread of basic education. Village work also included sanitation and some simple forms of medical relief. Separate organizations for carrying on these activities were created by the Congress, which functioned apart from the political plane, and which absorbed thousands of whole-time workers and a much larger number of part-time helpers. This quiet nonpolitical, constructive work was carried on even when political activities were at a low ebb; but even this was suppressed by government when there was open conflict with the Congress. The economic value of some of these activities was questioned by some people, but there could be no doubt of their social importance. They trained a large body of whole-time workers in intimate touch with the masses and produced a spirit of self-help and self-reliance among the people. Congressmen and -women also played an important part in trade-union and agrarian organizations, actually building up many of these. The largest and best organized trade union—that of the Ahmadabad textile industry—was started by Congressmen and worked in close co-operation with them.

All these activities gave a solid background to Congress work which was completely lacking in the religious-communal organizations. These latter functioned on the agitational plane only with fits and starts, or during elections. In them also was lacking that ever-present sense of risk and personal danger from government action which Congressmen had almost always to face. Thus there was a far greater tendency for careerists and opportunists to enter these organizations. The two Moslem organizations, the Ahrars and the Jamiat-ul-Ulema, however, suffered greatly from governmental repression because politically they often followed the same line as the Congress.

The Congress represented not only the nationalist urge of India, which had grown with the growth of the new bourgeoisie, but also, to a large extent, proletarian urges for social change. In particular it stood for revolutionary agrarian changes. This sometimes produced inner conflicts within the Congress, and the landlord class and the big industrialists, though often nationalistic, kept aloof from it for fear of socialistic changes. Within the Congress, socialists and communists found a place and could influence Congress policy. The communal organizations, whether Hindu or Moslem, were closely associated with the feudal and conservative elements and were opposed to any revolutionary social change. The real conflict had, therefore, nothing to do with religion, though religion often masked the issue, but was essentially between those who stood for a nationalist-democratic-socially revolutionary policy and those who were concerned with preserving the relics of a feudal regime. In a crisis, the

latter inevitably depend upon foreign support which is interested in preserving the status quo.[1]

The Muslim League

The Moslem League inevitably went more and more astray till it stood
openly against democracy in India and even for the partition of the
country. [It was] encouraged in these fantastic demands by British
officials, who wanted to exploit the Moslem League, as all other disruptive
forces, in order to weaken the Congress influence. It was astonishing that
just when it became obvious that small nations had no further place in
the world, except as parts of a federation of nations, there should be this
demand for a splitting up of India. Probably the demand was not seriously meant, but it was the logical consequence of the two-nation theory
that Mr Jinnah had advanced. The new development of communalism
had little to do with religious differences. These admittedly could be
adjusted. It was a political conflict between those who wanted a free,
united, and democratic India and certain reactionary and feudal elements
who, under the guise of religion, wanted to preserve their special interests.
Religion, as practiced and exploited in this way by its votaries of different
creeds, seemed to me a curse and a barrier to all progress, social and individual. Religion, which was supposed to encourage spirituality and
brotherly feeling, became the fountainhead of hatred, narrowness, mean-
ness, and the lowest materialism.[2]

The Question of Language—July 25, 1937

[Nehru's 1937 article, "The Question of Language", a copy of which he
had sent to Jinnah when it was first published, and which is mentioned
in the correspondence that follows, throws light on at least one pertinent
"communal" controversy that Nehru attempted to resolve.]

We have had during recent months a revival of the old controversy
between Hindu and Urdu, and high excitement has accompanied it and
charges and counter-charges have been flung about. A subject eminently
suited for calm and scholarly consideration and academic debate has been
dragged down to the level of the market-place, and communal passions

[1] D.I., pp. 395–99.
[2] T.F., p. 364–65.

have centred round it. Inevitably, many of the champions who have entered the field of battle have little to do with scholarship or the love of a language for its own sake; they have been chiefly concerned with Government orders and court procedure. Those who love language as the embodiment of culture, of airy thought caught in the network of words and phrases, of ideas crystallized, of fine shades of meaning, of the music and rhythm that accompany it, of the fascinating history and associations of its words, of the picture of life in all its phases, those to whom a language is dear because of all this and more, wondered at this vulgar argument and kept away from it.

And yet we cannot keep away from it or ignore it, for the question of language is an important one for us. It is not important because of that cry of the ignorant that India is a babel of tongues with hundreds and hundreds of languages. India, as everyone who looks round him can see, has singularly few languages considering its vast size, and these are intimately allied to each other. India has also one dominant and widespread language which, with its variations, covers a vast area and numbers its votaries by the hundred million. Yet the problem remains and has to be faced.

It has to be faced for the moment because of its communal and political implications. But that is a temporary matter and will pass. The real problem will remain: as to what policy we shall adopt in a scheme of general mass education and the cultural development of the people; how shall we promote the unity of India and yet preserve the rich diversity of our inheritance?

The question of language is ever one of great consequence for a people. Almost exactly three hundred years ago Milton, writing from Florence to a friend, emphasized this and said: "Nor is it to be considered of small consequence what language, pure or corrupt, a people has, or what is their customary degree of propriety in speaking it . . . for let the words of a country be in part unhandsome and offensive in themselves, in part debased by wear and wrongly uttered, and what do they declare, but, by no light indication, that the inhabitants of that country are an indolent, idly yawning race, with minds already long prepared for any amount of servility? On the other hand, we have never heard that any empire, any state, did not at least flourish in a middling degree as long as its own liking and care for its language lasted."

A living language is a throbbing, vital thing, ever changing, ever growing and mirroring the people who speak and write it. It has its roots in the masses, though its superstructure may represent the culture of a few. How, then, can we change it or shape it to our liking by resolutions or orders from above? And yet I find this widely prevalent notion that we can force a language to behave in a particular manner if we only will it so. It is true that under modern conditions, with mass education and mass propaganda through the Press, printed books, cinema, and the radio, a language can be varied much more rapidly than in past times. And yet that variation is but the mirror of the rapid changes taking place among the people who use it. If a language loses touch with the people, it loses its vitality and becomes an artificial, lifeless thing instead of the thing of life and strength and joy that it should be. Attempts to force the growth of a language in a particular direction are likely to end in distorting it and crushing its spirit.

What should be the policy of the State in regard to language? The Congress has briefly but clearly and definitely stated this in the resolution on Fundamental Rights: "The culture, language, and script of the minorities and of the different linguistic areas shall be protected." By this declaration the Congress is bound, and no minority or linguistic group can require a wider assurance. Further, the Congress has stated in its constitution, as well as in many resolutions, that, while the common language of the country should be Hindustani, the provincial languages should be dominant in their respective areas. A language cannot be imposed by resolution, and the Congress desires to develop a common language and carry on most of our work in the provincial languages would be pious wishes, ignored by the multitude, if they did not fit in with existing conditions and the needs of the situation. We have thus to see how far they so fit in.

Our great provincial languages are no dialects or vernaculars, as the ignorant sometimes call them. They are ancient languages with a rich inheritance, each spoken by many millions of persons, each tied up inextricably with the life and culture and ideas of the masses as well as of the upper classes. It is axiomatic that the masses can only grow educationally and culturally through the medium of their own language. Therefore it is inevitable that we lay stress on the provincial languages and carry on most of our work through them. The use of any other language will result in isolating the educated few from the masses and in retarding the growth of the people. Ever since the Congress took to the use of these provincial languages in carrying on its work we developed contacts with the masses rapidly and the strength and prestige of the Congress increased all over the country. The Congress message reached the most distant hamlet and the political consciousness of the masses grew. Our system of education and public work must therefore be based on the provincial languages.

What are these languages? Hindustani, of course, with its principal aspects of Hindi and Urdu, and its various dialects. Then there are Bengali, Marathi, and Gujrati, sister languages of Hindi and nearly allied to it. In the South there are Tamil, Telugu, Kannada, and Malayalam. Besides these there are Oriya, Assamese, and Sindhi, and Punjabi and Pushtu in the North-West. These dozen languages cover the whole of India, and of these Hindustani has the widest range and also claims a certain all-India character.

Without infringing in the least on the domain of the provincial languages, we must have a common all-India medium of communication. Some people imagine that English might serve as such, and to some extent English has served as such for our upper classes and for all-India political purposes. But this is manifestly impossible if we think in terms of the masses. We cannot educate millions of people in a totally foreign tongue. English will inevitably remain an important language for us because of our past associations and because of its present importance in the world. It will be the principal medium for us to communicate with the outside world, though I hope it will not be the only medium for this purpose. I think we should cultivate other foreign languages also, such as French, German, Russian, Spanish, Italian, Chinese, and Japanese. But English cannot develop into an all-India language, known by millions.[1]

The only possible all-India language is Hindustani. Already it is spoken by a hundred and twenty millions and partly understood by scores of millions of others. Even those who do not know it at all at present can learn it far more easily than a foreign language. There are many common words in all the languages of India, but what is far more important is the common cultural background of these languages, the similarity of ideas, and the many linguistic affinities. This makes it relatively easy for an Indian to learn another Indian language.

What is Hindustani? Vaguely we say that this word includes both Hindi and Urdu, as spoken and as written in the two scripts, and we endeavour to strike a golden mean between the two, and call this idea of

[1] See also Part One, Section 16.

17*

ours Hindustani. Is this just an idea with no reality for its basis, or is it something more?

There are many variations in Hindustani as spoken and written in various parts of Northern and Central India. Numerous dialects have arisen. But these are the inevitable consequences of want of education, and with mass education these dialects will tend to disappear and a certain standardization will set in.

There is the question of script. Devanagari and the Urdu script are utterly different from each other, and there is no possibility of either of them assimilating the other. Therefore wisely we have agreed that both should have full play. This will be an additional burden on those who have to learn both and it will encourage separatism to some extent. But we have to put up with these disadvantages, for any other course is not open to us. Both the scripts are part of the genius of our language, and around them have gathered not only literatures peculiar to the scripts, but also a wall of sentiment which is solid and irremovable. What the distant future will bring to us I do not know, but for the present both must remain.

The Latin script has been advocated as a solution of some of our linguistic difficulties. It is certainly more efficient than either Hindi or Urdu from the point of view of rapid work. In these days of the typewriter and duplicator and other mechanical devices the Latin script has great advantages over the Indian scripts, which cannot fully utilize these new devices. But in spite of these advantages I do not think there is the slightest chance of the Latin script replacing Devanagari or Urdu. There is the wall of sentiment, of course, strengthened even more by the fact that the Latin script is associated with our alien rulers. But there are more solid grounds also for its rejection. The scripts are essential parts of our literatures; without them we would be largely cut off from our old inheritance.

It may be possible, however, to reform our scripts to some extent. We have at present, besides Hindi and Urdu, the Bengali, Marathi, and Gujrati scripts, each of these three being very nearly allied to Devanagari. It should be easily possible to have a common script for these four languages. This need not necessarily be Devanagari exactly as it is written today, but a slight variation of it. The development of a common script for Hindi, Bengali, Gujrati, and Marathi would be a definite gain and would bring the four languages much nearer to each other.

I do not know how far it is possible for the Dravidian languages of the South to fit in with a northern script, or to evolve a common script for themselves. Those who have studied this might enlighten us on this point.

The Urdu script has to remain as it is, though some slight simplification of it might be attempted. It might easily absorb the Sindhi script, which is very similar to it.

Thus we ought to have later on two scripts: the composite Devanagari-Bengali-Marathi-Gujrati and the Urdu, and also, if necessary, a southern script. No attempt must be made to suppress any one of these, unless there is a possibility by general agreement of those concerned to fit in the southern languages with a northern script, which is likely to be Hindi or a slight variation of it.

Let us consider Hindustani both as the mother tongue of the North and Central India and as an all-India language. The two aspects are different and must be dealt with separately.

Hindi and Urdu are the two main aspects of this language. Obviously they have the same basis, the same grammar, the same fund of ordinary words to draw upon. They are, in fact, the same basic language. And yet the present differences are considerable, and one is said to draw its inspiration from Sanskrit and the other to some extent from Persian. To consider Hindi as the language of the Hindus and Urdu as that of the Muslims is absurd. Urdu, except for its script, is of the very soil of India and has no place outside India. It is even today the home language of large numbers of Hindus in the North.

The coming of Muslim rulers to India brought Persian as a Court language, and to the end of the Moghal period Persian continued to be so used. The language of the people in North and Central India continued to be Hindi throughout. Being a living language, it absorbed a number of Persian words; Gujrati and Marathi did likewise. But essentially Hindi remained Hindi. A highly Persianized form of Hindi developed round the imperial Courts, and this was called *Rekhta*. The word Urdu seems to have come into use during the Moghal period in the camps of the Moghals, but it appears to have been used almost synonymously with Hindi. It did not signify even a variation of Hindi. Right up to the Revolt of 1857, Urdu meant Hindi, except in regard to script. As is well known, some of the finest Hindi poets have been Muslims. Till this Revolt, and even for some time after, the usual term applied to the language was Hindi. This did not refer to the script, but to the language, the language of Hind. Muslims who wrote in the Urdu script usually called the language Hindi.

It was in the second half of the nineteenth century that the words Hindi and Urdu began to signify something different from each other.

This separatism grew. Probably it was a reflex of the rising national consciousness which first affected the Hindus, who began to lay stress on purer Hindi and the Devanagari script. Nationalism was for them inevitably at the beginning a form of Hindu nationalism. A little later the Muslims slowly developed their form of nationalism, which was Muslim nationalism, and they began to consider Urdu as their own particular preserve. Controversy centred round the scripts and their use in law courts and public offices. Thus the growing separatism in language and the conflict of scripts was the outcome of the growth of political and national consciousness, which to begin with took a communal turn. As this nationalism became truly national, thinking in terms of India and not in those of a particular community, the desire to stop this separatist tendency in language grew with it, and intelligent people began to lay stress on the innumerable common features of Hindi and Urdu. There was talk of Hindustani not only as the language of Northern and Central India, but as the national language of the whole country. But still, unfortunately, communalism is strong enough in India, and so the separatist tendency persists along with the unifying tendency. This separatism in language is bound to disappear with the fuller development of nationalism. It is well to bear this in mind, for only then shall we understand what the root cause of the evil is. Scratch a separatist in language and you will invariably find that he is a communalist, and very often a political reactionary.

Although the terms Hindi and Urdu were interchangeably used for a long time during the Moghal period, Urdu was applied more to the language of the mixed camps of the Moghals. Round about the Court and camp many Persian words were current, and these crept into the language. As one moves southwards, away from the centres of Moghal Court life, Urdu merges into purer Hindi. Inevitably this influence of the Courts affected the towns far more than the rural areas, and the towns of the North far more than the towns of Central India.

And this leads us to the real difference between Urdu and Hindi today—Urdu is the language of the towns and Hindi the language of the villages. Hindi is, of course, spoken also in the towns, but Urdu is almost entirely an urban language. The problem of bringing Urdu and Hindi nearer to each other thus becomes the much vaster problem of bringing the town and the village nearer to each other. Every other way will be a superficial way without lasting effect. Languages change organically when the people who speak them change.

While Hindi and Urdu of ordinary household speech do not differ much from each other, the gulf between the literary languages has grown in recent years. In written literary productions it is formidable, and this has led some people to believe that some evil-minded persons are the cause of it. That is a foolish fancy, though undoubtedly there are individuals who take delight in increasing separatist tendencies. But living languages do not function in this way, nor can they be twisted much by a few individuals. We have to look deeper for the causes of this apparent divergence.

This divergence, though unfortunate in itself, is really a sign of healthy growth. Both Hindi and Urdu, after a long period of stagnation, have woken up and are pushing ahead. They are struggling to give expression to new ideas, and leaving the old ruts for new forms of literary expression. The vocabulary of each is poor as far as these new ideas are concerned, but each can draw on a rich source. This source is Sanskrit in the one case and Persian in the other; and hence, as soon as we leave the ordinary language of the home or the market-place and enter more abstract regions, the divergences grow. Literary societies, jealous of the purity of the language they use, carry this tendency to extreme limits, and then accuse each other of encouraging separatist tendencies. The beam in one's own eye is not seen, the mote in the other's eye is obvious enough.

The immediate result of all this has been to increase the gulf between Hindi and Urdu, and sometimes it almost appears that the two are destined to develop into separate languages. And yet this fear is unjustified and there is no reason for alarm. We must welcome the new life that is coursing through both Hindi and Urdu, even though it might lead to a temporary widening of the gulf. Hindi and Urdu are both at present inadequate for the proper expression of modern ideas, scientific, political, economic, commercial, and sometimes cultural, and they are both trying hard, and with success, to enrich themselves so as to meet the needs of a modern community. Why should either be jealous of the other? We want our language to be as rich as possible, and this will not happen if we try to suppress either Hindi words or Urdu words because we feel that they do not fit in with our own particular backgrounds. We want both and we must accept both. We must realize that the growth of Hindi means the growth of Urdu and *vice versa*. The two will influence each other powerfully and the vocabulary and ideas of each will grow. But each must keep its doors and windows wide open for these words and ideas. Indeed, I would like Hindi and Urdu to welcome and absorb words and ideas from foreign languages and make them their own. It is absurd to coin new words from the Sanskrit or Persian for well-known and commonly used words in English or French or other foreign languages.

I have no doubt in my mind that Hindi and Urdu must come nearer to each other, and, though they may wear different garbs, will be essentially one language. The forces favouring this unification are too strong to be resisted by individuals. We have nationalism and the widespread desire to have a united India, and this must triumph. But stronger than this is the effect of rapid communications and transport and interchange of ideas and revolutionary changes going on in our political and social spheres. We cannot remain in our narrow grooves when the torrent of world change rushes past us. Education, when it spreads to the masses, will also inevitably produce standardisation and unification.

We must not, therefore, even look upon the separate development of Hindi and Urdu with suspicion. The enthusiast for Urdu should welcome the new spirit that is animating Hindi, and the lover of Hindi should equally appreciate the labours of those who seek to advance Urdu. They may work today along parallel lines somewhat separate from each other, but the two will coalesce. Nevertheless, though we tolerate willingly this existing separatism, we must help in the process of this unification. On what must this unity be based? Surely on the masses. The masses must be the common factor between Hindi and Urdu. Most of our present troubles are due to highly artificial literary languages cut off from the masses. When writers write, who do they write for? Every writer must have, consciously or subconsciously, an audience in his mind, whom he is seeking to influence or convert to his viewpoint. Because of our vast illiteracy, that audience has unhappily been limited, but even so it is big enough and it will grow rapidly. I am no expert in this matter, but my own impression is that the average writer in Hindi or Urdu does not seek to take advantage of even the existing audience. He thinks much more of the literary coteries in which he moves, and writes for them in the language that they have come to appreciate. His voice and his word do not reach the much larger public, and, if they happen to reach this public, they are not understood. Is it surprising that Hindi and Urdu books have restricted sales? Even our newspapers in Hindi and Urdu barely tap the great reading public because they, too, generally use the language of the literary coteries.

Our writers, therefore, must think in terms of a mass audience and clientele and must deliberately seek to write for them. This will result automatically in the simplification of language and the stilted and flowery phrases and constructions, which are always signs of decadence in a language, will give place to words of strength and power. We have not yet fully recovered from the notion that culture and literary attainments are the products and accompaniments of courtly circles. If we think in this way we remain confined in narrow circles and can find no entrance to the hearts and minds of the masses. Culture today must have a wider mass basis, and language, which is one of the embodiments of that culture, must also have that basis.

This approach to the masses is not merely a question of simple words and phrases. It is equally a matter of ideas and of the inner content of those words and phrases. Language which is to make [an] appeal to the masses must deal with . . . problems of those masses, with their joys and sorrows, their hopes and aspirations. It must represent and mirror the life of the people as a whole and not that of a small group at the top. Then only will it have its roots in the soil and find sustenance from it.

This applies not only to Hindi and Urdu, but to all our Indian languages. I know that in all of them these ideas are finding utterance, and they are looking more and more towards the masses. This process must be accelerated, and our writers should deliberately aim at encouraging it.

It is also desirable, I think, for our languages to cultivate contacts with foreign literatures by means of translations of both the old classics and modern books. This will put us in touch with cultural and literary and social movements in other countries and will strengthen our own languages by the infusion of fresh ideas.

I imagine that probably Bengali, of all Indian languages, has gone furthest in developing contacts with the masses. Literary Bengali is not something apart from and far removed from the life of the people of Bengal. The genius of one man, [Rabindranath] Tagore, has bridged that gap between the cultured few and the masses, and today his beautiful songs and poems are heard even in the humblest hut. They have not only added to the wealth of Bengali literature, but enriched the life of the people of Bengal, and made of their language a powerful medium of the finest literary expression in the simplest terms. We cannot produce geniuses for the asking, but we can all learn from this and shape our course accordingly. In this connection I should also like to mention Gujrati. I am told that Gandhiji's simple and powerful language has had a great influence on modern Gujrati writing.

Let us now consider the other aspect of Hindustani as an all-India language, bearing in mind that it is no rival to the great provincial languages and there is no question of its encroaching on them. For the moment let us set aside the question of script, for both scripts must have full play. We cannot, of course, insist on everyone learning both scripts; that would be an intolerable burden for the masses. The State should encourage both scripts and leave the persons concerned, or their parents, to choose between the two. Let us therefore consider the content of the language apart from its script.

Apart from its widespread range and dominance over India, Hindustani has certain other advantages as an all-India language. It is relatively easy to learn and its grammar is simple, except for the confusion of its genders. Can we simplify it still further?

We have a remarkably successful experiment to guide us, that of *Basic English*. A number of scholars, after many years' labour, have evolved a simplified form of English which is essentially English and indistinguishable from it, and yet which is astonishingly easy to learn. Grammar has almost disappeared except for a few simple rules, and the basic vocabulary has been reduced to about 850 words, excluding scientific, technical, and commercial terms. This whole vocabulary and grammar can be put down on one sheet of paper, and an intelligent person can learn it in two or three weeks. He will require practice, of course, in the use of the new language.

This experiment must not be confused with the many previous attempts to evolve a common world language—Volapuk, Esperanto, etc. All such languages, though simple, were highly artificial, and to learn them was an additional burden. The breath of life did not vitalize them and they could never become the languages of large numbers of people. Basic English, having all their advantages, does not suffer from this disadvantage, as it is a living language. Those who learn Basic English can not only have a simple and efficient means of communication with others, but they are already on the threshold of Standard English and can proceed further if they so wish.

My enthusiasm for Basic English might lead to the query, Why not have this as an all-India language? No, this cannot be, for the whole genius of this language is alien to our people and we would have to transplant them completely before we could impose this as an all-India language. The practical difficulties would also be far greater than in the case of Hindustani, which is already so widely known all over India.

But I think that where we teach English as a foreign tongue—and we shall have to do this on an extensive scale—Basic English should be taught. Only those who wish to make a special study of the language should proceed to Standard English.

Can we evolve a *Basic Hindustani* after the fashion of Basic English? I think this is easily possible if our scholars will turn their minds to this end. The grammar should be as simple as possible, almost non-existent, and yet it must not do violence to the existing grammar of the language. The essential thing to be borne in mind is that while this basic language is complete in itself for the expression of all non-technical ideas, it is yet a stepping-stone to the further study of the language. The vocabulary might consist of a thousand words or so, not chosen at random because they are common words in the Indian languages, but because they form a complete whole and require no extraneous assistance for all ordinary speaking and writing.

Such a Basic Hindustani should be the all-India language, and with a little effort from the State it will spread with extreme rapidity all over the country and will help in bringing about that national unity which we all desire. It will bring Hindi and Urdu closer together and will also help in developing an all-India linguistic unity. On that solid and common foundation, even if variations grow or diversions occur, they will not lead to separatism. Those who wish to add to their knowledge of Hindustani can easily do so; those who are content with knowing Basic Hindustani only can yet take part in the larger life of the nation.

I have said previously that we should not object to the development of Hindi or Urdu separately. The new words that come in from either direction will enrich our inheritance, if they are vital, living words forced on us by circumstances or coming up from the masses. But the formation of artificial words with no real sanction behind them has no such significance. To a large extent we have to form artificial words to meet the growing needs of our political, economic, scientific, and commercial life. In the formation of such words we should try to avoid duplication and separatism. We should be bold enough, I think, to lift bodily foreign technical words which have become current coin in many parts of the world, and to adopt them as Hindustani words. Indeed, I should like them to be adopted by all the Indian languages. This will make it easier for our people to read technical and scientific works in various languages, Indian and foreign. Any other course will lead to chaos and confusion in the mind of the student, who has to grapple with large numbers of technical terms, and who often has to read important books in other languages. An attempt to have a separate and distinct scientific vocabulary is to isolate and stultify our scientific growth and to put an intolerable burden on the teacher and taught alike. The public life and affairs of the world are already closely knit together and form a single whole. We should make it as easy as possible for our people to understand them and take part in them, and for foreigners to understand our public affairs.

Many foreign words can and should thus be taken in, but many technical words will have to be taken from our own language also. It is desirable that linguistic and technical experts should make a list of such words for common use. This will not only bring about uniformity and precision in matters where variety and vagueness are highly undesirable, but will also prevent the use of absurd phrases and expressions.[1]

[Commentary on Nehru's Essay on Language, by Gandhi—August 3, 1937.
"I have very carefully gone through . . . Nehru's essay on the Hindi-Urdu question. The question has latterly become an unfortunate controversy. There is no valid reason for the ugly turn it has taken. Be that as it may, Jawaharlal's essay is a valuable contribution to a proper elucidation of the whole subject considered from the national and purely educational point of view. His constructive suggestions, if they are widely accepted by persons concerned, should put an end to the controversy which has taken a communal turn. The suggestions are exhaustive and eminently reasonable."[2]]

Nehru–Jinnah Correspondence—1938

I. [To Jinnah—January 18, 1938.] We are eager to do everything in our power to put an end to every misapprehension and to endeavour to solve every problem that comes in the way of our developing our public life along right lines and promoting the unity and progress of the Indian people.[3]

II. [February 4, 1938.] I am sorry that my previous letter was difficult to understand. My purpose in writing it was, as I stated, to find out what our points of difference and agreement were. Presumably there are points of difference, as you have repeatedly criticised the Congress policy and practices. If these points of difference are noted down and our attention drawn to them, it would make their consideration easier.

It is possible that some of them may be due to misapprehension and this misapprehension might be removed; it is equally possible that some are more fundamental and then we could try to find a way out or, at any rate, know exactly how and where we stand. When there is a conflict of opinion, a clarification of the opposing opinions is an essential preliminary to their consideration. . . .

[1] U.I., pp. 241–55.
[2] B.O.L., pp. 246–47.
[3] B.S.W.J.N., pp. 193–94.

You have referred in your speeches to the Congress imposing Hindi-Hindustani and trying to crush Urdu. I presume you were misinformed for I am not aware of any attempt on the part of the Congress to injure Urdu. Sometime back I wrote an essay on 'The Question of Language' which represents, I believe, the Congress view-point. . . . If you disagree with the argument or conclusions of this essay, I shall be grateful to have your criticisms. . . .

I presume you are acquainted with the Congress resolutions and statements on minority and fundamental rights and regarding communal questions. . . .

The Congress policy as laid down in these resolutions may be incomplete or wrong. If so, we shall gladly consider suggestions to complete it or rectify it. Personally I do not see what more can be done by the Congress regarding religious or cultural matters. . . .

In considering wider political questions, the Congress has adhered to certain principles and policies for a number of years though minor variations have taken place from time to time. Our present policy in the legislatures and outside was defined by a comprehensive resolution passed by the Working Committee . . . last year. . . .

This included our objective of independence, our demand for a Constituent Assembly, our general attitude to the Constitution Act and . . . Federation, and our methods of work inside and outside the legislature. It referred also to our agrarian and labour programmes. Thus there appeared to be a very large measure of agreement between us not only in regard to fundamentals but even regarding many details.

In view of this agreement, it distressed and surprised me to find that there was so much conflict. I have tried, therefore, to find out what this conflict is about. I do not see how I can make any proposal, concrete or vague, when I do not know what the points [at] issue are. It is true that in reading your speeches I have come across various statements to the effect that the Congress is trying to establish a Hindu Raj. I am unaware of how this is being done or who is doing it. If any Congress Ministries or Congress organisations have made mistakes these should be pointed [out] to us. . . .

You state that you are fighting the Congress leadership which is misleading the Hindus. Further, you have said that you want to bring the Congress High Command to its senses. May I suggest that those who are privileged to advise or lead the Congress have no desire to fight anybody except British Imperialism? . . . Further . . . you said: "I have long, long ago, months ago now, thrown out a challenge to Pandit Jawaharlal Nehru and I throw out a challenge now to him to come and sit with us and let us formulate a constructive programme, which will give relief to the poor." It was to this challenge that I referred in my last letter. I do not remember on which previous occasion you had issued a similar challenge to me.

It is always helpful to discuss matters and problems face to face and, as I have said previously, we are always glad to do so. . . . Whenever necessity arises, every one of us will willingly welcome a talk. But even such a talk is likely to be vague and infructuous if some clarification of ideas does not take place previously. Correspondence helps in this process and sometimes is even preferable as it is more precise than talk. I trust, therefore, that you will help in clarifying the position by telling us where we differ and how you would like this difference to end. You have also criticised the Congress in vigorous language, as you were no doubt entitled to do. But are we not entitled to ask you to substantiate those criticisms in private at least, if not in public.[1]

III. [February 25, 1938.] I had no intention of flinging any complaints and grievances at you. In my attempt to find out what your complaints were, I read your speeches as reported in the newspapers. . . . I would indeed welcome a public treatment by you of the criticism made by you. But if you yourself are unwilling to write to the press on the subject, as you indicated in your letter, I put it to you that we are at least entitled to request you to substantiate the criticism in private.

If you have made no criticisms of the Congress, and the press reports are entirely wrong then, of course, no question of substantiation arises. All that need be done is to contradict the press reports. But if the criticisms have been made, as presumably they have been, then I would request you to justify them publicly or privately as you might choose. Personally I would prefer the former method.

I am afraid, I must confess, that I do not yet know what the fundamental points of dispute are. It is for this reason that I have been requesting you to clarify them. So far I have not received any help in this direction. Of course, we shall willingly meet you whenever opportunity arises. . . .

But when we meet, what are we to discuss? Responsible people with organisations behind them can hardly discuss anything in the air. Some clarification of the issues, some clear statement of what is wanted and

[1] Ibid., pp. 195-97.

what is objected to, is always desirable, otherwise we may not come to grips with the subject. . . .

It is thus highly desirable for us to define the issues first. This is also necessary as we may have always to consult many colleagues in regard to any matter affecting Congress policy. There is surely nothing undesirable or inappropriate about this defining of issues by correspondence. It is the usual method adopted between individuals and organisations. May I, therefore, beg of you to enlighten me ? [1]

IV. [March 8, 1938.] I am afraid our letters to each other repeat themselves. . . . It is not my desire, may I repeat, to carry on a controversy by correspondence, but only to find out what the main points [of] discussion [and] dispute are. It is surely usual for national issues to be formulated and clarified in this way to facilitate discussion. Both in national and international matters [men] . . . frequently [adopt] this course. . . . I go on requesting you to tell us what exactly are the points in dispute which have to be discussed and you go on insisting that this should not be done by correspondence.

At the same time you have pointed out that the main points in dispute have been constantly, and very recently, discussed in . . . Press statements and your public speeches. In my effort to discover [the] points of dispute I enumerated some of the criticisms which you were reported to have made in public speeches. In your reply you stated that you were misreported, but you did not say what the correct report should have been. Further, you said that these were minor and trifling matters, but again you did not point out what the major matters were. You will perceive my difficulty.

I hope I am not making any insinuations or innuendoes, as you suggest in your last letter. Certainly it is not my intention to do so, nor to raise trifling matters which are not germane to the present subject. But what are these matters which are germane? It may be that I am dense or not sufficiently acquainted with the intricacies of the problem. If so, I deserve to be enlightened. If you will refer me to any recent statement made in the Press or platform which will help me in understanding, I shall be grateful. . . .

You are perfectly right in saying that [disputes between the Muslim League and Congress have] . . . been tackled since 1925 repeatedly. Do you not think that this very history warns us not to approach it in a vague manner without clear ideas as to what we object to and what we want? . . .

[1] Ibid., pp. 199–200.

Vagueness, or an avoidance of real issues cannot lead to satisfactory results. It does seem strange to me that in spite of my repeated requests, I am not told what issues have to be discussed.[1]

(The sequence of certain passages in the above letter has been slightly altered, in view of the logic of the case being presented.)

[From Jinnah letter to Nehru—March 17, 1938: "I have received your letter of the 8th of March 1938. Your first letter of the 18th of January conveyed to me that you desire to know the points in dispute for the purpose of promoting Hindu-Muslim unity. When in reply I said that the subject-matter cannot be solved through correspondence and it was equally undesirable as discussing matters in the Press, you in your reply of the 4th of February formulated a catalogue of grievances with regard to my supposed criticism of the Congress and utterances which are hardly relevant to the question for our immediate consideration. You went on persisting on the same line and you are still of [the] opinion that those matters, although not germane to the present subject, should be further discussed which I do not propose to do as I have already explained to you in my previous letter.

"The question with which we started, as I understood, is of safe-guarding the rights and the interests of the Mussalmans with regard to their religion, culture, language, personal laws and political rights in the national life, the government and the administration of the country. Various suggestions have been made which will satisfy the Mussalmans and create a sense of security and confidence in the majority community. I am surprised when you say in your letter under reply, 'But what are these matters which are germane. It may be that I am dense or not sufficiently acquainted with the intricacies of the problem. If so, I deserve to be enlightened. If you will refer me to any recent statement made in the Press or platform which will help me in understanding, I shall be grateful.' Perhaps you have heard of the Fourteen Points.

"Next, as you say, 'Apart from this much has happened during these past few years which has altered the position.' Yes, I agree with you, and various suggestions have appeared in the newspapers recently. For instance, if you will refer to the *Statesman*, dated the 12th of February, 1938, there appears an article under the heading 'Through Moslem Eyes' (copy enclosed for your convenience). Next, an article in the *New Times* dated the 1st of March 1938, dealing with your pronouncement recently made, I believe at Haripura sessions of the Congress, where you are reported to have said: 'I have examined this so-called communal question through the telescope, and if there is nothing, what can you see.'

"This article in the *New Times* appeared on the 1st of March, 1938, making numerous suggestions (copy enclosed for your convenience). . . .

[Ultimately] I consider it is the duty of every true nationalist to which-ever party or community he may belong, to make it his business and

[1] Ibid., pp. 201, 203.

examine the situation and bring about a pact between the Mussalmans and the Hindus and create a real united front; and it should be as much your anxiety and duty as it is mine, irrespective of the question of the party or the community to which we belong. But if you desire that I should collect all these suggestions and submit to you as a petitioner for you and your colleagues to consider, I am afraid I can't do it nor can I do it for the purpose of carrying on further correspondence with regard to those various points with you. But if you still insist upon that, as you seem to do so when you say in your letter, 'My mind demands clarity before it can function effectively or think in terms of any action. Vagueness or an avoidance of real issues could not lead to satisfactory results. It does seem strange to me that in spite of my repeated requests I am not told what issues have to be discussed.' This is hardly a correct description or a fair representation, but in that case I would request you to ask the Congress officially to communicate with me to that effect and I shall place the matter before the Council of the All-India Muslim League as you yourself say that you are 'not the Congress President and thus have not the same representative capacity but if I can be of any help in this matter my services are at the disposal of the Congress and I shall gladly meet you and discuss these matters with you.' As to meeting you and discussing matters with you, I need hardly say that I shall be pleased to do so."[1]

The suggestions mentioned in Jinnah's letter (above) refer to his Fourteen Points of March 28, 1929 (a copy of which was enclosed in his March 17, 1938 letter to Nehru): "The League after anxious and careful consideration most earnestly and emphatically lays down that no scheme for the future constitution of the government of India will be acceptable to Mussulmans of India until and unless the following basic principles are given effect to and provisions are embodied therein to safeguard their rights and interests:

"(1) The form of the future Constitution should be federal with the residuary powers vested in the Provinces.

"(2) A uniform measure of autonomy shall be granted to all Provinces.

"(3) All Legislatures in the country and other elected bodies shall be constituted on the definite principle of adequate and effective representation of Minorities in every Province without reducing the majority in any Province to a minority or even equality.

"(4) In the Central Legislature, Mussulman representation shall not be less than one third.

"(5) Representation of communal groups shall continue to be by means of separate electorates as at present: provided it shall be open to any community, at any time, to abandon its separate electorate in favour of [a] joint electorate.

"(6) Any territorial redistribution that might at any time be necessary shall not in any way affect the Muslim majority in the Punjab, Bengal and the North-West Frontier Province.

[1] B.O.L., pp. 277–79.

"(7) Full religious liberty, i.e. liberty of belief, worship and observance, propaganda, association and education, shall be guaranteed to all communities.

"(8) No Bill or resolution or any part thereof shall be passed in any Legislature or any other elected body if three-fourths of the members of any community in that particular body oppose such a Bill, resolution or part thereof on the ground that it would be injurious to the interests of that community or in the alternative, such other method is devised as may be found feasible and practicable to deal with such cases.

"(9) Sind should be separated from the Bombay Presidency.

"(10) Reforms should be introduced in the North-West Frontier Province and Baluchistan on the same footing as in other Provinces.

"(11) Provision should be made in the Constitution giving Muslims an adequate share, along with the other Indians, in all the Services of the State and in local self-governing bodies having due regard to the requirements of efficiency.

"(12) The Constitution should embody adequate safeguards for the protection of Muslim culture and for the protection and promotion of Muslim education, language, religion, personal laws and Muslim charitable institutions and for their due share in the grants-in-aid given by the State and by local self-governing bodies.

"(13) No Cabinet, either Central or Provincial, should be formed without there being a proportion of at least one-third Muslim Ministers.

"(14) No change shall be made in the Constitution by the Central Legislature except with the concurrence of the States constituting the Indian Federation.

"The draft resolution also mentions an alternative to the above provision in the following terms:

"That, in the present circumstances, representation of Mussulmans in the different Legislatures of the country and other elected bodies through the separate electorates is inevitable and further, the Government being pledged over and over again not to disturb this franchise so granted to the Muslim community since 1909 till such time as the Mussulmans chose to abandon it, the Mussulmans will not consent to joint electorates unless Sind is actually constituted into a separate Province and reforms in fact are introduced in the North-West Frontier Province and Baluchistan on the same footing as in other Provinces.

"Further, it is provided that there shall be reservation of seats according to the Muslim population in the various Provinces; but where Mussulmans are in a majority they shall not contest more seats than their population warrants.

"The question of excess representation of Mussulmans over and above their population in Provinces where they are in a minority is to be considered hereafter." [1]]

---

[1] S.D.I.C. (Vol. I), pp. 246–47.

V. [April 6, 1938.] I am glad that you have indicated in your last letter a number of points which you have in mind. The enclosures you have sent mention these and I take it that they represent your view-point. I was somewhat surprised to see this list as I had no idea that you wanted to discuss many of these matters with us. Some of these are wholly covered by previous decisions of the Congress, some others are hardly capable of discussion.

As far as I can make out from your letter and the enclosures you have sent you wish to discuss the following matters:

1. The Fourteen Points formulated by the Muslim League in 1929.
2. The Congress should withdraw all opposition to the Communal Award and should not describe it as a negation of nationalism.
3. The share of the Muslims in the State Services should be definitely fixed in the Constitution by statutory enactment.
4. Muslim personal law and culture should be guaranteed by statute.
5. The Congress should take in hand the agitation in connexion with the Shahidganj mosque and should use its moral pressure to enable the Muslims to gain possession of the mosque.
6. The Muslims' right to call *Azan* and perform their religious ceremonies should not be fettered in any way.
7. Muslims should have freedom to perform cow-slaughter.
8. Muslim majorities in the Provinces, where such majorities exist at present, must not be affected by any territorial redistribution or adjustments.
9. The *Bande Mataram* song should be given up.
10. Muslims want Urdu to be the national language of India and they desire to have statutory guarantees that the use of Urdu shall not be curtailed or damaged.
11. Muslim representation in local bodies should be governed by the principles underlying the Communal Award, that is separate electorates and population strength.
12. The tri-colour flag should be changed or, alternatively, the flag of the Muslim League should be given equal importance.
13. Recognition of the Muslim League as the one authoritative and representative organization of Indian Muslims.
14. Coalition Ministries.

It is further stated that the formula evolved by you and . . . Rajendra Prasad in 1935 [in an unsuccessful attempt to find a basis of agreement to replace Britain's previous Communal Award] does not satisfy the Muslims now and nothing on those lines will satisfy them.

It is added that the list given above is not a complete list and that it can be augmented by the addition of further "demands". Not knowing these possible and unlimited additions I can say nothing about them. But I should like to deal with the various matters specifically mentioned and to indicate what the Congress attitude has been in regard to them.

But before considering them, the political and economic background of the free India we are working for has to be kept in mind, for ultimately that is the controlling factor. Some of these matters do not arise in considering an independent India or take a particular shape or have little importance. We can discuss them in terms of Indian independence or in terms of the British dominance of India continuing. The Congress naturally thinks in terms of independence, though it adjusts itself occasionally to the present transitional and temporary phases. It is thus not interested in amendments to the present Constitution, but aims at its complete removal and its substitution by a Constitution framed by the Indian people through a Constituent Assembly.

Another matter has assumed an urgent and vital significance and this is the exceedingly critical international situation and the possibility of war. This must concern India greatly and affect her struggle for freedom. This must therefore be considered the governing factor of the situation and almost everything else becomes of secondary importance, for all our efforts and petty arguments will be of little avail if the very foundation is upset. The Congress has clearly and repeatedly laid down its policy in the event of such a crisis and stated that it will be no party to imperialist war. Peace, therefore, and Indian independence is its basic policy. The Congress will very gladly and willingly co-operate with the Muslim League and all other organizations and individuals in the furtherance of this policy.

I have carefully looked through the various matters to which you have drawn attention in your letter and its enclosures and I find that there is nothing in them which refers to or touches the economic demands of the masses or affects the all-important questions of poverty and unemployment. For all of us in India these are the vital issues and unless some solution is found for them, we function in vain. The question of State Services, howsoever important and worthy of consideration it might be, affects a very small number of people. The peasantry, industrial workers, artisans and petty shopkeepers form the vast majority of the population and they are not improved in any way by any of the demands listed above. Their interests should be paramount.

Many of the "demands" involve changes of the Constitution which we are not in a position to bring about. Even if some such changes are desirable in themselves, it is not our policy to press for minor constitutional changes. We want to do away completely with the present Constitution and replace it by another for a free India.

In the same way the desire for statutory guarantees involves constitutional changes which we cannot give effect to. All we can do is to state that in a future Constitution for a free India we want certain guarantees to be incorporated. We have done this in regard to religious, cultural, linguistic and other rights of Minorities in the Karachi resolution on Fundamental Rights. We would like these fundamental rights to be made a part of the Constitution.

I now deal with the various matters listed above.

1. The Fourteen Points, I had thought, were somewhat out of date. Many of their provisions have been given effect to by the Communal Award and in other ways; some others are entirely acceptable to the Congress; yet others require constitutional changes which, as I have mentioned above, are beyond our present competence. Apart from the matters covered by the Communal Award and those involving a change in the Constitution, one or two matters remain which give rise to differences of opinion and which are still likely to lead to considerable argument.

2. The Congress has clearly stated its attitude towards the Communal Award, and it comes to this that it seeks alterations only on the basis of mutual consent of the parties concerned. I do not understand how anyone can take objection to this attitude and policy. If we are asked to describe the Award as not being anti-national, that would be patently false. Even apart from what it gives to various groups, its whole basis and structure are anti-national and come in the way of the development of national unity. As you know it gives an overwhelming and wholly undeserving weightage to the European elements in certain parts of India. If we think in terms of an independent India we cannot possibly fit in this Award with it. It is true that under stress of circumstances we have sometimes to accept as a temporary measure something that is on the face of it anti-national. It is also true that in the matters governed by the Communal Award we can only find a satisfactory and abiding solution by the consent and goodwill of the parties concerned. That is the Congress policy.

3. The fixing of the Muslims' share in the State Services by statutory enactment necessarily involves the fixing of the shares of other groups and communities similarly. This would mean a rigid and compartmental State structure which will impede progress and development. At the same

time it is generally admitted that State appointments should be fairly and adequately distributed and no community should have cause to complain. It is far better to do this by convention and agreement. The Congress is fully alive to this issue and desires to meet the wishes of various groups in the fullest measure, so as to give to all minority communities, as stated in No. 11 of the Fourteen Points, "an adequate share in all the services of the State and in Local Self-Governing Bodies having due regard to the requirements of efficiency". The State today is becoming more and more technical and demands expert knowledge in its various departments. It is right that, if a community is backward in this technical and expert knowledge, special efforts should be made to give it this education to bring it up to a higher level.

I understand that at the Unity Conference held at Allahabad in 1933 or thereabouts, a mutually satisfactory solution of this question of State services was arrived at.

4. As regards protection of culture the Congress has declared its willingness to embody this in the fundamental laws of the Constitution. It has also declared that it does not wish to interfere in any way with the personal law of any community.

5. I am considerably surprised at the suggestion that the Congress should take in hand the agitation in connexion with the Shahidganj mosque. That is a matter to be decided either legally or by mutual agreement. The Congress prefers in all such matters the way of mutual agreement and its services can always be utilized for this purpose where there is an opening for them and a desire to this effect on the part of the parties concerned. I am glad that the Premier of the Punjab has suggested that this is the only satisfactory way to a solution of the problem.

6. The right to perform religious ceremonies should certainly be guaranteed to all communities. The Congress resolution about this is quite clear. I know nothing about the particular incident relating to a Punjab village which has been referred to. No doubt many instances can be gathered together from various parts of India where petty interferences take place with Hindu, Muslim or Sikh ceremonies. These have to be tactfully dealt with wherever they arise. But the principle is quite clear and should be agreed to.

7. As regards cow-slaughter there has been a great deal of entirely false and unfounded propaganda against the Congress suggesting that the Congress was going to stop it forcibly by legislation. The Congress does not wish to undertake any legislative action in this matter to restrict the established rights of the Muslims.

8. The question of territorial redistribution has not arisen in any way. If and when it arises it must be dealt with on the basis of mutual agreement of the parties concerned.

9. Regarding the *Bande Mataram* song the Working Committee issued a long statement in October last to which I would invite your attention. First of all it has to be remembered that no formal national anthem has been adopted by the Congress at any time. It is true, however, that the *Bande Mataram* song has been intimately associated with Indian nationalism for more than thirty years and numerous associations of sentiment and sacrifice have gathered round it. Popular songs are not made to order, nor can they be successfully imposed. They grow out of public sentiment. During all these thirty or more years the *Bande Mataram* song was never considered as having any religious significance and was treated as a national song in praise of India. Nor, to my knowledge, was any objection taken to it except on political grounds by the Government. When, however, some objections were raised, the Working Committee carefully considered the matter and ultimately decided to recommend that certain stanzas, which contained certain allegorical references, might not be used on national platforms or occasions. The two stanzas that have been recommended by the Working Committee for use as a national song have not a word or a phrase which can offend anybody from any point of view and I am surprised that anyone can object to them. They may appeal to some more than to others. Some may prefer another national song; they have full freedom to do so. But to compel large numbers of people to give up what they have long valued and grown attached to is to cause needless hurt to them and injure the national movement itself. It would be improper for a national organization to do this.

10. About Urdu and Hindi I have previously written to you and have also sent you my pamphlet on *The Question of Language*. The Congress has declared in favour of guarantees for languages and culture. It wants to encourage all the great provincial languages of India and at the same time to make Hindustani, as written both in the *nagri* and Urdu scripts, the national language. Both scripts should be officially recognized and the choice should be left to the people concerned. In fact this policy is being pursued by the Congress Ministries.

11. The Congress has long been of [the] opinion that joint electorates are preferable to separate electorates from the point of view of national unity and harmonious co-operation between the different communities. But joint electorates, in order to have real value, must not be imposed on unwilling groups. Hence the Congress is quite clear that their introduction

should depend on their acceptance by the people concerned. This is the policy that is being pursued by the Congress Ministries in regard to local bodies. Recently in a bill dealing with Local Bodies introduced in the Bombay Assembly, separate electorates were maintained but an option was given to the people concerned to adopt a joint electorate, if they so chose. This principle seems to be in exact accordance with No. 5 of the Fourteen Points, which lays down that "Representation of communal groups shall continue to be by means of separate electorate as at present, provided that it shall be open to any community at any time, to abandon its separate electorate in favour of [a] joint electorate". It surprises me that the Muslim League group in the Bombay Assembly should have opposed the Bill with its optional clause although this carried out the very policy of the Muslim League.

May I also point out that in the resolution passed by the Muslim League in 1929, at the time it adopted the Fourteen Points, it was stated that "the Mussulmans will not consent to joint electorates unless Sind is actually constituted into a separate Province and reforms in fact are introduced in the North-West Frontier Province and Baluchistan on the same footing as in other provinces". Since then Sind has been separated and the North-West Frontier Province has been placed on a level with other Provinces. So far as Baluchistan is concerned the Congress is committed to a levelling up of this area in the same way.

12. The national tricolour flag was adopted originally in 1920 by the Congress after full and careful consultation with eminent Muslim, Sikh and other leaders. Obviously a country and a national movement must have a national flag representing the nation and all communities in it. No communal flag can represent the nation. If we did not possess a national flag now we would have to evolve one. The present national flag had its colours originally selected in order to represent the various communities, but we did not like to lay stress on this communal aspect of the colours. Artistically I think the combination of orange, white and green has resulted in a flag which is probably the most beautiful of all national flags. For these many years our flag has been used and it has spread to the remotest village and brought hope and courage and a sense of all-India unity to our masses. It has been associated with great sacrifices on the part of our people, including Hindus, Muslims and Sikhs, and many have suffered lathi blows and imprisonment and even death in defending it from insult or injury. Thus a powerful sentiment has grown up in its favour. On innumerable occasions . . . many leaders of the Muslim League today have associated themselves with this flag and emphasized its virtues

and significance as a symbol of Indian unity. It has spread outside the
Congress ranks and been generally recognized as the flag of the nation.
It is difficult to understand how anyone can reasonably object to it now.

Communal flags cannot obviously take its place for that can only mean
a host of flags of various communities being used together and thus
emphasizing our disunity and separateness. Communal flags might be
used for religious functions but they have no place at any national function
or over any public building meant for various communities.

May I add that during the past few months, on several occasions, the
national flag has been insulted by some members or volunteers of the
Muslim League. This has pained us greatly but we have deliberately
avoided anything in the nature of conflict in order not to add to communal bitterness. We have also issued strict orders, and they have been
obeyed, that no interference should take place with the Muslim League
flag, even though it might be inappropriately displayed.

13. I do not understand what is meant by our recognition of the
Muslim League as the one and only organization of Indian Muslims.
Obviously the Muslim League is an important communal organization
and we deal with it as such. But we have to deal with all organizations
and individuals that come within our ken. We do not determine the
measure of importance or distinction they possess. There are a large
number, about a hundred thousand, of Muslims on the Congress rolls,
many of whom have been our close companions, in prisons and outside,
for many years and we value their comradeship highly. There are many
organizations which contain Muslims and non-Muslims alike, such as
Trades Unions, Peasant Unions, Kisan Sabhas, Debt Committees,
Zamindar Associations, Chambers of Commerce, Employers' Associations, etc., and we have contacts with them. There are special Muslim
organizations such as the Jamiat-ul-Ulema, the Proja Party, the Ahrars
and others, which claim attention. Inevitably the more important the
organization the more the attention paid to it, but this importance does
not come from outside recognition but from inherent strength. And the
other organizations, even though they might be younger and smaller,
cannot be ignored.

14. I should like to know what is meant by coalition Ministries. A
Ministry must have a definite political and economic programme and
policy. Any other kind of Ministry would be a disjointed and ineffective
body, with no clear mind or direction. Given a common political and
economic programme and policy, co-operation is easy. You know probably that some such co-operation was sought for and obtained by the

Congress in the Frontier Province. In Bombay also repeated attempts were made on behalf of the Congress to obtain this co-operation on the basis of a common programme. The Congress has gone to the Assemblies with a definite programme and in furtherance of a clear policy. It will always gladly co-operate with other groups, whether it is in a majority or a minority in an Assembly, in furtherance of that programme and policy. On that basis I can conceive of even coalition Ministries being formed. Without that basis the Congress has no interest in a Ministry or in an Assembly.

I have dealt, I am afraid at exceeding length, with the various points raised in your letter and its enclosures. I am glad that I have had a glimpse into your mind through this correspondence as this enables me to understand a little better the problems that are before you and perhaps others. I agree entirely that it is the duty of every Indian to bring about harmonious joint effort of all of us for the achievement of India's freedom and the ending of the poverty of her people. For me, and I take it for most of us, the Congress has been a means to that end and not an end in itself. It has been a high privilege for us to work through the Congress because it has drawn to itself the love of millions of our countrymen, and through their sacrifice and united effort, taken us a long way to our goal. But much remains to be done and we have all to pull together to that end.

Personally the idea of pacts and the like does not appeal to me, though perhaps they might be necessary occasionally. What seems to me far more important is a more basic understanding of each other, bringing with it the desire and ability to co-operate together. That larger co-operation, if it is to include our millions, must necessarily be in the interests of these millions. My mind therefore is continually occupied with the problems of these unhappy masses of this country and I view all other problems in this light. I should like to view the communal problem also in this perspective for otherwise it has no great significance for me.[1]

VI. [April 16, 1938.] I am exceedingly sorry that anything that I have written to you should have caused you pain. It seems to be true that we approach public problems from different stand-points and inevitably I try to place my viewpoint before you and seek to gain your appreciation of it. To say anything that might pain you would defeat my own purpose, even apart from its impropriety. At the same time, I owe it to you, and to myself to endeavour to place frankly before you how my mind works and what my views are on the subject-matter under discussion. Our viewpoints might differ, but I do believe that the margin of difference can be lessened

[1] S.D.I.C. (Vol. I), pp. 423-29.

by a frank approach on either side. I have sought to make this approach in all sincerity and with every desire on my part not to say anything that might come in the way.

In my last letter I dealt with the various points mentioned in the extracts you had sent me, as I presume that, as you had drawn my attention to them, they might to a large extent represent what you had in mind. As you know, I have been trying to get at these points of difference and when I saw something concrete I [wanted] to give my reaction. . . . I tried to state what the Congress opinion has been. . . . There is no finality in day-to-day politics, although certain principles are supposed to govern policies. It is for the Congress, if it so chooses, to vary that policy. All I can do is to state what the past and present policy is.

I regret that you think that I write in an arrogant and militant spirit and as if I considered the Congress as the Sovereign Power, and that it is circumscribed in a hundred ways and further that it may have to go through the wilderness many a time again before it [achieves] its objective.

You have referred to my obsession with the international situation and the sense of impending catastrophe that possesses me. If I feel that way, as I do, I can hardly grow complacent or imagine that the Congress is a Sovereign Body. But when I discuss Congress policies, as a Congressman, I can only repeat what these are and not bring in my own particular [views] on the subject if these happen to be at variance with [a] Congress resolution.

You point out that the Congress has [stated] numerous falsehoods in regard to the Muslim League and some of its leaders. . . . I entirely agree with you that falsehoods, misrepresentations and insinuations are to be deprecated and countered wherever they might occur . . . [in] whatever the political complexion of [any] newspaper. There is no such thing as [a] Congress press over which the Congress has control, but it is true that many newspapers generally support the Congress. But whether we can influence them or not, we certainly want to stop all such false and misleading statements and to express our disapproval of them. In this matter I can only beg of you to point out specific instances so that we might take necessary action.[1]

Resumé of Attitude Toward Muslim League

In 1938, when Czechoslovakia had to face the Sudetenland crisis, the Nazi methods employed there were studied and referred to with approval

[1] B.S.W.J.N., pp. 216–17.

18 + N.

by Moslem League spokesmen. A comparison was drawn between the position of Sudetenland Germans and Indian Moslems. Violence and incitements in speeches and in some newspapers became marked. A Congress Moslem minister was stabbed, and there was no condemnation of this from any Moslem League leader; in fact it was condoned. Other exhibitions of violence frequently took place.

I was terribly depressed by these developments and by the general lowering of the standards of public life. Violence, vulgarity, and irresponsibility were on the increase, and it appeared that they were approved of by responsible leaders of the Moslem League. I wrote to some of these leaders and begged them to check this tendency, but with no success. So far as the Congress governments were concerned, it was obviously to their interest to win over every minority or other group, and they tried hard to do so. Indeed complaints arose from some quarters that they were showing undue favor to the Moslems at the expense of other groups. But it was not a question of a particular grievance which could be remedied, or a reasonable consideration of any matter. There was a regular rampage on the part of members or sympathizers of the Moslem League to make the Moslem masses believe that something terrible was happening and that the Congress was to blame. What that terrible thing was nobody seemed to know. But surely there must be something behind all this shouting and cursing, if not here then elsewhere. During by-elections the cry raised was "Islam in danger", and voters were asked to take their oaths on the holy book to vote for the Moslem League candidate.

All this had an undoubted effect on the Moslem masses. And yet it is surprising how many resisted it. The League won most by-elections, lost some; even when they won, there was a substantial minority of Moslem voters who went against them, being influenced more by the Congress agrarian program. But for the first time in its history the Moslem League got a mass backing and began to develop into a mass organization. Much as I regretted what was happening, I welcomed this development in a way, as I thought that this might lead ultimately to a change in the feudal leadership and more progressive elements would come forward. The real difficulty thus far had been the extreme political and social backwardness of the Moslems, which made them liable to exploitation by reactionary leaders.

Mr M. A. Jinnah himself was more advanced than most of his colleagues of the Moslem League. Indeed he stood head and shoulders above them and had therefore become the indispensable leader. From public platforms he confessed his great dissatisfaction with the opportunism, and sometimes even worse failings, of his colleagues. He knew well that a great part of the advanced, selfless, and courageous element among the Moslems had joined and worked with the Congress. And yet some destiny or course of events had thrown him among the very people for whom he had no respect. He was their leader, but he could only keep them together by becoming himself a prisoner to their reactionary ideologies. Not that he was an unwilling prisoner, so far as the ideologies were concerned, for despite his external modernism, he belonged to an older generation which was hardly aware of modern political thought or developments. Of economics, which overshadow the world today, he appeared to be entirely ignorant. The extraordinary occurrences that had taken place all over the world since World War I had apparently had no effect on him. He had left the Congress when that organization had taken a political leap forward. The gap had widened as the Congress developed an economic and mass outlook. But Mr Jinnah seemed to have remained ideologically in that identical place where he stood a generation ago, or rather he had gone further back, for now he condemned both India's unity and democracy. "They would not live," he has stated, "under any system of government that was based on the nonsensical notion of Western democracy." It took him a long time to realize that what he had stood for throughout a fairly long life was nonsensical.

Mr Jinnah is a lone figure even in the Moslem League, keeping apart from his closest co-workers, widely but distantly respected, more feared than liked. About his ability as a politician there is no doubt, but somehow that ability is tied up with the peculiar conditions of British rule in India today. He shines as a lawyer-politician, as a tactician, as one who thinks that he holds the balance between nationalist India and the British power. If conditions were different and he had to face real problems, political and economic, it is difficult to say how far his ability would carry him. Perhaps he is himself doubtful of this, although he has no small opinion of himself. This may be an explanation for that subconscious urge in him against change and to keep things going as they are, for an avoidance of discussion and calm consideration of problems with people who do not wholly agree with him. He fits into this present pattern; whether he or anybody else will fit into a new pattern it is difficult to say. What passion moves him, what objective does he strive for? Or is it that he has no dominating passion except the pleasure he has in playing a fascinating political game of chess in which he often has an opportunity to say "check"? He seems to have a hatred for the Congress which has grown with the years. His aversions and dislikes are obvious, but what does he like? With all his strength and tenacity, he is a strangely negative person whose appropriate symbol might well be a "no". Hence all attempts to understand his positive aspect fail, and one cannot come to grips with it.

Since British rule came to India, Moslems have produced few outstanding figures of the modern type. They have produced some remarkable men, but, as a rule, these represented the continuation of the old culture and tradition and did not easily fit in with modern developments. This incapacity to march with the changing times and adapt themselves culturally and otherwise to a new environment was not of course due to any innate failing. It derived from certain historical causes, from the delay in the development of a new industrial middle class, and the excessively feudal background of the Moslems, which blocked up avenues of development and prevented the release of talent. In Bengal the backwardness of the Moslems was most marked, but this was obviously due to two causes: the destruction of their upper classes during the early days of British rule, and the fact that the vast majority were converts from the lowest class of Hindus, who had long been denied opportunities of growth and progress. In northern India the cultured upper-class Moslems were tied up with their old traditional ways as well as the land system. In recent years there has been a marked change and a fairly rapid development of a new middle class among Indian Moslems, but even now they lag far behind Hindus and others in science and industry. The Hindus are backward also, sometimes even more hide-bound and tied up with traditional ways of thought and practice than the Moslems, but nevertheless they have produced some very eminent men in science, industry and other fields. The small Parsi community has also produced outstanding leaders of modern industry. Mr Jinnah's family, it is interesting to note, was originally Hindu [before becoming Moslem].

Both among Hindus and Moslems a good deal of talent and ability has in the past gone into government service, as that was the most attractive avenue open. With the growth of the political movement for freedom, that attraction became less, and able, earnest, and courageous persons were drawn into it. Thus many of the best types of Moslems came into the Congress. In more recent years young Moslems joined the Socialist and Communist parties also. Apart from all the ardent and progressive persons, Moslems were very poor in the quality of their leaders and were inclined to look to government service alone for advancement. Mr Jinnah was a different type. He was able, tenacious, and not open to the lure of office, which had been such a failing of so many others. His position in the Moslem League, therefore, became unique and he was able to command the respect which was denied to many others prominent in the League. Unfortunately his tenacity prevented him from opening his mind to any new ideas, and his unquestioned hold on his own organization made him intolerant both of his own dissidents and of other organizations. He became the Moslem League. But a question arose: as the League was becoming a mass organization, how long could this feudal leadership with outmoded ideas continue? [1]

[Congress repeatedly attempted to reduce communal tensions. Ironically, however, the very concessions it made to the Muslim League later were considered by many responsible Congress leaders actually to have encouraged the League in its quest for "territorial autonomy". The steady growth of the League inevitably proved disturbing to Congress leaders, already troubled by its hostility, and its divisive tendencies.

Nehru continued at this time to view the widening rift between Muslims and Hindus as stemming primarily from political and economic, rather than religious differences.]

7 | Science and its Political Implications

[Nehru's interest in science has been a dominant one throughout his life. Even in the midst of the political turmoil of the late 1930s, he addressed various science congresses in different parts of India. What he said at these meetings was not limited only to science. He attempted to awaken those attending the gatherings at which he spoke to the ways in which the great technological advances of the era might be applied in India; to the need for national planning, and to related goals of equal importance for the future well-being of India.]

[From Address to Indian Science Congress—December 26, 1937.] Most of us, unhappily, are too much engrossed in the business of politics to pay much attention to the finer and more important aspects of life. That is natural, perhaps, in a nation which struggles for national freedom and to rid itself of the bonds that prevent normal growth. Like a person in the grip of a disease, it can think only of how to gain health again, and this

[1] D.I., pp. 392–95.

obsession is a barrier to the growth of culture and science. We are entangled in our innumerable problems; we are oppressed by the appalling poverty of our people. But if we had a true standard of values we would realize that the Silver Jubilee of the Indian Science Congress this year is an event of outstanding importance. For that Congress represents science, and science is the spirit of the age and the dominating factor of the modern world. Even more than the present, the future belongs to science and to those who make friends with science and seek its help for the advancement of humanity. . . .

Though I have long been a slave driven in the chariot of Indian politics, with little leisure for other thoughts, my mind has often wandered to the days when as a student I haunted the laboratories of that home of science, Cambridge. And though circumstances made me part company with science, my thoughts turned to it with longing. In later years, through devious processes, I arrived again at science, when I realized that science was not only a pleasant diversion and abstraction, but was of the very texture of life, without which our modern world would vanish away. Politics led me to economics, and this led me inevitably to science and the scientific approach to all our problems and to life itself. It was science alone that could solve these problems of hunger and poverty, of insanitation and illiteracy, of superstition and deadening custom and tradition, of vast resources running to waste, of a rich country inhabited by starving people. . . .

I believe that without . . . planning little that is worth while can be done. But can [it] be done under present conditions, both political and social? At every step vested interests prevent planning and ordered development, and all our energy and enthusiasm is wasted because of this obstruction. Can we plan on a limited scale for limited objectives? We may do so in some measure, but immediately we come up against new problems and our plans go awry. Life is one organic whole and it cannot be separated into watertight compartments. The Mississippi Valley Committee, writing in their Letter of Transmittal to the Federal Administration of Public Works, U.S.A., refer to this planning business: "Planning for the use and control of water is planning for most of the basic functions of the life of a nation. We cannot plan for water unless we also reconsider the relevant problems of the land. We cannot plan for water and land unless we plan for the whole people. It is of little use to control rivers unless we also master the conditions which make for the security and freedom of human life."

And so we are driven to think of these basic conditions of human life, of the social system, the economic structure. If science is the dominating factor in modern life, then the social system and economic structure must fit in with science or it is doomed. Only then can we plan effectively and extensively.... I would ... like the State to send out promising Indian students ... to foreign countries for scientific ... technical training. For we have to build India on a scientific foundation, to develop her industries, to change the feudal character of her land system and bring her agriculture in line with modern methods, to develop the social services which she lacks so utterly today, and to do so many other things that shout out to be done. For all this we require a trained personnel.

I should like our Central and Provincial Governments to have expert boards to investigate our problems and suggest solutions. A politician dislikes and sometimes suspects the scientist and expert. But without that expert's aid that politician can achieve little.[1]

[From Address to National Academy of Sciences—Allahabad, March 5, 1938.] I ... have worshipped at the shrine of science and counted myself as one of its votaries.

Who indeed can afford to ignore science today? At every turn we have to seek its aid and the whole fabric of the world today is of its making. During the ten thousand years of human civilization, science came in with one vast sweep a century and a half ago, and during these one hundred and fifty years it proved more revolutionary and explosive than anything that had gone before. We who live in this age of science live in an environment and under conditions which are totally different from those of the pre-scientific age. But few realize this in its completeness, and they seek to understand the problems of today by a reference to a yesterday that is dead and gone.

Science has brought all these mighty changes and not all of them have been for the good of humanity. But the most vital and hopeful of the changes that it has brought about has been the development of the scientific outlook in man. It is true that even today vast numbers of people still live mentally in the pre-scientific age, and that most of us, even when we talk glibly of science, betray it in our thought and actions. Even scientists, learned in their particular subjects, often forget to apply the scientific method outside that charmed sphere. And yet it is the scientific method alone that offers hope to mankind and an ending of the agony of the world. This world is racked by fierce conflicts and they

[1] U.I., pp. 175-77.

are analyzed and called by many names. But essentially the major conflict is between the method of science and the methods opposed to science.

In the early days of science there was much talk of a conflict between religion and science, and science was called materialistic and religion spiritual. That conflict hardly seems real today when science has spread out its wings and ventured to make the whole universe its field of action, and converted solid matter itself into airy nothing. Yet the conflict was real, for it was a conflict between the intellectual tyranny imposed by what was deemed to be religion and the free spirit of man nurtured by the scientific method. Between the two there can be no compromise. For science cannot accept the closing of the windows of the mind, by whatever pleasant name this might be called; it cannot encourage blind faith in someone else's faith. Science therefore must be prepared not only to look up to the heavens and seek to bring them under its control, but also to look down, unafraid, into the pit of hell. To seek to avoid either is not the way of science. The true scientist is the sage unattached to life and the fruits of action, ever seeking truth wheresoever this quest might lead him. To tie himself to a fixed anchorage, from which there is no moving, is to give up that search and to become static in a dynamic world.

Perhaps there is no real conflict between true religion and science, but, if so, religion must put on the garb of science and approach all its problems in the spirit of science. A purely secular philosophy of life may be considered enough by most of us. Why should we trouble ourselves about matters beyond our ken when the problems of the world insistently demand solution? And yet that secular philosophy itself must have some background, some objective, other than merely material well-being. It must essentially have spiritual values and certain standards of behaviour, and, when we consider these, we enter immediately into the realm of what has been called religion.

But science has invaded this realm from many fronts. It has removed the line that was supposed to separate the world of things from the world of thought, matter from mind; it has peeped into the mind and even the unconscious self of man and sought the inner motives that move him; it has even dared to discuss the nature of ultimate reality. The reality of even a particle of matter, we are told, is not its actuality but its potentiality. Matter becomes just a "group agitation" and nature a theatre for such agitations or "for the inter-relations of activities". Everywhere there is motion, change, and the only unit of things real is the "event", which is, and instantaneously is no more. Nothing is except a happening. If this is the fate of solid matter, what then are the things of the spirit?

How futile the old arguments seem in view of these astonishing developments in scientific thought. It is time we brought our minds into line with the progress of science and gave up the meaningless controversies of an age gone by. It is true that science changes, and there is nothing dogmatic or final about it. But the method of science does not change, and it is to that we must adhere in our thought and activities, in research, in social life, in political and economic life, in religion. We may be specks of dust on a soap-bubble universe, but that speck of dust contained something that was the mind and spirit of man. Through the ages this has grown and made itself master of this earth and drawn power from its innermost bowels as well as from the thunderbolt in the skies. It has tried to fathom the secrets of the universe and brought the vagaries of nature itself to its use. More wonderful than the earth and the heavens is this mind and spirit of man which grows ever mightier and seeks fresh worlds to conquer.

That is the task of the scientist, but we know that all scientists are not fashioned in the heroic mould, nor are they the philosopher-kings of whom Plato told us in the days of old. Kingliness might not be theirs, but even philosophizing is often lacking, and the day's task follows a narrow sphere and a dull routine. As they specialize, and specialize they must, they lose sight of the larger picture and become pedants out of touch with reality. In India the political conditions under which we have had the misfortune to live have further stunted their growth and prevented them from playing their rightful part in social progress. Fear has often gripped them, as it has gripped so many others in the past, lest by any activity or even thought of theirs they might anger the Government of the day and thus endanger their security and position. It is not under these conditions that science flourishes or scientists prosper. Science requires a free environment to grow. When applied to social purposes, it requires a social objective in keeping with its method and the spirit of the age. . . .

We have vast problems to face and to solve. They will not be solved by the politicians alone, for they may not have the vision or the expert knowledge; they will not be solved by the scientists alone, for they will not have the power to do so or the larger outlook which takes everything into its ken. They can and will be solved by the co-operation of the two for a well-defined and definite social objective.[1]

[1] Ibid., pp. 178–81.

8 | Interpretation of India's Fight for Freedom—The Unity of India—Addressed to American Audience, January, 1938

Most Americans, bred in the democratic tradition, sympathize with India's struggle for freedom. They dislike empire and imperialism and the domination and exploitation of one nation by another. And yet they are perplexed when they consider the Indian problem, wondering whether it is possible to build a united and progressive nation out of the seemingly infinite diversity that makes up the fabric of Indian life. They have heard so much of the separatist elements, of the conflicts of religion and culture, of the variety of languages, of the mediæval conditions in the semi-feudal regions of the Indian States, of social cleavages, of the general backwardness of Indian life, that doubts assail them whether it is possible to harmonize all these in a free and independent India. Can democracy be built upon such insecure foundations? Could India stand together and free, if British rule were withdrawn?

These hesitations and perplexities are natural. The questions in which they originate must be considered by us dispassionately, and we must attempt to find the right answers. Freedom for a nation and a people may be, and is, I believe, always good in the long run; but in the final analysis freedom itself is a means to an end, that end being the raising of the people in question to higher levels and hence the general advancement of humanity. The vital and most important problem that faces us in India is the appalling poverty of the people. Will political independence help us to diminish this, as well as the numerous ills that flow from it?

It is well to remember that the British have been in effective control of India for more than a hundred and fifty years and that during this period they have had almost complete freedom to act in any manner they chose. No democratic or any other kind of control in fact existed, the British Parliament being too far away and too ignorant to intervene. India was, and is, a rich country, rich in agricultural resources, mineral wealth, human material; only her people are poor. It was indeed the wealth of India that attracted hordes of foreign adventurers to her shores.

With these resources and that human material, and following a century and a half of unchecked despotism, one is entitled to ask for substantial results. During this period Europe has changed out of recognition, Japan has transformed herself with amazing speed, America has become the wealthiest country in the world. But in India we still have grinding poverty, widespread illiteracy, a general absence of sanitation and medical relief—a lack, indeed, of all the good things of life. There are undoubtedly some good works which have followed British rule, notably in the field of irrigation. But how little they are compared to what might have been!

It is idle to blame the Indian people for this when those people have been allowed no say in the matter. The very backwardness of a people is a condemnation of its government. With this patent result of British rule in India, little argument is needed to demonstrate its failure. But even admitting the failure, it is true that our present problems are no nearer solution. It nevertheless is well to bear the fact in mind, for the very structure of British imperialist rule has been, and is, such as to aggravate our problems and not to solve any of them. And because these problems insistently demand solution we have to look for it outside the orbit of the British Empire.

India is smaller than the United States of America, yet it is a vast country and its population is far larger than that of the United States. Our problems therefore are continental. They are unlike those of the small countries of Europe. Till the advent of modern communications and modern methods of transport, it was very difficult for such a vast area to hold together politically for long. The United States grew and developed into a powerful unit, despite the vast area involved, because of the increase in transport and communications. If the United States had had a long history, going back hundreds and thousands of years before modern science and industry revolutionized life, probably the country would have been split up into many small national units, as happened in Europe. The fact that India was split up politically in the course of her long history was inevitable under the conditions then existing. Yet always the idea of the political unity of India persisted, and kings and emperors sought to realize it. Asoka indeed achieved unity two thousand years ago and built up an empire far greater than that of Britain in India today. It stretched right into Central Asia and included Afghanistan. Only a small part in South India remained outside, and this because of the horror of war and bloodshed that came over Asoka in the full flood of victory and conquest. Other rulers in the past tried to achieve the political unification of India and succeeded in some measure. But this desire for a unified political control of the whole country could not be realized in view of the lack of means and machinery. The coming of the British to India synchronized with the development in transport, communications and modern industry, and so it was that British rule succeeded at last in establishing political unity.

The desire for political unity, in India as in other countries before the advent of nationalism, was usually the desire of the ruler or the conqueror and not of the people as a whole. In India, where for long ages there had been a large measure of local self-government, the people were far more interested in their local freedom and rights than in the machinery of government at the top. Kings changed at the top, but the newcomers respected local rights and did not interfere with them. Because of this, conflicts between kings and people did not take place as in Europe; and later, under cover of this, kings gradually built up their autocratic power.

An all-India political unity thus was not possible in the past. What is far more important for us is to see what other more basic unifying or separatist features there were in Indian life. This will help us to understand the present and shape the future. Superficial observers of India, accustomed to the standardization which modern industry has brought about in the West, are apt to be impressed too much by the variety and diversity of India. They miss the unity of India; and yet the tremendous and fundamental fact of India is her essential unity throughout the ages. Indian history runs into thousands of years, and, of all modern nations, only China has such a continuous and ancient background of culture. Five to six thousand years ago the Indus Valley civilization flourished all over northern India and probably extended to the south also. Even then it was something highly developed, with millennia of growth behind it. Since that early dawn of history innumerable peoples, conquerors and settlers, pilgrims and students, have trekked into the Indian plains from the highlands of Asia and have influenced Indian life and culture and art; but always they have been absorbed and assimilated. India was changed by these contacts and yet she remained essentially her own old self. Like the ocean she received the tribute of a thousand rivers, and though she was disturbed often enough, and storms raged over the surface of her waters, the sea continued to be the sea. It is astonishing to note how India continued successfully this process of assimilation and adaptation. It could only have done so if the idea of a fundamental unity were so deep-rooted as to be accepted even by the newcomer, and if her culture were flexible and adaptable to changing conditions. . . .

This Indian background and unity were essentially cultural; they were not religious in the narrow sense of the word. That culture was not exclusive or intolerant to begin with; it was receptive and adaptable, and long ages of pre-eminence gave it deep roots and a solidarity which storms could not shake. It developed a beneficent attitude which, secure in its own strength, could afford to be tolerant and broadminded. And this very toleration gave it greater strength and adaptability. There was in it till almost the beginning of the Christian era a certain rationalism, something approaching a scientific outlook, which refused to tie itself down to dogmas. True, this culture and rationalism were largely confined to the upper classes, but they percolated down to the masses to some extent. Superstitions and dogmas and many an evil practice gradually crept in. Buddhism was a revolt against these. But the old way of life was still powerful, and it is one of the wonders of history how India succeeded in absorbing Buddhism without any physical conflict. Buddhism, which had spread throughout India and had made progress from Western Asia right across Central Asia to the Far East, gradually faded out of the land of its birth. The man who is supposed to be largely responsible for this was Shankaracharya, who lived in the eighth century after Christ. This amazingly brilliant young man travelled all over India arguing, debating, convincing large audiences, and in a few years (he died at the age of 32) changed the mental atmosphere of the country. The appeal was to reason and logic, not to force.

This practice of debate and conference over religious and other matters was common throughout India and there are records of many great gatherings from Kashmir in the north to the far south. Whatever the political divisions of the country, ideas spread rapidly and were hotly debated. India hung together culturally and the mental background of the people everywhere was much the same. Even the masses in different parts of the country were not dissimilar in thought and outlook. The chief places of pilgrimage fixed by Shankaracharya were situated at the four corners of India: Badrinath in the Himalayas in the north, Rameshwaram near Cape Comorin in the south, Dwarka in the west overlooking the Arabian Sea, and Puri in the east, washed by the waters of the Bay of Bengal. There was continuous intercourse between the peoples of the different regions. India as a whole was their holy land.

It is interesting to compare the intolerance of Europe in matters religious to the wide tolerance prevailing almost throughout history in India. Christianity came to India in the first century after Christ, long before Europe knew much about it, and found a welcome and a home.

There was no opposition whatever. Even now there flourish in India many early Christian sects which were crushed out of existence in Europe. There are the Nestorians, and various Syrian Christian sects. The Jews came to India also about eighteen hundred years ago or more, and were welcomed. They still carry on their community life and parts of an ancient city where they live are supposed to resemble old Jerusalem. The Zoroastrians also came to India, driven out of Persia, and made their home here, and have flourished ever since. The Moslems first came soon after the advent of Islam and they found ready admittance and welcome and full opportunities for propagating their faith. For centuries there was no conflict except on the frontiers; it was only when Moslems came as conquerors and raiders that there was conflict.

The coming of Moslem rule shook India. For a while there was a conflict between the old background and the new, but soon the old spirit of India began to assert itself and attempts began to be made to find a synthesis of the old and the new. Even in religion, most difficult subject of all, this attempt was repeatedly made by [Guru Nanak, founder of the Sikh religion], Kabir [famous Moslem poet] and others. The Moslem rulers generally accepted the background of Indian life and culture, varied by Persian cultural ideas. There was no difficulty whatever in the adaptation of old Indian arts to new ideas. New styles grew up in architecture and painting which were a true synthesis of the two and yet were essentially Indian. So also in music. Even in dress a certain uniformity crept in, and a common language developed.

Thus the whole history of India for thousands of years past shows her essential unity and the vitality and adaptability of her culture. This vitality took her message in art and thought and religion to the Far East; it took the shape of great colonizing expeditions to Malaysia, to Java and Sumatra and the Philippines and Borneo, as the remains of great monuments there, a thousand years old, bear testimony.

Behind this cultural unity, and giving strength to it, was the ceaseless attempt to find a harmony between the inner man and his outer environment. To some extent this was the outlook of the Middle Ages in Europe. And yet it probably was something more. The profit motive was not so obvious and riches were not valued in the same way as elsewhere. Unlike as in Europe, honour was reserved for the man of intellect and the man who served the state or society, and the great soldier or the rich man took second and third place. Perhaps it was this want of stress on the outer environment that made India politically weak and backward, while external progress went forward so rapidly in the West.

This past record of Indian cultural solidarity does not necessarily help us today. It is present conditions that we have to deal with, and memories of what has been may be of little avail. But though that is perfectly true, yet an ancient people has deep roots in the past and we cannot ignore them. Both the good and the bad that we possess have sprung from those roots; they give us strength and inspiration; they also burden us and tie us down to many a harmful tradition and evil practice. India undoubtedly deteriorated and the vital urge in her began to weaken. Her power to assimilate and absorb became feebler, and the flexibility of her thought and structure gave place to rigidity. What was dynamic became more and more static. The rationalism and the scientific basis of her thought continued for a favoured few, but for others irrationalism and superstition held sway. Caste, which was a division of society by occupation, and which at the start was far from rigid, developed a fearful rigidity and became the citadel of social reaction and a basis for the exploitation of the masses. For a long time India stagnated, the strength had gone out of her, and it was inevitable that she should fall an easy prey to the better-equipped and more vital and technically advanced nations of the West.

The immediate result of this was the growth of conservatism, a further shrinking of India inside her shell in self-defence. British rule forwarded this process by crystallizing many a changing custom and giving it the force of law. Even more important in keeping India back was the economic structure which British rule built up. The feudal Indian State system, the gilded Maharajas and Nabobs, and the big landlord system are essentially British creations in India. We have them, to our misfortune, still with us. But this desire of the British rulers to keep a semi-feudal structure in India could not hold back the impact of new ideas and new conditions. The British themselves thrived in the East on the strength of the great impulse given to the world by the advent of industrialism, and India herself was inevitably affected by this impulse. For their own purposes and in order to entrench themselves, they built railways and the other accompaniments of a modern administration. They tried hard to stop the industrial growth of India, desiring to keep her as a producer of raw materials only and a consumer of British manufactured goods. [This was still the essence of British policy in relation to industrial development in spite of the exigencies of the war.] But the industrial revolution had to spread to India, even though it came slowly because of the obstruction offered by the Government.

The British gave political unity to India. This had now become possible owing to the development of communications and transport. It was a unity of a common subjection, but it gave rise to the unity of common nationalism. The idea of a united and a free India gripped the people. It was not a superficial idea imposed from above, but the natural outcome of that fundamental unity which had been the background of Indian life for thousands of years. The difference that had crept in was the new emphasis on the political aspect. To combat this, the British Government tried to lay stress on the religious differences and adopted a policy which encouraged them and brought them into conflict with each other. It has had a measure of success, but nationalism, in India as in other countries of the East, is the dominant urge of the time and must triumph. This nationalism is being tempered today by the economic urge, but this is still further removed from the medieval outlook which thinks in terms of religious groupings in political affairs.

The growth of the powerful nationalist movement in India, represented by the National Congress, has demonstrated the political unity of India. The last two decades have seen vast upheavals, in the nature of a peaceful rebellion, taking place throughout the length and breadth of the country and shaking the foundations of British rule. This voluntary organization, commanding the willing allegiance of millions, has played a great rôle in fixing the idea of Indian unity in the minds of our masses. The capacity for united action and disciplined sacrifice for a national ideal which the people have shown has demonstrated not only the probability of Indian unity but its actual existence. In India today no one, whatever his political views or religious persuasions, thinks in terms other than those of national unity.

There are differences, of course, and certain separatist tendencies, but even these do not oppose national freedom or unity. [At the time this was written the object of the Moslem League was the national independence of India. It subsequently (1941) favored the division of India and the forming of a separate Pakistan.][1] [The separatist factions] seek to gain a special favour for their particular group and because of this they hinder sometimes the growth of the nationalist movement. Religious differences affect politics less and less, though still sometimes they distract attention. There is no religious or cultural conflict in India. What is called the religious or communal problem is really a dispute among upper-class people for a division of the spoils of office or of representation in a legislature. This will surely be settled amicably wherever it arises.[2]

[1] U.I., pp. 11-20. (Originally written for *Foreign Affairs*, U.S.A. Bracketed material based on footnotes, ibid., pp. 19-20.)
[2] Ibid., p. 20.

9 | Trip to Europe, 1938—Statements and Writings While Abroad During European Crisis—Return to India

Trip to Europe—1938

[Nehru was becoming increasingly restive about developments both at home and abroad. Early in June, 1938 (the year during which his mother died), he decided to depart for Europe to see his daughter, Indira, and "to freshen up my tired and puzzled mind".[1] On his way to Genoa, his ship stopped at Suez. He journeyed to Cairo, Alexandria and Port Said, again breaking journey in Egypt on his return to India later in the year.[2] From Genoa Nehru proceeded to Marseilles; next to Barcelona during the Spanish civil war at the invitation of the Republican Government; finally to London.[3]]

[To Gandhi—Allahabad, April 28, 1938.] As you know I have been greatly distressed at the turn events have taken in Congress politics during the last six months. Among the matters that have disturbed me is the new orientation of the Gandhi Seva Sangh. We are developing very rapidly on Tammany Hall lines and it is distressing to find that even the Gandhi Seva Sangh [Seva—Service; Sangh—from the Sanskrit, Sangha —Order] which might have set a standard to others and refused to become just a party organisation intent on winning elections by hook or crook, has descended to the common level. I feel strongly that the Congress Ministries are working inefficiently and not doing much that they could do. They are adapting themselves far too much to the old order and trying to justify it. But all this, bad as it is, might be tolerated. What is far worse is that we are losing the high position that we have built up, with so much labour, in the hearts of the people. We are sinking to the level of ordinary politicians who have no principles to stand by and whose work is governed by a day-to-day opportunism.

Partly of course this is due to a general deterioration all over the world, partly to the transition period through which we are passing. Nevertheless it does show up our failings and the sight is painful. I think there

[1] T.F., p. 363.
[2] B.O.L., p. 291.
[3] Ibid., p. 287.

are enough men of goodwill in the Congress to cope with the situation if they set about it the right way. But their minds are full of party conflicts and the desire to crush this individual or that group. Obviously bad men are preferred to good men because the former promise to toe the party line. When this happens there is bound to be deterioration.

For months past I have felt that I could not function effectively in India as things were going. I have carried on of course as one can always carry on. But I have felt out of place and a misfit. This was one reason (though there were others also) why I decided to go to Europe. I felt I could be more useful there and in any event I would freshen up my tired and puzzled mind. I have found [it] difficult to discuss any matter at length with you because I do not wish to tire and worry you in your present state of health. And then I have also felt that such discussions do not yield any worthwhile results.[1]

[On March 11, 1938, the Nazis invaded Austria. The Munich Pact, concluded on September 30, 1938, mistakenly was believed to guarantee "peace in our time".

An Anglo–German friendship pact was soon followed by one between France and Germany. Daladier, Chamberlain, Hitler and Mussolini agreed to a plan ceding the Sudetenland to the Reich. By March 14, 1939 the Republic of Czechoslovakia was dissolved.

With respect to Nehru's own attitude toward the concept of "collective security" at the time: "As far as I remember, the question [of collective security before World War II] had not arisen then in the form it arose later. The main danger lay from Nazi Germany and all my sympathies were entirely with its possible victims such as Czechoslovakia. I did feel then that Czechoslovakia should have been helped in every way and it seemed to me that the way England and France especially backed out of [doing] this at a moment of crisis was not right. To that extent it might be said that I was in favour of collective security, but the question did not come up clearly before me."[2]]

[Experiences in Europe.] My visit to Europe . . . coincided with a period of intense crisis in the international sphere, and I put myself psychologically in tune with this by going straight to Barcelona, that "flower of the fair cities of the world", as Cervantes called it. Alas, that this flower should be crushed today and enemy hands should hold this ancient home of liberty, which struggled for freedom even in the days of Ferdinand and Isabella! But when I visited this gracious city it was still the home of the unconquerable spirit of man which knows no defeat and

[1] Ibid., pp. 283–84.
[2] From letter to D.N., October 12, 1963.

reckons death and disaster as of little account in freedom's cause. Nightly I saw the bombs fall from the air, raining death and destruction on the populace. I saw the hungry crowds in the streets, the plight of the refugees; I visited the armies at the front and those brave young men of the International Brigade, so many of whom rest for ever in the soil of Spain. I came back full of the tragedy of Spain, which was being strangled not so much by enemies, but by those who called themselves the friends of democracy.[1]

I saw much else [in Spain] that impressed me powerfully; and there, in the midst of want and destruction and ever-impending disaster, I felt more at peace with myself than anywhere else in Europe. There was light there, the light of courage and determination and of doing something worth while.

I went to England and spent a month there and met people of all degrees and all shades of opinion. I sensed a change in the average man, a change in the right direction. But there was no change at the top where Chamberlainism sat triumphantly.[2]

Before Munich I met some of the members of the British Cabinet and other prominent politicians of England and ventured to express my anti-fascist and antinazi views before them. I found that my views were not welcome and I was told that there were many other considerations to be borne in mind.

In the summer before Munich, I was invited on behalf of the Nazi Government to visit Germany, an invitation to which was added the remark that they knew my opposition to Nazism and yet they wanted me to see Germany for myself. I could go as their guest or privately, in my own name or incognito, as I desired, and I would have perfect freedom to go where I liked. . . . I declined with thanks.[3]

[I did go] to Munich . . . just for a day on my way to Prague, in the Summer of 1938. The main purpose of my going there with Indira was to show her the Deutsches Museum. . . . I had no other engagement, but some Indian students met me, and I think I visited one of their rooms and spoke to them. . . . Even during my brief stay [in] Munich I

[1] U.I., pp. 113–14.
[2] T.F., p. 363.
[3] D.I., pp. 7, 6.

was ... oppressed by the Hitlerian atmosphere.... I had a feeling ...
that I was being watched continuously.

I [went to]... Prague.... I visited ... some of the Sudetenland
areas.... We went to Budapest from there.[1]

I went to Czechoslovakia and watched at close quarters the difficult
and intricate game of how to betray your friend and the cause you are
supposed to stand for on the highest moral grounds.[2]

During the Czechoslovak crisis what I saw of Franco-British statesmanship in Prague and in the Sudetenland, in London and Paris and in
Geneva, where the League Assembly was then sitting, amazed and disgusted me. Appeasement seemed to be a feeble word for it. There was
behind it not only a fear of Hitler but a sneaking admiration for him.[3]

What surprised me most was the utter collapse, in the moment of
crisis, of all the so-called advanced people and groups. Geneva gave me
the impression of archaeological remains, with the dead bodies of the
hundreds of international organizations that had their headquarters there,
lying about. London had exhibited tremendous relief that war had been
averted and cared for little else. Others had paid the price, and it did not
matter; but it was going to matter very much before a year was out.
The star of Mr Chamberlain was in the ascendant, though protesting
voices were heard. Paris distressed me greatly, especially the middle-class
section of it, which did not even protest overmuch. This was the Paris
of the Revolution, the symbol of liberty the world over.[4]

From Statements and Writings While Abroad
Address at Conference on Peace and Empire, Organized by India
  League and London Federation of Peace Councils—London,
  July 15 and 16, 1938

Peace and Empire—a curious combination of words and ideas fundamentally opposed to each other, and yet I think it was a happy idea to
put them together.... I do not suppose we can have peace in this world

[1] From letter to D.N., May 29, 1963.
[2] T.F., p. 363.
[3] D.I., p. 7.
[4] T.F., pp. 363-64.

unless we do away with imperialist ideas. Therefore the essence of the problem of peace is the problem of empire.

So long as empires continue to flourish we may have periods when open war between States does not take place, but even then there is no peace, for conflict and preparation for war continue. There is conflict between rival imperialist States, between the dominating power and the subject people, and between classes. The very basis of the imperialist State is coercion of subject peoples and their exploitation; inevitably this is resented and attempts are made to overthrow this domination. On this basis no peace can be founded.

Now you and I in these days of fascist aggression often labour to do something to check the fascist menace, but not always to check the imperialist idea too. Many people seek to distinguish between the two. They do not think much of the imperialist idea, but consider that we might carry on with it for a time, although we cannot possibly do with fascism. I wish you would consider that in this conference, and try to find out how far we can distinguish between the two.

Perhaps because I come from a country which is under imperialism, I attach a great deal of importance to this question of empire. But apart from that, I feel that you cannot distinguish between the two conceptions of fascism and empire, and that fascism is indeed an intensified form of the same system which is imperialism. Therefore, if you seek to combat fascism you inevitably combat imperialism.

We have to face an extraordinarily difficult and complex situation when the embattled legions of fascist reaction threaten the world and are often encouraged and supported by other imperialist Governments. The reactionary forces of the world gather together and consolidate themselves, and in order to face them and check them we must also forget our petty differences and hold together.

We find fascism spreading and all manner of propaganda going on in imperialist States and in other countries. Perhaps you know that in South America today there is tremendous propaganda on the part of the Fascist States. We also find imperialist countries gradually drifting towards fascism, although sometimes they talk the language of democracy at home. . . .

There is a kind of consolidation of the forces of reaction. How are we to meet this? By consolidating the forces of progress against reaction. And if those who represent the forces of progress are inclined to split up and argue too much about minor matters, and thereby endanger the major issue, then they will be incapable of effectively resisting the fascist and imperialist menace. At any time it would be a matter for your consideration, that we hold together. But with all manner of difficulties facing us, it becomes an imperative necessity.

Now only a joint front, not a national joint front, but a world joint front, can achieve our purpose. And out of the horrors we have gone through, the most hopeful signs that come to us are those which point towards the consolidation of the forces of progress and peace all over the world.

You will remember how in China there was internal conflict which weakened the nation. But when Japanese aggression came last year we beheld a people who had been bitterly fighting amongst themselves and destroying each other, who had built up enormous bitterness against each other, still being great enough to see the menace and to organize and unite themselves to fight it. Today, and for the last year, we have seen a united people in China fighting the invasion. In the same way, you will find in every country more or less successful attempts at unity growing up and you find all over the world these various national united groups looking for international solidarity.

In Europe and the West, where progressive groups have a longer history and different background, you have both advantages and disadvantages. But in Asia, where such groups have recently come into existence, the issue is often clouded by the nationalist issue, and one cannot think of it so easily in terms of internationalism, obviously because we have to think first of all in terms of national political feeling.

Even so, these modern developments, and especially what has happened in Abyssinia, in Spain and in China, have now forced people to think in terms of internationalism. We find a remarkable change in some of these countries of Asia, for even though we were engrossed in our struggles, we began to think more and more of the social struggles in other parts of the world, and to feel more and more that they affected us because they affected the entire world.

If we desire to resist the fascist menace effectively, we must equally oppose imperialism, or else we fail. The foreign policy of Britain is an example of this pitiful failure, for thinking in terms of imperialism it cannot resist fascist aggression or ally itself to the progressive forces of the world. And in so failing it is even helping in the disruption of its own empire which it seeks to preserve. We have here a significant example of the basic kinship of imperialism with fascism and of the contradictions which imperialism itself presents.

If we are convinced, as I take it most of us are, that imperialism is akin to fascism, and both are enemies of peace, then we must seek to remove both, and not try to distinguish between the two. Therefore, we have to seek to root out imperialism itself, and seek a complete freedom for all the subject peoples of the world.

Now we are often told that instead of the imperialist conception, we should develop the conception of the commonwealth of nations. This is a phrase which appeals to one, because we all want a commonwealth of nations in this world. But if we think in terms of an empire gradually being transformed into a commonwealth, almost retaining its own structure economically and politically, then it seems to me that we are likely to delude ourselves very greatly. We cannot have a real commonwealth of nations born of empire. It must have different parents.

In the British commonwealth you have a number of countries which are almost independent. But let us not forget that in the British Empire there is a vast area and a vast population which is completely subject, and if you think that this subject population is gradually going to become an equal partner in that commonwealth, you will find enormous difficulties. You will find that if that process is somehow achieved in a political way, there will be many economic bonds which are inconsistent with a free commonwealth, which will not permit real freedom for those subject people, but will prevent them from changing their economic order if they wish, and will prevent them from solving their social problems.

Every one of us, I suppose, is in favour of a real commonwealth of nations. But why seek to limit it to a few countries and nations? That means that you are building up one group to oppose another group. In other words, you are building on the conception of empire and one empire comes into conflict with another empire. That may reduce the danger of war within a group, but it increases the danger of war between groups.

Therefore, if we think in terms of a real commonwealth, we must necessarily abandon the ideas of imperialism, and build afresh on a new basis—a basis of complete freedom for all peoples. For the sake of such an order each nation should be prepared to shed, in common with others, some of the attributes of sovereignty. On this basis we can achieve collective security and establish peace.

Today in Asia, Africa and elsewhere, there are enormous populations which are subject, and until we get rid of that subjection, and imperialist ideas cease to exist, we will find this is a thorn in the side of peace.

The mandatory system in Africa and elsewhere is, I think, a very dangerous idea, because it covers a bad thing under a fair name. Essentially it is the imperialist system continuing in another guise. It is always dangerous to make one person the trustee of another, and allow him to profit by it. It may be that in some countries where you intend establishing complete freedom the same form of government may not be established as quickly in one place as in another, but you must start on the basis of complete freedom for every subject people, and then proceed in a practical way to help them if neccessary. Although, personally, I rather distrust these offers of help, occasionally they may be necessary. But I do not think you will find a way out through this mandatory system, for it is founded on the same basis as imperialism.

I mentioned to you the growing solidarity of the various peoples, their feeling of international fellowship and comradeship because of this crisis. The growth of this international fellowship would be jeopardized by the exclusion of nations who want to be friendly. The people of India have for ages past been on very friendly terms with the people of China. There has never been any conflict between them. May I venture to correct our friend who conveyed the greetings of the people of China? He said that the Chinese came to India in the twelfth century. He was out by one thousand years; they came one thousand years previously to India, and we still have records from their books of their visits. So we have had these long contacts, but apart from that, this recent crisis in China and the world has brought us much nearer to each other. We should like to hold together, we should like to work together for the peace and progress of the world. Why should we not be able to do so if we wish?

So if you look at the world as it is today, you may find countries who for some reason or another will not join a world order, but that is no reason why we should not start to build up that world order, and not limit it to a certain number of nations.

Therefore, a conception of a limited commonwealth must be combated and a conception of a larger commonwealth must grow up. Only then can we really achieve our aim of collective security. We want collective security, but I want to make my meaning quite clear. It is not the meaning that has been attached to it by Mr Neville Chamberlain. My idea of collective security, to begin with, is not to retain a *status quo* which is based on injustice. We cannot have security that way. The essential corollary is the removal of imperialism and Fascism.

We find today an extraordinary state of affairs in the world. We find people who are apparently intelligent following contradictory policies, and increasing the general mess and muddle of the world. In this country, in Britain, we have seen an extraordinary foreign policy developed. Most of you are opposed to it. Nevertheless, it is strange that such a thing should happen, and to an outsider, it is very, very difficult to understand it. It is difficult to understand it from any point of view. We see today a Government in Britain which presumably is interested in maintaining the British Empire, acting in a way which militates against the interests of that empire.

I am not interested in maintaining that empire, but I am interested in ending that empire in a proper way.

The general public may perhaps approve of this policy because of its confusion in regard to imperialism and fascism. This is a significant example of how imperialism, when driven into a corner, is bound to side with fascism. You cannot keep the two apart. When today these major issues confront the world, imperialists who have become more class conscious than ever seek the preservation of their class interests even at [a] risk to the safety and preservation of their imperial interests in the future.

We come, therefore, to this, that we have to base any policy that we evolve on true foundations, and to root out the real evil. The problem of Central Europe, Czechoslovakia, Spain, China and many other problems, we realize, ought to be taken together, and considered as a whole.

May I also remind you of another problem about which perhaps we do not think in this connection so often, but which is very much before us these days, the problem of Palestine? This is a peculiar problem and we are apt to think of it too much in terms of conflict between the Arabs and the Jews. May I remind you to begin with that right through two thousand years there has never been any real conflict between the Arabs and the Jews in Palestine? It is a problem which has recently arisen, since the war. It is fundamentally a problem created by British Imperialism in Palestine, and unless you keep that in mind, you will not solve it. Nor is it likely to be solved by British Imperialism.

It is true that this has become at the present moment rather a difficult problem because of the passions it has roused. What then is really the problem in Palestine? . . . It is essentially a struggle for independence. It is not a religious problem. . . .

British Imperialism played its hand so cleverly that the conflict became the conflict between Arabs and Jews, and the British Government cast itself in the rôle of umpire.

The problem of Palestine can only be solved in one way, and that is by the Arabs and Jews ignoring British imperialism and coming to an agreement with each other. Personally I think that there are many Arabs and Jews who desire to find a solution of the problem in this way. Unfortunately, recent events have created difficulties which have been played upon by imperialist elements, and it may be some time before the Arabs and Jews can come together, but it should be our business and duty to stress this viewpoint and to make it clear—(1) that you cannot solve this problem by trying to crush the Arab people; (2) that it will not be settled by British imperialism but by the two main parties coming together and agreeing to terms.

I do not propose to refer to the large numbers of countries which are subject countries, or countries which have other social troubles today, because almost every country has them. It may be that we can consider their problems later on, but I do think we must not forget the countries of Africa, because probably no people in the world have suffered so much, and have been exploited so much in the past as the people of Africa.

It may be that in the process of exploitation to some extent even my own countrymen have taken part. I am sorry for that. So far as we in India are concerned, the policy we wish to follow is this. We do not want anyone from India to go to any country and to function anywhere against the wishes of the people of that country, whether it is Burma, East Africa, or any other part of the world. I think the Indians in Africa have done a great deal of good work. Some of them have also derived a great deal of profit. I think Indians in Africa or elsewhere can be useful members of the community. But only on this basis do we welcome their remaining there, that the interests of the people of Africa are always placed first.

I suppose you realize that if India were free it would make a tremendous difference to the conception of empire throughout the world and all subject people would benefit thereby.

We think of India, China and other countries, but we are too often apt to forget Africa and the people of India want you to keep them in mind. After all, though the people of India would welcome the help and sympathy of all progressive people, they are today perhaps strong enough to fight their own battle, whilst that may not be true of some of the peoples of Africa. Therefore, the people of Africa deserve our special consideration.

Most of you will probably agree with the ideas I have put forward. Many people outside this hall may not agree with them. Many people may say that these are idealistic notions and have nothing to do with the modern world. I do not think there could be any more foolish notion than that. We shall only solve our problems today by proceeding in this way, and if you think we can solve them without raising these fundamental issues, you are highly mistaken.

Here is a small example of today in dealing with these problems. The example is of the Moors in Spanish Morocco. There was delay in dealing with their problem and the Fascist clique in Spain took advantage of this and deceived these poor unfortunate Moors by making them all manner of false promises and enlisting them on its side to attack the very people who were likely to give freedom to them. That kind of thing will happen again and again if this issue is not faced properly.

We can hardly expect a subject country to show enthusiasm about the freedom of others when its own people remain subject.

Therefore, in India, we have made it perfectly clear and the Congress has declared that it can play no part in any Imperialist war. So long as India is subject, it is an absurdity to expect it to give its men and resources in a cause which might be in favour of strengthening an empire. The right way to deal with the situation is to root out imperialism, to give complete freedom to the subject peoples and then to approach them in a friendly manner, to come to terms with them. If the approach is made in that manner, they will be friendly. Otherwise, there will be constant hostility, trouble and conflict, and when the crisis develops and peril comes, all manner of complications will arise and it is not easy to say what will happen. Therefore, I beg all of you to remember and realize that we are not dealing with distant idealistic solutions today, but with current problems, and if we neglect them and evade them we do so at our peril.[1]

From Speech as Representative of Indian National Congress at Conference Organized by International Peace Campaign on the Bombardment of Open Towns and the Restoration of Peace—Paris, July 23 and 24, 1938

I do not speak on behalf of kings and queens or princes, but I do claim to speak for hundreds of millions of my countrymen. We have associated ourselves with this work of peace most willingly because of the vital urgency of the problem. Also because, in any event, our past background, and our civilization, would have urged us to do so. For the spirit of India for long ages past, like that of our great sister nation China, has been a spirit of peace. Even in our national struggle for independence we have

[1] U.I., pp. 268–77.

always kept this ideal before us and adopted peaceful methods. So we gladly pledge ourselves to labour for peace. . . .

We have met here especially to discuss the aerial bombardment of open towns and civilian populations. Horror has piled on horror from day to day, and though the present is terrible to contemplate, the future seems to hold something that may be incredibly worse. Recently I visited Barcelona and saw with my own eyes its ruined buildings, its gaping chasms and the bombs hurtle through the air, bringing death and destruction in their train. That picture is imprinted in my heart, and each day's news of bombing in Spain or China stabs me and makes me sick with the horror of it. And yet over that picture there is another— that of the magnificent people of Spain who have endured and fought against these horrors for two long years with unexampled heroism and written with their own blood and suffering a history that will inspire ages to come. To these great men and women of Republican Spain I offer on behalf of the Indian people our respectful homage. And to the people of China also, knit to us by a thousand bonds since the dawn of history, we stretch out our hands in comradeship. Their perils are ours, their suffering hurts us, and we shall hold together, whatever good or ill fortune may befall us.

We are deeply moved by these aerial bombardments in Spain and China. And yet aerial bombing is no new thing for us. The evil is an old one, and because it went unchecked it has grown to those vast and terrible dimensions. Have you forgotten the bombing on the North-West Frontier of India, which has been going on now for many long years and still continues? There are no great cities there like Madrid and Barcelona and Canton and Hankow, but the villages of the Indian frontier also shelter human beings, men, women and children, and they also die and are maimed when bombs from the air fall on them. Do you remember that this question of aerial bombing was raised many years ago in the League of Nations, and the British Government refused to stop it on the frontier? This was called police action, and they insisted on its maintenance. The evil went unchecked, and if it has grown now is it surprising? On whom lies the responsibility?

The Prime Minister of Great Britain has recently offered to withdraw his reservation if there is general agreement in regard to the stoppage of aerial bombing. But that offer is an empty one, unless he takes action and stops all bombing on the frontier. Till then his protests against other people's bombing will have little meaning and less value.

The Dean of Chichester demanded yesterday at this Conference that no treaty should be made with countries that were carrying on aerial bombing, a sentiment that was rightly applauded. What of England then, which is still responsible for bombing on the frontier of India? Is it because the British Government cannot approach this question with clean hands, that they have developed an incredible foreign policy and now seek friendship and agreements with a Power that is most responsible for this bombing in Spain? I wish to dissociate India completely from this policy of encouraging the evil-doer and aggressor and to say that the people of India will be no party to it and will resist it whenever they have a chance to do so.

We have seen the tragic farce of non-intervention in Spain, which, under the cover of fair words and democratic procedure, has aided the insurgents and the invaders of Spain and prevented the people of the country from obtaining even the means of defence. The seas and a hundred doors are open for supplies to reach the insurgents, but the Pyrenees frontier is closed in the name of non-intervention, though women and children die through bombing or are starved from lack of food.

We blame and condemn the invaders and aggressors in Spain, but they have at least openly defied all canons of international law and decency and challenged the world to stop them. What of those Governments who, while bravely talking of peace and law, have submitted to this challenge, adapted themselves to each fresh act of aggression, and tried to make friends with the evil-doers? What of those who have criminally stood by and shown indifference when life and what was more sacred than life itself was crushed and dishonoured?

Even today the aggressor nations are far weaker in numbers and strength and resources than the other countries. And yet the latter appear helpless and incapable of taking effective action. Is it not so because their hands and feet are tied by their past and present imperialist policies? These Governments have failed; it is time that the people took action and compelled them to mend their ways. This action must be immediately to stop aerial bombardments, to open the Pyrenees frontier, to permit the means of defence and food to reach Republican Spain. If bombing is to continue, anti-aircraft guns and other apparatus meant for defence must be allowed to go through.

What vast destruction there has been during these last two years in Spain and China! The starving and the wounded, the women and the children cry aloud piteously for help, and it is the business of all decent and sensitive people all over the world to help. This is a world problem, and we must organize on a world basis. The real burden of the struggle has fallen on the people of the stricken countries; let us at least carry this small burden.

I am glad to tell this conference that the Indian National Congress has organized and is soon sending a medical unit to China. We have also met with considerable success in India in our boycott of Japanese goods, as the export figures demonstrate. A recent incident will indicate the strength of our feeling for the Chinese people. In Malaya the Japanese owned iron and tin mines which employed Chinese workers. These workers refused to help in producing munitions for Japan and left the mines. Thereupon Indian workers were engaged, but at our request they also refused to work there, although this meant privation and suffering for them.

And so the struggle goes on. How many of our friends and colleagues and dear ones have died in this struggle already, and not died in vain. How many of us ... gathered here may go the same way and not meet again? But whether we live or die, the cause of peace and freedom will remain, for that is greater than us—it is the cause of humanity itself. If that perishes, then all of us perish. If it lives, we live also, whatever fate may befall us. To that cause then let us pledge ourselves.[1]

[After speech.] What must we think of the Governments who do not know how to resist aggressors and allowed the Spanish nationalists to receive all necessary war material but insisted that the Pyrenean frontier should be closed against Republican Spain? Aid for the victims of aggression should be organized on a world basis.[2]

Nationalism and the Mass Struggle in India—August, 1938

[An especially cogent summary of the period, published in England.]

The Congress, being a nationalist movement, inevitably has all kinds of people in it. Of course all those who are absolutely pro-imperialist are out of it, because it is an essentially anti-imperialist organisation. But it has people who are very moderate in politics and very reactionary in social matters, and it has at the other extreme a fair number of Socialists, some Communists and others who have recently been co-operating with

[1] Ibid., pp. 278–83.
[2] I.A.A., p. 68.

it. But the Congress also consists of a very large middle section which is certainly anti-imperialist, which is vaguely favourable to Socialism and which is pro-peasant because of our work [with] the peasantry and generally pro-worker too. It is this section which ultimately decides what policy should be. Ordinarily this great middle section goes to the "left", and fairly far to the left if there is nothing to pull it back. Naturally the small right wing tries to pull it back and has some power to do this.

It should be remembered that the terms "left" and "right" are some-what loosely used in India and have not the same significance as in the West. Thus a person may be very "left" or advanced in a political and nationalist sense and yet "right" in a social sense. He may be a good anti-imperialist and may have a record of effective struggle against the British Government. He is respected for this and commands influence. This seeming contradiction arises from the fact that there are two parallel movements—the political and the social. The problem in India is to co-ordinate and integrate these two.

Apart from these sections there is Mr Gandhi, who occupies a peculiar position. He does not belong to the right wing, although they always seek his support, as only if they can get it does the right wing count in the Congress. There is no doubt that Mr Gandhi has changed the whole Congress, the whole nationalist movement in India. He has given it tremendous mass backing and tremendous mass strength. He has awakened people in India to an extraordinary extent and awakened them more or less in a revolutionary direction. He has adopted revolutionary methods, but he also attaches the greatest importance to passive and non-violent methods. He obstructs anything which he fears will lead to violence, but apart from that his tendency has always been towards the "left". Whatever views may be held about him, there is no doubt that he is a tremendous power in India to-day. His popularity among the Indian people is no less than it ever was, except among certain "leftist" elements.

In the last two or three years there has been a crystallisation of Socialist opinion in the Congress. This resulted largely from the increase in the numbers of Congress and came primarily from contact with the masses. But intellectually it also arose from the fact that many people went to prison and there read a large number of books. When they were released they discussed matters among themselves and gradually a certain socialist group came into existence. Three or four years ago this gave rise to the Congress Socialist Party. This took place during a period of reaction while the right group in the Congress was in the ascendancy. The Congress

Socialist Group immediately came into conflict with this right group, but in such a way that it antagonised the large middle group and did not succeed, as it might have done, in carrying this large anti-imperialist group with it. About two years ago this antagonism lessened to some extent. The feeling grew that we must work together on an anti-imperialist basis, that otherwise each group was weak and powerless. We had to put this programme on anti-imperialism and independence in the forefront and for the rest to carry on propaganda. This was the position for a year or two prior to the elections.

After the elections the Congress had to face actual problems. It was not so easy to pass a resolution that would please everybody. The acceptance of office by Congress ministers resulted in two different tendencies. On the one hand there was a tremendous feeling of awakening among the people, both the peasantry and the workers, a feeling as if a great burden had been removed and that big things were going on. This resulted among the workers in big strikes, and among the peasantry in a ferment which took the form not of any particular action but of large demonstrations and a new aggressiveness which they developed in dealing with their landlords or landlords' agents or with the police. They were not so easily cowed. . . . Where previously they might have put up with a beating from a policeman, now if he even spoke to them offensively they would take umbrage and report the matter. Now, they thought, we have our own ministers; they must come to right things. Among the workers, too, there was the growing feeling that they were not going to be suppressed in the way they used to be. In several big strikes, for instance, the strikers knew very well that the police would not take the same action as in the past.

On the other hand there was obviously a tendency for the Congress leaders to become slightly more compromising. They were dealing with day-to-day problems, meeting the Governor and others and trying to find a way out which usually took the form of some kind of a middle way. Sometimes when there was a conflict, the Governor gave way. But on two or three occasions the Governor did not give way and the Ministers resigned. The issue was not, perhaps, a very vital one, but the importance was psychological. One such issue was the release of political prisoners. The ministers resigned, but when they had done so, the Governor reversed his decision and gave way. The simple reason was that the Governor and the Viceroy and the British Government were afraid of a conflict. They saw that the nationalist movement had grown much stronger than it had ever been before and much better organised and were unwilling to fight it. There was also the influence of the international situation. It was very much against [the] interests [of the above officials] to seek a conflict in India with the international situation in its present state. They therefore adopted the very unusual course for the British Government and actually climbed down.

One result of these resignations was that ... the same ministers [had to be accepted. Fresh elections could not be held] because these would have resulted in a bigger majority for Congress and an election campaign which would have again roused the masses. The only alternative [in view was] to set aside the constitution and govern directly under martial law. That would have meant increasing ... conflict, and [the British officials] accordingly accepted the situation and drew back.

One of the fundamental [aspects] of the Indian situation as far as the British Government is concerned is that along with the growth of the nationalist movement the international situation puts that movement in a very strong position. It is uncertain, of course, how far that situation will be used, but everybody in India realises that to some extent it will be used. We have laid stress on two main things. First of all if any attempt is made to supplement [the] constitution by bringing in Federation it will lead to conflict. We are all opposed to Federation which we look upon as the worst part of the constitution. Secondly, we have laid stress on the fact that if there is any outside crisis and war, we are not going to be ordered out for the British Government. It is for the Indian people to decide whether they take part in war or not. It may further be said that they propose to take no part in imperialist war. That is a matter which is exercising the minds of British officials in India who are wondering what, in a moment of crisis, India may do.

As far as our internal problems are concerned, they are getting very complex and difficult; more and more social questions are appearing within the nationalist movement. On the one hand there is this disrupting tendency, which is inevitable to some extent. On the other there is a powerful urge to keep united. If we do not keep united as an anti-imperialist front, we shall become weak and unable to carry on [an] effective struggle against British imperialism. So far this urge for unity has been much stronger than the other. I think it is likely to continue and I believe that it is right that it should continue as such. Although there is a great deal of criticism of each other, every group recognises that we must hold together.

The peasant movement in India, as has been pointed out, has grown more aggressive and more self-reliant. This took the form of big demands.

19+N.

As a matter of fact some parts of Congress had been thinking in terms of peasant demands for many years. Here it may be pointed out that Congress demands many things. It is a national organisation spread out right from the northern frontier to the south. In almost every village some traces of it can be found, some members of it and a committee, but the situation varies in different provinces. There is a fair measure of provincial autonomy, though in matters of policy the national bodies have the decisive authority. Some provinces are more pro-peasant and pro-worker than others, as, for instance, the United Provinces. There the Congress movement is itself largely a peasant movement, with the result that no separate peasant movement of any consequence has arisen, whereas in other parts peasant movements have developed because the peasantry did not find the same field within the Congress. Generally speaking, the Congress programme was very pro-peasant, but when the Ministries began to function, difficulties of two kinds appeared. One was due to the mixed character of Congress, which even includes some landlords with the exception of the very big ones. This acted as a check on legislation. Also there was the fact that there are two houses, an upper house elected by a very restricted franchise and consisting generally of big landlords, and a more popular house. The upper house would certainly reject any big agrarian measure that came before it. Therefore in a province such as, for instance, Bihar, it was decided that the best course was to pass a moderate measure of agrarian reform quickly. A compromise measure was agreed [upon] with the upper house and became law, but the peasantry was not wholly satisfied ... and the peasant movement came into conflict with the Congress movement. In the United Provinces, on the other hand, a more far-reaching measure was put forward which is still being discussed in the Assembly. It is bound to result in conflict between the two houses, but what form this will take cannot be foretold. But there the measure has the support of the peasants.

This land problem is fundamental in India and cannot be solved under the present land system. The Ministries can go on functioning and can tackle other problems, but while this problem is postponed it becomes more acute. The ministers have tackled it partly because they promised to do so, and also for the reason that they personally want the support of the peasants in any future conflict.

In the same way the question of industrial workers has been tackled. Various committees were appointed and on the whole their reports were favourable to the workers. They recommended rises in wages and improvements in many other directions. In Bombay ... the most industrialised province, the employers reluctantly accepted the recommendations of the Government and the committee and gave a rise in wages. In the United Provinces, however, the committee appointed by the Government recommended more or less the same changes as in Bombay, but the employers thereupon retorted with an aggressive memorandum rejecting everything recommended and criticising the Government very strongly as a partial body. Thereupon a big strike took place . . . which has apparently now been settled and the rise in wages has been granted.

Generally speaking, then, both the peasantry and the workers have gained something in standards, but, what is more important, they have gained considerably in strength and are more prepared to enter into big disputes. On the other hand, psychologically speaking, the Congress and the Congress Ministers have become less revolutionary sitting as ministers and carrying on the day-to-day work in co-operation with British officials. The two processes work simultaneously, the masses becoming more aggressive and more revolutionary-minded and the leaders less so. But ultimately what will count is the masses and their problems.

That, then, is the position in India to-day. There are internal conflicts developing inside Congress, but at the same time there is a stronger desire to prevent a split. On the other hand, the conflict with British Imperialism is developing on the question of Federation, and if there is an international crisis, the attitude of Congress will also lead to a conflict. It is unlikely that the British Government will do anything much in India, but it is possible that if they went far in the way of changing the present Federation scheme and the general government of India, they might win certain groups in Congress to their side. Even, however, if there is no major conflict, Congress Ministries cannot go on functioning very long, unless big changes occur. So many other matters come up that give rise to conflict with prominent British Government officials that the present constitution is likely to break down. The biggest issues will then arise in India.

India is thus, like the rest of the world, far from static, and all manner of dynamic possibilities confront her. Her present constitution, imposed upon her by British imperialism, is essentially unstable and cannot last. Her people are engrossed in their manifold problems, and yet realise more and more that these problems are connected with international developments. Because of the strength they have developed, they face the future with a measure of confidence and look forward to the day when full power will come to them to enable them to solve their social problems and play an effective part in evolving peace and freedom in the world.[1]

Betrayal of Czechoslovakia—Letter to "Manchester Guardian" —September 8, 1938

As an Indian, intensely interested in Indian independence and world peace, I have followed recent developments in Spain and Czecho-Slovakia with anxious interest. For some years past the Indian National Congress has criticized and dissociated itself from British foreign policy, which has seemed to us consistently reactionary and anti-democratic, and an encouragement to Fascist and Nazi aggression. Manchuria, Palestine, Abyssinia, Spain agitated the people of India. In Manchuria the foundations were laid for encouraging triumphant aggression, all covenants and rules of international law were ignored, and the League of Nations sabotaged. With all our sympathy and goodwill for the Jews in their distress in the face of fierce and inhuman persecution in Europe, we considered the struggle in Palestine as essentially a national struggle for freedom which was suppressed by violence by British Imperialism in order to control the route to India. In Abyssinia there was a gross betrayal of a brave people. In Spain little was left undone which could harass the Republic and encourage the Insurgents. Having decided that the Spanish Government should lose or was going to lose, the British Government tried in a variety of ways to hasten the desired end, and even insult, injury and gross humiliation by the Insurgents were endured.

The fact that everywhere this policy has been a disastrous failure has not deterred the British Government from pursuing it. The consequences of the rape of Manchuria we see all around us in the world today. The problem of Palestine grows worse from day to day; violence counters violence and the Government uses ever-increasing military forces and coercion in an attempt to subdue a people. It is not always remembered that the problem is largely the creation of the British Government and it must shoulder the responsibility for much that has happened. Abyssinia, as your correspondent points out, still remains unconquered and is likely to remain so. In Spain a heroic people have refused to fall in with the wishes of the British Government and have demonstrated that they will not be and cannot be crushed or subdued.

It is a remarkable record of failure. And yet the Government of Great

[1] L.M. (Aug., 1938), pp. 478–82.

Britain is not capable of learning from it and mending its ways. It pursues even more intensively its policy of encouraging aggression and giving support to General Franco and the Fascist and Nazi powers. No doubt it will carry on in this way, if allowed to do so, till it puts an end to itself as well as the British Empire, for overriding every other consideration are its own class sympathies and leanings towards fascism. That will certainly be a service it will render, howsoever unwittingly, to the world, and I would be the last person to object to an ending of imperialism. But I am deeply concerned with the prospect of world war and it distresses me exceedingly to realize how British foreign policy is directly leading to war. It is true that Herr Hitler has the last and determining word in this matter, but Herr Hitler's decision itself will largely depend on the British attitude. This attitude has so far done everything to encourage him and to bully and threaten Czecho-Slovakia. So, if war comes, the British Government can have the satisfaction or otherwise of feeling that they were largely responsible for it, and the people of Britain, who have put this Government in power, can draw what comfort they can from this fact.

I had thought that nothing that the Government did could surprise me (unless it suddenly turned progressive and worked for peace). But I was mistaken. Recent developments in Czecho-Slovakia, and the way the British Government, directly and through its mediators, has bullied and threatened the Czech Government at every turn, has produced a feeling of nausea in me, and I have wondered how any Englishman with any trace of liberal instincts or decency could tolerate this. I have wondered still more how those who talk so loudly of peace could have supported, actively or passively, this obvious invitation to war.

Recently I spent some time in Czecho-Slovakia and came into contact with numerous people, both Czech and German. I returned full of admiration for the admirable temper of the Czechs and the democratic Germans who, in face of grave danger and unexampled bullying, kept calm and cheerful, eager to do everything to preserve peace, and yet fully determined to keep their independence. As events have shown, they are prepared to go to extraordinary lengths to satisfy every minority claim and preserve peace, but everybody knows that the question at issue is not a minority one. If it was a love of minority rights that moved people, why do we not hear of the German minority in Italy or the minorities in Poland? The question is one of power politics and the Nazi desire to break up the Czecho-Soviet alliance, to put an end to the one democratic State in Central Europe, to reach the Rumanian oil fields and wheat, and thus to dominate Europe. British policy has encouraged this and tried to weaken that democratic State.

In any event, we in India want no fascism or imperialism, and we are more convinced than ever that both are closely akin and dangers to world peace and freedom. India resents British foreign policy and will be no party to it, and we shall endeavour with all our strength to sever the bond that unites us to this pillar of reaction. The British Government has given us an additional and unanswerable argument for complete independence.

All our sympathies are with Czecho-Slovakia. If war comes, the British people, in spite of their pro-Fascist Government, will inevitably be dragged into it. But, even then, how will this Government, with its patent sympathies for the Fascist and Nazi States, advance the cause of democracy and freedom? So long as this Government endures, Fascism will always be at the doorstep.

The people of India have no intention of submitting to any foreign decision on war. They alone can decide and certainly they will not accept the dictation of the British Government, which they distrust utterly. India would willingly throw her entire weight on the side of democracy and freedom, but we heard these words often twenty years ago and more. Only free and democratic countries can help freedom and democracy elsewhere. If Britain is on the side of democracy, then its first task is to eliminate empire from India. That is the sequence of events in Indian eyes, and to that sequence the people of India will adhere.[1]

[Nehru's mounting despair about the international situation caused him to write a number of increasingly vehement articles during 1938.]

London in Suspense—September 28, 1938

After the mysterious happenings behind the scenes of the past few weeks, the journeying to and fro, the appeals and the ultimatums, the mounting danger of war, Mr Neville Chamberlain at last was to make a public pronouncement. . . . It struck me as singularly ineffective. There was no reference to the vital issues at stake, to the naked sword that was being flashed before the world and terrorising humanity, to the way of violence that was becoming the law of nations and which Mr Chamberlain himself had been encouraging by his activities. There was hardly a

[1] U.I., pp. 284–87.

mention of the proud and gallant nation [Czechoslovakia] that was being offered as a sacrifice to the blood lust of the beasts of prey that surrounded it. The reference to it was a disparaging one—"a far-away country of whose people we know nothing". No hint at the dignity and courage and love of peace and freedom and calm determination and tremendous sacrifices of these far-away people, who had been coerced and abandoned so faithlessly by their friends. Nothing was said of the incessant threats and insults and lies that had flown unceasingly from Nazi quarters. Only a brief, apologetic reference to Herr Hitler's "unreasonableness".

I felt depressed and my heart was heavy within me. Was virtue always to be treated so, unless it was accompanied by the big battalion? Was evil ever to triumph?

I thought that perhaps Mr Chamberlain would do greater justice to his theme the next day in Parliament. Perhaps, at last, he would give credit where it was due, and speak the truth without fear of . . . Hitler. Zero hour was approaching; it was time that the truth was out. But at the back of my mind I did not believe this for Mr Chamberlain's past stood up before me and was witness to his partiality for fascism and its works.

Meanwhile there was a digging of trenches in the parks and open spaces, and anti-air-craft guns were being mounted. A.R.P.—air-raid precautions—stared at us from every hoarding, and in innumerable improvised depots men and women tried on gas masks, true emblems in all their ugliness of this savage age of violence. People went about their businesses, but their faces were strained and full of apprehension. There was sorrow in many homes as their loved ones were summoned to put themselves in readiness for the coming war. . . .

I am pressed by people to get a gas mask. The idea seems ridiculous to me. Am I to go about with a snout and the appearance of a beast? I am not adverse to risk and danger and a few days in Barcelona gave me some taste of air-raids. I do not believe in the efficacy of gas masks and if danger comes, the mask will be poor protection. Perhaps its main purpose is to give confidence to the wearer and keep up public morale. No one knows how he will function face to face with extreme danger, yet I imagine that I shall not easily lose my head.

Still the curiosity to see a gas mask at close quarters overcomes me and I decided to go to one of the A.R.P. Depots. I am fitted and later fetch a gas mask.

President Roosevelt has sent another message to Herr Hitler—a digni-fied, moving appeal in which the real point at issue is stressed. What a vast difference between what he says and how he says it and Mr Neville Chamberlain's pronouncements! Even the printed word of President Roosevelt shows that there is a man behind it. What does reason matter or fear of consequences to Hitler? Is Hitler absolutely mad that he should risk his astonishing diplomatic victory, obtained no doubt under threat of violence, by plunging into war? Does he not know that defeat and disaster will certainly be his lot in a world war; that many of his own people will turn against him? Or perhaps he has taken the true measure of Mr Chamberlain and M Daladier and knows exactly how far they can go....

Somehow I feel (or is it my imagination) that ... [Chamberlain] was not big enough for the task he undertook, and this complex comes out repeatedly in his words and manner. He is excited and proud about his personal intervention, his talks with Hitler, the part he is playing in world affairs. Though Prime Minister of Britain, he is not used to these high tasks and the intoxication of the adventure fills him. . . . There [is] neither warmth, nor depth of intellect in what Mr Chamberlain [says]. It [is] very evident that he [is] not a man of destiny.

My thoughts flew to his meeting with Hitler and I thought how overwhelmed he must have been by Hitler, overwhelmed not only by the frequent ultimatums of the latter, but by the dynamic and passionate and somewhat neurotic personality. For Hitler, for all his evil bent and distorted intent, has something elemental about him and Mr Chamberlain is of the earth, earthy. But even Mr Chamberlain could have met that elemental force with another force, also elemental but far more powerful, the force of organised democracy, the will of millions of people. He did not possess that power, nor did he seek to possess it. He moved in his narrow sphere and thought in limited terms, and never tried to develop or represent the urge that moves millions. It was inevitable, under the circumstances, that in the clash of wills he must go down before Hitler.

But was there even a clash of will? There was no hint of such real clash in what Mr Chamberlain said, as there had been none in his deeds. He approached Hitler with sympathy and a large measure of approval and agreement. There was no talk of high principles, of freedom, of democracy, of human right and justice, of international law and morality, of the barbarity of the way of the sword, of the sickening lies and vulgarity of the high priests of Nazism, of the unparalleled coercion of minorities in Germany, of refusal to submit to blackmail and bullying. On principles there was hardly any dispute, only some details were discussed. It is evident that Mr Chamberlain's outlook, allowing for his English environment, was not so different from Hitler's.

In that long speech of his there was much in praise of Hitler, of his sincerity, of belief in his bonafides, of his promise not to seek further territory in Europe. There was no mention of President Roosevelt and his striking messages. There was no mention of Russia, although Russia is intimately concerned with the fate of Czechoslovakia.

And what of Czechoslovakia herself? There was mention of course, but not a word about the unparalleled sacrifices of her people, of their astonishing restraint and dignity in face of intolerable provocation, of their holding aloft the banner of democracy. It was an astonishing and significant omission, deliberately made.

Mr Chamberlain's speech held the audience. Not because of the excellence of the argument or the personality of the speaker, but because of the vital importance of the subject. He led up to a dramatic conclusion. He was going to Munich tomorrow and so were Signor Mussolini and M Daladier. And as a great favour Hitler had made a striking concession —he would defer mobilisation for twenty-four hours!

Mr Chamberlain succeeded in rousing the House by this element of drama and by the hope it brought of the possible avoidance of war. The strain of the last few days lessened and relief appeared in all the faces.

It was good that war had been pushed off, even though this might be only for a day or two longer. It was terrible to contemplate that war, and any relief from it was welcome.

And yet, and yet, what of Czechoslovakia, what of democracy and freedom? Was there going to be another betrayal again, the final murder of that nation? This sinister gathering of four at Munich, was it the prelude to the Four-Power Pact of Fascism-cum-Imperialism to isolate Russia, to end Spain finally, and to crush all progressive elements? Mr Chamberlain's past record inevitably makes one think so.

So tomorrow Chamberlain meets Hitler and Mussolini. One was too much for him, what will be his fate with these two strong men? Perhaps Mr Chamberlain and Monsieur Daladier will, under cover of intricate words, agree to everything that Hitler says, and then, as another of his great favours, Hitler will consent to postpone war by a few days or weeks. That will indeed be a great triumph and Hitler ought to be hailed then as the prophet of peace. The Nobel Peace Prize might still be awarded to him, though Mr Chamberlain will be a hot competitor.[1]

[1] C.S.W., pp. 103-11.

19*

India in Relationship to World Crisis—The Choice Before India —September 28, 1938

In this grave hour, when the fates of nations hang in the balance and world war threatens humanity, the people of India cannot remain passive spectators of the march of historic events. They stand to gain or lose from them, as do others; and they have to decide how best to serve the cause of freedom that is dear to them. To wait on others to decide for them, or not to decide at all, is to prove unworthy of our historic destiny. All the peoples of the world desire peace, but individuals and those in power and authority are driving the world to terrible war even though they talk glibly of peace. The people of India are even more committed to the way of peace than other peoples.

The Congress has clearly laid down the principle which must govern our action in times of world crisis and war. By those principles we must stand. But the time is fast approaching for the application of those principles in the light of events and recent developments. A negative attitude of protest or the mere enunciation of a principle is not enough when a positive policy and constructive action become necessary. Our movement long ago passed the stage of protest in our national affairs and we took to constructive action. In foreign affairs also we are passing that purely agitational stage, and India's voice counts today and is listened to with attention in international gatherings. It becomes essential, therefore, that we should fashion our policy accordingly and link our national struggle with that policy. . . .

Fascism crushed all progressive elements and set up new standards in cruelty and inhumanity. It gloried in brutality and openly aimed at war. Imperialist Powers talked in terms of democracy but aided and abetted fascism and helped it to grow. International morality decayed, all idea of collective action for peace was given up, and an unabashed gangsterism among nations grew up and was tolerated. Yet it was clear that only by collective action could the aggressor be stayed and peace maintained. A surrender to violence and aggression was no basis for peace, for . . . aggression and blackmail grew by every surrender and brought world war ever nearer. It was not difficult for this aggression to be checked and peace ensured if those Powers who believed in peace acted together, for their strength was far greater than that of the Fascist aggressor. But many of these very Powers who talked of peace and democracy were imperialist and they sympathized with fascism and encouraged it.

The British Government has a special responsibility for the growth of fascism and thus for bringing war nearer. They tolerated aggression in Manchuria, took part in the betrayal of Abyssinia, and indirectly aided the Fascist rebels in Spain. Their general policy was one of consistently encouraging Fascism and Naziism. They did not succeed in Spain because the people of Spain refused to fall in with their wishes and fought with unsurpassed courage and determination for their freedom.[1]

Governments have power to shape a country's policy and to give it a right or wrong turn. But in moments of crisis, of war, and potential war, popular forces emerge and grow and make a vital difference. They change governments or compel them to act in a different way. It is these progressive forces that we see growing up around us, and if the crisis develops into war or otherwise they will grow all the more. We have to reckon with these forces, to welcome them, and to co-operate with them. It is fear of these that has prevented the British Government from co-operating with the Soviet Union in ensuring peace and has made them seek alliance with the Nazis even at the cost of weakening their empire.

Yet there are obvious dangers with an imperialist and reactionary government exploiting for its own purposes in war-time the slogan of democracy. Do we not have now even Hitler and Mussolini giving their approval to the principle of self-determination, choosing to forget what they have done and are doing to many of their own people? Have we forgotten the fine phrases and slogans used by the British Government during the last war? Obviously we cannot be taken in by phrases again and allow ourselves to be exploited for imperialist purposes. We cannot be parties to the horror and disillusion of the last war.

It is true that this very memory of the past will cling to us and be a constant reminder to us of what we should not do. It is true also that there is a greater realization of the issue today, a vaster mass consciousness, a greater vigilance among the people. The existence of the Soviet Union itself and the astonishing fight for democracy in Spain are significant. And yet who can say that vast numbers of people will not be misled again and their courage and sacrifice and idealism not exploited for base ends, leaving after the holocaust of war the same misery, the same injustices, imperialism and fascism?

How to avoid this terrible danger and yet how not to be a mere spectator when the most vital issues are at stake? It is a question most difficult to answer for every person who cares for freedom and democracy and

[1] U.I., pp. 294–95.

world peace and order. For us in India the difficulty is no less. We sympathize with all our heart with Czecho-Slovakia in her struggle for freedom, we realize the world significance of it, the momentous consequences which flow from it. We want to help her in her struggle to the best of our ability, for thereby we help the cause of freedom and democracy throughout the world. We want to combat fascism. But we will not permit ourselves to be exploited by imperialism, we will not have war imposed upon us by outside authority, we will not sacrifice to preserve the old injustices or to maintain an order that is based on them. We will not and cannot forget our own struggle for freedom. Slogans which may sound pleasant to the ear but have little reality behind them or vague promises which have been broken often before, cannot determine our course of action. Will anyone dare to ask us to fight for democracy and deny us that democracy?

It is a terrible predicament and a difficult question to answer. Yet the answer must be given, and given in clear language. The Congress, in its resolutions, has already clearly indicated what this answer must be. We have to amplify this and apply it, in terms of constructive statesmanship, to the needs of the hour.

Whether there is war or a so-called peace which is continuous conflict and a herald to war, we must be clear what we are aiming at and fight for that. We must not permit vague slogans or what are termed military necessities to take away such liberties as we possess and to divert us from our objective. We must have no imperialist settlement at the end, but the liquidation of imperialism itself. We must have a real League of Nations controlling armaments and air services, and collective security based on freedom and social justice. And those who have the conduct of war or peace must be people who believe in these objectives.

If I were an Englishman I would not trust the present British Government in war or peace, and I would not like to commit myself to their care to be used and exploited as they wish. Their talk of peace and democracy has been pure bluff. They could have ensured peace by co-operating with France, the Soviet Union, and the United States of America, and as for democracy, they have done their utmost to slay it in Central Europe. I would demand that this Government must go. So long as it remains I would fear betrayal.

But as an Indian I must confine myself to India. It is time that the problem of our independence was faced and settled finally. We have had enough delay, and if every group of people are considered worthy of self-determination, the three hundred and seventy millions of India have waited long enough for it. There is no other way of settling this question except by recognition of our right to independence, and through a constituent assembly. The proposed Federation is dead; let there be no further talk of it. We have bigger questions to decide, vaster problems to settle, and the sooner we set about them the better. More and more people, even in England, have come to realize that it is both good politics and good sense to have a friendly and free India by their side rather than a hostile India ever giving trouble and weakening them in times of crisis. As a prelude to the new age of freedom and democracy, for which we work and for which we may have to fight, India must have the full sense of freedom.

But we are in the midst of a crisis, and intricate schemes cannot be evolved in a day. What can be done without delay? India's right to independence must be recognized, as also the fact that her constitution will be drawn up by a constituent assembly elected by adult franchise. A committee consisting of representatives of the people should be set up to work out the details for the election of this assembly. And immediate steps should be taken for the transitional period so that a popular direction is given to affairs. With this background, questions of trade and economic relations between India and England will be considered in a friendly spirit, and I have no doubt that India will seek to do justice to all just interests of the British people in India.

An India with her freedom assured to her, and working for the establishment of a democratic State, will be a pillar of strength to freedom and democracy elsewhere, and will throw in her weight and resources, in war or peace, for the defence of democracy. She will most willingly join forces in the defence of Czecho-Slovakia, to combat fascism, to work for a settlement to do away with the injustices of the past and the present and lay the foundations of a true world order. Then India and England, if England also pursues the paths of freedom and justice, will co-operate together for peace and the good of humanity.[1]

India and the Munich Crisis—October 23, 1938

Today the prestige of England and France has vanished utterly from all over the East. Unfortunately even the progressive forces in these countries have suffered because of this and little reliance is placed on them. When crisis came they failed to make any impression or even to

Ibid., pp. 297–300.

pull together, and even now the lesson has not been sufficiently learnt. India feels more than ever that the only way to gain her objective of independence is by her own organised strength and will to freedom, through such sacrifices as may be demanded of her. She is not weak today; she is self-reliant and is conscious of her growing strength, and she has learnt not to surrender to evil or to superior physical might, whatever the consequences.

Inevitably we shall rely on ourselves but it is foolish to think on narrow national lines in this world today, especially after Munich and the triumphant domination of fascism over Europe. If the progressive forces all over the world cannot even now pull together they are doomed to annihilation and they will deserve that doom. Therefore India must necessarily pursue this policy of cooperation with those who stand for freedom. What will others do?

Recent events have demonstrated with startling clarity that freedom is indivisible. We cannot have a static world in which freedom and democracy exist in some parts and a total denial of freedom in other parts. There will be conflict between the two, for the very presence of democratic freedom is an offence in the eyes of fascism and ultimately undermines it. Therefore there is a continuous attempt by fascism to put an end to free conditions in other countries. This can either be met by a policy of surrender and a progressive suppression of liberties or by facing aggression and refusing to submit to it. The policy of the British Government is apparently the former one, or perhaps this is not surrender for them as they themselves approve of fascism. This simply cannot be the policy of those who care for freedom and democracy. What are these to do?

"To resist is to conquer" is the slogan of the Spanish Republic and they have lived up magnificently to that slogan. Alone in Europe, they have shown that democracy, if it so wills, can defend itself successfully even against overwhelming odds. Powerful States have collapsed and proud empires have been humbled by methods of gangsterism. But the people of Spain stand unconquered and unsubdued, and out of the very horror they have gone through, they have built up a new Spain which fills all friends of democracy with hope.

If we are to face fascism, it is in that spirit that we have to do it. To hold hard to our principles and to freedom and to refuse to surrender, even unto death. But if we compromise with those principles, and carry on our own imperialism while we combat fascism, we lose both friends and supporters as well as all the strength and enthusiasm that comes from fighting for a worthy cause. If England really fought for democracy, she would have the world's sympathy and support. But who would sympathise with an imperialist England fighting to keep her colonies?

The weakness of England and France during the recent crisis was their imperialism. Imperialism cannot champion democracy; it cannot fight fascism effectively as at heart it sympathises with it. The Empire of England, as that of France, will fade away before long but if the present policy continues they will not only end but end in further dishonour and will give place to fascist empires.

Collective security was meant to check violent aggression on the part of nations. It has failed, because it had an imperialist basis, and so long as that foundation endures, it will not function effectively. And yet collective security is essential if a rational and peaceful world order is to be evolved.

A new Europe is rising up before our eyes, a new world, and we have to understand them and adjust ourselves accordingly. Events are marching ahead and changing the shape of things as we have known them. There seems to be too much of the frightened and helpless spectator about the champion of freedom and democracy in Europe today. He has lost all initiative and can only bemoan his lot. It is time that this defeatist attitude was ended and the issues faced squarely and action taken.

The spread of fascism must be countered both at home and abroad. It can only be checked by encouraging democracy everywhere and placing our reliance on it. As an Indian I desire passionately the freedom of India and I shall go on working for it. But I feel now more than ever that this is necessary from the wider international viewpoint, in order to combat fascism. Only a free and democratic India can help democracy elsewhere. A subject India dominated by imperialism will be a burden which ever grows heavier and thus weakens the democratic front. British imperialism is now facing a difficult problem of its own creation in Palestine, and a sorry mess they have made of it. They will not solve it by methods of terrorism. They will not solve any of their imperialist problems by coercion. This policy will only lead to their own weakening and the strengthening of fascist elements in those countries, as we see in the Arab world today. And India is a much vaster undertaking than little Palestine.

The only possible policy, if Britain believes in democracy, is to shed imperialism utterly and rapidly and replace it by free democratic institutions in these countries, which, instead of weakening it, will then be powerful allies. An independent democratic India will be a tower of strength against fascism in Europe or Asia. . . .

To ask India to accept present conditions and to co-operate with Britain in sustaining a vanishing democracy, is to refuse to understand the mind and temper of India or the march of events in Europe. We must look [at] things straight and get out of . . . mental ruts which have brought so much evil in their train. India believes in freedom and democracy and wants to give her support to any system that insures them. She holds out her hand of fellowship to all who believe in them in England or elsewhere. But only a free India can do so, and Indian freedom thus becomes a vital factor in world politics.[1]

India and England—October 28, 1938

Two and a half years ago I visited England and met many people . . . belonging to various parties and groups. They showed a courteous interest in the Indian problem and expressed sympathy for our cause. I appreciated the courtesy and welcomed the sympathy.

And yet, inevitably, I attached no great importance to either, for I was fully conscious of the indifference and apathy to India of people generally and even of those whose business it is to consider such problems.

I found a general desire not to think about India, to shirk the issue. It was too complicated and in a world full of troubles, why add to them? The Government of India Act had just been passed and, unsatisfactory as it was, it had one merit at least. It postponed the issue for a while and gave an excuse for not thinking about it.

I was not disappointed for I had not expected much more, and for many years we had trained ourselves in India not to rely on others but to develop our own strength. I went back to India. Our problem did not vanish because people in England were not thinking about it. It grew and we grew with it.

Meanwhile, the international situation became ever more critical and we came to realise that the Indian problem was a part of this world problem and that we in India could make a difference if crisis or war came. That realisation has grown with us and with others and has raised the Indian national struggle for independence to the international plane.

During my present visit to England I have again had the privilege of meeting old friends and new and spoken about India to numerous gatherings.

I found still a certain apathy and considerable ignorance, and inevitably

[1] C.S.W., pp. 113-18.

the urgent problems of Spain and China and Central Europe absorbed attention. And yet I found a vital difference and a new and more realistic way of looking at the Indian problem.

Perhaps this was due to a realisation of the great strength of the Indian national movement today, perhaps to the gravity of the international situation and the apprehension that India might add to the danger of it when crisis came. Perhaps this very gravity, this sense of impending catastrophe, had forced people out of the old mental ruts and made them think afresh in terms of reality.

For the reality is this: that India wants, and is determined to achieve, full independence; that the problem of our appalling poverty clamours for solution, and that this will not be solved till the people of India have power in their hands to shape their political and economic destiny as they will and without interference from outside; that the organised strength of the Indian people has grown greatly in recent years and it is difficult for outside authority to check for long their march to freedom; that the international situation indirectly helps greatly the Indian national movement.

Even the Conservative die-hard has to acknowledge that this in essence is a true analysis of the Indian situation. India is bound to achieve her independence, preferably with the goodwill of others, but even if that goodwill is denied her. And so almost everybody to-day talks in terms of Indian independence.

Looked at in this perspective, the questions of Provincial Autonomy and Federation become minor issues in a larger context. They may, of course, provoke a major conflict, but the real question is, and will remain, independence, and every step we may take, every tactic we might adopt, will be considered and decided with reference to this question alone. Does it strengthen us and bring independence within our grasp?

If obstruction is offered, if attempts are made to impose anything on us, our reaction is bound to be hostile. The result ultimately will be the same, for forces beyond human control are working to that end, but that result may be one brought about in friendliness and goodwill and leading to friendship and co-operation, or it may have a background of ill-will and conflict darkening the future and creating barriers to healthy co-operation.

I believe it is an appreciation of all this that has brought about a welcome change in the outlook of many people here. They realise that in a dynamic situation mere passivity and indifference do not pay, while an active policy might well be advantageous.

England and India have an unfortunate background of hostility and conflict. It is not easy for an Indian to forget this, and yet in these pregnant days of world conflicts and Fascist aggression and an ever-present possibility of terrible war, if we continue to think and function in the narrow terms of the past, we do so at our peril. We must rise above them and take the larger view.

I trust that it may be possible in the future for India and England to co-operate together as equals for the common good. But that co-operation is impossible under the shadow of Empire. That Empire will have to be liquidated and India will have to gain her independence before real co-operation is possible.

As an Indian nationalist I have nothing to say to England, for we can only think of her in terms of imperialism. I can only work for building up and increasing our own strength and relying on it to gain our objective. . . .

As a Socialist, I have even more to say to my comrades here. British Labour in the past has wobbled dangerously on imperial issues and more particularly on India. Its record is bad. But in these times of peril, none of us dare wobble or equivocate. And so it is time that British Labour acted up to the principles it has enunciated, and, as it happens, even expediency demands such action.

Labour, which is anti-Fascist, must also equally be anti-Imperialist. It must stand for the ending of Empire. It must clearly declare for the independence of India and for the right of the people there to frame their own constitution through a Constituent Assembly, and it must be prepared to do everything in its power to bring this about.

We are not concerned over-much with the Federation, for we want the whole of the Government of India Act to go and to be replaced by a constitution of our own making.

The time has passed for minor remedies and the world rushes to catastrophe. We may yet avert this if the progressive forces of the world work together. India can play her part in this company, but only a free India can do so. British Labour working to this end will lay the foundations of future friendship and co-operation between the peoples of England and India.

It is gratifying to note that the leaders of British Labour are thinking on these lines. It is still more pleasing to find the rank and file of the Labour movement responding enthusiastically to this call of freedom.

The world marches rapidly to-day and no one knows what to-morrow will bring. India also is changing and going ahead, and all our planning may be out of date soon. But a basis of goodwill between the progressive forces in India and England will lay the foundations for future co-operation for our mutual good and to the advantage of world peace and freedom.[1]

Return to India, *1938*

I returned . . . [to India from Europe in late 1938] sad at heart with many illusions shattered.[2]

[A postscript—from letter to Indira, November 14, 1938.]

We live in an age of revolution, a revolution which started when the War broke out in 1914, and continues from year to year with the world in the throes of conflict everywhere. The French Revolution of one hundred and fifty years ago gradually ushered in an age of political equality, but the times have changed, and that by itself is not enough to-day. The boundaries of democracy have to be widened now so as to include economic equality also. This is the great revolution through which we are all passing, the revolution to ensure economic equality, and thus to give democracy its full meaning, and to bring ourselves in line with the advance of science and technology.

This equality does not fit in with imperialism or with capitalism, which are based on inequality and the exploitation of nation or class. Therefore it is resisted by those who profit by this exploitation, and when the conflict grows, even the conception of political equality and parliamentary democracy is repudiated. That is fascism, which in many ways takes us back to the Middle Ages. It exalts the domination of Race, and in place of the divine right of an autocratic king has the divine right of an all-powerful Leader. The growth of fascism during the last five years and its attack on every democratic principle and conception of freedom and civilization have made the defence of democracy the vital question to-day. The present world conflict is not between communism and socialism on the one hand and fascism on the other. It is between democracy and fascism, and all the real forces of democracy line up and become anti-fascists. . . .

But behind this democracy lies inevitably the idea of an extension of democracy, and for fear of this, reactionaries everywhere, even though

[1] Ibid., pp. 119-25.
[2] T.F., p. 364.

paying lip-service to democracy, give their sympathy or allegiance to fascism.[1]

[After arrival in Bombay—November 17, 1938.] One thing I want to emphasize is that the world today is witnessing a revolutionary change. Only those nations which are strong and united, forgetting dissensions, can attain freedom and retain it.

The biggest problem for us is to attain our freedom and remove our poverty. It is our first duty but even then we cannot forget the happenings in Spain, China and Palestine. Those events are bound to have repercussions in this country.[2]

[1] G.W.H., pp. 955-56.
[2] I.A.A., pp. 69-70.

PART FIVE

1939—A Crucial Year

Today there is a mighty awakening among the people of the [Indian] States. When, in after years, the history of India comes to be written, the year 1938 will stand out as the year of this awakening. The historian of that distant future will not wonder at this awakening; but he will marvel that the millions who inhabit the Indian States submitted for generations to intolerable and appalling conditions, and that a system of government which had long vanished in other parts of the world still continued in India.

The year 1938 has become history, and we stand on the threshold of 1939. The movement for freedom gathers pace, and the whole of India looks with sympathy and understanding on this great struggle.[1]

*

Two Statements by Gandhi:

I. "Pandit Jawaharlal Nehru has compelled me to study, among other things, the implications of a Constituent Assembly. When he first introduced it in the Congress resolutions, I reconciled myself to it because of my belief in his superior knowledge of the technicalities of democracy. But I was not free from scepticism. Hard facts have, however, made me a convert and, for that reason perhaps, more enthusiastic then Jawaharlal himself. For I seem to see in it a remedy, which Jawaharlal may not, for our communal and other distempers, besides being a vehicle for mass political and other education.

"The more criticism I see of the scheme, the more enamoured I become of it. It will be the surest index to the popular feeling. It will bring out the best and the worst in us."[2]

II. "Believe me if Jawaharlal is not in jail today, it is not because he is afraid of it. He is quite capable of mounting the gallows with a smile on his lips."[3]

[1] U.I., p. 27.
[2] S.D.I.C. (Vol. II), p. 477.
[3] Quoted in G.I.A., p. 408.

On the Eve of War—On Chamberlain— Further Homage to the Spanish and Chinese Republics—India Looks at the World

I

On the Eve of War

[Although the international crisis overshadowed all else in 1939, there were vast problems demanding attention within India. As the clouds of war loomed ever larger, Nehru spoke with fresh intensity and a mounting sense of urgency about the issues at stake, both abroad and at home. (Because of the crucial nature of the events that occurred throughout the year, an entire Part is devoted to 1939.)]

On Chamberlain—Allahabad, January 7, 1939

Mr Neville Chamberlain [talks] of peace and appeasement and [brings] war nearer; he [talks] of democracy and [does] everything to strangle it. Ordinarily, Governments [are] afraid of defeat in war, but recently they [have] had the queer spectacle of the British Government being afraid of victory. As someone [has] said, Mr Chamberlain snatched defeat out of the jaws of victory; or he was so afraid that war might result in the ending of the Nazi regime and Fascism that he was prepared to put up with losses to the British Empire.

Mr Chamberlain's policy [has] not been one of being frightened by German might, but one of deliberate support for the Nazi policy. The events of 1938 as well as earlier [have shown] how the British Government [has] almost consistently supported Fascism and Nazism, despite temporary conflicts.[1]

[1] I.A.A., pp. 72–73.

599

Further Homage to the Spanish and Chinese Republics—
January 24, 1939

In this age when black reaction grips the world, and culture and civilisation decay, and violence seems to reign unchecked, the magnificent struggles of the Spanish and Chinese Republics against overwhelming odds have lightened the darkness of many a wanderer through the pathless night. We sorrow for the incredible horrors that have taken place, but our hearts are full of pride and admiration for the human courage that has smiled through disaster and found greater strength in it, and for the invincible spirit of man that does not bend to insolent might, whatever the consequences. Anxiously we follow the fate of the people of Spain, and yet we know that they can never be crushed, for a cause that has this invincible courage and sacrifice behind it can never die. Madrid and Valencia and Barcelona will live for ever more, and out of their ashes the Spanish Republicans will yet build up the free Spain of their desire.

We who struggle for our own freedom are deeply moved by this epic struggle of the Spanish Republic, for the freedom of the world is imperilled there. The frontiers of our struggle lie not only in our own country but in Spain and China also.

Meanwhile millions of refugees starve in Republican Spain and women and children face not only the enemy bombs from the air but death through lack of food. India cannot remain indifferent to this terrible tragedy and we must make every effort to send them food and succour.

I congratulate those who [are aiding] the Spanish people in their dire distress. We can do little for these brave torch-bearers of freedom, but we can at least send them [our] tribute to their magnificent courage and to the cause to which they have offered their immeasurable sacrifice. [1]

India Looks at the World—January 25, 1939

Nationalism is in ill odour today in the West and has become the parent of aggressiveness, intolerance, and brutal violence. All that is reactionary seeks shelter under that name—fascism, imperialism, race bigotry, and the crushing of that free spirit of inquiry which gave the semblance of greatness to Europe in the nineteenth century. Culture succumbs before its onslaught and civilization decays. Democracy and freedom are its pet

[1] C.S.W., pp. 57–58.

aversions, and in its name innocent men and women and children in Spain are bombed to death, and fierce race persecution takes place.

Yet it was nationalism that built up the nations of Europe a hundred years or more ago and provided the background for that civilization whose end seems to be drawing near. And it is nationalism which is the driving-force today in the countries of the East which suffer under foreign domination and seek freedom. To them it brings unity and vitality and a lifting of the burdens of the spirit which subjection entails. There is virtue in it up to a certain stage; till then it is a progressive force adding to human freedom. But even then it is a narrowing creed, and a nation seeking freedom, like a person who is sick, can think of little besides its own struggle and its own misery.

India has been no exception to this rule, and often, in the intensity of her struggle, she has forgotten the world and thought only in terms of herself. But, as strength came to her, and confidence born of success, she began to look beyond her frontiers. The increasing interest she has taken in the problems of the world is a measure of the growth of her nationalist movement. Perhaps nothing is so surprising in India today as this anxious interest in foreign affairs and the realization that her own struggle for freedom is a part of the world struggle. And this interest is by no means confined to the intelligentsia, but goes deep down to the worker, the petty shopkeeper, and even, to a certain extent, to the peasant. The invasion of Manchuria by Japan caused a wave of sympathy for China, and Japan, which had so far been popular with Indians, began to be disliked. The rape of Abyssinia by Italy was deeply felt and resented. The tragic events of Central Europe produced a profound impression. But most of all India felt, almost as a personal sorrow, the revolt against the Republic of Spain and the invasion of China, with all their attendant horrors. Thousands of demonstrations were held in favour of Spain and China, and out of our poverty we extended our helping hand to them in the shape of food and medical missions.

This reaction in India was not due primarily to humanitarian reasons, but to a growing realization of the significance of the conflicts in the world and to an intelligent self-interest. We saw in fascism the mirror of the imperialism from which we had suffered, and in the growth of fascism we saw defeat for freedom and democracy, for which we struggled. With our long experience of British Imperialism, we distrusted the assurances, so often given, of British support of collective security and the League of Nations. Because of this we followed, perhaps with greater clarity than elsewhere, the development of British foreign policy towards co-operation with the Fascist Powers, and our opposition to British Imperialism became a part of our opposition to all imperialism and fascism.

To this British foreign policy we were entirely opposed, and yet, as [part] of the Empire, we were bound by it. By resolution and public declaration we dissociated ourselves from it and endeavoured, in such ways as were open to us, to develop our own foreign policy. The medical mission that we sent to China or the foodstuffs that went from India to Spain were our methods of asserting our foreign policy and dissociating ourselves from that of Britain. We laid down, further, our line of action in the event of world war breaking out. It was for the people of India to determine whether India would join a war or not, and any decision imposed upon us by Britain would be resisted. Nor were we prepared on any account to permit our resources to be exploited for an imperialist war.

The Indian nationalist movement has stood for many years for full independence and the severance of our tie with the British Empire. Recent events in Europe have made this an urgent necessity for us, for we cannot tolerate association with British foreign policy and the possibility of our resources being utilized for wrong ends. We must control our foreign policy, our finances, and our defences, and have perfect freedom to develop our own contacts with other countries.

Foreign affairs are thus casting their long shadow over the Indian national struggle, and the growing consciousness of this makes India look at the world with ever-increasing interest. She thinks of the day, which may not be long distant, when she will be a free country, and already she prepares mentally for that change. The British Empire is fading away before our eyes, and everyone knows that it cannot hold India in subjection for long. Responsible statesmen in England no doubt realize this, and yet it is exceedingly difficult for them to give up the assumptions and mental atmosphere of a century ago, and adapt themselves to what logic tells them is the inevitable end.

That is the dilemma of Britain today. There are only two courses open to her in regard to India. The natural and the logical course is to recognize what must be and adapt herself gracefully to it. This means the immediate recognition of India's right to self-determination on the basis of complete freedom and the drawing up of India's Constitution by a Constituent Assembly consisting of her elected representatives. Such a decision, and immediate steps taken to implement it, would immediately bring about a psychological change, and the old atmosphere of conflict and hostility would give place to a spirit of co-operation. India, achieving her independence in this way, would not look unfavourably to certain privileges in the matter of trade and commerce being granted to Britain. She might even accept certain financial burdens which in justice should not fall on her. We would be willing to pay this price for freedom with peace, for the cost of conflict will, in any event, be much greater. India would also be a friend and colleague in world affairs, provided Britain stood for freedom and democracy.

The other course is to keep India in subjection and attempt to impose vital decisions on her. This would inevitably lead to a major conflict with Indian nationalism. It might delay Indian freedom for a while, but certainly it would not delay it for very long; and it is possible that the conflict itself might precipitate matters. It was no easy matter for the British Government to suppress the last civil disobedience movement. Today the Congress and the national movement are far stronger than they have ever been, and Britain, on the other hand, thanks to Mr Chamberlain's policy, is dangerously near to impotence in foreign affairs. That does not mean that Britain cannot strike hard at India. She can certainly do so, but it will be a very difficult task to undertake, and if international crisis intervenes, as it well might, a perilous one. It is not surprising, therefore, that the British Government have no desire whatever to force a conflict in India. They would welcome a settlement with India, if this could be obtained without giving up their vital and vested interests. But any settlement means, in fact, a settlement with the National Congress. This, if it is genuinely attempted and is to be successful, means facing up to all the implications of the first of the two courses outlined above. British Imperialism, by its very nature, is unable to do this. The British Government will therefore at all costs avoid the first course.

That is the dilemma, and there is no middle course, except one of marking time. But time runs fast in this age of dictators, and events follow one another with a startling rapidity. At any moment the edifice of "appeasement" which Mr Chamberlain has built up so laboriously, even at the cost of what nations and individuals hold most dear, might collapse and bring catastrophe. What of India then? What will India do? That is the question that often worries British statesmen. For it will matter a great deal what India does. India will make a difference.

It is not as if India were waiting for a chance to profit by England's difficulty. Even during the Czecho-Slovakian crisis Mr Gandhi made it clear that we do not blackmail or bargain. But it is manifestly absurd to imagine that India would in any way help a Government which was not only keeping her in subjection, but was also following a foreign policy which she detests and abhors. It is equally out of the question that we should forget our objective of independence and suspend our struggle simply because England was in difficulties. We shall pursue our path, and it seems inevitable that this will bring us into conflict with the British Government, for we shall resist anything that is imposed upon us against our will.

Even apart from the European or Far Eastern situation, internal conditions in India will not permit of marking time for long. There is an apparent quiet on the surface, and in a great part of India, Congress Governments are functioning in the Provinces, but there is an ominous rumbling, and signs are already visible pointing to an approaching crisis.

So the British Government cannot easily mark time for long. And yet they cannot make up their minds about India or any other problem and drift helplessly to disaster. They seem to have lost the capacity to think or act, and perhaps that is the surest sign of the decay of the British ruling classes, which have so long wielded power and controlled the Empire. Their attitude to India cannot be considered by itself; it is part of their general world policy. A support of fascism in Europe does not fit in with the establishment of a free, democratic State in India. If the latter was aimed at it would mean the liquidation of British Imperialism the world over, the strengthening of democracy in England, and an unrelenting opposition to fascism and all it stands for. It would mean the end of Governments like the one under which England has the misfortune to suffer today.

It is clear, therefore, that under existing circumstances the British Government will not adopt the first course mentioned above. They will incline more towards the second course, and yet they will hesitate to adopt it and will try to find some middle way. That middle way is to aggravate some of our internal problems so that we may weaken and be in a mood to compromise with them. If it fails then, subject to the international situation and several other factors, they will adopt the method of repression. Even so they will try to avoid a direct conflict, and will largely function through and behind various reactionary forces in India, notably the Indian Princes and the communalists. We see the development of this line of action today. . . .

The Hindu-Muslim problem has during the past year and a half assumed a new aspect, and is undoubtedly obstructing political progress. It is largely psychological, due to an apprehension in the minds of the Muslims that, under a democratic system, they might be ignored by a

Hindu majority. The problem is a serious one and, because of its psychological basis, difficult to tackle. And yet it has no deep roots and it must not be confused with the conflicts of nationalities in Europe. For the vast majority of Muslims and Hindus are of the same races, with much the same customs and language. The increasing importance of economic problems, which affect both alike, is the surest way of liquidating this problem. Meanwhile a tactful and generous approach will help in toning it down.[1]

2	Independence Day Message—Meaning of Struggle for Freedom—The Indian States and Federation—Communalism Government of India Act

Message on India's Independence Day—January 26, 1939

Eight years have passed since we took [the Independence Day] pledge for the first time, years heavy with sorrow for us and struggle, but also with a measure of triumph and achievement. But though success has come to us, we know its meager worth, and the promised land has yet to be reached when this pledge of ours will redeem itself.

And the world? War rages in the Far East and in Spain to the accompaniment of incredible and inhuman atrocities, and the black night of reaction covers Europe. Multitudes, tortured beyond endurance, become refugees and wander from one country to another, seeking home and shelter, and finding none.

What then does our pledge mean to us today, what significance does it have? Has it grown stale and meaningless through too much repetition, or is it still the vital spark of old which fired us to action and brave endeavor? Have we grown tired and complacent, tied up with offices and the petty routine of administration, thinking in terms of compromise? Have we forgotten that we still form [part] of a slave Empire which exploits

[1] U.I., pp. 335–41.

us and keeps us embedded in dire poverty, and which strangles freedom wherever in this world it fights for breath? Is it in this Empire that we will find redemption of our pledge?

There are some amongst us, whose memory is of the shortest, who have already forgotten the pledges they took and the many brave resolutions that they made. But we do not forget and we will not allow others to forget. We have pledged ourselves to win full independence, to put an end to imperialism in India, to sever our connection with the Empire that encircles us. By that pledge we stand.

We stand by it even more than we did eight years ago, for that Empire has added to its sins by the butchery of democracy and freedom in Central Europe . . . [in] Spain, and . . . in Palestine. We will not forget this, and in war or peace, we shall fight this policy which hands over the world to fascism.

We stand by that pledge even more today because we have seen what petty change has come to us by provincial autonomy, and how imperialism still sits entrenched in the citadels. We see how India's will is repeatedly ignored in the interests of British finance and industry. We see from day to day the employment of British power to crush the people of the states. Ranpura is a wilderness today, and armed troops gather there from distant parts of India in order to terrorize the people of the Orissa states. In Jaipur, an English prime minister dares to challenge not only the people of the state but the Congress organization itself, a challenge that will be accepted. Everywhere it is becoming apparent that the struggle in the states is not with the helpless rulers but with the grim might of British imperialism.

Is this the way in which the British Government seeks the co-operation of the nationalist movement in the provincial autonomy and endeavors to prepare the ground for federation? We have had enough of this foolery and the sooner it is ended the better.

The time has gone by for empty and misleading tasks. We are up against the hard realities of the situation, and the pledge we take today tells us what path we have to tread and what our inevitable goal is. There is going to be no federation in India of England's choosing. We will have no federation except a federation of a free India. To think or talk in other terms is to betray our pledge and to dishonor ourselves and our cause.

There will be no federation, and the provincial autonomy of today must itself fade away and give place to an independent India, a bulwark of democracy and freedom, opposing fascism and imperialism alike. That is the meaning of the pledge.

And so we take the pledge, realizing its full significance and preparing ourselves for all that it involves. There is no peace or quiet for us or anyone else in the world today. We have to keep our knapsacks on our backs and be ready for the order to march. The peoples of Europe, in the vicious grip of fascism and its allies, the governments of England and France, stumble helplessly and seek in vain a path through the darkness that envelops them. But our path is clear.[1]

Meaning of Struggle for Freedom—February–March, 1939

Many people talk about the weakness and vulnerability of British Imperialism today and imagine that if we shout loudly enough or threaten persistently, the walls of that citadel will fall down. British Imperialism is weak today and the Empire of Britain seems to be fading away before our eyes. The forces of evil and reaction dominate the world and are triumphantly aggressive, and British Imperialism lines up with them. But it is by no means so weak or vulnerable as our wishes lead us to think; outside the scriptures, shouting has not been known to bring down the walls of citadels or cities. We dare not underrate the strength of our adversary. If we win it will be by our own strength, not the weakness of our opponent, for however weak he might be, he will always know how to profit by our lack of strength.

It is a patent fact today that the British Government cannot hinder our progress to independence if we can hold together and act in a disciplined and united manner. It is only our own weaknesses and lack of unity and discipline that give it the chance to hold us down and frustrate us. We are strong enough today, potentially; how can we convert that potentiality into actuality?

Long years of struggle and training have hardened us and disciplined our minds and bodies. Instead of loose talk we speak the language of action, and even our mildest whispering has weight because it has the promise of action behind it. Success has come to us in some measure, and that very success has made people forget that training and discipline which laid the foundation for it. It is strange how short our memories are, how soon we forget.

A generation has gone by since the Congress took to this new path of disciplined and peaceful struggle. Many of our dearly loved captains and comrades are no more, and we, who still linger on, feel lonely as our old

[1] Quoted in N.R.S., pp. 164–66.

companions in the struggle drop out. New people come and fill the ranks and grow rightly impatient at the slowness of change. They are eagerly welcomed with their fresh enthusiasm and desire to achieve. They represent Today more than we do, and Tomorrow is theirs. But these newcomers have no memory of that training and discipline of the long years of trouble. Will they profit by the experience of the passing generation, or will they stumble along and themselves learn in that bitter school? The world is heavy with sorrow and tragedy stalks everywhere. Abyssinia, Spain, China, Palestine—can we forget them? Can we forget the mad folly of our communal troubles? There is no easy walk-over to freedom anywhere, and many of us will have to pass through the valley of the shadow again and again before we reach the mountain-tops of our desire.

Dangers and difficulties have not deterred us in the past; they will not frighten us now. But we must be prepared for them like men who mean business and who do not waste their energy in vain talk and idle action. The way of preparation lies in our rooting out all impurity and indiscipline from our organization and making it the bright and shining instrument that will cleave its way to India's freedom.[1]

The Indian States and Federation

[Proposals to establish an Indian Federation, comprising such Indian States as might accede thereto and the Provinces of British India (constituted as autonomous Provinces), had been discussed by representatives of the British Government, of the Parliament of the United Kingdom, of British India and of the Princes and Rulers of the Indian States. Although a Constitution for a Federation of India had been approved by Parliament and embodied in the Government of India Act of 1935, it was provided by that Act that the Federation should not be established until such date as the British Crown might so decree.[2] As previously indicated, Nehru was opposed to the basis on which Federation was desired by the British Government.]

[May, 1939.] Vital economic problems press for solution and they can be tackled only in a small and sometimes ineffective way, since the power to deal with them fundamentally is lacking under the present constitution with its numerous reservations and safeguards for existing vested interests. Thus social cleavages are appearing, and these have a tendency to disrupt the national movement. They will probably not [cause] disruption, [since] the sense of unity [concerning] the political objective of independence

[1] U.I., pp. 130–32.
[2] Based on S.D.I.C. (Vol. II), pp. 755–56.

is very great. Foreign observers, used to bitter class conflicts, are astonished at the way the Congress has held together and effectively disciplined, in a single movement, various classes and groups whose interests conflict with one another. . . .

The Indian States have rather suddenly come into the center of the national political struggle, and their people are astir from Kashmir in the North to Hyderabad and Travancore in the South. In many States active struggles, involving civil disobedience, are proceeding. In some, popular victories have already been won. The most noticeable feature of these struggles is the part played by the British government in crushing the popular movement and bolstering up the feudal Princes. Indeed it has become obvious that the real resistance comes either from the British government or British officers employed by the States. The Princes count for little. The Congress had so far adopted a cautious policy in regard to the States, but, with this new development, it is taking a much more active part and, in particular, is opposing British interference and support of the old feudal order. It is quite possible that this conflict might spread from the States to the rest of India and become a major national conflict, involving even the Congress Ministries in the Provinces.

Provincial autonomy came nearly two years ago, and already it seems largely to have exhausted its potentialities. Federation is yet far off, although there is often talk of it. As proposed, it is wholly rejected by the Congress and [by] even the principal Muslim organization, and if it is [to be imposed] it will certainly be resisted. The Viceroy and the British Ministers say that it is coming, but they go on postponing it for fear of the conflict that seems inevitable. They still hope that some compromise might be arrived at, but there is likely to be none on the basis of this federation or anything like it. Recent developments in the States also make it exceedingly unlikely that this federation will ever function in India.

Thus India presents today a strange picture of the provinces under Congress governments cooperating in many matters with the British government but with frequent friction between them, of a continuing background of hostility between the national movement and British imperialism, of major problems all heading for a crisis and a conflict. But the long shadow of Europe reaches us here and affects our movement as well as British policy toward us, and what happens in the world outside will influence greatly events in India. And so India looks at the world anxiously and with deepest interest and prepares for the day when she may have to make great decisions.[1]

[1] A. (May, 1939), pp. 254-55.
20+N.

[Government in the Indian States.] There are about six hundred States in India—big ones and small ones and tiny ones, which one cannot even place on the map. They differ greatly among themselves and some have advanced industrially and educationally, and some have had competent Rulers or Ministers. The majority of them, however, are sinks of reaction and incompetence and unrestrained autocratic power, sometimes exercised by vicious and degraded individuals. But whether the Ruler happens to be good or bad, or his Ministers competent or incompetent, the evil lies in the system. This system has vanished from the rest of the world and, left to itself, it would have vanished from India also long ago. But in spite of its manifest decay and stagnation, it has been propped up and artificially maintained by British Imperialism. Offspring of the British power in India, suckled by imperialism, for its own purposes, it has survived till today, though mighty revolutions have shaken the world and changed it, empires have collapsed and crowds of princes and petty Rulers have faded away. That system has no inherent importance or strength, it is the strength of British imperialism that counts. For us in India, that system has in reality been one of the facets of imperialism. Therefore, when conflict comes, we must recognize who our opponent is.

We are told now of the so-called independence of the States and of their treaties with the Paramount Power, which are sacrosanct and inviolable and apparently must go on for ever and ever. We have recently seen what happens to international treaties and the most sacred of covenants when they do not suit the purposes of imperialism. We have seen these treaties torn up, friends and allies basely deserted and betrayed and the pledged word broken by England and France. Democracy and freedom were the sufferers and so it did not matter. But when reaction and autocracy and imperialism stand to lose, it does matter, and treaties, however moth-eaten and harmful to the people they might be, have to be preserved. It is a monstrous imposition to be asked to put up with these treaties of a century and a quarter ago, in the making of which the people had no voice or say. It is fantastic to expect the people to keep on their chains of slavery, imposed upon them by force and fraud, and to submit to a system which crushes the life-blood out of them. We recognize no such treaties and we shall in no event accept them. The only final authority and paramount power that we recognize is the will of the people, and the only thing that counts ultimately is the good of the people.

A new theory of the independence of the States has been advanced in recent years, and it has been advanced by the very power that holds them in an iron grip and keeps them in subjection. Neither history nor constitutional law gives any justification for this, and if we examine the origins of these States, most of their Rulers would be reduced to the status of feudal barons. But we need not trouble ourselves with legal research, as the practice and facts are plain enough. This practice has been for the British Power to dominate these States completely and its slightest gesture is a command to them, which they disobey at their peril. The Political Department of the Government of India pulls the strings and the puppets dance to its tune, the local Resident is the master of the situation; and latterly the practice has grown of British officials being imposed as Ministers of the Rulers of the States. If this is independence, then it will be interesting to learn how it differs from the most abject subjection. There is no independence in the States, and there is going to be none, for it is hardly possible geographically and it is entirely opposed to the conception of a united free India. It is conceivable and desirable in the case of the larger States for them to have a great deal of autonomy within the framework of an Indian Federation. But they will have to remain integral parts of India and the major matters of common concern must be controlled by a democratic Federal Centre. Internally, they will have responsible government.

It is clear that the problem of the States would be easy of solution if the conflict was confined to the people and the Ruler. Many of the Rulers, left to themselves, would ultimately line themselves with the people and if they hesitated to do so, the pressure from below would soon induce them to change their minds. Not to do so would imperil their position and the only alternative would be complete removal. The Congress and the various Praja Mandals have so far made every effort to induce the Rulers to side with their people and establish responsible government. They must realize that for them not to agree to do so will not stop the coming of freedom to their people; their opposition will only place an insurmountable barrier between them and their people, and an arrangement between the two will then become exceedingly difficult. The map of the world has changed many times during the last hundred years; empires have ceased to be and new countries have arisen. Even now, before our very eyes, we see this map changing. It requires no prophet to say with confidence that the Indian States system is doomed even as the British Empire, which has so long protected it, is doomed. It is the path of prudence as well as of wisdom for the Rulers to line themselves with their people and share with them in the new freedom, and instead of being despotic and disliked Rulers, with a precarious tenure, to be proud and equal citizens of a great commonwealth. A few of the Rulers of the States have realized this and have taken some steps in the right direction. . . .

But, unhappily, most of them stick to their old ways and show no signs of change. They demonstrate afresh the lesson of history that when a class has fulfilled its purpose and the world has no need of it, it decays and loses wisdom and all capacity. It cannot adapt itself to changing conditions. In a vain attempt to hold on to what is fading away, it loses even what little it might have retained.

What is the nature of the conflict today? This must be clearly understood. It varies slightly from State to State, but the demand everywhere is for full responsible government. Yet the conflict is not at present to enforce that demand, but to establish the right of organizing people for that demand. When this right is denied and civil liberties are crushed, no way is left open to the people to carry on what are called constitutional methods of agitation. Their choice then is either to submit and give up all political and even public activity, and to suffer a degradation of the spirit and a continuation of the tyranny that oppresses them, or to resort to direct action. This direct action, according to our code, is perfectly peaceful *Satyagraha* and a refusal to submit to violence and evil, whatever the consequences. The immediate issue today is, thus, one of civil liberties in most of the States, though the objective everywhere is responsible government.

The freedom of the people of the States is a big enough thing, yet it is part of the larger freedom of India, and till we gain that larger freedom, it is struggle for us. If the Federation is imposed upon us, we shall fight it and sweep it away. Wherever the British Power intervenes against the people in the States, we shall have to face it. The time approaches when the final solution has to come—a Constituent Assembly of all the Indian people, framing the constitution of a free and democratic India.[1]

Communalism

The communal problem faces us threateningly, and yet it grows ever clearer that in its essence it is a political problem and not just a communal one. Bloody riots have occurred . . . and open and unabashed provocation to murder and violence has had free field. Strange stories come of incompetence and mischief-making and toleration of this new phase of

[1] S.D.I.C. (Vol. II), pp. 759–61. (For an historical summary of evolution of Indian States, see Appendix.)

violence. A few riots need not frighten us, distressing as they are. Let us not forget that the vast majority of our population lives peacefully and is unaffected by the mischief of a few. But even so we must discover the secret springs behind these disturbances and take steps to put an end to this growing violence and terrorism. All men and women of goodwill, to whatever party or group they might belong, must desire this. Those who are in official charge of the functions of government in local areas must realize their responsibilities and appreciate that their failure to curb this violence is a black stain on their record and reputation. It is possible that the best of administrators might be overwhelmed temporarily by the course of events. It is also possible, and the presumption is not unjustified, that incompetence or mischief often lies behind these disturbances. We can tolerate neither incompetence nor mischief-making, nor can we drift along while these flourish.

Our problems fill our minds. Yet the problem of problems today, overshadowing all else, is the growth and triumph of gangsterism in international affairs. The lights go out in Europe and elsewhere, the shadows increase, and in the darkness freedom is butchered and brutal violence reigns. Tragedy envelops us, heart-breaking tragedy, as we see the death of nation after nation.[1]

Government of India Act

We have been recently told on behalf of the British Government that the Government of India Act holds and will continue. If that is the British answer to us, then our path is clear; it is one of resistance to British Imperialism whatever the consequences might be. It is whispered also that an attempt is being made to restrict the powers of the Provincial Governments in the event of war, by giving executive authority in the Provinces to the Central Government. If this attempt is made, it will be fought to the uttermost.

It has not been our policy or habit to bargain or blackmail in times of crisis. We function differently, and we shall continue this policy whether war comes or not. But we can only function in terms of the dignity and freedom of the Indian people, and no other conditions are acceptable to us. The issues before us are not academic; they are of the Here and Now, vital for the interests of India, of England, and the world. We offer our co-operation for freedom and democracy well realizing the imminent peril

[1] U.I., pp. 148–49.

of today. But we offer the co-operation of a free people and not of a slave nation. The conspiracy against freedom, in the name of "appeasement" or a bogus peace, has gone far enough, and it is time it was halted, if the world is not to perish in widespread catastrophe.[1]

[The British Government amended the Government of India Act in 1939, 1940 and 1941, in order to restrict the powers of Provincial administrations, while increasing those of the Viceroy and the Central Government. It also suspended representative government in the majority of provinces.[2]]

3 | Tripuri Congress Session—Letters to Bose Brothers—Further Letters and Statements of the Period

Tripuri Congress Session

At the Tripuri Congress [Session of 1939] there were unseemly scenes. I was at that time very low in spirits, and it was difficult for me to carry on without a breakdown. Political events, national and international happenings, affected me, of course; but the immediate causes were unconnected with public affairs. I was disgusted with myself, and in a press article I wrote: "I fear I give little satisfaction to . . . [my colleagues], and yet that is not surprising, for I give even less satisfaction to myself. It is not out of this stuff that leadership comes, and the sooner my colleagues realize this the better for them and me. The mind functions efficiently enough, the intellect is trained to carry on through habit, but the springs that give life and vitality to that functioning seem to dry up."

Subhas Bose resigned from the presidency and started the Forward Bloc, which was intended to be almost a rival organization to the Congress. It petered out after a while, as it was bound to do, but it added to the

[1] Ibid., pp. 150–51.
[2] Ibid., based on footnote, pp. 150–51.

disruptive tendencies and the general deterioration. Under cover of fine phrases, adventurist and opportunist elements found platforms, and I could not help thinking of the rise of the Nazi party in Germany. Their way had been to mobilize mass support for one program and then to utilize this for an entirely different purpose.

Deliberately I kept out of the new Congress Executive.[1]

[Nehru and Gandhi were both fundamentally opposed to a number of the political views of Subhas Bose, who had been Congress President in 1938.

Although, at times, Nehru appeared to be more in agreement with Bose than with Gandhi, his basic attitude toward what was loosely termed "progressivism", as toward most other questions, was, in fact, quite different from that of Bose. Jawaharlal's approach to Congress policy was essentially Gandhian. Although at one point, Nehru attempted to bring Bose and Gandhi more closely together, his own position tended to become increasingly distant from that of Bose.

Bose was re-elected Congress President for the Tripuri Session of March, 1939, despite Gandhi's and Nehru's opposition. A stormy struggle followed, in which Gandhi's policies finally triumphed. Bose subsequently resigned as President.

During the Tripuri Session, Nehru moved a strong resolution on March 12, in opposition to Britain's foreign policy.]

[From Statement on Resolution of March 12.] India [must take] a keen interest in foreign policy because it [affects our] interests considerably. India [has] to pay special attention to British foreign policy because unfortunately she [is] still part of the British Empire. She [has] no direct voice in this policy and she [is] often misrepresented....

[I cannot] but condemn in the strongest terms the betrayal of Czechoslovakia by England and France. The League of Nations at Geneva [is] nothing but a tombstone of peace....

If Republican Spain [has] failed ... it [is] not because of the arms supplied by Italy and Germany but because of the plotting of the British and French Governments, which were determined to kill it and succeeded in doing so....

India cannot be a party to this kind of murder of democracy. India must dissociate itself from British foreign policy and line up with those countries which love freedom and democracy.

India is on the threshold of freedom, and she is bound to play an important role in the world's history. Therefore, she cannot remain indifferent.[2]

[1] T.F., p. 365.
[2] I.A.A., pp. 73–74.

Letters to Bose Brothers—1939

[The following excerpts from letters to Sarat Bose (brother of Subhas), as well as to Subhas, suggest the nature of Nehru's continuing differences with the latter. Because of Subhas Bose's pro-Axis leanings during World War II—purportedly to defeat Imperialism—controversy between the two men became ever more sharply accentuated.]

[From letter to Sarat Chandra Bose—Allahabad, March 24, 1939.] There are, as we all know, differences of opinion amongst leading Congressmen on matters of policy and programme and we have often given expression to our respective view-points, although we have succeeded in pulling together. Generally speaking, Gandhiji's programme has been followed by the Congress and his leadership accepted. Personally I do not see any harm in . . . differences, provided the common link remains and we act in unison. . . .

[Recently] I wrote . . . [to Subhas Bose] as follows: "Public affairs involve principles and policies. They also involve an understanding of each other and faith in the *bona fides* of colleagues. If this understanding and faith are lacking, it is very difficult to cooperate with advantage. As I have grown in years I have come to attach more and more importance to this faith and understanding between colleagues. What am I to do with the finest principles if I do not have confidence in the person concerned? The party rivalries in many provinces illustrate this and we find extreme bitterness and often an utter lack of scruple among people who are ordinarily honourable and straight. I cannot stomach this kind of politics and I have kept absolutely aloof from them for these many years. I function individually without any group or any second person to support me, although I am happy enough to possess the confidence of many. I feel that this provincial deterioration is now being transferred or extended to the all-India plane. This is a matter of the most serious concern to me.

"So we come back to this: behind the political problems, there are psychological problems, and these are always more difficult to handle. The only way to do so is perfect frankness with each other and I hope therefore that all of us will be perfectly frank."

I had hoped that it would be possible, in these days of internal and external crisis, to have a large measure of cooperation among Congressmen. . . . It seems to me obvious that the essential preliminary to any action or Leftist programme is that we should function effectively. If we do not do so then all programmes are futile and lead nowhere. And yet it is just this absence of functioning that is creeping upon us slowly but surely. . . .

I feel as strongly as ever that it is essential for us to be clear in our own minds about the policy and programme to be pursued. More especially the so-called Left should be clear. It is dangerous for the Left to be vague and to allow itself to drift to adventurist positions. . . . I find many people who call themselves Leftists suggesting methods and policies which are very Rightist and moderate.[1]

[The following letter lends insight into the generous manner in which Nehru periodically has replied to even his most severe critics. His attitude concerning the importance of maintaining Congress unity, and of standing firmly with Gandhi, whatever their differences, also is clearly stressed. Nehru's opposition to Bose—who already had served as Congress President—stemmed essentially from fear that Bose might utilize his potential power in destructive fashion; from dismay at Bose's misunderstanding of Gandhi's ideas, and the need for Congress Unity; from a sense of foreboding about Bose's uncritical attitude towards Nazism and Fascism, as well as his basically unsound ideas concerning ostensibly progressive programs of action.]

[To Subhas Chandra Bose—Allahabad, April 3, 1939.] First of all I should like to say how glad I am that you have written to me fully and frankly and made it clear to me how you feel about me and about various incidents. Frankness hurts often enough, but it is almost always desirable, especially between those who have to work together. It helps one to see oneself in proper perspective from another's and a more critical viewpoint. Your letter is very helpful in this respect and I am grateful to you for it.

It is not an easy matter to answer a letter which runs into twenty-seven typed sheets and is full of references to numerous incidents as well as to various policies and programmes. I am afraid therefore that my reply will not be as full and detailed as it might be. To endeavour to deal with all these matters properly one would have to write a book, or something like it.

Your letter is essentially an indictment of my conduct and an investigation into my failings. It is, as you will well realise, a difficult and embarrassing task to have to reply to such an indictment. But so far as the failings are concerned, or many of them at any rate, I have little to say. I plead guilty to them, well realising that I have the misfortune to possess them. May I also say that I entirely appreciate the truth of your remark that ever since you came out of internment in 1937, you treated me with

[1] B.O.L., pp. 324–25, 327–28.

20*

the utmost regard and consideration, in private as well as in public life. I am grateful to you for this. Personally I have always had, and still have, regard and affection for you, though sometimes I did not like at all what you did or how you did it. To some extent, I suppose, we are temperamentally different and our approach to life and its problems is not the same.

I shall now deal with your letter and take up the paragraphs one by one.

I forget what I told you when you saw me in Allahabad on my return from Europe last November. . . . Probably . . . that my own future course of action would depend on Gandhiji's reactions to various matters. You will remember what I told you before and after Haripura. I was greatly troubled . . . about my association with the Working Committee . . . and I wanted to leave. This was because I . . . felt . . . that I was performing no useful function there. Also that Gandhiji was thinking in terms of what he called a "homogeneous" committee and I could not see myself forming part of it. The choice before me then became one of withdrawing myself quietly from it and cooperating with it from outside, or of challenging Gandhiji and his group. I felt that it would be injurious [to] the interests of India and our cause for me or you to create this definite split. It is of course absurd to say that there should be unity at any cost. Unity may be harmful and injurious at times and then it must go. It all depends on the circumstances then prevailing, and I was convinced at the time that the pushing out, or the attempt to push out, of Gandhiji and his group would weaken us greatly as a critical moment. I was not prepared to face that contingency. At the same time I disliked many of the developments that were taking place and disapproved of the general attitude of Gandhiji in regard to certain matters. . . .

I went to Europe and when I came back I was faced by the old problem again. It was then that you met me and probably I told you what I had in mind. My own mind was clear but my action would depend on Gandhiji's reactions to the situation. If he still held to the "homogeneous" idea, then I was out of it. If not, then I would try to cooperate as a member of the Working Committee. I was not prepared to do anything to split the Congress on this issue. I was full of the developing crises in India and outside and felt that we might have to face a big struggle in the course of a few months. That struggle, without Gandhiji's active participation and leadership, was not likely to be an effective one.

My conception of this struggle was not on the basis of Federation. I wanted the Congress to treat Federation as almost a dead issue and to concentrate on the demand for self-determination and [a] Constituent

Assembly, and further to place this in relation to the world crisis. I felt that too much positive stress on fighting Federation helped in keeping this issue alive and prevented us from thinking, and later acting, on the more fundamental plane. When I was in England you issued a statement to the effect that you would fight Federation to the last and that if the Congress accepted it, you would still fight it. Now this statement of yours had exactly the contrary effect in England. Everybody said that if the Congress President is thinking in terms of resigning on the issue of Federation, Congress must be on the point of accepting it. I felt helpless and could not easily meet this argument.

I framed two resolutions on this basis. There was nothing extraordinary about them except that the stress was different. All our resolutions for the Working Committee, as you know, have to be framed with a view to being agreed to by other members. It is easy enough to draft something which pleases one better, but which does not meet with the approval of others. My idea in placing these resolutions before the W.C. was to prepare the ground, as well as the mind of the country, for a more comprehensive and far-reaching resolution at the next Congress. However my resolutions were not agreed to and I was told that they should be considered at Congress time.

It was at this meeting of the W.C. that I proposed a resolution about the Jews. You will remember that just previously there had been a terrible pogrom in Germany against the Jews and the world was full of this. I felt that we must express our opinion in regard to it. You say that you were "astounded when I produced a resolution . . . seeking to make India an asylum for the Jews". I am surprised to learn that you felt so strongly about this. . . .

You say that "in the habit of interfering from the top, no Congress President can beat" me. I realise that I am an interfering sort of a person, but so far as the work of the A.I.C.C. is concerned I do not recollect having interfered with the work of the office of the A.I.C.C. though I sought to influence it frequently. My deliberate policy was (as circulars to this effect were issued) not to interfere and in provincial matters even for the A.I.C.C. office not to interfere, unless there was no other way out. . . .

May I explain a little further what has troubled my mind very greatly during the past two months or so ? I was against your standing for election[1] for two major reasons: it meant under the circumstances a break with Gandhiji and I did not want this to take place. (Why this should have

[1] For re-election as Congress President.

necessarily happened I need not go into. I felt that it would happen.) It would mean also, I thought, a set-back for the real Left. The Left was not strong enough to shoulder the burden by itself and when a real contest came in the Congress, it would lose and then there would be a reaction against it. I thought it probable that you would win the election . . . but I doubted very much whether you could carry the Congress with you in a clear contest with what is called Gandhism. Even if by any chance you secured a majority in the Congress, this would not represent a strong enough backing in the country without Gandhiji and effective work, and even more so preparation for a struggle would be very difficult. There were so many disruptive tendencies already existing in the country and instead of controlling them, we would add to them. All this meant weakening our national movement just when strength was necessary.

These were my two main reasons for my opposition to your re-election. What some Bombay friends told you was not wholly correct. What I said was that if you stood for certain definite Leftist principles and policies, then there might be some point in your seeking re-election, as the election would then be an education in ideas and policies. But an election on a more or less personal basis did not even have this merit. In any event I did not think your standing for election desirable for the reasons I have given above. . . .

I saw also that you were closely associated with a number of odd individuals who were apparently influencing you considerably. These individuals were, some of them, personally desirable but they did not represent to my mind any Leftist opinion, or any organised opinion. That is why I call them adventurist in the technical political sense. A spirit of adventure is of course a very desirable thing in an individual or a nation. But in a political contest the word has a certain meaning, not by any means dishonourable to the person concerned. I did not at all like this adventurist tendency and considered it harmful to our cause. The association of vague Leftist slogans with no clear Leftist ideology or principles has in recent years been much in evidence in Europe. It has led to Fascist development and a straying away of large sections of the public. The possibility of such a thing happening in India possessed my mind and disturbed me. The fact that in international affairs you held different views from mine and did not wholly approve our condemnation of Nazi Germany or Fascist Italy added to my discomfort, and looking at the picture as a whole, I did not at all fancy the direction in which apparently you wanted us to go. . . .

To my misfortune, I am affected by international happenings more than

I should be. A very grave crisis had arisen in Europe which might have led to war. I felt that we should not passively await events. . . .

There is no need for me to discuss my own failings which you point out. I admit them and regret them. You are right in saying that as President I functioned often as a secretary or a glorified clerk. I have long developed the habit of being my own secretary and clerk, and I fear I encroach in this way on others' preserves. It is also true that because of me Congress resolutions have tended to become long and verbose and rather like theses. In the Working Committee, I fear, I talked too much and did not always behave as I should.

I objected to your use of the words Left and Right because I thought that you were using them vaguely and loosely. Of course there is such a thing as a Left and a Right. It exists in the Congress and in the country. But unless the terms are used concisely they might and do create confusion. . . .

Am I a Socialist or an individualist? Is there a necessary contradiction in the two terms? Are we all such integrated human beings that we can define ourselves precisely in a word or a phrase? I suppose I am temperamentally and by training an individualist, and intellectually a socialist, whatever all this might mean. I hope that socialism does not kill or suppress individuality; indeed I am attracted to it because it will release innumerable individuals from economic and cultural bondage. But I am a dull subject to discuss, especially at the tail end of an inordinately long letter. Let us leave it at this that I am an unsatisfactory human being who is dissatisfied with himself and the world, and whom the petty world he lives in does not particularly like.

I dare not now, in the early hours of the morning, write about my views in regard to national or international affairs. I am not silent about them as a rule. As you have observed, I talk rather a lot and write even more. I shall leave it at that for the present. But I would add that while I champion lost causes frequently and condemn countries like Germany and Italy, I do not think I have ever given a certificate of good conduct to British and French Imperialism.[1]

Further Letters and Statements of the Period

[Gandhi had written to Nehru from Wardha on February 3, 1939: "After the [Bose] election [before the Tripuri Congress Session] and the manner

[1] B.O.L., pp. 350–52, 354–57, 361–63.

in which it was fought, I feel that I shall serve the country by absenting myself from the Congress at the forthcoming session. Moreover my health is none too good. I would like you to help me. Please do not press me to attend." [1]]

[From letter to Gandhi—Allahabad, April 17, 1939.] You have been greatly distressed at developments in Congress during the last many months and you have condemned corruption, etc. I think every sane element in the Congress, whatever his political views, is eager to deal with this problem. I have been paying a great deal of attention to many factors outside the Congress and I must say that I am alarmed at the trend of events and the development of new forces. I am not merely referring to the communal question. There are deeper forces at work. If at this juncture the Congress weakens and disrupts, the consequences may well be disastrous. We must hold together. I would beg of you, therefore, to make up your mind to settle this matter, even though that way of settlement may not be to the liking of all of us. Only so can we go in the direction of our choice. Otherwise we are stuck up.

A word about myself. It is my misfortune to be too much of an individualist. I found it very difficult to pull on, in the later days, at the Working Committee meetings and probably I became a nuisance to my colleagues also. And this not through any lack of goodwill on either side. Hence I felt that I should not continue in it. For even more potent reasons I felt it difficult to think of joining a Committee of a different kind formed by Subhas. My feelings are still the same. But in view of this deadlock that has arisen, if a way out is found and my presence in the Committee is considered helpful, I shall agree to serve as such. This is not a prospect that I cherish. But I do feel that I cannot shirk this responsibility if it is offered to me under the present extraordinary circumstances. [2]

[From statement at Tripuri Congress Session, 1939—On continuing preoccupation with village industries.] Some people think that the revival of khadi and other village industries would put back the clock of our country's progress and that India's salvation can only come through a process of large-scale industrialization. I call myself a socialist and as such I do believe that ... large-scale industries have a place in this country. Anything that increases the material well-being of the country is bound to have ... repercussion on the people. But we shall never be able to move

[1] Ibid., p. 317.
[2] Ibid., pp. 380-81.

the India of the rural masses through mere multiplication of big factories. It can only be reached through khadi and village industries. By all means, let us have big factories . . . for production of things that cannot be manufactured in our villages. Let the big manufacturer and . . . small artisan function, each in his own place and within his respective legitimate sphere. There is no inherent conflict between the two and there need be none. Those who call khadi worthless prove their own worthlessness. They will never really understand our country's problems.[1]

[Nehru made numerous other statements favoring the use of khadi, even though at times he disagreed with Gandhi about the degree to which it should be emphasized.]

[During the thirties.] The cloth we wear is *khadi*. It is hand spun and hand woven, and is thus entirely a product of the cottages and mud-huts of India. . . . I should like to point out . . . that [our *khadi*] movement and . . . *charkha* [spinning wheel] are not meant to compete with the big machine. Many people fall into this mistake, and imagine that the *charkha* means a going back to the Middle Ages, and the discarding of machines and all that industrialism has brought us. This is all wrong. Our movement is decidedly not against industrialism as such or machines and factories. We want India to have the best of everything, and as rapidly as possible. But having regard [for] existing conditions in India, and especially the terrible poverty of our peasantry, we have urged them to spin in their spare time. Thus not only do they better their own conditions a little, but they help in lessening our dependence on foreign cloth, which has taken so much wealth out of our country.[2]

I have stated often enough . . . that I do not consider Khadi [a] final solution of our economic ills and therefore I seek elsewhere for that final solution. But still I believe that situated as we are today, Khadi has a definite value, political, social and economic, and must therefore be encouraged.[3]

[Despite Nehru's intermittent, partial reservations about the *khadi* movement Gandhi stated on July 30, 1937: "Your calling khadi 'livery of freedom' will live as long as we speak the English language in India. It needs a first-class poet to translate into Hindi the whole of the thought

[1] T.D.G. (Vol. V), p. 64.
[2] G.W.H., p. 349.
[3] H.I.N.C. (Vol. II), p. 26.

behind that enchanting phrase. For me it is not merely poetry but it enunciates a great truth whose full significance we have yet to grasp." [1]]

4 | On the Eve of World War II

[February–March, 1939.] In view of the crisis and . . . rapid developments in Europe most of us, I suppose, were forced to think out afresh what [our] political faith should be. Perhaps this sense of crisis and tension was not so obvious in India and events did not compel us to examine our premises afresh. Our Socialist friends in India have not reacted sufficiently to changing conditions. The Communists in Europe might change, under the compulsion of events, but not so the Communists of India.

I had been considerably upset by the course of events in the Soviet Union, the trials and the repeated purges of vast numbers of Communists. I think the trials were generally bona-fide and there had been a definite conspiracy against the régime and widespread attempts at sabotage. Nevertheless, I could not reconcile myself to what was happening there, and it indicated to me ill-health in the body politic, which necessitated an ever-continuing use of violence and suppression. Still the progress made in Russian economy, the advancing standards of the people, the great advance in cultural matters and many other things continued to impress me. I was eager to visit the Soviet Union, but unfortunately my daughter's illness prevented me from going there.

Whatever doubts I had about internal happenings in Russia, I was quite clear in my mind about her foreign policy. This had been consistently one of peace and, unlike England and France, of fulfilling international obligations and supporting the cause of democracy abroad. The Soviet Union stood as the one real effective bulwark against Fascism in Europe and Asia. Without the Soviet Union what could be the state of Europe today? Fascist reaction would triumph everywhere and democracy and freedom would become dreams of a past age.

On Spain, on Czecho-Slovakia, and right through the September

[1] B.O.L., p. 245.

crisis, the [British] Communist Party seemed to me to take the straightest line. Their analysis of the situation almost always turned out to be correct, and even when the nerves of most of the progressive groups were shattered, the Communists as a rule kept their heads and continued to function. They had the capacity to learn from events and to shape their policy accordingly, unlike the British Labour Party, which has shown an astounding inability to understand a changing world.

The events in Europe, the growth of Fascism, the Spanish Revolution, and most of all the deliberate encouragement of the Nazi and Fascist Powers by the so-called democratic Governments of England and France, impressed upon me that the dominant urge of owning classes is to protect their own vested interests. When nationalism means protection of their interests, then they are nationalists and patriots; but when these interests are endangered, then nationalism or patriotism has little value for them. The ruling classes of Britain and France are even prepared to endanger the security of their empires rather than co-operate for the defence of democracy with Soviet Russia, for such co-operation might release forces which would undermine their privileged position. Democracy means nothing to them, nor freedom, though they talk loudly of them; their main concern is the protection of their vested interests and privileges. That they might lose these anyhow, even by the policy they pursue, is their misfortune.

The Marxian philosophy appeals to me in a broad sense and helps me to understand the processes of history. I am far from being an orthodox Marxist, nor does any other orthodoxy appeal to me. But I am convinced that the old Liberal approach in England or elsewhere is no longer valid. *Laissez-faire* is dead, and unless far-reaching changes are made with reasonable speed, disaster awaits us, whether we live in England or India. Today the community has to be organized in order to establish social and economic justice. This organization is possible on the Fascist basis, but this does not bring justice or equality, and is essentially unsound. The only other way is the Socialist way.

Liberty and democracy have no meaning without equality, and equality cannot be established so long as the principal instruments of production are privately owned. Private ownership of these means of production thus comes in the way of real democracy. Many factors go to shape opinion, but the most important and fundamental of them is the property relation, which ultimately governs our institutions and our social fabric. Those who profit by an existing property relation do not, as a class, voluntarily agree to a change which involves a loss of power and privilege. We have reached a stage when there is an essential contradiction between the existing property relation and the forces of production, and democracy cannot effectively function unless this relation is transformed. Class struggles are inherent in the present system, and the attempt to change it and bring it in line with modern requirements meets with the fierce opposition of the ruling or owning classes. That is the logic of the conflicts of today, and it has little to do with the goodwill or ill-will of individuals, who might in their individual capacities succeed in rising above their class allegiance. But the class as a whole will hold together and oppose change.

I do not see why under Socialism there should not be a great deal of freedom for the individual; indeed, far greater freedom than the present system gives. He can have freedom of conscience and mind, freedom of enterprise, and even the possession of private property on a restricted scale. Above all, he will have the freedom which comes from economic security, which only a small number possess today.

I think India and the world will have to march in this direction of Socialism unless catastrophe brings ruin to the world. That march may vary in different countries and the intermediate steps might not be the same. Nothing is so foolish as to imagine that exactly the same processes take place in different countries with varying backgrounds. India, even if she accepted this goal, would have to find her own way to it, for we have to avoid unnecessary sacrifice and the way of chaos, which may retard our progress for a generation.

But India has not accepted this goal, and our immediate objective is political independence. We must remember this and not confuse the issue, for else we will have neither Socialism nor independence. We have seen that even in Europe the middle classes are powerful enough to suppress today any movement aiming at vital social change, and when danger threatens have a tendency to go to Fascism. The middle classes in India are relatively at least as strong, and it would be the extremity of folly to estrange them and force them into the opposing ranks. Our national policy must therefore be one which includes a great majority of them on the common basis of political independence and anti-imperialism, and our international policy must be one of anti-Fascism.

Marxism and Socialism are not policies of violence, though, like most other groups, capitalist or Liberal, they envisage the possibility of violence. Can they fit in with the peaceful methods of the Congress, not only as a temporary expedient, but in a straightforward bona-fide manner? It is not necessary for us to discuss the whole philosophy underlying the doctrine of non-violence or to consider how far it is applicable to remote and extreme cases. For us the problem is that of India and of India of today and tomorrow. I am convinced that the way of non-violence is not merely the only feasible course for us, but is, on its merits, the best and most effective method. I think that the field of its application will grow as its effectiveness is recognized. But here in India large numbers of people have recognized it, and it has become the solid foundation of our movement. It has proved effective enough already, but it is quite possible, with further experience, to extend its applications in a variety of ways. It is easy to belittle it and point to its failures, but it is far easier to point out the innumerable failures of the method of violence. We have seen power-fully armed countries collapse and sink into servitude without a struggle. India, with all her lack of armed might, would never have succumbed in this way.

There are peculiar dangers in India in the use of the violent method. It cannot be used in a disciplined or organized manner. It will come in the way of mass organization and mass action, and it is bound to lead to inter-nal conflicts on a big scale, resulting in chaos and the collapse of our movement. I am not optimist enough to imagine that out of this chaos a free, united, and advanced India will emerge.

No one in India thinks in terms of this type of violence. It is out of the question. But there is a feeling that a violent mentality increases the militancy of the masses and is therefore to be vaguely encouraged among the industrial workers or even the kisans. This is folly, and if continued the consequences are likely to be disastrous. So long as a Government deals gently with it, it flourishes, but a determined Government can crush it easily and completely demoralize the workers. Strength comes not from occasional exhibitions of individual or group violence, but from mass organization and the capacity for mass action, which, to be effective in India, must be peaceful action. . . .

Any Socialist or Communist who pays lip service to non-violence and acts differently does injury to his ideals and makes people think that his acts do not conform to his professions.[1]

[The Spanish war terminated on March 29, 1939, with Franco as victor.]

[Destiny—April 16, 1939.] The Ides of March brought disaster to Europe and to democracy, and Czecho-Slovakia vanished from the map of the world. Yet war did not come. Stunned and full of fear, the countries of

[1] U.I., pp. 115-20.

Europe waited for yet another spring of the beast of prey. . . . We were told that the spring campaigns and offensives were over and peace would reign in Europe till the far-off autumn at least. But autumn was still far off when Easter came with its message of good-will, and Good Friday saw the rape of Albania. Yet war did not come.

War has not come yet, but who can tell when it will descend on us? Who dare say that peace is assured till the autumn or even till the hot summer envelops us? There is marching and stamping of millions of armed men in Europe, and night and day men and women turn out engines of destruction and dig trenches and erect barricades, and the sky is covered with the messengers of death. Who dare say that the thin thread that holds back these forces will not snap and unleash destruction and doom on hapless mankind? Peace, so-called peace, holds today; what of tomorrow or the day after?

Like some pre-ordained tragedy, inevitable and inescapable, war pursues us and will seize us by the throat. We cannot escape our destiny.[1]

[A problem for India—May 24, 1939.] The tragedy of Spain and much that has happened in the West has been a personal sorrow to me, leaving a deep and lasting impress. But Spain is far, and the problems of India fill my mind and distress me. It is not external difficulty that troubles, but the whole background of India with its conflicts and disruptive forces, its pettiness and mutual suspicion. [We have no faith today in one another], and every foolish statement and wild charge is believed. Vulgarity, that most distressful symptom, creeps into our public life in the Congress and even more outside it. Policies and programmes and high principles have their importance; they are vital and urgent. But behind them all lies the human material without which these principles and policies can have little meaning.[2]

[May, 1939.] Our war resistance policy is of vital importance to us. It has been adopted because of our love of freedom and democracy and our insistence on Indian independence. Now that very policy might be given a twist and made to fit in with Fascist desires. The Fascist Powers would very much like India to be a thorn in the side of England when war comes, so that they might profit by the situation we create. There is nothing that we would dislike so much as to play into the hands of the Fascist Powers, just as we dislike being exploited by imperialist Britain. Our anti-war

[1] Ibid., p. 152.
[2] Ibid., pp. 160–61.

policy must therefore be based on freedom and democracy and opposition
to Fascism and imperialism.[1]

[The wooing of Russia—May 30, 1939.] Twenty years ago the young
Soviet Republic was assailed on all sides by powerful nations—England,
the United States, France, Japan. Within her own territories counter-
revolution, aided from abroad, raised its ugly head. Without an army,
without money, without technical resources or industry, and faced by
utter disorganisation following war and defeat and revolution, she hung
on the brink of collapse and her enemies counted the hours when they
would finally triumph over her. Even her friends thought it an impossible
venture, doomed to disappear. But the indomitable will and genius of a
great man embodying a new life and a new hope, triumphed over these
amazing odds, and Soviet Russia lived.

Yet they looked upon her with contempt and disdain, an untouchable
among nations, of the pariah breed that had dared to challenge her
betters. They would not recognise her or deal with her, and insulted her
and put every difficulty in her way. She still lived on, ignoring these gibes
and intent on creating that new life which had inspired her to this great
endeavour. Trial and misfortune came her way and often she erred and
suffered for error. But still she went on with faith and energy building the
world of her dreams.

Perhaps the dreams did not quite come true, the reality was somewhat
different from the picture in the mind. Yet a new world did come into
existence, a brave new world with life and hope and security and opportunity for the millions that inhabited her broad territories. Industry spread
with lightning speed, new cities sprang up, agriculture changed its aspect
and collective farms replaced the outworn methods of yesterday, literacy
became wide-spread, education and culture grew, the sciences were wooed
and their planned methods applied to a nation's regeneration.

The world was interested. What was this strange phenomenon of rapid
progress and lack of unemployment, when the rest of the world was
crushed and throttled by the great depression and unemployment grew
everywhere? The statesmen and the chancellories did not approve of this
abnormal behaviour. It was a bad example for their own people. They set
about intriguing to get the Soviet into trouble; they irritated her by offensive behaviour; they tried to entangle her into war. But she ignored these
insults and refused to be drawn into war. Full of her gigantic programme

[1] Ibid., p. 164.

of national reconstruction, she pursued the policy of peace in foreign affairs, deliberately and consistently.

Meanwhile she built her army and air-force, and, as these grew, respect for her also grew even among those who disliked her. But with respect there grew also fear and so they still intrigued and tried to isolate her and to encourage the new fascist Powers against her. The upholders of democracy in Europe made love to the Nazis and the Fascists, put up with their aggressions, brutalities and vulgar insolence, betrayed those who had relied upon them, were treacherous to their friends and allies, all in the hope of crushing the Soviet and turning Nazi aggression against her. They ignored her at Munich although she was an ally of France as well as of the very country they had met to dismember. To the last the Soviet was faithful to her allies and commitments.

Eight months have passed since Munich and the policy of "appeasement" has had full play. And now the gods laugh. There is no longer any ignoring of Soviet Russia. She has suitors galore, each one trying to win her favour. Even Hitler, the great enemy of Communism, is respectful to her and seeks accommodation. France and England pursue her and in soft words try to hide their previous dislike of her. Suddenly Soviet Russia has gained the whip hand in international affairs and it is her decision that will make a vital difference.

For Soviet Russia today is the most powerful country in the Eurasian continent. She is powerful not only because of [her] great army and . . . air force but because of her enormous resources and the strength of the socialist structure she has built up. Hitler's Germany, with all her armed might, has feet of clay and no sustaining strength for war or peace. She is old already and requires frequent tonics to keep her going. These tonics have come to her through each fresh aggression and through the goodwill of England and France. Her resources are limited, her money power strained to the utmost. France, with her fine army, counts but she has already taken a back seat among the Powers. England, with her great empire, where is she today? She has great resources but great weaknesses also; the days of her pride and domination are past. . . .

It is a strange thought that the only effective bulwark against Nazi aggression in Europe is the Soviet. Without Soviet help most of the other countries might even collapse without a struggle. Without that help England's guarantee to Poland or Rumania means little.

There are only two Powers in the world today which count in the ultimate analysis—the United States of America and the Soviet Union. The United States are almost unapproachable and their resources are enormous. The Soviet Union is not so favourably situated geographically but is yet almost unbeatable. All other Powers are of the second rank compared to these two and have to rely on alliances for their protection. And as time passes the disparity will increase.

And so Soviet Russia, with all her communism, is wooed by those who hated her, and the gods laugh.[1]

[Of China—June 15, 1939.] The news agencies feed us with news of Europe and of what Herr Hitler says or Mr Neville Chamberlain denies. We hear little about China except that an air raid has taken place and there have been hundreds or thousands of casualties. It is one of our many unfortunate disabilities that we depend almost entirely for our foreign news service on a British agency which looks at news not from our point of view, but definitely from the British imperialist view-point. Its offices in London decide what is good for us to have, and a restricted measure of this is poured out to us from day to day.... Reuters ... still think that we wait eagerly for the golden words that fall from the mouths of the big officials of the India Office. Meanwhile real world news for which we hanker is denied to us.

Any person who has travelled East to Malaya or Java knows the tremendous difference between the news supply there and in India. Fresh news pours in there about China, the Far East, America and even Europe, and not only fresh news but a fresh outlook, which is a pleasant change after the Reuter service. This fresh news comes through the American agencies which unfortunately do not reach India.

So we hear little in India about China. Fortunately the *Herald* has made a particular feature of news from China and although it does not get them telegraphically, it publishes frequently special articles on conditions in China. There is no lack of news if only we can get it, for China today is news in every sense of the word.

She is news because what is happening in China is of enormous significance to the world, to Asia, and to India. China is one of the key countries of the world, and in the world perspective, she counts more than the small warring countries of Europe. In any event, to Asia and to us in India, she and her future are of prime importance.

China is news also because of the vast scale of horrible destruction that the Japanese armies have perpetrated there. Do we realise what the small news items that we read mean? Daily bombing of great cities, the killing of tens of thousands, the cruelty and inhumanity of modern warfare.

[1] C.S.W., pp. 129-33.

But, above all, she is news because of her heroic resistance and the way she has overcome the tremendous difficulties she had to face. Only a great people could have done that, a great people, not merely because they are the heirs to a great past, but because they have established their claim to the future. It is difficult in this changing world to prophesy, but every indication points to China emerging victorious from her present trials. In a military sense, she is stronger today, after two years of warfare, than she was at the commencement of the war. She is hardened, better organised, better equipped, and she has developed a kind of warfare which suits her technical inferiority and her wide spaces. The morale of her people is excellent, and the army and the peasantry pull together in a common undertaking. Most of the old generals, timid, compromising and incompetent, have given place to younger men trained in the hard field of experience. The old ones were politically irremovable to begin with, but when disasters came and their incompetence was manifest they had to go.

Today it is well recognised in foreign military circles, and this includes the German war chiefs, that unless something very extraordinary occurs, China will win, though it may take her time to do so. The Chinese people and their leaders do not underrate their task. They take the long view and say that, so far as they are concerned, the war has just begun.

What extraordinary event can occur which might imperil China's chances? It is highly unlikely that Japan by herself can succeed in crushing Chinese resistance. But if the United States of America or England deliberately adopted an anti-Chinese policy, it might make a difference. The United States will not do so for it will go counter to their whole Far Eastern policy. What of England? The England of Mr Neville Chamberlain is capable of anything. Today however she is definitely pro-Chinese. What she will be tomorrow only Mr Chamberlain knows.

Behind the war and inhumanity and violence, there is something happening in China which is of vital significance. A new China is rising, rooted in her culture, but shedding the lethargy and weaknesses of ages, strong and united, modern and with a human outlook. The unity that China has achieved in these years of trial is astonishing and inspiring. It is not merely unity in defence, but a unity in work and in building up. Behind the war-fronts, in the vast undeveloped hinterland of China, there are vast schemes afoot which are changing the face of the country. In spite of continuous danger of bombing from the air, industries are growing up, and what is especially interesting, a scheme of cooperatives for the small and cottage industries is taking rapid shape, even within ear-shot of the guns. The great advantage of these cottage and small industries is that they can be quickly established in the devastated regions, and can be moved if danger threatens.

This is the new China that is growing up in the smoke of war and in the midst of devastation on an unparalleled scale. We have much to learn from her.[1]

[Mao Tse-Tung sent the following communication to Nehru on May 24, 1939 (from Yenan, Shensi, China): "We have had the pleasure and privilege of receiving the Indian Medical Unit . . . and the messages from the Indian National Congress to the Chinese people, greeting and encouraging them in fighting the Japanese imperialists.

"We wish to inform you that the Indian Medical Unit has begun their work here and have been very warmly welcomed by all members of the 8th Route Army and their spirit of sharing such common hardships with us has made a profound impression on all who come in touch with them.

"We take this opportunity to thank your great Indian people and the Indian National Congress for the medical and material aid that you have given and hope that in the future the Indian National Congress and the Indian people will continue to help and aid us and thus together drive out the Japanese imperialists.[2]"]

[Nehru had made the following statement at a Provincial Conference in the Punjab, as early as April 11, 1928.] Your gallant soldiers have been exploited enough in the past not in India only, but in the four quarters of the world. Even to-day they are made to do the dirty work of British imperialism in China, in Persia and in Mesopotamia, and they are used to suppress people who are our friends and neighbours and who have done us no harm. It is time that we put an end to this shameful exploitation of the courage of our manhood. We are told that we are not capable of defending our country against . . . foreign invasion, but our soldiers are capable enough of defending the British Empire, in Europe, in Asia and in Africa. You know how our man-power and our wealth [were] exploited by the British during the last war. You know also the measure of return that we got for our help. . . .

If the British Government embarks on any warlike adventure and endeavours to exploit India, it will be our duty to refuse to take any part in such a war or to co-operate . . . in any way whatsoever. This will be no easy matter. It will mean our having to face and endure fines and hardship, but if we have the courage to face them and the capacity to endure them to the end, and the statesmanship not to compromise, we shall

[1] Ibid., pp. 11–15.
[2] Quoted in B.O.L., pp. 385–86.

emerge triumphant from this ordeal, and our dear country which has so long suffered alien domination will be free again.[1]

<table>
<tr><td rowspan="1">5</td><td>Trip to China: World War II—On World Union and Collective Security— Events at Beginning of War— Congress Working Committee Resolution on the War—Commentary on the War and on Congress Working Committee Resolution</td></tr>
</table>

Trip to China—August, 1939 : World War II

[The Russo-German ten-year non-aggression pact was signed on August 24, 1939. (Nehru's reaction to the pact is described in Part VI.) The Anglo-Polish mutual assistance agreement was announced August 25. Hitler invaded Poland on September 1, 1939. Russia invaded Poland on September 17, 1939; Finland in November, 1939.]

The situation in Europe in August 1939 was threatening, and I did not want to leave India at a moment of crisis. But the desire to visit China, even for a short while, was strong. So I flew to China, and within two days of my leaving India I was in Chungking. Very soon I had to rush back to India, as war had at last descended upon Europe. I spent less than two weeks in free China, but these two weeks were memorable ones both personally for me and for the future relations of India and China.

As I flew to China, my mind went back to the long line of illustrious pilgrims and travellers who had journeyed between India and China for thousands of years. Across vast deserts and mighty mountains, they had

[1] B.A.I., p. 143.

marched for many months and sometimes for years, encountering dangers and perils, but full of enthusiasm and the spirit of adventure, for they were the bearers of the treasures of thought and culture from one country to another. In those far-off days they had forged the imperishable links which bound India and China together. I imagined myself as one of a long line, yet another link joining together these two Ancients in history and civilization, who had found re-birth and youthful vitality again, and were facing the future with hope and confidence.

Almost my first experience in Chungking was of an air-raid, and these were repeated nightly while I was there. I was interested in the behavior of the Chinese crowds and I watched with admiration how calm and untroubled they were when death threatened them from the skies. I saw the life in the city being carried on almost normally in spite of the terrible strain of the war. I visited factories, summer schools, military academies, youth camps, and universities, torn from their ancient roots, finding a new life and vitality under bamboo shelters. I was fascinated by the growth of the village co-operative movement and cottage industries. I met scholars, statesmen and generals, the leaders of the new China, and, above all, I had the privilege of meeting on several occasions the supreme leader of China, Generalissimo Chiang-Kai-shek, who embodies in himself the unity of China and her determination to be free. It was my privilege also to meet the first lady of the land, Madame Chiang, who has been a continuous source of inspiration to the nation.

But though I met men and women of note and distinction, I was always trying to understand the people of China. I had read much about them and of their magnificent record of culture, and I was eager to sense the reality. I found not only a race wise and profound, deep in the lore of its own great past, but also a vital people, full of life and energy, adapting themselves to modern conditions. On the face of even the man in the street there was the imprint of ages of culture.

I found, to my joy, that my desire that China and India should draw closer to each other was fully reciprocated by China's leaders. Often, as we sat in a dug-out and enemy planes were bombing the city, we discussed the past and the present of our two countries and the bright promise of their future co-operation.

I returned to India full of this thought, and the vague ideas I had nourished for many years now began to take definite shape in my mind. There had been much talk in the West of a Federation of Europe, and of a Federal Union which seemed to exclude India and China. I had dreamed of a wider federation, comprising all of the nations and peoples of the world. Perhaps the time for that was not yet. But if there were to be regional federations, then surely there must be an Eastern Federation of China and India and other eastern countries.[1]

[Reaction to Chinese journey upon return to India—from Associated Press Interview—September 9, 1939.] [My] visit . . . [to China] has been very worth while even though it was [made] at a very inopportune moment. I was astonished and gratified at the desire of the Chinese people and their leader for a close and friendly relation with the people of India. I bring innumerable messages of greetings and good wishes from the leaders of China and India. I have been charged by the Chinese Generalissimo to convey his greetings and good wishes to Gandhiji and Dr Rabindranath Tagore. . . . I would have been held up in China but for the courtesy of the Chinese Government who put a plane at my disposal. I saw numerous air raids in China but I have not seen a single person getting excited.[2]

On World Union and Collective Security

I.

My . . . picture of the future is a federation which includes China and India, Burma and Ceylon, Afghanistan and possibly other countries. If a world federation comes, that will be welcome.[3]

II. [May 31, 1939.]

One of the tragedies of history is the slowness with which people's minds adapt themselves to a changing environment. The world changes from day to day, not so our minds which are peculiarly static and insist on imagining that today is the same as yesterday and tomorrow will not differ greatly. This lag between our minds and reality prevents us from solving the problems of the day and produces war and revolution and much else that afflicts the world. The great French Revolution came, bringing a tremendous release from mental bondage and for nearly a hundred years its ideas governed radical thought in Europe. And yet even before that Revolution . . . passed into history, another revolution of vital import had begun in Western Europe and was silently changing the face of things. This was the industrial revolution which has changed the

[1] T.F., pp. 367–68.
[2] B.A.I., p. 163.
[3] T.F., p. 367.

world more than anything that has happened in recorded history. This mighty change was hardly noticed even by those who lived through its early stages, and the thinkers of the first half of the nineteenth century still clung to the ideas of the French Revolution. It was these ideas, already out of date to a great extent, which were of the essence of the mental atmosphere of that century of change.

So it has been throughout history, so it is today, and even the prospect of approaching catastrophe does not push us out of our mental ruts, or does so at too slow a pace to prevent that catastrophe. The war of 1914–18 and the Russian Revolution might have been considered a big enough knock in the head to make even the dull of mind think furiously. But it was not, and most people went back to the old ruts and grew angry at those who thought differently. The events that followed during the next twenty years shook everyone up, [namely] failure of the capitalist structure and the great depression and unemployment, the rise of Fascism and Nazism and the growth of gangsterism in international affairs. Yet the shake was not enough. Then came the past year with all its horror and tragedy. That seems to have made some difference to many people, but do they yet realise that the remedy for the disease must be a radical one and nothing else will cure our distemper?

In India, even more than in Europe, we are wedded to the old process of thought, and though externally we differ from each other, the background is essentially the same. That is perhaps inevitable as our main pre-occupation must needs [be] ... nationalism and the desire to be rid of British Imperialism. There is a vast difference of class and approach between the Liberal in India, fearful of change, and the votaries of revolutionary violence, who hate present conditions and seek to change them at any cost. Between the two extremes most groups of Congressmen come in. And yet great as the difference is between these various groups and individuals, and governed as they are in their reactions by class and other considerations, still most of them function in much the same mental atmosphere. They quarrel amongst themselves in opposing camps, but essentially they talk the same language and accept the same postulates. That is the trouble with our Congress Governments also, which have the additional disadvantage of having to function completely in the old medium.

It is this old medium, this old method of approaching our problems, which is hopelessly out of date and incapable of producing solutions. The old political and economic structure is rotten and moth-eaten and all the king's horses and all the king's men cannot hold it together for long. We

discuss the problem of the States [though it involved] bargaining or give
and take between the rulers and the people, with the paramount power
taking a share of the spoil. But the states simply cannot fit [into] the
modern world and no amount of argument or soft words can change that
fundamental fact. . . . Systems like individuals have their span of life and
they cannot go beyond it.[1]

III. [June 1, 1939.]

We have in recent years tried to consider the Indian problem in its
relation to the world problem. Even if we had not done so, events would
have forced us and others to this consideration. Everyone must realise
that we have reached a stage when separate national solutions of any
problem are ruled out as they come into conflict with a real solution. We
must think in terms of the world, which has narrowed down so greatly in
our own day and become an organic whole, each part of it sensitive to the
other parts. More and more people realise this now and yet, as always, our
minds lag behind reality. Peace is indivisible, they say; so is freedom, so
is India, so is the world in any vital matter today.

Our freedom and our independence must therefore be thought of in
terms of the world and of world cooperation. The days of isolated national
existence are past beyond recall and the only alternative to world cooperation is world disruption and war and continuous conflicts between nations
till they are all involved in a common ruin.

It is difficult to conceive of effective world cooperation at present because there are forces and powerful nations which are bent on following a
contrary policy. Yet it may be possible to have the right objective and to
lay the foundations of such cooperation even now, though it may not be
world wide to begin with. Intelligent opinion all over the world and vast
numbers of people are eager and anxious for this to happen, but governments, vested interests and groups come in the way.

A faint glimpse of this world cooperation came to President Wilson
twenty years ago and he sought to realise it. But the war treaties and the
statesmen of that generation scotched the idea, and the great pile of the
League of Nations rises mournfully today in Geneva, like a mausoleum,
enshrining the dead body of a great hope. It had to die [since] it started
[as] an attempt to stabilise something which could not endure, [in order]
to protect the imperialisms and special interests of the victor nations. Its

[1] N.H., May 31, 1939. (From Ms copy.)

cry for peace meant the continuation of an unjust *status quo* all over the world, its democracy was a cloak for the subjection of many peoples and nations. It had to die because it was not brave enough to live. There can be no resurrection of that dead body. But there can be a resurrection of the idea that the League enshrined, not in the limited, twisted and perverse way that took shape in Paris and Geneva, but [in a manner] fuller, more powerful and organic and based on collective peace, freedom and democracy. On no other basis can it seek rebirth or find sustenance.

During the last few years there has been much talk of collective security but England and France killed it and with it the League. Faced by new dangers, threatening their very existence, they are trying to find allies in case of war. But even now they do not think in terms of real collective security for peace.

This idea of collective security failed for various reasons. The main reason for this failure was its alliance with imperialism. Collective security is intimately allied to democracy and freedom and in a world where these do not exist except in limited areas, it is bound to fail. The crux of the question thus becomes ... the liquidation of imperialism and the independence of India.

Many people are being driven to the conclusion that a closer cooperation between nations is essential for peace and progress. Vaguely they hanker after a world commonwealth which is something much more than a League of Nations. Some ardent Britishers imagine that the British Empire or Commonwealth of Nations offers a nucleus for this, forgetting that the basis of this empire is imperialism and exploitation of subject peoples. Even apart from the dependent part of the Empire, the semi-independent Dominions are loosening their bonds and tend to drift out of the imperial circle. ... In case of war, it is exceedingly doubtful if the British Empire, as such, will survive.

There are ... suggestions that the nations of the British Empire should draw closer to each other and have a federal legislature. This can either mean a federation of the white part of the Empire to dominate over the rest, or the complete liquidation of imperialism in India and the British colonies. In the latter event India, by virtue of her potential resources and manpower, is likely to have a powerful influence over the other parts, [of] which [the] other parts may not approve. ... In any event India cannot think in terms of the British Empire or Commonwealth and the whole logic of history and fact is opposed to our association with [so] limited [a] group .... Today with the situation in South Africa, where our countrymen are being humiliated and crushed, it is an insult for any one to suggest to us that we should continue as a member of this group.

But the fact remains that world co-operation must come and the independence of all nations must be curbed in the interests of world order and peace. That co-operation cannot and should not be confined to the British group even if that [were] possible. Indeed to attempt to confine it so is to defeat its very purpose.

A recent book, Clarence Streit's "Union Now", which has attracted considerable attention, deals with this problem. Mr Streit recommends a union of the so-called democracies. He mentions fifteen members to begin with: the United States of America, the United Kingdom, France, Canada, Australia, Ireland, South Africa, New Zealand, Belgium, Holland, Switzerland, Denmark, Norway, Sweden, and Finland. These countries are supposed to form a Federal Union with a parliament and not merely a league or an alliance.

This conception is certainly an advance over the idea of the British Empire but it suffers from two grave defects—the exclusion of the Soviet [Union], China and India as well as some other countries, and the silence about imperialism. That exclusion is presumably not intended to last but even so it is a bad beginning, full of dangerous possibilities. Many of the countries of this Union are already semi-fascist and imperialist. They might drift towards the fascist countries and come to terms with them and oppose the Soviet [Union] and the freedom movements in China and India. No progressive Union has a chance of survival today without the inclusion of . . . Soviet [Russia].

Nor can a real Union be formed except on the basis of the ending of imperialism, otherwise the Union becomes one of imperialist powers for the protection of their vested interests in subject countries. Even that they will not succeed in doing, as they will quarrel among themselves. Out of imperialism peace does not come; it is the parent of war.

A world Union is necessary today. Unhappily it will not come because those in authority are children of the old world which has ceased to be and cannot think or act in terms of the new. It will not come before the world is shattered again by war and millions have perished. But it will come because there is no other way out. Such a Union can have nothing to do with imperialism or fascism and must be based on the fullest democracy and freedom, each nation having autonomy within its borders, and submitting in international matters to the Union Legislature to which it sends its representatives. Inevitably it will have to work under a planned and socialised economy in order to end the conflicts of today.

To such a Federal Union India would gladly belong and contribute to her utmost for the peace and progress of the world.[1]

Events at Beginning of War

[Nehru was in China when Hitler invaded Poland. Lord Linlithgow, Viceroy of India, promptly declared India to be at war on September 3, the same day on which both Great Britain and France declared war on Germany. Without consulting either a single Indian national leader— or any leader of the eleven provinces enjoying provincial autonomy in India—the British plunged India into a world war against totalitarian oppression, at a moment when her own freedom seemed more cruelly remote than ever before. In addition to which an amendment to the Government of India Act of 1935 was rushed through the British Parliament in eleven minutes, empowering the Viceroy to override the provisions of the Act even with respect to provincial autonomy. The same day a Defence of India Ordinance was issued by the Viceroy, considerably curtailing the civil liberties of the Indian people.[2]

On September 11, 1939, a week after Britain had declared war in behalf of India, the Viceroy announced the postponement of plans to complete "federation" within India until after the war.

On September 14, the Congress Working Committee met to consider the current situation. In conformity with its policy, it made the first of many strong protests it was to issue during the war period. Although Nehru consistently favored supporting the Allies in opposition to the Axis powers throughout the war, he found it impossible to approve of India's becoming involved in the war effort short of her own freedom being guaranteed. In view of his passionate concern about the international situation his dilemma was agonizing.]

[From statement at time of outbreak of war.] Freedom is too precious to be bargained for, but it is too precious also to be ignored or put aside because the world has gone awry.... If we participate in the joint effort for freedom, that effort must be really joint, based on consent as between free equals. Otherwise it has no meaning, no value. Even from the point of view of success in the war, that free joint participation is of importance. From the wider point of view of the [objectives] ... the war is supposed to achieve, our freedom is essential.[3]

[When Nehru became the major draftsman of the September 14, 1939 Congress Working Committee Resolution relating to the war, Gandhi

[1] N.H., June 1, 1939. (From Ms copy.)
[2] T.T.N., p. 81.
[3] T.A.Y. (Vol. V–VI, 1940–41), p. 512.
21 + N.

stated: "The author of the statement is an artist. Though he cannot be surpassed in his implacable opposition to imperialism in any shape or form, he is a friend of the English people. Indeed he is more English than Indian in his thoughts and make-up. He is often more at home with Englishmen than with his own countrymen. And he is a humanitarian in the sense that he reacts to every wrong, no matter where perpetrated. Though, therefore, he is an ardent nationalist, his nationalism is enriched by his internationalism. Hence, the statement is a manifesto addressed not only to his own countrymen, not only to the British Government and the British people, but is addressed also to the nations of the world, including those that are exploited like India. He has compelled India, through the Working Committee, to think not merely of her own freedom, but of the freedom of all the exploited nations of the world."[1]

Gandhi's statement about Nehru was highly flattering, yet there were inevitable differences between the two men regarding how best to handle the extremely grave situation that had arisen. Moreover, although the Congress Working Committee approved the September 14 Resolution, a number of issues were involved concerning which there was by no means unanimous agreement. This was so despite the fact that all concerned deeply resented Britain's declaring India at war, without her consent. In any event, if the Committee's deliberations and activities were to have any effect whatever, it was of paramount importance that it have firm leadership and clear unity of purpose.

Since Gandhi had been unable to convert either Nehru or the Working Committee to his own point of view about the current situation, and since it was Nehru's Resolution that had been adopted, it was clearly Nehru—who was not Congress President at the time—who must be placed in a position of unquestioned authority. There was no one else on the Committee who held similar views who also possessed comparable ability as potential "helmsman".

The dilemma of Congress, especially with respect to whether to attempt to negotiate various questions relating to independence—in view of the war crisis—or whether and to what extent to cooperate in the war effort, was to remain a difficult one: "[Gandhi] pointed out the . . . fact that his shoulders were not strong enough for negotiation and that Jawaharlal must bear the burden. . . . The old-time adherents of Gandhi felt that they could not go all the way with him or with Jawaharlal. . . . It was therefore necessary that Gandhi and Jawaharlal should agree and lead or the latter should have full play." It was Gandhi who decided that Jawaharlal should have "full play".

Because of the constitutional difficulties involved in making Nehru President, "an alternative proposal to constitute a War-Committee was mooted only to be approved. . . . [Jawaharlal] was to be its President and would select his own colleagues."[2]

[1] T.D.G. (Vol. V), p. 166.

[2] H.I.N.C. (Vol. II), pp. 132–33. (A full summary of Congress discussions in September, 1939, is to be found in H.I.N.C.)

*From Congress Working Committee Resolution on the War—
September 14, 1939*

"The Working Committee have given their earnest consideration to the grave crisis that has developed owing to the declaration of war in Europe. The principles which should guide the nation in the event of war have been repeatedly laid down by the Congress, and only a month ago this committee reiterated them and expressed their displeasure at the flouting of Indian opinion by the British Government in India. As a first step to dissociate themselves from this policy of the British Government, the Committee called upon the Congress members of the Central Legislative Assembly to refrain from attending the next session. Since then the British Government have declared India as a belligerent country, promulgated Ordinances, passed the Government of India Act Amending Bill, and taken other far-reaching measures which affect the Indian people vitally, and circumscribe and limit the powers and activities of the provincial governments. This has been done without the consent of the Indian people whose declared wishes in such matters have been deliberately ignored by the British Government. The Working Committee must take the gravest view of these developments.

"The Congress has repeatedly declared its entire disapproval of the ideology and practice of Fascism and Nazism and their glorification of war and violence and the suppression of the human spirit. It has condemned the aggression in which they have repeatedly indulged and their sweeping away of well-established principles and recognised standards of civilised behaviour. It has seen in Fascism and Nazism the intensification of the principles of Imperialism against which the Indian people have struggled for many years. The Working Committee must therefore unhesitatingly condemn the latest aggression of the Nazi Government in Germany against Poland and sympathise with those who resist it. . . .

"In Manchuria the British Government connived at aggression; in Abyssinia they acquiesced in it. In Czechoslovakia and Spain democracy was in peril and it was deliberately betrayed, and the whole system of collective security was sabotaged by the very powers who had previously declared their firm faith in it.

"Again it is asserted that democracy is in danger and must be defended and with this statement the Committee are in entire agreement. The Committee believe that the peoples of the West are moved by this ideal and objective and for these they are prepared to make sacrifices. But again and again the ideals and sentiments of the people and of those who have sacrificed themselves in the struggle have been ignored and faith has not been kept with them.

"If the war is to defend the *status quo*, imperialist possessions, colonies, vested interests and privileges, then India can have nothing to do with it. If, however, the issue is democracy and a world order based on democracy, then India is intensely interested in it. The Committee are convinced that the interests of Indian democracy do not conflict with the interests of British democracy or of world democracy. But there is an inherent and ineradicable conflict between democracy for India or elsewhere and imperialism and fascism. If Great Britain fights for the maintenance and extension of democracy, then she must necessarily end imperialism in her own possessions, establish full democracy in India, and the Indian people must have the right of self-determination by framing their own constitution through a Constituent Assembly without external interference and must guide their own policy. A free democratic India will gladly associate herself with other free nations for mutual defence against aggression and for economic co-operation. She will work for the establishment of a real world order based on freedom and democracy, utilising the world's knowledge and resources for the progress and advancement of humanity.

"The crisis that has overtaken Europe is not of Europe only but of humanity and will not pass like other crises or wars leaving the essential structure of the present-day world intact. It is likely to refashion the world for good or ill, politically, socially and economically. This crisis is the inevitable consequence of the social and political conflicts and contradictions which have grown alarmingly since the last Great War, and it will not be finally resolved till these conflicts and contradictions are removed and a new equilibrium established. That equilibrium can only be based on the ending of domination and exploitation of one country by another, and on a reorganization of economic relations on a juster basis for the common good of all. India is the crux of the problem, for India has been the outstanding example of modern imperialism and no refashioning of the world can succeed which ignores this vital problem. With her vast resources she must play an important part in any scheme of world reorganization. But she can only do so as a free nation whose energies have been released to work for this great end. Freedom today is indivisible and every attempt to retain imperialist domination in any part of the world will lead inevitably to fresh disaster.

"The Working Committee have noted that many rulers . . . of Indian States have offered their services and resources and expressed their desire to support the cause of democracy in Europe. If they must make their professions in favour of democracy abroad, the Committee would suggest that their first concern should be the introduction of democracy within their own states in which today undiluted autocracy reigns supreme. The British Government in India is more responsible for this autocracy than even the rulers themselves, as has been made painfully evident during the past year. This policy is the very negation of democracy and of the new world order for which Great Britain claims to be fighting in Europe.

"As the Working Committee view past events in Europe, Africa and Asia, and more particularly past and present occurrences in India, they fail to find any attempt to advance the cause of democracy or self-determination or any evidence that the present war declarations of the British Government are being, or are going to be, acted upon. The true measure of democracy is the ending of imperialism and fascism alike and the aggression that has accompanied them in the past and the present. Only on that basis can a new order be built up. In the struggle for that new world order, the Committee are eager and desirous to help in every way. But the Committee cannot associate themselves or offer any co-operation in a war which is conducted on imperialist lines and which is meant to consolidate imperialism in India and elsewhere.

"In view, however, of the gravity of the occasion and the fact that the pace of events during the last few days has often been swifter than the working of men's minds, the Committee desire to take no final decision at this stage, so as to allow for the full elucidation of the issues at stake, the real objectives aimed at, and the position of India in the present and in the future. But the decision cannot long be delayed as India is being committed from day to day to a policy to which she is not a party and of which she disapproves.

"The Working Committee therefore invite the British Government to declare in unequivocal terms what their war aims are in regard to democracy and imperialism and the new order that is envisaged; in particular, how these aims are going to apply to India and to be given effect to in the present. Do they include the elimination of imperialism and the treatment of India as a free nation whose policy will be guided in accordance with the wishes of her people? A clear declaration about the future, pledging the Government to the ending of Imperialism and Fascism alike, will be welcomed by the people of all countries, but it is far more important to give immediate effect to it, to the largest possible extent, for only this will convince the people that the declaration is meant to be honoured. The real test of any declaration is its application in the present, for it is the present that will govern action today and give shape to the future.

"War has broken out in Europe and the prospect is terrible to contemplate. But war has been taking its heavy toll of human life during recent years in Abyssinia, Spain and China. Innumerable innocent men, women and children have been bombed to death from the air in open cities. Cold-blooded massacres, torture and utmost humiliation have followed each other in quick succession during these years of horror. That horror grows, and violence and the threat of violence shadow the world and, unless checked and ended, will destroy the precious inheritance of past ages. That horror has to be checked in Europe and China, but it will not end till its root causes of Fascism and Imperialism are removed. To that end the Working Committee are prepared to give their co-operation. But it will be infinite tragedy if even this terrible war is carried on in the spirit of imperialism and for the purpose of retaining this structure which is itself the cause of war and human degradation.

"The Working Committee wish to declare that the Indian people have no quarrel with the German people. But they have a deep-rooted quarrel with systems which deny freedom and are based on violence and aggression. They do not look forward to a victory of one people over another or to a dictated peace, but to a victory of real democracy for all the people of all countries and a world freed from the nightmare of violence and imperialist oppression.

"The Committee earnestly appeal to the Indian people to end all internal conflict and controversy and, in this grave hour of peril, to keep in readiness and hold together as a united nation, calm of purpose and determined to achieve the freedom of India within the larger freedom of the world".[1]

Commentary on the War and on Congress Working Committee Resolution of September 14, 1939

Soon after the outbreak of the war various individuals, high and not so high, expressed their opinions on Nazi aggression, and there was widespread condemnation of it. There was also considerable sympathy for the Polish people in their sad plight. Mahatma Gandhi spoke forcibly and other leaders condemned Nazi aggression. It is evident that the British authorities were greatly relieved by these various statements and came to the conclusion that India could be taken for granted in anything they did in connection with the war or in this country. They did not realize that our condemnation of Naziism and of the invasion of Poland could not alter our established policy of opposition to imperialism, and the latter, perforce, continued. They did not appreciate that Congressmen have developed a certain discipline among themselves and, in courtesy to their colleagues and in deference to their organization, they refrain from giving pointed expression to their individual views on vital matters which involve action. They forgot that we have cultivated a habit of being moderate in language but strong in any action that we might decide upon. In particular, they have not, in spite of a quarter of a century's experience, understood that behind the friendliness and courteous approach of Gandhiji there is the man of steel who does not bend on any vital matter affecting India's freedom.

Then came the Congress Working Committee's statement of September 14 crystallizing nationalist opinion and giving clear expression to it. That statement immediately evoked a remarkable response in India. What innumerable people had been feeling vaguely in their minds and hearts was clarified and put down in stately language. Doubts were resolved, many a perplexity vanished, for it seemed that the people of India had found voice and pointed to the world the inevitable path which had to be followed if our present-day problems were to be solved. And the world listened in spite of attempts of censors and the like to suppress this remarkable appeal. The progressives in England hailed it; in democratic America it received considerable publicity; even in war-ridden Europe

[1] I.W.F., pp. 30–35.

it evoked a response. People of suppressed and subject nations saw in it a charter for the oppressed. It was in tune with the spirit of the times.

All that has happened since then has been a logical development of that invitation of the Congress Working Committee for a clarification of war aims. Lord Zetland's[1] speech, the A.I.C.C. meeting, the Viceroy's statement, the Muslim League's resolutions, the House of Commons' debate, and now the war resolutions in the Provincial Assemblies and the inevitable resignations of the Congress Ministries, have all followed each other in ordered sequence, throwing a flood of light on the Indian scene.

What does this light show us? First of all, the high statesmanship and wisdom of the Congress, which stands justified today before India and the world. Holding to its ideals and its previous declarations, it has applied them to changing and difficult circumstances, and thus demonstrated that it has the capacity to be idealistic and practical at the same time. The freedom of India, for which it stands, has been woven into the larger picture of world freedom and war and peace aims, and a practical solution offered for the world's ills.

Secondly, the true nature of this war has become evident. The reply of the British Government to the Congress shows, beyond a doubt, that they are moved now, as before, by a desire to preserve their imperialist interests. This is no democratic war in which the forces of democracy are ranged on one side against the forces of Naziism and reaction on the other. True, there are some democratic forces on the side of the Allies, but the Governments that control the destinies of England and France are the old discredited Governments which must bear responsibility for the present unhappy state of Europe. We cannot forget Munich and Spain. Today the French Government is a citadel of reaction, and need we say more about the British Government than that Mr Neville Chamberlain is still the Prime Minister? We knew all this. And yet it was necessary that all doubt should be removed from the minds of the people and that reality should emerge out of the fog of war.

That reality has come, and it is not beautiful to look at, and not all the fine phrasing of Sir Samuel Hoare can rejuvenate the aged and the decrepit. Imperialism is a tottering structure today, wholly out of place in modern conditions, but the British ruling class still think in its terms and seek to preserve it. They are even afraid to make a clear declaration about India's freedom. This Imperialism is not in love with the minorities or even the Princes (though it utilizes both to serve its main purpose); it is

[1] British Secretary of State for India. (Nehru's statement concerning Lord Zetland's attitude is to be found in Part Five, Section 8.)

mainly concerned with British financial and other vested interests in India.

It is an axiom of Indian politics that there can be no compromise between imperialism and Indian nationalism and freedom. Whatever the phase of our struggle, that hostility has persisted. The Congress offer was that imperialism should be ended, the independence of India recognized, and thus age-long hostility should give place to friendship and co-operation between the two countries. That offer has been rejected, and we go our separate ways till fate or circumstance unites us again.

Thirdly, the position of the Muslim League has been cleared up beyond any possibility of misunderstanding. We had welcomed the League's acceptance of independence as its objective three years ago and the widening of the basis of its membership. But we were soon to realize that the old politically reactionary outlook still held the field. Under cover of communal propaganda the Muslim masses were prevented from realizing this. We are not for the moment discussing the communal demands of the League. They may be right or wrong. It is conceivable for a person to be a communalist and yet an ardent believer in political freedom, though at some stage or other a conflict will arise between these two loyalties. The Congress has often erred in the petty issues of politics, but it has always shown an unerring instinct whenever a major issue arose. The League, on the other hand, has a remarkable record of being wrong on the major issues, though it may occasionally be right on some trivial matter.

It is a tragedy that at this supreme crisis in our national history the League should have sided with full-blooded reaction. We do not believe that many of its own members agree with this attitude. We are certain that the Muslim masses are firm adherents of Indian freedom. In some communal matter the League may represent them, but it certainly does not do so in matters political.[1]

6 | War Aims and Peace Aims

I. [September 21, 1939.] Before we consider war aims and peace aims, let us define our approach to the problem. In India today the war is still a

[1] U.I., pp. 343-46.

far-away affair, exciting enough, but something apart from us, affecting us little. This is not so in Europe and elsewhere, for there it is constant sorrow and misery, and imminent danger and death and destruction, and a tension that breaks the heart, for innumerable multitudes. There is no home in Europe which is free from this gnawing fear and this sinking of the heart, for the world they have known has come to an end and horror has descended upon them, horror almost without end for themselves, for their dear ones, for much they have valued in life. Brave men and women, pawns in the hands of elemental forces which they cannot control, face the issue with courage, but the only hope that illumines their minds for a while is the hope of a better future for the world, so that their sacrifice may not have been in vain.

Let us think of these people in various countries, whether that country is Poland or France or England or Russia or Germany, with respect and full sympathy. Let us not presume to make fun of their suffering or say anything unthinkingly which hurts those who have to carry this heavy burden. We have had an old quarrel with England, though not with the people of England. That quarrel will end with our freedom. Only then can we make friends on equal terms with England. But for the English people in their present misfortune, as for other peoples, we have only sympathy and goodwill. We also know that whatever their imperialist Government may have done or may do in the future, there is a large fund of sympathy for freedom and democracy today among the English people. It is for these ideals that they fight. These ideals are ours also, though we fear that Governments may belie their words and their professions. Imperialism holds sway still in many parts of the world, and notably in India. And yet 1939 is not 1914. This quarter of a century has brought mighty changes in the world and in India, changes not so much in the outer structure, but in minds of people and in their desire to change this outer structure and put an end to an order based on violence and conflict.

In India we are very different from what we were in 1914. We have gained strength and political consciousness and a capacity for united action. In spite of our manifold difficulties and problems, we are no weak nation today. Our voice counts to some extent, even in international affairs. If we had been free we might have even succeeded in preventing this war. Sometimes the Irish analogy is placed before us. While we may learn much from Ireland and her struggle for freedom, we must remember that we are placed differently. Ireland is a small country which is geographically and economically tied to Britain. Even an independent Ireland cannot make much difference to world affairs. Not so India. A free India, with

21 *

her vast resources, can be of great service to the world and to humanity. India will always make a difference to the world; fate has marked us for big things. When we fall, we fall low; when we rise, inevitably we play our part in the world drama. . . .

What will be the end of the war? How long will it last? What will Soviet Russia do? Will Herr Hitler seek peace after crushing Poland? We do not claim to have an answer to these and many other questions, and those who seek to answer them have, perhaps, little justification for doing so. We are, however, convinced that this war, if it does not annihilate modern civilization, will revolutionize the present political and economic order. We cannot conceive of empires and imperialism continuing in the old way after the war.

Soviet Russia is at present a mystifying factor in the world situation. It is obvious that whatever Russia does will have important and far-reaching results. But as we do not know what she is going to do, we have to leave her out of our present calculations. The Russo-German Pact came as a shock and a surprise to many. There was nothing surprising in it except the manner of doing it and the moment chosen for it. At any other time it would have naturally fitted in with Soviet foreign policy. But there can be little doubt that at that particular moment it brought dismay to many friends of Russia. There seemed to be too much over-reaching, cynicism, and opportunism about it. That criticism applied to Hitler also, who overnight had dropped his fierce anti-Communism and apparently made friends with the Soviet. A cynic said that Russia had joined the Anti-Comintern Pact; another that Hitler was turning Communist as well as a patron of the Jews. All this seems to us fantastic nonsense, for there can be, and there is going to be, no real alliance between Hitler and Stalin. But both are willing enough to play at the game of power politics. Russia has suffered enough at the hands of England to resent it bitterly.

The Soviet's march into Eastern Poland was another shock. But it is yet difficult to say whether this was to counter the German army or to weaken the Poles or merely to take advantage of a particular situation from the nationalist point of view. From the meagre information that we possess it seems, however, that Russia's advance into Poland has certainly come in the way of German designs. It has prevented German occupation of Eastern Poland and cried a halt to the German army. More important still is the occupation of the entire Polish-Rumanian frontier by the Soviet army. This has made it certain that Germany cannot take possession of the Rumanian oil-fields which she coveted, and probably that she cannot draw upon the vast wheat supplies of Rumania. The Balkans are saved from German aggression, and Turkey breathes with relief. All this may mean little today, but in the future, as the war progresses, it will have a vital significance. It may be thus that Soviet Russia has rendered a great service to the cause of the Western Allies, and Bernard Shaw's dictum that Stalin has made a cat's-paw of Hitler has some truth in it.

Herr Hitler has ominously hinted in his Danzig speech that he has some terrible secret weapon which he will not hesitate to use, howsoever inhuman it might be, if circumstances compel him to do so. What this novel terror is, no one knows. It might well be an idle boast. There are terrors enough for humanity in the armoury of every Great Power today, more weapons will be forged as the war proceeds and all the powers of science are harnessed to quench the insatiable thirst for blood. We cannot say which side will have the advantage in this gruesome competition.

The aeroplane has, so far, not been the vital factor which some people expected it to be, though it is murderous and destructive enough. Perhaps we have not yet seen full use made of it. But all the experience in Spain and China, as well as the growth of the means of defence against air attack, indicate that the air arm will not be the deciding factor.

There is a chance, it is said, that Hitler may try for peace after his Polish campaign is over, or Signor Mussolini might act on his behalf in this respect. But there will be no peace then, for peace means the triumph of Hitler and the submission of England and France to his might. There may still be some advocates of "appeasement" in England or France, but the temper of their people will not permit it. There is also a chance—a more probable one—of internal trouble in Germany, which might shorten the war. But on that, too, it is unsafe to rely, at any rate in the early stages of the war. The war is thus likely to be a long one running into two or three years.

There are too many uncertainties in war for prophecy to be made. Yet the human mind must look ahead and try to peep through the veil of the future. That future seems to indicate that the area of the war will spread and more and more nations will be dragged in. It will, in effect, become a world war where neutrals hardly count, and it will go on year after year, destroying and killing and reducing the world to waste and ruin till the common-sense of war-worn humanity rebels against it and puts an end to it.

In this long war the advantages are all on the side of the Western Allies. Their economic and financial resources are far greater than those of Germany, and they will have a great part of the world to draw upon. In spite of German submarine activity or attack from the air, the sea routes will be more or less controlled by them. America and Asia and Africa will supply them with many of their needs, while Germany's sources of supply are strictly limited. We ignore for the present the part that Soviet Russia might play. This can be of tremendous importance both in the military and economic sense, but we think it highly unlikely that Russia will aid Nazi Germany.

If other countries join the war, the only possible allies for Germany are Italy and Japan. Japan will be immobilized to some extent by Soviet Russia, and her Chinese campaign has sobered her. Italy will make a difference in the Mediterranean, but not a vital one. . . .

On the side of the Western Allies there would be a tremendous acquisition of strength if the United States of America joined them. There is at present a marked isolationist tendency in the United States, but far stronger than that is the anti-Hitler and anti-Nazi feeling. On no account will America tolerate a victory for Hitler. It is extremely likely, therefore, that in the later stages of the war the United States will join England and France. Even before [that occurs, America] will help . . . [supply] their war needs, and, as in the last war, this very help will become an inducement to join [in the war effort, itself].

Whatever the more fundamental reasons for the war, the conflicts between rival imperialisms, the final cause was Nazi aggression. The last eighteen months of continuing Nazi aggression in Central Europe have embittered vast numbers of people all over the world against Nazi Germany, which has become in their eyes the embodiment of evil in the international sphere. This is a powerful psychological factor in favour of the Western Allies. Recent reports of internal trouble in Germany proper may be exaggerated, but such trouble is always likely, more especially if the war drags on and adds to the burdens and miseries of the people. It is certain that there will be continual trouble in Bohemia and Moravia and probably Slovakia. The people of Czecho-Slovakia, easily subdued because of their friends' betrayal, will take their revenge now.

All this indicates that in a long war—and the war is likely to be a long one—the scales will be heavily balanced in favour of the Western Allies. But that advantage will be theirs only if their war and peace aims are for real freedom and democracy and self-determination, so that the peoples of the world may know and believe that the objective is worth the terrible price they pay. It is not for the continuation of imperialism that they will fight and make sacrifices. And it is the peoples of the world who will have the final say, not the Governments that have misled them for so long. If

Governments do not fall in with their wishes, they will have to go and give place to others.[1]

II. [September 23, 1939.] What are the professed war aims of the Western Allies? We are told that they fight for democracy and freedom, for the ending of the Nazi régime and Hitlerism, for the liberation of Poland. Mr Chamberlain has now added that Czecho-Slovakia must also be freed. We agree. But all this is not enough, and hence the importance of the invitation extended by the Working Committee to the British Government to state fully and unequivocally what their war and peace aims are.

Let us carry the argument further. If Hitlerism is to go, it necessarily follows that there should be no truce or pacts with any Fascist [Powers, including those other than Germany].... Japanese and Italian aggression should not be recognized, and our policy should be directed to assist China, in so far as we can, in her struggle for freedom. It means, further, that the policy applied to Fascism should be extended to imperialism, and both should be ended. In any event, and even apart from international developments, we must have a free and independent India. But for the present we consider Indian freedom in its world context of imperialism....

A statement of war aims should thus include: the liberation of countries taken by Hitler, the ending of the Nazi régime, no truce or pacts with Fascist Powers, and the extension of democracy and freedom by the winding up of the imperialist structure and the application of the principle of self-determination. There should, of course, be no secret treaties, no conquests, no indemnities or reparations, no bargains over colonial areas. In the colonies also the principle of self-determination should be applied, and steps should be taken to democratize them. All discrimination based on race must go. We can admit no peace settlement over the bodies of colonial peoples.

It is in no spirit of bargaining that we make these suggestions, nor is there the slightest desire to take advantage of another's difficulty. We sympathize with that difficulty, but that sympathy cannot make us forget our own difficulties and disabilities. If we desire the freedom of Poland or Czecho-Slovakia, much more do we desire the freedom of China, and it is not just narrow self-interest that induces us to give first place to the freedom of India. Freedom can have no meaning for us if we ourselves do not possess it, and it would be a hollow mockery if we shouted for the freedom of a distant land and submitted to subjection ourselves. But even

[1] U.I., pp. 306–12.

looking at it from the point of view of the war, such freedom is essential in order to make this a popular war, which can move the people to courage and sacrifice for a cause which they consider theirs. As this war goes on from month to month and year to year, and weariness comes over the peoples of all countries, it is this urge to defend one's own hard-earned freedom that will tell in the end. The war will not be won by mercenary armies with mercenary motives, howsoever efficient they might be.

Coming to India, the first step to be taken by the British Government is to make a public declaration recognizing India as a free and independent nation which can draw up her own Constitution. We must recognize that this declaration cannot be given full effect immediately, but it is essential, as the Working Committee have pointed out, that it should be applied, in so far as is possible, in the present. For it is that application that touches the minds and hearts of the people and impresses the world. It is this present that will govern the conduct of the war and give it that vitality which can only come from the yoking of the popular will to a great task. Whatever we do must be of our free will and choice, and only then will the effort be really joint, for it will then be based on the free co-operation of partners in a common undertaking.

Unhappily, the British Government, as is its way, has taken action already which makes reasonable approach from us difficult. They passed the Government of India Act Amending Bill through the House of Commons in all its stages in exactly eleven minutes, though they knew full well that we were entirely opposed to it. Here in India legislation and ordinances have been similarly rushed through. The India Office and the Government of India still live in an age that is long past; they neither grow, nor learn, nor remember. Even the shock of war has not had much effect on their mental processes or their ancient ways. They take India for granted, not realizing that nothing can be taken for granted in this cataclysmic age, much less India, which, though quiet on the surface, is shaken by all manner of forces and vital urges.

Yet, in spite of this difficulty of approach, the Working Committee have, in the spirit of true statesmanship, stretched out their hand and offered their co-operation to the British people and all other people who struggle for freedom's cause. But India can only co-operate with dignity and freedom, or else she is not worth co-operation. Any other way is that of imposition, and we can no longer endure this.

How and to what extent is it necessary and possible to give present application to Indian freedom? It is clear that whatever we do must be of our free will and based on our decision. In matters pertaining to the war there must be equality of action, even though this cannot be put on the Statute Book. India may be technically at war, but there is no war situation in this country, and there is absolutely no reason why our normal legislative or judicial processes should be replaced by abnormal measures. These abnormal measures have been passed. They must remain dead letters, and all necessary steps should be taken through the Provincial Legislatures and the Provincial Governments. The Amending Act passed by the British Parliament should also remain a dead letter, and in so far as the Provincial Governments are concerned, their powers and activities should in no way be limited. Such limitations and safeguards as exist in the Constitution should not be applied. So far there is little difficulty.

But it is essential that even during this interim period India's representatives should have effective control over the policies and activities in the centre in regard to external affairs, armed forces, and financial matters. Only in this way can a policy based on real consent be carried through. For this purpose some *ad hoc* machinery will have to be devised. Amendments of the present Act are not desirable. The Act will have to go as a whole when the Constitution of India's making takes its place. Meanwhile effective interim arrangements can be made by consent.

It is clear that if India's war policy is to have popular backing and support, it must be carried out by popular representatives in whom the people have confidence. It is no easy matter to live down the prejudice of generations and to make our people look upon the effort as their own. This can only be done by taking them into our confidence, by explaining our policies, and by convincing them that it is to their advantage as well as for the world's good. That is the way democracy functions. We shall have to know the larger policies governing the war also, so that we can justify them before our people and the world.

A war policy for a nation must inevitably first take into consideration the defence of the country. India must feel that she is taking part in her own defence and in preserving her own freedom as well as helping in the struggle for freedom elsewhere. The army will have to be considered a national army and not a mercenary force [owing] allegiance to someone else. It is on this national basis that recruitment should take place, so that our soldiers should not merely be cannon-fodder, but fighters for their country and for freedom. In addition to this it will be necessary to have a large-scale organization for civil defence on a militia basis. All this can only be done by a popular Government.

Even more important is the development of industries to supply war and other needs. Industries must develop on a vast scale in India during wartime. They must not be allowed to grow in a haphazard way, but should be planned and controlled in the national interest and with due safeguards for workers. The National Planning Committee can be of great assistance in this work.

As the war progresses and consumes more and more commodities, planned production and distribution will be organized all over the world, and gradually a world-planned economy will appear. The capitalist system will recede into the background, and it may be that international control of industry will take its place. India, as an important producer, must have a say in any such control.

Finally, India must speak as a free nation at the Peace Conference.

We have endeavoured to indicate what the war and peace aims of those who speak for democracy should be, and, in particular, how they should be applied to India. The list is not exhaustive, but it is a solid foundation to build upon and an incentive for the great effort needed. We have not touched upon the problem of a reorganization of the world after the war, though we think some such reorganization essential and inevitable.

Will the statesmen and peoples of the world, and especially of the warring countries, be wise and far-seeing enough to follow the path we have pointed out? We do not know. But here in India let us forget our differences, our Leftism and Rightism, and think of these vital problems which face us and insistently demand solution. The world is pregnant with possibilities. It has no pity at any time for the weak or the ineffective or the disunited. Today, when nations fight desperately for survival, only those who are far-seeing and disciplined and united in action will play a rôle in the history that is being made.[1]

[Statement as Chairman of Congress War Sub-Committee, September 29, 1939.] It [has been] made perfectly clear by the Working Committee, as well as by . . . Congress leaders, that we [are] not out to bargain or . . . take advantage of England's difficulty. But it [is] essential, in our opinion, both from the point of view of India and the world, that [Britain's] war aims should be clarified, and people made to believe in their reality and their *bona fides*. It is astonishing that a request of this kind should be called inopportune and ill-timed. . . . Must vast numbers of human beings suffer unto death without even knowing definitely what they die for?

Every war in the past has begun with fervent declarations invoking justice and honour and right as against unjust aggression and might. And

[1] Ibid., pp. 312–17.

yet, when [a] war has ended, there has been little difference, and the fervent declarations have been forgotten. . . . Are we to continue to suffer under systems which are essentially based on violence and aggression ? . . .

It is because we feel that large numbers of British people have the same world ideas [that] many of us possess in India that we have offered them our co-operation in the realization of these ideals. But if the ideals are not [the same], what do we fight for ? [1]

[Message to English people—cabled to *News Chronicle*, London, October 5, 1939.] The spell of violence and inhuman warfare holds Europe and threatens the fabric of civilisation all over the world. Behind the clash of arms there is a deeper clash of ideas and aims and the future of the world hangs in the balance. History is being made not only on the battlefields but in the minds of men, and the vital question for all of us is whether that history is . . . to be different from that of past ages and whether this terrible war will make [an] essential difference to human freedom and end the very causes of war and human degradation. To India with her thirst for freedom and horror of war and violence, this question is of paramount importance. She has reacted strongly against the philosophy and methods of fascism and Nazi aggression and brutality and seen in them the negation of all she stands for. World peace for her means freedom and democracy and the ending of the domination of one nation over another. So India condemned aggression in Manchuria, Abyssinia, Czechoslovakia, and was deeply distressed at events in Spain and the brutal Nazi invasion of Poland. India will therefore gladly [use] her resources for a new order of peace and freedom.

If [our idea] of peace is the objective then war and peace aims must be clearly defined and [present] action . . . must conform to them . . . If this war is for democracy and self-determination and against Nazi aggression, it cannot be fought for territorial annexations, indemnities or reparations, for keeping colonial peoples in subjection, and for maintaining the imperialist system.

For this urgent reason the Congress has invited the British Government to state its war and peace aims clearly and in particular how these apply to the imperialist order and to India. [2]

[From Statements on Congress War Crisis Resolution.]

[October 9, 1939.] During the last few years the Congress has passed a

[1] I.A.A., pp. 328–29.
[2] C.S.W., pp. 177–78.

number of resolutions on war. It is said that these resolutions can have but one meaning and that is to declare ourselves against war but that is not the only policy that follows from the resolution. The statement of the Working Committee is not inconsistent with any of the principles laid down in these resolutions. It is for us to consider whether it is worth while to choose a certain course which obviously has [caused] difficulties [or] an alternative [course that would involve functioning along agitational lines, which would perhaps prevent our being effective at the international level]. We must have strength to face difficulties and overcome them in any course we may adopt. The statement of [the] Working Committee has taken note of possible difficulties in [deciding] upon a course which, I think, is far-seeing and right [under] the circumstances.[1]

[October 11, 1939.] Only a free India can decide whether we can participate in the war [or] not. We want a declaration whether the principles of democracy, liberty and self-determination for which [it] is claimed [the war is being] fought will be applicable to India also.[2]

[October 25, 1939.] The alternatives to democracy in India are Fascism, Sovietism or India's continued subjection to foreign rule. . . . Recently the democratic ideal has been criticised by various people in India. I do not know if they have thought of the inevitable consequences of giving up that ideal. I cannot conceive of any objective other than democracy in [India at the present time]. With proper protection and safeguards for the minorities . . . everyone concerned [will be benefited]. Of course the majority will remain a majority, as nothing can convert a majority into a minority except . . . rule by a Fascist or military clique. So far as the Muslims are concerned, it is a little misleading to talk in terms of majorities and minorities. A religious group seventy million strong cannot be considered a minority. As [the group is] spread out in India in certain provinces [it is] in a majority and in such provinces . . . minority [problems differ entirely from those in] the rest of India. It is quite inconceivable to me that in these circumstances either the Hindus can [persecute] the Muslims or the Muslims [can persecute] the Hindus. I would add, or [that] the Hindus and Muslims together [could persecute] anybody else as [a] religious group. The Sikhs are very small in number but I do not think there is the slightest chance of their being tyrannized over by anybody. It is unfortunate that [the] communal question has taken [a] new shape and is being used as a barrier to India's freedom. Nothing has surprised me

[1] B.A.I., p. 169.
[2] Ibid., p. 169.

and pained me so much during the last year or two, as the amazing charges brought against the Congress and Congress Governments [that they have suppressed] Muslims and [committed] atrocities against them. The Congress Governments have made many mistakes, as was natural, in regard to various departments of Government, but I am personally quite convinced that in regard to the treatment of minorities, they have taken the greatest care possible not to offend against any minority rights or privileges. We have so often asked for an impartial enquiry into the vague charges brought forward and our offer still remains unaccepted . . . yet totally unfounded statements continue to be made. So far as the Congress is concerned, it is prepared today as it has always been prepared, to consider the communal or minority question in all [of its aspects, in order] to put an end to all misapprehensions and arrive at a satisfactory settlement. But the Congress cannot consider any proposal which goes against India's unity and freedom and which is opposed to all democratic ideals. . . .

Our fight is against British Imperialism. We do not propose to fight any countryman of ours or any organisation of Indians, if any Indian or any organisation in India allies itself with British Imperialism, but I am sure India [would] survive such a misfortune. . . .

One of the great advantages of a crisis like the present one is that it forces people and organizations to show [their true nature]. It becomes impossible . . . to play with vague phrases and indulge in brave talk, because such talk [has] to be followed by action. So in the present instance this crisis [could] result in removing [the] fog from Indian politics [that] has confused . . . issues for so long, and the public [might finally] understand . . . the real [objectives] of individuals and organizations.[1]

7 | New British Proposals—First Reaction to Viceroy's Declaration, October, 1939

New British Proposals

[On October 17, 1939, the Viceroy, Lord Linlithgow, announced that the 1935 Government of India Act would be modified to the extent deemed

[1] Ibid., pp. 172–74.

desirable by the British. Only dominion status, but not complete independence, would be granted to India after the war. At that time provisions of the 1935 India Act could be reassessed. In addition to the points mentioned by Nehru in the following passage, the British offered to include a greater number of Indians in the Viceroy's Executive Council. Minorities were to be protected. The latter guarantee was especially provoking to Nehru and other Congress leaders of like mind, since Congress itself stood for full protection of all minorities.

With respect to the Congress desire for self-government, Lord Linlithgow declared that the situation must be faced in terms of "world politics", "political realities" and "practical considerations".]

First Reaction to Viceroy's Declaration—October 17, 1939

The Viceroy has spoken and the British Government has given answer to India's questions. What were those questions that the Congress put, not on behalf of itself only, not only on behalf of the hundreds of millions of India, but for vast numbers of human beings all over the world, who were sick and weary of war and violence, of fascism and imperialism and all their ugly and numerous progeny, and hungered for a new order and peace and freedom? "The Working Committee invite the British Government to declare in unequivocal terms what their war aims are in regard to democracy and imperialism and the new order that is envisaged, in particular, how these aims are going to apply to India and to be given effect to in the present. Do they include the elimination of imperialism and the treatment of India as a free nation whose policy will be guided in accordance with the wishes of her people?"

We have the answer now. The Viceroy "is authorised by His Majesty's Government to say that at the end of the war they will be very willing to enter into consultation with representatives of several communities, parties and interests in India and with the Indian Princes with a view to securing their aid and co-operation in framing such constitutional modifications as may be deemed desirable." Further he announces the immediate establishment of a consultative group of all major political parties in British India and of the Indian Princes which will associate public opinion with the conduct of the war. In order to comfort us still further, we are told that the pledge given in the preamble of the Act of 1919 still holds.

We would hesitate ordinarily to comment in haste on these pronouncements for the gravest issues are at stake, and it is right and proper that India's rejoinder should be given by the Congress Working Committee. We presume that the Committee will meet soon and give the only lead to the country that seems possible now. But while it is our privilege to carry the message of the Congress, and to discipline ourselves and the nation in the pursuit of our objectives and ideals, we may not remain silent even for a day when a challenge has been thrown out to the Indian people and to the ideals we have cherished for so long.

The last six weeks have seen the elimination of a nation from the map of Europe and the crushing of a proud people. That has been a major occurrence, full of tragedy, and yet it is but a minor prelude to the vast and cataclysmic changes that are taking place before our eyes. Hitler, who dreamed of dominion over Europe and possibly the world, has been compelled by force of circumstances to give up that dream and to submit to the superior might of Soviet Russia. The South-East of Europe lies beyond his reach now, the Baltic States and the Baltic Sea are dominated by Russia. Half Poland has gone and Nazi Germany, with all her armed might, plays second fiddle and lives in fear of what may come.

This is the beginning, the first fruits of the war. What will follow in the months and years to come we can only dimly see now, but only the blind can imagine that the present-day world of empires and colonies and dependencies will survive this holocaust of war. . . .

Every man and woman of intelligence has some realisation of these profound changes that are taking place in this era of war and revolution. But not so the British Government and not the Government of India. They live in Whitehall and New Delhi apart from humbler, though perhaps more intelligent folk, and they neither see nor remember. In 1939 they remind us of a preamble of the Act of 1919. For them these twenty years have been but a bad dream that is no more, and though the world may crash and go to pieces, who dare touch the sanctums of Whitehall or New Delhi? But we remember that even in 1919 the preamble was indignantly rejected by the Indian people, that three times since then we have faced the might of the British Empire, unarmed and peaceful and clad in simple homespun, but strong in the strength of our millions, and proud of the spirit of our people and of the ideals we cherished. We remember that in 1935 yet another Act was imposed upon us and the old Act of 1919 was consigned to oblivion. This new Act also we rejected. And now the old preamble of 1919 is fished out of the dustbin and presented to us by His Excellency the Viceroy as a gift worthy of England, fighting for democracy, and worthy of India, insistent on independence.

Need we examine any other parts of the Viceroy's statement? We ask for independence and are promised a consultation at the end of the war for such constitutional modifications as may be deemed desirable.

Perhaps we were foolish in asking our questions. Yet we do not think so, for there is no one in India now, and few, we imagine, in the world who will be deceived by British professions of a war for democracy and freedom. We know now, beyond a peradventure, that Britain clings to her imperialism and fights to preserve it, howsoever her statesmen may cover this ancient habit of theirs by soft and pleasing words. What of the British Labour Party now and all those radicals and lovers of freedom in England who talk so eloquently of the brave new world that is coming? What of America, that great land of democracy, to which imperialist England looks for support and sustenance during this war? Does Britain think that the people of the United States will pour their gold and commodities to make the world safe for British imperialism? What of the free dominions of the British Commonwealth, who have been charmed by brave phrases and made to come to Britain's aid? How will they like this exposure of the reality that lies behind those phrases? The aims and objectives of this terrible war are clear at last, at least in so far as the present British Cabinet is concerned. Let no man doubt them.

The Congress asked a question, but in asking that question it also gave its own answer. That answer stands. We can never be parties to supporting imperialism. The issues are clear and so are we in our minds. This is not a matter for Congressmen only but for all of us, whether we belong to the Muslim League or Hindu Mahasabha or Sikh League or any other organisation of Indians. For India's honour and India's freedom are involved and nothing else can count when these supremely vital issues are at stake.

The Viceroy has told us to think of the unity of India. His Excellency's reminder was not necessary. But even the unity of India cannot be purchased at the cost of India's freedom. We want no union of slaves in bondage. We want a united India but a free India, and we have no shadow of doubt that we shall get what we want. Meanwhile we may have to go into the wilderness again, as we have so often done in the past. If the fates so will it, we shall do so gladly, rejoicing that yet again we have been privileged to serve the cause that is dearer to us than everything else. And in doing so we shall help in building the new world order for which millions crave—an order of peace and freedom from which fascism and imperialism have been eliminated, and the days of war and violence are no more.[1]

[1] C.S.W., pp. 182-87.

8 | Congress Rejection of Viceroy's Proposals—More about Viceroy's Statement—On Lord Zetland's Statement

[As the following statements indicate, in the wake of declarations made by the Viceroy in October and November, 1939, Congress-British as well as Congress-Muslim League differences were greatly exacerbated.

In Nehru's view the British were utilizing the pretext that the communal problem—rather than British policy, itself—was responsible for the resignation of Congress provincial ministries. It was claimed by the British that communal friction also was a basic reason for not granting India her independence. Hence British policy served primarily to intensify Congress leaders' burning desire for a Constituent Assembly, at which plans for a free, united, democratic and secular state finally might be formulated.]

Resolution Rejecting Viceroy's Proposals Passed by Congress Working Committee, Wardha—October 22, 1939

"The Working Committee are of the opinion that the Viceroy's statement [of October 17] in answer to the Congress invitation for a clear declaration of ... British war aims, particularly in their application to India, is wholly unsatisfactory and calculated to rouse resentment among all those who are anxious to gain—and are intent upon gaining—India's independence. This invitation was made not only on behalf of the people of India, but also on behalf of the millions of people all over the world who are weary of war and violence and the Fascist and Imperialist systems which exploit nations and peoples, and are ultimately the causes of war. ... [These peoples] yearn for a new order of peace and freedom.

"The Viceregal statement is an unequivocal reiteration of the old imperialistic policy.

"The Committee regard the mention of the differences among several parties as a screen to hide the true intentions of Great Britain.

"What the Committee had asked for was a declaration of war aims as a test of Britain's *bona fides* regarding India, irrespective of the attitude of the opposing parties or groups.

"The Congress has always stood for the amplest guarantee of the rights of minorities. The freedom the Congress claimed was not for the Congress or any particular group or community but for the nation and for all communities in India that go to build that nation. The only way to establish this freedom and to ascertain the will of the nation as a whole is through the democratic process which gives a full opportunity to all.

"The Committee must, therefore, regard the Viceroy's statement as in every way unfortunate. In the circumstances, the Committee cannot possibly give any support to Great Britain, for it would amount to an endorsement of the imperialist policy which the Congress has always sought to end. As a first step in this direction, the Committee call upon the Congress Ministries to tender their resignations.

"The Committee earnestly appeal to the nation to end all internal controversies in this hour of great crisis and call upon all Congress Committees and Congressmen generally to be prepared for all developments and eventualities and to show restraint of word and deed, so that nothing may be said or done which is not in keeping with India's honour or the principles for which the Congress stands.

"The Committee warn Congressmen against any hasty action in the shape of civil disobedience, political strikes and the like.

"The Committee will watch the situation and the activities of the British Government in India and will not hesitate to guide the country to take further steps whenever the necessity for this arises.

"The Committee desire to impress upon all Congressmen that a programme of resistance commensurate with the magnitude of the issue before the country requires perfect discipline within the Congress ranks and the consolidation of the Congress organization.

"The Working Committee realise that the non-violent resistance offered by the Congress in the past has sometimes been mixed with violence.

"The Committee desire to impress upon all Congressmen that any resistance that may have to be offered must be purged of all violence and to remind them of the pledges taken to this effect as early as 1921 . . . and repeated on many subsequent occasions." [1]

More about the Viceroy's Statement—October 26, 1939

The Viceroy's statement betrays the same old colour of British Imperialism, the same old sweetness without grace and the same old insincere verbiage. But let British Imperialism remember that Congressmen also have their old methods, their old colours and their old temper and urge for irresistible action. . . . If it becomes a question of choosing between complete destruction of our twenty years' work and immediately coming into conflict with British Imperialism, we would prefer not to be led away by the fact that the Congress was pursuing parliamentary activities but to remember that it is essentially pledged to India's Independence and would take steps to win it. [2]

[1] I.A.A., pp. 142-43.
[2] B.A.I., p. 174.

On Lord Zetland's Statement, *1939*

[Certain remarks made by Lord Zetland, British Secretary of State for India—like the Viceroy's declarations of October and November—greatly aroused Nehru. The allegedly "reactionary and provocative character" of the Zetland pronouncements also "compelled the Congress to wash its hands of all connection with war and administration". [1]]

Lord Zetland occupies a high office. But many of his recent utterances can hardly be termed responsible or helpful. I have no desire to discuss his latest speech in any detail. He has raised some novel points and arguments and laid stress on the minorities question specially. No one in India can possibly ignore this question and all of us are obviously desirous of solving it to the satisfaction of the various parties concerned.

How is it to be solved within the context of democracy? Obviously, the fundamental principles governing any consideration of any aspect of the Indian problem are democracy and unity of India. The suggestion put forward by the Congress that all these matters should be decided by a Constituent Assembly meets in principle all the difficulties raised. This does not mean that all our problems are simple of solution or that there will not be complications and difficulties to face. But it does offer not only a suitable method but the only way within the context of democracy. The mass of people [would] elect their representatives [by adult suffrage]; all the principal minorities [would be] represented and have a voice in the shaping of India's future. In regard to their particular problems it may be said that a minority's rights might be over-ridden by majority vote. That [would be solved] by the suggestion that such rights should be settled by agreements. If there [were no agreement about specific issues] . . . the only proper course [would be to refer problems to independent arbitration at] the League of Nations or the International Court at the Hague. Nothing could be fairer than this and no minority can possibly object to it. It avoids the possibility of the majority forcing its will on a minority in regard to the minorities' special rights and interests. It avoids also the absurdity of a minority imposing its will on a majority. The importance of the Constituent Assembly procedure is to [obtain] the . . . opinion of the masses: Hindus, Muslims, Sikhs, etc., through their elected representatives. The question [would] not arise then of [whom] the Congress . . . or the Muslim League or any other party [would represent]. If these

[1] H.I.N.C. (Vol. II), p. 135.

organisations command the confidence of the people their nominees will be elected to the Constituent Assembly.

I agree with Lord Zetland that it is a little absurd to consider the Muslims in India as a minority. Not only their great numbers but the fact that in large areas of the country they are in a majority makes it clear that no minority question really arises. Ordinarily speaking, such numbers warrant no protection, as they can well look after their own interests. As a matter of fact in predominantly Muslim areas like the Punjab, Bengal, Sind, the N.W.F.P. and Baluchistan the minorities are non-Muslims and many of them have demanded protection. If India is looked at as a whole these various factors balance one another and prevent misbehaviour of any religious or racial groups.

Lord Zetland unfortunately still thinks in terms of a bygone age and has a semi-feudal outlook on life. He does not realise that new forces are convulsing India. Even among the Muslims the mass of the people are claiming their own rights from [the] upper class and sometimes their semi-feudal leaders. The problems of India are essentially economic though a continuous attempt is made and has again been made by Lord Zetland to make them appear to be racial and minority problems. Lord Zetland possibly still thinks of the Princes of India as . . . hereditary rulers and of the Rajputs and other [groups] as the obvious military class. But things are very different in the India of to-day and all this attempt to hide the real issues cannot last long in this dynamic situation.

I can well understand the opposition of the British Government to the idea of [a] Constituent Assembly because such an Assembly necessarily puts an end to British Imperialism. Between the position of Indian nationalism and that of . . . British Imperialism there is no common factor. If the British Government is unable to agree to India determining her future we are equally unable to agree to the British Government interfering in any way in such a decision. We agree to differ and the future will decide whose will prevails. There is no other way of having a free constitution [in] India, [for] every other method involves a measure of dictation from abroad. . . . The days of small groups at the top deciding the fate of India cannot last.[1]

[1] From Ms (1939).

Further Communal Developments— Comments on Viceroy's Statement in Conjunction with Jinnah and Communalism—Plan for Talks with Jinnah—Correspondence with Jinnah— Other Correspondence

9

Further Communal Developments, Autumn, 1939

[Before] the resignation of the Congress governments in the provinces . . . the Congress . . . [attempted] to approach Mr M. A. Jinnah and the Moslem League. Mr Jinnah was invited to attend the first meeting of the Congress executive after the commencement of the war. He was unable to join us. We met him later and tried to evolve a common policy in view of the world crisis. Not much progress was made, but nevertheless we decided to continue our talks. Meanwhile the Congress governments resigned on the political issue which had nothing to do with the Moslem League and the communal problem. Mr Jinnah, however, chose that moment for a fierce attack on the Congress. . . . He followed this up by very unbecoming remarks on nationalist Moslems in the Congress and especially on the [Moslem] Congress president, Maulana Abul Kalam Azad, who was greatly respected among Hindus and Moslems alike.[1]

From Comments on Viceroy's Statement in Conjunction with Jinnah and Communalism—November, 1939

The Viceroy [has] . . . dwelt upon the entire disagreement between representatives of the major political parties on fundamental issues [converting the question at issue into a communal one].[2]

This seems to me an entire misapprehension of the situation and I am not aware of any such disagreement on fundamental issues. But there is a fundamental disagreement between the Congress and the British Government and it was because of this that the Viceroy's proposals could not be considered by us.[3]

[1] D.I., p. 399.
[2] H.I.N.C. (Vol. II), p. 151
[3] I.A.A., p. 331.

It was agreed between Mr Jinnah and me that the communal question should be discussed fully by us at an early, convenient date.[1]

[Further reply to Viceroy concerning communalism—November 6, 1939.] For several days we lived in an air of mystery and picked up tit-bits of news and anticipations of the doings of the High Commands and the Men of Note who had foregathered in New Delhi. And now we have had a spate of information—letters and statements and even a radio broadcast by the Viceroy. His Excellency has spoken and written in moving terms and yet he will forgive us, we hope, if we are not moved overmuch by his statement. We are bad boys, we are told, who will not compose our [communal] differences in spite of every attempt of the British Government and every appeal addressed to us by the Viceroy. We have our faults and our failings, as we are only too painfully aware, but must we consider the British Government the White Angel of Peace that it claims to be? We have some experience of this Government, stretching over an odd hundred and eighty years, and it is hard to forget this. We have some knowledge of how the communal question took shape in India and was nurtured, and grew and grew, under the benign influence of successive Viceroys and governments. It is evident that the old tradition still holds and finds expression in British policy in India. The Viceroy has spoken, [also] the Marquis of Zetland . . . Sir Samuel Hoare, and others of high or low degree. . . . Through all [such] utterances runs the old thread of the White Man's Burden and of British statesmen and administrators grappling with the internal troubles of this unhappy land.

What happened in Delhi? The Viceroy met Mahatma Gandhi, Shri Rajendra Prasad and Mr Jinnah and put forward a proposal that if they could agree about the provinces, the problem of the Centre could be tackled with greater ease. It would appear that the Viceroy looked upon the crisis as something that had taken place between Mr Jinnah and the Congress with which he had no direct concern except in the capacity of a benevolent arbitrator. What exactly had happened in the provinces which required adjustment? The Congress Governments had resigned but they did not resign on any communal issue. They resigned because of British policy with which they did not agree and from which they wished to dis-sociate themselves. The conflict was with the British Government. . . .

If Mr Jinnah controlled British policy and could speak on its behalf, he might have been able to help. But he is himself an opponent and critic of that policy and has his own grievances against the British Government.

[1] H.I.N.C. (Vol. II), p. 151.

What then was to be done about the Provincial Governments? It is beyond our capacity to understand what the Viceroy expected from his visitors, unless we presume that he has not followed or understood recent developments.

There has seldom been such widespread resentment in India as was noticed when British policy was stated by the Viceroy two weeks ago. Apart from a few individuals who, however eminent, have no representative character, everyone reacted strongly against that statement. The Muslim League, let us remember, did not approve of it; the Hindu Mahasabha criticised [it]; even the Liberal Federation was unkind to it. The Congress reaction was the strongest of all and resulted in the resignation of the Congress Governments.

And yet in spite of all this, the Viceroy meets our leaders and, ignoring everything, asks them to go ahead with the Provincial Governments. If there were not tragedy behind all this, we would be inclined to appreciate the humour of it. But it is tragic that His Excellency should endeavour to play this role and imagine that we can be made to play fast and loose with our innermost convictions and with our firm resolves. It is still more tragic to realise that not all the catastrophic changes that have happened and are happening in Europe have effected the complacency of the British ruling class, or made it think in terms other than those of divide and rule. But the plane of catastrophe moves east and complacency and self-deception will not stop its progress.

It is clear that the conflict in Delhi was centred round the declaration of war aims and Indian freedom that the Congress demanded and the British Government was not prepared to make. That was the straight issue and it should have been faced frankly and in a straight-forward manner. Till this is settled satisfactorily, everything else is subsidiary. Till this "main and moral" obstruction is removed, there is no going back of the Congress Ministries, nor any co-operation with the British Government. Till then we dissociate ourselves completely with British policy and war effort.

Let us also be clear in our minds that there is no obstruction on the Indian side to such a declaration. The Muslim League may not agree with us in some matters, but the League stands for independence and Indian freedom. Mr Jinnah, so far as we know, approves of such a declaration though he may not attach the same importance to it as we do. The Congress President has now made clear that the Constituent Assembly that we demand "will be formed on the widest possible basis of franchise and by agreement in regard to communal representation". Further "that there must be full protection of minority rights and interests and this protection should be by agreement between the parties concerned". That surely removes every vestige of apprehension from the minds of minorities. There will be many difficult matters for us to consider and settle but the principles are firmly established and agreed to. There is no major communal difficulty about the framing of India's constitution by such a Constituent Assembly.

And so the whole fabric of communal disunion as a bar to India's progress, conjured up by the Viceroy, fades away and vanishes at the touch of reason and reality. The only reality that counts today is Britain's carrying on a war, which becomes more and more imperialistic, and her refusal to declare her war aims explicitly. If that is so, we have made our decision and by that we shall stand.[1]

Plan for Talks with Jinnah

[During the autumn of 1939 it was hoped that talks would be held between Congress and Muslim League leaders. Nehru was appointed Congress delegate to renew negotiations with Jinnah. Their conversations of the preceding year had proved abortive. Informed that the League was currently in a more receptive mood, Nehru wrote, after meeting with the Muslim League leader, Liaquat Ali Khan: "Very feelingly he began his conversation with the remark that if only our Leaders would rise to the Great Occasion we could successfully exploit this great opportunity to win our freedom. After all . . . [existing] communal differences were not insuperable." Nehru was told further that, in speaking of him, Jinnah had professed affection, coupled with high regard for his character and integrity. The League leader had proclaimed it a tragedy that the Hindu-Muslim problem could not be settled in a friendly spirit.

The proposed conversations between Nehru and Jinnah never took place, however, Jinnah changing his mind about having the talks. Instead, he issued an appeal for a Day of Deliverance from what he termed the tyranny, oppression and injustice of Congress rule, "referring to the resignation of the Congress ministries."[2]

As one considers Nehru's pre-Independence optimism that hostilities between India's various communal groups inevitably would be terminated —or his equally intense faith that Jinnah could not possibly gain support for creation of a separate Pakistan—one tends to comprehend something basic concerning the man's character. Due to Nehru's own honesty and constructive approach to problems, it was virtually impossible for him, throughout his career, to distrust others. Because of his own attitude about

[1] C.S.W., pp. 218–22.
[2] M.B., p. 264.

the necessity to create a peaceful, united, secular and democratic India, he simply could not believe that others might be possessed of a conversely, negative or destructive philosophy about so important a subject. (Even in conjunction with imperialism, it was the principle, and only rarely the individuals involved, who aroused his ire. With regard to Franco, or the Nazis and Fascists, his opposition was, of course, total. But even during the period following Independence—not covered in these volumes—in view of his own long-standing expressions of friendship, it was initially inconceivable to Nehru that Communist China, for example, could become aggressive and markedly belligerent toward India.)]

Correspondence with Jinnah

[Letter to Jinnah, written immediately after the Viceroy's statement— Lucknow, October 18, 1939.] I entirely agree with you that it is a tragedy that the Hindu-Muslim problem has not so far been settled in a friendly way. I feel terribly distressed about it and ashamed of myself, in so far as I have not been able to contribute anything substantial towards its solution. I must confess to you that in this matter I have lost confidence in myself, though I am not usually given that way. But the last two or three years have had a powerful effect on me. My own mind moves on a different plane and most of my interests lie in other directions. And so, though I have given much thought to the problem and understand most of its implications, I feel as if I was an outsider and alien in spirit. Hence my hesitation.

But that does not come in the way of my trying my utmost to help to find a solution and I shall certainly do so. With your goodwill and commanding position in the Muslim League that should not be so difficult as people imagine. I can assure you with all earnestness that all the members of the Working Committee are keenly desirous of finding a solution. It is a matter of enormous surprise and regret to me that we have so far failed in this endeavour. For, after all, the actual matters in dispute should be, and indeed are, easily capable of adjustment.

I shall therefore try to meet you as early as possible ... Will you please let me know your programme? When we meet I shall gladly discuss all the aspects of the question. But I suppose it will be better at a later stage for some representatives of the League to meet Congress representatives.

At the present moment, as you will no doubt appreciate, my mind is full of the rapid developments that are taking place. I do not know where they will land us in the course of the next few weeks. The Viceroy's statement has been astonishing in its imperialist challenge to all of us. As far as I can see there is no course open to the Congress except to reject his suggestions in their entirety, and this will necessarily have far-reaching consequences for us as well as others. I do not know what you and your colleagues in the Muslim League will decide, but I earnestly trust that you will also express your strong disapproval of the Viceroy's statement and refuse to cooperate with him on the lines he has suggested. I feel strongly that our dignity and self-respect as Indians have been insulted by the British Government. They take us for granted as hangers-on of their system, to be ordered about when and where they will.[1]

[A second letter to Jinnah—Allahabad, December 9, 1939.] Two days ago I sent you a letter informing you that I intended going to Bombay soon and hoped to meet you there. Yesterday morning I read in the newspapers your statement fixing December 22nd as a day of deliverance and thanksgiving as a mark of relief that the Congress Governments have at last ceased to function. I have read this statement very carefully more than once and have given twenty-four hours' thought to the matter. It is not for me, in this letter, to enter into any controversy about facts or impressions or conclusions. You know my views about these, formed, I hope, in all earnestness and with a desire to find the truth. It may be that I am mistaken, but I have sought more light and that light has not come.[2]

[From Jinnah's appeal (December 2, 1939): "I wish the [Mussalmans] all over India to observe Friday the 22nd December as the 'Day of Deliverance' and thanksgiving as a mark of relief that the Congress regime has at last ceased to function. I hope that the provincial, district and primary Muslim Leagues all over India will hold public meetings and pass the resolution with such modification as they may be advised, and after Juma prayers offer prayers by way of thanksgiving for being delivered from the unjust Congress regime."[3]

From Jinnah letter to Nehru, sent from Bombay, on December 13, 1939. (This document assumes a most curious character, in view of both the previous communications and those that follow.) "I am in receipt of your letter of the 9th December. I did not know where to address my reply to you as your movements were reported in the press. The latest

[1] B.O.L., pp. 402–03.
[2] Ibid., p. 413.
[3] E.I.P., p. 352.

announcement is that you are arriving in Bombay on the 14th of December and I am therefore sending this letter to your Bombay address. I quite agree with you 'that there must be some common ground for discussion, some common objective aimed at, for that discussion to yield fruit.' That is the very reason why I made it clear in our conversation at Delhi in October last to Mr Gandhi and yourself: First, that so long as the Congress is not prepared to treat the Muslim League as the authoritative and representative organisation of the Mussalmans of India it was not possible to carry on talks regarding the Hindu-Muslim settlement as that was the basis laid down by the working committee of the All India Muslim League. . . .

"The Muslim League was also not satisfied with the declaration made by the Viceroy [on October 17, 1939]. If happily we could settle the Hindu-Muslim question then we would be in a position to evolve an agreed formula for a demand of a declaration by His Majesty's Government that would satisfy us. [My suggestions made in Delhi were acceptable to neither Mr Gandhi nor yourself] but you were good enough to express your wish that you would like to meet me again and I said that I would be always glad to see you. In reply to your letter of the 1st December expressing your wish to see me in Bombay I informed you that I shall be in Bombay till the 3rd week of December and I shall be glad to see you."[1]]

[Third letter to Jinnah—Bombay, December 14, 1939.] Thank you for your letter of the 13th December. . . . I sent you my last letter from Allahabad after reading and giving full thought to your statement about the celebration of "a day of deliverance and thanksgiving" by the Muslims. This statement had distressed me greatly as it made me realise that the gulf that separated us in our approach to public problems was very great. In view of this fundamental difference, I wondered what common ground there was for discussion and I put my difficulty before you. That difficulty remains.

In your letter you have emphasized two other preliminary conditions before any common ground for discussion can arise. The first is that the Congress must treat the Muslim League as the authoritative and representative organisation of the Mussalmans of India. The Congress has always considered the League as a very important and influential organisation of the Muslims and it is because of this that we have been eager to settle any differences that may exist between us. But presumably what you suggest is something more and involves some kind of repudiation by us of or dissociation from other Muslims who are not in the League. There are, as you know, a large number of Muslims in the Congress, who

have been and are our closest colleagues. There are Muslim organisations
. . . apart from trade unions and peasant unions which have many Muslims
as their members. As a general rule, many of these organisations and individuals have adopted the same political platform as we have done in the
Congress. We cannot possibly dissociate ourselves from them or disown
them in any way.

You have rightly pointed out on many occasions that the Congress does
not represent everybody in India. Of course not. It does not represent
those who disagree with it, whether they are Muslims or Hindus. In the
ultimate analysis it represents its members and sympathisers. So also
the Muslim League, as any other organisation, represents its own members and sympathisers. But there is this vital difference that while the
Congress by its constitution has its membership open to all who subscribe
to its objective and methods, the Muslim League is only open to Muslims.
Thus the Congress constitutionally has a national basis and it cannot give
that up without putting an end to its existence. There are many Hindus,
as you know, in the Hindu Mahasabha who oppose the idea of the Congress
representing the Hindus as such. Then there are the Sikhs and others
who claim that they should be heard when communal matters are considered.

I am afraid therefore that if your desire is that we should consider the
League as the sole organisation representing the Muslims to the exclusion
of all others, we are wholly unable to accede to it. It would be equally at
variance with facts if we made a similar claim for the Congress, in spite of
the vastness of the Congress organisation. But I would venture to say that
such questions do not arise when two organisations deal with each other
and consider problems of mutual interest.

Your second point is that the Muslim League cannot endorse the
Congress demand for a declaration from the British Government. I
regret to learn this, for [it] means that, apart from communal questions,
we differ entirely on purely political grounds. The Congress demand is
essentially for a declaration of war aims and more especially for a declaration of Indian independence and the right of the Indian people to frame
their own constitution without external interference. If the Muslim League
does not agree to this, this means that our political objectives are wholly
dissimilar. The Congress demand is not new. It is inherent in article one
of the Congress and all our policy for many years past has been based on it.
It is inconceivable to me how the Congress can give it up or even vary it.
Personally I would be entirely opposed to any attempt at variation. But
this is not a personal matter. There is a resolution of the All India Congress

Committee, endorsed by a thousand meetings all over India, and I am powerless to ignore it.

It thus seems that politically we have no common ground and that our objectives are different. That in itself makes discussion difficult and fruitless. What led me to write my last letter to you also remains—the prospect of a celebration of a day of deliverance by the Muslims, as suggested by you. That raises very vital and far-reaching issues, into which I need not go now, but which must influence all of us. That approach to the communal problem cannot be reconciled with an attempt to solve it.

I feel therefore that it will serve little purpose for us to meet at this stage and under these conditions with this background. I should like to assure you however that we are always prepared to have free and frank discussions of the communal or other problems as between the Congress and the League. . . .

It has been our misfortune that charges are made in a one-sided way and they are never inquired into or disposed of. You will appreciate that it is very easy to make complaints and very unsafe to rely upon them without due inquiry.[1]

[From Jinnah's December 15, 1939 letter to Nehru: "[As] you make it clear that you are wholly unable to treat with the Muslim League as the authoritative and representative organisation of the Mussalmans of India, may I know in these circumstances what do you expect or wish me to do ?"[2]]

[Fourth letter to Jinnah—Bombay, December 16, 1939.] Thank you for your letter of December 15th.

I realise the difference you have pointed out. Of course the Muslim League cannot oppose the idea of any declaration to be made by the British Government. The only question can be about the nature and content of that declaration. What the Congress had asked for was an enunciation of war aims and a recognition of India's independence and the right of her people to frame their constitution, a right that must necesarily be inherent in independence. All these are basic principles which flow from our objective of independence, and as the Muslim League has the same declared objective, there should be no difference of opinion about them. In the application of these principles many important matters will no doubt have to be considered. But so far as the basic demands are concerned, they

[1] Ibid., pp. 415-17.
[2] Ibid., p. 418.

are of the very essence of Indian nationalism. To give them up or to vary them materially is to knock down our case for independence.

In regard to the war also the Congress has repeatedly declared its policy during the last eleven years. The present declaration is a logical outcome of that policy. I have personally had some share in shaping this policy and I have attached importance to it. You will appreciate that it is exceedingly difficult, apart from the question of desirability, to vary such long-established and fundamental policies. These policies are political in their essence and, I would venture to say, are the only policies which flow from a demand for Indian freedom. Details may be considered and discussed, their application should be worked out in mutual cooperation and, in particular, the interests of various groups and minorities should be considered carefully and protected. But to challenge the very basis of that declaration is to demonstrate that there is a great difference in political outlook and policies. This, as such, has nothing to do with the Hindu-Muslim problem. It is because of this that I feel that there is little in common in our political objectives.

May I say again that no one on our behalf, so far as I know, challenges or minimises the authority, influence and importance of the Muslim League. It is for this reason that we have been eager to discuss matters with it and to arrive at a satisfactory solution of the problems that confront us. Unfortunately we never seem to reach even the proper discussion of these problems as various hurdles and obstructions, in the shape of conditions precedent, come in our way. These conditions precedent, as I have ventured to point out to you, have far-reaching significance. I do not know why they should be allowed to obstruct all progress or prevent us from considering these problems. It should not be difficult to remove these hurdles and come to grips with the subject itself. But as these hurdles continue and others are added to them, I am compelled to think that the real difficulty is the difference in political outlook and objectives.

At the present moment, the decision to have an all-India demonstration on December 22nd has added a psychological barrier which effectively prevents mutual approach and discussion. I regret this exceedingly and have earnestly wished that you would see your way to remove this barrier which is leading and can only lead to ill-will. I still hope that you may be able to do so.

I do wish to assure you that for my part I do not want to leave any stone unturned which can lead to mutual understanding and settlement. But you will not have me, as I do not want to have you, leave integrity of mind and purpose in pursuit of anything. Nothing worthwhile can be gained that way. I have deep political convictions and I have laboured in accordance with them these many years. I cannot leave them at any time, much less now when the world is in the throes of a terrific crisis.[1]

[Further observation on Jinnah and the Muslim League.] The "Day of Deliverance" was rather a flop, and counter demonstrations among Moslems took place in some parts of India. But it added to bitterness and confirmed the conviction that Mr Jinnah and the Moslem League under his leadership had no intention whatever of coming to any settlement with the Congress, or of advancing the cause of Indian freedom. They preferred the existing situation.[2]

Other Correspondence

[Letter to Asaf Ali—Allahabad, November 16, 1939.] It is difficult to speculate about future happenings in the war. But one thing seems to me certain. Any combination—anti-Soviet or otherwise—will not be of long duration. They have upset the apple-cart in Europe and it is going to be very difficult to set it up again. In India there is no going back to the pre-war conditions and Congress is not going to resume governments in the Provinces on the old conditions.

I do not know what exactly you envisage in regard to communal talks with Jinnah. I am perfectly ready, as I told Jinnah, and I wait to hear from him. But essentially there is no communal difficulty in the way as between Jinnah and us. [There is a] political difficulty. He cannot reconcile himself to any action of the kind that the Congress is used to. Therefore to talk in terms of united political action on the basis of the settlement of the communal problem is to ignore this basic reality. I do not mean that the Hindus and Muslims cannot have united action. I think they can and will to a large extent. But this at the present moment does not depend on any communal issue.[3]

[Letter to Mahadev Desai—December 9, 1939.] Your letter of the 5th. . . . It is not a question of our acknowledging the Muslim League in a particular way. It involves far reaching implications and the giving up of all basic principles in the Congress. It means the complete disruption of the Congress.

[1] Ibid., pp. 418–19.
[2] D.I., p. 399.
[3] B.O.L., pp. 407–08.

You must have seen Jinnah's new statement. There is a limit even to
political falsehood and indecency but all limits have been passed. I do not
see how I can even meet Jinnah now. Only two days ago I wrote to him
that I would be going to Bombay soon and I hoped to meet him then.
Since yesterday I have given a great deal of thought to the matter and I
have decided to send another letter to him. . . . Stafford Cripps has been
here. . . . [He] has been having long talks with [various British leaders,
including Halifax]. . . . I might mention that while Cripps is thoroughly
straight and his abilities unquestioned, his judgement is not always to be
relied upon.[1]

10 | Resignation of Congress Ministries—War Issues—Which Way? What Means?

Resignation of Congress Ministries

[By November 15, 1939, Congress Party ministries in eight Provinces had
resigned, one after the other, in protest against the Viceroy's Statement
of October, 1939.]

When the Congress governments resigned early in November 1939, there
was many a sigh of relief; the government offices were henceforth closed
punctually at four in the afternoon, and reverted to their previous aspect
of cloistered chambers where quiet prevailed and the public was not welcome. Life went back to its old routine and slow tempo, and the afternoons
and evenings were free for polo and tennis and bridge and the amenities
of club life. A bad dream had faded, and business and play could now be
carried on as in the old days. True, there was a war on, thus far only in
Europe, and Poland had been crushed by Hitler's legions. But all this was
far away, and anyway it was a phony war. While soldiers did their duty
and fought and died, here also duty had to be performed, and this duty was
to bear the White Man's Burden worthily and with dignity.

[1] Ibid., pp. 412-13.

The brief period during which the Congress governments functioned in the provinces confirmed our belief that the major obstruction to progress in India was the political and economic structure imposed by the British. It was perfectly true that many traditional habits and social forms and practices were barriers to progress and they had to go. Yet the inherent tendency of Indian economy to expand was not restricted so much by these forms and habits as by the political and economic stranglehold of the British. But for that steel framework, expansion was inevitable, bringing in its wake many social changes and the ending of outworn customs and ceremonial patterns. Hence attention had to be concentrated on the removal of that framework, and the energy spent on other matters bore little result and was often like plowing the sands. That framework was itself based on and protected the semifeudal land tenure system and many other relics of the past. Any kind of democracy in India was incompatible with the British political and economic structure, and conflict between the two was inevitable. Hence the partial democracy of 1937–39 was always on the verge of conflict. Hence also the official British view that democracy in India had not been successful, because they could only consider it in terms of maintaining the structure and values and vested interests they had built up. As the kind of tame and subservient democracy of which they could have approved was not forthcoming, and all manner of radical changes were aimed at, the only alternative left to the British power was to revert to a purely authoritarian regime and put an end to all pretensions of democracy. There is a marked similarity in the development of this outlook and the birth and growth of fascism in Europe. Even the rule of law on which the British had prided themselves in India gave place to something in the nature of a state of siege and rule by ordinance and decree.[1]

War Issues

[The Congress position regarding the war was further clarified in a Working Committee Resolution on November 24, 1939.]

"The Working Committee has noted with pleasure the response of the country to the policy enunciated by it regarding the war in Europe and its repercussions in India. This policy, based on numerous declarations of the Congress, was laid down in the statement issued by the Committee on September 14, and subsequent events have amply justified its wisdom and

[1] D.I., pp. 383–84.
22*

expediency. The course of the war and the policy pursued by the British and French Governments, and in particular, the declarations made on behalf of the British Government in regard to India, seem to demonstrate that the present war, like the world war of 1914–18, is being carried on for imperialist ends, and British imperialism is to remain entrenched in India. With such a war and with this policy the Congress cannot associate itself, and it cannot countenance the exploitation of India's resources to this end.

"The Working Committee's unequivocal demand was for a declaration of war aims in regard to democracy and imperialism and, in particular, how these aims were going to be applied to India. These aims could only be considered worthy if they included the elimination of imperialism and the treatment of India as an independent nation, whose policy would be guided in accordance with the wishes of her people.

"The answer to this demand has been entirely unsatisfactory and an attempt has been made on behalf of the British Government to create misunderstanding and to befog the main and normal issue. In justification of this refusal to make a declaration in terms of the Working Committee's resolution, communal pleas have been advanced and the rights of minorities and of the Princes pleaded as a barrier to India's freedom.

"The Committee wishes to declare, with all emphasis, that no communal considerations arise in meeting the demand of the Congress, and the minorities, whatever their other differences might be, do not oppose India's right to freedom and independence.

"The Princes are represented by, and are the emblems of, the Paramount Power in India. In the end, it will be the people of the Indian States who will determine what part they will take in a free India, though the British Government have consistently ignored their wishes in a matter which vitally affects them.

"In any event, the wishes of those who may oppose India's independence are, and must be, irrelevant to the declaration of the British Government's intentions. The Committee can only interpret this attempt to avoid a statement on war aims and Indian freedom, by taking shelter under irrelevant issues, as a desire to maintain imperialist domination in India in alliance with the reactionary elements in the country.

"The Congress has looked upon the war crisis and the problems it raises as essentially a moral issue, and has not sought to profit by it in any spirit of bargaining.

"The moral and dominant issue of war aims and India's freedom has to be settled satisfactorily before any other subsidiary question can be considered.

"In no event can the Congress accept the responsibility of government, even in the transitional period, without real power being given to popular representatives.

"The Committee wishes to declare again that the recognition of India's independence and the right of her people to frame their constitution through a Constituent Assembly is essential, in order to remove the taint of imperialism from Britain's policy and to enable the Congress to consider further co-operation. It holds that a Constituent Assembly is the only democratic method of determining the constitution of a free country and no one who believes in democracy and freedom can possibly take exception to it. A Constituent Assembly alone is the adequate instrument for solving communal and other difficulties.

"This, however, does not mean that the Working Committee will relax its efforts for arriving at a solution of the communal problem. This assembly can frame a constitution in which the rights of accepted minorities would be protected to their satisfaction and in the event of some matters relating to minority rights not being mutually agreed to they can be referred to arbitration.

"The Constituent Assembly should be elected on the basis of adult suffrage, the existing separate electorates being retained for such minorities as desire them. The number of members in the assembly should reflect their numerical strength.

"The declarations made on behalf of the British Government, being inadequate, have compelled the Congress to dissociate itself from the British policy and war effort and, as a first step in non-co-operation, to bring about the resignations of all Congress Governments in the provinces. That policy of non-co-operation continues, and must continue, unless the British Government revises its policy and accepts the Congress contentions.

"The Working Committee would, however, remind Congressmen that it is inherent in every form of satyagraha that no effort is spared to achieve an honourable settlement with the opponent. While a Satyagrahi is ever ready for a non-violent fight, if it has to come, he never relaxes his efforts for peace and always works for its attainment. The Working Committee will, therefore, continue to explore the means of arriving at an honourable settlement, even though the British Government has banged the door in the face of the Congress.

"The Committee must, however, resist, by the non-violent methods of the Congress, all attempts to coerce the people of India along paths which are not of their choice, and everything that is against the dignity and freedom of India.

"The Working Committee appreciates and expresses its pleasure at the readiness expressed by Congressmen for launching civil disobedience should this become necessary. But civil disobedience requires the same strict discipline as an army organized for armed conflict. The army is helpless unless it possesses its weapons of destruction and knows how to use them. So also, an army of non-violent soldiers is ineffective unless it understands and possesses the essentials of non-violence. . . ."[1]

"We are not out to bargain because one does not bargain about one's freedom. We are not out to embarrass at a moment of peculiar difficulty, because that has not been India's way. But we are out to assert and gain our freedom and we cannot give that up because the war situation has developed to England's disadvantage.

[1] I.A.A., pp. 144–46.

"It must be remembered also, in spite of everything that is happening abroad, that there has been no change in British policy in India. Many of our comrades are in prison and they continue to be sent to prison. We are treated as a hostile people and then it is expected that because of the fear of consequences we should help in the maintenance of the British Empire. Whatever the consequences, we cannot help an Empire to maintain its hold over us."[1]

[From United Press Report of speech—Allahabad, November 24, 1939.] The fact is clear that the attitude of the British Government has cut the ropes which bound us in some measure in an uneasy alliance with them in the Provincial Governments. There can be no going back . . . on the old conditions. We [are] launched on a new adventure and we shall see it through.

As is often the case . . . [the British have] tried to belittle India's demand and to divert the issue. It is not our custom to bargain or to seek jobs, howsoever high. We do not claim anything for ourselves or even the Congress. What we claim is for the Indian people.

Lord Zetland has said that [ours] is an impossible demand. We have nothing further to say to Lord Zetland and in future we shall address ourselves to our own people. . . . We are prepared for all eventualities and consequences. We are not in a hurry but we are deadly serious and there should be no mistake about that.[2]

Which Way? What Means?—November 15, 1939

Again we are standing on the threshold of great happenings. Again our pulses quicken and our toes are a-quiver, and the old call comes to our ears. We pack up our little troubles and store away our domestic worries, for what do they matter when that call comes to make us forget all else when India, whom we have loved and sought to serve, whispers to us and casts her magic spell on our little selves?

Yet some are impatient and in the pride of their youth they make accusation. Why this delay? Why do we go so slow when the blood tingles in our veins and life calls to us to march? Do not worry, young manhood and womanhood of India; do not fret or grow impatient. The time will come all too soon when you will have to shoulder this heavy burden; the call to march will also come, and the pace may be swifter than you imagine. For

[1] Ibid., p. 335. (A later corroboration of Congress' 1939 stand on the war.)
[2] Ibid., p. 332.

the pace is set today by a world rushing headlong into the unknown future, and none of us, whether we wish it or not, can stand when the very ground shakes underneath our feet.

The time will come. May it find us ready, stout of heart and swift of limb and calm of mind and purpose. May we know well then the path we have to travel so that no doubts might assail us, no divided counsels weaken our resolve.

We know our goal, our objective, our heart's desire. Of that there need be no further argument. But what of the way we have to travel, the methods we adopt, the means that govern our actions? Surely that, too, is not a matter for argument; for long years we have blazed the trail and fashioned the way so that others may follow on the well-trodden path. Twenty years ago many might have doubted the efficacy of this strait and narrow way, but today we have long experience to guide us, our own successes and failures to teach us. In spite of attempts to divert us from it, we have stuck to it with firm resolve, and the millions of India have understood its significance and efficacy and are wedded to it as never before. The Congress continues to declare its firm faith in it; for it there is no other way.

And yet it is necessary that we do not take too much for granted, and that in this hour of destiny we examine afresh its implications and accept them with all our heart and mind. This is no time for theory or idle speculation; action awaits us and action demands concentration of mind and effort and cannot permit the philosophy of doubt or the luxury of debate in the midst of action. Much less can it permit individuals or groups to neutralize that very action by their contrary methods and by their challenging the very roots of that action.

It is necessary that we examine this question frankly and come to clear and final decisions, for a new generation has arisen which has no roots in our past experience and speaks a different language, and there are some who openly or secretly, and from even the shelter of our organization, express contempt for our methods and means. It may be, as we well believe, that these doubters and dissidents are few and cannot make much difference to a vast nation-wide movement. But it is possible that they might produce confusion in many minds and lead to happenings which injure our cause. Therefore there must be clarity and decision. We can take no unnecessary risks in the struggle ahead of us.

Nineteen years ago the Congress adopted non-violence as its method of action, and in these years that have passed we have experimented with it on many an occasion. We impressed the world, but, what is more important, we impressed ourselves and drew amazing strength from what we did and how we did it. The old choice of a subject people—submission or violent revolt—no longer applied to us. We had a potent weapon, the value of which grew with our growing strength and understanding of it. It was a weapon which might be used anywhere, but it was peculiarly suited to the genius and present condition of India. Our own example is there to justify it and to comfort and cheer us. But world events during the past few years have demonstrated the futility and brutality of the methods of violence.

Few of us, I suppose, can say that the era of violence is over or is likely to end soon. Today violence flourishes in its intensest and most destructive and inhuman form, as never before. Yet its very virulence is a sign of its decay. It will die or it will kill a good part of the world.

> *The sword, as ever, is a shift of fools*
> *To hide their folly.*

But we live in an age of folly and madness, and our rulers and those who govern human affairs are the true products of this age. From day to day we face this terrible problem: how to resist violent aggression? For the alternative is often no other than meek submission and surrender to evil. Spain resisted with violence, and, though she succumbed in the end, her people set a magnificent example of courage and heroic endurance. Forsaken by their friends, they checked for two and a half years the tide of Fascist aggression. Who will say, even today after their defeat, that they were wrong? For they had no other honourable course left open to them. The method of non-violence was not in their minds and was, under the circumstances, out of their reach. So also in China.

Czecho-Slovakia, with all her armed might and undoubted courage, succumbed without a fight. True, she did so because her friends betrayed her. But still the fact remains that all her armed might proved of no avail to her in her time of need. Poland was utterly vanquished in three weeks of struggle, and her great army and fleets of aeroplanes vanished into nowhere.

The way of violence and armed might is only feasible today, even in the narrowest interpretation of immediate success, when the armed forces are superior or equal to those opposed to them. Otherwise there is surrender without a fight or a collapse after the briefest of struggles, bringing utter defeat and demoralization in their train. Petty violence is completely ruled out, as it has not even the virtue of holding out a bare possibility of success, and it brings all the horrors of defeat and disruption.

What the future will bring to India is beyond our ken. If that future is still one of armed national forces, it is difficult for most of us to conceive of a free India without a national army and all the other apparatus for defence. But we need not consider that future now. We have to deal with the present.

In this present these doubts and difficulties do not arise, for our course is clear and our path marked out. This is the way of non-violent resistance to all obstructions to Indian freedom, and there is no other way. Let us be quite clear about it, for we dare not proceed to action with our minds being pulled in different directions. I am not aware of any other way offering us a ghost of a chance of effective action. Indeed, there will be no real action at all if we think of other ways.

I believe there is general agreement among Congressmen on this question. But there are a few, somewhat new to the Congress, who, while apparently agreeing, plan differently. They realize that there can be no national and nation-wide movement except through the Congress. All else would be adventurism. They want, therefore, to utilize the Congress and at the same time to break through it in directions which are opposed to Congress policy. The proposed technique is to embed themselves in the Congress and then to undermine its basic creed and method of action. In particular, the continuance of the technique of non-violence is to be combated, not obviously and patently, but insidiously and from within.

Now it is open to any Indian to put forward his own proposals and ideas, to work for them and convert others to his viewpoint, and even to act up to them if he thinks that it is vital to do so. But it is not open to him to do so under cover of something else. That would be misleading the public, and out of such deception mass movements do not arise. That would be treachery to the Congress and sabotage of a movement in full flood. If there is ideological conflict, it is all to the good that this should see the light of day and the people should understand it and decide. This should be so at any time, much more so on the eve of great happenings. No organization can tolerate internal sabotage when it is thinking in terms of coming to grips with a powerful adversary. We cannot have indiscipline in our own ranks or a division of counsel when action calls us.

It becomes essential for us, therefore, to decide this issue with all clarity and definiteness. We have, of course, decided it so far as the Congress is concerned, and we propose to hold by that decision. Any other course is ineffective and fraught with peril to the nation. It is not difficult for us, if we were so minded, to produce chaos in India, but out of chaos freedom does not necessarily, or even usually, emerge. In India there are obvious possibilities of chaos, leading to the most unfortunate of consequences. We cannot always predict the consequences of our action, especially when we are dealing with the masses. We take risks and must take them. But it would be inconceivable folly to do something which adds to these risks enormously, puts obstructions in the way to our freedom, and takes away that moral stature from our movement which has been our pride these many years. When the world is a-wearying of the methods of violence, for us even to think of a reversion to them would be tragedy indeed.

We must therefore stick, stoutly and wholeheartedly, to the method of non-violence and reject all substitutes that might be offered to us. We must remember that it is not possible to have a variety of methods functioning side by side, for each weakens and neutralizes the other. We must, therefore, choose wisely and abide by our choice, not spoiling it by flirtation with other ways. Above all, we must realize that non-violence is non-violence. It is not just a word to be used mechanically when our minds function differently and our mouths utter other words and phrases opposed to it and our actions belie it. We have to be true to it in every way if we are to be just to it, to ourselves, and to our cause.[1]

I I After Resignation of Congress Ministries —Postscript to 1939

After Resignation of Congress Ministries

The constitution was suspended, and autocratic rule was re-established. The old constitutional conflict of Western countries between an elected parliament and the king's prerogative, which had cost the heads of two kings in England and France, took shape in India. But there was something much more than this constitutional aspect. The volcano was not in action, but it was there and rumblings were heard.

The impasse continued, and, meanwhile, new laws and ordinances descended upon us by decree, and Congressmen and others were arrested in ever-growing numbers. Resentment grew and a demand for action on

[1] U.I., pp. 352–56.

our side. But the course of the war and the peril of England itself made us hesitate, for we could not wholly forget the old lesson which Gandhiji had taught us, that our objective should not be to embarrass the opponent in his hour of need.

As the war progressed, new problems arose, or the old problems took new shape, and the old alignments seemed to change, the old standards to fade away. There were many shocks, and adjustment was difficult.[1]

The Congress ministries had resigned . . . because they could not accept the Viceroy's mandates or the British Government's policy. But the assemblies were still there. The Viceroy or the governors could have dissolved them and had a fresh election. But they knew well that such an election would result in an overwhelming majority in favor of . . . Congress governments that had resigned. No other ministry was possible, as it could not command a majority. . . . The only course was [to suspend] provincial assemblies, [to hold] no fresh elections, and [for] the Viceroy and governors to exercise dictatorial powers. It was a clear case of conflict between the people and parliament on the one side and the King's representatives on the other. One party had to be suppressed or to give in. Parliament was suppressed. . . .

Our course was clear. Yet we restrained and held ourselves, even though many among us were indignant with us, even though many colleagues of ours found their way to prisons for the offense of explaining our policy to the people. We were hesitant because we hoped against hope that England's Government, including some progressive and labor elements, might, in this hour of supreme trial, shake itself out of its deadening imperialism and act according to its professions.[2]

Postscript to 1939

Early in 1940, soon after the resignation of the Congress ministries, the then Congress president, Dr Rajendra Prasad, wrote to Mr M. A. Jinnah and also made a public statement inviting the Moslem League to place any charges against the Congress governments before the federal court for inquiry and decision. Mr Jinnah declined this offer and referred to the possibility of a royal commission being appointed for the purpose. There was no question of any such commission being appointed, and only the

[1] T.F., pp. 369-70.
[2] Ibid., pp. 377-78.

British government could do so. Some of the British governors who had functioned during the regime of the Congress governments declared that they had found nothing objectionable in the treatment of minorities. Under the act of 1935 they had been especially empowered to protect minorities if any such need arose.[1]

["The change in Jinnah's attitude," as Brecher has observed, "is difficult to explain, but most well-informed persons are agreed that the Viceroy sought to weaken the Congress at this time and to strengthen the League."[2]
It is generally agreed that the 1939 resignation of Congress Ministries was of direct benefit to the Muslim League. V. P. Menon has noted that when the Congress resigned provincial office, the Viceroy's "attitude automatically changed.... [He] began to lean more on the support of the ... League.... For all practical purposes Jinnah was given a veto on further constitutional progress.... The Viceroy even discouraged the efforts of certain well-wishers to bridge the gulf between ... Congress and the Government."[3]]

12 | The National Planning Committee, 1938—Developments Concerning Planning in 1939

The National Planning Committee, 1938

[Just as Nehru had exerted the most important influence in Congress and in the country at large, in making India aware of both international issues and the need for a Constituent Assembly, so he was the first and most forceful exponent in the country of national planning. Even before 1938 he felt strongly that a National Planning Committee should be created When he urged that such a committee be formally appointed in 1938, and the Congress approved his suggestion, he was asked to be its chairman. Later, as Prime Minister, he was to play a decisive role in helping to formulate, inaugurate and implement free India's several Five-Year-Plans.]

[1] D.I., p. 392.
[2] M.B., p. 264.
[3] T.P.I., pp. 69–72.

[As Chairman of the Committee—1938.] The economy based on the latest technical achievements of the day must necessarily be the dominating one. If technology demands the big machine, as it does today in a large measure, then the big machine with all its implications and consequences must be accepted. Where it is possible, in terms of that technology, to decentralize production, this would be desirable. But, in any event, the latest technique has to be followed, and to adhere to out-worn and out-of-date methods of production, except as a temporary and stopgap measure, is to arrest growth and development.[1]

Toward the end of 1938 a National Planning Committee was constituted at the instance of the Congress. It consisted of fifteen members plus representatives of provincial governments and such Indian states as chose to collaborate with us. Among the members were well-known industrialists, financiers, economists, professors, scientists, as well as representatives of the Trade Union Congress and the Village Industries Association. The non-Congress provincial governments (Bengal, Punjab, and Sind), as well as some of the major states (Hyderabad, Mysore, Baroda, Travancore, Bhopal) co-operated with the committee. In a sense it was a remarkably representative committee cutting across political boundaries as well as the high barrier between official and nonofficial India—except for the fact that the Government of India was not represented and took up a non-co-operative attitude. Hardheaded big business was there as well as people who are called idealists and doctrinaires, and socialists and near-communists. Experts and directors of industries came from provincial governments and states.

It was a strange assortment of different types, and it was not clear how such an odd mixture would work. I accepted the chairmanship of the committee not without hesitation and misgiving; the work was after my own heart, and I could not keep out of it.

Difficulties faced us at every turn. There was not enough data for real planning, and few statistics were available. The Government of India was not helpful. Even the provincial governments, though friendly and co-operative, did not seem to be particularly keen on all-India planning and took only a distant interest in our work. They were far too busy with their own problems and troubles. Important elements in the Congress, under whose auspices the committee had come into existence, rather looked upon it as an unwanted child, not knowing how it would grow up and rather suspicious of its future activities. Big business was definitely

[1] Quoted in M.J.N., p. 428.

apprehensive and critical, and probably joined up because it felt that it could look after its interests better from inside the committee than from outside.

It was obvious also that any comprehensive planning could only take place under a free national government, strong enough and popular enough to be in a position to introduce fundamental changes in the social and economic structure. Thus the attainment of national freedom and the elimination of foreign control became an essential prerequisite for planning. There were many other obstacles—our social backwardness, customs, traditional outlook, etc.—but they had in any event to be faced. Planning, thus, was not so much for the present as for an unascertained future, and there was an air of unreality about it. Yet it had to be based on the present, and we hoped that this future was not a distant one. If we could collect the available material, co-ordinate it, and draw up blueprints, we would prepare the ground for the real, effective future planning, meanwhile indicating to provincial governments and states the lines on which they should proceed and develop their resources. . . .

The original idea behind the Planning Committee had been to further industrialization—"the problems of poverty and unemployment, of national defence and of economic regeneration in general cannot be solved without industrialization. As a step towards such industrialization, a comprehensive scheme of national planning should be formulated. This scheme should provide for the development of heavy key industries, medium scale industries and cottage industries. . . ." But no planning could possibly ignore agriculture, which was the mainstay of the people. Equally important were the social services. So one thing led to another, and it was impossible to isolate anything or to progress in one direction without corresponding progress in another. The more we thought of this planning business, the vaster it grew in its sweep and range, till it seemed to embrace almost every activity. That did not mean that we intended regulating and regimenting everything, but we had to keep almost everything in view even in deciding about one particular sector of the plan. The fascination of this work grew upon me, and, I think, upon the other members of our committee also. But at the same time a certain vagueness and indefiniteness crept in; instead of concentrating on some major aspects of the plan we tended to become diffuse. This also led to delay in the work of many of our subcommittees which lacked the sense of urgency and of working for a definite objective within a stated time.

Constituted as we were, it was not easy for all of us to agree to any basic social policy or principles underlying social organization. Any attempt to discuss these principles in the abstract was bound to lead to fundamental differences of approach at the outset and possibly to a splitting up of the committee. Not to have such a guiding policy was a serious drawback, yet there was no help for it. We decided to consider the general problem of planning as well as each individual problem concretely and not in the abstract, and allow principles to develop out of such considerations. Broadly speaking, there were two approaches: the socialist one aiming at the elimination of the profit motive and emphasizing the importance of equitable distribution, and the big-business one striving to retain free enterprise and the profit motive as far as possible and laying greater stress on production. There was also a difference in outlook between those who favored a rapid growth of heavy industry and others who wanted greater attention to be paid to the development of village and cottage industries, thus absorbing the vast number of the unemployed and partially employed. Ultimately there were bound to be differences in the final conclusions. It did not very much matter even if there were two or more reports, provided that all the available facts were collected and co-ordinated, the common ground mapped out, and the divergences indicated. When the time would come for giving effect to the plan, the then existing democratic government would have to choose what basic policy to adopt. Meanwhile a great deal of essential preparation would have been made and the various aspects of the problem placed before the public and the various provincial and state governments. . . .

We fixed a ten-year period for the plan, with control figures for different periods and different sectors of economic life. Certain objective tests were also suggested: (1) The improvement of nutrition—a balanced diet having a calorific value of two thousand four hundred to two thousand eight hundred units for an adult worker. (2) Improvement in clothing from the then consumption of about fifteen yards to at least thirty yards per capita per annum. (3) Housing standards to reach at least one hundred square feet per capita. Further, certain indices of progress had to be kept in mind: (a) Increase in agricultural production, (b) Increase in industrial production, (c) Diminution of unemployment, (d) Increase in per capita income, (e) Liquidation of illiteracy, (f) Increase in public utility services, (g) Provision of medical aid on the basis of one unit for thousand population, (h) Increase in the average expectation of life.

The objective for the country as a whole was the attainment, as far as possible, of national self-sufficiency. International trade was certainly not excluded, but we were anxious to avoid being drawn into the whirlpool of economic imperialism. We wanted neither to be victims of an imperialist power nor to develop such tendencies ourselves. The first charge on the country's produce should be to meet the domestic needs of food, raw materials, and manufactured goods. Surplus production would not be dumped abroad but be used for exchange of such commodities as we might require. To base our national economy on export markets might lead to conflicts with other nations and to sudden upsets when those markets were closed to us.

So, though we did not start with a well-defined social theory, our social objectives were clear enough and afforded a common basis for planning. The very essence of this planning was a large measure of regulation and co-ordination. Thus while free enterprise was not ruled out as such, its scope was severely restricted. In regard to defense industries it was decided that they must be owned and controlled by the state. Regarding other key industries, the majority were of [the opinion] . . . they should be state-owned, but a substantial majority of the committee considered that state control would be sufficient. Such control of these industries, however, had to be rigid. Public utilities, it was also decided, should be owned by some organ of the state—either the central government, provincial government, or a local board. It was suggested that something of the nature of the London Transport Board might control public utilities. In regard to other important and vital industries no special rule was laid down, but it was made clear that the very nature of planning required control in some measure, which might vary with the industry.

In regard to the agency in state-owned industries it was suggested that as a general rule an autonomous public trust would be suitable. Such a trust would insure public ownership and control and at the same time avoid the difficulties and inefficiency which sometimes creep in under direct democratic control. Co-operative ownership and control were also suggested for industries. Any planning would involve a close scrutiny of the development of industry in all its branches and a periodical survey of the progress made. It would mean also the training of the technical staffs necessary for the further expansion of industry, and the state might call upon industries to train such staffs.

The general principles governing land policy were laid down: "Agricultural land, mines, quarries, rivers and forests are forms of national wealth, ownership of which must vest absolutely in the people of India collectively." The co-operative principle should be applied to the exploitation of land by developing collective and co-operative farms. It was not proposed, however, to rule out peasant farming in small holdings, to begin with at any rate, but no intermediaries of the type of taluqdars, zamindars, etc. should be recognized after the transition period was over. The rights and titles possessed by these classes should be progressively bought out. Collective farms were to be started immediately by the state on cultivable waste land. Co-operative farming could be combined either with individual or joint ownership. A certain latitude was allowed for various types to develop so that, with greater experience, particular types might be encouraged more than others.

We, or some of us at any rate, hoped to evolve a socialized system of credit. If banks, insurance, etc. were not to be nationalized, they should at least be under the control of the state, thus leading to a state regulation of capital and credit. It was also desirable to control the export and import trade. By these various means a considerable measure of state control would be established in regard to land as well as in industry as a whole, though varying in particular instances, and allowing private initiative to continue in a restricted sphere.

Thus, through the consideration of special problems, we gradually developed our social objectives and policy. There were gaps in them and occasional vagueness and even some contradiction; it was far from a perfect scheme in theory. But I was agreeably surprised at the large measure of unanimity achieved by us in spite of the incongruous elements in our committee. The big-business element was the biggest single group, and its outlook on many matters, especially financial and commercial, was definitely conservative. Yet the urge for rapid progress, and the conviction that only thus could we solve our problems of poverty and unemployment, were so great that all of us were forced out of our grooves and compelled to think on new lines. We had avoided a theoretical approach, and as each practical problem was viewed in its larger context, it led us inevitably in a particular direction. To me the spirit of co-operation of the members of the Planning Committee was peculiarly soothing and gratifying, for I found it a pleasant contrast to the squabbles and conflicts of politics. We knew our differences, and yet we tried and often succeeded, after discussing every point of view, in arriving at an integrated conclusion which was accepted by all of us or most of us.

Constituted as we were, not only in our committee but in the larger field of India, we could not then plan for socialism as such. Yet it became clear to me that our plan, as it developed, was inevitably leading us toward establishing some of the fundamentals of the socialist structure. It was limiting the acquisitive factor in society, removing many of the barriers to growth, and thus leading to a rapidly expanding social structure. It was based on planning for the benefit of the common man, raising his standards greatly, giving him opportunities of growth, and releasing an enormous amount of latent talent and capacity. And all this was to be attempted in the context of democratic freedom and with a large measure of co-operation of some at least of the groups who were normally opposed to socialistic doctrine. That co-operation seemed to me worth while even if it involved toning down or weakening the plan in some respects. Probably I was too optimistic. But as long as a big step in the right direction was taken, I felt that the very dynamics involved in the process of change would facilitate further adaptation and progress. If conflict was inevitable, it had to be faced. But if it could be avoided or minimized, that was an obvious gain. Especially as in the political sphere there was conflict enough for us, and in the future there might well be unstable conditions. A general consent for a plan was thus of great value. It was easy enough to draw up blueprints based on [an idealistic] conception. It was much more difficult to get behind them that measure of general consent and approval which was essential for the satisfactory working of any plan.

Planning, though inevitably bringing about a great deal of control and co-ordination and interfering in some measure with individual freedom, would, as a matter of fact, in the context of India today, lead to a vast increase of freedom. We have very little freedom to lose. We have only to gain freedom. If we adhered to the democratic state structure and encouraged co-operative enterprises, many of the dangers of regimentation and concentration of power might be avoided.

At our first sessions we had framed a formidable questionnaire which was issued to various governments and public bodies, universities, chambers of commerce, trade unions, research institutes, etc. Twenty-nine subcommittees were also appointed to investigate and report on specific problems. Eight of these subcommittees were for agricultural problems; several were for industry; five for commerce and finance; two for transport; two for education; two for public welfare; two for demographic relations; and one for woman's role in planned economy. There were in all about three hundred and fifty members of these subcommittees, some of them overlapping. Most of them were specialists or experts in their subjects—businessmen; government, state, and municipal employees; university professors or lecturers; technicians; scientists; trade unionists, and public men. We collected in this way much of the talent available in the country. The only persons who were not permitted to co-operate with us, even when they were personally desirous of doing so, were the officials and employees of the Government of India. To have so many persons associated in our work was helpful in many ways. We had the advantage of their special knowledge and experience, and they were led to think of their special subjects in relation to the wider problem. It also led to a greater interest in planning all over the country. But these numbers were disadvantageous also, for there was inevitable delay when busy people spread out all over a vast country had to meet repeatedly.

I was heartened to come into touch with so much ability and earnestness in all departments of national activity, and these contacts added to my own education greatly. Our method of work was to have an interim report from each subcommittee, which the Planning Committee considered, approving of it or partly criticizing it, and then sending it back with its remarks to the subcommittee. A final report was then submitted, out of which arose our decisions on that particular subject. An attempt was being made continually to co-ordinate the decisions on each subject with those arrived at on other subjects. When all the final reports had been thus considered and disposed of, the Planning Committee was to review the whole problem in its vastness and intricacy and evolve its own comprehensive report, to which the subcommittees' reports would be added as appendices. As a matter of fact that final report was gradually taking shape in the course of our consideration of the subcommittees' reports.

There were irritating delays, chiefly due to some of the subcommittees not keeping to the timetable fixed for them, but on the whole we made good progress and got through an enormous amount of work. Two interesting decisions were made in connection with education. We suggested that definite norms of physical fitness for boys and girls be laid down for every stage of education. We also suggested establishment of a system of compulsory social or labor service, so as to make every young man and woman contribute one year of his or her life, between the ages of 18 and 22, to works of national utility, including agriculture, industry, public utilities, and public works of all kinds. No exemption was to [be] allowed except for physical or mental disability.[1]

Developments Concerning Planning in 1939

[Effect of the war on planning in India.] When World War II started in September 1939, it was suggested that the National Planning Committee should suspend its activities. In November the Congress governments in the provinces resigned and this added to our difficulties, for under the absolute rule of the governors in the provinces no interest was taken in

[1] D.I., pp. 399–407.

our work. Businessmen were busier than ever making money out of war requirements and were not so much interested in planning. The situation was changing from day to day. We decided, however, to continue and felt that the war made this even more necessary. It was bound to result in further industrialization, and the work we had already done and were engaged in doing could be of great help in this process. We were dealing then with our subcommittees' reports on engineering industries, transport, chemical industries, and manufacturing industries, all of the highest importance from the point of view of the war. But the government was not interested in our work and in fact viewed it with great disfavor. During the early months of the war—the so-called phony period—their policy was not to encourage the growth of Indian industry. Afterward, the pressure of events forced them to buy many of their requirements in India, but even so they disapproved of any heavy industries being started in India. Disapproval meant virtual prohibition, for no machinery could be imported without government sanction.[1]

[From statement on National Planning Committee—1939.] National planning is of vital importance to a nation at any time. In war time, this subject becomes even more important. Our [Planning] Committee thus has an even more important task before it now than it had when it was formed. . . . India is on the eve of industrial development on a big scale and we must be prepared for this.[2]

[From letter to Krishna Kripalani—Anand Bhawan, September 29, 1939.] It seems to me obvious that certain key and vital industries, defence industries, and public utilities must be on a large scale. There are certain others which may be on a large scale or a small scale or on a cottage scale. A difference of opinion might arise in regard to the latter. Behind that difference there is a difference of outlook and philosophy and, as I understood Mr. [X.], he laid stress on this difference of outlook. His point was that the modern large scale capitalist system ignored the problem of distribution and was based on violence. With this I entirely agree. His solution was that with the development of cottage industries there was a much fairer distribution and the element of violence was much less. I agree with that too but it does not go far enough. Violence and monopoly and concentration of wealth in a few hands are produced by the present economic structure. It is not large scale industry that brings any injustice and

[1] Ibid., p. 407.
[2] I.A.A., p. 328.

violence but the misuse of large scale industry by private capitalists and financiers. It is true that the big machine multiplies the power of man exceedingly both for construction and destruction, both for good and for ill. It is possible, I think, to eliminate the evil use and the violence of the big machine by changing the economic structure of capitalism. It is essentially private ownership and the acquisitive form of society that encourage a competitive violence. Under a socialist society this evil should go, at the same time leaving us the good which the big machine has brought.

It is true, I think, that there are certain inherent dangers in big industry and the big machine. There is a tendency to concentrate power and I am not quite sure that this can be wholly eliminated. But I cannot conceive of the world or of any progressive country doing away with the big machine. Even if this was possible, this would result in lowering production tremendously and in thus reducing standards of life greatly. For a country to try to do away with industrialisation would lead to that country falling a prey, economically and otherwise, to other more industrialised countries, which would exploit it. For the development of cottage industries on a wide-spread scale, it is obvious that political and economic power is necessary. It is unlikely that a country entirely devoted to cottage industries will ever get this political or economic power, and so in effect it will not even be able to push cottage industries as it wants to.

I feel therefore that it is inevitable and desirable to encourage the use and development of the big machine and thus to industrialise India. I am convinced at the same time that no amount of industrialisation in this way will do away with the necessity of developing cottage industries on a large scale in India, and this not merely as feeders but as independent units. I do not know what science may achieve in the course of the next generation or two but as far as I can see cottage industries will be essential for India in addition to large scale industries, which should be encouraged in every way. The problem, therefore, becomes one of coordination between the two. It is a question of planning by the State. It cannot be successfully tackled under the present anarchic capitalist system satisfactorily.

I have tried to explain briefly my own views on this subject. I cannot presume to interpret anyone else's views. But I do feel that it is easily possible for me to cooperate fully with the advocates of cottage industries, even though I might not accept their fundamental outlook.

Unfortunately we are not dealing with a socialist state at present but are passing through a transition stage when the capitalist system is cracking up. This gives rise to innumerable difficulties. In any event it is clear that the principles to be applied even today should be those laid down by the Congress, that is, the State should own or control key industries and services, transport, etc. If the term key industries is held to include all vital industries we get a large degree of socialisation. I would add further as a necessary corollary to our policy that where there is any conflict between a privately owned large scale industry and cottage industry, the State should own or control that large scale industry. The State would then have the power and liberty to adopt any policy which it lays down and it can coordinate the two.

With considerable experience of Congress policies during the last twenty years, I can say with confidence that they have been of great economic and social advantage to India. It is perfectly true that the Congress proceeded on the assumption that large scale industries were strong enough to look after themselves and therefore more attention should be given to cottage industries. This must be considered in a proper context. We were a non-official organisation and the economic structure of the State was entirely outside our control. Encouraging large scale industries under these circumstances meant encouraging private vested interests, often foreign vested interests. Our objective was not only to increase production by utilising the wasted man power of India as well as the wasted time of a large number of people, but also to create self-reliance among the masses of India. The Congress achieved a great measure of success in this.

This subject cannot be considered in the air as a matter of pure theory but must be related to the circumstances and the facts of life as they exist in a country. We can never ignore the human factors. In China today there is no particular bent towards cottage industries.[1]

[In addition to the ideas expressed above, it might be noted that at no time did Nehru believe in jeopardizing already-existing, large-scale industry—which, in his view, was bound to be outmoded in short-order, in any event—in favor of creating a merely theoretical, socialistic society. What he did increasingly desire, over the years, was to make certain that not-yet-existing key-industries—for which sufficient private capital was not available, but whose existence could potentially improve the well-being of the Indian populace as a whole—be brought into being, under public auspices. It was in this connection that he favored public initiative. Otherwise, he feared that needed facilities might not be created at all, or be permitted to be utilized by—or gain profit for—merely a privileged minority.]

[1] B.O.L., pp. 391-93.